The Making of a Global Digital Rulebook

Thibaut Kleiner · Andrea G. Rodríguez
Editors

The Making of a Global Digital Rulebook

Digital Sovereignty and International Action in the EU

palgrave
macmillan

Editors
Thibaut Kleiner
European Commission
Brussels, Belgium

Andrea G. Rodríguez
Centre for European Policy Studies (CEPS)
Brussels, Belgium

ISBN 978-981-95-9225-8 ISBN 978-981-95-9226-5 (eBook)
https://doi.org/10.1007/978-981-95-9226-5

Cover credit: Andrej Aleksandrov

This Palgrave Macmillan imprint is published by the registered company Springer Nature Singapore Pte Ltd.
The registered company address is: 152 Beach Road, #21-01/04 Gateway East, Singapore 189721, Singapore

If disposing of this product, please recycle the paper.

Acknowledgements

We would like to thank our contributors for putting their trust in this project—the book you hold in your hands. We are deeply grateful for their willingness to endure weekend emails, sudden calls and texts, late-afternoon meetings and—most importantly—for jumping off the cliff with us for the idea that in uncertain times the only way forward is more Europe.

We also want to thank the conversations with friends, peers and colleagues that sparked so many ideas brought to life in this book. In particular, we want to thank Roberto Viola, Neelie Kroes, Günther Oettinger and Anthony Whelan for their inspiration in drafting this book; Zrinka Reisinger, Silvana Enculescu and Barbara Bajor-Szewczyk for their constant help throughout the project; and the many individuals in the EU institutions that were involved one way or another in actually making the EU digital rulebook. We also want to thank Alejandra Bringas for her unwavering support over the years and commitment to making Europe a place where AI is governed with the highest levels of transparency and accountability. To Virag Turcsan, for her critical insights and understanding when things get hard. To Sofia Martinez and Saskia Santana for their inspiring leadership and example.

Lastly, we would like to sincerely thank our families for their patience, understanding and support—tolerating late work hours and endless discussions about the book over lunches, dinners, afternoon walks and weekend plans. Thank you for listening to unfinished chapters, playing devil's advocate when necessary and standing by us every step of the way.

Contents

Editors and Contributors

About the Editors

Thibaut Kleiner is the Director for Future Networks in the Directorate for Communications, Networks, Content and Technology of the European Commission, the executive arm of the European Union. He has a long experience in the EU institutions, having joined the European Commission in 2001. After ten years in competition policy, he has worked in the digital policy area since 2011. In that capacity, he has shaped the agenda of the Commission in the digital field. Thibaut is also Visiting Professor at the College of Europe. An economist by training, he holds a Master from HEC Paris and a PhD from the London School of Economics. He has contributed to many books and articles throughout his career.

Andrea G. Rodríguez is a deep tech ecosystem builder and digital policy researcher. She is an Associate Researcher at the Centre for European Policy Studies (CEPS) in Brussels and Director for Quantum Technologies in ADIGITAL. Previously, she worked as Chair of the Governing Board at IMPAQT, a quantum technology consortium based in Delft (The Netherlands) and held many think tank and academic roles in the Catholic University of Lille (ESPOL), Barcelona's CIDOB, or the EPC in Brussels. Currently, Andrea also takes part in many advisory and working groups, increasing Europe's leverage in emerging technologies vis-à-vis geopolitical giants.

Contributors

Kyriakos Baxevanidis European Commission, Brussels, Belgium

Lucas Bersegol European Space Policy Institute (ESPI), Vienna, Austria

Sara Dalledonne European Space Policy Institute (ESPI), Vienna, Austria

Giovanni De Gregorio Católica Global School of Law, Lisbon, Portugal

Fabian Delcros European Commission, Brussels, Belgium

Peter Eberl European Commission, Brussels, Belgium

Alicia García-Herrero Bruegel, Brussels, Belgium;
Hong Kong University of Science and Technology, Hong Kong, Hong Kong

Anna Herold European Commission, Brussels, Belgium

Thibaut Kleiner European Commission, Brussels, Belgium

Cornelia Kutterer MIAI (Chair Legal and Regulatory Implications of AI), University of Grenoble, Grenoble, France

Kristo Lehtonen The Finnish Innovation Fund (Sitra), Helsinki, Finland

Stefan Lindström Finnish Ministry of Foreign Affairs, New Delhi, India

Viivi Lähteenoja University of Helsinki, Helsinki, Finland

Ludwig Moeller European Space Policy Institute (ESPI), Vienna, Austria

Gary Ng Natixis, Paris, France;
Central European Institute of Asian Studies, Bratislava, Slovakia

Alberto Palomo Gaia-X European Association for Data & Cloud AISBL, Brussels, Belgium

Eric Peters European Commission, Brussels, Belgium

Andrea Renda Centre for European Policy Studies (CEPS), Brussels, Belgium

Raquel Jorge Ricart Centre for European Policy Studies (CEPS), Brussels, Belgium

Andrea G. Rodríguez Centre for European Policy Studies (CEPS), Brussels, Belgium

Tim Rühlig European Union Institute for Security Studies (EU ISS), Paris, France

Esteve Sanz European Commission, Brussels, Belgium

Chloe Teevan European Centre for Development Policy Management (ECDPM), Maastricht, Netherlands

Paul Timmers University of Leuven, Leuven, Belgium

Sabina Tsakova European Commission, Brussels, Belgium

Goran Zeković European Commission, Brussels, Belgium

List of Figures

List of Tables

CHAPTER 1

Introduction to "The Making of a Global Digital Rulebook"

Thibaut Kleiner and Andrea G. Rodríguez

> It's time to give Europe a soul.
> Jacques Delors, Former President of the European Commission (1985–1995)

In the afternoon of an Autumn day in Brussels, after finishing a panel discussion, we sat down over a cup of coffee to chat about recent developments in European digital policy. The Spanish Presidency had just managed to conclude negotiations on the Artificial Intelligence Act, meaning that virtually all legislative files proposed by the European Commission in the past years would soon be law.

This was a remarkable feature that few observers had seemed to notice, we thought, but they had noticed even less that there was a bigger

T. Kleiner (✉)
European Commission, Brussels, Belgium
e-mail: thibaut.kleiner@ec.europa.eu

A. G. Rodríguez
Centre for European Policy Studies (CEPS), Brussels, Belgium
e-mail: andrea.rodriguez@ceps.eu

T. Kleiner and A. Garcia Rodriguez (eds.), *The Making of a Global Digital Rulebook*, https://doi.org/10.1007/978-981-95-9226-5_1

story behind individual policies. Our conversation, which was meant to be a regular catch-up between a think-tanker and a policymaker, ended up becoming the genesis of this book. We realised that there is something untold in EU digital policy relevant for the whole of the European project. How was it possible that the EU institutions had managed to adopt so many policies and legislations and to be given so much power in the digital field, which is so close to the heart of national sovereignty and sensitive for competitiveness, democracy and the whole of society? This story—*the making of the EU digital rulebook*—was not only worth telling, it was worth investigating, we thought, because it may bring some clues for other policy areas and beyond for the future of the EU.

Several conversations and sketches over paper came after that initial conversation, which resulted in the production of this volume. We decided to gather a team of experts, half with an academic background and the other half with a policy background, and to challenge them to tell us their version of the story from the perspective of the field they know best. Three aspects were particularly important: first, we wanted to come to terms with the concept of digital sovereignty, which we believed had an important role in the recent developments of the EU digital policy. Second, we wanted them to highlight the inherent tensions between interest groups that occupied their field. Third, we wanted to account for the relationship of the digital policy agenda with European integration in general and to relate it to the international context.

These questions, in our view, could provide a framework of analysis to evaluate how the EU managed to create a comprehensive regulatory and policy framework in all things digital, something that we felt should be of interest to students, practitioners and anyone interested in EU affairs. We had not anticipated that the second Trump administration would turn hostile to these EU digital policies nor that some EU companies would call for a pause in the implementation the EU digital rulebook. But by studying the underpinnings of the EU policymaking, we also discovered some of the mechanisms that explain its resilience (Fig. 1.1).

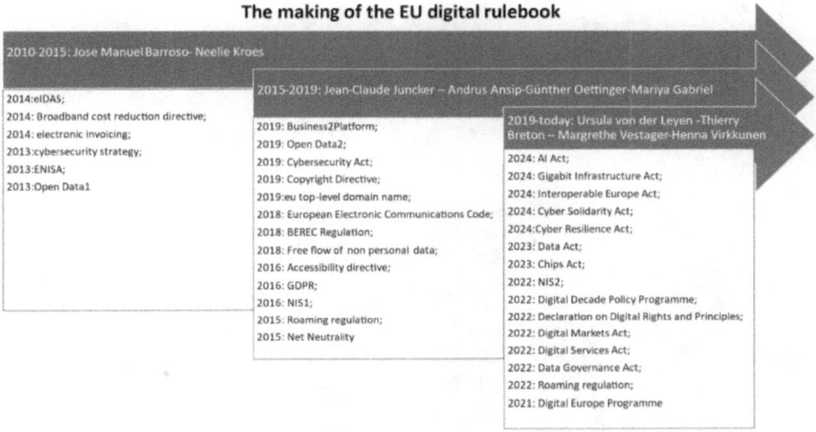

Fig. 1.1 Timeline of the EU digital legislations

The Digital Policy Space as a New Object of Investigation

EU digital law and policy is a fairly recent area of scholarly investigation. Policy insiders know that digital is important. However, this is still largely overlooked by the broader public. There are still too few university courses teaching digital policy, and students are often missing out on an area that has become a centrepiece for policymakers around the globe. In 2008, Facebook provided a service for just 100 million active users globally; this increased 30 times in the following 25 years to reach today more than 3 billion globally, out of which 255 million were in the EU (Meta, 2025). Here, according to Eurostat, a very small proportion of the population is not using the Internet today, and usage has increased tremendously over time. 65% of the EU population is doing banking online, and 60% participate in social networks (Fig. 1.2).

Interest in digital policy from an academic perspective has surged as technology started to gain importance in the economy, social relations and global geopolitics. Before 2010, there was little if not a consolidated

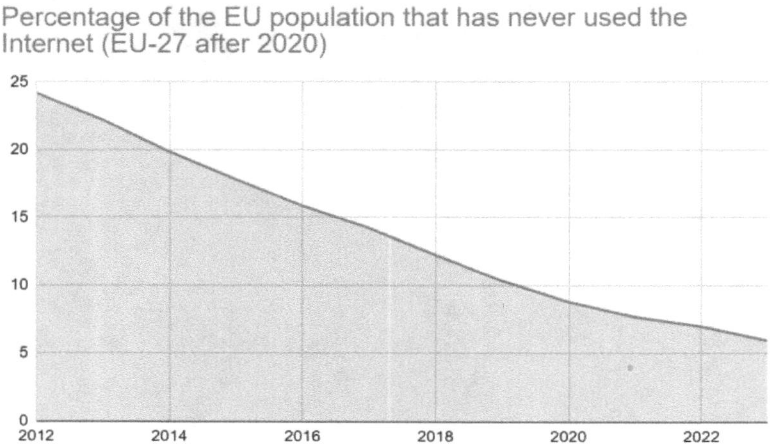

Fig. 1.2 Percentage of EU population that has never used the Internet according to Eurostat

digital policy agenda, and it was, therefore, something that remained at in the margins of the spotlight. The single market, the harmonisation of rules and eventually monetary policy in the advent of the 2007–2008 fiscal crises were the areas in which the EU was considered a serious player—not on digital.

However, since the mid-2010s, the publication of volumes analysing the EU digital policies has surged. Nevertheless, they have mostly focused on particular aspects in which digitalisation has a transformative effect, from the review of the economic impact of digital data to the legal analysis of the digital agenda passing by the democratic effect of new technologies or even the impact of such on global geopolitics. New studies on the EU digital agenda are published respecting academic siloes, which often miss out on the "bigger picture".

For instance, from a legal perspective, Marco Inglese (2019) critically analyses how the EU's collaborative economy challenges traditional legal frameworks, which paves the way for new regulatory approaches. These new approaches to regulation are necessary to enhance clarity and predictability. With a focus on the platform economy, Inglese surveys the controversial aspects of the digital single market and advocates in favour of an EU legislative intervention to be able to create a level-playing field for companies entering the digital single market.

From an economic perspective, Mario Mariniello (2022) offers a comprehensive overview of the factors leading up to the birth of the digital economy in the EU. Published after the COVID-19 pandemic, Marinello reflects on the role of digital technologies in today's economic and social life. He argues that digital infrastructure is key for the creation of digital markets, which are, therefore, essential to the creation of a digital society. Moreover, Antonio Manganelli and Antonio Nicita argue that there is no such thing as a digital market (Manganelli & Nicita, 2022), but rather that digitalisation extends across all economic sectors that, one way or another, become influenced by data. Furthermore, they argue that the EU is facing multiple challenges regulating the transition to the new digital economy with a focus on the platform economy.

From a governance perspective, Mirela Mărcuţ observes the opportunities and challenges of the EU digital agenda. She argues that the fact that the digital space lacked a clear regulatory framework was an incentive for EU member states to delegate the regulation of the digital space to the European Union (Mărcuţ, 2020). Moreover, the central role of national and EU regulatory authorities in shaping the digital single market is "a sign of the Europeanization of digital policies" (Mărcuţ, 2020, p. 130).

Lastly, from a geopolitical perspective, Anu Bradford explores the influence of Europe's digital policy in the global landscape. Bradford argues that the EU's market size and regulatory rigour drive the creation of global standards (Bradford, 2020). Non-EU countries, in their pursuit of benefitting from the European market, adapt their regulatory frameworks so they become interoperable with the European. Further work (e.g. Bradford, 2023) describes the US, the EU and Chinese approaches to regulation. In her work, she highlights the frictions that arise from these clashing ideologies, a dynamic that leads to a "regulatory competition" that further increases geopolitical tension.

Key Questions and Thesis of the Book

This book aims to depart from academic silos and seeks to address EU digital policy from multiple angles to provide readers with a multidisciplinary perspective. More precisely, we tried to challenge a set of experts in digital law and policy to come to terms with a paradox: in a period where politicians have been increasingly involved with digital trends, technologies and problems and where nationalism has been tightening, the EU's digital agenda has become a paradoxical example of advanced EU integration. The Commission has become, for instance, the de facto global regulator of online platforms and is leading the governance of AI, data and electronic identity and cybersecurity standards. It has established boards that coordinate with Member States in all areas of the digital space, from audiovisual to privacy to economic governance.

How did the EU manage to deliver such an integrated set of rules and policies in the digital space? What were the key factors that facilitated the development of an EU digital policy over the past years, and what does it tell us about institution building and market creation? In particular, we were triggered by a specific concept that has been used by EU policymakers recently and that we asked the authors to investigate further: the concept of digital sovereignty. The object of the book is that digitalisation has an impact on the political and societal integration of the European Union far beyond the achievements of the (digital) single market.

Sovereignty is a form of legitimate controlling power; it has been mostly understood in the context of national sovereignty and embodied by the control of the State over territory, resources and people. However, the digital age has forced us to rethink the concept of sovereignty (Floridi, 2020). The term *digital sovereignty* has been used by governments to convey the idea that states should reassert their authority over the internet and protect their citizens and businesses from the manifold challenges to self-determination in the digital sphere (Pohle & Thiel, 2020).

The use of the concept of EU digital sovereignty in EU political discourse (Broeders et al., 2022) is something that we found symptomatic of a paradigm change (Stengg, 2024). It reflects the claim that the EU has power and, therefore, that it is not merely a market but can define its interests and organise its will. Digital sovereignty refers to a change in perspective whereby power is not limited to a territory but addresses the functional sovereignty relating to the power of online actors on economy and society, notably through the control of data, and where the state is the guarantor of citizens' and consumers' rights against the hegemonic power of digital giants (Chander & Sun, 2023).

Digital sovereignty also has to do with the values underpinning the digital private order developed by Internet giants and has an intrinsic international dimension. The Internet has been mainly influenced by the US in terms of language, applications, etc., and, as a result, as a vehicle for a strongly capitalist, individualistic and techno-positivistic view, which was able to spread worldwide via the technologies themselves and through dominant business models (Foster & McChesney, 2011). However, China has mounted a rival approach with its centralised and authoritarian focus and its ability to develop endogenous digital platforms. It is, therefore, not surprising that the EU's digital sovereignty framework also should contain specific values and societal references.

The book posits that EU digital policies have experienced some evolutions and acceleration towards greater EU integration, thanks notably to the development of a more constitutional approach to EU digital law and the development of a vision of digital sovereignty that is more unique to the EU and provides common identity and common objectives in addition to—and instead of—only trying to build a common market. Our thesis is that the EU institutions have managed to increase EU integration (and their powers and international influence) in the digital space by supplementing the single market logic with objectives linked to rights and values. We tried to investigate this thesis through the various chapters, covering the full spectrum of the EU digital rulebook.

Framework of Analysis I: European Integration and the EU's Digital Policy Agenda

In that context, it is useful to introduce the book by reminding us about key perspectives on European integration (Rosamond, 2000):

- **Functionalism**, the original "Monnet" approach, starts with concrete projects of cooperation, which then spill over into other areas and lead to broader political integration. Crises and incremental steps in solving practical problems lead to deeper integration. This approach may also benefit from supranational institutions promoting integration. Neo-functionalism, a term associated with Haas (1958), asks how cooperation in specific sectors could lead to greater economic and political integration, also paying attention to the role of supranational institutions like the European Commission but also of sub-national interest groups and pressure groups.

  This theory remains a relevant framework for analysing developments in the European digital policy agenda, such as regulations affecting artificial intelligence. However, it is debatable to what extent the resulting structures truly constitute supranational institutions. The relationship between the different factors affecting digital policy—as will be shown by the different case studies offered in this volume—does affect the resulting structures.
- **Intergovernmentalism** considers that national governments are at the heart of the process and advance cooperation based on their national interests. Intergovernmentalism argues that the nation-state is not becoming obsolete due to European integration. Milward (2000) argued that national governments, rather than being weakened by European integration as some of their sovereignty was delegated to the EU, became strengthened by the process because, in some policy areas, it is in the member states' interest to pool sovereignty.

  Scholars of neo-intergovernmentalism, like Moravcsik (1998), consider that the spillovers and further integration from concrete projects are not automatic but rather influenced by national governments who adjust the pace and scope of integration. This is true in the case of policy areas such as cybersecurity, in which European harmonised action has certainly had a positive impact in securing the continent's network and information systems and mitigating cross-border cyber threats.
- **Institutionalism** emphasises the importance of institutions in the process of European integration. Institutionalism looks at different levels of interactions: institutions/rules, organisations/groups and individuals (Sweet et al., 2001). A key feature of historical institutionalism is path dependency, whereby decisions made about

institutions in the past impact significantly on the outcomes of the future and are difficult to reverse.

- **Social constructivism** emphasises the role of ideas, identities and norms to develop common narratives and shared values that influence national governments and foster greater cooperation and convergence. Risse explains that constructivism is based on a social ontology which insists that human agents do not exist independently from their social environment and its collectively shared systems of meanings (culture in a broad sense) (Risse, 2004). Looking at identity formation, language and discourses is an important element here (Christiansen et al., 1999).

  The European Union's digital policy couldn't be understood without the socio-philosophical context in which it was born. As opposed to the market-driven digital policy of the United States or the regime preservation-driven approach of China (Bradford, 2023), the EU stands as a unique entity combining market creation/intervention under a value-based approach. What constitutes a truly European approach to digital policy is precisely the fact that it does not have a specific country's interest at heart—it would be hard with 27 individual sovereign entities—but that sovereignty is spread out into the 450 million European citizens that the EU regulates.
- **Multi-level governance** argues that policymaking and integration in the EU are much too complicated to be explained by static integration theories. Key writers Hooghe and Marks defined Multi-Level Governance as the dispersion of authority across multiple levels of political governance, with either hierarchical or polycentric models (Hooghe & Marks, 2001). It is following this approach that we propose a complex volume written by expert voices that try to detangle the complex network of actors and institutions influencing digital policy in the EU.

The Framework of Analysis II: The Landscape of Forces

To be able to appreciate the development of the EU digital policies, it is also useful to have some analytical framework in terms of those who are making it. To that extent, we have proposed to the authors of this book a representation and categorisation of the interest groups that are influencing policy and law-making. EU institutions are not very well known, and it is useful to briefly recall how EU legislation is developed, most commonly through the so-called ordinary legislative procedure.

The EU legislative process primarily involves three main institutions: (i) the European Commission, which is the executive body of the EU and has the exclusive right of initiative to propose new legislation. The Commission proposes legislation based on the EU treaties and is also in charge of ensuring that the EU laws are properly enforced and implemented; (ii) the European Parliament, composed of directly elected members from each EU member state, debates, amends and votes on legislation. In practice, rapporteurs have a significant role in shaping the Parliament's positions, working with shadow rapporteurs, submitting their amendments and agreements to votes in committees and plenaries and negotiating with the Council based on a mandate; (iii) the Council of the European Union (Council of Ministers) represents the governments of the member states. The Council also debates, amends and votes on proposed legislation. In practice, rotating presidencies—changing every six months—are in charge of conducting negotiations based on a mandate.

There are several types of EU legislative acts, with different binding powers, the most common being directives, which set the goals and overall obligations but leave it to the Member States to decide about the form of implementation through national transposition. Digital legislation has, however, recently mostly taken the form of regulations, which are directly applicable across the EU without needing national implementation. The ordinary legislative procedure is the most common and significant legislative process in the EU and follows certain steps:

1. Proposal by the European Commission:
   - The Commission drafts and presents a legislative proposal, often after consultations and impact assessments with stakeholders, experts and sometimes citizens.
2. First Reading by the European Parliament and the Council:
   - European Parliament: The proposal goes to the relevant committee within the Parliament, which debates and can propose amendments. The full Parliament then votes.

- Council of the EU: After the Parliament, the proposal (with or without amendments) goes to the Council, which may adopt the Parliament's position or amend it further.
- Negotiations between Council and Parliament operate through so-called trilogues, where the Commission assists the co-legislators as an "honest broker" to try and find compromises.

3. Second Reading:
   - If the Council and the Parliament do not agree on the text during the first reading, the proposal goes through a second reading in both bodies.
   - If both Parliament and the Council approve the text at this stage, the legislation is adopted. If they cannot agree, the proposal moves to the next stage.
4. Conciliation Committee:
   - A Conciliation Committee, composed of equal members from the Council and Parliament, is convened to negotiate a compromise.
   - If a compromise is reached, both the Parliament and the Council must approve it in a final vote.
5. Adoption of Legislation:
   - If all parties agree, the law is adopted and becomes part of EU legislation, binding on all member states.

Through the legislative process, however, interest groups are active, trying to influence the law-making for their benefit. At the stage of the Commission's proposal, policy differences, sometimes represented through the various Directorates Generals of the Commission, can confront their priorities, whereas consultations and impact assessments help inform the content of the initiatives. In the subsequent negotiations within the Council and Parliament and between institutions, similar policy debates may resurface, as well as additional issues linked to specific national interests or the interests of special groups like industry or non-governmental bodies. Given the very global nature of the digital domain, foreign countries may also try to influence the legislative process, as well as multinationals.

To account for this rich field of influence in digital policymaking and to try and identify trends and specificities, a graphic framework has been proposed for this volume, called the Landscape of Forces.

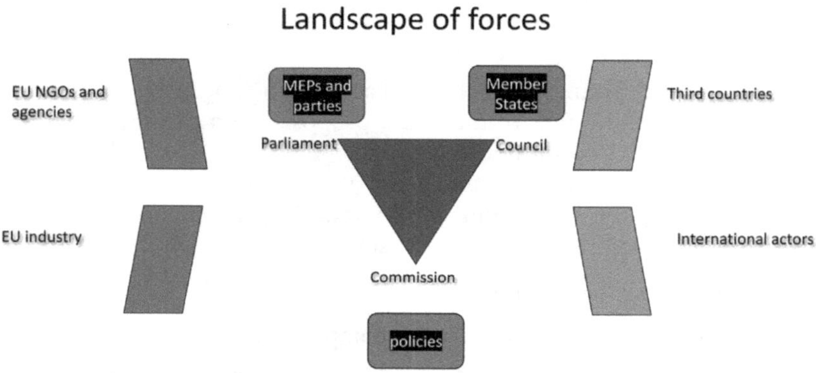

The Making of a Global Digital Rulebook

Digital policy, as compared to other areas of EU policymaking, has been a recent addition to the EU policy playbook and has grown to become a central piece of EU action, having spillover effects over the rest of policy areas: from agriculture to the relationship with non-EU countries. However, it has experienced a massive development in the past years, with a flurry of policies and legislation being adopted that cover the full ground of the digital space. Scholars and legal advisors have even developed trackers to have a complete picture of the digital legislation that has been developed over the past years. Zenner et al. (2024) have, for instance, developed for the think tank Bruegel a comprehensive dataset on EU legislation for the digital world based on twelve categories: (1) research and innovation; (2) industrial policy; (3) connectivity; (4) data and privacy; (5) intellectual property rights (IPR); (6) cybersecurity; (7) law enforcement; (8) trust and safety; (9) e-commerce and consumer protection; (10) competition, (11) media; and (12) finance. Legal consultant Digitbeetle provides a tracker of 22 digital legislations

(Digibeetle, 2024), and consultant Taylor Wessing has developed a catalogue of digital legislation using another set of twelve categories (Wessing, 2024). Because Zenner, Scott Marcus and Sekut have a very broad scope, they end up counting more than 100 pieces of digital legislation. They, however, also recognise that the core of the recent proposals relates to online platforms, data, AI, electronic identity and cybersecurity while also pointing at previous legislations, including media copyright and telecommunications. These areas constitute the EU digital rulebook, and they are the focus of the investigation of this volume, together with emerging policy areas such as quantum and space.

The book explains how the adoption of the EU digital rulebook was made possible. It aims to uncover the underlying dynamics and the complex relationship between the actors that have influenced the emergence and development of a particular sub-field of digital policy. Through a series of case studies meticulously analysed by experts in these policy areas, the book offers a unique mix of insider information and perspective. The authors of this volume represent more than 11 EU nationalities, providing a diversity of experiences, academic backgrounds and professions that enrich the perspective around the thesis of the book. The connecting thread of this conversation is the reflection on how the process of digitalisation, the securitisation of digital technologies and the erosion of the international rule-based order with the heightening of geopolitics have made the EU increasingly develop its digital policy agenda with a renewed "sovereign" lens.

The book is divided as follows. *Part I* sets up the foundations of the EU digital policy agenda. In Chapter 2, Thibaut Kleiner offers a historical review of the genesis and evolution of the digital policy agenda, exposing the emergence of digital sovereignty as a new narrative of EU policymaking in that area. In Chapter 3, Viivi Lähteenoja investigates the philosophical underpinnings of what we call "EU values" and explores the relationship of value-based rulemaking with sovereignty. In Chapter 4, Eric Peters breaks down the concept of "strategic autonomy" and "digital sovereignty" from a political science perspective, contextualising its evolution with the advancements of the EU economic governance of the digital space.

Part II of the book deep dives into the successes and challenges of the EU digital agenda following a case-study approach. In Chapter 5, Peter Eberl and Kyriakos Baxevanidis present a historical overview of the developments of telecommunications policy and describe recent advancements in the light of recent disruptive geopolitical events and new technologies. Chapter 6, Alberto Palomo analyses data as the backbone of the digital economy and relates the advancements of the data strategy with a renewed push for digital industrial policy. He explains the emergence of data-driven business models in Europe and develops the case for European data spaces.

In Chapter 7, Goran Zeković explains the emergence of a legal framework for European digital identity. In Chapter 8, Paul Timmers develops the emergence, evolution and consolidation of European cybersecurity policy, analysing its main pillars and offering new perspectives on the way forward. In Chapter 9, Anna Herold and Sabina Tsakova develop the genesis and evolution of European audiovisual and media policy from its inception to the present.

Chapter 10 discusses, from a legal perspective, the emergence of a normative framework regulating digital platforms. In it, Cornelia Kutterer and Giovanni de Gregorio offer a detailed evolution of platform regulation in the EU, showing the attempt of the EU to embrace a more constitutional perspective.

In Chapter 11, Esteve Sanz describes the multi-stakeholder model of Internet governance and reflects on the innovations facilitating the emergence of Web 4.0. In Chapter 12, Alicia Garcia Herrero and Gary Ng describe the importance of having a robust and secure semiconductor supply chain and offer a comparative policy analysis between China and the European Union, reflecting on how global geopolitics can impact the global semiconductor supply chain.

Chapters 13, 14 and 15 are dedicated to emerging technologies. In Chapter 13, Andrea Renda analyses and contextualises the emergence of the EU Artificial Intelligence Act, distinguishing four historical periods between 2015 and 2024. In Chapter 14, Ludwig Moeller, Sara Dalledone and Lucas Bersegol describe the role of space in the EU's digital policy agenda and analyse the factors of disruption. Under the lens of digital sovereignty, they analyse the key governance challenges for Europe moving forward. Chapter 15 deals with quantum technologies. In it, Andrea G. Rodríguez describes the European approach to quantum technologies, distinguishing three stages from 2016 to 2024 and analysing "smart competition" as the means to ensure strategic autonomy.

Part III deals with the international dimensions of Europe's digital policy. In Chapter 16, Chloe Teevan describes the strategic dimension of the Global Gateway, offering a critical view of its emergence and the challenges and successes so far of the initiative. In Chapter 17, Kristo Lehtonen and Stefan Lindström offer a timeline of EU-US relations in the context of digital sovereignty increasingly becoming a central piece in Europe's policy and action. They offer EU-US data relations as a case study and argue that 2024 inaugurates a new wave in the EU's strategic thought with a renewed interest in data governance and a more assertive industrial policy.

Chapter 18 describes the geostrategic importance of the Indo-Pacific for the EU's digital policy. In this chapter, Raquel Jorge Ricart argues that while the EU is increasing its efforts to approach the region, there are still questions about the extent to which it can influence policy and strategic choices in the Indo-Pacific. Chapter 19 discusses EU relations with China and the emergence of China as a technological powerhouse. Tim Rühlig dissects the EU's de-risking strategy *vis-à-vis* China and compares both powerhouses. Lastly, Fabian Delcros defends in Chapter 20 the need for the EU to be a relevant actor in multinational fora to achieve its digital policy ambitions.

Bibliography

Bradford, A. (2020). *The Brussels effect: How the European Union rules the world*. Oxford University Press.

Bradford, A. (2023). *Digital empires: The global battle to regulate technology*. Oxford University Press.

Broeders, D., Csernatoni, R., Irion, K., Kaminska, M., Monti, G., Robles-Carrillo, M., & Timmers, P. (2022, December 5). *Digital sovereignty: From narrative to policy?* https://eucyberdirect.eu/research/digital-sovereignty-narrative-policy

Chander, A., & Sun, H. (2023). *Data sovereignty—From the Digital Silk Road to the return of the state*. Oxford University Press.

Christiansen, T., Jørgensen, K. E., & Wiener, A. (1999). The social construction of Europe. *Journal of European Public Policy, 6*, 528–544.

Digibeetle. (2024). *EU digital and data legislation tracker*. https://digibeetle.eu/legislation-tracker/

Floridi, L. (2020, August 12). The fight for digital sovereignty: What it is, and why it matters, especially for the EU. *Philosophy & Technology, 33*, 369–378.

Foster, J. B., & McChesney, R. W. (2011). The Internet's unholy marriage to Capitalism. *Monthly Review, 62*(10).

Haas, E. B. (1958). *The uniting of Europe : Political, social, and economic forces, 1950–1957*. Stanford University Press.

Hooghe, L., & Marks, G. (2001). *Multi-level governance and European integration*. Row Man and Littlefield.
Inglese, M. (2019). *Regulating the collaborative economy in the European Union digital single market*. Springer.
Mărcuţ, M. (2020). *The governance of digital policies: Towards a new competence in the European Union*. Palgrave Pivot.
Manganelli, A., & Nicita, A. (2022). *Regulating digital markets: The European approach*. Palgrave McMillan.
Marinello, M. (2022). *Digital economic policy: The economics of digital markets from a European Union perspective*. Oxford University Press.
Meta. (2025, August 25). *Digital Services Act—Information on average monthly active recipients in the European Union*. https://transparency.meta.com/reports/regulatory-transparency-reports/
Milward, A. (2000). *The European rescue of the nation-state*. Routledge.
Moravcsik, A. (1998). *The choice for Europe: Social purpose and state power from Messina to Maastricht*. Cornell University Press.
Pohle, J., & Thiel, T. (2020, December 17). Digital Sovereignty. *Internet Policy Review, 9*(4).
Risse, T. (2004). Social constructivism and European integration. In A. Wiener & T. Diez (Eds.), *European integration theory* (pp. 159–176). Oxford University Press.
Rosamond, B. (2000). *Theories of European integration*. Bloomsbury Publishing.
Stengg, W. (2024). *Digital policy in the EU: Towards a human-centred digital transformation*. Edward Elgar Publishing.
Sweet, S. A., Sandholtz, W., & Fligstein, N. (Eds.). (2001). *The institutionalization of European space*. Oxford University Press.
Wessing, T. (2024). *Digital legislation tracker*. https://www.taylorwessing.com/en/online-services/digital-legislation-tracker
Zenner, K., Scott Marcus, J., & Sekut, K. (2024, June 6). *A dataset of EU legislation for the digital world*. https://www.bruegel.org/dataset/dataset-eu-legislation-digital-world

CHAPTER 2

A Brief History of EU Digital Law and Policy—From ESPRIT to the Digital Decade

Thibaut Kleiner

Brexit means Brexit.
Theresa May, Former UK Prime Minister (2016–2019)

Introduction

To understand EU digital law and policy, it is useful to start with some historical perspective and analyse how it has developed and which dynamics were at play in that process. The European Union (EU) is a

Disclaimer: The author is an official of the European Commission. The information and views set out in this chapter are those of the author and do not necessarily reflect the official opinion of the Institution.

T. Kleiner (✉)
European Commission, Brussels, Belgium
e-mail: Thibaut.kleiner@ec.europa.eu

T. Kleiner and A. Garcia Rodriguez (eds.), *The Making of a Global Digital Rulebook*, https://doi.org/10.1007/978-981-95-9226-5_2

recent political experiment and still a fragile one, as can be seen from the decision of the UK to leave the Union in 2016 ("Brexit"). Digital technologies are also recent, and the appreciation of their impact on the economy and society only became widespread a few years ago. It is, therefore, particularly relevant to look at the digital space as an interesting and important example of how European integration has increased over time.

EU law and policy are reaching a state where, comparatively, the governance of the digital space is more integrated in the EU than it is in the USA, where different States have adopted different stances on important issues from privacy to electronic identity and the federal State appears unable or unwilling to adopt national legislation, nor to force a deregulation agenda. This does not mean that the EU is a fully functioning and integrated entity yet. Differences do remain between national markets, and innovation is localised and not scaling up as fast as it could. However, successive strategies have tried to build a potential path towards reversing the comparative decline of European technological leadership in Information and Communication Technologies and managed to develop a coherent set of rules and narratives that today make the EU arguably the leading regulator of the digital space worldwide, even though this is also challenged notably by the US administration under President Trump.

This chapter looks at these successive strategies, trying to analyse their underpinnings and their achievements and to assess what they say about EU integration. It shows that EU digital policy started with a focus on technological competitiveness and the promotion of pro-market deregulatory approaches before the failure of policies focused on Member States' actions and the failure of market forces to deliver results pushed the Commission to create a new policy space around digital topics and eventually to build a programmatic, legislative effort and a single market integration agenda. The chapter shows, however, that a clear narrative based on common values and principles has eventually emerged, superseding a pure single market approach, calling for digital sovereignty and promoting the European way to digital transformation as a means of European integration.

Let the Market Rule: 1980–2000

Arguably, there was not much of a digital policy domain in the EU for a long time until 2010 and the Digital Agenda. The Directorate General in Charge of Information and Communication Technologies in the European Commission was established in 1986 with a focus on Research and Development. At that time, the European Union only had 12 Member States, with Spain and Portugal joining in January 1986, and the President of the European Commission, Jacques Delors, was building a case in favour of a single market. The digital sector—mostly understood as telecommunications and computing, as the Internet was still in its infancy and the World Wide Web had not been invented yet—was identified as strategic for EU competitiveness but also one where market forces were best left to their own devices. Still, EU leaders tried to take some initiatives to boost the sector's performance through research funding and a deregulation agenda.

Davignon and the ESPRIT Programme

The origins of some EU policies for the digital sector did not start with regulation but rather with an industrial perspective. In the early 1980s, the then Commissioner in charge of industry, Etienne Davignon, expressed worries about Europe's IT industries, which were falling dangerously behind their American and Japanese rivals. Whereas Europe had significant companies like Siemens or Nixdorf from Germany or Philips from the Netherlands, Olivetti from Italy, and Bull from France, it was losing ground internationally. 8 out of 10 computers sold in the EU at the time were imported from the USA, and 9 out of 10 videotape recorders sold in the EU were imported from Japan. The global market share of the European IT industry had shrunk to 10%, and European companies commanded less than 40% of their indigenous markets (European Commission, 2019).

In late 1981, Commissioner Davignon invited the directors of the twelve largest European IT companies to a roundtable to discuss the future of the industry in Europe. "Gentlemen, if you want Europe's information industry to have a chance to survive, you must make joint efforts and put your pre-competitive projects in common. If you do this, the Commission will fund up to 50% of the costs of these research projects in the areas which you consider strategic", Davignon told the 12 company directors (European Commission, 2019). Industry was able to respond to the call and present a work plan for a collaborative research and development programme, while the European Commission created the "Information Technology and Telecommunications Task Force". In 1983, the pilot phase was launched, and a proposal was made to establish a funding programme. However, this initiative was met with resistance, notably from Germany and the UK, who feared that this initiative would undermine their national programmes and who did not want to give up either money or power to set European priorities in IT research. The Commission was able to overcome this opposition, notably by reducing the budget of the proposed programme and thanks to this institutional entrepreneurship, the European Strategic Program for Research in Information Technology (ESPRIT) was born in 1984 with a budget of 1.5 billion euros over four years; half of that amount coming from the European Commission and half from project participants.

The ESPRIT programme had the primary goal of boosting Europe's competitiveness and addressing technological gaps in areas like software engineering and microelectronics. The programme aimed to promote collaborative research and development efforts among European countries, fostering innovation, knowledge exchange and the development of a skilled workforce between universities and industry. It played a pivotal role in elevating Europe's standing in the global information technology landscape and led to significant commercial results (European Commission, 1997).

ESPRIT spanned from 1984 to 1998 over four EU Research and Development (R&D) framework programmes, and it established an important track record for both university and industrial research, supporting both concrete projects and research infrastructures. Many research and development areas were covered: advanced microelectronics, software technologies, data processing, office systems, computer-integrated manufacturing and engineering, IT applications and even artificial intelligence. Projects were selected by replying to open invitations to tender and financed using shared-cost contracts. Community support was normally 50% of total expenditure. Participants could be companies (including SMEs), universities and other bodies established in the Community. Each project had to involve at least two independent industrial partners from a minimum of two Member States.

ESPRIT led to significant success for EU research and innovation in several areas. For instance, in telecommunication, it helped Europe to take the lead in mobile telephony and audio-visual standards.

The case of the GSM standard One remarkable result of ESPRIT's activities was to establish EU leadership in telecommunication standards. The case of the GSM standard is particularly interesting in that context. At the beginning of the 1980s, when mobile telephony was developed, it was based on analogue technology, and several systems were not compatible with each other and were quite expensive. To support the deployment of this promising technology, the European Commission developed the vision of a Single Market for mobile telecommunication. It published a Green Paper in 1987, where it called for the creation of a European Telecommunications Standards Institute (ETSI).

In 1988, ETSI was created, and it received funding from the ESPRIT programme to develop a pan-European common standard for mobile communication. It was built on an expert group that had started operating a few years earlier, the Groupe Speciale Mobile-GSM, hence the name of the forthcoming standard. It took the approach to use an open approach where all relevant experts, also involving American companies, for instance, would be involved.

The EU's research programmes also funded tests and the scientific verification of the work, and the Commission lobbied the Member States to adopt the standard and to establish a dedicated spectrum for mobile communication for the whole EU. Interestingly, to deliver pan-European coverage, the spectrum was released essentially in exchange for a coverage obligation rather than paying money to governments through spectrum auctions. The Commission agreed on a timetable to release the GSM networks across the whole of the EU, which took place in 1991. This initiative to have a common pan-European standard, GSM, with a complete roll-out strategy proved to be a real success. The adoption of mobile phones was very fast in the 1990s in the EU, paving the way to industrial leadership of the European telecom industry (Gros & Magliano, 2024).

A Legislative Agenda Focused on the Deregulation of Telecommunication Markets

The dominant belief among EU policymakers during the 1980s and 1990s was that market forces are the key to success in the information age and that policies linked to digital technologies should focus on economic prosperity (Shahin & Finger, 2009). Such an agenda was very much in tune with the US approach. When the Commission proposed legislation, it was rather to ensure that market conditions were fair and to avoid past regulations that would impede the development of free markets. This is best illustrated by the main legislative efforts of the Commission at the time in the telecom markets.

In the 1970s, the US authorities started to attack the monopoly that AT&T had enjoyed for a good century over virtually all aspects of telecommunications. Some markets were opened for terminal equipment and long-distance calls. The Department of Justice, in 1974, argued that local exchanges, which were regulated locally by the various states, were an essential facility and could be used to monopolise the other telecom markets. The lawsuit led to the break-up of AT&T in 1984, with seven "baby Bells" being created.

Due to a lack of local competition, though, Congress adopted the Telecommunications Act in 1996, introducing competition in the local loop, with obligations to interconnect and provide unbundled access to networks. Most importantly, it gave additional powers to the Federal Communications Commission (FCC).[1] The 1996 Telecommunications Act empowered the FCC to implement local competition provisions, thus creating a single regulatory framework for the whole of the USA. The US experience was an important inspiration for the overall objectives and philosophy of the European liberalisation efforts but also differed strongly in the more centralised model it promoted, compared to a more decentralised one in the EU (Mayer-Schönberger & Strasser, 1999).

In Europe, there had been national monopolies for telecommunication services. The UK started in the 1980s to liberalise its national market. In 1987, the Commission adopted a Green Paper arguing in favour of

[1] The FCC is an independent US government agency overseen by Congress, and it is responsible for implementing and enforcing America's communications law and regulations who regulate interstate and international communications by radio, television, wire, satellite and cable in all 50 states, the District of Columbia and US territories.

telecom liberalisation to support competitiveness. However, to succeed in abolishing national monopolies was not an easy achievement. It took nine years and the combined weight of three Commissioners, Peter Sutherland for competition, Lord Cockfield for the Single Market and Karl-Heinz Narjes for industry and information technology, to take the first directive through the Commission. Member States attacked it in front of the Court, but eventually, the Court sided with the Commission, and in February 1996, the Council and Parliament had confirmed that there were less restrictive means to safeguard public service in telecommunications than maintaining monopoly rights (Ungerer, 2018). Liberalisation in the EU required several directives adopted from 1990 to 1998 to liberalise successively telecom infrastructure and cable television, value-added and data services, telecom terminal equipment, authorisation of licences, application on open network provision to facilitate access of new entrants to existing infrastructure and the universal service directive.

Importantly, the use of directives to achieve the EU liberalisation agenda meant that Member States had some leeway to implement the EU objectives, and some of them used it to adjust the rules to their national specificities and preferences. While this may have offered more flexibility and some advantage in fine-tuning the regulation locally, it also meant that the degree of uniformity across the Union has been less than in the USA, and markets are still today considered to operate on a national basis. This being said, given also the difficulty of breaking national monopolies in the EU, these developments highlight the pro-market agenda at the time, with DG Competition at the helm of these efforts. The results of the liberalisation efforts of the 1990s were spectacular, with a sharp decline in prices, more choice and opportunities for new services, notably mobile telephony and the Internet.

2000–2010: Optimism, Nations Rule and Limits to the Market

EU policies led to considerable success in the telecom markets in the late 1990s and to wild hopes of leading the world in the information society, only to eventually disappoint. Technological progress and the widespread diffusion of new technologies that were thoughts of science-fiction, like mobile phones and the new opportunities coming from the Internet, went together with a pro-market agenda, where the State is best placed when not getting involved. The Lisbon strategy embodied the expectations that the EU would rise further on the back of this policy agenda. The reality was. However, different and blind faith in private companies could only recess, paving the way to a policy change.

E-commerce

During the late 1990s, the EU experienced accelerated uptake of the Internet. The Internet was perceived as one of the biggest technological breakthroughs, creating new business models and a new way of selling goods and services through e-commerce. The ease of creating new sites on the World Wide Web (WWW) facilitated the creation of many dot-com companies, and investors wanted to capitalise on the hype. For instance, the web browser developer Netscape staged its initial public offering (IPO) on Nasdaq on 9 August 1995. Despite operating at a loss and having no discernible revenue streams, the stock was listed at $28 on the first morning of the offering but soon hit $58.25 on that day, meaning that its market capitalisation sat above $2.5 billion (International Banker, 2021). This US trend also spread to Europe, with firms like Boo.com launching new e-commerce websites and spending vast amounts of advertising (Malmsten, 2001).

The e-commerce directive was introduced in the EU in 2000 to establish common rules in the emerging field of e-commerce. It sought to eliminate barriers to cross-border services to foster an integrated single market and boost consumer confidence in e-commerce transactions. One important provision included the limited liability of intermediaries and the country-of-origin principle, meaning that online service providers would be subject to the laws and regulations of their home country instead of all those where they would operate. The EU approach was again inspired by the USA, where the federal government had established that Internet service providers have immunity from liability for third-party content under section 230 of the Telecommunications Act of 1996. As the chairman of the FCC said in his speech before the World Economic Development Forum in September 1999: "Our hands-off approach wasn't entirely a choice. The reality is that the Internet grew so fast that policymakers could not have written a code to govern it even if they wanted to" (Kennard, 1999).

The USA also established a broad framework for the Internet, whereby the Federal Trade Commission would protect consumers on issues like online advertising privacy and fraud, with a specific focus on children thanks to the Children's Online Privacy Protection Act (COPPA), complemented by specific laws on various aspects, like a legal framework for electronic contracts and signatures adopted in 2000. The EU approach in the 2000s, following US leadership and different from today, was therefore very minimalist in terms of putting obligations on online businesses and rather tried to avoid national barriers to the growth of the Internet and e-commerce.

Internet Governance

This pro-market approach can also be found in Internet governance. The birth of the Internet has been amply documented (Internet Society, 1997), and the role of European pioneers has been significant therein. It is overlooked that Europe could have led the Internet revolution—notably in France, where Pouzin had designed in the 1970s a radically innovative new system that was a key inspiration for the Internet. Unfortunately, Europe's telecommunication operators slashed a way of transferring data that was radically different and more difficult for them to monetise (The Economist, 2013), displaying a strategy—preserving rents instead of innovating—that would endure until today. However, from the mid-1990s onwards, when it was clear that the Internet was going to win, the Commission started to support its adoption, notably by embracing the privatisation exercise that occurred in the USA and led to the massive expansion and adoption of the Internet.

The Internet was born from academic networks and defence contracts. The National Science Foundation Network (NSF) was created in the USA in the 1980s as a backbone to connect researchers to supercomputers for free, and when the World Wide Web protocol was invented in 1991, it embraced it and provided the first freely available Web browser. Some commercial firms started to build an Internet backbone and provide access to the network on the back of the growing number of personal computers that could be connected to the Internet. In 1995, the NSF awarded contracts for three network access points to provide connection points between commercial networks and one routing arbiter to ensure an orderly exchange of traffic across the Internet. The NSF decided to transfer in 1998 the network access points and routing arbiter functions to the commercial sector. As a result, the Internet became organised around

13 root servers. This provided a solution to scale the infrastructure layer of the Internet.

As regards the other layer of the Internet—the web applications and domain registration—the growth became unmanageable by a single entity operating for free (there were 7500 domain names in 1993, 120,000 in 1995, and 2 million in 1998). In 1998, the US government formalised an agreement with the non-profit Internet Corporation for Assigned Numbers and Names (ICANN) for oversight of domain name registration, thus providing a centralised function for the governance of the Internet through a private entity. This privatisation of the Internet was in line with the neoliberal globalisation process of the time and was rationalised through the growing demand for domain registration and the need to manage large amounts of user-generated content (Radu, 2019).

Interestingly, the EU did not oppose this privatisation in the hands of US companies and this lack of rivalry for an infrastructure that could have been considered an essential facility. Rather, it supported private sector leadership on the basis that it continues to deliver important public policy objectives, notably regarding backbone infrastructures, technical standards and allocation of IP addresses (European Commission, 2009). In the context of the World Summit on the Information Society (WSIS) between 2003 and 2005, the European Union sided with the USA and promoted a multi-stakeholder model for Internet governance, where the role of governments is limited. The EU approach continued to be pro-market and aligned with the USA, even though this would durably favour the US digital ecosystem, a reality still experienced today.

The World Summit on the Information Society (WSIS) The WSIS summit was organised through the Geneva conference in 2003 and the Tunis conference in 2005. Many countries, as a result of the geopolitical suspicion after the Iraq War in the early 2000s, requested the internationalisation of the US supervision of ICANN (Kurbalija, 2024). The 2003 summit failed to agree on the future of Internet governance, and as a result of the discussions in Geneva, a Working Group on Internet Governance was established, and it published its report just before the WSIS in Tunis. The Tunis gathering involved a large number of participants (1500 people from International Organizations, 6,200 from NGOs, 4800 from the private sector, and 980 from the media), and the issue of Internet governance was the most controversial one. On one side, developing countries, as well as Russia and China, wanted to change the relationship between ICANN and the US Department of Commerce and wanted governments to have more control over the Internet (multilateral approach). On the other side, developed countries around the United States, as well as academics, companies and NGOs, were keen to preserve the private nature of the Internet (multi-stakeholder approach). The EU and its Member States had a pivotal role in that context and helped forge a compromise whereby the possibility for an internationalisation of the status of ICANN would remain open, and the contract with the US government would remain in place for the time being while improvements were retained. The Tunis agenda was designed whereby Internet governance was established as a multi-stakeholder process where roles and responsibilities were defined for governments, private sector and civil societies (WSIS, 2005). It also created the Internet Governance Forum, as a United Nations body, to facilitate policy discussions in the future. Thanks to the EU, the vision of China and Russia did not prevail, and Internet governance was not put under the government's control.

The Lisbon Strategy: National Governments First

In 2000, at the extraordinary meeting of the European Council of 23 and 24 March 2000 in Lisbon, the heads of state and government of the 15 countries of the EU defined a new strategic objective to strengthen employment, economic reform and social cohesion, which is known as the Lisbon strategy. The origins of the Lisbon strategy did not come from the European Commission but rather can be linked to two national leaders: British Prime Minister Tony Blair and Spanish Prime Minister Jose Maria Aznar. Both shared a belief that the answer to Europe's economic problems lay in the adaptation of Europe's social model through microeconomic reforms aimed at raising competitiveness and productivity. They were aided in their quest by a sympathetic Portuguese Council presidency headed by Antonio Guterres, who endorsed their plan for a special summit to agree upon a new strategy (James, 2012).

As is often quoted from the Council conclusions, the EU "set itself a new strategic goal for the next decade: to become the most competitive and dynamic knowledge-based economy in the world capable of sustainable economic growth with more and better jobs and greater social cohesion". Information technologies were at the heart of this goal. The

EU set to itself the following targets for 2010: (1) annual economic growth of around 3% of GDP; (2) the creation of 20 million new jobs; (3) raising the employment rate from 61% to "as close as possible" to 70%; (4) raising the employment rate for women from 51% to "more than" 60%; (5) raising the employment rate of older workers to 50%; (6) raising research and development spending to approach 3% of GDP.

The Lisbon strategy was first and foremost an experiment of intergovernmental, whereby national governments would deliver reforms and, through soft measures (like reports providing naming and shaming transparency), be held to account, whereas the role of the Commission would be limited to one of a secretariat, merely helping on the process—the Open Method of Coordination—and background analysis. Member States did not want more structural mechanisms of policy coordination and convergence and did not provide the Commission with many tools to assist in ambitious goals.

However, the Lisbon strategy became rapidly criticised for its bureaucratic nature and for the lack of tangible progress it allowed regarding its targets and the overall EU competitiveness. Most importantly, for the purpose of this book, it is remarkable that the original strategy, even though it made a lot about the information society, did not give any specific place to individual digital technologies, even though these are at the very heart of competitiveness. Instead, the goals were set at a very macro level and rapidly appeared as overly ambitious and abstract and not adequate for each Member State, given important differences in development and profile. To that extent, the existence of different models of capitalism and intrinsic institutional constraints for reform were largely ignored by the strategy.

The Lisbon strategy was given a second chance with the 2005 Kok report, which emphasised some improvements and, most interestingly, put the finger on the importance of ICT for the objectives of the strategy and the need to focus more on them, including by improving the regulatory framework, increasing R&D in that sector and adapting education and training systems (Welfens, 2008). Even though the Lisbon strategy did not bring the expected results, and the 2000s are sometimes referred to as "the lost decade for EU competitiveness", the Open Method of Cooperation is considered to have advanced more of a common culture and fostered common narratives among government officials. This would prove useful to foster a more cohesive vision for the digital space in the next decades.

Failing Digital Champions Led to a New Paradigm of Legislation

It is sometimes difficult to remember that the EU was one day the world's leading producer of mobile phones. But in the late 1990s and 2000s, on the back notably, of the early mover advantage provided by the GSM standard and the benefits of telecom liberalisation, European companies were ruling the world in terms of connectivity and devices.

In 2000, Nokia, Ericsson and Siemens together represented almost 50% of global market shares (Statista.com, 2015). In 1999, Nokia7119 was launched, being the first mobile phone with a WAP Browser and the coolest reputation thanks to fun games and ringtones. The industry had launched an annual conference in the glitzy city of Cannes, 3GSM—which would become the Mobile World Congress a few years later the event was famous for its optimistic exuberance. The Dotcom boom was also experienced in the EU with perceived limitless opportunities for some new companies like lastminute.com, priceminister.com or Boo.com.

In other digital domains, the EU was not doing everything wrong either, with leading software manufacturers (SAP), service providers (Cap Gemini), telecom operators (Vodafone) and media (Vivendi-Universal). EU research was at the forefront of several emerging technologies like digital radio, digital TV, the MP3 standard to digitalise music, etc. However, beyond the enthusiasm and the hype, the situation in the EU ICT industry was not everywhere glorious, and the gap between the Internet and computing, as well as structural weaknesses in terms of innovation funding, were already serious flaws. As discussed above, the ICT sector was largely untouched by governments, but this also meant it was not nurtured by any industrial policy. Even though the patent holder for MP3, the standard used for digital music, was largely the Fraunhofer Institute, a German research centre, it was Apple, in California, that had exploited to its fullest benefit the iPod and its iTunes music store.

The failure of Nokia mobile The story of Nokia is very illustrative of the problem with the EU digital sector at the time. Nokia was a dominant player in the mobile phone industry for most of the 1999–2010 period, experiencing substantial market shares. In the late 1990s, Nokia launched very innovative feature mobile phones that were very much liked for their reliability, user-friendliness and fun. It was also able to produce a range of mobile phones catering for various market segments. In 2000, its global market share was 30%. In the mid-2000s, thanks to its product quality and brand building, it had established itself as a clear market leader, reaching up to 40% of the worldwide market in 2008, thanks to famous models like the Nokia 1100. It had also developed smartphones with more advanced features for business users, competing here also with Blackberry, from Canada. In 2007, however, Apple launched the iPhone, and Nokia's Symbian operating system was not up to the task against iOS and Android in adjusting to tactile screens and app stores. Nokia's market shares started to decline, even though it was still retaining some leading position. In 2011, it entered into a strategic partnership with Microsoft, adopting the Windows phone operating system. Unable to adjust to the shift of smartphones faced with delayed response against the touchscreen trend and unable to build an ecosystem of developers to provide a convincing app offer, Nokia further lost market shares to the point that its Devices and Services division was acquired by Microsoft, leaving Nokia to only operate in the network system market. This failure was symbolic of the perceived inability of large European incumbents to adapt and innovate in the digital sector. It also tainted the faith in markets to deliver results in the interests of EU citizens, something also experienced at the time in the financial sector. The failure of Nokia and of the Lisbon strategy provided the basis for a re-think of EU digital policies and an opportunity to form the digital space as a new agenda for the EU.

Another failure of the EU digital sector was the inability of telecom operators to win the hearts of customers. The deregulation agenda of the 1990s was producing effects through increased competition that was largely imposed on telecom operators by the EU national regulators, including promoting the entry of new competitors. Whereas prices of fixed and mobile communication went down significantly through the 2010s, travellers across the EU were sometimes faced with a telephone bill shock because of roaming fees—additional charges for using a mobile phone outside the country of your provider. It was possible to use your phone in another EU country—a benefit of the single market and common EU standards—but it came with a hefty price tag and messages of warning whenever you would cross a border, with some doubts that the surcharges reflected real additional costs. This was an issue and a disappointment towards free markets. Viviane Reding, the Commissioner in charge of ICT from 2005 to 2010, would not miss the opportunity to address this problem.

DG Competition was looking at how to incentivise the market players to reduce roaming charges by examining market transparency mechanisms as ways to incentivise new cross-border packages. However, Commissioner Reding surprised even her services by announcing in 2006 that she would propose legislation to limit the roaming charges. This move can be considered a vote of defiance against the abilities of market forces to deliver on their own. And the first step in a series of initiatives by the EU executive to deliver free roaming, a file that would occupy headlines for at least ten years. Telecom giants would attack the measure, but the Court of Justice in 2010 concluded that it was legal to restrict prices of roaming, notably because it was about cross-border practices (Euractiv, 2010). This paved the way for further initiatives to abolish roaming charges and led to the famous "roam-like-at-home", with a new Commissioner in charge of the Digital Agenda (see Chapter 5 of this book).

The Digital Agenda

Arguably, EU digital policy started in earnest with the Digital Agenda launched in 2010 as one of the seven flagship initiatives of the Europe 2020 Strategy and the first initiative of the Barroso II Commission, adopted just a few months after it took office. This comprehensive strategy, for the first time, developed a holistic view of the digital space, encompassing supply and demand and organising various policy tools to boost competitiveness and market integration. The genesis of the Digital Agenda is to be found in the failure of the Lisbon strategy and disillusionment with market forces in the aftermath of the financial crisis. It addressed, however, fundamental issues that continue to be relevant almost fifteen years after its adoption.

Scepticism with Incumbents

The Digital Agenda was designed at a time of fading faith in the market following the 2008 financial crisis. More precisely, Neelie Kroes, the Dutch Vice-President of the Commission in charge of the Digital Agenda, sometimes nicknamed Steelie Neelie, had been competition Commissioner in her previous mandate. She had expressed disappointment with the banking elites that had not anticipated the financial crisis, and that did not take responsibility for the enormous costs[2] that resulted from their recklessness for the European economy and society. Vice-President Kroes was, therefore, sceptical about incumbent players, be it bankers... or telecom operators. Those were perceived as not able to innovate compared to Internet and Over-The-Top service providers, and instead as trying to keep some of their former monopoly rents and to rip off customers, e.g. with roaming charges. In a famous speech at the end of her mandate (Kroes, Speech—Adapt or die: What I would do if I ran a telecom company, 2014), she advised the incumbent telecom operators to "adapt or die", highlighting her reluctance to prompt lame-ducks through regulation.

By contrast, and maybe not surprisingly, she became a strong advocate of digital startups, the newcomers spurring innovation and challenging established players. This may explain that the Digital Agenda was not designed as a traditional industrial strategy to protect and reinforce incumbent market operators or declining champions—like Nokia—but rather an attempt to boost the whole digital sector and to promote a vibrant framework that would benefit all dimensions of the digital economy, and eventually society as a whole. The underpinning reasoning of it was that "successful delivery of this Agenda will spur innovation, economic growth and improvements in daily life for both citizens and businesses". The Digital Agenda, contrary to the approach of the 2000s and the Lisbon strategy, recognised, therefore, the importance of digital technologies well beyond the purely economic sphere and indeed for society.

Startup Europe In the early 2010s, the EU experienced renewed interest in startups. The dotcom bubble had been forgotten, and the failure of Nokia had illustrated the importance of building startup ecosystems and open innovation models to be successful in the Internet era. Several cities across the Union, like London, Paris, Munich or Berlin, were starting to develop relevant startup ecosystems. In that context, Neelie Kroes, the

[2] During the 2008–2010 financial crisis, 20 bank debt guarantees and 15 bank recapitalisation schemes and 44 cases of individual bank aid cases were dealt with by the European Commission under the state aid rules. At the height of the crisis, the effectively committed aid amounted to some 13% of the GDP of the EU. See: (Lannoo & Napolli, 2010).

European Commission's Vice-President in charge of the Digital Agenda, launched the Startup Europe initiative in 2012, promoting policies for startups and gathering a group of tech entrepreneurs to provide her advice (the Startup Europe Leaders Club) to work together on recommendations to boost digital startups in the EU. Her role in boosting startups gained attention when she started to also support concrete initiatives, like the efforts of France Digitale, also launched in 2012, to fight a new tax scheme introduced in France that would make stock options less attractive a means of remuneration in the country (a movement known as 'Les Pigeons'). Neelie Kroes would also take a position in support of online platforms against lawmakers trying to prohibit platform economy business launches.

In 2012, on the stage of Le Web, one of the largest tech gatherings at the time, in the outskirts of Paris, she announced a EUR 100 Million scheme to support startups as part of the Future Internet initiative and asked Loic Le Meur, the master of ceremony, what he would do to support startups if he were in her position, thus reverting the accusation that not enough was done for tech entrepreneurs in the EU. A tour around Europe was subsequently organised to promote startups in various cities in an effort that culminated with the publication in December 2012 of the Startup Manifesto, which advocated several measures developed by the Startup Europe Leaders Club in areas from skill development to data policy and digital governments. The Manifesto was presented to the President of the European Council and EU heads of state and governments at the European Council.

Neelie Kroes would go on supporting startup ecosystems until the end of her mandate and beyond, becoming the Startup Envoy of the Netherlands in 2015 and chairing their Startup Delta initiative to promote startups in the kingdom. Today, it is recognised that the EU startup ecosystems have become first-class and rivals with the USA, China or India in several areas, from Fintech to social entrepreneurship, as can be seen from the annual reports on the State of European Tech.

A New Holistic Paradigm

It is true that by 2010, digital technologies had acquired a growing importance in people's daily lives. Facebook has more than half a billion subscribers already. With smartphones and the Internet being more accessible, new services were available, in particular around media services, with Internet downloads, often piracy, having reduced by half the music sales and licensing revenues of music companies. Online content, often user-generated, on new platforms like social media or YouTube was changing the business models of media outlets. Companies were starting to use cloud services and analytics for their businesses, and e-health and e-governments were new policy areas for governments. And harmful content and cybercrime were mushrooming. In short, society could not be considered immune from the impact of digital technologies.

The Digital Agenda in that context was rather clear that its aims were beyond competitiveness: "The overall aim of the Digital Agenda is to deliver sustainable economic and social benefits from a digital single market based on fast and ultra-fast Internet and interoperable applications". It echoed Germany's strategy, presented a few months earlier in 2009, to use open data and digital technologies to boost performance but went further in its scope. The promoted objective was to use Information and Communication Technologies (ICT) for greater goods, in terms of not only competitiveness but also overall social benefits, putting Digital at the heart of the European ambitions for 2020. It is also good to remember that the Arab Spring took place in the same period, and social media were identified as powerful vehicles for freedom of speech (Smidi & Shahin, 2017). The digital space was therefore not considered any more as merely a sector where the EU should improve its performance, but rather a core feature of the whole economy and society too (Fig. 2.1).

The Digital Agenda was expressed as a virtuous circle, where the creation of content and cross-border services, accelerated thanks to a pan-European infrastructure, would spur additional demand for these services and content, further requiring improvements in connectivity, etc. The link between supply and demand was made, as well as the importance of a European single market. This holistic approach was new compared to past attempts that only tried to optimise market functioning. The Commission underlined the well-known issues that had affected the performance of the European ICT industry (like insufficient deployment of fibre networks or insufficient R&D) but also included considerations regarding the demand side, and notably the marked problem that 30% of Europeans had still never used the Internet in 2010 as well as legal barriers. A series of issues were singled out as key elements to tackle, as illustrated in the graph above.

The Commission designed a scoreboard to monitor the 101 specific policy actions that the Digital Agenda initiated. Besides 31 legislative

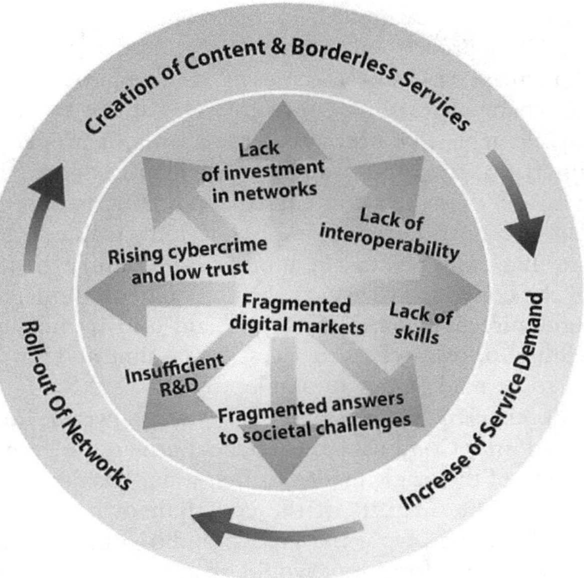

Fig. 2.1 Digital services and markets by the European Commission (2010)

proposals, several actions involved self-regulation, for instance, regarding the protection of children or the building of industrial alliances, e.g. for e-health or cloud computing, highlighting an attempt not to only engage in legislation.

Mixed Results

The Digital Agenda contained many initiatives and was very ambitious in its reach. It recognised that to spur the benefits of the single market, new rules were needed to create a market and that laissez-faire approaches were not adequate anymore. Overall, however, and maybe because it tried to cover so much ground, the Commission only had partial success in delivering this agenda.

On the supply side, the starting point was with content and services. Before streaming platforms emerged, the only way to access digital content across EU borders was very much through illegal means (illegal copies, downloads or streaming). In that context, Kroes was aiming to emulate the US approach and facilitate legal access to content to stem piracy and increase volumes of content consumption. This, however, would mean changing existing copyright rules at the time, and notably, the licensing elements that prevented access without proper licence from one EU country to the other. In the EU, content owners, from authors to film studios, license their content out on a country-by-country basis, which means that distributors in one EU country may not hold a licence to distribute that same content in another EU country. Kroes promoted a reform of the copyright rules, which she branded "outdated" since the EU copyright directives dated to 2001, and also wanted to introduce new possibilities for researchers to access data online and for public sector information to be made freely re-usable.

This comprehensive reform approach was, however, met with the resistance of another Commissioner, Michel Barnier, the French Commissioner in charge of the single market at that time. Barnier was much more concerned about the interests of the copyright owners, maybe because many of them stemmed from the French audio-visual and media sector, and he feared that a reform that would change licensing regimes would put content owners in a detrimental position against online platforms and content distributors. As a result, the two Commissioners, Kroes and Barnier, were involved in some in-fighting about the lead on the copyright file, and ultimately, this prevented any serious proposal from emerging (Hirst, 2014). That was the first setback for the Digital Agenda.

More successful was, however, the sister project dealing with content that Kroes initiated and that dealt with open data. The idea behind open data is that public sector data is a trove that should be opened and provided for free to innovators so that they can use it and offer new services and applications. After all, the data has been collected and paid for through taxpayers, so why should it not be used freely by economic actors? There is, however, some copyright issue involved: data always has an owner, and it can be used only based on some licensing modality. Vice-President Kroes was active in promoting data as the new gold (Kroes, Neelie Kroes Vice-President of the European Commission responsible for the Digital Agenda Data is the new gold Opening Remarks, Press Conference on Open Data Strategy Brussels, 12th December 2011, 2011) of the digital economy, and she proposed an open data package to increase the possibilities for web entrepreneurs, businesses, journalists, academics and all citizens to generate new and rich content by obliging EU institutions and most public authorities in Europe to share their data and making public data automatically re-usable. This proposal was not as controversial as a full copyright reform but would nevertheless have some possible costs for some administrations that were generating revenues from selling data.

The terms of the licensing agreements also generated some discussions with legal communication. After some negotiations, the Public Sector Information directive was however adopted, and open data could be generalised across the Union, with marked success for the national institutes that promoted it and companies that could develop new services. While several startups have flourished in the EU that use government data for innovative businesses (ODINE, 2024), the initiative also benefited large companies like Google, which use public information to power their maps and other online services. The Digital Agenda was successful here again, promoting disruptive opportunities and challenging the status quo.

As regards the demand side aspects of the digital economy, the Digital Agenda made a comprehensive attempt to grow Internet usage by citizens, with the slogan "every European digital", by businesses and notably SMEs and by governments. Vice-President Kroes decisively put digital policies on the agenda of national and local administrations, notably by appointing a series of Digital Ambassadors, thus following the UK example, and organising conferences and digital assemblies around the EU to promote the benefits of going online. At the end of her mandate, there were fewer "digital virgins"—people who had never been on the Internet—a number reduced from 30% to less than 20% of the population, with significant progress in countries like Greece, Romania, Ireland, Portugal, the Czech Republic and Croatia, whereas regular Internet users narrowed 75% (European Commission, 2014). Progress was less impressive for SMEs, with a mere 14% of SMEs using the Internet as a sales channel in 2014, only two points up in four years.

Kroes also launched initiatives in favour of e-government, with an action plan adopted in 2010 enabling citizens and businesses to use online facilities to, for example, register a business, apply for and access social security and health benefits, enrol in a university or bid to provide goods and services for public administrations (European Commission, 2010). The goal was to boost Europe's competitiveness and allow public authorities to offer improved services more cost-effectively at a time of budget constraints. Unfortunately, progress remained slow in this area, too, despite initiatives like the European public cloud and the funding of pan-European infrastructures in favour of e-signature and e-invoicing or a legislative proposal for electronic identity. The importance of digital services was not sufficiently coming across at the national level in a period where the aftermath of the financial crisis was still being felt.

Emblematic of this was the failure to get the budget required for the ambitious plans of the Digital Agenda. Whereas Vice-President Kroes had put forward a proposal for the Connecting Europe Facility to deploy broadband networks and digital services across the continent, with a required budget of 9 billion euros, the political compromise among Member States only delivered a mere 1 billion euros budget for these activities in the Multiannual Financial Framework 2014–2020. A clear disappointment which made the ability of the EU to support the deployment of digital technologies limited and which may have triggered its need to resort to legislation as a policy tool for action.[3]

As regards legislation, one area where the Digital Agenda not only unearthed new grounds but also delivered successful outcomes was in the area of cybersecurity. This was traditionally a sector where the EU had very little say, if any, given the proximity of cybersecurity with national intelligence and security services. However, Neelie Kroes was able to build momentum around several connected files to eventually establish the Commission's role more promisingly. She first developed a coalition of prominent businesses in favour of the protection of children online and enhanced EU funding for a network for Safer Internet national centres, outlining in a strategy of a Better Internet for Children (European Commission, 2012) the objectives to deliver not only safety and security but also more positive content and education. This echoed another initiative in favour of digital education (European Commission, 2013).

Secondly, she reformed the Commission's agency dealing with cybersecurity, ENISA, located in Heraklion (Greece), giving it new tasks beyond education and making it more central in supporting a network of expertise among Member States, notably thanks to the opening of a branch in Athens. The first Cybersecurity Strategy was proposed, with the High Representative Ashton and Commissioner for Home Affairs Malmström teaming up with Vice-President Kroes. Most importantly, Kroes proposed

[3] This echoes the analysis of Majone who considers that lack of an ability by the Commission to tax and spend drives its focus on regulation see: (Majone, 1996).

for the first-time legislation in the field of cybersecurity (the Network Information Security directive), a bold move aimed at securing minimum capabilities among Member States and exchange of reactive information among them, as well as obligations in terms of cyber risk management for critical infrastructures. In that context, she also drew some partnerships with the US government, agreeing that the EU would align with the USA and make October cybersecurity month, while the USA would adopt Safer Internet Day in February. The Network Information Security Directive (Directive 2016/1148, 2016), proposed in 2013, was ground-breaking in a context where Member States were not always trusting each other, let alone the Commission (see Chapter 8 of this book). It was proposed in a favourable context linked with the Snowden revelations that the US government was engaged in mass surveillance using digital technologies. The directive would take several years to be adopted, in 2016, but it highlighted a successful result for Vice-President Kroes.

Less successful was, however, the attempt of the Commissioner to reform telecommunication markets. Proposed at the very end of her mandate as a package deal, the Telecom Single Market Regulation was an ambitious proposal to come to terms with barriers to intra-EU activities of telecom operators to boost their investments and capabilities to deploy high-speed broadband. The proposal contained innovative provisions for spectrum management, as well as proposals for abolishing roaming, and it proposed harmonised rules for net neutrality within the EU. The package was, however, met with resistance from national regulators and national administrations, who felt their position would be undermined by a proposal to create more pan-European structures of telecom regulation. The incumbent telecom operators were not very supportive either, as they were seeing reduced revenues from the end of roaming charges and net neutrality, more calls for investment in broadband networks, and increased cross-border competition without a clear path to higher profits. In the end, time was not sufficient to have the proposal adopted through the parliament and the package deal was undone, with roaming and net neutrality being salvaged as separate proposals and the rest buried until the next Commission would reshape it (see Chapter 5 of this book).

In conclusion, the Digital Agenda can be characterised as a genuinely ground-breaking initiative, which was the real beginning of proper digital law and policy and shaped it durably for the years to come. It started with a relevant problem analysis and proposals but was probably too ambitious and not sufficiently supported by national governments and industry to deliver on its full scope. A lot was initiated, and a lot was delivered, but despite some bright spots, the overall result was rather one of unfinished business.

The Digital Single Market

The Juncker Commission came to power at the end of 2014 with a clear manifesto of 10 priorities that had been used during the parliamentary elections to give the new Commission's president the democratic legitimacy of a Spitzenkandidat and a clear majority in the European Parliament. The Digital Single Market strategy was maybe less pioneering than the Digital Agenda, but it offered an effective platform for the Commission to embark on a successful legislative programme; it obtained real breakthroughs, notably on copyright and telecom, two of the left-overs of the Digital Agenda, as well as cybersecurity and it positioned the EU as the lead regulator for digital matters.

A More Focused and Result-Oriented Strategy

In 2014, the EU was still struggling to get economic growth back on track, and the euro area was under pressure. The digital sector was seen as one where growth was happening and where the EU could do better (Cerulus & Kayali, 2019). As Jean-Claude Juncker explained in the televised debate between all lead candidates, he wanted to replace debt with ideas and the digital single market (Juncker, 2014, minute 8), thus highlighting an economic focus for his plans in continuation with the digital agenda. But the digital single market was, first and foremost, a regulatory agenda. The leftovers from the Digital Agenda also had to be tackled, notably in the telecom or copyright domains, and major proposals had still to be endorsed by the EU co-legislators, notably the General Data Protection Regulation, Telecom legislation and the Network Information Security directive. It was, therefore, logical for Juncker to want to pursue the legislation that had started and put digital policies at the top of his manifesto.

Juncker entrusted the Estonian former Prime Minister and recently elected Member of the European Parliament, Andrus Ansip, with the Digital Single Market vice-president portfolio. In that role, Ansip had to work with the German Commissioner Günther Oettinger, former Minister-President of the Baden-Württemberg region, who would be in charge of Digital Economy and Society. The Digital Single Market strategy (DSM) was published in 2015. The initial focus of the agenda on growth was clear from the very definition provided for the Digital Single Market, but so was also the regulatory ambition: "a Digital Single Market is one in which the free movement of goods, persons, services and capital is ensured and where individuals and businesses can seamlessly access and exercise online activities under conditions of fair competition, and a high level of consumer and personal data protection, irrespective of their nationality or place of residence".

The plan restated the fundamentals of an internal market while recognising new realities requiring specific public regulations and the necessity to regulate the relations between the various players (Bertarini, 2023). The DSM started with a reminder of Juncker's political priorities, which notably underlined the economic potential of digital technologies to generate up to EUR 250 billion of additional growth by 2020 and outlined the serious groundwork that had been done to prepare the initiative, mentioning various studies and consultations of Member States and Parliament in a companion staff working document. To that extent, the DSM was a good illustration of the *Better Regulation* approach that the Commission was promoting, more generally (European Commission, 2024a), and that required justifications before actions were launched. Given the criticism about the way the Telecom Single Market proposal had been proposed at the end of the previous college, the DSM was at least properly learning from past mistakes and was trying to involve Member States and stakeholders instead of simply resorting to the Commission's leadership.

In the genesis of the DSM strategy, both offensive and defensive elements were present. In 2015, digital technologies were already widespread in the EU, and they had shown their benefits in terms of providing access to new services and opportunities from notably large social media platforms. The offensive aspect was to use the scale of the European single market to create more growth and allow the development of bigger companies and the digitalisation of the economy. But negative consequences were also identified, from the spreading of illegal and harmful content, especially for children, to cybercrimes and various online consumer abuses. Not surprisingly, Member States started to adopt some national measures to tackle these issues. It became increasingly clear that two trends had to be tackled: (i) more legislation was emerging at the national level, with the risk of undermining the EU Single Market, and (ii) Member States were too small to effectively regulate large online players and the EU level was better suited.

At the national level, Germany adopted its Digital Agenda 2014–2017, covering a very large area of policies and legal areas. Importantly, Germany outlined that "German policies relating to digitisation will be guided by the core values and accepted rules on which our coexistence is based. Our value systems are based on our constitution. The freedom of the individual must continue to be protected in a digital world. Data protection, the integrity of networks and the transparency of data usage serve to safeguard our democracy and must be championed more vocally at both a European and a global level. Therefore, we must continue to ensure that our existing value systems are not lost in the digital world and that they continue to provide a framework for our future coexistence" (Federal Government of Germany, 2014). France had started a large public consultation to prepare its Law on the Digital Republic, with a wide area of topics to be addressed (Vie publique, 2019). It was considering regulation on copyright and cybersecurity.

Similar trends could be witnessed around the Union. For the EU, these national initiatives were a direct threat as they could lead to the creation of new barriers to trade and undo the digital remit that had been tackled over the years through the single market programme. The challenge was also about sovereignty in terms of who would write the rule book for digital interactions: governments or (foreign) online platforms.

A more offensive agenda for the EU was to show its value-added as a force to protect citizens and enhance the power of national governments. This ability for governments to rule over large platforms was being tested regularly. For instance, when Spain 2014 introduced a law requiring that online platforms, such as Google, would pay a fee to the association of Spanish editors when it would post links and excerpts of news articles, Google simply decided to snub the government and withdraw its services from Spain, while keeping it in other jurisdictions. This was a clear indication of the inability of a national government to impose its will on large platforms (NB: Interestingly, eight years later, on the back of the EU Copyright Directive, which introduced a similar mechanism for the whole of the Union, Google was back in Spain) (Lippolis, 2023).

National governments were facing difficulties with platforms like Uber, Amazon and Airbnb, which were escaping taxation and disrupting local businesses. For instance, in 2014, taxi drivers around major cities in the EU organised gridlocks and protests against Uber (Topping et al.,

2014). The Digital Single Market strategy was, therefore, an opportunity to show that EU-wide approaches and legislations were more effective counterweights to the market power of these large digital players.

In terms of focus, the DSM strategy learned from the experience of the Digital Agenda. It was a more compact and targeted proposal, with only 16 actions and three pillars, compared to the more than a hundred items of the Digital Agenda. Again, lessons had been drawn from the previous cycle. The key message of the DSM was rather straightforward: "Europe has the capabilities to lead in the global digital economy, but we are currently not making the most of them. Fragmentation and barriers that do not exist in the physical Single Market are holding the EU back" (COM(2015) 192 final, 2015a). The strategy proposed to move forward in three areas:

- Better access for consumers and businesses to online goods and services across Europe;
- Creating the right conditions for digital networks and services to flourish;
- Maximising the growth potential of our European Digital Economy.

To that extent, the DSM was rather business-friendly in its original design and oriented towards growth and jobs, and it is not surprising that it received support from trade associations, such as Business Europe (Business Europe, 2017). Rapidly, however, the priorities shifted towards legislation. The DSM proposed to put forward 16 actions, out of which 13 legislative proposals, most of them in 2016, which represented a significant effort in producing legislation in several areas. This included protective measures for consumers and measures to enhance pan-European offers through new copyright, telecom and audio-visual laws. This shock of legislation was coming on top of ongoing proposals that were leftovers from the previous College.

Early Successes

The DSM was overall successful as the Juncker Commission delivered all but one of its actions (the e-privacy regulation was proposed but not brought to a positive outcome). It benefited from the dynamics created by the Digital Agenda, which pioneered the idea that the digital space required some control and that pan-European efforts would be helpful to deliver a boost to national economies and control large digital players.

The initial boost for the DSM strategy, however, came from successfully concluding proposals coming from the previous Commission. The roaming and Net Neutrality provisions were agreed upon in June 2015 (European Commission, 2015b), barely one month after the strategy was adopted. The two measures were the only elements that could be rescued from the Telecom Single Market proposal of the previous Commission. Their adoption was a nice way to set the scene for the DSM, though.

The roaming regulation is one of the all-time successes of the EU (Blackman et al., 2018), very concretely demonstrating the value-added of EU regulation in bringing concrete benefits to consumers and contributing to the borderless feeling that the single market is meant to embody. Not surprisingly, it led to a very positive reception.

The Net Neutrality regulation established that all data traffic on a network should be treated indiscriminately, and Internet providers should not block, slow down or speed up content delivery at their discretion. This measure first pioneered in the USA (and then cancelled by President Trump, who had ascended to power in 2016) was also an important result for Internet content providers and for democracy in general and was also praised by activists.

Soon after, a breakthrough was obtained regarding the General Data Protection Regulation (GDPR), and a political agreement was reached between the Council and Parliament in December after 11 trilogue meetings, which is a very high number, highlighting the controversy of the proposal. The GDPR was hailed as a world-first to protect online privacy and would soon become a source of inspiration for the whole world.

Last among the leftovers from the Digital Agenda, the Network and Information Security Directive was adopted in July 2016, requiring that cybersecurity measures be taken across critical sectors and that national governments establish a minimum level of security and mandatory reporting of incidents (Clifford Chance, 2016). It was another major success for the EU to establish pan-European rules in an area so far closely guarded by national governments.

These legislative successes boosted the Commission's abilities to not only develop legislation but also build experience in terms of how to get those proposals to be rapidly adopted. In line with its plans, the Commission made several proposals in 2015 and 2016, intending to have them adopted by the end of 2017—as highlighted in its mid-term review of the

DSM (COM(2017) 228 final, 2017a). In 2015, it proposed harmonisation of different Value-Added-Tax regimes as well as the parcels directive to address obstacles for cross-border e-commerce. The same year, it proposed the cross-border portability of online content services, followed by a regulation to prevent geo-blocking, so that consumers would be able to access their online subscriptions to films, sports events, e-books, video games or music services when travelling in other EU countries.

From Market to Fundamental Rights

Interestingly, however, the focus of attention on these proposals shifted progressively, with more proposals being made by the Commission that addressed societal rather than pure economic issues. Whereas the Digital Single Market started with an economic/growth focus and included elements focusing on competitiveness like the policy linked to the "digitalisation of industry" or the "5G action plan", the rhetoric of the EU institutions started to shift in 2017 towards protecting consumers and tackling multiple risks coming from the digital world, with a focus on regulation (Heidebrecht, 2023).

Instead of promoting business integration and economic growth, the key benefits of the digital single market were presented as addressing citizens and consumers. For instance, in their press release on the adoption of the end of roaming, the EU institutions said, "The European Union is about bringing people together and making their lives easier. The end of roaming charges is a true European success story" (Council of the European Union, 2017). For the adoption of the telecommunication code, the Council declared, "Consumers will be better-protected thanks to the Code" (Council of the European Union, 2018).

The years of this shift in narrative correspond to an important change in the EU: the UK, a proponent of the single market and opponent to any form of deeper integration, had decided in 2016 to leave the Union. In the White Paper on "The Future of Europe" (COM(2017) 2025 final, 2017b), it was already noticeable that alternative paths were outlined whereby the focus was put on European values as the main vehicle for European unity,[4] at a time when the Brexit vote was questioning the integrity of the European integration process.

[4] The White Paper makes clear that no matter which scenarios for the future are preferred, common values will apply to the EU. "We want a society in which peace,

The French President, Emmanuel Macron, in his speech on Europe at the Sorbonne in 2017 that addressed European sovereignty and included digital technology as a key to it, expressed the wish to use regulations to protect companies and citizens and move away from a Darwinian situation: "And today, this digital continent has no standards, or more precisely, it has a law: the survival of the fittest. It is Europe's responsibility to define its regulatory framework so as not to effectively be subject to the survival of the fittest here" (Ouest France, 2017). Values and regulations were therefore put forward to address imbalances, moving away from the usual narrative of market integration as a key to prosperity. President Juncker, in his State of the Union 2017, expressed a priority to "better protect Europeans in the digital age".

The shift towards tackling societal problems and not only economic benefits was also the result of a series of crises that could be seen from the digital environment. Several scandals and controversies occurred in the 2014–2017 period. The Snowden revelations uncovered that large online platforms were channels of US mass surveillance. Several data breaches, from dating apps (Hern et al., 2015) to online games, showed the vulnerability of users to cyber-attacks and the absence of control over criminals and hackers. The Cambridge Analytica (Confessore, 2018) whistleblower showed that personal data could be used for political profiling and influence, with dramatic consequences for the US and UK democracies.

Facebook also had to admit it had conducted an emotional contagion experiment—and that it might be in line with its terms of reference (Meyer, 2014). Controversies went in many more directions. Google was subject to an antitrust case by the Commission for abuse of its dominant position, a case that lasted many years and, in the end, was considered as not having tamed Google dominance (Dorpe & Nylen, 2020), nor having prevented competitors to Google from disappearing from the market, despite a heavy fine in 2017 of more than 2 billion euros (European Commission, 2017c). Apple was accused of illegal State aid through extremely favourable tax conditions offered by Ireland. YouTube

freedom, tolerance and solidarity are placed above all else. We want to live in a democracy with a diversity of views and a critical, independent and free press. We want to be free to speak our mind and be sure that no individual or institution is above the law. We want a Union in which all citizens and all Member States are treated equally. We want to create a better life for our children than we had for ourselves. Regardless of which of the scenarios presented here ends up closest to reality, these values and aspirations will continue to bind Europeans and are worth fighting for". (emphasis added).

was accused of amplifying terrorist content on its platform (Whittaker et al., 2021). The list could continue, but it is illustrative of the breadth of problems identified and linked to digital activities.

A third element also came from a pragmatic realisation that consensus among Member States could be reached more effectively based on common values and the taming of large digital players originating from the USA. This could be seen through concrete examples, like data protection or copyright.

After several years of negotiations and revisions, the GDPR was adopted on 14 April 2016, and it came into effect on 25 May 2018. The GDPR replaced the Data Protection Directive 95/46/EC and introduced more robust and consistent data protection rules throughout the EU. It was designed to give individuals greater control over their data and to address the challenges posed by the increasingly digital and interconnected world. Concluding the GDPR legislation was not easy. Lobbying was fierce and unprecedented (D'Cunha, 2020). It took over two years and three months and 3999 amendments—plenty of them helpfully drafted by corporate lobbyists—for the European Parliament to settle on its preferred text in March 2014 (D'Mello, 2018). The proposal was legitimised through the Snowden scandal based on fundamental rights rather than economic benefits, referring to the Charter of Fundamental Rights and building consensus among Member States based on common values and digital constitutionalism (de Gregorio, 2021).

Another significant legislative battle took place around the Copyright Directive between 2016 and 2019, with a fierce attempt from large technology companies to derail the proposal, with Google reportedly spending millions of euros lobbying the Parliament against this law (Smirke, 2018). Whereas the Communication of the Commission preparing the proposal had an economic logic and expressed the view that: "A copyright framework that offers a high level of protection is the basis of the global competitiveness of Europe's creative industries" (COM(2015) 626 final, 2015c), the final press release by the Council upon adoption of the Directive gave less prominence to economic benefits and stated that: "we will therefore unlock the opportunities of the digital world, both for creators, whose rights should be fully respected and for the European citizens, who should take advantage of the benefits brought by the Digital Single Market". In the process, a confrontation had taken place whereby large (non-EU) platforms were arguing that the copyright would kill the Internet, and (EU) rights holders were asking for fair remuneration. And the European Parliament, in its very tight final vote, had shown its democratic maturity and its ability to prioritise European interests in front of American platforms (see Chapter 9).

A fourth element in the shift away from the market and towards values and citizens also came from a change in the Commission, with a new Commissioner, Mariya Gabriel, from Bulgaria, who was appointed in 2017 in the digital portfolio after Vice-President Georgieva moved to the World Bank prompting Commissioner Oettinger to replace her and to leave his post. Commissioner Gabriel, a former MEP from the Committee on Civil Liberties, Justice and Home Affairs, had a different profile from her predecessor.

Whereas Commissioner Oettinger had insisted on the digitalisation of industry, Commissioner Gabriel had more interest in societal issues. As she answered in her hearing in front of the Parliament: "I will pay special attention to the challenges that digital transformation poses for our European society and its social model. We must, firstly, ensure that digital innovations bring maximum benefits to all our citizens while respecting European democratic and social values" (European Parliament, 2017). This change of leadership contributed to a change of focus in the narrative of the Digital Single Market and paved the way to further integration not through economic convergence but rather through shared values for the benefit of consumers and citizens.

In conclusion, the Digital Single Market was a turning point for the EU in its ability to adopt legislation for the digital space. It was a significant success in terms of delivery of its programme, in contrast to the Digital Agenda, with all proposals but one having been adopted by the end of the Juncker Commission. This was achieved through further emphasis on legislation, EU values, fundamental rights and benefits for citizens rather than a focus on market integration and economic growth. It put the Union on course to becoming the leading regulatory force in the digital space.

Completing the Cycle: Shaping Europe's Digital Future and the Digital Decade Policy Programme

The election of Ursula von der Leyen as President of the Commission came as a surprise, as she had not been running the European parliamentary elections. A leading German politician, born in Brussels from one of the first German high-ranking civil servants in the European Commission, she speaks fluent German, French and English, having studied in London and lived in the USA. The vision she presented in her political priorities before her confirmation by the European Parliament (Leyen, 2019) was full of optimism and confidence, presenting the EU as an "aspiration of a world full of new technologies and age-old values. Of a Europe that takes the global lead on the major challenges of our times".

The digital transformation was introduced among President von der Leyen's six political priorities as a Europe fit for the digital age, where she outlined the playbook for her mandate: "To release that potential, we have to find our European way, balancing the flow and wide use of data while preserving high privacy, security, safety and ethical standards. We already achieved this with the General Data Protection Regulation, and many countries have followed our path". What was interesting was the assertiveness of a genuinely European perspective on digital transformation.

The structure of her Commission reflected the importance of the digital file, with an Executive Vice-President, Margrethe Vestager, from Denmark, tasked with leading it and a Commissioner, Thierry Breton, from France, in charge of the single market and supervising DG Connect, the department responsible for everything digital in the Commission. Commissioner Breton was not the first choice for Commissioner for this portfolio, but he was called upon after Sylvie Goulard failed to be confirmed by the Parliament on the back of accusations of conflicts of interest with the US digital sector.

Breton had hands-on experience in the digital sector as he came directly from the industry and had been CEO of the IT multinational Atos for more than ten years. He resigned from his position at Atos and sold all his shares in the company to take his position in the Commission. In his hearing in front of the Parliament, Thierry Breton explained, "We have to work on our technological sovereignty", and he stressed the need to regulate tech and cyberspace and to address the challenges arising from competition from outside the EU. This focus on sovereignty and regulation echoed the French President's Sorbonne speech of 2017. The concept of digital sovereignty was also put forward by Germany, which, in July 2020, in its official programme for its presidency of the European Council, announced its intention "to establish digital sovereignty as a leitmotiv of European digital policy" (Germany's Presidency of the Council of the European Union, 2020, p. 8).

By contrast, in her hearing, Executive Vice-President Vestager put more emphasis on consumers and pledged not to make Europe more like China or the USA but more like itself, here echoing von der Leyen. She also kept the competition portfolio and her pro-market credentials, which were also reflected in her presentation. She was also more programmatic and confirmed the plans announced by the President, e.g. regulation on platforms on Artificial Intelligence. The notion of "sovereignty" contains both power and legitimacy (Floridi, 2020), both industrial strength and values. The assertiveness of both Breton and Vestager reflected this complementarity, and their respective focuses offered a common basis for the two heads of the EU executive in the digital realm. And they got rapidly into a delivery mode with a hasty series of announcements, strategies and new legislations.

A Tale of Two Strategies: The European Path to the Digital Transformation

Interestingly, the strategy of the von der Leyen (VDL) Commission regarding digital transformation was outlined in two steps. First, the "shaping Europe's digital future" strategy was adopted a few months after the inauguration of the VDL Commission. One year later, the 2030 Digital Compass communication was adopted, which provided a complementary, less programmatic and more architectural strategy for EU policy for the next decade. In parallel, the EU discourses about digital sovereignty were reinforced and made this concept more central to the EU strategy.

The Communication "Shaping Europe's Digital Future" (European Commission, 2020a) came in February 2020, two months after the Communication on the European Green Deal, and outlined the list of proposals that would be made in that area. The text was rather focused and simple, by comparison with the Digital Single Market strategy and the Digital Agenda, and was not based on long consultations or impact assessments. It proposed to focus on three priorities: (i) technology that works for people, (ii) a fair and competitive economy, and (iii) an open, democratic and sustainable society. These were translated into 15 initiatives. In addition, it had a section on "Europe as a digital leader" with three initiatives. The plan was, therefore, less about grand statements and more about a business-like plan for actions, but it already underlined key themes that would imprint on the rest of the mandate.

A few of the initiatives mentioned were only mere implementations of the funding programmes decided in the multiannual financial framework, like "Building and deploying cutting-edge joint digital capacities" or "Destination Earth", an initiative to develop a high-precision digital model of Earth. At the same time, the strategy contained important guiding elements and underlined notably that competition policy alone cannot address all the systemic problems that may arise in the platform economy, thus anticipating the Digital Markets Act. Or it underlined the objective of developing a "European way to digital transformation which enhances our democratic values, respects our fundamental rights, and contributes to a sustainable, climate-neutral and resource-efficient economy, very much anticipating the declaration on Digital Rights and Principles that would come a few years later". However, it is fair to say that this initial strategy did not at all mention the concept of digital sovereignty.

On the same day as the communication on shaping Europe's digital future was adopted, however, the data strategy was also proposed, at the initiative of Commissioner Breton, with more details on facts, figures and how it would be delivered through a combination of legislation and industrial policy, creating a single market for data and funding data spaces. Interestingly, this initiative referred to technological sovereignty and was linked to the industrial strategy of the EU (COM(2020) 66 final, 2020b). Commissioner Breton explained that most of the data was in the hands of few companies, and he wanted to change that: "My goal is to prepare ourselves so the data will be used for Europeans, by Europeans and with our values" (Espinoza & Fleming, 2020).

Soon after, the Commission made proposals for the Data Governance Act, a cross-sectoral instrument that aims to regulate the re-use of publicly/held protected data by boosting data sharing through the regulation of novel data intermediaries and by encouraging the sharing of data for altruistic purposes (European Commission, 2022). It also created the Data Governance Board with Member States' representatives designated to assist the Commission. The Data Governance Act was negotiated rapidly and entered into force in 2023. The Data Act (European Commission, 2023a) was proposed in 2023 to empower users of data—notably from connected devices—to access the data they generate and to create fair conditions for the exploitation of the data. It was negotiated in less than a year to become applicable in 2025 (see Chapter 6).

Another policy document that was rapidly delivered in 2020 was the White Paper on Artificial Intelligence. It launched a public consultation on key elements of the EU policy on AI. In particular, it put forward a European approach to AI, "which aims to promote Europe's innovation capacity in the area of AI while supporting the development and uptake of ethical and trustworthy AI across the EU economy. AI should work for people and be a force for good in society" (COM(2020) 65 final, 2020c). It also underlined that the strategy should "increase Europe's technological sovereignty in key enabling technologies and infrastructures for the data economy".

However, while the von der Leyen Commission had started to deliver some of its initiatives in the digital remit, the COVID-19 pandemic changed the dynamics and created a new impetus necessary to respond to the new situation. The extreme measures that were adopted across the EU to slow down the COVID-19 spreading, and notably the confinement of whole populations, created a new situation where digital technologies became even more essential, given that they could be operated remotely. Online services were, during the confinement, the only means for companies and public services to continue functioning, and this prompted not only an acceleration of the digitalisation of the EU economy and society but also revealed worrying dependencies.

For instance, automotive production lines had to slow down and sometimes even stop due to a shortage of chips and the industry called for more production in the EU (ACEA, 2021). Similar dependencies suddenly were becoming transparent for several services that the EU would need but not produce or control. This is what Commissioner Breton made clear in a speech at the Hannover Messe organised in 2020 in digital format due to the coronavirus pandemic: "We need to be realistic, without naivety: The coronavirus crisis will accelerate major trends at work on our planet. It confronts us with our overreliance on others in critical areas – both geopolitically and economically. It invites us to take a fresh look at Europe's place in the world. [...] It is time to take our destiny into our own hands. [...] Data, microelectronics and connectivity are the cornerstones of our digital sovereignty" (Breton, 2020).

As a result, the Commission put forward a second strategy in 2021: the Digital Compass communication. Producing two digital strategies in such a short timeframe highlighted the unprecedented pace of change in the importance of technology and the growing prominence of the considerations relating to dependency and sovereignty. This time, the objective was to establish a longer-term plan and a vision until 2030 with the 2030 Digital Compass: the European Way for the Digital Decade.

While the first strategy of the von der Leyen Commission aimed to *develop* a European way of digital transformation, the Digital Compass *defined* this European way and outlined a comprehensive plan to deliver it. In short, the communication explains that "The European way to a digitalised economy and society is about solidarity, prosperity, and sustainability, anchored in the empowerment of its citizens and businesses, ensuring the security and resilience of its digital ecosystem and supply chains". It explains that two dimensions are required: (i) an industrial agenda to develop technology and digital infrastructures and address dependencies and promote leadership; (ii) principles, rules and values intrinsic to the European way (COM(2021) 118 final, 2021). These two dimensions were delivered through two policy vehicles: the Digital Decade Policy Programme and the Declaration on Digital Rights and Principles.

The Digital Decade

In January 2021, the European Commission proposed a Declaration on Digital Rights and Principles (2023/C 23/01, 2023a). The declaration was prepared through wide-ranging public consultation, a Eurobarometer survey, workshops and analysis, including input from targeted groups—in particular, people with disabilities, older people, consumer groups, people in rural communities and digital rights advocates. It was subsequently negotiated between the three institutions, and it was solemnly signed and proclaimed by the presidents of the three institutions (Palmer, 2022) in December 2022 as the EU's commitment to a secure, safe and sustainable digital transformation that puts people at the centre, in line with EU core values and fundamental rights. The declaration is structured around six themes:

1. Putting people and their rights at the centre of the digital transformation
2. Supporting solidarity and inclusion
3. Ensuring freedom of choice online
4. Fostering participation in the digital public space
5. Increasing the safety, security and empowerment of individuals
6. Promoting the sustainability of the digital future

It explicitly refers to digital sovereignty in its preamble: "The EU way for the digital transformation of our societies and economy encompasses in particular digital sovereignty openly, respect for fundamental rights, the rule of law and democracy, inclusion, accessibility, equality, sustainability, resilience, security, improving quality of life, the availability of services and respect of everyone's rights and aspirations. It should contribute to a dynamic, resource-efficient, and fair economy and society in the EU".

Commentators broadly welcomed the declaration and noticed that the declaration was largely in line with previous EU legal documents but also underlined that through the negotiations with Parliament and Council, the Preamble included an extensive reference to the "union of values", which was considered a "significant, even if only symbolic, departure from the approach that sees digital matters solely through the lens of the Digital Single Market" (Warso, 2022). Scholars see the declaration as a step forward within the process of constitutionalisation of the digital environment in Europe (Cocito & de Hert, 2023).

The second leg of the new EU strategy was delivered with the Digital Decade Policy Programme, which was signed in December 2022. The 2030 Digital Compass communication had proposed a compass made of four cardinal points: digital skills, digital infrastructures, digitalisation of business and digitalisation of the public sector, and announced targets that would underpin these four areas and give objectives for the whole of the EU. It also announced a Policy Programme to deliver a governance mechanism for the digital decade and a declaration on Digital Rights and Principles. It finally promoted multi-country projects as a concrete mechanism to foster cross-border projects and collaboration between Member States.

The plan was made tangible thanks to the Recovery and Resilience Facility (Regulation (EU) 2021/241, 2021), created to address the economic recession caused by the COVID-19 pandemic through EU-level borrowing, and notably the obligation to dedicate 20% of this facility to digital investments—a boost of around 120 billion euros. The "Path to the Digital Decade" set out the concrete digital targets which the Union as a whole is expected to achieve by the end of the decade. These digital targets for 2030 are based on the same four cardinal points: digital skills, digital infrastructures, digitalisation of businesses and public services. The Digital Decade Policy Programme 2030 then established a governance framework to achieve common objectives and targets at the level of the

EU through an annual cooperation mechanism involving the Commission and Member States. It includes measurement of progress towards the 2030 targets, a yearly report on the State of the Digital Decade to assess progress and provide recommendations and created a new legal structure to support the implementation of multi-country projects, the European Digital Infrastructure Consortium (European Commission, 2023b).

Interestingly, the policy programme introduces in Article 3 its general objectives and spells out that one of them is to "ensure the Union's digital sovereignty openly, in particular by secure and accessible digital and data infrastructures capable of efficiently storing, transmitting and processing vast volumes of data that enable other technological developments, supporting the competitiveness and sustainability of the Union's industry and economy, in particular of SMEs, and the resilience of the Union's value chains, as well as fostering the startup ecosystem and the smooth functioning of the European digital innovation hubs". It is also made clear in this article that the Member States shall take account of the Declaration on Digital Rights and Principles, thus confirming the two aspects of sovereignty: in terms of economic power and resilience and in terms of identity and values. With this overarching plan, the Commission had provided a narrative for its action and distinguished itself from the USA and China, defining its distinctive path for digital transformation. But to bring flesh to the bone, it was also needed to deliver a series of legislations and policies. And this is precisely what the Union did over two years.

Delivering the EU Digital Rule Book

In parallel with making the European way to digital transformation more explicit, the EU advanced very concretely in ticking the box of all meaningful areas of digital legislation during the von der Leyen Commission. Building on the strong basis of the Digital Single Market strategy, it continued delivering proposals and having them adopted by the Council and Parliament.

The EU adopted ground-breaking regulations in several areas: platform legislation, with the Digital Services Act and the Digital Markets Act; cybersecurity with the NIS2, the Cyber Resilience Act, the Cyber Solidarity Act; Artificial Intelligence with the AI Act, data—through Data Governance Act and Data Act, digital identity with the EU Digital Identity Wallet, media with the European Media Freedom Act (see part II of the book). This came on top of already adopted legislation in the area of telecommunication, copyright, data and audio-visual. These legislative acts were designed using regulations as legal vehicles instead of directives, the main instrument in the 1990s and 2000s. Regulations are directly applicable legal acts; they offer a legal framework that applies in the same manner in the whole of the Union, thus avoiding in principle differences in interpretation and disparities in the implementation of the law. They are, however, normally more difficult to design and to get adopted precisely because they require the acceptance of Member States without them being able to bring national nuances in the way that directives would allow.

To that extent, the design of recent EU laws deserves to be mentioned in terms of how it gave the Commission an increasingly central role while also preserving Member States' responsibilities by creating a large number of boards. For instance, in the area of platform regulation, the Digital Services Act and the Digital Markets Act have created national authorities to supervise platforms, but they gave the Commission the primacy of implementation (European Commission, 2024b). Similarly, the AI Act led to the creation of the AI Office, giving the Commission the prime role when dealing with Generative AI while also creating national authorities. This two-tier system can also be found in other areas of recent legislation, with the Data Governance Board, the EMFA Board and the CHIPS Board.

Compared to the initial steps in regulating the digital space, this model is a marked evolution. The models of governance identified in the chapter started from largely a laissez-faire approach, moving then to a more self-regulatory approach to one characterised by more brutality (Miadzvetskaya, 2023)—using fines as a means to gain power and central oversight at the EU level.

The new model of governance resulting from the most recent EU digital laws is a hybrid construct. It gives primacy to the Commission and boosts its federal character, but at the same time, it preserves a role for the Member States, highlighting the need for continued internal legitimacy still required for the EU institution. The way the EU power is exerted over online private actors is through the threat of fines, which is legitimised through a system of due diligence and legal scrutiny by the Courts, very much like has been applied in competition policy.

This new generation of digital legislation also contains innovative approaches in its regulatory technique. Contrary to more classic legislation, like telecom, where regulators tell operators what to do, the approach followed by platform, AI or cyber regulation companies is based on auditable self-enforcement of obligations. The burden is for market actors to show compliance with legal obligations based on standards, codes of conduct, reports and other types of guidance and interpretation. Regulators only verify compliance, may dispute adequacy and may resort to hefty fines in case of breach. Here again, a centralised and uniform regulation is combined with decentralised modes of delivery.

This regulatory agenda not only produced a quasi-federal role for the EU in the digital space but it was also used to deliver sovereignty in terms of competitiveness and economic power. This is another originality of the recent legislative agenda that regulations were used to deliver industrial policy. This is very clear with the European Chips Act (European Commission, 2023c), which aims to support large-scale production capacity building and innovation to address semiconductor shortages and strengthen Europe's technological leadership. With more than € 43 billion of public and private investments, it introduced a set of measures to prepare, anticipate and swiftly respond to any future supply chain disruptions, building notably on the European Semiconductor Board to coordinate between the Commission, Member States and stakeholders. One could have expected such an industrial policy agenda to be delivered without the need for legislation. This would overlook the tensions between governments and limitations for budgetary support in that area (see Chapter 12). Regulation was found as a mechanism to create consensus and trust between national governments and to build a stronger industrial policy agenda.

Further initiatives were developed in the area of cloud computing,[5] quantum[6] and AI (European Commission, 2024c, which aimed at boosting EU technological leadership in line with the objectives and targets of the 2030 Digital Compass. As outlined in the story of the von der Leyen Commission, the institution considered it has delivered: "We set a clear vision at the start of the mandate: ensure that our society benefits from technology and that innovation boosts our competitiveness while minimising risks for citizens. We fulfilled our mandate" (European Commission, 2024d), putting an emphasis not only on legislation but also on significant results in terms of deployment of its digital infrastructures like 5G connectivity, investments in supercomputers and more generally in R&D.

Importantly, this regulatory agenda was designed with global interactions in mind, highlighting the external legitimacy of EU digital sovereignty being at play. At the Davos Forum in 2021, von der Leyen offered to join forces with partners to codify the digital space: "Together, we could create a digital economy rulebook that is valid worldwide. It goes from data protection and privacy to the security of critical infrastructure. A body of rules based on our values: human rights and pluralism, inclusion, and the protection of privacy". Embracing the "Brussels effect", European leaders have kept underlining that the EU legislative agenda would be fit for the rest of the world, too.

In short, the Commission has been extremely successful in driving a regulatory agenda that delivered a new digital sovereignty for the Union and new levels of integration. It was strongly based on a European vision for digital transformation that reinforced the consistency between the

[5] The EU has developed a cloud strategy with a number of initiatives, notably the setting up of the European Alliance on Industrial Data, Edge and Cloud aims to shape the next generation of secure, low-carbon and interoperable cloud and edge services and infrastructure; an Important Project of Common European Interest that will federate energy-efficient and trustworthy cloud infrastructures and related services and the funding of SIMPL, an open source, sustainable and secure middleware that will enable cloud-to-edge federations and be the core software powering Data Spaces otherwise funded by the EU and a cloud rulebook to facilitate procurement of cloud services.

[6] The EU has taken a series of initiatives in this area, providing 1 billion euro funding through the Quantum Flagship, and establishing a Joint Undertaking for the development of a quantum communication infrastructure covering the whole EU (EuroQCI). In 2023, a number of Member States signed a joint declaration aiming at making the EU the ultimate 'quantum valley' in the world the leading region globally for quantum excellence and innovation.

various legislations (Roberts et al., 2021) to the point that it may appear as a proper rule book. The EU was successful in bringing this agenda to all areas of the digital space, including for industrial policy purposes. It used hybrid forms of governance to underpin internal legitimacy and international assertiveness to promote external legitimacy. However, with the return of Donald Trump as President of the USA in 2025, and stark support for the US "tech bros", the CEOs of the leading US digital companies, this regulatory agenda has found a clear challenger in terms of its implementation. In August and December 2025, the Trump administration and the Office of the U.S. Trade Representative issued official statements and social media posts threatening to impose tariffs and export restrictions on countries, primarily in the EU and the UK, that implement digital taxes or regulations deemed discriminatory towards American tech companies.

And digital regulation has also been subject to a call for simplification, with notably the Draghi report pointing at a lack of EU competitiveness in the digital sector and hinting as excessive regulation. The proposal for a digital omnibus end 2025 has thus been presented by some as the end of the so-called Brussels effect with in its place a US deregulatory agenda having the upper hand (Politico, 2025). The European Commission has defended its sovereign right to establish its own rules, and even though it remained prudent in using the full scope of its powers, did not stop enforcing its rules, adopting a number of decision and fines totalling 3.5 billion in 2025 alone (Soares, 2026). The Commission also repeatedly explained that the simplification agenda was in the interest of European industry, and its competitiveness and not a reaction to demands from the USA. In parallel, the call for digital sovereignty has intensified, with a shift towards home-grown industrial capabilities in the digital area, and not just regulatory power, as illustrated by the Franco-German summit on Digital Sovereignty in December 2025. The 2025 AI Continent Action Plan, as well as industrial proposals in 2026 for quantum, microelectronics and cloud illustrate this shift in focus.

Towards a Digital Union?

The historical overview of the development of the EU digital law and policy offers a rich perspective not only on the successive attempts and developments of many areas. It shows a clear evolution whereby a series of stages could be identified: i) a large laissez-faire agenda, copied from US policies and focusing on technology and market creation through deregulation; ii) failure of a Member States-led agenda to become the most successful knowledge economy in the world; iii) creation of an EU policy space for the digital agenda with mixed results; iv) acceleration of a regulatory agenda to develop a single digital market that succeeded on the back not of some market integration narrative but rather one based on shared values for the benefit of consumers and citizens; v) delivery of a comprehensive rule book and economic governance aiming at EU digital sovereignty and global regulatory leadership[7]; vi) challenges in implementation and opposition from the US authorities, and reinforced industrial efforts towards digital sovereignty.

The chapter also highlighted how the EU was able, over time, to increase its powers quite significantly and how the Commission has become the effective global regulator of some of the most powerful economic entities in the world, supervising the behaviour and market practices of large online platforms and providers of Artificial Intelligence, and developing standards for the whole digital sector. These increased powers are greater than what the Commission could achieve with the GDPR or with telecom regulation, where national authorities have the upper hand. These powers can, however, be considered as hybrid as they are shared to some extent because Member States are represented in boards and have some control at the national level, too. The Commission's powers are, therefore, possibly more tolerated than desired, and they are used to enhance national outreach, too. And their legitimacy is attacked notably by the US administration, which tries to use trade coercion and to leverage tech dependencies to weaken their effects.

In many ways, the culmination of efforts in the digital area comes close to a situation that one could characterise as a Digital Union, with all the parameters of an integrated market, with common rules, common narratives and an EU-level governance. The massive scope of EU digital regulation, which by now touches upon virtually all areas of the digital space, from cybersecurity to media, and the increased consistency of the narrative based on digital sovereignty has made this policy area a remarkable case of European integration and a source of inspiration for many jurisdictions. Admittedly, the ability of the EU to effectively implement its legislative powers still has to be tested, notably in front of threats from

[7] Interestingly, this analysis broadly corresponds to the stages that De Gregorio (2020) identified in his thesis of digital constitutionalism.

the USA and of a simplification agenda that could undo some of the digital rulebook components.

These historical developments offer telling lessons for the analysis of European integration. First of all, the chapter could verify the validity of the functionalist analysis of integration in the sense that digital policies only emerged in earnest in front of crises: the digital agenda was born from the failure of the Lisbon strategy and the failure of European companies like Nokia in the ICT sector; legislations for cybersecurity rules and data protection or platforms were addressing identified problems affecting citizens and consumers—from surveillance to cyber-attacks and illegal content. The success of the GDPR was also an opportunity for spillover in other areas of digital policy, going into AI or platform regulation, and subsequently, one trilogue at a time, the EU remit would soon cover the full spectrum of the digital space.

The chapter also showed that intergovernmentalist approaches are not absent from the historical development of EU digital law and policy. Failure to build a telecom single market or success in setting up an AI office or a Joint Undertaking for joint purchasing of supercomputers highlights that the interest of the national authorities is part of the story. Member States were ready to use the EU institutions to magnify their might in front of very powerful economic actors in the digital sector, which they could not tame by themselves alone. Boards made of national representatives were created in all policy areas to maintain some role at the national level. It remains to be seen, however, if Member States will be able to keep their influence or whether the degree of EU integration in so many areas and the core role of the Commission will not be conducive to increasing centralisation of power in a way reminiscent of what happened for competition law, for instance, and reduce intergovernmental explanations and rather promote institutional theories, especially if the Digital Decade policy programme is successful in organising the EU economic governance of the digital sector. Reciprocally, failure by the EU level to effectively implement its new set of digital rules could lead to the national level authorities taking back power.

However, and even though lack of competitiveness and dependencies towards the USA and China has also emerged as another narrative most recently, the most striking element in this historical overview is perhaps the importance of the EU narrative that developed based on a common EU identity and the progressive definition of a European way of digital transformation based on common values, such as those provided in the EU Declaration on Digital Rights and Principles. This showed that constructivist theories of European integration are much needed to understand the success of the EU in the area of digital policies.

The use of concepts like digital sovereignty by the policymakers themselves and the attempt to develop a European approach distinct from those of competing regions, like the USA or China, was instrumental in convincing lawmakers to agree on new legislation and to move together in a more constitutionalist path, whereby technology and regulation are derived from common principles. The chapter showed that these common narratives and shared values played an essential role in accelerating EU integration in the digital space and providing legitimacy to the legislative agenda that would spill over into several related areas. These narratives were also underpinning a global ambition to adopt first-of-a-kind regulations with the hope that others would follow.

To conclude, one should also recognise that the history of the EU digital law and policy is still in the making. There are significant implementation challenges ahead, and the success in advancing EU integration in that field will need to be confirmed through concrete results. The EU digital sector has not become more competitive globally yet; the EU has not advanced massively towards the 2030 targets of the Digital Compass, and the "Brussels effect"—while tangible for data protection and noticeable at the level of global policy debates—is increasingly put into question. Conversely, EU integration in the digital sector may also lead to further spillovers, not only in remaining areas of national dominance in the digital sector (like telecom) but also in other sectors, like cleantech or defence. In her political guidelines, the re-elected President of the European Commission Ursula von der Leyen explained that her mandate will decide whether Europe will shape its future or let it be shaped by events or by others. The ability of the Union to defend its digital sovereignty, in terms of the implementation of its rulebook, as well as in its capacity to reduce its technological dependencies, will be a key test for the European project as a whole.

Bibliography

ACEA. (2021, October 21). *Chip shortage: Auto industry calls for more EU-made semiconductor*. https://www.acea.auto/message-dg/chip-shortage-auto-industry-calls-for-more-eu-made-semiconductors/

Atomico. (2024). *Welcome to the State of European Tech 2024, the definitive take on Europe's tech ecosystem*. https://www.stateofeuropeantech.com/

Bertarini, B. (2023). *European Union digital single market: Legal framework and challenges*. FrancoAngeli. https://www.econstor.eu/bitstream/10419/279839/1/1865944661.pdf

Blackman, C., Forge, S., Gouarderes, F., & Cujkova, J. (2018, November). *Roaming: One year after implementation*. https://carloscoelho.eu/ed/files/roaming-one-year-after-implementation.pdf

Breton, T. (2020, July 15). *Speech by Commissioner Thierry Breton at Hannover Messe Digital Days*. https://ec.europa.eu/commission/presscorner/detail/en/speech_20_1362

Business Europe. (2017, May 4). *Letter to Mr Andrus Ansip*. https://www.businesseurope.eu/sites/buseur/files/media/public_letters/imco/2017-05-04_mbe-a.ansip_-_dsm_midterm_review.pdf

Cerulus, L., & Kayali, L. (2019, July 18). *The Juncker Commission's digital legacy*. https://www.politico.eu/article/juncker-commission-digital-legacy-policies-tech-social-media-data/

Clifford Chance. (2016, September). *NIS Directive adopted: Cyber-security taken to the next level*. https://www.cliffordchance.com/content/dam/cliffordchance/briefings/2016/09/nis-directive-adopted-cybersecurity-taken-to-the-next-level.pdf

Cocito, C., & de Hert, P. (2023). The transformative nature of the EU Declaration on digital rights and principles: Replacing the old paradigm (Normative equivalency of rights). *Computer Law & Society Review, 50*.

Confessore, N. (2018, April 4). *Cambridge Analytica and Facebook: The scandal and the fallout so far*. https://archive.is/Vc1ea#selection-4661.0-4661.68

Council of the European Union. (2017, June 14). *End of roaming charges in the EU: Joint statement by the European Parliament, the Council and the Commission*. Retrieved from Press releases: https://www.consilium.europa.eu/en/press/press-releases/2017/06/14/joint-statement-end-of-roaming-charges-in-eu/

Council of the European Union. (2018, December 4). *Better connectivity: EU adopts telecoms reform*. https://www.consilium.europa.eu/en/press/press-releases/2018/12/04/better-connectivity-eu-adopts-telecoms-reform/

D'Cunha, C. (2020, November 2). *The GDPR was the most lobbied law in EU history. DSA: Hold my beer*. https://www.linkedin.com/pulse/gdpr-most-lobbied-law-eu-history-dsa-hold-my-beer-christian-d-cunha/

de Gregorio, G. (2021). The rise of digital constitutionalism in the European Union. *International Journal of Constitutional Law, 19*(1), 41–70.

D'Mello, Y. (2018, May 3). *How did we get there, a brief history of the GDPR*. https://aithority.com/technology/analytics/how-did-we-get-here-a-brief-history-of-the-gdpr/

Dorpe, S., & Nylen, L. (2020, October 22). *Europe failed to tame Google. Can the US do any better?* https://www.politico.eu/article/europe-failed-to-tame-google-can-the-us-do-any-better/

Espinoza, J., & Fleming, S. (2020, January 14). *Europe urged to use industrial data trove to steal march on rivals.* https://www.ft.com/content/8187a268-3494-11ea-a6d3-9a26f8c3cba4

Euractiv. (2010, June 9). *EU wins roaming battle against telecoms giants.* https://www.euractiv.com/section/digital/news/eu-wins-roaming-battle-against-telecoms-giants/

European Commission. (1997). *ESPRIT success stories for the information society.* https://cordis.europa.eu/article/id/9407-esprit-success-stories-for-the-information-society

European Commission. (2009, June 18). *Communication from the Commission to the European Parliament and the Council: Internet governance: The next steps.* https://eur-lex.europa.eu/LexUriServ/LexUriServ.do?uri=COM:2009:0277:FIN:EN:PDF

European Commission. (2010, December 15). *Digital Agenda: eGovernment Action Plan to smooth access to public services across the EU.* https://ec.europa.eu/commission/presscorner/detail/en/ip_10_1718

European Commission. (2012). *Communication from the Commission to the European Parliament, the Council, the European Economic and Social Committee and the Committee of the Regions European Strategy for a Better Internet for Children.* https://eur-lex.europa.eu/legal-content/EN/ALL/?uri=CELEX:52012DC0196

European Commission. (2013, September 25). *Commission launches 'Opening up Education' to boost innovation and digital skills in schools and universities.* https://ec.europa.eu/commission/presscorner/detail/en/ip_13_859

European Commission. (2014, May 28). *Scoreboard 2014—Progress Report Digital Agenda Targets 2014.* https://digital-strategy.ec.europa.eu/en/library/scoreboard-2014-progress-report-digital-agenda-targets-2014

European Commission. (2015a, May 6). *Communication from the Commission to the European Parliament, the Council, the European Economic and Social Committee and the Committee of the Regions A Digital Single Market Strategy for Europe.* https://eur-lex.europa.eu/legal-content/EN/TXT/?uri=celex%3A52015DC0192

European Commission. (2015b, June 30). *Commission welcomes agreement to end roaming charges and to guarantee an open Internet.* https://ec.europa.eu/commission/presscorner/detail/en/ip_15_5265

European Commission. (2015c, December 9). *Communication to the Council, the Parliament, the Economic and Social Committee and the Committee of the Regions: 'Towards a modern, more European copyright framework'*. https://eur-lex.europa.eu/legal-content/EN/TXT/?uri=COM%3A2015%3A626%3AFIN

European Commission. (2017a, May 10). *Communication from the Commission to the European Parliament, the Council, the European Economic and Social Committee and the Committee of the Regions on the Mid-Term Review on the implementation of the Digital Single Market Strategy A Connected Digital S*. https://eur-lex.europa.eu/legal-content/EN/TXT/?uri=COM%3A2017%3A228%3AFIN

European Commission. (2017b, March 1). *White paper on the future of Europe: Reflections and scenarios for the EU27 by 2025*. https://eur-lex.europa.eu/legal-content/EN/ALL/?uri=celex:52017DC2025

European Commission. (2017c, June 27). *Antitrust: Commission fines Google €2.42 billion for abusing dominance as search engine by giving illegal advantage to own comparison shopping service—Factsheet*. https://ec.europa.eu/commission/presscorner/detail/en/memo_17_1785

European Commission. (2019). *25 years of digital Europe—The EU's role in high-tech development*. https://ec.europa.eu/information_society/doc/digitaleurope-historial.pdf

European Commission. (2020a). *Shaping Europe's digital future*. https://commission.europa.eu/document/download/84c05739-547a-4b86-9564-76e834dc7a49_en?filename=communication-shaping-europes-digital-future-feb2020_en.pdf

European Commission. (2020b, February 19). *Communication from the Commission to the European Parliament, the Council, the European Economic and Social Committee and the Committee of the Regions A European Strategy for Data*. https://eur-lex.europa.eu/legal-content/EN/TXT/?uri=CELEX%3A52020DC0066

European Commission. (2020c, February 19). *White paper on artificial intelligence. On artificial intelligence—A European approach to excellence and trust*. https://commission.europa.eu/system/files/2020-02/commission-white-paper-artificial-intelligence-feb2020_en.pdf

European Commission. (2021, March 3). *Communication from the Commission to the European Parliament, the Council, the European Economic and Social Committee and the Committee of the Regions 2030 Digital Compass: the European way for the Digital Decade*. https://eur-lex.europa.eu/legal-content/en/TXT/?uri=CELEX%3A52021DC0118

European Commission. (2022). *Data Governance Act explained*. https://digital-strategy.ec.europa.eu/en/policies/data-governance-act-explained

European Commission. (2023a). *Data Act explained*. https://digital-strategy.ec.europa.eu/en/factpages/data-act-explained

European Commission. (2023b). *European Digital Infrastructure Consortium (EDIC)*. https://digital-strategy.ec.europa.eu/en/policies/edic

European Commission. (2023c, November 30). *European Chips Act—Questions and answers*. https://ec.europa.eu/commission/presscorner/detail/en/qanda_23_4519

European Commission. (2024a). *Better regulation: Why and how*. https://commission.europa.eu/law/law-making-process/planning-and-proposing-law/better-regulation_en

European Commission. (2024b, February 23). *Questions and answers on the Digital Services Act*. https://ec.europa.eu/commission/presscorner/detail/en/qanda_20_2348

European Commission. (2024c, January 24). *Commission launches AI innovation package to support Artificial Intelligence startups and SMEs*. https://ec.europa.eu/commission/presscorner/detail/en/ip_24_383

European Commission. (2024d). *Keeping our promise to Europe: The story of the von der Leyen Commission*. https://commission.europa.eu/document/download/37fb50d6-73e1-426c-bd4a-87c44c8763d9_en?filename=Keeping-our-promise-to-Europe_brochure.pdf

European Parliament. (2017). *Hearing of Commissioner-Designate Ms Mariya Gabriel; Written questions and answers*. https://www.europarl.europa.eu/cmsdata/121420/Annex%20EN%20version.pdf

European Union. (2016, July 17). *Directive 2016/1148 of 6 July 2016 concerning measures for a high common level of security of network and information systems across the Union*. https://eur-lex.europa.eu/legal-content/EN/TXT/PDF/?uri=CELEX:32016L1148

European Union. (2021, February 18). *Regulation (EU) 2021/241 of the European Parliament and of the Council of 12 February 2021 establishing the Recovery and Resilience Facility*. https://eur-lex.europa.eu/legal-content/EN/TXT/?uri=celex%3A32021R0241

European Union. (2023, January 23). *European Declaration on digital rights and principles for the digital decade*. https://eur-lex.europa.eu/legal-content/EN/TXT/?uri=OJ%3AJOC_2023_023_R_0001

Federal Government of Germany. (2014). *Digital Agenda 2014–2017*. https://www.bmi.bund.de/SharedDocs/downloads/EN/publikationen/2014/digital-agenda.pdf?__blob=publicationFile

Floridi, L. (2020). The fight for digital sovereignty: What it is, and why it matters, especially for the EU. *Philosophy & Technology, 33*, 369–378.

Germany's Presidency of the Council of the European Union. (2020). *Together for Europe's recovery: Programme for Germany's Presidency of the Council of the European Union*. https://www.eu2020.de/blob/2360248/e0312c50f910931819ab67f630d15b2f/06-30-pdf-programm-en-data.pdf

Gros, D., & Magliano, D. (2024, July). *Mobile Telecom in Europe: Urban legend or case study in market fragmentation?* https://iep.unibocconi.eu/sites/default/files/media/attach/PB22_Report%20Telecom_%20Gros-Magliano.pdf

Heidebrecht, S. (2023). From market liberalism to public intervention: Digital sovereignty and changing European Union digital single market governance. *JCMS: Journal of Common Market Studies, 62*, 205–223.

Hern, A., Fishwick, C., & Weaver, M. (2015, July 21). *Ashley Madison customer service in meltdown as site battles hack fallout*. https://www.theguardian.com/technology/2015/jul/21/ashley-madison-customer-service-meltdown-hack-fallout

Hirst, N. (2014, March 5). *Cross-border content complications*. https://www.politico.eu/article/cross-border-content-complications/

International Banker. (2021, September 21). *The dotcom bubble burst in 2000*. https://internationalbanker.com/history-of-financial-crises/the-dotcom-bubble-burst-2000/

Internet Society. (1997). *A brief history of the Internet*. https://www.internetsociety.org/internet/history-internet/brief-history-internet/

James, S. (2012). The origins and evolution of the Lisbon Agenda. In *The EU's Lisbon strategy, evaluating success, understanding failure* (Vols. 8–29). Palgrave MacMillan.

Juncker, J.-C. (2014). *Statement of Jean-Claude Juncker during the Eurovision televised debate of 15 May 2014 between the Spitzenkandidaten*. https://audiovisual.ec.europa.eu/corporateplayer/index.html?video=I-089480&language=undefined

Kennard, W. (1999, September 23). *Vision to mission: A blueprint for architects of the global information infrastructure*. Speech before the World Economic Development Forum. Davos.

Kroes, N. (2011, December 12). *Neelie Kroes Vice-President of the European Commission responsible for the Digital Agenda Data is the new gold Opening Remarks, Press Conference on Open Data Strategy Brussels, 12th December 2011*. https://ec.europa.eu/commission/presscorner/detail/en/SPEECH_11_872

Kroes, N. (2014, October 1). *Speech—Adapt or die: What I would do if I ran a telecom company*. https://ec.europa.eu/commission/presscorner/detail/de/SPEECH_14_647

Kurbalija, J. (2024, May 4). *15 years of the World Summit on the Information Society (WSIS)*. https://www.diplomacy.edu/blog/15-years-world-summit-information-society-wsis/#2_About_WSIS

Lannoo, K., & Napolli, C. (2010, October 29). *Bank state aid in the financial crisis*. https://www.ceps.eu/ceps-publications/bank-state-aid-financial-crisis-fragmentation-or-level-playing-field/

Leyen, U. (2019). *A union that strives for more: My agenda for Europe*. https://commission.europa.eu/document/download/063d44e9-04ed-4033-acf9-639ecb187e87_en?filename=political-guidelines-next-commission_en.pdf
Lippolis, A. S. (2023, August 31). *Google News in Spain: The legacy of its shutdown and the impact of its reopening*. https://thefix.media/2023/8/31/google-news-in-spain-the-legacy-of-its-shutdown-and-the-impact-of-its-reopening
Majone, G. (1994). The rise of the regulatory state in Europe. *West European Politics, 17*(3), 77–101.
Majone, G. (Ed.). (1996). *Regulating Europe*. Routledge.
Malmsten, E. (2001). *Boo Hoo: A dot.com story from concept to Catastrophe*. Penguin Random House Business Books.
Mayer-Schönberger, V., & Strasser, M. (1999, Summer). A closer look at telecom deregulation: The European advantage. *Harvard Journal of Law & Technology, 12*(3).
Meyer, M. N. (2014, June 30). *Everything you need to know about Facebook's controversial emotion experiment*. https://www.wired.com/2014/06/everything-you-need-to-know-about-facebooks-manipulative-experiment/
Miadzvetskaya, Y. (2023). Data Governance Act: On international transfers of non-personal data and GDPR. *Mimesis. European Data Protection Law Review, 9*(1), 13–26.
ODINE. (2024). *Stories*. https://opendataincubator.eu/stories/
Ouest France. (2017, September 26). *Sorbonne speech of Emmanuel Macron—Full text/English version*. https://international.blogs.ouest-france.fr/archive/2017/09/29/macron-sorbonne-verbatim-europe-18583.html
Palmer, S. (2022, December 15). *The EU just signed its Declaration on Digital Rights and Principles—But what is it?* https://www.euronews.com/my-europe/2022/12/15/the-eu-just-signed-its-declaration-on-digital-rights-and-principles-but-what-is-it
Politico. (2025, November 25). Brussels is done being the world's digital policeman by Pieter Haeck and Ellen O'Regan. https://www.politico.eu/article/brussels-police-world-digital-tech-us-china-regulations/
Radu, R. (2019). Privatization and globalization of the Internet. In R. Radu (Ed.), *Negotiating internet governance* (pp. 75–112). Oxford University Press.
Roberts, H., Cowls, J., Casolari, F., Morley, J., Tddeo, M., & Floridi, L. (2021). *Safeguarding European values with digital sovereignty: An analysis of statements and policies*. https://policyreview.info/articles/analysis/safeguarding-european-values-digital-sovereignty-analysis-statements-and-policies
Shahin, J., & Finger, M. (2009). The history of a European information society: Shifts from government to governance. In J. Tuptimhin & P. Russell (Eds.), *Global e-governance: Advancing governance through innovation and leadership* (pp. 62–83). IOS Press.

Soares, J. (2026, January 13). *€3.77bn in fines: Last year's Big Tech bill in Europe.* https://euperspectives.eu/2026/01/last-years-big-tech-bill-in-europe/#
Smidi, A., & Shahin, S. (2017, June). Social media and social mobilisation in the Middle East. *India Quarterly. Special Issue: The Middle East, 73*(2), 196–209.
Smirke, R. (2018, March 7). *Music Chiefs Slam Google lobbying spend ahead of EU copyright vote.* https://www.billboard.com/pro/google-lobbying-dollars-eu-copyright-vote-uk-music/
Startup Manifesto. (2013). *Help internet-driven economic growth transform the lives of millions.* https://static1.squarespace.com/static/5d6c0364248be40001e27464/t/5d6c05e898811e000186b749/1567360488288/manifesto.pdf
Statista.com. (2015, March 3). *Global market share held by mobile phone vendors 1997–2014.* https://www.statista.com/statistics/271574/global-market-share-held-by-mobile-phone-manufacturers-since-2009/#statisticContainer
The Economist. (2013, November 28). *The Internet fifth man.* https://www.economist.com/technology-quarterly/2013/11/28/the-internets-fifth-man
Topping, A., Kassam, A., & Davies, L. (2014, June 11). *Angry cab drivers gridlock Europe in protest at 'unregulated' taxi app.* https://www.theguardian.com/uk-news/2014/jun/11/cab-drivers-europe-protest-taxi-app-uber-london-madrid
Ungerer, H. (2018). *Liberalisation of telecommunications in the Nineties—When European competition policy went to its limits.* https://ec.europa.eu/competition/compat60/memories/pdf/006-ungerer.pdf
Vie publique. (2019, June 19). *République numérique: qu'a changé la loi du 7 octobre 2016?* https://www.vie-publique.fr/eclairage/20301-loi-republique-numerique-7-octobre-2016-loi-lemaire-quels-changements
Warso, Z. (2022, December 2). *A right to participation in the Digital Public Space?* https://openfuture.eu/blog/a-right-to-participation-in-the-digital-public-space/
Welfens, P. (2008). Digital EU Integration and the Lisbon Process. In P. Welfens (Ed.), *Digital integration, growth and rational regulation.* Springer.
Whittaker, J., Looney, S., Reed, A., & Votta, F. (2021). Recommender systems and the amplification of extremist content. *Internet Policy Review, 10*(2). https://policyreview.info/articles/analysis/recommender-systems-and-amplification-extremist-content
WSIS. (2005, November 18). *Tunis agenda for the information society.* https://www.itu.int/net/wsis/docs2/tunis/off/6rev1.html

CHAPTER 3

European Values: Sovereignty in EU Digital Law and Policy

Viivi Lähteenoja

Introduction

In recent decades and in the wake of intensifying datafication of society and societies, brought to public attention in force by the Snowden revelations in 2013 (Hintz et al., 2018), policymakers in the European Union (later EU) have increasingly turned their attention to the governance of the digital economy and society. At the same time, rising international tensions, together with disruptive digital transformation, are putting increasing pressure on the EU's geopolitical positioning. The result of these two developments can be seen in the relatively recently increased rhetoric of "digital sovereignty" by EU politicians and policymakers (Timmers, 2019). Scholars have gone as far as describing this trend as a sign of "the EU's efforts to maximise its digital sovereignty" (Roberts et al., 2021) and predicted that there's no end in sight for it (Pohle & Thiel, 2020, pp. 2–3).

In the various definitions and descriptions of technological or digital sovereignty, the term is invariably linked to the EU's ability to uphold,

V. Lähteenoja (✉)
University of Helsinki, Helsinki, Finland
e-mail: viivi.lahteenoja@helsinki.fi

T. Kleiner and A. Garcia Rodriguez (eds.), *The Making of a Global Digital Rulebook*, https://doi.org/10.1007/978-981-95-9226-5_3

defend, and promote its values. The president of the European Commission (later EC) Ursula von der Leyen called it the ability that "Europe must have to make its own choices, based on its values, respecting its own rules" (Leyen, 2020). In a speech entitled "Digital sovereignty is central to European strategic autonomy", the president of the European Council Charles Michel referred to Europe's ability "to better defend our interests and our values" (Michel, 2021). Additionally, the European Parliamentary Research Service, in a paper entitled "Digital sovereignty for Europe", urged the EU "to promote more actively European values and principles in areas such as data protection, cybersecurity and ethically designed artificial intelligence" (Madiega, 2020). In short, it has been found that "digital sovereignty is seen as a basis for strengthening the EU's role in an interconnected world, promoting its core interests, and protecting the fundamental values upon which the Union is based" (Roberts et al., 2021, p. 3).

In order to be able to promote and protect European values through sovereignty, "we should of course know what the values we speak of are" (Dijck, 2020). Two documents that contain explicit lists of European values are the Treaty on European Union (later TEU) and the European Declaration on Digital Rights and Principles for the Digital Decade (later the Declaration). The former contains an enumeration of the values on which the EU has been founded: "The Union is founded on the values of respect for human dignity, freedom, democracy, equality, the rule of law and respect for human rights, including the rights of persons belonging to minorities. These values are common to the Member States in a society in which pluralism, non-discrimination, tolerance, justice, solidarity and equality between women and men prevail" (326 OJ § (2012), art. 2). The latter lists six principles: I. putting people at the centre of the digital transformation, II. solidarity and inclusion, III. freedom of choice, IV. participation in the digital public space, V. safety, security and empowerment, and VI. sustainability. Presumably, these are the values to which EU policy documents, as well as in speeches by EU politicians and policymakers, refer to when they speak of the EU upholding, defending, and promoting "European values".

There clearly exists a strong link between the idea of shared or common European values, such as the ones codified in the TEU and the Declaration, and the concept of digital sovereignty, as it has been seen to emerge in twenty-first-century EU rhetoric. "Digital sovereignty is – especially in Europe – now often used as a shorthand for an ordered, value-driven, regulated and therefore reasonable and secure digital sphere. It is presumed to resolve the multifaceted problems of individual rights and freedoms, collective and infrastructural security, political and legal enforceability and fair economic competition" (Pohle & Thiel, 2020, p. 19). Given that the concept occupies such a central role in EU policy-making, it will be interesting and worthwhile to explore philosophically the nature of digital sovereignty. It is the purpose of this chapter to provide this kind of exploration. By the end of our journey, we will be able to recognise some of how today's digital sovereignty in the EU is part of a historical continuum with rich and deep roots in the continent's past.

After this introduction, the first half of this chapter sketches out some contours of the philosophical shape of (digital) sovereignty through descriptions of some scenes in the history of European sovereignty (Section 2). In the second half of this chapter, we will explore contemporary digital sovereignty as a kind of attempt to build out a "digital constitution" for the EU. We will use the Declaration, one of the key digital policy documents of the 2020s on the European values that digital sovereignty seeks to protect, as a case study (Section 3). Finally, this chapter concludes with some remarks and open questions about the future of EU digital sovereignty (Section 4).

Scenes From the History of European Sovereignty

Digital sovereignty has been the subject of researchers' and analysts' attempts at definition in at least four ways. Some have studied it specifically in the EU context and attempted to build a definition using an inductive, bottom-up approach based on existing legal and policy documents (Burwell & Propp, 2020) (Leonard & Shapiro, 2016). Others have approached the topic from the point of view of describing the conceptual confusion and discursive practices around digital sovereignty (Couture & Toupin, 2019). Yet others have attempted to build out a positive conceptual definition and framework for understanding digital sovereignty (Roberts, et al., 2021). Finally, the concept has been discussed by and in the context of indigenous peoples, especially in the Americas and Oceania (Kukutai & Taylor, 2016).

Seeking clarity in definitions is certainly justified given how inconsistently the term is used in different EU policy context, none of which seems to give a clear definition (Roberts et al., 2021, p. 3). However, this chapter is less interested in a precise definition of the term. Rather, we seek to understand some of the many roots of today's European notions of digital sovereignty via an examination of moments in the continent's history. The insights hopefully gained from this examination can then be used as a lens through which to understand the aims and motivations of EU politicians and policymakers in promoting digital sovereignty today and in the foreseeable future.

Sovereignty Before Sovereignty

Although the term sovereignty did not become established as a political concept until much later, similar ideas have existed throughout European history (and elsewhere). One striking feature of these ideas is their *organic* nature: the understanding that a state (or similar) is a natural thing with parts, and of which the sovereign is the head.

It has not been uncommon throughout history for the state to be described in bodily terms, but the European "body politic" has deep roots in Ancient Greek political theory (Paris, 2020, p. 459), most notably in the city/soul analogy by Plato (Neu, 1971). In his *Republic*, Plato describes his utopian city-state via an analogy of the human soul, where the different parts of society perform distinct roles as parts of an organic whole. After Plato, Aristotle developed a deeply natural political theory. "Man is by nature a political animal", he writes on the very first pages of his *Politics* (Aristotle, 1984). And sovereign power was firmly placed at the head of this body politic, the state (Merriam, 2001).

This Greek "organicism", the understanding of the state as an organic thing with sovereignty as its unifying principle, was deeply influential on Roman political theorising (Paris, 2020) as well as Roman law (Merriam, 2001). The Roman Republic especially during Cicero's life was the time during which the notion of state as a body became fleshed out, so to speak, in detail (Walters, 2020).

Greek and Roman notions of the organic body of the state with a sovereign at its head were, in turn, a major influence on Christian theology. "Traditionally, Christian ethicists accepted in the wake of Aristotle biological insights as a basis for their virtue ethics against the background of a belief in the *scala naturae*" (Tavernier, 2014).

In Christian theology, the duty of all mankind was to obey and to act as befit their station in "the organic constitution of the universe" (Formigari, 1973), the hierarchy of the *scala naturae*, or the Great Chain of Being.

This chain dictated the proper place of everything in this world and the next: at the top was God, from whom the chain descends through His angels to His representatives on earth in the clergy and kings, and then lower classes of humans, before reaching animals and finally minerals of the earth.

On the one hand, God is the source of all earthly powers, as St Paul writes in Romans 13:1: "Let everyone be subject to the governing authorities, for there is no authority except that which God has established. The authorities that exist have been established by God".[1] In other words, God is the supreme sovereign, and all other sovereigns are so by His grace alone, and all Christians are to be subject to these earthly sovereigns, such as kings and emperors.[2]

On the other hand, St Paul conceives of the Christian church as a mystical, organic body at the head of which was Christ (Hicks, 1963). During the Middle Ages, this notion of the "two bodies" of Christ became an established doctrine: the "natural" body of Christ that is part of the Eucharist, and the "mystical" body of Christ that is the collective, social, and enduring structure of the church. This latter idea, that of a persistent body of people, became transferred onto the sphere of politics and hence the "body politic".

As we go on to examine modern and then contemporary notions of digital sovereignty, we will find echoes of the very same organicism that has been a feature of European notions of supreme authority since ancient Greek thought.[3]

[1] New International Version (NIV).

[2] See also King James VI and I and Johann P. Sommerville, eds., 'Speech to Parliament of 21 March 1610', in *King James VI and I: Political Writings*, Cambridge Texts in the History of Political Thought (Cambridge: Cambridge University Press, 1995), 179–203, https://doi.org/10.1017/CBO9780511809743.012: 'The state of monarchy is the supremest thing upon earth. For kings are not only God's lieutenants upon earth, and sit upon God's throne, but even by God himself they are called gods'

[3] An additional remark on the rhetoric of "bodies" and sovereignty. The organic body as a metaphor for a sovereign being bears interesting resemblance to the language of digital sovereignty. When individuals are concerned, the most commonly used term associated with their digital sovereignty is arguably "consent". In the current data protection regime of the EU, informed consent is something that is often required for processing of personal data to be legal. If there is no legal grounds, like consent, to process personal data, that processing is illegal. The other major context where consent plays an important part as demarcating the legal from the illegal is bodily autonomy. Globally, legislators are increasingly defining the lack of consent as the criterion for the crime of rape. Both kinds

Modern Sovereignty

The modern concept of sovereignty is usually traced back to the processes leading up to the Peace of Westphalia in 1648 and to the works of people like the French theorist Jean Bodin and the English philosopher Thomas Hobbes. In their writings, sovereignty gained prominence as a critical feature of, and is articulated primarily in terms of, the state. "The modern polity is known as the state, and the fundamental characteristic of authority within it, sovereignty" (Philpott, 2020). This is in contrast to earlier notions of sovereignty, which were not so connected with a specific nation or place, but rather were considered universal and to flow from the nature of God in the Middle Ages, or from what Aristotle would have called "the unmoved mover", the originator of the universe.

It is from the modern era that the core meaning of sovereignty is derived from, as we understand it today: sovereignty is "supreme authority over a territory".

Although now territorially bounded, Bodin embraced the earlier organic notions of sovereignty and envisioned that it united the ruler and the ruled into a single body. Further, that body was above any human law, and in fact the source of all human law. However, like Hobbes, he also believed that the sovereign was still subject to *divine* law and therefore accountable to God, a kind of absolute hierarchy that is another feature carried over from earlier notions of sovereignty.

This notion of an absolute hierarchy with God at the top was later challenged by 1700s social-contract theorists like John Locke and Immanuel Kant. In effect, they reversed the logic of the Great Chain and posited that it is *individuals* who have natural rights and so sovereignty, and not God. The state is therefore sovereign only when, and because, individuals collectively delegate their sovereignty to a government. Individuals can also revoke this delegation of their sovereignty should the state violate their natural rights. In other words, "individual rights [are] ontologically prior to states" (Paris, 2020, p. 458).

of consent are also commonly criticised for not being fit for (legal) purpose. The kind of "informed" consent that the GDPR, for example, requires is hardly ever present when we just want to get the annoying popup out of the way so we can keep browsing. Similarly, consent-based approaches to criminal law around sexual offences have been criticised for placing an unreasonable burden of proof on the accused in criminal cases. How is it possible to prove consent after the fact? Perhaps consent is not the appropriate legal criterion for either kind of crime.

An effect of this Enlightenment-era reversal, linked also with contemporary medical discoveries, was the mechanisation of the previously organic body politic—just as the human body was being increasingly studied as a kind of machine (Ihalainen, 2009). Instead of divine will, this new body was governed by the rational decisions of the individuals who made it up (Cohen, 1997). This striking new individualism will play a significant part in analysing contemporary digital sovereignty as well.

The modern idea of sovereignty also assumes a kind of equality between sovereign states, at least insofar as they are sovereign states (Paris, 2020). This equality and the multiplicity of sovereign states imply the principle of non-intervention and the resulting distinction between internal and external sovereignty. These two are not mutually exclusive kinds of sovereignty, but rather always coexist at the same time. Internal sovereignty refers to the supreme right of the sovereign to act within its borders, and external sovereignty refers to others respecting this right, that is, the principle of non-interference in the internal affairs of a sovereign state. We will see how this distinction between internal and external sovereignty will be especially relevant to EU digital policy as they require a different kind of legitimation and can be asserted in different ways.

Modern sovereignty is fundamentally "constitutional independence", in which "constitutional" refers to a constitution in the sense of "the body of principles and basic rules in the light of which [the state] is to be governed" (James, 1999, p. 461). In this way, sovereignty in this sense is always a *legal* condition of a state. It does not mean that to be sovereign is lawful and to be otherwise is unlawful. Rather, sovereignty is legal insofar as any constitution is a body of principles and basic rules which has the *force* of law (James, 1999, p. 462).

A constitution, in the above sense, does not necessarily need to be written down and exist *de jure*, but it must be de facto respected. Although just about every sovereign state today has a written constitution (Great Britain being a notable exception), it will become important for us to understand contemporary digital sovereignty that constitutions come in many shapes and only require that they are respected *as if* they were law.[4]

[4] Another remark on a similarity in the languages of sovereignty and governing the digital. Especially in the writings of Hobbes, there is a concept that is tightly connected with sovereignty and that shares some of its characteristics, and that is private property.

To summarise, modern sovereignty is first and foremost the property of the state. It is the result of a set of individuals, within certain geographical boundaries, delegating their individual sovereignties to their governments, which makes the state sovereign. These individuals are rational agents who, together, form the mechanism that is the modern body politic. Modern sovereignty is constitutional independence: because states are internally sovereign, that is, they are free to govern within their borders in whichever way, they must also be externally sovereign: free from the interference of others in their internal affairs. The constitution which defines them is that set of rules that have the force of law, whether legally codified or merely observed in practice. Each of these features will show up in some way in our analysis of the pursuits of European digital sovereignty.

Sovereignty After Sovereignty

Finally, we consider the contemporary shape of sovereignty. Most commonly, the term sovereignty denotes a variant of the modern notion of political authority, which has the core meaning of "supreme authority within a territory" (Philpott, 2020). Contemporary European digital sovereignty can be considered to belong to a period in the history of sovereignty that began after the Second World War and in which the role of the state—previously the prime example of the embodiment of sovereignty—is being increasingly limited and different types of non-state actors can increasingly assume the mantle of sovereignty. Examples of these non-state actors are the EU itself, as well as large technology companies with global reach.

We saw earlier how territoriality, or being geographically bound, emerged as a key ingredient of the modern concept of sovereignty. But with the contemporary de-emphasis on the state as the prime locus of sovereignty, and the emergence of non-state actors like the EU and

There are interesting parallels to be drawn between notions of "data sovereignty" and "data ownership", two ideas that often seem to go hand in hand. The rhetoric of "owning one's data" or "getting back control of one's own data" is particularly prevalent in US contexts, but it is also used in Europe. Attempts at applying legal property rights to data have not seen much success, and the current era of LLMs illegally using copyrighted material and violating other intellectual property rights suggests that "property" might not be the most effective way of dealing with rights over data and the digital.

Big Tech companies, some scholars of digital sovereignty are explicitly distancing themselves from the territoriality involved in earlier definitions.

Roberts et al. write: "We also move away from traditional notions of (digital) sovereignty as necessarily being defined by a fixed physical geography and instead view digital sovereignty as something that can be held across political communities and spatial networks that are not limited to the nation-state (Agnew, 2005). This is in recognition of the fact that not all historical polities have been territorially organised, and that contemporary governance of the digital is, in many areas, not territorially bound. In short, we assume that the concept of "sovereignty" has finally and completely detached itself from that of "sovereign"" (Roberts et al., 2021, p. 5).

In addition to letting go of the territoriality of modern sovereignty, the absoluteness of contemporary sovereignty is also shifting. The "supremacy" of the authority of a sovereign state in its internal affairs is no longer absolute. An example of this is the EU itself. Member states of the EU have supreme authority within their territories—but not over everything. While member states are sovereign over governing their defence, they are not all sovereign over governing their currencies. This shift in the absoluteness of sovereignty is also evident in the increasing pressure to make exceptions to one of the formerly basic tenets of sovereignty and contemporary international relations that relies on it, namely non-intervention. Examples of the violation of this principle—non-intervention by other states in the internal affairs of another—abound in recent history: Iraq, the former Yugoslavia, Bosnia, Kosovo, Somalia, Rwanda, Haiti, Cambodia, Liberia, Libya and more. These interventions have been sanctioned by international bodies like the UN Security Council or unilaterally conducted.

In sum, contemporary sovereignty is no longer intrinsically connected with the state and specifically the territorial aspects of traditional state actors. Rather, non-state actors like the EU and multinational technology companies also exhibit characteristics or deploy the rhetoric of sovereignty. Second, sovereignty is not absolute nor does non-intervention necessarily hold any more. International bodies like the UN and NATO are themselves made up of sovereign states and they can and have sanctioned interventions into the internal matters of sovereign states. These are features that will also play a part in understanding contemporary digital sovereignty.

Summary

To conclude the first part of this chapter, we can now summarise in brief the kinds of features that European sovereignty has picked up during its evolution from the earliest Greek philosophers to contemporary EU politicians and policymakers.

From pagan Antiquity and the Christian thought of the Middle Ages, sovereignty today retains the idea that it is a natural, organic thing that is the proper subject of sovereignty, and of which the sovereign is a part—the head.

Modern sovereignty added the notions of geographical borders and individuals within those borders as primary holders of sovereignty, on whose behalf and legitimised by whom the sovereign state functions, somewhat like a natural machine akin to the human body. It is the set of rules within a state, observed even if not always recorded, that constitute the sovereignty of that state. Further, that sovereignty over the internal affairs of the state is to be respected by other sovereign nations, between whom the international affairs of trade and war and negotiation take place.

Finally, arriving at contemporary sovereignty, we find certain earlier aspects negated or negotiated. The territoriality and absolutism so intrinsic to modern sovereignty are fading as international cooperation on human rights intensifies and developments like European integration progresses. Further, market giants like US-based technology companies become peers of sovereign states in matters of international concern.

We can see how the concept of sovereignty has shifted throughout its history and today presents itself as a kind of mosaic composed of parts of its history, with gaps where older parts have fallen out. The picture that forms looks different depending on how much one zooms in or out.

On the level of the individual, we see the individual as the ontologically prior being: the proper subject of sovereignty that stems from the fundamental essence of what it is to be human, a fundamental right. In fact, however, we individuals living in governed societies delegate this sovereignty to our respective constitutions. We respect and live by a certain set of rules, codified into law or not, and we entrust to others the governance of these rules. But it is impossible to give up sovereignty: we still retain all our rights as human beings, to things like bodily autonomy and security of person and to things like private property, even if we count on the state and its police and judicial systems, say, to protect these rights.

On the level of the state, sovereignty is being circumscribed by international commitments such as to human rights and obligations to interfere in the internal affairs of sovereign states in defence of these rights. On the other hand, increasing European integration is also pulling in the direction of limiting the sovereignty of EU member states. This trend has not gone unnoticed within these states, and anti-EU sentiment that objects to limits on state sovereignty to pursue one's own interests in one's own ways is present in many of them.

On the level of the EU, sovereignty shows up as doubly challenging, as both internal and external legitimacy of a bloc like the EU can be questioned. Internally, considerations like member state autonomy pose real questions to EU sovereignty especially in times of crises such as the COVID-19 pandemic and the climate crisis, and armed conflicts like Russia's attack on Ukraine. Externally, the EU seems to be only somewhat sovereign, in that it can negotiate and trade with sovereign nations, but not, for example, declare war on one.

Finally, on a global level, states are no longer the only actors with features akin to sovereignty. Global technology conglomerates are the custodians of de facto rules that we individuals follow in very much the same way as we follow the rules of our constitutions that our legitimate representatives govern. They are negotiation partners and in many ways peers of sovereign states in international affairs. Examples are easy to find. During COVID-19, different states (and the EU) negotiated with Apple and Google over contact-tracing apps. Ukraine, on the other hand, has a negotiating partner in Starlink, the US company that currently provides much of the country's connectivity in lieu of its own, mostly destroyed, infrastructure.

Having now concluded our tour of scenes from the history of European sovereignty, and examined the mosaic it presents from various distances, it is time to turn to the digital decade in the EU and the politics and policymaking of specifically digital sovereignty in the 2020s.

Towards a New Digital Constitution?

In the first half of this chapter, we've discussed some of the salient features of European sovereignty throughout the continent's history and the layered picture they paint today. In this second half, we turn our attention to the EU regulator and legislator in the 2020s and what can be said of their vision of and for European digital sovereignty. But first, as a case study, we will use the 2022 Declaration on European Digital Rights and Principles (European Commission, 2022) and analyse it in the light of the features of sovereignty we have observed in the first half.

Declaration on European Digital Rights and Principles

The Declaration on European Digital Rights and Principles of 2022 is a short document at only six pages and 2161 words total. It opens with a proclamation of intent: "We aim to promote a European way for the digital transition, putting people at the centre. It shall be based on European values and benefiting all individuals and businesses". It then goes on to detail, in a dedicated chapter for each, six principles. These are: I. putting people at the centre of the digital transformation, II. solidarity and inclusion, III. freedom of choice, IV. participation in the digital public space, V. safety, security and empowerment, and VI. sustainability.

Its contents display signs of three interesting tensions and asymmetries: (a) between legalistic prescription and inspirational description, (b) between a positive "ability to" and a negative "safety from" outlook, and (c) between emphases on people, businesses, and the planet. Let us examine each of these in more detail.

Legalistic Prescription and Inspirational Description

According to paragraph (7) of the Preamble, the Declaration "builds on primary EU law, in particular in the Treaty on European Union, the Treaty on the Functioning of the European Union, the EU Charter of Fundamental Rights and the case-law of the Court of Justice of the EU, as well as in secondary law. It also builds on and complements the European Pillar of Social Rights".

The Declaration is, in other words, a very *legalistic* document. This is not surprising, as one of the key elements of modern sovereignty, as we saw above, is precisely its nature as a *legal* condition. The Declaration can be seen as an attempt to *constitute* and prescribe a certain set of rules which all those within its borders ought to respect and which the EU in turn promises to govern with the legitimacy we, individuals, have (arguably) delegated to the EU. In a sense, the Declaration is also a *claim* to sovereignty.

This characterisation of the Declaration as a legalistic document can be contrasted with an *inspirational* tone that it also adopts in part. Paragraph (4) of the Preamble contains the phrase "respect of people' rights and aspirations" which describes these two modes: legalistic rights and inspirational aspirations.

Inspirational description can be found in each of the Declaration's chapters. The structure of the chapters follows the same pattern throughout the Declaration. After the title of the chapter, or subsection of a chapter, a sentence with "should" is presented, that describes a desired state of affairs. "Technology should serve and benefit all Europeans ..." (ch. I), "Everyone should have access to technology that aims at uniting, and not dividing, people" (ch. II), and so on. As is easy to see, these "should" statements describe an aspirational world, not the current one.

After each "should" sentence, the rest of the chapter (or subsection of a chapter) continues with the phrase "We commit to" followed by a set of bullet-pointed statements of intent: "strengthening the democratic framework for a digital transformation" (ch. I), "making sure that technological solutions respect people's rights" (ch. II), and so on.

These bullet-pointed items exemplify what Pohle and Thiel call the "prescriptive and normative" nature of claims to specifically *digital* sovereignty: "rather than referring to existing instruments or specific practices, they usually formulate aspirations or recommendations for action" (Pohle & Thiel, 2020, p. 8). So although the Declaration begins with a very legalistic tone, it goes on to rely mostly on aspirational "should" language and recommendations for overall good approaches without setting down in detail what the rules are that this sovereignty claim asserts the EU will govern.

It should be noted here, of course, that the Declaration accompanies a slew of actual laws passed in order to realise some of the aspirational "shoulds" of the Declaration, such as the Data Governance Act, the Digital Markets Act, the Digital Services Act, the Interoperable Europe Act, the revised eIDAS and NIS regulations, the Data Act, and the AI Act. Viewed as an accompaniment to these legal initiatives, and alongside the substantial investment through various instruments into the further development of the digital single market, it is unlikely that the Declaration was ever intended to be other than mainly inspirational and aspirational.

Positive "Ability To" and Negative "Safety From" Outlooks

The Declaration is characterised by references to safety and security (together 27 instances) and safeguards and protections (together 20 instances). These themes can be contrasted with mentions of empowerment (eight instances), choice (seven instances), and sovereignty and self-determination (together one instance), which are far less prevalent throughout the document. These two clusters of concepts, which can be characterised respectively as "negative" (or "protection from") and "positive" ("ability to"), seem then to exhibit a significant asymmetry in the contents of the document.

The two outlooks, positive and negative, can be viewed as an attempt to strike the appropriate balance between what in modern sovereignty discourse was referred to as "internal" and "external" sovereignty. Viewed in this light, it is interesting to note that internal considerations—what the EU and its citizens should be able to do within their sphere of sovereignty—receive such little emphasis (16 mentions of the keywords altogether) compared to the external considerations—what the EU and its citizens should be safe from (47 mentions of the keywords altogether). In other words, exerting and asserting the EU's sovereignty externally—that is, having it respected by other sovereign actors—seems to have been the primary anxiety and preoccupation of the authors of the Declaration. While states like China and Russia are obvious candidates for the source of such anxiety, it is important again to consider the Declaration in its wider context, the wave of regulation following the 2020 European strategy for data (European Commission, 2020). Arguably that set of regulations is not intended to target states such as China and Russia, rather it is US-based technology giants who are at their cross-hairs.

Here we encounter again one of the novel aspects of contemporary and digital sovereignty: the establishment of multinational corporations as trade and negotiation partners in international relations. What is the EU to do if corporations from a sovereign state meddle in its internal affairs? Asserting digital sovereignty only works if it is considered legitimate by other parties. In fact, the home state of these corporations may consider targeting them by regulation interference in *its* internal affairs. And asserting digital sovereignty only works if the other parties are in some salient way peers and so capable of respecting the sovereignty of the other. This may or may not be the case for large technology companies: can they be considered sovereign or not? Don't we, users of the services provided by these companies, follow their rules? Don't we, in this way, delegate to them our sovereignty to govern those rules as the digital constitution of our globalised online society? Scholars tend to be reluctant to grant these companies "real" sovereignty, at least according to their preferred definition of it (Roberts et al., 2021), and there is indeed something unsettling about it. Is not sovereignty after all something belonging to a *natural* body politic, not a faceless, soulless conglomerate with only *legal* personhood? But having said that, will not a pragmatic approach be quite clear on the matter: if it walks like it's sovereign and quacks like it's sovereign, then is it not sovereign? And what are we to read into the fact that the very word "corporation", defined as a "body corporate", derives from the Latin verb "corporate", which means "to form into a body"?

Emphases on People, Businesses, and the Planet

The third interesting asymmetry we can find in the Declaration is that it seeks to strike a balance between three broad types of considerations: "human" and "societal" considerations, "business" and "economic" considerations, and "environmental" and "sustainability" considerations. The last is mostly confined to its own chapter (VI, the last one), but the other two appear, often together, throughout the document: "individuals and businesses" appear as a pair twice and "economy and society" as a pair six times.

The repeated recurrence of economic considerations alongside societal ones is interesting, especially in the light of the anxieties of outside threats discussed above. Not only are people and their fundamental rights in society to be protected, but also the viability of the economy and its denizens, private companies. But how can European companies flourish if the market they operate in is monopolised by foreign alternatives? This seems to be at the crux of much of the 2020s digital law and policy in the EU and it is natural that the tendency is evident also in the Declaration. After all, the values-based approach to regulation is relatively new for the EU and contrasts with the earlier focus on specifically competition and competitiveness as the main drivers of EU policymaking. The processes culminating in the GDPR can be seen as the watershed moment in this shift towards "human" and "societal" considerations taking up more space but, as we see here in the Declaration, emphasis on competitiveness (a value in itself) has not by any means disappeared.

European Digital Sovereignty Now?

It is clear that new technologies are constantly asking new kinds of questions about us as individuals and societies. And how we respond to these questions tells a lot about us as individuals and societies. The EU response since the GDPR has been focused, but not exclusively, on values-based regulation. As the vehicle for asserting a host of European values in an increasingly digitalising world, the old concept of sovereignty has been selected as fit for the task at hand—updated with various prefixes such as "digital", "data", and "tech". A new vision for the old continent.

Claims to sovereignty, like the EU's, can be categorised into types based on who is being claimed sovereign: individuals, states, or companies (Pohle & Thiel, 2020, p. 8). Ideas linked to individual digital sovereignty have been at the forefront of EU digital law and rhetoric from at least the GDPR onwards. The GDPR casts all of us as "data subjects", a conveniently ambiguous term in English with connotations of being both subject to data collection and subjects who exercise agency.

The "human-centric" approach in the Declaration as well as countless other policy documents takes the individual as the point of origin for rights and agency over personal data. In the Enlightenment sense of sovereignty, this means that our individual rights and agency—our digital sovereignty—is and must be both *natural* and *ontologically primary* to any other sovereignty claims. In other words, data rights are as fundamental as (other) human rights and apply to all people by virtue of them being humans, and any other claim to digital sovereignty must be legitimised as the collective delegation of our individual sovereignties to this claimant. "Understood as democratic sovereignty, it encompasses popular sovereignty and citizens' right to exercise self-determination by making use of their inalienable rights" (Pohle & Thiel, 2020, p. 3).

State claims to sovereignty are the most common ones since the Westphalian model took over the world. Specifically digital sovereignty refers especially to a state's ability to control its digital infrastructures and technology deployment (Pohle & Thiel, 2020, p. 8). Digital sovereignty claims like these can be legitimised and motivated by real or perceived threats to the state's political ideology and system, like in China, or likewise real or perceived threats to the state's national security and related infrastructural control, like in the USA (Pohle & Thiel, 2020, pp. 8–9). The EU has markedly chosen "a third way", which prioritises data protection of its citizens and businesses.

Finally, companies' claims to sovereignty are an interesting case and can be analysed in two ways. First, there's the sovereignty of *the economic sector* of a state or bloc like the EU. In the EU, this kind of sovereignty claim sits at the intersection of individual and state sovereignty: "the goal [is] to achieve more independence from foreign technologies and to promote the innovative power of the domestic industry" on the other hand and "the aim [is] to protect consumers by offering technological services that respect user rights and domestic laws and norms such as data protection regulations" (Pohle & Thiel, 2020, p. 11). We see here again the twinning of "people and businesses" that we detected also in the Declaration.

On the other hand, we can also speak meaningfully of a kind of sovereignty claim that some large, multinational corporations can have. Such platforms have a set of features that positions them particularly well to assert, or tacitly assume, sovereignty. Arguably the most important feature is that they have direct and at times intimate connections to individuals as consumers, "to a large number of consumers who rely on the platform as it becomes integrated into the fabric of their daily lives" (Culpepper & Thelen, 2019). We, as consumers, become dependent on the convenience offered by these platforms to the extent that we exert political pressure on their behalf and against the regulator who seeks to restrain them, even to the point that, "to the extent that people come to prefer what powerful platforms want, they become tacit or even active supporters of policies that may harm their [own] objectively defined material interests" (Culpepper & Thelen, 2019, p. 11).

At least in certain contexts, our consumer identities as, for example, iPhone users (as opposed to Android users) will certainly be more salient to us than our identities as citizens of this or that EU member state. As loyal users of these platform companies' services, we effectively delegate our digital sovereignty to them in a way analogous to the way in which, in a state, we delegate our sovereignty to the government. Whether or not this delegation is constitutive of legitimacy is another question, but it has been pointed out that "unethical outcomes can arise if the EU is unable to introduce sufficiently strong regulatory measures on account of the perceived 'pseudo-' or merely 'quasi-legitimacy' held by technology companies through their ubiquity, scope, and their users' loyalty or reliance on them" (Roberts et al., 2021, p. 19).

The sovereignty claims of large platforms and the multinational corporations behind them pose a dilemma for the proponents of EU digital sovereignty. It is clear that people in the EU depend on the infrastructure-like services provided by these companies and have consumer identities linked with them. In some very real way, we follow the de facto laws that we allow, and in a sense mandate, these companies to govern. They are the constitution of our activities insofar as we inhabit the digital sphere. As such, these companies have a certain claim to sovereignty over us.

So what can EU digital sovereignty do to ensure that Europeans and European values are respected and protected in the digital world? It is evident that EU policymaking is recognising that "as the capacity and complexity of digital technologies continue to grow, it will be increasingly necessary to introduce new and better measures to ensure that the interests of EU citizens are protected, and European values are safeguarded" (Roberts et al., 2021, p. 20). If we take the commitment to EU digital sovereignty seriously, and keep with our understanding of sovereignty as a kind of constitutional independence, one such measure will be the formation of a digital constitution for the EU, one that has a stronger appeal to legitimacy than that of those de facto constitutive rules of platform actors. The Declaration can serve as an inspirational basis for one such constitution, and arguably the regulation and investments of the 2020s are already putting one in place.

But are measures we have today sufficient to form those rules that might establish the EU digital constitution? Arguably not, and for anything more drastic, amending the existing EU Treaties might be necessary (Roberts et al., 2021, p. 20). And of course, any overt moves towards a digital constitution for the EU will face criticism. For example, there are "longstanding questions over the institutional legitimacy of EU policy making" (Roberts et al., 2021, p. 18) in the first place. Digital constitutionalism for the EU can also be critiqued as accelerating tighter European integration, which is a notoriously fraught issue. Third, attempts at constructing a digital constitution for the EU can be accused of protectionist tendencies in mandating data localisation. And finally, it can be argued that a digital constitution is conceptually unnecessary since it relies on a claim of "cyber exceptionalism". The exceptionalist claim is that "the digital realm is qualitatively distinctive from the analogue world and that digital spaces therefore need to be treated differently from all previous technological innovations" (Pohle & Thiel, 2020, p. 4). But if this claim does not hold, why would we need a separate constitution for cyberspace?

Summary

To summarise this second half of this chapter, we can see that the Declaration of Digital Rights and Principles is a policy document that is highly aspirational in nature, though it is grounded in earlier, very legalistic mechanisms. It is also only a part of the puzzle, where other policy elements such as new and revised regulations as well as funding instruments provide the rest of the full picture of the ambition for the EU's digital decade. The Declaration places considerable emphasis on protections and safeguards, as opposed to empowerment and freedoms. What are to be protected are people and businesses, and what they are to be safeguarded from seem to be largely large, non-EU companies, as opposed to sovereign states.

Further, digital sovereignty is the EU's answer to questions that new technologies are asking us as citizens, consumers, and human societies. It is the way in which the EU seeks to assert and defend its values in an increasingly interconnected but fragmented world. In this context, digital sovereignty must contend with three different kinds of claims to it with varying degrees of legitimacy: claims by individuals as data subjects, claims by the EU to over its digital infrastructure and technology deployment, and claims by large online platform companies as controllers of the rules that form the de facto constitution of the digital sphere. Policy documents like the Declaration can be seen as continuation of a sustained effort to create a legitimate European digital constitution. Arguably, this effort has not yet had its intended effect, and whether it can or even should succeed is still very much an open issue.

Concluding Remarks

It has been argued in recent years that the EU "lacks a clear, coherent vision of digital sovereignty, with different actors from different EU institutions emphasising different domains in which, and mechanisms by which, digital sovereignty should be sought and strengthened" (Roberts et al., 2021, p. 18). This lack of clarity and coherence makes it difficult to discern if digital sovereignty measures are in fact succeeding (Roberts et al., 2021, p. 5).

The lack of a rigid and doggedly followed formulation of the vision behind the EU's new sovereignty may not, on the other hand, be only a problem. As any EU policymaker will have heard a million times, innovation thrives in places where there's room to move and grow, not in legislative straitjackets. Like sovereignty itself, it's something organic, it needs space to breathe.

The choice of sovereignty as *the* model to assert the EU's values, independence, and autonomy in a globalising world cuts two ways. It must be legitimate to both internal and external stakeholders: member states and

EU citizens as well as the international community of sovereign states and non-state actors with considerable power to interfere in the internal affairs of sovereign states. Paris writes: "States seeking to change the prevailing standards of state behaviour by advancing new sovereignty norms face a … paradox: how to do so in a way that resonates with other states and domestic audiences. One solution is to retrieve older understandings from "deeper" in the tool-kit—that is, versions of sovereignty that have established meanings, even if they have been in partial abeyance" (Paris, 2020, p. 463). In this chapter, we have explored some of these older understandings of sovereignty and how they inform contemporary notions and rhetoric of digital sovereignty in the EU.

The rhetoric of digital sovereignty is arguably also an example of a "strategic narrative" in the sense that it is "a means by which political actors attempt to construct a shared meaning of the past, present, and future of international politics to shape the behaviour of domestic and international actors" (Miskimmon et al., 2017, p. 6). This narrative construction supports efforts to establish the legitimacy of joint rules that could serve as the "digital constitution" of the EU.

In the modern sense of sovereignty, a constitution is what constitutes a thing as a sovereign state and so it is easy to see efforts in this direction as contributing to the increased integration of the EU towards a more unitary shape. "Historically, the most enthusiastic supporters of European integration have … come from Catholic Christian Democratic parties, whose ideals are rooted in mediaeval Christendom", where as we have seen, "only God was sovereign and His divine law – a universal set of values – governed all leaders" (Philpott, 2020). In this way, the EU's rhetoric of digital sovereignty as the guarantor and custodian of European values can be seen to form a natural continuation to European integration efforts.

Now the big question that remains is that of power over the future: *who* decides how the EU's ambitions for a new digital constitution and sovereignty will shape up, and *how* will they decide? As one of the core European values, robust and effective democracy must be the only way forward. But it is not clear that this will be the case. As Pohle and Thiel assert: "we believe that much more reflection and debate is needed on how sovereign powers can be held democratically accountable with regard to the digital. … Digital sovereignty is not an end in itself. Instead, we have to put even more thought into the procedural framework of how sovereign power can be held accountable and opened up to public reflection and control in order to truly democratise digital sovereignty" (Pohle & Thiel, 2020, pp. 13–14).

To conclude, a final remark on what the EU's digital sovereignty might mean for the rest of the world. If internally, it must be thoroughly democratised and democratic, what must it be externally? Should the EU, for example, "strengthen its global reach in that domain [controlling large technology companies] by elaborating legal instruments capable of extending their application beyond the Union's borders; the … GDPR approach could represent a benchmark in this respect" (Roberts et al., 2021, p. 19)? The basic principle of modern sovereignty is that of non-intervention: no sovereign state shall interfere in the internal affairs of another sovereign state. This would suggest that such aggressive measures as proposed by Roberts et al. would be in breach of the commonly accepted rules of international politics.

However, as we have seen, recent history has shown time and again that sovereign states and their internal affairs have been subject to interference by others. In addition, not all who interfere in the internal affairs of the EU are sovereign states. Is it therefore permissible to target these actors—large platform companies—even beyond the borders of the EU? When does such activity cross into meddling in the internal affairs of their home states?

It should also be noted that in no place in this chapter have we touched on the Global Majority countries, or indeed anyone outside the trio of China, Russia, and the US. Yet EU policymakers and politicians, when they speak of digital sovereignty, do often refer to "the Brussels effect", the EU's "unilateral power to regulate global markets" (Bradford, 2020, p. 14), and specifically the reach of the influence of the GDPR. This rhetoric of the EU as a "regulatory superpower" often contains notions of a role as leader and inspiration that the EU can play for the rest of the world.

It was Europe who spread the Westphalian model of sovereign states to the rest of the world as former European colonies increasingly claimed their own statehood in the nineteenth and twentieth centuries (Paris, 2020, p. 457). Now, the EU is proclaiming a new kind of sovereignty, the digital kind. This outward-facing proclamation can be seen as a kind of "norm entrepreneurship". In the literature on the emergence and development of international norms, norm entrepreneurs seek to "convince a critical mass of states... to embrace" (Finnemore & Sikkink, 1998, p. 895) a norm. And especially in the case of sovereignty, there's a strategic advantage in promoting norms that "align with – and thus help to legitimize – [one's] own policies and behaviour" (Paris, 2020, p. 454). Thus it is not surprising that the spectres of imperialism and colonialism by Europe and the West hover eerily in the background whenever EU digital sovereignty is advertised as an inspiration for the world.

Indeed, regulatory or constitutional design may not be enough to ensure the accountability and overall desirable effects of digital sovereignty. But as a final, hopeful note, this author joins the political philosopher and oftentimes critic of sovereignty Bertrand de Jouvenel in placing my hope for what can truly channel sovereignty today in "the shared moral concepts of the citizenry, which act as a constraint upon the choices of the sovereign" (Philpott, 2020).

Bibliography

Agnew, J. (2005, June 1). Sovereignty regimes: Territoriality and state authority in contemporary world politics. *Annals of the Association of American Geographers, 95*(1), 437–461.

Aristotle. (1984). In J. Barnes (Ed.), *The complete works of Aristotle: The revised Oxford translation*. Princeton University Press.

Bradford, A. (2020). *The Brussels effect: How the European Union rules the world*. Oxford University Press.

Burwell, F., & Propp, K. (2020, June 22). The European Union and the search for digital sovereignty: Building "Fortress Europe" or preparing for a new world? https://www.atlanticcouncil.org/in-depth-research-reports/issue-brief/the-european-union-and-the-search-for-digital-sovereignty/

Cohen, B. I. (1997). The body politic before and after the scientific revolution. In P. H. Theerman & K. Hunger Parshall (Eds.), *Experiencing nature: Proceedings of a conference in honor of Allen G. Debus* (pp. 1–41). Springer Netherlands.

Consolidated version of the Treaty on European Union. (2012). http://data.europa.eu/eli/treaty/teu_2012/oj/eng.

Couture, S., & Toupin, S. (2019, October 1). What does the notion of "sovereignty" mean when referring to the digital? *New Media & Society, 21*(10), 2305–2322.

Culpepper, P. D., & Thelen, K. (2019, June 11). Are we all amazon primed? Consumers and the politics of platform power. *Comparative Political Studies*.

Dijck, J. (2020, April 1). Governing digital societies: Private platforms, public values. *Computer Law & Security Review, 36*.

European Commission. (2020). *European data strategy*. https://ec.europa.eu/info/strategy/priorities-2019-2024/europe-fit-digital-age/european-data-strategy_en

European Commission. (2022, January 26). *Declaration on European digital rights and principles*. https://digital-strategy.ec.europa.eu/en/library/declaration-european-digital-rights-and-principles

Finnemore, M., & Sikkink, K. (1998). International norm dynamics and political change. *International Organization, 52*(4), 887–917.

Formigari, L. (1973). Chain of being. In *Dictionary of the history of ideas*.

Hicks, R. I. (1963). The body political and the body ecclesiastical. *Journal of Bible and Religion, 31*(1), 29–35.

Hintz, A., Dencik, L., & Wahl-Jorgensen, K. (2018). *Digital citizenship in a Datafied society*. Polity Press.

Ihalainen, P. (2009). Towards an immortal political body: The state machine in eighteenth-century English political discourse. *Contributions to the History of Concepts, 5*(1), 4–47.

James, A. (1999, August 1). The practice of sovereign statehood in contemporary international society. *Political Studies, 47*(3), 457–473.

Kukutai, T., & Taylor, J. (2016). *Indigenous data sovereignty: Toward an agenda*. ANU Press.

Leonard, M., & Shapiro, J. (2016, June 25). *Strategic sovereignty: How Europe can regain the capacity to act*. https://ecfr.eu/publication/strategic_sovereignty_how_europe_can_regain_the_capacity_to_act/

Leyen, U. (2020). *Op-Ed by Commission President von der Leyen*. https://ec.europa.eu/commission/presscorner/detail/en/AC_20_260

Madiega, T. (2020). *Digital sovereignty for Europe. EPRS Ideas Paper. Towards a More Resilient EU*. https://www.europarl.europa.eu/RegData/etudes/BRIE/2020/651992/EPRS_BRI(2020)651992_EN.pdf

Merriam, C. E. (2001). *History of the theory of sovereignty since Rousseau*. Batoche Books.

Michel, C. (2021). *Digital sovereignty is central to European strategic autonomy—Speech by President Charles Michel at "Masters of Digital 2021" Online Event*. https://www.consilium.europa.eu/en/press/press-releases/2021/02/03/speech-by-president-charles-michel-at-the-digitaleurope-masters-of-digital-online-event/.

Miskimmon, A., O'Loughlin, B., & Roselle, L. (2017). *Forging the world: Strategic narratives and international relations*. University of Michigan Press.

Neu, J. (1971, July). Plato's analogy of state and individual. *Philosophy, 46*(77), 238–254.

Paris, R. (2020, July). The right to dominate: How old ideas about sovereignty pose new challenges for world order. *International Organization, 74*(3), 453–489.

Philpott, D. (2020, Fall). *Sovereignty*. (E. N. Zalta, Ed.). https://plato.stanford.edu/archives/fall2020/entries/sovereignty/.

Pohle, J., & Thiel, T. (2020, December 17). Digital sovereignty. *Internet Policy Review, 9*(4).

Roberts, H., Cowls, J., Casolari, F., Morley, J., Taddeo, M., & Floridi, L. (2021, September 30). Safeguarding European values with digital sovereignty: An analysis of statements and policies. *Internet Policy Review, 10*(3).

Speech to Parliament of 21 March 1610. (1995). In King James VI and I, & J. P. Sommerville (Eds.), *King James VI and I: Political writings* (pp. 179–203). Cambridge University Press.

Tavernier, J. (2014). Morality and nature: Evolutionary challenges to Christian ethics. *Zygon: Journal of Religion and Science, 49*(1), 171–189.

Timmers, P. (2019, December). Challenged by "digital sovereignty". *Journal of Internet Law, 23*(6).

Walters, B. (2020). *The deaths of the republic: Imagery of the body politic in Ciceronian Rome*. Oxford University Press.

CHAPTER 4

Digital Sovereignty as a Laboratory for EU Strategic Autonomy

Eric Peters

It will still take a long time to show that sovereignty withers when it is frozen in the forms of the past. For it to live, it is necessary to transfer it, as the frameworks of action expand, into a larger space where it merges with others destined for the same evolution. None is lost in this transfer; on the contrary, all are strengthened.

Jean Monnet, Memoirs, 1976.

We must make this Europe's Digital Decade. Europe must now lead the way on digital–or it will have to follow the way of others, who are setting these standards for us. This is why we must move fast. None of this is an

Disclaimer: The author is an official of the European Commission. The information and views set out in this chapter are those of the author and do not necessarily reflect the official opinion of the Institution.

E. Peters (✉)
European Commission, Brussels, Belgium
e-mail: Eric.peters@ec.europa.eu

T. Kleiner and A. Garcia Rodriguez (eds.), *The Making of a Global Digital Rulebook*, https://doi.org/10.1007/978-981-95-9226-5_4

end in itself–it is about Europe's digital sovereignty, on a small and large scale.

President Von der Leyen, State of the Union address, September 2020.

Introduction

As illustrated by Jean Monnet's quote in his Memoirs, the question of sovereignty has been central to European construction since its inception in the 1950s (Dinan, 2014). However, most of the political debate, including in the context of the European Defence Community project, has focused on the freely consented delegation by Member States of their sovereignty by negotiations of specific competence attributions and underpinned with common institutions (such as economic governance with common monetary policy and single market, Schengen).

Recently, the external dimension of EU sovereignty—referring to the Union's ability to act independently on the global stage and safeguard its resilience against external shocks—has become a central focus of European policy. This shift is a response to a series of geopolitical challenges and crises, including the COVID-19 pandemic, which underscored the urgent need for the EU to secure critical supply chains and adopt a more self-reliant approach in key sectors such as health, digital technology and energy. These developments have driven the EU to prioritise strategic autonomy, aiming to reduce dependencies and enhance its capacity to withstand external disruptions.

After a period of restraint of public authorities to regulate the Internet in the first decade of this century, the critical importance of digital technologies in driving economic growth, ensuring security, setting global standards, promoting integration and responding to geopolitical challenges has led to a major shift, with the rise of digital policies which have been a laboratory for advancing sovereignty, to secure the EU's economic future, protect its citizens and assert its influence on the global stage.

This chapter will detail the origins of the mechanism through which the EU has advanced its sovereignty agenda in the digital realm, notably through the preparation, negotiation and implementation of the 2030 Digital Decade Strategy (L 323/4, 2022).

Setting the Scene–From Sovereignty to Digital Sovereignty

The EU'S Primary Objective: Defend the Interests of its Citizens

The European Union (EU) has consistently advocated for global economic integration, not as an end in itself, but as a strategic means to achieve critical objectives aligned with its broader interests. This approach, rooted in a commitment to peaceful cooperation and a rules-based international order, has solidified Europe's position as a leading global trading power and contributed significantly to its prosperity. However, it is crucial to recall the foundational objective of the European project as outlined in the Treaty on the European Union (TUE).

Article 3 of the TUE articulates the EU's overarching mission: to protect and promote the interests of its citizens across various dimensions—security, economic well-being, social justice, cultural identity and global engagement. Each clause underscores the EU's commitment to ensuring that its citizens can flourish within a safe, equitable and prosperous environment, reinforcing the principle that the Union's actions are fundamentally centred on the well-being and protection of its people. Article 3 also mandates that the EU employs all appropriate means to pursue these objectives within the scope of its competencies. This legal framework not only delineates the EU's areas of action but also highlights its proactive stance in addressing the needs and interests of its citizens.

When the interests of EU citizens diverge from broader global policy objectives—such as in the context of globalisation increasingly characterised by fewer protections and fair rules or amid rising geopolitical tensions—the Treaty mandates that the EU prioritises its own interests to safeguard and empower its citizens. Far from being naive, the EU has consistently and effectively adapted to the shifting global landscape since its inception. During the rise of rules-based globalisation following World War II and the establishment of global markets ensuring secure supply chains, it was in the EU's interest to promote its integration into international investment and trade flows. This strategy enabled the EU to import inexpensive goods while exporting high-value products, as demonstrated in the Global Agenda 2006 (COM (2006) 567 final, 2006),[1] where 30% of the world's product value originated from the EU.

The same principle applies to the EU's approach to competition policy, particularly in an increasingly insecure and unstable global environment. This approach requires reframing concerns about consumer prices within a broader context that includes the EU's capacity to act, investment in critical technological infrastructures (such as semiconductors and batteries) and the ability to respond effectively to crises like the COVID-19 pandemic (Jones, et al., 2021).

The growing emphasis on sovereignty, particularly in the economic domain, reflects the EU's recognition of the need to recalibrate its policy priorities in response to emerging risks and geopolitical shifts, ensuring that its strategies align with the best interests of its citizens. The EU's agility and effectiveness in pursuing its interests are rooted in its dynamic and adaptive strategies, which are deeply embedded in the principles enshrined in the TUE. These strategies encompass a blend of legislative initiatives, strategic partnerships and diplomatic engagements. By fostering a robust internal market, investing in innovation and digital transformation and enhancing its defence capabilities, the EU is increasingly demonstrating its commitment to safeguarding the future of its citizens and businesses in a more conflictual and risk-laden geopolitical environment. This recalibration of dependencies and investment in industrial capacities is central to the ongoing discourse on sovereignty and strategic autonomy, where digital policies play a crucial role.

Sovereignty and Strategic Autonomy as Policy Concepts

The European Union (EU) frequently invokes the concepts of 'sovereignty' and 'strategic autonomy' within its legal and policy texts

[1] 'European manufacturing industry has broadly maintained its share of GDP in volume in the face of globalisation. Its output has increased by 40% over the last two decades. Despite rapid economic change and the emergence of a new range of competitors in particular China, Brazil and India, the EU's position on world markets remains almost unchanged, while the US and Japan have lost ground. Analysis shows that this good performance is mainly due to the ability of EU companies to sell products at premium price due to quality, branding and related services. These "upmarket" products now account for a third of world demand and represent half of European exports, not only in luxury consumer goods, but across the whole range of EU exports'.

to articulate its renewed vision for the Union's role on the global stage and its internal governance.

Sovereignty in the EU context traditionally referred to the shared sovereignty among Member States, enabling them to collectively wield greater influence and address transnational challenges more effectively than they could individually. This shared sovereignty is enshrined in treaties, notably the Treaty on the European Union (TUE). However, there has recently been a significant shift towards viewing sovereignty not only as an internal (re-)distribution of competencies but in its primary sense in political theory developed since Jean Bodin (Bodin, 1986 [1576]): an ability to act autonomously and assertively on the global stage linked with a capacity to take legitimate action within a territory. This external dimension of sovereignty includes the EU's capacity to act and to master its own destiny, including representing and defending its interests internationally ensuring its strategic presence and influence worldwide. This recent dimension of EU's sovereignty has been coined mainly between 2017 and 2019, notably by President Macron, Chancellor Merkel and President Von der Leyen (Germany's Presidency of the Council of the European Union, 2020; Leyen, 2019; Macron, 2017; Merkel, 2018) with the notion of sovereignty spreading into EU legal texts and leading to further analysis by think tanks (e.g. Leonard et al., 2019).

Strategic autonomy, on the other hand, has emerged since 2013 from the security and defence sphere in response to global geopolitical shifts (Borell, 2020; Damen, 2022). It emphasises the EU's aim to reduce dependencies on external actors and bolster its own capabilities in critical areas like defence, technology and supply chains (Council of the European Union, 2016)[2] and, more recently, in economic fields (monetary, trade, health). It has thus developed a common vision of the threats through the Strategic Compass (EEAS, 2022). Strategic autonomy is certainly not a short-term endeavour but a gradual, long-term process aimed at empowering Europeans to take greater control of their own affairs. In order to defend the EU's interests and values in an increasingly challenging world, the EU has progressively recognised the necessity to increasingly rely on itself to secure its future.

[2] The Council conclusions on implementing the EU Global Strategy in the area of Security and Defence Council of 14 November 2016 refer notably to the EU's 'capacity to act autonomously when and where necessary and with partners wherever possible'.

Since 2019, the terms 'EU's sovereignty' and 'EU's strategic autonomy' have been used somehow interchangeably in the economic realm by EU institutions, with a preference of liberals for the notion of 'open strategic autonomy' while those favouring a more assertive industrial policy do usually have a preference for the word 'sovereignty'. But in reality, both describe the Union's capacity to act independently and assertively and to protect itself from external risk and influences. For instance, the EU's Global Strategy and the Commission's communications on industrial policy (COM (2021) 350 final, 2021) outline steps to achieve strategic autonomy, ensuring the EU can act independently and uphold its interests and values in a complex, interdependent world. Similarly, the European Commission's White Paper on Artificial Intelligence (COM (2020) 65 final, 2020) highlights the importance of digital sovereignty, emphasising the need for the EU to develop its own technological capabilities to ensure security, privacy and competitiveness. Together, these concepts shape the EU's efforts to create a resilient, self-reliant Union capable of navigating and thriving amidst global uncertainties.

Key Features of Sovereignty/Strategic Autonomy

The pursuit of EU sovereignty and strategic autonomy, including in the digital age, necessitates a policy framework that includes the following elements.

First, the role of frontiers remains crucial, as it establishes the territorial limits that differentiate the interests and protection needs of the population within from those of the outside world. Sovereignty and frontiers are intrinsically linked; the concept of sovereignty fundamentally depends on the demarcation and control of these borders, which define the physical and jurisdictional boundaries within which a state exercises its sovereign authority. This delineation is vital for maintaining the integrity of a political entity's territory, ensuring the enforcement of its laws and safeguarding its collective interests. In a broader geopolitical context, frontiers also symbolise the limits of influence and control, marking the extent to which a political entity can project power and uphold its sovereignty against external challenges. The concept of borders, which was not a central focus during the first seven decades of EU integration—marked by the continuous expansion of territorial scope without a clear and explicit delineation of the ultimate limits to enlargement—has now gained renewed importance in the ongoing debate on sovereignty. This renewed focus has significant implications for the scope of EU policies, both those active within the Union and those governing its citizens, as well as for determining who participates in policymaking discussions—whether it be the 27 Member States, the EEA or potentially even broader settings.

Second, a crucial element is the collective representation of policy issues, risks and threats facing the EU and its economy. This involves not only identifying common objectives but also devising coordinated action measures to address these challenges effectively. It includes selecting relevant policy areas and determining the appropriate policy mix for collective response. This strategic vision is exemplified in documents such as the Strategic Compass for EU Security and Defence and the Digital Decade Policy Programme for digital transformation. Achieving this vision requires gathering and analysing underlying facts, building expertise and enhancing the capacity of the political ecosystem, which includes both public and private actors.

Third, the development of industrial and technological capacities and the mitigation of dependencies are fundamental to both sovereignty and strategic autonomy. The private sector plays a pivotal role in producing the technologies and infrastructures essential for a well-functioning economy. Reducing reliance on external actors for critical resources, technologies and capabilities is vital for maintaining strategic autonomy. This is achieved through investments in European industries, diversification of supply chains and the promotion of indigenous innovation. The EU's initiatives to establish a European battery industry and its push for semiconductor self-sufficiency are prime examples of this strategy. Similarly, enhancing collective capabilities in defence, technology and cybersecurity—through mechanisms such as the European Defence Fund and the Horizon Europe research programme—reflects this comprehensive approach.

Fourth, the effective capacity to act, including through regulations, is another crucial aspect. This means not only acting together as Member States but also ensuring that public authorities have the capacity to ensure alignment of all actors effectively, including the private sector, with broader public policy objectives. This is particularly important in contexts where large digital players seek—and sometimes succeed—to leverage their power and capacities to operate autonomously, illustrating the famous word of Peter Thiel ('competition is for losers'). The General Data

Protection Regulation (GDPR) is a clear instance of the EU asserting its regulatory power to protect citizens' data privacy against global digital giants. This regulatory capacity ensures that the EU can set and enforce standards that align with its values and strategic objectives.

Finally, legitimacy and governance of public action are crucial to ensuring an effective capacity to act through legitimate means. This involves the democratic legitimacy of EU institutions and decision-making processes, transparency and accountability, articulated with respect to the rule of law. Ensuring that the EU's actions are perceived as legitimate and necessary by its citizens and Member States is essential for the effectiveness and sustainability of its policies. This legitimacy is underpinned by the principles outlined in the EU treaties and the operational frameworks of its institutions but also in the policy frameworks that are designed and explicated for forging collecting consensus (common objectives, monitoring process, governance of the decision-making, stakeholder consultations), as well as on the strong link that can be established between policy objectives, action taken and the rule of law and fundamental rights.

Sovereignty and EU Integration—A Paradigm Shift

This chapter looks in more detail into the roots and drivers of the emergence of the EU's sovereignty agenda. The last two decades have seen the EU grappling with a series of disruptions that have profoundly influenced its approach to sovereignty and shaped the overall context in which the notion of digital sovereignty has developed. These disruptions have highlighted the need for the EU to reassert the nature and cost of its dependencies on the rest of the world and to adapt to a rapidly changing global landscape.

The Weakening of Twentieth-Century Globalisation

One of the most profound disruptions in recent years has been the unravelling of globalisation as it was shaped at the start of the twenty-first century. The traditional rules-based international order has come under considerable strain, with multilateral institutions weakening, multilateral negotiations stalling and enforcement mechanisms failing. This has severely limited the prospects for the continued development of global exchanges under a framework of fair rules and consensus among members of multilateral fora. A clear example of this is the Doha Development Agenda, the last round of World Trade Organization (WTO) negotiations launched in 2001, which stalled in 2007 and has since seen its dispute settlement body effectively paralysed over the past decade.

The COVID-19 pandemic further exposed the fragility of global systems, starkly highlighting the vulnerabilities of disrupted global flows. Nations experienced acute shortages of critical supplies as global logistics networks broke down, revealing the increased risks associated with overreliance on extended supply chains. The inability of global markets to manage and mitigate these risks has prompted a shift towards more assertive public interventions, often through 'command and control' mechanisms.

A Growing Focus on Security

Another significant disruption has been a growing focus on security. Since 2014 and more recently since 2022, Russia has posed a direct threat to EU security through its aggressive actions, with the annexation of Crimea, war in Ukraine and cyber-attacks against EU Member States. In the context of a heating technological race, the relationship with China has increasingly presented a geopolitical challenge for the EU, particularly in areas such as 5G technology. Concerns over espionage and cyber security have led the EU to scrutinise and, in some cases, ban Chinese technology firms like Huawei from participating in critical infrastructure projects. Developed in this context, the EU's 5G Security Toolbox (COM (2020) 50 final, 2020) provides guidelines for Member States to mitigate risks associated with the deployment of 5G networks.

These developments have happened in a context of uncertainty regarding transatlantic relations and flickering US commitment to European security. The relationship between the EU and the USA has faced challenges, particularly concerning security and technological sovereignty. The American pivot to Asia (Clinton, 2011), incidents such as the Obama-era spying revelations and the unpredictability, if not antagonistic European policy of the Trump administration have been a series of wake-up calls for the EU to develop its own capacities in strategic sectors. In many ways, these developments have been seminal for the decision of Member States to secure their industrial basis and foster EU-grown technologies as they set up the Euro HPC (European High-Performance Computing) programme aiming at establishing sovereign high-performance computing capabilities within Europe and by European companies.

The Impact of Brexit Negotiations

Brexit and its consecutive negotiations with the EU have also played a crucial role in the shift of the EU's approach to sovereignty.

The negotiation was the first of its kind. Indeed, trade agreements and accession negotiations are usually operated while keeping strict control over the possible impacts on the single market, these negotiations being essentially limited and under a well-controlled extension of the rules defined among Member States. The Brexit negotiation was testing the EU's priority and had the potential to undermine the Member States.

The Brexit negotiations forced EU institutions to address a broader set of interests beyond the mere limitation of the economic cost and optimisation of gains linked to the establishment of trade frontiers as usually operated in a classical trade agreement (Gostyńska-Jakubowska & Ondarza, 2020). The Brexit process, including the negotiation of the new trade agreement finalised in December 2020, triggered the necessity for EU institutions and their negotiation teams to change their negotiation culture and approach, considering and following greater strategic objectives, including political and social dimensions in its policymaking, where strategic long-term interest may trump immediate economic losses. This has been notably the case of the negotiations on the Northern Ireland Protocol, which involved complex considerations of political stability, border security, the rights of citizens and the preservation of the EU's internal market.

Brexit has also forced the EU to reevaluate and strengthen its internal cohesion and unity after the negotiations. The EU has taken steps to ensure that the remaining Member States remain committed to the European project. For example, the EU has intensified its efforts to promote deeper economic integration among the remaining members through initiatives such as the Recovery and Resilience Facility (RRF), which aims to support economic recovery post-COVID-19 while promoting green and digital transitions.

In this context, the negotiation of Brexit has implied a sharp shift in the design, conduct and implementation of the negotiation from EU institutions (COM/2021/262 final, 2021) infiltrated into the Commission's teams from political layers to desk officers.

The Rise of Digital Technologies

The intensification of the digital transformation and the rise of a 'digital age' has been a game changer in renewing the political appetite and approach to sovereignty (Floridi, 2020). In many ways, the digital revolution has dissolved traditional borders, raising critical questions about security and data control within frontiers. It also has considerably blurred the role and importance of private companies having the power to intervene in areas usually restricted to public action (health, security, geolocalisation and mapping), to define the direct environment of citizens' online lives and to directly interface with them a great part of their awake time.

Firstly, the dissolution of frontiers in the digital age means that actors can access people and businesses directly, bypassing traditional state controls, distance and physical obstacles. This raises significant issues regarding interference and the effective capacity of the state to act. For example, social media platforms based outside the EU can influence the core of democracy through public opinion and electoral outcomes within Member States. The spread of disinformation and foreign interference in democratic processes has underscored the need for the EU to assert greater control over digital content and platforms. The EU's efforts to tackle these challenges include initiatives such as the Code of Practice on Disinformation, which seeks to hold platforms accountable for the spread of fake news.

Secondly, the rise of a powerful private sector that is dominantly based in the USA poses significant challenges to the EU's sovereignty. Tech giants like Google, Facebook and Amazon have the capacity to define the digital environment, including its use. The concept of 'code is law' (Lessig, 2000) highlights how these companies' algorithms and policies effectively set the rules for behaviours online, often without oversight or accountability. This has led to concerns about privacy, data security and market dominance (Chander & Sun, 2023). The first line of action of the EU has been to respond by regulating foreign actors with far-reaching regulations. This has been reflected by the adoption of the GDPR, which set a global benchmark for data protection, emphasising the need for stringent privacy standards and user consent, as well as the Digital Services Act (DSA) and the Digital Market Act (DMA) that aim to curb the power of 'Big Tech' and ensure a fair and competitive digital market. However, effectively and timely regulating these companies remains very challenging due to their power and the rapid evolution of their technology, which makes ex-post decisions 'too little too late'.

More generally, the rise of digital technologies has raised concerns about the long-term impacts of the US's assertive promotion of its strategic interests, which might not always align with the EU's. Since the advent of the digital age, the USA has maintained a strong grip on the development of the Internet and its regulatory framework, pursuing strategic geopolitical and economic goals and seeking to maintain its dominance on the global stage. As globalisation faded, together with the prospect of integrating developing and emerging countries into the liberal democratic fold, the Internet was seen as a new and efficient means to achieve these objectives by directly accessing and influencing citizens worldwide, beyond and sometimes against their government. This US approach has been implemented through a mix of policies, including limited liability for online platforms, the promotion of multistakeholder governance and the backing of online anonymity. For example, the USA has heavily influenced global policies through its domestic regulations, such as Section 230 of the Communications Decency Act enacted in 1996, which shields online platforms from liability. This regulation served as a model for the EU's E-Commerce Directive in 2000, whose central rule—limited liability and interdiction of general monitoring—was maintained if not reinforced in the DSA. Additionally, the USA has shaped global internet governance through multistakeholder forums, maintaining de facto, even if indirectly, its dominance in the management of the Internet and its governance. The EU's efforts to regulate large tech companies through initiatives like the DSA and the DMA represent an attempt to seek to accommodate this, ensuring some ex-post obligations to correct the effects of the lack of responsibility limitation, to create a safer and more transparent online environment, reflecting European values of privacy and consumer protection.

Last but not least, the EU's diminishing role as a tech leader bears the risk of strategic irrelevance. The EU is increasingly less central to the innovation and design of the digital environment. 80% of the technologies and services needed for Europe's digital transformation are designed and manufactured in third countries, and the share of European platforms has failed to exceed 5% of global value for ten years (European Commission, 2024a). More generally, Europe lags behind the USA and China in critical areas such as artificial intelligence (AI), 5G networks and semiconductor production.

The intrinsic dynamic of the 'winner-takes-all' digital ecosystem gives an additional advantage to established leaders, which could be strengthened at a time when generative AI can provide systemic dominance over weaker rivals. Occupying the technological frontier is the ultimate weapon to achieve digital sovereignty critically. But after decades of insufficient investments and a lack of coordinated strategy, it would require massive investment in R&D, structuring projects and attracting brains to rebalance what currently amounts only to half that of the USA. Despite the target of 3% of GDP that has been set—but never achieved—for more than two decades, the EU's global share of R&D has fallen from 41% to 31%.

The Draghi report published in September 2024 has brought forward supplementary evidence on the worrying position of the EU. Roughly a third of startups founded in Europe since 2008 that went on to be unicorns—those valued at $1 billion or more—left the bloc, with the majority coming to the USA. The report stresses that the USA is home to 22 of the 50 companies with the world's biggest research and development budgets, while Europe has only 12. Over 70% of AI models built since 2017 are from the USA and 15% stem from China. All six of the most valuable companies in the USA—all of which are worth more than $1 trillion—have been created in the last 50 years, while no European company valued at more than $100 billion has been started in that period (Draghi, 2024).

In many ways, the EU's deteriorating position reflects a past lack of brinkmanship as compared with the strategic plans set up by the EU's main competitors to regain sovereignty (Alcidi, et al., 2023). Major global powers have implemented policies prioritising domestic interests, each ing different narratives to justify similar actions. The USA, under the 'America First' banner initiated by the Trump administration, shifted towards protecting domestic objectives, a trend exemplified by the Inflation Reduction Act (IRA), which promotes domestic interests even at the expense of global partners. China, through its 'dual circulation strategy' and 'Made in China 2025' industrial policy, has pushed towards self-sufficiency and has adopted a more assertive stance towards Western economies. India's own 'Make in India' initiative also aligns with this trend.

Conclusion

The development of digital technologies and services provides an injunction and a test bed for the EU to redefine its sovereignty objectives, principles and actions. This is a crucial area where the EU realises the increasing cost of its dependencies and the need to invest much more in managing these risks, thus becoming 'digitally sovereign', i.e. having the 'ability to act independently in the digital world' (Bendiek & Stuerzer, 2023) and to address concerns over the economic and social influence of non-EU technological companies. The initial strategy of achieving these objectives through regulation—ensuring that foreign actors comply with EU values—has proven insufficient and frequently too slow to keep up with the rapid pace of technological advancements, demonstrating that regulatory measures alone are not enough.

The overall context has been fostering a growing recognition that the EU needs to adopt a comprehensive approach. This involves significant investment in digital technologies and infrastructures, explicit acknowledgement of the interlinkages between different policy areas and robust governance processes to ensure the legitimacy and efficacy of collective action at the EU and Member State levels. By adopting such a multifaceted strategy, the EU would seek to act based on its own strategic considerations and to better protect and promote the interests of its citizens while reinforcing its sovereignty in an increasingly complex and interconnected world.

The Digital Decade: An Original Attempt to Adapt the Digital Policies to the New Sovereignty Context

Genesis

The Political Guidelines setting out President Von der Leyen's policy priorities in July 2019 constitute a clear step change in the importance given by the Commission to digital issues with a clear focus on 'twinning the green and digital transition'. This is also the first reference to 'digital sovereignty' in such a strategic document of the Commission.[3]

The 'Shaping Europe's Digital Future' Communication, which was the instrument designed to implement the 2019–2024 Commission's digital agenda, was primarily focused on setting standards and regulations. The approach was chiefly seeking efficiency ('the EU's digital strategy aims to make this transformation work for people and businesses'), emphasising the opportunities of the digital transformation and with an EU-centred angle, with limited reference to the position of the EU in the global digital ecosystem and on EU's position in the technological race.

The COVID-19 Crisis Time

The COVID-19 crisis has crystallised several evolutions that were creeping in the 2010s into disruptive challenges, thereby reinforcing the necessity for a new EU's digital policy approach.

First, the COVID-19 pandemic significantly heightened the EU's sense of vulnerability across several dimensions, exposing the fragility of existing systems and dependencies on non-European technologies and supply chains. The pandemic-induced lockdowns in key manufacturing hubs, particularly in China, led to severe shortages of essential components like semiconductors, underscoring the EU's reliance on a few foreign suppliers and the need for a more resilient supply chain within Europe. The crisis highlighted the EU's dependency on non-European technology providers, posing severe risks to economic stability and security, notably linked to security vulnerabilities in 5G networks and potential espionage. The pandemic also revealed the vulnerability of our democratic fabric with the surge in disinformation on health issues, particularly through digital platforms, which undermined public health efforts and sowed distrust in institutions.

More generally, the COVID-19 crisis shed light on how the key problems facing the EU's citizens and Member States are no longer internal to the European space but external (Leonard & Shapiro, 2019). Traditionally, the EU's primary focus was on internal issues—economic integration, political stability and regulatory harmonisation aimed at fostering peace

[3] 'It may be too late to replicate hyperscalers, but it is not too late to achieve technological sovereignty in some critical technology areas', Ursula von der Leyen Political Guidelines, 2019.

and prosperity within its borders. The pandemic itself was a clear example of how global health challenges transcend borders and require coordinated international responses. The pandemic's impact on global trade disrupted European economies, affecting many sectors, from manufacturing to tourism. Europe's reliance on external sources for energy supplies, such as natural gas from Russia, has further reinforced the need to better anticipate and manage external risks of disruptions in energy supplies.

Third, digital transformation has taken centre stage in people's lives and businesses, with digital technologies becoming essential. With lockdowns forcing businesses to close physical offices, remote work became the norm, often without possible offline alternatives. The use of conference platforms grew exponentially, demonstrating the critical role of digital tools in maintaining business continuity. Schools and universities shifted to online learning, underscoring the importance of digital infrastructure and skills. However, this shift also highlighted the digital divide, with many students lacking access to necessary devices and reliable internet connections. This happened in a context where the EU's digital ecosystem was far from punching above its weight for designing the future digital environment through Web3, 6G or the so-called Metaverse (virtual spaces). The EU continued to suffer from several actors having reached global critical mass, as highlighted by the decreasing value of its online platform ecosystem, from 4% in the mid-2010s to less than 3% today. The current digital environment in which European citizens spend a substantial part of their lives is thus largely defined and designed by non-European actors abroad. This is all the more important now that a new acceleration of digital transformation has been in the making with virtual spaces or the rise of AI.

These geopolitical, economic, social and environmental realities intersected with the digital transformation in two ways: they were accelerated by digitalisation, and at the same time, digital tools became the instruments that policymakers could use to intervene with more efficient processes, data-based solutions and better-informed decisions, as exemplified by the COVID-19 certificate application and its underlying digital infrastructure.

The Digital Decade's Political Premises

It is, therefore, no coincidence that the announcement of the Digital Decade by President Von der Leyen coincided with COVID-19. As the pandemic forced nations into lockdowns and remote work setups, the digital transformation shifted from an important to an essential nature for all aspects of life. In the 2020 State of the Union address, President Von der Leyen said: 'We must make this Europe's Digital Decade. We need a common plan for digital Europe with clearly defined goals for 2030, such as connectivity, skills and digital public services. And we need to follow clear principles: the right to privacy and connectivity, freedom of speech, free flow of data and cybersecurity'.

While the digital policy was put as one of the six strategic priorities of VDL back in 2019 with a specific status of a 'twin transition' with the fight against climate change, it lacked a proper governance mechanism, as well as a concrete legally binding commitment from Member States to put it on a par with climate change policy and to ensure that this European ambition was translated into action.

The COVID-19 crisis raised this awareness at the highest level, increasing the political capital which political parties afforded the EU's digital transformation. President Von der Leyen's announcement thus reflected a clear push of the European People's Party (EPP) to increase the EU's ambitions for digital policy. This, indeed, was the main point of the EPP intervention in the debate that followed the 2020 State of the Union speech as portrayed by the party chairman, Manfred Weber:

> I want to focus my contribution on our main title – how can we address the fears of Europeans after the crisis or during the crisis? How can we answer this? And our main message is that we have to now show credibility. For the European People's Party, the headline of the upcoming weeks is jobs, jobs and jobs.... For us, credibility means immediately starting the digital catch-up. You spoke about this. But, I must ask, where are the initiatives from the Commission? We have had green papers, we have had white papers, but no real progress has been made. And that is what we need. We can probably even have a kind of Digital Act like we do the Climate Act to prioritise things – investment in infrastructure and investment in technologies

President Ursula von der Leyen announced the Digital Decade as a visionary initiative aimed at accelerating the EU's digital transformation and reinforcing its global competitiveness. This marked a pivotal moment in EU digital policy, signalling a decisive shift towards prioritising digital innovation, sovereignty and resilience.

The announcement of the Digital Decade Policy Programme thus represented a watershed moment in EU digital policy, marking a strategic pivot towards a more resilient, innovative and digitally empowered Europe. It did not only reflect the lessons learned from the COVID-19 crisis; it also charted a course towards a future where digital transformation is not merely a necessity but a driver of prosperity, security and progress. In a time of doubts and fears, propelled by the rise of inflation and a looming energy crisis, the EU also had to ensure that people would benefit from a positive economic environment and more job creation to deliver on its promise of prosperity for all. In this regard, accelerating the deployment of digital technologies, which was meant to bring in €2.2 trillion additional GDP for the EU by 2030 (European Commission, 2020), was essential.

After 20 years of digital policy initiatives that were set out to respond to specific new issues (e.g. protection of privacy, net neutrality, protection of copyright), it was time to take stock and design a comprehensive framework that would respond to EU strategic interests and to the need to project EU values with a more ambitious and integrated approach for digital policy.

The Digital Compass Communication and the Digital Decade Policy Programme

The Digital Compass, announced by President Ursula von der Leyen, was the vehicle to outline and detail the vision and renewed approach in response to the European Council's (hereinafter: the Council) invitation to 'set a clear roadmap for the EU at a horizon 2030', emphasising the need for a comprehensive and forward-looking approach to digital policy, recognising the transformative potential of digitalisation across all sectors of the economy and society.

From the outset, the Communication includes one of the boldest assertions on digital sovereignty. It calls for Europe to become 'digitally sovereign' and to anchor this endeavour in clear goals and principles, notably 'by building and deploying technological capabilities in a way that empowers people and businesses to seize the potential of the digital transformation, and helps build a healthier and greener society' (COM/2021/118 final, 2021).

- **Comprehensiveness**: The Digital Compass Communication presents a holistic strategy that encompasses the key aspects of the digital ecosystem and technologies.
- **Investing in digital technologies and infrastructures.** The Communication recognises the need to complete regulation with massive investments in resilient, secure and trustworthy infrastructures and technologies for ensuring the respect of European rules and values and improving the EU's capacity to shape its future, including its prosperity and security.
- **Anchored into values.** Communication is an important step to describe more clearly the values and principles that are at the basis of the European approach to digital transformation, including ethical concerns and citizens' rights online.
- **Stressing cooperation.** Cooperation is a cornerstone of Communication, including enhanced collaboration among Member States and Public-Private Partnerships.

Proposing concrete instruments:

- *Digital Rights Principles* The Digital Decade Communication emphasises the importance of upholding fundamental rights in the digital sphere. Building on the experience of the European Pillars of Social Rights, the Communication announces an inter-institutional solemn Declaration (COM(2022) 28 final, 2022) between the European Commission, the European Parliament and the Council, which would entail the different rights and principles recapitulating the citizens' rights included in primary and secondary legislation as well as the principles that need to be applied to reflect European values (i.e. human-centric, sustainability, security, freedom of expression, protection of privacy in the digital age).
- *Targets* The Digital Decade Communication sets out specific targets to guide the EU's digital transformation efforts. These 12 targets

include basic digital skills, ICT specialists, gigabit connectivity, semiconductors, edge nodes, quantum technologies, digitalisation intensity of SMEs, the take up of AI, Cloud and data analytics by businesses, number of 'Unicorns',[4] digitalisation of key public services for citizens, access to e-Health records and electronic identification.

- *Monitoring* Based on the Digital Economic and Society Index (DESI) (European Commission, 2022) monitoring system set up by the Commission in 2014, which would be enhanced to be adjusted to the Compass scope and content.
- *Governance* Effective governance structures are essential for coordinating and implementing the Digital Decade's objectives. The Communication outlines a governance framework that brings together stakeholders from across the public and private sectors, as well as civil society and academia.
- *Multi-country projects (MCPs)* The Communication emphasises the importance of pooling resources and expertise to tackle common challenges for projects that Member States alone could not achieve. MCPs under the Digital Decade may focus on a wide range of areas, including digital infrastructure development, digital skills training and the deployment of emerging technologies.

Overall, the Digital Decade Communication represented a bold and ambitious vision for Europe's digital future. By prioritising innovation, inclusion and sustainability, the EU is thus invited to embark on a transformative journey and to position itself as a global leader in the digital age, with the overarching objective to remain in control of its future.

The Digital Decade Policy Programme

In September 2021, the Commission proposed the 'Path to the Digital Decade', a draft Decision of the Council and European Parliament, to be adopted under normal procedure, implementing the Digital Compass Communication. The text was adopted after a very rapid negotiation with a political agreement after three trilogues on 14 July 2022. The Decision forms the framework of the Digital Decade, together with the Declaration

[4] Privately-owned startup businesses worth more than $1 billion

on Digital Rights and Principles signed on 14 December 2022 and which entered into force on 8 January 2023.

Elements of the Proposal

The Digital Decade Policy Programme (DDPP) reflects in a legal text the main elements of the Digital Compass while detailing cooperation obligations (Article 1) and setting out a robust governance mechanism, thus putting digital policy on par with the EU climate change policy framework.

The DDPP sets a number of general objectives, which cover the whole scope of the EU's digital transformation: building a human-centred digital space, protecting fundamental rights, addressing divides, resilience, competitiveness, digital sovereignty, democracy and public services, sustainability, as well as efficiency and coherence of digital policies.

The DDPP also includes 12 common quantitative targets that are measured by 17 key performance indicators (KPIs) with over 30 indicators in total at the EU and Member State level (see above).

Critically, Member States are requested to set out their contribution to the EU's digital transformation through 'national Digital Decade strategic roadmaps'. These roadmaps must outline concrete measures, policies and investment plans that each country intends to implement to achieve the 2030 objectives. Roadmaps play a key role both in ensuring the integration of digital issues and integrated adherence of all national actors, and in giving a comprehensive view of the actions taken by each Member State on digital transformation.

Every year, the Commission shall issue a report on the 'State of the Digital Decade' to assess Member States' progress, highlight best practices and identify areas that require improvement. These annual reports also include recommendations. The Digital Decade Board, made of experts and high-ranking officials from each Member State, acts as their central coordination point on digital policies and is used to exchange best practices and discuss issues of common interest. This governance and cycle enable a strategic piloting of the EU digital transformation.

One of the key features of the DDPP refers to the policy recommendations that the Commission can adopt, notably in case a Member State does not amend its national roadmap in accordance with recommended policies, measures and actions nor provide sufficient explanations as to why it intends not to address the recommended actions. The Member State concerned is required to take such a recommendation into utmost account and explain how it intends to implement it.

The DDPP also proposes to create a brand-new legal framework that aims to facilitate and accelerate the launch and implementation of Multi-Country Projects (MCPs).

Negotiations and Broader Policy Perspectives

Since the inception of the work on the Digital Decade, launched with the 2020 State of the Union address, EU institutions, particularly the co-legislators, have been highly supportive. This support facilitated an exceptionally swift negotiation process, lasting only 10 months and involving just two substantive trilogues (negotiation meetings involving the Commission, the Council and the European Parliament). The discussions primarily focused on several key elements: the level of ambition for the targets—viewed by some as too high, while others feared these targets could exacerbate the digital divide across the Member States; the need to reinforce aspects related to the single market and the green transition greatly supported by the European Parliament; the importance of streamlining the governance mechanism to avoid complex, burdensome processes and duplication with the European Semester and the Recovery and Resilience Facility (RRF) underlined by the Council; and the functionality and added value of European Digital Innovation Hubs (EDIHs), as well as their governance and connection with other initiatives.

In this regard, the Parliament and the Council positions differed on a number of issues:

- *Link to the Declaration on Digital Rights and Principles*. The Council sought to remove the reference to the Declaration in the context of the monitoring, while the Parliament was seeking to keep the Commission proposal, further reinforcing the language through the addition of a recital.
- *Targets and objectives*. The Parliament sought to adjust some of the targets (connectivity, business, public services), added a target on cloud infrastructure and brought a sustainability dimension to some of them. The Council aimed at only limited amendments to the Commission proposal (target on public services) but was seeking to

gain flexibility for the obligation linked to the achievement of the targets.

- Key performance indicators (KPIs) for measuring the progress. The Parliament suggested defining the KPIs through a delegated act, while the Council kept the Commission's proposal to use an implementing act given their different role in each comitology procedure.
- Recommendations. The Parliament supported the provision, giving the Commission the possibility to issue recommendations on national roadmaps, contrary to the Council.
- Spectrum. The Council successfully removed all provisions on the spectrum, a constant position to oppose any harmonisation in this area, despite the Parliament's support to keep them.

The European Parliament was particularly vigilant in ensuring that the Digital Decade framework could encompass and guide all policy dimensions of the digital transformation. It emphasised the importance of setting and monitoring targets, pooling financial resources and promoting initiatives in critical areas, such as semiconductors, digital skills and online public services. Additionally, the Parliament advocated for the inclusion of subnational governance levels, particularly regions, in the planning process, stressing the regional dimension of national roadmaps.

This development and implementation of the Digital Decade within the EU has taken place against a complex and highly strategic political backdrop, where the need to reinforce the EU's digital sovereignty has been felt as paramount. On this aspect in particular, this initiative has garnered strong backing from Council,[5] which views it as essential for ensuring Europe's autonomy in critical digital infrastructures, reducing dependency on external technologies and safeguarding the EU's digital ecosystem from geopolitical influences. The European Parliament has also broadly supported the Digital Decade, seeing it as a crucial mechanism to increase policy coherence across Member States and to unify

[5] See notably the Council Conclusions from 1 to 2 October 2020, which highlight the need to 'reduce strategic dependencies' and 'strengthen Europe's autonomy in the digital field' by advancing digital sovereignty. Also the 2023 Opinion of the European Economic and Social Committee on Digital Sovereignty, 'despite significant progress to enhance the EU's digital sovereignty, there is still heavy reliance on non-EU-based tech companies. This is limiting the EU's leadership and strategic autonomy in the digital world, and in turn limiting the EU's economic growth potential' (European Economic and Social Committee, 2022).

Europe's approach to the digital transition. However, this push for digital sovereignty has not been without controversy or opposition.

Externally, the USA and China, both global digital powerhouses, have expressed concerns through diplomatic channels and think tanks about the potential protectionist underpinnings of the EU's digital sovereignty agenda. These concerns often revolve around fears that the EU's policies could lead to a more fragmented global digital market and reduce the influence of non-European technology firms within Europe. Criticism has also emerged from within the EU, particularly from transatlantic think-thanks (e.g. Burwell & Propp, 2020) or industry groups like Digital Europe,[6] which argue that the focus on sovereignty might stifle innovation and limit access to cutting-edge technologies developed outside the EU. These groups contend that Europe risks isolating itself technologically and economically if it prioritises sovereignty over collaboration and global integration.

Moreover, critics within the EU warn that the emphasis on digital sovereignty could lead to a regulatory environment that is overly restrictive, potentially hampering the competitiveness of European companies on the global stage. They argue that rather than focusing solely on sovereignty, the EU should strive for a balanced approach that ensures security and independence while remaining open to international cooperation and innovation.

Despite these challenges, the political momentum behind the Digital Decade reflects a broader consensus within the EU that achieving digital sovereignty is not just an economic imperative but a strategic necessity in an increasingly digital world where power dynamics are shifting rapidly. This context underscores the Digital Decade's role as a pivotal tool in the EU's quest to assert its influence and leadership in the global digital arena.

[6] Digital Europe's Position Paper (March 2021) provides a critical analysis of the EU's digital sovereignty strategy, arguing that the focus on autonomy should not come at the expense of openness and global cooperation. They emphasise that while sovereignty is important, Europe must remain engaged in the global digital economy to foster innovation and competitiveness.

Achievement and Issues

Although it is too early to draw conclusions about the DDPP's contribution to the EU's digital sovereignty, the first years of implementation have started to shape an innovative framework for digital policymaking at the EU and national level, enabling progress on all key sovereignty dimensions.

The Collective Representation of the EU's Interests in its Digital Transformation

The DDPP has enabled a comprehensive representation of the critical issues facing the EU as an independent entity. Negotiated under a limited and sector-specific legal basis (Article 173.3, which pertains to industrial policy for competitiveness and excludes any harmonisation of Member States' laws and regulations), the DDPP has effectively established a framework for cooperation that is remarkably comprehensive. It touches on a wide range of measures, policies and actions relevant to the EU, including areas where the Union has only limited competence, such as digital skills.

The first reports on the 'State of the Digital Decade' have become pivotal references for digital policymaking, providing an exhaustive overview of the EU's digital transformation along with clear policy directives. These reports underscore that a successful digital transformation for the EU is not a given. The annual State of the Digital Decade reports identify priority policy challenges, such as underinvestment in R&D, the rise of security threats and disinformation, and investment gaps in areas like skills, smart greening and gigabit infrastructures. The reports also highlight key drivers, such as the need for enhanced digital skills and the training of ICT experts, and areas of progress, including the development of e-government services and connectivity networks.

Additionally, this comprehensive representation extends to policy areas that used to be overlooked, such as space, security and defence—which are aspects of the EU's digital transformation. It covers their opportunities, risks and achievements.

Unlike previous frameworks for discussing Europe's digital transformation, this collective representation is strictly focused on the EU27, marking a significant shift from the earlier era of the Digital Economy and Society Index (DESI) and the Digital Single Market strategy, which included about 35 countries, including members of the European Economic Area (EEA) and those in the process of accession. The Digital Decade Board now exclusively includes the EU27, reflecting this important change.

Building Industrial and Technological Capacities and Addressing Dependencies

The DDPP has enabled the preparation, monitoring and reinforce investments in the digital industry and infrastructures. Despite recent efforts in critical digital technologies (HPC, 5G, Chips Act), the State of the Digital Decade reports has resonated as 'wake-up calls' faced by monitoring insufficient progress, opening the perspective of missing the objectives and targets by 2030 in many areas. They have stressed the need for collective action notably to strengthen competitiveness by deepening the single market (e.g. follow up to the Connectivity White Paper (European Commission, 2024b) dedicated to open the debate on the modernisation of the telecommunication regulatory framework), to accelerate the development of the European-based digital industry, infrastructures and services (e.g. leveraging procurement), and mobilising investments on human capital, infrastructure development and deployment, start-up ecosystems (EU and Member State funding, capital market) where a major gap still exists with the USA and China starting with R&D efforts and patents.

The Digital Decade has also enabled the adoption of a more strategic and systemic approach to industrial development, ensuring a greater understanding of the interlinkages between layers (fundamental research, R&D, development of infrastructure) and sectors (for instance, between cloud, edge nodes, connectivity and AI-based software or the identification of driver factors such as connectivity or skills for achieving targets). As a consequence, it has broadened the scope and intensified synergies between policy strands (regulation, funding, cooperation). Developing a robust generative AI ecosystem indeed requires the EU to master the entire technological value chain across all layers, including ensuring the simultaneous development of all interdependent components, the chips and high-performance computing capacities crucial for training models and foundational data for AI systems, and the researchers and specialists who develop these systems. Additionally, it involves cultivating a skilled workforce capable of deploying AI in business, including SMEs, and establishing a robust connectivity infrastructure which encompasses data centres.

Last but not least, the Digital Decade enables, for the first time, to review comprehensively the actions taken at the Member State level in all digital areas. In their national roadmaps, Member States have identified 1623 measures aimed at achieving the Digital Decade targets and objectives, amounting to EUR 251.9 billion in investments (including EUR 168 billion from the public budget, which amounts to 1% of the EU's GDP). The proposed measures focus mainly on semiconductors (public budget EUR 40 billion, 24%), connectivity (EUR 29 billion, 17%) and basic digital skills (EUR 25 billion, 15%). While references to general objectives in national roadmaps are less developed than the specific targets, they still encompass 414 measures addressing competitiveness (public budget EUR 56.8 billion), technological leadership (EUR 22.3 billion) and cybersecurity (EUR 5.9 billion).

Effective Capacity to Act, Including through Regulations, Is another Crucial Aspect

Ensuring an alignment of private sector decisions with the EU's strategic interests is a key requirement for reinforcing its digital sovereignty (Smuha, 2023). In this respect, the Digital Decade provides for a clear contribution not only to steer and take stock both on the formal implementation of regulations (e.g. DSA, DMA, AI Act) but also, and more importantly, to assess the concrete effects of these regulations, e.g. effective protection of people, administrative burden created, and to analysis interfaces between industrial policy and the single market regulation. Such monitoring contributes to identifying blind spots and regulations that lack effectiveness, for instance, in the case of rising disinformation or the impact of digital technologies on mental health.

Moreover, this contribution to regulations' implementation is reinforced by two critical aspects that further strengthen their connection with the political and societal reality on the ground. First, it is accompanied by the analysis of the perception by citizens of their needs in terms of protection and empowerment in the context of digital technologies as well as on the priorities to act for the EU (in terms of fostering European champions and preserving children's health). Second, the Digital Decade governance mechanism continuously updates the political justification of those regulations as part of the political priorities that are adjusted every year depending on the political context—the rise of conflicts, the evolution of societies and the economic context, thus reinforcing every year EU action into the realities of the times.

The EU's effective capacity to act is also reinforced by the identification of concrete actions and measures that the Member States and the EU can leverage through the recommendations or by sharing best practices. Numerous examples in reports and discussions with the Digital Decade Board include actions and measures to accelerate the dissemination of digital technologies across society and regions, tackle digital divides and foster digital ecosystem initiatives (AI factories, EDIHs, EDICs, Smart Cities). Examples extend to concrete measures to accelerate the smart green transition, i.e. by setting greening targets, developing large pilots and boosting collaboration (e.g. via code of conduct), mobilising green finance for digital, while ensuring that people and their rights are at the heart of digital transformation, such as through the fight against disinformation, safe and healthy online spaces for all, and the protection of children online.

Legitimacy and Governance of Public Action

As Europe seeks to solidify its position as a global leader in digital innovation, the Digital Decade plays a crucial role in reinforcing the legitimacy and governance of digital policy.

Firstly, the Digital Decade establishes clear and ambitious objectives and targets for digital infrastructure, skills, business and public services. By setting these benchmarks, the EU provides a transparent roadmap for Member States, businesses and citizens to follow, fostering a shared sense of purpose and accountability. This transparency is key to building trust among these stakeholders, as it ensures progress can be measured and that adjustments can be made when necessary. Importantly, in turn, transparency reinforces the legitimacy of policy.

Furthermore, the Digital Decade emphasises a cohesive approach to digital governance as well as enables endorsing digital sovereignty—not just under a Westphalian context[7] brought to the EU sphere, but

[7] The Westphalian system, also known as Westphalian sovereignty, is a principle in international law that each state has exclusive sovereignty over its territory. The principle developed in Europe after the Peace of Westphalia in 1648, based on the state theory of Jean Bodin and the natural law teachings of Hugo Grotius.

rather under a network of actors and levels acting in coordination with complementary roles and action geared towards common objectives. The framework developed by the Decade harmonises the approaches taken at the national, regional and even local levels (a city can indeed decide to adopt objectives and set up projects consistent with the Digital Decade). This provides common references and builds a political discourse, thereby creating a common narrative on sovereignty through an inclusive and collective process.

The improved consistency in terms of monitoring and analysis enhances the EU's ability to effectively enforce digital policies. Indeed, the involvement of Member States in the governance process through regular monitoring and reporting ensures that digital policies are implemented uniformly, preventing discrepancies that could undermine the legitimacy of the initiative. The Digital Decade Board, by imposing a single representative responsible for covering all dimensions of the Digital Decade, helps integrate digital issues at the national level, fostering cooperation and collaboration between the different ministries and authorities.

Additionally, the Digital Decade supports the EU's broader objectives of promoting digital sovereignty and ethical technology development. By prioritising the development of home-grown digital technologies and ensuring that these technologies align with European values such as privacy, inclusivity and human rights, the EU reinforces its legitimacy *vis à vis* its citizens.

Overall, the Digital Decade strengthens the legitimacy and governance of digital policy in the EU by providing a clear, unified framework for digital transformation, promoting regulatory cohesion and aligning digital developments with European values. This initiative ensures that Europe can navigate the complexities of the digital age while upholding the principles that define its governance and legitimacy.

Conclusion—Future Challenges

The Digital Decade represents a significant leap in the EU's approach to policymaking, embodying an innovative shift towards a more integrated, future-oriented strategy for digital governance. Unlike previous initiatives, the Digital Decade introduces a comprehensive framework that sets measurable targets across multiple domains—ranging from digital infrastructure to skills development and public services—ensuring a holistic approach to Europe's digital transformation. By integrating regular monitoring and dynamic policy adjustments, this forward-looking strategy allows the EU to respond agilely to technological advancements and emerging challenges. Moreover, the Digital Decade pioneers a collaborative governance model, where Member States actively participate in the implementation and evaluation process, fostering a sense of shared responsibility and collective progress. This innovation in policymaking not only strengthens the EU's internal cohesion; it also positions us as a global leader in setting standards for the digital age. Finally, the Digital Decade sets new ground for other policy areas, providing a blueprint for how the EU can tackle complex, cross-border challenges with a unified, agile and forward-thinking approach.

Regarding digital policymaking, one of the key effects of the Digital Decade is to show that in the long run, the success of Europe in driving a successful digital transformation will depend on continuous, bold efforts on all fronts: appropriate design and implementation of regulation, investments, cooperation and to coordinate these efforts across EU countries. A lot will depend on the leadership that will be deployed by Member States, leveraging fully the infrastructure set up by the Decade. A lot will also depend on the way the Decade will be integrated into the new leadership priorities under President Von der Leyen for the European Commission's forthcoming mandate (2024–2029). In this respect, the first signals sent in the Political Guidelines (Leyen, 2024) are very positive: they make a clear reference to digital targets and priorities, reflecting the 2024 State of the Digital Decade report on, e.g. technological leadership, the dissemination of digital technologies and AI innovation leadership. These political messages aligned with the Digital Decade were further reinforced by the Draghi report (Draghi, 2024), which has heavily drawn on the State of the Digital decade 2024 in its analysis, conclusions and recommendations.

However, the Digital Decade is only one—if important—step. Implementing a policy to establish the EU as a technological supremo will necessitate both internal and geopolitical transformations. Beyond very significant budgetary efforts for enabling the EU to catch up on critical technologies and infrastructures, it will be crucial to bolster and mobilise the defence industry, which must be equipped for true strategic autonomy and for managing the resulting impacts, even with the EU's closest allies. Overcoming these significant challenges is essential to adopting a European 'power policy' centred on technology, akin to the US' longstanding approach. The 'Sputnik moment' revitalised the US's approach in response to the technological threat from the USSR, and more recently, it has focused on dominating the digital space as a means of global influence.

The convergence of the analysis of the 2024 State of the Digital Decade report and the 2024–2029 Political Guidelines is a clear positive signal towards a possible acceleration of collective action in the second part of this Decade to respond to the aforementioned wake-up calls. In this respect, the review of the Digital Decade planned for 2026 will be an important milestone to further the Decade's toolbox, increase its ambition and facilitate the development of measures by the EU and Member States. In this context, it will be particularly important to reinforce the links between strategic objectives and single market regulation with R&D and industrial policies. It will also be crucial to adjust the monitoring and analytical tools that the EU and Member States have at their disposal to prepare and nurture the next Decade, notably regarding the evolution of vulnerabilities and capacities of EU technologies and infrastructures, to be able to adjust and drive policymaking as recommended also in the Draghi report (Draghi, 2024)

This evolution is critical for the EU and the future of its citizens, as stated by Italian philosopher Luciano Floridi: 'Digital sovereignty is not just a matter of interest for some specialists. It is already affecting everybody. And this is why it is essential to design it as well as possible, together' (Floridi, 2020).

References

Alcidi, C., Kiss-Galfalvi, T., Postica, D., Righetti, E., Rizos, V., & Shamsfakhr, F. (2023, December 14). *What ways and means for a real strategic autonomy of the EU in the economic field?* CEPS https://www.ceps.eu/ceps-publications/what-ways-and-means-for-a-real-strategic-autonomy-of-the-eu-in-the-economic-field/

Bendiek, A., & Stuerzer, I. (2023). The Brussels effect, European regulatory power and political capital: Evidence for mutually reinforcing internal and external dimensions of the Brussels effect from the European digital policy debate. *Digital Society, 2*(5) https://pmc.ncbi.nlm.nih.gov/articles/PMC9868500/#CR6

Bodin, J. (1986 [1576]). Six livres de la république. Gallimard.

Borell, J. (2020, December 3). *Why European strategic autonomy matters.* European External Action Service https://www.eeas.europa.eu/eeas/why-european-strategic-autonomy-matters_en

Burwell, F., & Propp, K. (2020, June 22). *The European Union and the search for digital sovereignty: Building "Fortress Europe" or preparing for a new world?, Issue brief*. Atlantic Council https://www.atlanticcouncil.org/in-depth-research-reports/issue-brief/the-european-union-and-the-search-for-digital-sovereignty/

Chander, A., & Sun, H. (Eds.). (2023). *Data sovereignty: From the digital silk road to the return of the state*. Oxford University Press.

Clinton, H. (2011, October 11). America's Pacific century. *Foreign Policy*.

Council of the European Union. (2016, November 14). *Council conclusions on implementing the EU global strategy in the area of security and defence*. Consilium https://www.consilium.europa.eu/media/22459/eugs-conclusions-st14149en16.pdf

Damen, M. (2022, July 8). *EU strategic autonomy 2013–2023: From concept to capacity*. European Parliamentary Research Service https://www.europarl.europa.eu/thinktank/en/document/EPRS_BRI(2022)733589

Dinan, D. (2014). *Europe recast: A history of the European union*. Palgrave Macmillan.

Draghi, M. (2024). *The future of European competitiveness–A competitiveness strategy for Europe*. Obtenido de https://commission.europa.eu/topics/strengthening-european-competitiveness/eu-competitiveness-looking-ahead_en

EEAS. (2022). *Strategic compass for security and defence*. https://www.eeas.europa.eu/eeas/strategic-compass-security-and-defence-1_en

European Commission. (2020, February 19). *White Paper on Artificial Intelligence-A European approach to excellence and trust.*. Retrieved from https://eur-lex.europa.eu/legal-content/EN/TXT/PDF/?uri=CELEX:52020DC0065

European Commission. (2022). *The Digital Economy and Society Index (DESI)*. Shaping Europe's digital future https://digital-strategy.ec.europa.eu/en/policies/desi

European Commission. (2024a). *State of the digital decade 2024 report*. Obtenido de shaping Europe's digital future https://digital-strategy.ec.europa.eu/en/factpages/state-digital-decade-2024-report

European Commission. (2024b, February 21). *White Paper-How to master Europe's digital infrastructure needs?* Retrieved from Shaping Europe's digital future https://digital-strategy.ec.europa.eu/en/library/white-paper-how-master-europes-digital-infrastructure-needs.

European Commission. (26 de 2021). *Communication from the Commission to the European Parliament, the Council, the European Economic and Social Committee and the Committee of the Regions—European Commission Guidance on strengthening the code of practice on disinformation*. Obtenido de https://eur-lex.europa.eu/legal-content/EN/ALL/?uri=COM%3A2021%3A262%3AFIN

European Economic and Social Committee. (2022, October 26). *Digital sovereignty: A crucial pillar for EU's digitalisation and growth*. https://www.eesc.europa.eu/en/our-work/opinions-information-reports/opinions/digital-sovereignty-crucial-pillar-eus-digitalisation-and-growth

Floridi, L. (2020August 12). The fight for digital sovereignty: What it is, and why it matters, especially for the EU. *Philosophy & Technology, 33*, 369–378.

Germany's Presidency of the Council of the European Union. (2020). *Together for Europe's recovery: Programme for Germany's Presidency of the Council of the European Union* Germany Presidency of the Council of the European Union. https://www.eu2020.de/blob/2360248/e0312c50f910931819ab67f630d15b2f/06-30-pdf-programm-en-data.pdf

Gostyńska-Jakubowska, A., & Ondarza, N. (2020). *The Barnier method: Lessons learned from the EU'S institutional approach to the Brexit negotiations*. European policy Centre..

Jones, E., Menon, A., & Weatherill, S. (Eds.). (2021). *The Oxford handbook of the European Union*. Oxford University Press.

Leonard, M., & Shapiro, J. (2019, June 25). *Strategic sovereignty: How Europe can regain the capacity to act*. European Council of Foreign Relations https://ecfr.eu/publication/strategic_sovereignty_how_europe_can_regain_the_capacity_to_act/

Leonard, M., Pisani-Ferry, J., Ribakova, E., Shapiro, J., & Wolff, G. (2019, June). *Redefining Europe's Economic Sovereignty*. European Council on Foreign Relations https://ecfr.eu/wp-content/uploads/2_Redefining_Europes_economic_sovereignty.pdf

Lessig, L. (2000, January 1). *Code is Law: On liberty in cyberspace*. Harvard Magazine https://www.harvardmagazine.com/2000/01/code-is-law-html

Leyen, U. (2019). *A Union that strives for more: My agenda for Europe*. Retrieved from European Commission https://commission.europa.eu/document/download/063d44e9-04ed-4033-acf9-639ecb187e87_en?filename=political-guidelines-next-commission_en.pdf

Leyen, U. (2024). *Europe's Choice—Political Guidelines for the Next European Commission 2024–2029*. European Commission: https://commission.europa.eu/document/download/e6cd4328-673c-4e7a-8683-f63ffb2cf648_en?filename=Political%20Guidelines%202024-2029_EN.pdf

Macron, E. (2017, September 26). *Initiative pour l'Europe*. Élysée. https://www.elysee.fr/emmanuel-macron/2017/09/26/initiative-pour-l-europe-discours-d-emmanuel-macron-pour-une-europe-souveraine-unie-democratique

Merkel, A. (2018, May 10). *Rede von Bundeskanzlerin Dr. Angela Merkel bei der Verleihung des Internationalen Karlspreises an Staatspräsident Emmanuel Macron*. Bundesregierung https://www.bundesregierung.de/breg-de/service/newsletter-und-abos/bulletin/rede-von-bundeskanzlerin-dr-angela-merkel-1122402

Smuha, N. A. (2023). *Digital sovereignty in the European Union: Five challenges from a normative perspective. ERA conference proceedings*. KU Leuven.

CHAPTER 5

European Integration: The Case of Electronic Communications

Peter Eberl and Kyriakos Baxevanidis

"Monopolies are not good for innovation. They have a tendency to try to preserve the status quo. But the Internet has always been about permissionless innovation". Vint Cerf, one of the "fathers of the Internet".

Disclaimer: The authors are officials of the European Commission. The information and views set out in this chapter are those of the authors and do not necessarily reflect the official opinion of the Institution.

P. Eberl (✉) · K. Baxevanidis
European Commission, Brussels, Belgium
e-mail: Peter.eberl@ec.europa.eu

K. Baxevanidis
e-mail: Kyriakos.baxevanidis@ec.europa.eu

T. Kleiner and A. Garcia Rodriguez (eds.), *The Making of a Global Digital Rulebook*, https://doi.org/10.1007/978-981-95-9226-5_5

Introduction

The electronic communications sector has evolved dramatically over the past four decades due to fast technological and commercial innovation. It has expanded from mainly copper-based fixed-line voice telecommunications to 5G and 6G mobile communications and fibre networks that carry predominantly data traffic. Nowadays, electronic communications networks and services constitute the infrastructure of the Internet and are the backbone of the digital economy and society.

The technological and commercial evolution has always been accompanied by regulatory measures that enabled innovation and reacted to new developments. Building and constantly upgrading the electronic communications infrastructure requires significant investments, which can be best achieved in competitive markets: creating and maintaining effective competition that fosters and facilitates investments has always been a main objective of the regulation of this sector. Spectrum policy has played an essential role in this context. Other important objectives have been the internal market, the protection of end-users, in particular consumers, and the resilience of electronic communications networks and services.

As a pioneer of competition-based regulation in the European Union, the electronic communications sector has inspired subsequent regulation in other areas, such as platform regulation. Moreover, the regulatory framework for electronic communications is closely intertwined with other areas of Union legislation, for instance, on consumer or data protection, resulting in a constant exchange of regulatory approaches. The EU's regulatory policies have thus prioritised competition and market access, with positive effects in terms of benefits for consumers. Conversely, the EU telecommunication market is more fragmented compared to regions like the US, where a few large players dominate, and is more a collection of national markets than a genuine single market. EU integration in this sector strikes out, therefore, as much less complete than in other digital markets. This chapter sets out the historical background and evolution of the regulatory framework for electronic communications before having an outlook on future challenges and developments. In addition to providing an analysis of the key parameters of the legal framework, it tries to identify parameters hindering a single telecommunication market.

Historical Background

Throughout most of the twentieth century, the telecommunications sector around the world was characterised by national monopolies. In Europe, most of these monopolies were State-owned or publicly controlled. The break-up of AT&T's monopoly in the US in 1984 also triggered in the European Union a process of liberalisation and regulation of the sector.[1] Starting in 1990 (Commission Directive 90/388/EEC, 1990), exclusive and special rights, which had legally protected the monopolies, were gradually abolished, culminating in the full liberalisation in 1998 (Commission Directive 96/19/EC, 1996). This opening to competition was done by Commission Directives based on Article 86 (3) TEC (now Article 106 TFEU). However, experience in the US and the UK demonstrated that the mere abolishment of monopoly rights was not sufficient to create effective competition. Therefore, in parallel to the liberalisation process, the European Union set up a harmonised framework of applicable rules based on the internal market provision Article 95 TEC (now Article 114 TFEU) (Council Directive 90/387/EEC, 1990).

This resulted in a regulatory framework of 20 Directives, which were consolidated in 2002 into five Directives that comprised the relevant sector-specific rules, namely:

- Framework Directive 2002/21/EC, which defined the concept of electronic communications services based on the conveyance of signals, including signals used for the conveyance of broadcasting services. The Framework Directive further aligns more closely the significant market power (SMP) concept to the dominance concept used in competition law.
- Access Directive 2002/19/EC, which covered access obligations that could be imposed on providers with significant market power:
- Authorisation Directive 2002/20/EC, which governed the general authorisation and the rights of use for radio frequencies and numbers;

[1] Groundbreaking for the applicability of competition law was the ECJ's so-called "BT judgment" of 20.03.1985; case 41/83 (Italy/Commission), Rec. 1985, p. 873. On 30.06.1987, the Commission published its Greenbook on the development of the common market for telecommunications services and equipment.

- Universal Service Directive 2002/22/EC, which contained provisions on universal service and end-user rights;
- ePrivacy Directive 2002/58/EC, which protects the confidentiality of electronic communications.

These Directives were complemented by a revised Commission Directive 2002/77/EC on competition in electronic communications markets, and Regulation (EC) 2887/2000 on unbundled access to the local loop, which aimed at facilitating market entry by granting cost-oriented access to the "last mile". In addition, Regulation (EC) 1211/2009 established the Body of European Regulators for Electronic Communications (BEREC) and the Agency for Support for BEREC (BEREC Office). BEREC acts as a forum for cooperation among the national regulatory authorities (NRAs) and between NRAs and the Commission with a view to ensuring the consistent implementation of the regulatory framework. It replaced the European Regulators Group for Electronic Communications Networks and Services (ERG) that had been set up by Commission Decision 2002/627/EC.

The regulatory framework of 2002 was amended and updated in 2009 through Directive 2009/140/EC, amending the Framework Directive, the Access Directive and the Authorisation Directive, and Directive 2009/136/EC, amending the Universal Service Directive and the ePrivacy Directive.

The framework for market regulation had been complemented by the Commission Recommendation on relevant markets (C(2003) 497, 2003) and by the Commission Guidelines for market analysis and the assessment of significant market power (2018/C 159/01, 2018), both based on Article 15 of the Framework Directive. The Recommendation and the Guidelines have been updated periodically since then and applied in their most recent form also under the EECC (C(2020) 8750, 2020).

The market analysis is performed by the Member States' national regulatory authorities (NRAs) in close coordination with the Commission and BEREC. NRAs have to submit relevant draft measures to the Commission and the NRAs of other Member States for comments ("Article 7 procedure").[2] The Commission may veto a draft measure if it creates a barrier to the single market or in case of serious doubts as to its compatibility with

[2] Now Article 32 and 33 EECC.

Union law. It is important to notice that the structures of national markets were fairly different at the outset. For instance, not all Member States had cable networks, which developed into competing infrastructures for broadband provided by former national monopolies. Most importantly, national regulators also adopted different approaches to regulating fibre. Some (like Germany) imposed an obligation to supply active fibre-access products, while others (notably, France, Portugal, and Spain) promoted infrastructure competition by requiring that the incumbent make only ducts and poles available to competitors (Cave et al., 2019). Similarly, Member States adopted different approaches in the way they licensed spectrum for 3G and 4G; some used auctions and others beauty contests, which resulted in big national diversities.

This overview shows that telecom regulation is one of the oldest and most established forms of digital legislation in the EU. National regulators have been established for a very long time, and regulation operates along national logic, which has displayed significant differences.

International Roaming

One illustration of the difficulty of building a telecom single market is illustrated by the case of roaming. The markets for international roaming (within the EU) presented several particularities that ultimately led to the adoption of the first Roaming Regulation in 2007.

International roaming enables a customer of a mobile network operator (MNO) to make and receive calls, send and receive data, or access other mobile services when travelling outside the geographical coverage area of its home network using the infrastructure of a "visited" network. In order to provide their customers with the possibility of international roaming, MNOs conclude international roaming agreements with MNOs in the visited country (wholesale agreements). International roaming customers thus purchase the service from their home operator but are connected to the network of a foreign operator when roaming abroad. International roaming differs from international calls: while international calls are made from the customer's home network to destinations abroad, roaming calls are made by the customer while abroad; they may be directed to destinations in the visited country, the home country, or other countries.

Although the wholesale market for international roaming was covered under the 2002 regulatory framework in the Commission's Recommendation on relevant markets, prices, both at the wholesale and retail levels, were significantly above costs. In 2006, at €1.15 per minute, the average retail charge for a roamed call was more than five times higher than the actual cost of providing the wholesale service and 50% higher than the average inter-operator tariff. Retail roaming charges were roughly four times higher than domestic tariffs. In addition, there was a lack of transparency; in particular, many consumers were not aware of the high charges for receiving calls abroad, which were estimated to be at least four times the average cost to the operator.[3]

The Commission had also conducted competition investigations under both Article 81 TEC (now Article 101 TFEU) and Article 82 TEC (now Article 102 TFEU), which, however, did not solve the pricing issue.

In light of these findings, the Commission presented a proposal for the first Roaming Regulation based on Article 95 (now Article 114 TFEU) in July 2006, which, after adoption by the European Parliament and the Council, entered into force on 30 June 2007 (Regulation (EC) No 717/2007, 2007). The Regulation focused on international roaming voice calls and introduced price caps for outgoing and incoming international roaming calls within the European Union. At the retail level, the so-called "Euro Tariff" price cap was initially set at 0.49 € per minute (excluding VAT) for outgoing roaming calls and at 0.24 € per minute (excluding VAT) for incoming roaming calls.

The wholesale cap for charges among operators was initially set at 0.30 € per minute. A glide path in the Roaming Regulation further reduced both the retail and wholesale caps in 2008 and 2009. In addition, the Roaming Regulation imposed transparency obligations on the customer's home network operator, including price information on the applicable roaming tariffs when the customer enters a foreign country. The Roaming Regulation was initially applicable for three years and requested the Commission to review the functioning of the Regulation and to assess whether its duration or scope should be extended.

[3] A common position of the European Regulators Group (the predecessor of BEREC), referred to in the Commission's impact assessment, indicated that high retail charges appeared to result from high wholesale charges and high retail mark-ups, with little pass-through of reductions in wholesale charges.

The Court of Justice of the European Union confirmed in its judgement of 8 June 2010 that the object of the Roaming Regulation was to improve the conditions for the functioning of the internal market and that it could thus be adopted on the basis of Article 95 TEC (Vodafone Ltd and Others v Secretary of State for Business, Enterprise and Regulatory Reform, 2010). The Court explained that, in the absence of the Roaming Regulation, there would have been a risk of significant distortions of competition and disruption of the orderly functioning of the Community-wide roaming market.

In addition, the Court found that also the regulation of retail markets by an intervention, limited in time, to protect consumers against excessive prices was proportionate. The Court stated that regulation of the wholesale market alone would not have produced direct and immediate effects for consumers. However, from the Court's emphasis on the limited time period of the regulatory intervention, it emerged that extensions of the Roaming Regulation require an assessment of the competitive situation in the roaming markets.

Following the Commission's review and proposal, the European Parliament and the Council adopted an amending Regulation that entered into force on 1st July 2009 (Regulation (EC) 544/2009, 2009). It extended the duration of the Roaming Regulation to June 2012 and included retail and wholesale price caps for SMS and a wholesale cap for regulated data roaming (initially at 1.00 € per MB, subject to a glide path with gradual reductions to 0.50 € per MB in 2011). The price caps for outgoing and incoming calls were further reduced at both retail and wholesale levels. In addition, consumers were protected from "bill shocks" by a cut-off mechanism once their data roaming bill reached € 50 unless they had chosen another cut-off limit.

In June 2012, the Roaming Regulation was recast ("Roaming III Regulation") and introduced a retail price cap for data roaming (initially 0.70 € per MB, gradually decreasing to 0.20 € per MB in 2014) (Regulation (EU) 531/2012, 2012). In addition, the retail and wholesale price caps for international roaming calls and SMS were gradually further reduced.[4] The Roaming III Regulation also introduced an option (as of

[4] Retail caps: for outgoing calls 0.29 € in 2012, 0.19 € in 2014; for incoming calls: 0.08 € in 2012, 0.05 € in 2014; SMS: 0.09 € in 2012, 0.06 € in 2014. Wholesale caps: for outgoing calls 0.14 € in 2012, 0.05 € in 2014; for SMS: 0.03 € in 2012, 0.02 € in 2014).

July 2014) for consumers to choose a separate roaming contract or a provider at their destination.

Telecoms Single Market Proposal, Open Internet Regulation, and "Roam-Like-at-Home"

In May 2010, the European Commission launched the "Digital Agenda for Europe" that set out as priorities inter alia creating a digital single market and increasing Europeans' access to fast and ultra-fast Internet (COM/2010/0245 final, 2010). Due to limited progress on these objectives, the Commission proposed, in September 2013, a Regulation aiming to complete the European single market for electronic communications and to achieve a Connected Continent (COM/2013/0627 final–2013/0309 (COD), 2013). The Commission proposal was designed to complement the existing regulatory framework, last revised in 2009. It covered a broad range of areas, in particular (1) a single authorisation; (2) harmonisation of spectrum rules and virtual broadband access products; (3) enhanced end-user rights, including on switching and international intra-EU calls; (4) net-neutrality provisions; and (5) amendments to the Roaming III Regulation.

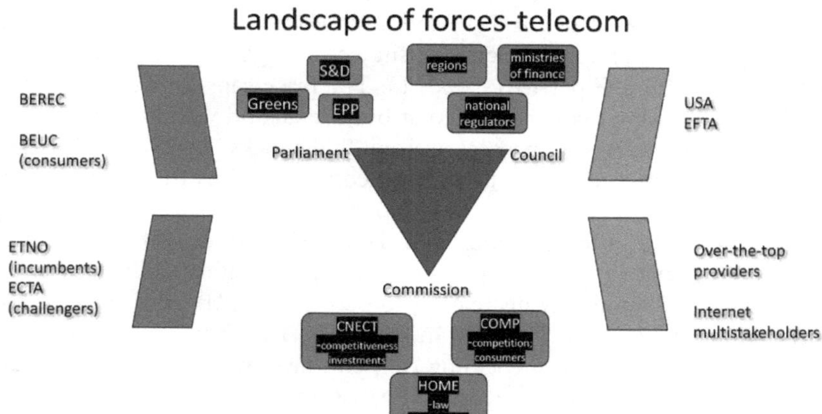

However, the proposal for a "European Single Market for Electronic Communications to achieve a Connected Continent", introduced in

2013, faced numerous obstacles that ultimately led to its partial implementation rather than full success. As can be seen from the landscape of forces, several streams of influence can be identified around the regulation of telecom markets. In the first place, and as explained above, the sector already contains a number of institutional actors in the EU, such as national regulators organised in BEREC, who could praise themselves for having brought positive results to consumers in terms of low prices and broadband access. It is not hard to see why national regulators and BEREC could see in the attempt to build a single market some kind of existential threat to their activities. However, they criticised the proposal based on a series of technical arguments, arguing that it may create unnecessary complexity and uncertainty, and limit innovation and competition, and that some of the proposals would be counterproductive, and attacking the idea that global competitiveness should be an objective of the regulation in addition to the competition, with the risk of undermining the substantial achievements of the existing legislative framework (BEREC, 2013)

This risk towards consumer benefits was echoed by associations like BEUC. While national actors rejected the power grab at play in the proposal and the plans for pan-European consolidation to increase the competitiveness of the industry, other commentators also attacked the proposal for not being radical enough and not proposing a pan-European telecoms regulator or pan-European spectrum licences (Conradi & Amin, 2014). Achieving consensus among the 28 member states proved difficult, as different countries had varying priorities and economic interests. Some member states were reluctant to cede national control over key regulatory areas like spectrum management, a sensitive issue because it relates to national security, economic interests, and government revenues (in the form of spectrum auctions).

Telecom companies were divided, too, between incumbent players who supported the proposal and challenger telecom operators, represented by the lobby group, the European Competitive Telecommunications Association, who did not support the thrust of increased consolidation. The complexity of the proposal was also raised to criticise it as an increasing bureaucratic burden. International actors focused on some elements of the proposal, like Net Neutrality, which had repercussions on Internet governance, and generally, service providers were trying to escape falling into the scope of the legislation.

Finally, the timing of the proposal was also a factor. It was introduced late in the legislative cycle, just before the European Parliament elections in 2014 and the change in the European Commission. The political momentum was lost as a result, and priorities shifted under the new administration. With limited time for thorough negotiations and debate, only certain elements of the proposal gained approval before the end of the legislative session.

As a result, just before the European Parliament elections in May 2014, the European Parliament's first reading position of April 2014 focused on the coordination of spectrum, net neutrality, and the abolishment of roaming retail charges in the EU, thus leaving aside a number of other elements of the Commission's proposal. The Council's general approach of March 2015 contained only provisions on net neutrality and roaming. Following the trilogue negotiations and its adoption, the Regulation entered into force on 29 November 2015 (Regulation (EU) 2015/2120, 2015). It enshrined the open internet provisions in European law and abolished roaming charges in the EU from 15 June 2017.

Open Internet

Regulation (EU) 2015/2120 introduced provisions ensuring the open Internet. This topic has been discussed as "net neutrality" worldwide since the late 2000s, including within the ITU at the World Conference on International Telecommunications in Dubai in December 2012. The topic is closely related to the debate on financial contributions to the huge investments needed to build and upgrade modern electronic communications infrastructures, which re-emerged 10 years later. The potential threat by electronic communications network providers to use traffic management measures to strengthen their bargaining position vis-à-vis content providers played an important role in this debate. The Netherlands (Staatsblad 2012, 235, 2012) were the first Member State to adopt national net neutrality legislation in May 2012 (entry into force in June 2012), and Slovenia followed in December 2012 (ZEKom-1, 2012). This development illustrated a concrete risk of fragmentation of the internal market.

The open Internet rules have applied since 30 April 2016 and cover both fixed-line and mobile Internet access services. They do not apply to IP interconnection and to non-public networks such as closed private or corporate networks.

The core provision is Article 3: paragraph 1 establishes a right of end-users to access and distribute lawful content of their choice via their internet access service,[5] while paragraph 3 lays down the rules for non-discriminatory traffic management. Internet access service providers shall treat all traffic equally when providing Internet access services, without discrimination, restriction or interference, and irrespective of the sender and receiver, the content accessed or distributed, the applications or services used or provided, or the terminal equipment used. This means that providers shall not block, slow down, alter, restrict, interfere with, degrade or discriminate between specific content, applications or services, or specific categories thereof. These traffic management rules protect all end-users, both as sender and as receiver, including content providers, where they send traffic via an internet access service.

Pursuant to the second subparagraph of Article 3(3), equal treatment does not exclude reasonable traffic management to optimise the overall transmission quality and thus contribute to the efficient use of network resources provided that any differentiation is based on objective technical quality requirements and not commercial considerations, is transparent, non-discriminatory, and proportionate, does not involve any monitoring of the specific content of traffic (such as "deep-packet inspection"), and is not maintained for longer than necessary.

The Regulation contains an exhaustive list of three exceptions where blocking, throttling, etc., are permitted, namely where and as long as necessary to:

(1) comply with legal obligations under Union law, or under national legislation that complies with Union law, to which the internet access service provider is subject;
(2) preserve the integrity and security of the network, of services provided via that network, and of the terminal equipment of end-users; and

[5] Article 3(1): "End-users shall have the right to access and distribute information and content, use and provide applications and services, and use terminal equipment of their choice, irrespective of the end-user's or provider's location or the location, origin or destination of the information, content, application or service, via their internet access service. This paragraph is without prejudice to Union law, or national law that complies with Union law, related to the lawfulness of the content, applications or services".

(3) prevent impending network congestion and mitigate the effects of exceptional or temporary network congestion, provided that equivalent categories of traffic are treated equally. As the third exception is limited to "exceptional and temporary" congestion, it does not apply in case of frequent or recurring congestion, for instance, due to insufficient investments in capacity.

Article 3(2) deals with commercial practices and agreements on commercial and technical conditions, such as price, speed or data volumes, including so-called zero-rating. Those agreements and practices must not limit the exercise of rights of end-users or circumvent other provisions of the Regulation.

Article 3(5) foresees the possibility of providing so-called "specialised services" where optimisation is necessary to meet service requirements for specific levels of quality (for instance, regarding latency) for specific content, applications or services such as managed IP-TV or eHealth services. Where those "specialised services" are offered by providers of electronic communications services to the public, including internet access service providers, they are subject to certain safeguards in order to avoid degradation of the internet access service. In particular, specialised services shall not be offered or usable as a substitute to internet access services, and there must be sufficient network capacity to provide specialised services in addition to any internet access service so that their provision is not to the detriment of the availability or general quality of internet access services for end-users.

Pursuant to Article 5, national regulatory authorities play an important role in the implementation of the open Internet provisions. They have been granted additional investigation and enforcement powers. Consequently, BEREC also plays a very important role in the consistent application of the open Internet rules. In accordance with Article 5(3), BEREC issued, after consulting stakeholders and in close cooperation with the Commission, guidelines on 30 August 2016 (BEREC, 2016).

The Court of Justice ruled in several cases on preliminary questions relating to the open internet provisions, in particular on "zero-rating" or "zero tariffs" (Joined Cases C-807/18; C-39/19, 2020; C-854/19; C-5/20; C-34/20, 2021). These are commercial agreements or practices falling into the scope of Article 3(2) where data traffic associated with a service or an application provided by a partner of the internet access service provider is not counted towards the data volume purchased by the end-user. In its judgement of 2 September 2021, the Court found that such commercial practices draw a distinction within internet traffic on the basis of commercial considerations and are therefore contrary to the general obligation of equal treatment of traffic, without discrimination or interference, as required by the Regulation on open internet access (C-854/19; C-5/20; C-34/20, 2021).

Roam-Like-at-Home

Regulation (EU) 2015/2120 also amended the Roaming III Regulation. It abolished retail roaming charges in the EU as of 15 June 2017 and introduced the roam-like-at-home principle. This means that end-users pay the same price for calls, texts, and mobile data when they are travelling in the EU, as they pay in their home Member State. As a transitional measure, retail roaming caps were further lowered as of April 2016. Wholesale roaming charges remained regulated. In order to avoid a negative impact (such as a "waterbed effect") on domestic tariffs and markets, two safeguards were introduced. First, providers are permitted to apply a fair use policy to avoid abusive or anomalous usage of roaming services by customers. Second, a provider may apply to the national regulators for a sustainability derogation in specific and exceptional circumstances, namely where the provider cannot recover the cost of its roaming services from its roaming revenues. Where such a derogation is granted, the provider may apply a surcharge as authorised by the regulator.

Both the Roaming Regulations, and ultimately Roam-like-at-home, and the open internet rules have strengthened the digital single market considerably. The reduction and abolition of retail roaming charges benefited both consumers and business users of communications services. As demonstrated in several BEREC and Commission reports, the significant unit price reduction for calls and SMS, and in particular for data, was largely outweighed by an exponential increase in the volumes of consumption. It is likely that the abolition of roaming costs will foster economic cross-border activities and increase the spending of travellers for other goods and services in the visited country.

The common Union rules for the open internet prevent legislative fragmentation, which benefits not only internet access service providers but also consumers and business customers, be it receivers or senders of content. Moreover, the open internet rules offer protection to vulnerable small- and mid-sized content providers against blocking, throttling or discrimination of their services, including as regards cross-border delivery of their services.

European Electronic Communications Code of 2018

As announced during the trilogue negotiations on Regulation (EU) 2015/2120, the Commission proposed an overhaul of the electronic communications framework in September 2016. The proposal led to the European Electronic Communications Code (EECC), which was adopted on 11 December 2018 and entered into force nine days later. It is a "recast" directive that consolidates four directives of the previous regulatory framework, namely the Framework Directive 2002/21/EC, the Access Directive 2002/19/EC, the Authorisation Directive 2002/20/EC and the Universal Service Directive 2002/22/EC.[6] Member States had 24 months to transpose the EECC. It was accompanied by a revised BEREC Regulation, which entered into force the same day as the EECC (20 December 2018) (Regulation (EU) 2018/1971, 2018).

The EECC pursues four—equivalent—main objectives:

- Promote connectivity, access to and take-up of very high-capacity networks by all citizens and businesses of the Union;
- Promote effective and sustainable competition;
- Contribute to the development of the internal market for electronic communications networks and services, and
- Strengthen the rights of end-users, including those with disabilities.

The EECC is structured in four parts: (1) Framework/ general rules, (2) Networks, (3) Services, and (4) Final provisions.

The general rules part covers, inter alia, the definitions where the scope of electronic communications is extended to include also so-called over-the-top communications services such as messaging services, voice-over-IP communications, or Internet-based email services. The revised definition creates a level playing field both in terms of protection of the end-users of the respective communications services and in terms of regulatory obligations applicable to the providers. This extension is achieved

[6] The ePrivacy Directive (2002/58) which was part of that framework, was not included. Instead, the Commission adopted a proposal for an ePrivacy Regulation in January 2017.

through the concept of "interpersonal communication services", which are one category of electronic communications services.[7] As many of these services are provided without direct payment by the end-user but are rather financed by advertising, the EECC clarifies, based on established CJEU case law, that remuneration of the service provider may occur by a third party and not necessarily by the service recipient.[8] The new definitions of electronic communications services and interpersonal communications are relevant for other Union legislation, such as the NIS2 Directive (Directive (EU) 2022/2555, 2022) and the Digital Markets Act. As regards the enforcement of the EECC, the independence, competencies, and enforcement powers of the national regulatory authorities are reinforced. The general authorisation regime is maintained, and the information that national regulatory authorities may request from providers has been harmonised.

Networks

The EEEC's network part focuses mainly on spectrum and access.[9]

Spectrum

As stated in the Code,[10] radio spectrum is a scarce public resource with an important public and market value. It is an essential input for radio-based electronic communications networks and services and, insofar as it relates to such networks and services, should, therefore, be efficiently allocated and assigned by relevant regulatory or other competent authorities in accordance with harmonised objectives and principles governing their action as well as with objective, transparent, and non-discriminatory criteria, taking into account the democratic, social, linguistic, and cultural interests related to the use of radio spectrum.

Radio spectrum policy is an area of shared competence between the EU and Member States. The EU adopts rules, in particular, for the EU-wide designation of frequency bands under harmonised technical conditions.

[7] Article 2(5) and 2(4) EECC.

[8] Recital 16 EECC.

[9] The network part also covers rights of way.

[10] Recital 107 of the Code.

Member States' action focuses on the implementation of spectrum authorisation, management, and use. However, the way spectrum is managed and used in one Member State has an impact on the internal market as a whole, for example, through disparate starting times in the development of new wireless technologies or new services or harmful cross-border interference, with further possible repercussions for EU competitiveness, resilience, and technological leadership. While, in this context, it makes sense that more coordinated ways among all Member States to maximise the social and economic value of spectrum and enhance terrestrial and satellite connectivity across the entire EU are sought, national defence, security, and market interests largely prevented past attempts of the Commission (including through initial proposals of the Code) for more EU coordination, convergence, and certainty in spectrum.

Decision No 676/2002/EC established the legal framework of radio spectrum in the Union, while Decision 243/2012/EU established a multiannual Radio Spectrum Policy Programme (RSPP) that set the strategic priorities (general principles and key policy objectives) of the radio spectrum policy in the EU. The Code further promoted the effective, efficient, and coordinated use of radio spectrum in the Union with a focus on provisions and principles on coherent radio spectrum authorisation across the Member States of the Union.

In this context, the Code notably includes provisions that reinforce cross-border cooperation in dealing with radio-frequency harmful interference issues, establishes a voluntary peer-review process among Member State authorities when new spectrum assignments are prepared, sets a framework for adoption of Commission Recommendations as to the most appropriate authorisation regime in relation to a specific (harmonised, each time) spectrum band, sets a framework of transfer or lease of individual rights of use for radio spectrum while empowering the Commission to adopt relevant implementing measures specifying relevant details of transfer or lease, sets common deadlines in the EU concerning the assignment of the 5G pioneer spectrum bands, and sets provisions for the deployment of small-area wireless access points (small antennas used for the transmission of high-throughput information at close distances). The Code further sets a new legal basis for the functioning of the Radio Spectrum Policy Group (RSPG)—a high-level group of Member State experts that advises the Commission on radio spectrum policy matters.

Access
The EECC's access provisions aim at facilitating the rollout of very high-capacity networks through increased competition and predictability for investment. The emphasis is on access to civil infrastructure (such as masts, ducts, and cabinets) with a view to lowering significantly the deployment costs for very high-capacity networks. The EECC promotes sustainable competition through new rules on symmetric regulation to overcome technical or economic bottlenecks, in particular, for in-house wiring.

The principle of asymmetric access regulation based on market analysis and significant market power (SMP) is maintained.[11] Article 67 incorporates the three-criteria test from the Recommendation on relevant markets in electronic communications. Prior to the adoption of proposed market access remedies, the national regulatory authority has to consult the Commission, BEREC, and the national regulatory authorities in other Member States.[12] National regulatory authorities may impose on providers with SMP obligations in terms of transparency,[13] non-discrimination,[14] accounting separation,[15] access to civil engineering,[16] access to network elements and associated facilities,[17] price control and cost accounting,[18] and functional separation.[19]

However, some derogations are introduced in order to foster investment. For instance, Article 76 of EECC promotes risk-sharing and predictability through rules on co-investment in new, very high-capacity networks. This provision concerns scenarios where a provider with SMPs opens the deployment of very high-capacity networks to other providers of electronic communications networks or services. Subject to certain conditions, access regulation on the provider with SMP may be rolled back by the national regulatory authority, under close supervision by

[11] Articles 63 and 67 EECC.

[12] Article 32 EECC replacing Article 7 of the Framework Directive.

[13] Article 69 EECC.

[14] Article 70 EECC.

[15] Article 71 EECC.

[16] Article 72 EECC.

[17] Article 73 EECC.

[18] Article 74 EECC.

[19] Article 77 EECC.

the Commission and BEREC, in order to safeguard the internal market. Similarly, a lighter access regime applies where a provider with SMP is a "wholesale-only" provider, i.e., without retail activities in the downstream markets.[20]

Furthermore, the EECC introduces single termination rates to be determined by the Commission at the EU level.[21] This measure replaces national termination rates, thereby reducing the regulatory burden and eliminating cross-border distortions. In addition, national regulatory authorities were empowered with tools to provide investment certainty in less attractive areas by mapping network investment intentions ("geographical surveys of network deployments").[22] Finally, Article 59(2)(c) EECC noteworthily introduces the possibility of imposing interoperability obligations on providers of number-independent interpersonal communications services, which reach a significant level of coverage and user uptake. The rationale of this provision is to enable intervention where increased use of number-independent interpersonal communications services might entail a lack of sufficient interoperability between communications services or might put at risk access to emergency services (which at that time depended largely on end-users using number-based interpersonal communications services).[23] Today, as regards designated gatekeepers, Article 7 DMA lays down a more detailed provision with the same goal of achieving interoperability of number-independent interpersonal communications services.

Services

The focus of s the EECC's services part is on universal service obligations and end-user rights.[24]

Universal Service

The EECC strengthens the universal service, ensuring the availability and affordability of adequate broadband internet access service and voice

[20] Article 80 EECC.

[21] Article 75 EECC.

[22] Article 22 EECC.

[23] See recital 149 EECC.

[24] The services part also comprises a title on numbering resources.

communications, at least at a fixed location. Member States shall define the adequate broadband internet access service with a view to ensuring the bandwidth necessary for social and economic participation in society.[25] The adequacy of the broadband internet access service requires that every citizen must be able to access and use basic services, which are determined in a list that the Commission updates periodically.

As regards affordability, Member States have to assess whether retail prices for adequate broadband internet access service and voice communications services prevent consumers with a low income or special social needs (including older people, end-users with disabilities, and consumers living in rural or geographically isolated areas) from accessing such services. If so, Member States have to take measures to ensure the affordability of those services for such consumers, at least at a fixed location. Universal service may be provided by any technology at a fixed location, such as the consumer's home. In addition, Member States may ensure affordability of adequate broadband internet access and voice communications services beyond a fixed location, i.e., to citizens on the move, where they consider that this is necessary to ensure the consumers' full social and economic participation in society.[26] Particular attention should be paid in this context to ensuring that end-users with disabilities have equivalent access.

Ensuring affordability may involve special tariff options or specific packages, which should, in principle, be offered by all providers in order to maintain choice and avoid market distortion.[27] If the net cost of a universal service obligation constitutes an unfair burden for a provider, Member States may, upon request, either compensate that provider from public funds under transparent conditions or share the net cost of the universal service obligations between providers of electronic communications networks and services.[28] Any such compensation or cost-sharing mechanism has to comply with State aid rules.[29]

[25] Article 84(3) EECC.

[26] Recital 214 EECC.

[27] Recital 220 et seq. RRCC.

[28] Article 90 EECC.

[29] See also recital 239 EECC.

End-User Rights

The EECC modernises the end-user provisions of the Universal Service Directive to address issues of consumer and other end-user protection. The EECC introduces maximum harmonisation for end-user rights, which means that Member States cannot silverplate the provisions (with few exceptions). The new provisions include a non-discrimination clause and more transparency (including price and quality comparison). Importantly, providers of electronic communications networks and services have to provide enhanced contract information, including a mandatory contract summary that presents the essential elements of the contract in an easily understandable form. The new provisions contain a new provision on bundles and facilitate switching and portability, permitting end-users to terminate a contract that has been automatically prolonged. The EECC also strengthens the rights of end-users with disabilities, complementing the European Accessibility Act (Directive (EU) 2019/882, 2019).

The EECC also updates and strengthens the security provisions of the Framework Directive to ensure that providers of electronic communications networks and services enhance their resilience against cyber-attacks and other incidents. Such enhanced resilience is crucial to protect the end-users and everyone relying on well-functioning electronic communications networks and services, including critical infrastructures and essential or important services. Articles 40 and 41 of the EECC align the terminology and some concepts to the NIS 1 Directive while respecting the particularities of the electronic communications sector. The EECC security provisions apply to all electronic communications networks and services, including all interpersonal communications services (number-based and number-independent). Article 40 (3) introduces a new approach to inform users who are potentially affected by a significant threat of possible protective measures or remedies which the users can take. The EECC security provisions in Articles 40 and 41 have been incorporated into the NIS 2 Directive (EU) 2022/2555. Pursuant to Article 43 of the NIS 2 Directive, they have been deleted with effect from 18 October 2024.

Last but not least, the EECC strengthens the protection of citizens in emergency situations. First, in case of emergency communications, the precision of the caller localisation is improved through the use of device-based data.[30] Second, Member States are obliged to ensure that, when public warning systems regarding imminent or developing major emergencies and disasters are activated, warnings are transmitted by providers of mobile number-based interpersonal communications services to the end-users concerned.[31] Member States may determine that public warnings be transmitted by other services provided that the effectiveness of the public warning system is equivalent in terms of coverage and capacity to reach end-users.

Moreover, consumers have been protected through a price ceiling for international intra-EU communications since May 2019. This provision was not included in the Commission EECC proposal but was included during the trilogue negotiations upon request of the European Parliament (which had opposed a similar provision in the Commission's Telecoms Single Market proposal of 2014). As the price ceiling is to be directly applicable (and the EECC is a Directive), it was inserted in a provision of the BEREC Regulation[32] (Article 50) that amended Regulation (EU) 2015/2120 and introduced a definition of 'regulated intra-EU communications' and a new Article 5a therein. From 15 May 2019, retail prices (excluding VAT) charged to consumers for regulated intra-EU communications were not allowed to exceed EUR 0,19 per minute for calls and EUR 0,06 per SMS message. Article 5a of the amended Regulation (EU) 2015/2120 was initially applicable until 14 May 2024; however, Article 17 (4) of the Gigabit Infrastructure Act (Regulation (EU) 2024/1309, 2024) extended its applicability until 30 June 2032. In addition, Article 17 (2) of the Gigabit Infrastructure Act amended Article 5a of Regulation (EU) 2015/2120 in order to prohibit providers, from 1 January 2029, from applying different retail prices to consumers for domestic communications and intra-EU communications, subject to prior adoption of technical safeguards such as sustainability, fair use and anti-fraud measures.

[30] Article 109 EECC.

[31] Article 110 EECC.

[32] Regulation (EU) 2018/1971 was adopted at the same time as the EECC.

Implementation of the Code and Main Follow-Up Policy Initiatives

The effect-taking of the Code as of 21 December 2020 has been a milestone for the European electronic communications ecosystem. It has established a modern pro-investment framework that has enabled new action and the further evolution of the legislative framework in specific fields. Some key telecommunication policy actions following the effect-taking of the Code are provided below.

Initiatives that Reinforce the Single Market to the Benefit of European Consumers

Since the introduction of Roam-Like-at-Home in June 2017, EU citizens can stay connected without paying additional charges when travelling in the EU and the European Economic Area (EEA). This has made travelling much easier, as citizens no longer need to worry about high roaming charges or make additional efforts to buy local SIM cards when travelling in the EU. In 2022, the roaming rules were prolonged for another 10 years and are now explicitly ensuring that consumers should have the same quality of mobile services abroad as they normally have at home. Additionally, mobile operators are now obliged to protect their customers by providing them with clear information about any services that are not regulated and that can cause surcharges, such as calls to premium numbers and roaming when on ships and planes. The roaming rules also lower wholesale charges (the cost to operators for using networks abroad to provide services to their customers when they are abroad), ultimately benefiting consumers. These rules are also being extended to neighbouring countries such as Ukraine and Moldova. With several voluntary agreements between EU operators and foreign operators, citizens can already use roaming services at lower prices in Ukraine, Moldova, and the six Western Balkan countries. The Commission is further working towards the inclusion of those countries under internal market roaming rules.

Further rules adopted in 2024 under the Gigabit Infrastructure Act set a path to phase out the surcharges for international calls within the EU.

Enablement of Top-Performing Networks Through Fibre and 5G Rollout

The 2023 Report on the state of the Digital Decade underlined fibre coverage at 56% of all households (41% of households in rural areas) and basic 5G population coverage in the EU currently at 81% (51% of the population in rural areas).

Varying national and local administrative hurdles often pose obstacles in network deployments. A new piece of legislation (the "Gigabit Infrastructure Act") updated and reinforced earlier frameworks with the aim to reinforce/incentivise network investments and rollout by addressing persistent administrative barriers in network deployments. These include simplifying and digitising permit granting procedures as well as setting deadlines by national/local authorities, accessing information on existing infrastructure and planned civil works, encouraging co-deployment and infrastructure (e.g., fibre in buildings) sharing, and improving overall coordination among all relevant actors.

With regard to mobile networks, the need for efficient and effective management of radio spectrum—the essential and scarce resource for wireless connectivity—has led to the adoption and implementation of Union legislation that enabled the deployment of wireless services at higher speed and capacity as well as better performance and security, both for terrestrial and aeronautical/maritime communications. Examples include the harmonisation across the Union of all bands for the provision of 5G services, the enablement of 5G use onboard aircraft and vessels in the EU, the enablement of local/WiFi connectivity services as well as short-range communications in support of Internet of Things applications. Regarding international negotiations and agreements on radio spectrum management (with the main aim to avoid cross-border harmful interferences to wireless communications) under the auspices of the International Telecommunications Union (ITU), the Council adopted a Decision laying down the EU position for the 2023 negotiations[33] on agenda items relevant to the Union's law, policies, and programmes, which addressed radio spectrum usage for space, terrestrial, maritime, and

[33] Such international negotiations are following a four-year-cycle and are taking place under the so-called World Radio Communication Conferences (WRC). Latest event has been the WRC-23 one (that took place in November-December 2023 in Dubai, UAE, to be followed by the WRC-27 (2027) event.

other services. This laid the basis for a successful outcome for the Union at the international spectrum discussions in 2023 (WRC-23).

Targeted Support to Cross-Border Infrastructure Deployment and Access

Through the Connecting Europe Facility (CEF) programme (European Commission, 2021), the Union is supporting the development of high-performing, sustainable, and efficiently interconnected trans-European networks in the field of digital services. This has led to the deployment of strategic backbone EU cross-border networks, including submarine cables, 5G-based systems to enable use cases functioning as early socio-economic drivers (5G smart communities) in public administrations, healthcare centres, schools, and other education and training institutions, and 5G-based systems covering cross-border segments of transport corridors.

For example, the WiFi4EU programme has been supporting the deployment of hotspots in Europe's most remote communities for free Internet access to the public. It has helped until early 2024, in this context, some 7,200 local authorities to establish free WiFi service in public spaces. The initiative connects, in early 2024, European citizens with over 9,000 wireless networks encompassing some 93,300 hotspots.

Fibre networks provide the fastest, most secure, and most environmentally sustainable means of connectivity. A challenge arises when fibre is to be deployed in remote and rural areas where, notably, the cost of deployment is a preventive factor. In response to this, the Union's Connecting Europe Broadband Fund (CEBF) has been investing since 2018 in the deployment of high-quality fibre-to-the-home (FTTH) networks across (by early 2024) 1 800 000 residential, business, and public administration premises, mostly in rural areas.

A New Telecommunications Landscape as a Result of Recent Disruptive Geopolitical Events and Technological Developments

The period following the implementation of the Code has been anything but smooth or linear. It has been characterised by turbulent events—notably the COVID-19 pandemic and the war of aggression of Russia against Ukraine in Europe—that have changed the course not only of Europe but of the world's history.[34] The above events and the confinement measures due to COVID-19 created a heavy reliance on telecommunications for almost all activities. These events highlighted both the power/role and also some vulnerabilities of Europe's digital networks due notably to digital divides in Europe.

The recent geopolitical developments highlighted further the importance of security and resilience of infrastructures against both human-made and natural hazards, as well as the complementary role of terrestrial, satellite, and submarine connectivity solutions for uninterrupted availability of service under all circumstances. In a rapidly changing security landscape, a strategic Union-wide approach to security and resilience of critical digital infrastructures is essential for the EU's economic security, building on the solid existing legislative framework, notably the NIS2 Directive, the Directive on the resilience of critical entities (Directive (EU) 2022/2557, 2022), and the Council Recommendation on a Union-wide coordinated approach to strengthen the resilience of critical infrastructure (European Council, 2022).

In parallel, digital networks are undergoing a technological transformation where connectivity is converging with cloud and edge computing capabilities, and the value chain is shifting to new business models and markets based, notably, on Artificial Intelligence, Virtual Worlds (else metaverse), App Economy, Internet of Things (IoT), automation, or new forms of content delivery such as high-quality video streaming. These applications are fast spreading across various industrial and societal areas (such as mobility, energy, manufacturing, the environment, healthcare, creative industries, etc.) and require a continuous exponential increase in data processing, storage, and transmission. The ability to process and transport large amounts of data created by millions of devices across the entire global Internet has led to the remote storage and processing of data in the cloud, between the cloud and the end-user, and close to the end-user (edge computing). This has led to the virtualisation of electronic communications network functions in software and a shifting of these functions to the cloud or the edge.

These developments make it imperative to ensure that the EU network infrastructure is ready for these geopolitical and technological changes.

[34] Due partly to those events, there are EU Member States that even in early 2024 have not fully transposed the Code into their legal system.

This is on the understanding that the future competitiveness of all sectors of Europe's economy depends on advanced digital network infrastructures and services, as they form the basis for global GDP growth between EUR 1 and 2 trillion (McKinsey Global Institute, 2020) and the digital and green transition of our society and economy. From a societal perspective, the availability of high-quality, reliable, and secure connectivity for everybody and everywhere in the EU, including in rural and remote areas, is indispensable.

The above connectivity challenge is only part of a broader strategic goal of a twin digital-green transition in Europe where not only digital infrastructures but also digital skills and the digital transformation of our public services and businesses are considered, and all of these are carried out in a sustainable manner in line with the Green Deal plan of the Union (European Commission, 2024).

To address this major challenge, the Union launched in 2021 the Digital Decade Vision (COM(2021) 118 final, 2021) as a compass towards the new strategic goal, and in 2022, an implementation strategy (the Digital Decade Policy Programme, Decision (EU) 2022/2481, 2022) to reach this strategic goal. These initiatives represent the first effort ever of the Union to set policy objectives and quantitative targets for 2030 across all key digital areas, as well as an implementation strategy to reach them.

The central role of digital infrastructures and connectivity, in particular, was highlighted, among others, in two more recent high-level policy initiatives in Europe, namely the Draghi report on "The future of European competitiveness" and the more focused Letta report on Europe's single market (entitled: "Much more than a Market")—both published in 2024 (Draghi, 2024; Letta, 2024). More specifically, the first one was commissioned to the former Italian Prime Minister and President of the European Central Bank, Mario Draghi, by the European Commission to reflect on the future of European competitiveness, and the second was commissioned to the former Italian Prime Minister Enrico Letta by the European Council, to examine the future of the EU single market including the market for electronic communications.

In the broad context of the future of European competitiveness, Professor Draghi makes an alarming call on the need for Europe to refocus its collective efforts on closing the innovation gap with the US and China. In this context, advanced digital technologies are singled out as the area where Europe profoundly lags on innovation (while a lagging digital sector affects almost all other sectors). The lack of a true single market, including on connectivity (that prevents notable companies from reaching size, which in turn leads to lower technology adoption according to evidence provided in his report) and the related lack of sufficient investment in connectivity are, according to Mr. Draghi, among the key barriers to innovation in Europe.

Professor Letta's report focuses on barriers to the single market for electronic communications. It outlines a comprehensive plan for relaunching the Single Market as a catalyst for prosperity and competitiveness. It emphasises six broad action areas: (1) leveraging research, innovation and education, (2) addressing the funding challenge for EU's strategic objectives, (3) scaling and market integration, (4) ensuring sustainability and inclusivity, (5) governance, and (6) the international dimension of the Single Market. Professor Letta's analysis and proposed measures are endorsed and further expanded in some cases by Professor Draghi (making the two reports highly complementary).

Overall, the two reports broadly endorse the Commission's Digital Decade 2030 initiative, while most of the analysis and proposed solutions under the Single Market part of the Draghi and Letta reports on electronic communications are similar to the ones discussed in the Commission's White Paper "How to master Europe's digital infrastructure needs" (presented later in this chapter) that presents considerations about a future legislative framework for electronic communications, with some proposals of the Draghi/Letta reports being even bolder than the scenarios of the White Paper (discussed later in this chapter). Both reports also fully share the need for urgent action.

A New Digital Decade 2030 Vision and Implementation Strategy for Europe

The Digital Decade vision and implementation strategy (https://digital-strategy.ec.europa.eu/en/policies/europes-digital-decade) represent the first effort ever of the Union to set policy objectives and quantitative targets for 2030 across the whole digital landscape. It also sets a binding commitment from EU Member States to cooperate to achieve these objectives, including through a specific monitoring and cooperation mechanism. The Digital Decade represents an agreement between the Union and the Member States to work together towards a fast and well-managed digital transition. It strengthens the Union's sovereignty (Timmers, 2023) and competitiveness, making sure that humans are at the centre of this transition and contributing to a sustainable economy in line with the Union's climate objectives (Green Deal).[35]

The Digital Decade's objectives and targets focus on four key areas (also called cardinal points), namely, digital skills, digital infrastructure—including connectivity, the digitalisation of businesses, and online public services.

Under the digital infrastructure cardinal point, the Digital Decade Policy Programme sets a series of objectives and targets to promote the development of resilient, secure, performant, and sustainable digital infrastructures in the Union, including a digital target for the Commission and Member States to achieve by 2030 gigabit connectivity for all and coverage by a next-generation wireless high-speed network with performance at least equivalent to that of 5G (5th generation mobile networks) in all populated areas.

The chart below, prepared by the Commission services, shows the share of the 2030 digital infrastructure (including connectivity) targets achieved by end 2024 and functions as a benchmark for future action.

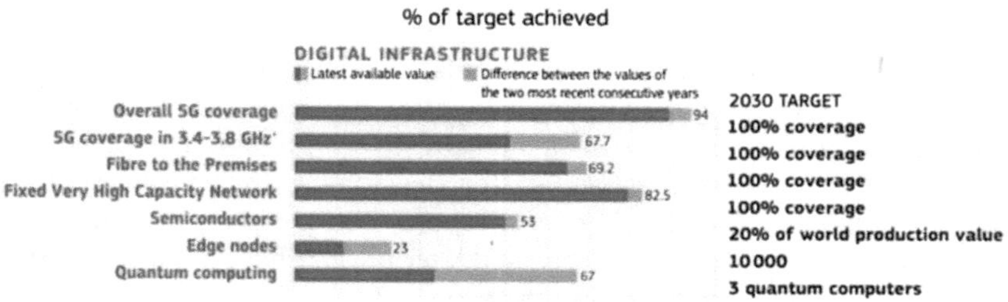

While the first phase of the Digital Decade process has been successfully implemented (with key actions ranging from setting plans and monitoring progress to deploying large-scale multi-country projects in support of achieving the Digital Decade targets), there is still a long way to go until the decade's end, including a possible revision of its targets midway (in 2026).

[35] In parallel to the adoption of the Digital Decade Policy Programme, the EU institutions made on 15 December 2022, a solemn "European Declaration on Digital Rights and Principles for the Digital Decade", according to which people are at the centre of the digital transformation in the European Union and all businesses, including SMEs, should benefit from it.

Hand-in-hand with Europe's plans to reach the Digital Decade targets also goes the implementation of a major support programme to help Europe recover from the devastating effects of the pandemic. In this context, the Union put together in 2022 an unprecedented and bold financial package (of around EUR 723 billion, of which at least 20% is earmarked for digital targets) for the Union's Member States to invest in national reforms and projects to recover from the recent health and geopolitical crisis. The digital department of the Commission has been coordinating the successful implementation of the digital part of the so-called Recovery and Resilience Facility (RRF), supporting all 27 Member States to be on a stable path to meet the common Digital Decade targets. By early 2024, Member States have exceeded the digital target set by the RRF Regulation, devoting about 26% of their Recovery and Resilience Plans to digital-related measures.

Status of Connectivity in Europe Assessed Against the Digital Decade Targets and Investment Needs

Since the establishment of the Digital Decade process, progress in telecommunications in Europe has been measured against the relevant digital decade targets. The 2025 State of the Digital Decade report (European Commission, https://digital-strategy.ec.europa.eu/en/policies/2025-state-digital-decade-package, 2023) (figures reflecting the status by the end of 2024) shows that at the current state of the Digital Decade, the EU is still far from achieving the Digital Decade connectivity targets. Fibre networks, which are critical for delivering gigabit connectivity, only reach 69.2% of households and it is estimated that at the current pace, full coverage would only be achieved by 2051. While 5G population coverage stands at 94.3%, the deployment of 5G stand-alone networks (that ensure full-fledged 5G functionality and relevant quality of service—instead of only patchy upgrades of 4G networks) is lagging behind with only 2% of the 5G-users connected via stand-alone infrastructure. 5G is still falling short in quality with regard to end-users' expectations and industry needs, as well as in addressing the divide between rural and urban areas. The EU is lagging behind in terms of coverage compared to the US, where 97% of the population is covered by 5G.

Reaching the current Digital Decade targets for Gigabit connectivity and 5G may require a total investment of up to EUR 148 billion if fixed and mobile networks are deployed independently, and a stand-alone 5G offering European citizens and businesses the full capabilities that can be offered by 5G mobile networks is deployed. A further EUR 26–79 billion of investments may be required under different scenarios to ensure full coverage of transport corridors, including roads, railways, and waterways, bringing the required total investment needs for connectivity alone to over EUR 200 billion.

Additionally, for future upgrades, e.g., 6G or WiFi 6, the required network densification is likely to increase by a factor of 2–3 by the end of the decade, at least in high-density demand areas. Furthermore, beyond terrestrial connectivity, further investments are required for the integration of advanced satellite services, providing complementary solutions for backhaul device connectivity in remote areas not covered by terrestrial technologies or to ensure service continuity in case of crisis or disaster relief.

However, the bulk of investments in electronic communications infrastructure come and will continue to come from private investors. In this context, the current financial situation of the EU electronic communications sector raises concerns about its capacity to find funding for the substantial investments that are needed to catch up with the technological shift. Crucial, in turn, for the future of connectivity is the perception of the attractiveness of advanced digital networks by private investors.

A modern regulatory framework that incentivises, among others, the transition from legacy copper networks to fibre networks, the development of 5G and other wireless networks and cloud-based infrastructures, as well as the scale-up of operators within the single market, and which takes account of emerging technologies and latest geopolitical developments, is key to ensuring that Europe has the advanced, secured communications and computing infrastructure it needs. Short of that, the EU risks missing its 2030 digital targets and falling behind other leading regions as regards to competitiveness, economic growth and related user benefits. From the above, a clear need appears to review the current telecommunications regulatory framework and identify areas that could be improved to meet the new challenges of the single market in telecommunications in Europe.

Considerations About a Future Legislative Framework for Electronic Communications

As discussed earlier, one of the main objectives of the Code has been to promote connectivity by putting in place a regulatory framework conducive to more investment in very high-capacity networks. While reinforcing investment objectives, the Code also aims at promoting competition (both at the infrastructure as well as at the services level), contributing to the development of the internal market and promoting end-user benefits. All these principles remain valid, but in addition, due to recent technological developments and new global challenges, the Commission is considering whether incorporating wider dimensions, such as sustainability, industrial competitiveness, and economic security, into the policy framework would be appropriate.

In this context, the Commission run from February to May 2023 a broad-scale exploratory consultation on "The future of the electronic communications sector and its infrastructure", the input which formed to a large extent the basis of a White Paper that was launched on 21 February 2024 and that was entitled "How to master Europe's digital infrastructure needs?". The focus of the above White paper has been to take stock of the current situation on connectivity technologies and market and discuss possible scenarios of future policy action to notably address Europe's connectivity infrastructure needs in the path towards achieving the Digital Decade targets under the current geopolitical setting (Letta, 2024).

The White Paper (https://digital-strategy.ec.europa.eu/en/library/white-paper-how-master-europes-digital-infrastructure-needs) is another attempt to advance towards a European telecom single market, echoing the attempt made by the Commission in 2013, ten years earlier. It is noticeable, however, that no legislative proposal was made by the von der Leyen Commission, as the White Paper is only a series of proposals subject to further consultation. In fact, it appears that the executive has hesitated and declined the option of making such a legislative proposal, whereas announcements had been made by the Commissioner in charge, Thierry Breton. In an interview with a French newspaper in the summer of 2023, he announced a legislative proposal that should arrive by the end of 2023 and focus on several areas: research and development in the telecom sector, new legislation to establish a single market for telecommunication infrastructures favouring investment and quality of service, and the emergence of pan-European leaders by lifting obstacles to consolidation (Breton, 2023a, 2023b). He outlined further his idea in a message on social media in October 2023 (Breton, 2023a, 2023b). However, no legislative proposal eventually emerged. The hesitation in making a legislative proposal shows that the Commission was not confident about its chances of success and that, again, some opposition to the proposal could be felt. This came from stakeholders (Hartmann, 2024a, 2024b), with some NGOs even accusing him of bias towards telecom incumbents in a letter to the Parliament (e.g., EpicenterWorks, 2024), while resistance to some ideas could be heard from European as well as from national regulators (Hartmann, 2024a, 2024b).

In the above context, the White Paper identifies the scope of policy action in some key areas as regards connectivity markets.

- In light of the recent developments in the telecommunications market, and in particular the quick progress of convergence between electronic communications networks and the cloud, a rethinking of the scope of application of the electronic communications regulatory framework could be considered in particular as concerns the application of the same applicable rules to different networks or network segments involved in data exchange between users. It is difficult to justify the rationale for any different today applicable rules (for instance, as regards lawful interception).
- In the same context, the recent technological changes create an opportunity for alignment of the operations of electronic communications and cloud services with the development of pan-European core network operators. For example, the cloudification of 5G networks can provide significant benefits to the electronic communications network providers and allow them to leverage the same economies of scale of cloud providers by, inter alia, unifying the core network functionality of several national electronic communications networks in the cloud. However, when it comes to electronic communications networks, this integration of functionalities in centralised cloud data centres that provide cross-border core network functionalities currently faces several legal barriers due to non-harmonised legal frameworks in the MS, inter alia, in the area of authorisation including for the usage of radio spectrum.

- On the service side, a consistent provision of Network as a Service (NaaS)[36]—based applications relying on stand-alone 5G core networks,[37] network slicing, and spectrum resources available across Member States could provide a new business case for cross-border operations.
- On the network side, the main recent changes in the overall global architecture of the internet and of interconnection are caused and driven by the expansion of their own backbone and delivery infrastructures by the content application providers (CAPs). This leads to a very direct and cooperative interaction between CAPs and Internet Service Providers (ISPs) as they have to agree on technical and commercial conditions for transit and peering bilaterally (e.g., on the locations of traffic handover, the level of transit prices, on the question of settlement-free or paid peering or on quality and efficiency aspects). There are very few known cases of intervention (by a regulatory authority or by a court) into the contractual relationships between market actors that generally function well, and so do the markets for transit and peering. However, it cannot be excluded that the number of cases in the future will increase. Should this be the case, subject to careful assessment, policy measures could be envisaged to ensure swift resolution of disputes.
- Areas of focus (not being an exclusive list) for possible future legislative action, in this context, are those of authorisation, barriers to core network centralisation, radio spectrum, switch-off of copper networks and migration to fibre ones, an access policy to a full fibre environment, and sustainability networks.

The White Paper proposes a number of possible scenarios at the Union level to complete the digital networks single market, notably on the scope of the telecom regulation, provisions regarding copper switching, harmonisation of radio spectrum policies, and facilitating the greening of digital networks. Similar recommendations appeared in both the Draghi

36 There are definitions from many sources of the NaaS term converging basically to the fact that NaaS is a cloud model that enables users to easily operate the network without establishing, owning, or maintaining their own infrastructure.

37 Standalone 5G networks: with a core network infrastructure separate from previous generations and supporting only 5G network operations.

and Letta reports, with bottom-line reports recommending more coordination at the EU level as opposed to 27 different, in general, national systems.

The Commission, after a significant period of consultation, made a proposal for a Digital Networks Act in January 2026. The proposal contains a series of innovative measures. Notably, it proposes to establish obligations and cooperation mechanisms aimed at ensuring the availability and capabilities of networks in situations of crisis, including the continuity of emergency communications and public warnings.

It also establishes a single passport for the provision of electronic communications networks and services. This means that telecom operators would be able to provide their services freely throughout Europe without having to seek authorisations in each national market, thanks to harmonised conditions and obligations. This new mechanism, while not centralising authorisation at European level, should facilitate operations across borders. The DNA makes clear, though, that national authorities would keep control as regards cybersecurity and would be able to block numbers in case of fraud or misuse. The DNA also promotes a more pan-European approach for spectrum management, notably through a spectrum Single Market procedure. Importantly, the DNA also provides some incentives for investment, through a framework to manage the transition from legacy copper networks to fibre-to-the-home networks, based on a national process with national plans to be notified to the Commission and a deadline for copper switch-off set at 2035. The DNA also proposes to create a new body (the Office of Digital Networks, enhancing the existing BEREC secretariat) to provide administrative and support services to both BEREC and the Radio Spectrum Policy Body (RSPB), with a view to enabling better coordination and more coherent outcomes. All in all, the proposal is aligned with a number of ideas explored in the White Paper, but it also preserves national structures. It offers harmonised rules to cope with remaining national regulatory structures, while still being based on national authorities and introducing loose supervision from the enhanced Office for Digital Networks. The act also goes around national regulation thanks to a passporting mechanism, which however preserves the control of national authorities.

Conclusion

A milestone for electronic communications in Europe has been achieved with the effect of the Code as of 21 December 2020. The framework is, however, far from other digital legislation in leaving the bulk of the power at the national level. The telecom domain appears relatively immune so far to calls for greater market integration, let alone for a consensus on digital sovereignty understood as industry competitiveness and EU-level regulation. The consensus among national regulators, and many times repeated by BEREC, is that the EU approach should focus on competition and consumers. Paradoxically, this is very much in line with a human-centric model as it benefits consumers through notably low prices and diversity of choice, but it does not solve the debate of the past twenty years about the need for the EU telecom sector to invest more and to innovate more, and with the EU targets for 2030 of universal high-speed broadband access for all, which is a pre-condition for participating in the digital economy and society.

The period, however, of transposition and implementation of the Code was characterised by major health and geopolitical events that have been changing the course not only of Europe but of global history. The European response to those challenges, including electronic communications policy, has been bold, including setting up support programmes to exit the crisis and the establishment of decade-long high-level targets and a strategy to reach them across the whole digital spectrum (with electronic communications being a core element in this process).

The proposal for a Digital Networks Act offers an opportunity to make out of national telecom markets more of a single European market. As it is not the first time that such an attempt was made, and as previous attempts were not fully successful, it will be interesting to watch how Council and Parliament will react and whether new structures, such as the Office of Digital Networks, or possibilities of a single passport, will be retained.

Bibliography

BEREC. (2013). *BEREC views on the proposal for a Regulation "laying down measures to complete the European single market for electronic communications and to achieve a Connected Continent"*. Retrieved from https://www.berec.europa.eu/sites/default/files/files/document_register_store/2013/10/BEREC_views_on_Regulation_Proposal_to_complete_the_single_market_2013-10-17_2.pdf

BEREC. (2016, August 30). *BEREC Guidelines on the Implementation by National Regulators of European Net Neutrality Rules*. Retrieved from https://www.berec.europa.eu/en/document-categories/berec/regulatory-best-practices/guidelines/berec-guidelines-on-the-implementation-by-national-regulators-of-european-net-neutrality-rules

Breton, T. (2023a, October 10). *A 'Digital Networks Act' to redefine the DNA of our telecoms regulation*. Retrieved from LinkedIN: https://www.linkedin.com/pulse/digital-networks-act-redefine-dna-our-telecoms-thierry-breton/

Breton, T. (2023b, June 15). La Commission soutient les Etats membres qui bannissent Huawei. (F. Schmitt, & N. Madelaine, Interviewers) https://www.lesechos.fr/tech-medias/hightech/thierry-breton-la-commission-soutient-les-etats-membres-qui-bannissent-huawei-1952702

Cave, M., Genakos, C., & Valletti, T. (2019). The European framework for regulating telecommunications: A 25-year appraisal. *Review of Industrial Organization, 55*, 47–62. https://doi.org/10.1007/s11151-019-09686-6

Conradi, M., & Amin, R. (2014, April). The most ambitious plan in 26 years of telecoms market reform? No way! *Computer Law & Security Review, 30*(2), 199–200.

Draghi, M. (2024). *The future of European competitiveness—A competitiveness strategy for Europe*. Obtenido de https://commission.europa.eu/topics/strengthening-european-competitiveness/eu-competitiveness-looking-ahead_en

Državni zbor Republike Slovenije. (2012, December 20). *U K A Z o razglasitvi Zakona o elektronskih komunikacijah (ZEKom-1)*. Retrieved from https://www.uradni-list.si/glasilo-uradni-list-rs/vsebina/111442

EpicenterWorks. (2024, January 26). *Letter to members of the European Parliament industry capture of commissioner Thierry Breton*. Retrieved from https://epicenter.works/fileadmin/user_upload/Breton-warning-MEPs.pdf

European Commission. (1987). *Towards a dynamic European economy, Green Paper on the development of the common market for telecommnications services and equipment*. Retrieved from https://eur-lex.europa.eu/legal-content/en/HIS/?uri=CELEX:51987DC0290

European Commission. (1990, June 28). *Competition in the markets for telecommunication services*. Retrieved from https://eur-lex.europa.eu/legal-content/EN/TXT/?uri=CELEX%3A31990L0388

European Commission. (1996, March 13). *Commission Directive 96/19/EC of 13 March 1996 amending Directive 90/388/EEC with regard to the implementation of full competition in telecommunications markets*. Retrieved from https://eur-lex.europa.eu/eli/dir/1996/19/oj

European Commission. (2002a, July 29). *2002/627/EC: Commission Decision of 29 July 2002 establishing the European Regulators Group for electronic communications networks and services (Text with EEA relevance)*. Retrieved from https://eur-lex.europa.eu/legal-content/EN/ALL/?uri=celex:32002D0627

European Commission. (2002b, September 16). *Commission Directive 2002/77/EC of 16 September 2002 on competition in the markets for electronic communications networks and services (Text with EEA relevance)*. Retrieved from https://eur-lex.europa.eu/legal-content/EN/TXT/?uri=celex%3A32002L0077

European Commission. (2003, February 11). *Commission Recommendation of 11 February 2003 on relevant product and service markets within the electronic communications sector susceptible to ex ante regulation in accordance with Directive 2002/21/EC of the European Parliament and of the Council on a*. Retrieved from https://eur-lex.europa.eu/legal-content/EN/TXT/?uri=CELEX%3A32003H0311

European Commission. (2010, May 19). *Communication from the Commission to the European Parliament, the Council, the European Economic and Social Committee and the Committee of the Regions A Digital Agenda for Europe*. Retrieved from https://eur-lex.europa.eu/legal-content/en/ALL/?uri=celex%3A52010DC0245

European Commission. (11 de September de 2013). *Proposal for a Regulation (of the European Parliament and of the Council laying down measures concerning the European single market for electronic communications and to achieve a Connected Continent, and amending Directives 2002/20/EC, 2002/21/EC and 2002*. Obtenido de https://eur-lex.europa.eu/legal-content/EN/TXT/?uri=CELEX:52013PC0627

European Commission. (2018, May 7). *Communication from the Commission — Guidelines on market analysis and the assessment of significant market power under the EU regulatory framework for electronic communications networks and services*. Retrieved from https://eur-lex.europa.eu/legal-content/EN/TXT/?uri=CELEX%3A52018XC0507%2801%29

European Commission. (18 de December de 2020). *Commission Recommendation (EU) 2020/2245 of 18 December 2020 on relevant product and service markets within the electronic communications sector susceptible to ex ante regulation in accordance with Directive (EU) 2018/1972 of the European Parliament and o*. Obtenido de https://eur-lex.europa.eu/legal-content/EN/TXT/?uri=CELEX%3A32020H2245

European Commission. (2021a). *Communication from the Commission to the European Parliament the Council, the European Economic and Social Committee and the Committee of the Regions. 2030 Digital Compass: the European way for the Digital Decade*. Brussels: European Commission.

European Commission. (2021b). *Connecting Europe Facility—CEF Digital*. Retrieved from https://digital-strategy.ec.europa.eu/en/activities/cef-digital

European Commission. (2022). *Roaming: connected anywhere in the EU at no extra charge*. Retrieved from Shaping Europe's digital future. https://digital-strategy.ec.europa.eu/en/policies/roaming

European Commission. (2023, September 27). *2023 Report on the state of the Digital Decade*. Retrieved from https://digital-strategy.ec.europa.eu/en/library/2023-report-state-digital-decade

European Commission. (2024). *The European Green Deal: Striving to be the first climate-neutral continent*. Retrieved from https://commission.europa.eu/strategy-and-policy/priorities-2019-2024/european-green-deal_en

European Council. (1990, June 28). *Council Directive 90/387/EEC of 28 June 1990 on the establishment of the internal market for telecommunications services through the implementation of open network provision*. Retrieved from https://eur-lex.europa.eu/legal-content/EN/TXT/?uri=CELEX%3A31990L0387

European Council. (2022, December 8). *Council Recommendation of 8 December 2022 on a Union-wide coordinated approach to strengthen the resilience of critical infrastructure*. Retrieved from https://eur-lex.europa.eu/legal-content/EN/TXT/?uri=CELEX%3A32023H0120%2801%29

European Union. (18 de December de 2000). *Regulation (EC) No 2887/2000 of the European Parliament and of the Council of 18 December 2000 on unbundled access to the local loop (Text with EEA relevance)*. Obtenido de https://eur-lex.europa.eu/legal-content/EN/TXT/?uri=CELEX%3A32000R2887

European Union. (2002, March 7). *Directive 2002/19/EC of the European Parliament and of the Council of 7 March 2002 on access to, and interconnection of, electronic communications networks and associated facilities (Access Directive)*. Retrieved from https://eur-lex.europa.eu/legal-content/EN/ALL/?uri=CELEX:32002L0019

European Union. (7 de March de 2002). *Directive 2002/20/EC of the European Parliament and of the Council of 7 March 2002 on the authorisation of electronic communications networks and services (Authorisation Directive)*. Obtenido de https://eur-lex.europa.eu/legal-content/EN/TXT/?uri=celex%3A32002L0020

European Union. (7 de March de 2002). *Directive 2002/21/EC of the European Parliament and of the Council of 7 March 2002 on a common regulatory framework for electronic communications networks and services (Framework Directive)*. Obtenido de https://eur-lex.europa.eu/legal-content/EN/TXT/?uri=CELEX%3A32002L0021

European Union. (2002, March 7). *Directive 2002/22/EC of the European Parliament and of the Council of 7 March 2002 on universal service and users' rights relating to electronic communications networks and services (Universal Service Directive)*. Retrieved from https://eur-lex.europa.eu/legal-content/en/TXT/?uri=CELEX%3A32002L0022

European Union. (2002, July 12). *Directive 2002/58/EC of the European Parliament and of the Council of 12 July 2002 concerning the processing of personal data and the protection of privacy in the electronic communications sector (Directive on privacy and electronic communications)*.

European Union. (2007, June 27). *Regulation (EC) No 717/2007 of the European Parliament and of the Council of 27 June 2007 on roaming on public mobile telephone networks within the Community and amending Directive 2002/21/EC*. Retrieved from https://eur-lex.europa.eu/legal-content/en/ALL/?uri=CELEX%3A32007R0717

European Union. (2009a, November 25). *Directive 2009/136/EC of the European Parliament and of the Council of 25 November 2009 amending Directive 2002/22/EC on universal service and users' rights relating to electronic communications networks and services, Directive 2002/58/EC concerning the p*. Retrieved from https://eur-lex.europa.eu/legal-content/EN/TXT/?uri=celex%3A32009L0136

European Union. (2009b, November 25). *Directive 2009/140/EC of the European Parliament and of the Council of 25 November 2009 amending Directives 2002/21/EC on a common regulatory framework for electronic communications networks and services, 2002/19/EC on access to, and interconnection of, e*. Retrieved from https://eur-lex.europa.eu/legal-content/en/ALL/?uri=CELEX%3A32009L0140

European Union. (2009c, November 25). *Regulation (EC) No 1211/2009 of the European Parliament and of the Council of 25 November 2009 establishing the Body of European Regulators for Electronic Communications (BEREC) and the Office (Text with EEA relevance)*. Retrieved from https://eur-lex.europa.eu/legal-content/EN/TXT/?uri=celex%3A32009R1211

European Union. (2009d, June 18). *Regulation (EC) No 544/2009 of the European Parliament and of the Council of 18 June 2009 amending Regulation (EC) No 717/2007 on roaming on public mobile telephone networks within the Community and Directive 2002/21/EC on a common regulatory framework fo*. Retrieved from https://eur-lex.europa.eu/legal-content/EN/TXT/?uri=CELEX%3A32009R0544

European Union. (2012, June 13). *Regulation (EU) No 531/2012 of the European Parliament and of the Council of 13 June 2012 on roaming on public mobile communications networks within the Union (recast)*. Retrieved from https://eur-lex.europa.eu/legal-content/EN/TXT/?uri=celex%3A32012R0531

European Union. (2015, November 25). *Regulation (EU) 2015/2120 of the European Parliament and of the Council of 25 November 2015 laying down measures concerning open internet access and amending Directive 2002/22/EC on universal service and users' rights relating to electronic communications*. Retrieved from https://eur-lex.europa.eu/eli/reg/2015/2120/oj

European Union. (2018, December 11). *Regulation (EU) 2018/1971 of the European Parliament and of the Council of 11 December 2018 establishing the Body of European Regulators for Electronic Communications (BEREC) and the Agency for Support for BEREC (BEREC Office), amending Regulation (EU)*

20. Retrieved from https://eur-lex.europa.eu/legal-content/EN/TXT/?uri=CELEX%3A32018R1971

European Union. (2019, April 17). *Directive (EU) 2019/882 of the European Parliament and of the Council of 17 April 2019 on the accessibility requirements for products and services*. Retrieved from https://eur-lex.europa.eu/eli/dir/2019/882/oj

European Union. (2022a, December 14). *Decision (EU) 2022/2481 of the European Parliament and of the Council of 14 December 2022 establishing the Digital Decade Policy Programme 2030*. Retrieved from https://eur-lex.europa.eu/legal-content/EN/TXT/?uri=CELEX%3A32022D2481

European Union. (2022b, December 14). *Directive (EU) 2022/2555 of the European Parliament and of the Council of 14 December 2022 on measures for a high common level of cybersecurity across the Union, amending Regulation (EU) No 910/2014 and Directive (EU) 2018/1972, and repealing Directive (E*. Retrieved from https://eur-lex.europa.eu/eli/dir/2022/2555/oj

European Union. (2022c, December 14). *Directive (EU) 2022/2557 of the European Parliament and of the Council of 14 December 2022 on the resilience of critical entities and repealing Council Directive 2008/114/EC*. Retrieved from https://eur-lex.europa.eu/eli/dir/2022/2557/oj

European Union. (2024, April 29). *Regulation (EU) 2024/1309 of the European Parliament and of the Council of 29 April 2024 on measures to reduce the cost of deploying gigabit electronic communications networks, amending Regulation (EU) 2015/2120 and repealing Directive 2014/61/EU (Gigabit*. Retrieved from https://eur-lex.europa.eu/legal-content/EN/TXT/?uri=CELEX%3A32024R1309

Hartmann, T. (2024a, September 27). *Institutional fight over EU telecoms rules laid bare at Brussels conference*. Retrieved from Euractiv: https://www.euractiv.com/section/digital/news/institutional-fight-over-eu-telecoms-rules-laid-bare-at-brussels-conference/

Hartmann, T. (2024b, July 31). *Telecoms stakeholders urge Breton to reconsider some stances in light of Commission appointment*. Retrieved from Euractiv: https://www.euractiv.com/section/digital/news/telecoms-stakeholders-urge-breton-to-reconsider-some-stances-in-light-of-commission-appointment/

Letta, E. (2024). *Much more than a market — Speed, Security, Solidarity. Empowering the SIngle Market to deliver a sustainable future and prosperity for all EU Citizens*. Brussels: European Commission.

McKinsey Global Institute. (2020, February 20). *Connected world: An evolution in connectivity beyond the 5G revolution*. Retrieved from https://www.mckinsey.com/industries/technology-media-and-telecommunications/our-insights/connected-world-an-evolution-in-connectivity-beyond-the-5g-revolution

Staatsblad van het Koninkrijk der Nederlanden. (2012, May 10). *Wet van 10 mei 2012 tot wijziging van de Telecommunicatiewet ter implementatie van de herziene telecommunicatierichtlijnen*. Retrieved from https://zoek.officielebekendmakingen.nl/stb-2012-235.html

Telenor Magyarország, Joined Cases C-807/18; C-39/19 (Court (Grand Chamber) September 15, 2020).

Timmers, P. (2023). Sovereignty in the digital age. In H. Werthner, C. Ghezzi, J. Kramer, J. Nida-Rümelin, B. Nuseibeh, E. Prem, & A. Stanger (Eds.), *Introduction to digital humanism* (pp. 571–592). Springer.

Vodafone and Telekom Deutschland, C-854/19; C-5/20; C-34/20 (Court (Eighth Chamber) September 2, 2021).

Vodafone Ltd and Others v Secretary of State for Business, Enterprise and Regulatory Reform., C-58/08 (High Court of Justice (England & Wales), Queen's Bench Division (Administrative Court)—United Kingdom. June 8, 2010).

CHAPTER 6

Decrypting and Implementing the EU Data Strategy

Alberto Palomo

Introduction

Perhaps the most famous EU legislation in the digital policy field has been the General Data Protection Regulation (GDPR), which, according to its proponents, has changed the way citizens and companies think about data and serves as an international benchmark for a trustworthy digital market (Albrecht, 2016), thus epitomising the 'Brussels effect' (Bradford, 2020). But data has a more general significance for the EU digital economy and society. The history of computing has inevitably been associated with data, and, in particular, the capacity to transform and store it. This is because, alongside the chronological development of more effective and efficient computational methods and tools (both in the form of hardware and software), the ubiquitous challenge of how to sustainably source, store, manage, and capitalise on datasets has long been withstanding.

Being able to access and control the wealth of data created by Europe's digital economy has become a question of sovereignty, closely interlinked with the digital transformation of the continent and a key ingredient

A. Palomo (✉)
Gaia-X European Association for Data & Cloud AISBL, Brussels, Belgium
e-mail: alberto.palomo@cantab.net

T. Kleiner and A. Garcia Rodriguez (eds.), *The Making of a Global Digital Rulebook*, https://doi.org/10.1007/978-981-95-9226-5_6

for Europe to lead in emerging technologies like artificial intelligence (Chander & Sun, 2023). To analyse the importance of data in making the EU digital rulebook, it is thus not enough to look at law-making. One must also examine how the data economy can flourish in the EU and enact sovereignty aspirations by looking at data-driven business models and at the progress made in implementing the EU Data Strategy (European Commission, 2020).

In 2020, the European Commission published its Data Strategy to foster the creation and reuse of data in the EU, ensure data sovereignty, and drive innovation. The Strategy foresees the creation of a single market for data and proposes a governance framework and a network of 'data spaces' to drive the digital transformation in the EU. Likewise, it aims to increase investments in digital infrastructure and promote digital literacy and skills. The European Data Strategy shows the strategic values of digital data and the ambitions of a geopolitically driven European Commission to ensure companies and citizens have access to tools to improve business operations and everyday lives. The 2025 Data Union strategy amplified this approach with a focus on Artificial Intelligence.

This chapter investigates the role of data in the digital economy, as well as its importance for the EU in terms of economic opportunities, business models, and sovereignty. It looks at the underpinnings of the EU Data Strategy and proposes solutions to advance it through data spaces and a new model of trust building. In particular, it unfolds specificities that could very well characterise an EU model of competitiveness based on decentralised agreements, open standards and trust frameworks.

Data as the Backbone of the Digital Economy: Underpinnings of the EU Data Strategy

To analyse the EU Data Strategy, it is essential to understand the importance of data for the digital economy and its impact on new business models. Data can be formally defined as a symbolic representation (numerical, alphabetical, algorithmic, spatial, etc.) of an attribute or a qualitative or quantitative variable describing empirical facts, events, and/or entities (Wikipedia, 2024). According to this definition, data existed long before any form of automatic computational capabilities, but it was the advent of digital computers[1] that brought an exponential increase in the capabilities for processing it.

However, digital is no longer about software only, but rather about the use of data (Parsons, 2017). Moreover, contrary to the adage 'data is the new oil' (University of Sheffield, 2024), data is really more like sand in that it takes a lot of capital, Research and Development efforts, and well-coordinated industrial and logistical processes to extract value out of it (O'Reilly, 2021). This is because data sourcing, consolidation, and contextualisation can be cumbersome and slow. But once a critical maturity point is reached, it generates an endless manna of information available for actionable insights.

Data is accumulated primarily in two ways: either by sensor-based retrieval (automatically, once the sensor is set up) or manually by insertion. Typically, the first is more volumetric and is quite useful for transactional purposes, but it is harder to extrapolate beyond its origins because it is very specific and usually lacks context, and thus often challenging to interrelate with other types of data. On the contrary, the manual alternative tends to collect data of higher representative value precisely because its time-consuming sourcing nature is justified by design.

However, the large digital platforms born around the mid-2000s to early 2010s have been able to become aggregators of data: they provide a (often free) business-to-consumer (B2C) service whereby the latter inserts (or generates) the data the platform later capitalises on. And it has been proven that these platforms, especially the ones with the most comprehensive and up-to-date data, can use it to build a significant advantage over their competitors. This creates a sort of 'flywheel effect' because data prowess generates economies of scale and scope, thus resulting in market concentration (Furman, 2019) and possibly a decline in innovation and customer choice (Boissay et al., 2021) which has been subject to regulation by the European Union (see Chapter 10).

[1] Originally of an electromechanical nature, from the late 1930s and early 1940s, it was the democratisation of transistors in the late 1950s and integrated circuit technology in the 1960s that led the way for the 1970s revolution of the microprocessor and its natural extension, the microcomputer.

Data for the European Economy

For peer-to-peer data transactions, the pecuniary valuation of data is still an open challenge. Yet, very few doubt that, at a large scale, there are benefits from curating and transforming data. Since 2013, the European Commission has tracked digitalisation in the EU and the effects of the data economy (European Commission, 2021). The study measures aspects like the number of data professionals, the value of the data market, the quantity of data suppliers and data that companies use, as well as the overall impact of the data economy on the EU's GDP.

Key findings in 2023 indicate (IDC & the Lisbon Council, 2024) that the value of the data economy, measuring the overall impact of the data market on the economy as a whole, exceeded the threshold of €544B in 2023, with a growth of 9.3% compared to 2022. This positive growth trend is confirmed by the value of the data market, which shows a growth rate higher than that of total IT spending, at 11.1% year-on-year and €82B. Regarding supply and demand, data providers are estimated at over 238,000 units, with a growth of 9.2% year-on-year. Data users also increased, rising to over 604,000 units and recording a growth of 3.5% compared to the previous year. These figures also confirm the consolidation of digital tools and data in European companies, including SMEs.

Likewise, revenues generated by data providers increased by 9.3% to nearly €93B, with Germany, France, and Italy showing the largest share of data revenue by country, representing 2/3 of the total figures. According to the latest estimates, the number of data professionals also reached 7.7 M in 2023, which corresponds to 4.3% of the total workforce, with an increase of 4.7% from 2022. However, there is a continued imbalance between the demand and supply of data skills in Europe, as the estimated shortfall reached about 363,000 unfilled positions, or 4.7% of the total demand (a slight decrease from 4.9% in 2022). The data skills gap is nonetheless expected to persist, indicating a need for more targeted education and training programmes.

In short, these findings indicate that the European data economy's impact on its GDP has been positive, but also highlight the many challenges going ahead, from the lack of professionals to power imbalances that, in recent years, have attracted the attention of policymakers in Brussels. Moreover, it has opened a debate on not only how data is extracted and used but also *who* extracts data and *where* it is stored, as well as *why* it has been used. This has been at the heart of the justifications for the General Data Protection Regulation. But it also sparked concerns in terms of economic power and democratic control. The growing importance of data for the European economy and the asymmetrical participation of European companies vis-à-vis American or Chinese giants have also sparked discussions about the ethics of the data economy and, most importantly, the role of data in achieving Europe's digital sovereignty ambitions.

Digital Sovereignty and Data Sovereignty

With this in mind, the European Commission published in February 2020 a timely and ambitious European Data Strategy (European Commission, 2020) to make the union a world leader in terms of a society powered by data. The strategy outlines that its vision stems from European values and fundamental rights and the conviction that the human being is and should remain at the centre. However, its core focus is market-driven: the strategy aims to create a genuine single market for data, open to data from across the world—where personal as well as non-personal data are secure, and businesses have easy access to an almost infinite amount of high-quality industrial data. It then outlines the problems hampering this vision: availability of data, data interoperability and quality, imbalance of market power, data governance, data infrastructures and technologies, skills and data literacy, and cybersecurity. It also makes proposals to use legislation, as well as funding to meet its objectives. To that extent, the industrial angle of the strategy is quite prominent, and the Commission explains that it will use its funding to strengthen Europe's technological sovereignty for the data-agile economy.

The Commission is explicit that 'the European strategy for data aims at creating a single market for data that will ensure Europe's global competitiveness and data sovereignty' (European Commission, 2020). 'Digital sovereignty' is a topic firmly brought to prominence following the COVID-19 pandemic, and though there are many definitions (see Chapter 4), it generally refers to the ability of a state or organisation to govern, control, and manage its digital infrastructure, data, and technologies, independently from external influences. Closely related is the concept of data sovereignty (Hummel et al., 2021), which has been used increasingly to qualify a situation where the control of data flows via national jurisdiction. Digital sovereignty is linked (Michel, 2021) to the concept of European strategic autonomy,[2] and it echoes a series of policies aiming at reinforcing industrial capabilities.

In the specific case of data, digital sovereignty covers the protection of EU fundamental rights and values as well, and notably privacy, as the promotion of EU economic interests, faced with the concentration of data gathering by non-EU entities. Executive Vice President Vestager has explained that large online platforms create challenges for competition and that smaller players may not have access to the data they would need to compete (Mc Mahon, 2021). In its judgement, the EU Court of Justice acknowledged that in the context of the examination of an abuse of a dominant position by an undertaking, it may be necessary for the competition authority of the Member State concerned also to examine whether that undertaking's conduct complies with rules other than those relating to competition law, such as the rules laid down by the GDPR (Cole & Salis, 2024). This points to the need for digital sovereignty not only to look at how data is used by private entities in line with EU values but also at the impact of it in terms of economic power.

The Data Strategy was first and foremost designed around the creation of a single market for data supporting a European human-centric approach. It proposed to create incentives for data sharing, establishing practical, fair, and clear rules on data access and use, which comply with European values and rights such as personal data protection, consumer protection, and competition rules, thus delivering on the objective of strengthening data and digital sovereignty.

New Data-Based and Data-Driven Business Models

Data innovation is often articulated around the so-called 'data-based business models', a subset of the overarching 'digital business models'. Both are closely linked, but whereas data-based business models focus on developing new products and services based on data (out of which to generate business value or profit), digital business models typically deal with the integration of digital technologies into traditional business processes like communication, operations or sales (Schäfer, 2023). Both leverage digital

[2] Defined as the political, institutional and material ability of the EU and its Member States to manage their interdependence with third parties, to ensure the well-being of their citizens and to implement self-determined policy decisions (Helwig & Sinkkonen, 2022).

tools and platforms to provide products and services to clients, whether these be customers or internal stakeholders, yet the first is more specific as it includes analysing (often large) datasets and transforming, collating or combining data to generate wisdom or new datasets.

In this sense, one can further split data-based business models across those where the output is an actual data product[3] or those where the analysis leads to identifying patterns and thus signalling new potential opportunities, generating insights like those described earlier in the chapter. This second subtype is often called 'Data-driven business models' as they are characterised by using data as a further resource to improve existing business processes. An example of a data-driven business model is profiling the conversations with customers happening within the company's digital channels to identify efficiencies in existing business lines.

On the contrary, models based on data products are strictly bound to data.[4] These are disruptive in the sense of representing new artefacts and thus the potential of new business opportunities, while data-driven models will typically aim for incremental improvements on preexisting lines.[5] Both approaches are crucial in today's digital economy as they help companies improve competitiveness[12]. For example, some of the domains in which to apply them include:

- *Customer Satisfaction/Loyalty and Personalised Offers* Data business models allow the analysis of customer behaviour and preferences, which leads to offering personalised services and recommendations. Netflix is famously known for this (Netflix, 2024), as the streamer collects a lot of user analytics to understand viewers' watching behaviour and preferences. Based on these data points, the platform suggests unique personalised entertainment options to each of its customers. This significantly increases customer satisfaction and drives client retention. Additionally, many of the fidelity programmes

[3] Defined as a collection of data accompanied by the metadata describing its characteristics, as well as the computer code necessary for its consumption.

[4] Indirectly, in some scenarios, as for example Machine Learning models result from training distinct algorithms over datasets, and—as such—the shape of the model is proportional to the specific data points employed in the process.

[5] Although actionable business intelligence can also generate impactful changes.

(Dunne & Gopinatha, 2021), for example, the ones from retailers and supermarkets, also involve a data analysis perspective.

- *Risk Management and Forecasting* Detailed data analysis enables a more accurate risk assessment and forecasting. This is not particularly new, as what is nowadays the 'Data Science' profession owes a lot of its curriculum to the field of Statistics. Yet, the amount of data and the capabilities of the tools available today are several orders of magnitude larger or more powerful than just a few years back, and it is also not uncommon that any kind of large-sized organisation would hold a team dedicated to this topic now, whereas before it was observed mostly only across very specific industries. An example of this is that of retailers and banks, who now use data analytics to detect and prevent fraudulent activities: by classifying digital activities across different dimensions, (semi)automatic IT systems can assign a risk score to each of the transactions across e-retail or via credit cards, serving to identify unusual patterns and behaviours, and flagging some for further inspection, or just blocking those deemed riskier and more likely to be fraudulent.
- *Cost Efficiency and Resource Optimisation* This is one of the most common types of applications because it does not necessarily require the development of complex algorithmic models or procuring a highly-skilled workforce. Even the simplest forms of data analysis will typically help assess the operational status of an organisation and put the focus on areas where to make better use of resources. For example, shipment and logistic operators are using data-driven analytics to optimise the maintenance of their fleets (Annata, 2023), including carrying out preventive maintenance via the frequent (in some cases, even real-time) analysis of machine data. This not only increases safety and a more reliable operational model for the company but also allows for better scheduling and mitigates unexpected operational halts, which are typically quite costly, both financially and reputationally. And—again—the growth of our capacity to source and transform machine data has taken this application scope to a whole new level. The question of ownership and rights over machine-generated data is the main driving force behind the recent European Data Act (European Commission, 2024).
- *Market Research and Product and Service Innovation* Since data enables informed decisions, it can also be used to select new products and services to develop, as well as how to market and price them. For

example, Coca-Cola has been known to launch new flavours based on the collection and analysis of data on their customers' use of beverage fountains (Harvard Digital Innovation and Transformation, 2020).

Likewise, Uber's whole business model is dependent on the adequate management of data, especially as it pertains to connecting drivers with passengers. But beyond that transactional purpose, it has an automated analytics system that helps direct drivers to specific geographic areas where passengers are more likely to need transportation services (Patel, 2024). This is achieved by gathering demand data from different locations and generating a probabilistic 'temperature map' for drivers, which is key to their success as a business, as otherwise supply and demand would not be fine-tuned.

Technological Innovation for New Data Business Models

As alluded to above, technological innovation is a crucial factor for the development and success of these new data-based and data-driven business models. Some of the key technologies driving these innovations include:

- *Artificial Intelligence (AI)* This is today's forefront of data innovation. In a more general sense, it is an academic field with a history already spanning several decades. However, it has developed profoundly within the last few years, specifically by advancing recipes known as Deep Learning. By processing vast amounts of data across human brain-inspired algorithms (backpropagation on multi-layered artificial neural networks), the resulting models have been found to excel at traditional human-like cognitive behaviour like recognising images, hearing and speaking, translating languages, or being able to create new text, images or music.
- *Machine Learning (ML)* This is a complex technology at the intersection of Computing and Mathematics. It is composed of different heuristic techniques that help to analyse data points by developing statistical models that enable computers to perform tasks without explicit instructions. Instead, ML systems learn from data

and improve their performance over time, and can be split across the following classes:

- Supervised Learning implies training the model based on data that has been previously labelled, meaning its input comes with the correct output, and there is a loss function being minimised while the model gets trained in steps. Ultimately, the trained model can make predictions on its own, with a certain degree of accuracy. A classic example of a supervised learning algorithm is *linear regression* or *decision trees*.
- Unsupervised Learning, on the other hand, has some basic tutelage in the form of a general category for training algorithms. Said algorithm is given data without labels, and the model gets constructed by finding its patterns and relationships within the data. A classic example of an unsupervised learning algorithm is *clustering*, or *principal component analysis* (PCA).
- Reinforcement Learning is a specific class of models that learns by interacting with an environment and receives rewards or penalties based on its actions. With enough training and under the right conditions, it can become quite successful at very complex competitive tasks, for example, beating the World Go or chess champions (Somers, 2018). A classic example of a reinforcement learning algorithm is *Q-learning* for policy creation.
- *Big Data Analytics* This technology precedes the current wave of AI by several years, and it was sparked by fostering the ability to process and analyse large datasets by splitting them into smaller batches and parallelising their computation before consolidating individual results into a final one. What originally started with only offline analysis soon later also permitted real-time analysis. As commented above, Big Data technologies help businesses gain insights from diverse data sources, improving everything from customer segmentation to supply chain management (Ferro & Pizzamiglio, 2023). It is also not uncommon that the paradigm of splitting datasets is combined with ML algorithms (especially as some of these compute very large amounts of data points) when the specific algorithm can be parallelised since some cannot by design.
- *Graphic Processing Units (GPU) and High-Performance Computing (HPC)* A GPU is a specialised electronic circuit designed to accelerate the processing of images and videos. Its name is a reference to its ability to render graphics in games, video editing, and other

intensive graphic-related tasks. This is because generating graphics involves computing large matrices, and these graphic cards contain thousands of smaller cores working together to process multiple tasks simultaneously, making them highly efficient for the parallel processing of matrix calculations.

Furthermore, they can also be capitalised for the training of artificial neural networks at the heart of Artificial Intelligence (AI). And since AI training is an extremely laborious task, GPUs provide the ability to build large and exotic models like the ones recently in vogue. That has driven very positive financial prospects for the corporations involved in their design and manufacture, with Nvidia, for example, recently becoming one of the world's largest companies by market capitalisation.

Similarly, the field of HPC involves using computer clusters and supercomputers to solve complex computational problems at high speeds. This is typically achieved by aggregating computing power to deliver much higher performance than a typical workstation can provide, enabling the processing of large data sets and complex calculations, and thus it is used across scientific fields like molecular research, earth and sea modelling, weather forecasting, or complex financial modelling.

HPC's architecture is made up of the individual servers or computers that perform the calculations (with each node typically containing multiple processors and may also include GPUs for specialised tasks); a network to interconnect the nodes through a high-speed network, allowing them to communicate and share data efficiently (crucial for parallel processing); storage to handle the vast amounts of data they process; and the specialised software for managing and orchestrating the HPC tasks (including the operating systems, job schedulers, parallel programming libraries and computational algorithms and tools). Finally, due to the high energy consumption and heat generation, cooling systems are required to maintain optimal operating temperatures and prevent hardware damage. All these elements work together to enable HPC systems to tackle complex problems that would be infeasible for regular computers.

- *Cloud Computing* Given the specialised hardware, software and concrete setup required for large computing loads, cloud platforms have emerged (Red Hat, 2024) as a solution to provide flexible and scalable infrastructure for storing and processing data. They enable businesses to access powerful computing resources on demand, facilitating the implementation of data-driven strategies (Assur & Rowshankish, 2022). It offers a wide range of benefits, including:

- Cost-effectiveness, with Pay-as-you-go service models aimed at reducing IT overhead, thus saving the user time, money, and—mostly—nuisance.
- Easily adjust resources to meet changing demands (whether this means handling peak traffic or expanding the organisation's operations globally).
- Improved performance and reliability, with cloud providers ensuring high availability for access to applications and data from anywhere and at any time. Precisely, this access-from-anywhere was one of the original value propositions of a model that allows remote work and easier cross-collaboration. Additionally, cloud providers take care of updates, so users do not have to.
- Economies of scale translate into a faster time-to-market of innovative applications and services, which in turn offers agility and flexibility to customers, allowing them to easily test new ideas and technologies without a significant upfront investment.
- Security to protect against cyber threats and compliance with local and global regulations and codes of conduct.

- *Edge Computing* Similarly, computing 'at the edge' is a decentralised paradigm where processing power and storage are moved closer to the data sources. So instead of relying solely on centralised cloud data centres, this model brings computing near devices and end-users, and this turns in reduced latency (which helps real-time applications), increasing bandwidth efficiency (having offloaded processing tasks from centralised data centres) as well as improved reliability, since the edge provides redundancy and fault tolerance. Moreover, some of the additional key gains include enhanced data privacy, as local processing minimises information transfer, and native support for IoT devices since these often generate large amounts of data and require low-latency processing (see below).
- *Internet of Things (IoT)* This refers to the interconnected network of physical objects embedded with sensors, software, and other technologies that enable them to collect and exchange data. These

devices can range from everyday items like smartphones and appliances to industrial machinery and infrastructure components, and they generate massive amounts of data which can be analysed (Manyika, et al., 2023).

All of these technologies are transforming how businesses and non-profit institutions operate, enabling them to harness the full potential of their data. Organisations that manage to effectively integrate these innovations into their business and operational plans can gain a very significant competitive advantage.

Two Paradigms to Make the Most of Data

As explained above, data can have significant benefits. However, these are not immediate and require efforts and dedicated tools to transform data into value. This is why, recently, data was also interpreted 'as the new oxygen' of the information society (Botin, 2022) since—depending on its context and use—it can be useful or it can be worthless; it can also become very expensive or even harmful when highly concentrated. In that context, two paradigms have emerged to make data valuable.

Because beyond guaranteeing data quality, value extraction is also highly dependent on the ability to contextualise and calibrate it. This is because capitalising on data is not typically a fully deterministic process but rather an educated trial-and-error effort at the intersection of statistics, data transformation skills and business acumen. Different interpretations can be reached by way of data pooling, statistical reduction, and insight generation, highly dependent on the data one starts from. In this sense, parametrisation of the data sourcing, assuring quality control of the transformation pipeline, and selecting an adequate semantic gauge for the intersection of the various datasets are all critical elements for any data calibration process. Yet, these can all be demanding tasks.

In that context, the first paradigm to extract value from data corresponds to the one developed by large online platforms, which is based on scale. Having a larger and more granular repository of datasets is usually conducive to a deeper cognisance, more so if these cover different yet complementary domains. Large platforms typically collect consumer data from the Internet in a rather indiscriminate manner and large volumes. According to Simple Analytics, a European privacy-friendly competitor to Google Analytics, 66% of the websites on the Internet use an analytics tool, and more than 86% of those use Google Analytics. They explain that Google Analytics collects data through short lines of JavaScript or HTML code called tags. These tags are placed on a web page and collect data points when triggered by a specific event—for instance, when a visitor views a page, clicks on a link or plays an embedded video. As a result, Google can develop metrics about webpages and, thanks to cookies, can also relate events—e.g. page view, clicks, playing a video or a transaction—to individuals (Iron Brands, 2024). It can also link data across its many services, thus obtaining fine-grained information about websites and users. The more personalised information is, however, unavailable if the user has disabled cookies through ad-blockers and cookie banner opt-outs, which lowers the quality of the data that Google Analytics can collect. And the approach of collecting massive amounts of data makes it sometimes cumbersome and untargeted (Fig. 6.1).

A second paradigm to extract value from data has emerged that is more attuned to the European and privacy-enhancing approach and more suited to industrial data, too. A very natural and cost-effective alternative for accessing large quantities of purposeful data relies on leveraging prior efforts, tapping into preexisting stacks of well-governed data sources. In this manner, critical mass can be reached by interconnecting different

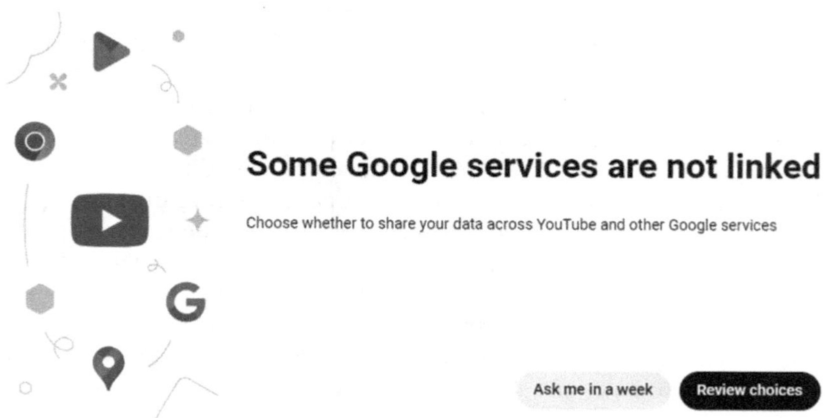

Fig. 6.1 Example of an online platform's claim for disaggregated services

datasets, which typically gets dubbed as 'data-sharing'.[6] This alternative is more tailored to specific data use cases and requires more advanced calibration, as well as a more sophisticated data governance framework, given that the data is decentralised in several entities and subject to local preferences. This paradigm is the one promoted by the Commission for its data spaces. By promoting distribution and reducing reliance on a central point of control, decentralisation aims to enhance transparency, resilience, and democratisation in various systems and applications. It is also linked to 'data sovereignty', 'data level playing field' and 'public-private governance' (Page & Cecconi, 2023). These two paradigms can be reflected in a landscape of forces (Fig. 6.2).

For the European Data Strategy to be effective, data-sharing plays a critical role, as it underpins the creation of a single data market permitting that data flows freely, not only geographically, but also across sectors and for the benefit of companies, third-sector organisations, researchers, as well as public administrations.

The concept of 'Data Ecosystems' relates to this objective. There are several definitions for it, each highlighting different aspects of

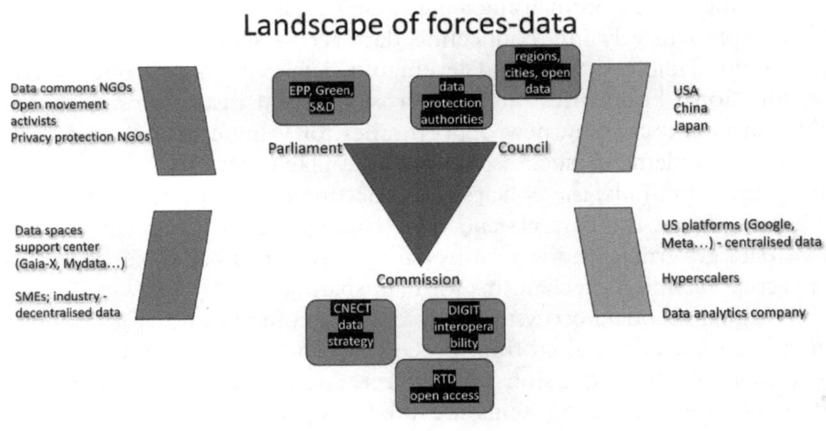

Fig. 6.2 Landscape of forces

[6] Truthfully, the sharing of data should not necessarily entail copying it, as there are alternative and more state-of-the-art techniques by which one can leverage the benefits of accessing the data without replication.

how data is managed and utilised. For example, the Harvard Business School (Stobierski, 2021) considers a data ecosystem composed of various programming languages, IT packages, algorithms, cloud-computing services, and any other general infrastructure that an organisation uses to collect, store, analyse, and leverage data. On the other hand, McKinsey thinks of them as centred around a platform that combines data from numerous providers and builds value through the usage of processed data. In this interpretation (Abdulla et al., 2021), a successful data ecosystem balances the creation of economies of scale by attracting participants and generating clear benefits, as well as cultivating a collaboration network where a vast number of heterogeneous stakeholders join forces to pursue complementary objectives.

Meanwhile, the IT research firm Gartner (2024) thinks of data ecosystems as comprehensive systems simplifying the management and use of data across various applications, offering streamlined data use, pre-integrated solutions, and unified management. In any case, and regardless of differences in conceptualisation, these three definitions agree on the criticality of integrating different tools and systems to effectively manage and leverage data.

This implies operationalising a methodological and structural paradigm for comprehensively interconnecting data across silos. In this way, data ecosystems enable sharing and leveraging data not only through intra-organisational boundaries but also across different institutions, fostering innovation and creating new opportunities for value creation. And thus, it comprises elements such as the list of available data sources, the data integration methods, the policies and procedures ensuring the quality and cybersecurity of the datasets and their compliance with regulations (vis-a-vis data governance), the various data analytics tools at stake, as well as the actual technical mechanisms for data-sharing.

The goal of a data ecosystem is to create a cohesive and efficient environment for collecting, storing, processing, and analysing data in a way that drives informed decision-making. Yet, unlike more traditional monolithic systems, data ecosystems are predicated on reusing data. This is the differentiating factor because, unlike oil (or other critical resources), data is a non-rivalrous asset. This means it can be used concurrently by different entities, with everyone benefitting from its access. This being the case, how come there is not a thriving Data Economy and data-driven society already?

First and foremost, dealing with data is an arduous task, both conceptually and technically. We briefly discussed the evolution of information systems, which since the 1970s has seen an ever-increasing spectrum of data methods and tools. Data storage remained costly for a long time, and—moreover—the technical capabilities of systems mostly focused on structured data, with its natural limitations. It has only been relatively recently, with the advent of commodity off-the-shelf distributed computing paradigms, that we have seen a democratisation of Big Data also covering unstructured data sources. Moreover, an optimal modern-day data environment will typically source data from different contexts, and thus, informational systems ought to be interconnected in some form or another. Data replication or consolidation is the simplest paradigm of all, but that also lacks real-time synchronicity, and any more advanced form requires extensive technical wisdom, for which talent remains scarce.

Secondly, effective data-based problem-solving is an elusive complex. The modernly called field of 'Data Science' is a combination of statistical knowledge, business acumen, and computational prowess, and for a good reason: most advanced data analysis today relies on transforming large quantities of data points by way of computer tools to make them fit into statistical frameworks with the intent to satisfactorily answer business-driven questions. This is usually a rather heuristic process, even more so when engaging in predictive tasks (i.e. looking into the future).

Finally, with data holding so much potential for influence and impact, its management comes with a great responsibility. There are different kinds of risks associated with dealing with data, including forfeiting organisational advantages if competitors can gain access to one's valuable wisdom, or the aforementioned inadequate business insight-generation due to data quality issues, a loss of oversight due to multiple and siloed data sources, or just unfit statistical modelling. It gets even worse in the case of losing control of data, typical of cybersecurity incidents, and with a heavy impact on organisational reputation or costs incurred in compliance or regulatory breaches. These can all in some way be traced back to the concept of 'Trust' and having confidence that the usage of data will happen according to guidelines and with benefits outweighing burdens.

Digital Infrastructures

Organisations are typically cautious in sharing data (FutureCIO, 2024). This explains why the European Data Strategy looks to mitigate this market failure, empowering the European data economy with a focus on industrial and corporate data. The Strategy has two complementary pillars. First, it drives the creation of distributed data ecosystems, pooling many different data resources to generate enough critical mass to become useful. This embodies the second paradigm of data valuation outlined above. It facilitates capillarisation and uptake across a varying set of stakeholders and geographies, including the small and medium-sized enterprises that make up a very large portion of the European economy.

The second side to the Strategy lies in the abilities and tools necessary to leverage the large repositories of datasets and resources sitting within the aforementioned data ecosystems. With the cloud offering the agility, flexibility, cost-effectiveness, and rapid scaling benefits highlighted earlier, the 'as a service' model becomes a natural complement to capitalise on data. The Strategy thus becomes a synergetic duo of data-as-raw-materials alongside tools-as-a-service, and one of the key core attributes of the Strategy is the explicit interconnection between these two angles (Fig. 6.3).

This interconnection is threaded alongside four different domains: funding innovative computing infrastructures, championing operational cloud enablers, creating legal frameworks for accessing and reusing data, and rolling out the common European data spaces. On the first of these, the *Important Project of Common European Interest on Next-Generation Cloud Infrastructure and Service* (IPCEI-CIS) (European Commission, 2024a) aims to develop a European data processing ecosystem that is interoperable and openly accessible. With 19 participant companies from 7 member states, the project will receive €1200 M in public funding,

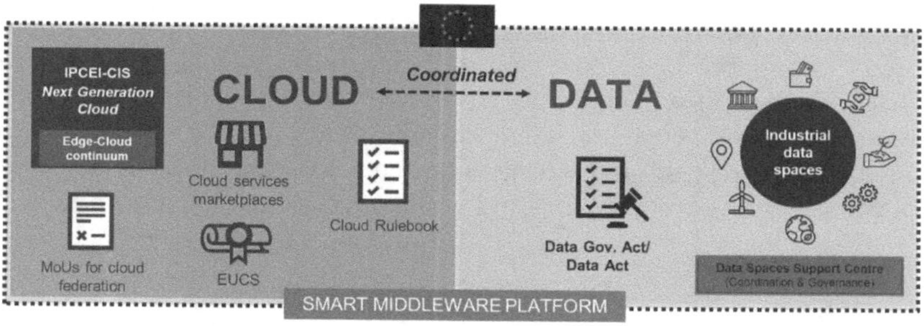

Fig. 6.3 Smart middleware platform

unlocking an additional €1400 M in private investments. The goal of the project is to create a multi-provider cloud-to-edge continuum, a federated, energy-efficient, trustworthy, and permeating computational fabric facilitating high availability and low-latency access to data processing capabilities. This relies on deploying 10,000 climate-neutral, highly secure edge nodes across all of the EU's geography and developing orchestration software as well as data-sharing tools.

On the governance side of these digital technologies, the Commission has promoted several initiatives, including the *European Memorandum of Understanding on Cloud Federation*. Signed by 27 EU Member States in October 2020, it is aimed at enhancing Europe's cloud infrastructure by building the next generation of cloud services (European Commission, 2020a). Key aspects of this document include the desire to combine private, national, as well as European Union funds to deploy a resilient, secure, and competitive cloud infrastructure that supports the needs of businesses and the public sector. Also, to have it span all over the continent, a joint technical solution and policy norms are necessary to foster interoperable EU cloud services. Moreover, this is part of a broader effort to ensure that Europe can support emerging technologies, including AI and 5G/6G.

Likewise, it has propelled the creation of a Cloud Rulebook, a comprehensive framework designed to guide cloud service users and providers. By creating a unified set of both binding and non-binding rules that cover aspects such as data protection, cybersecurity, and interoperability, this ensures secure, sustainable, and interoperable cloud services across Europe. The rulebook also provides guidelines for the public procurement of data processing services, helping public authorities to make informed decisions when selecting cloud service providers. This is also related to the EU's *Cybersecurity Certification Scheme for Cloud Services* (EUCS), a standardised certification process for the cybersecurity of cloud services. This is provided by the European Union Agency for Cybersecurity (ENISA) under the EU Cybersecurity Act (Regulation (EU) 2019/881, European Union, 2019a).

At last, these cloud governance tools are topped with the funding of a digital services marketplace (codename DOME for 'Distributed Open Marketplace for Europe'), which aims to federate the fragmented cloud and edge digital services market. This involves creating a single, cohesive marketplace where services from different providers and countries can be accessed and integrated seamlessly. It was officially launched in July 2024, providing a unified platform for different cloud, edge, and AI services belonging to providers accredited via verifiable credentials by EU legislation. This promotes transparent transactions under a common framework, thus enhancing digital trust across the union as part of the EU's broader strategy to enhance digital integration and competitiveness in the global market.

A crucial characteristic of the European Data Strategy is creating a thorough interconnection between these cloud and data pillars, each full of initiatives on their own. This is the purpose of the Smart Middleware Platform (project codename: Simpl), an open-source, modular, scalable software stack developed by the Commission to support data access and interoperability across European data spaces (European Commission, 2024c). Simpl sits on top of cloud or edge infrastructure and facilitates the creation and operation of data spaces by enabling seamless data-sharing and integration and anchors them to use cases by interconnecting datasets and various infrastructure elements. The project itself is composed of three different offerings: Simpl-Open, which is the open-source software stack pegging data spaces to cloud-to-edge federations; Simpl-Labs, an environment for experimenting with said software; and Simpl-Live, made of specific instances of the stack, tailored to sectoral data spaces. By design, data spaces funded by the Commission ought to employ the software pieces from Simpl.

Finally, data spaces sit on top of these infrastructures and create a space for data exchanges between participants. The financial support from European authorities for the creation of these data spaces comes through various sources, including (i) the Digital Europe Programme, with over 12 M € funding for projects aimed at both designing and creating data spaces (European Union, 2024), (ii) the Horizon Europe overall programme for research and innovation, that has included the development of technologies and solutions for data management, privacy preservation, and data interoperability (Pezuela & Alonso, 2023), and (iii) ad-hoc calls for proposals like that within the Internal Security Fund for projects focused on a data space for innovation (European Commission, 2023).

Regulatory Tools

Part of the EU's broader efforts to create a single market for data is geared towards ensuring that data can be used transversely, securely, and efficiently. That is why the adopted Data Governance Act aims to increase trust, remove barriers to data-sharing, and enhance data availability (Regulation (EU) 2022/868, European Union, 2022). It includes measures to facilitate the reuse of public sector data that cannot be made publicly available just as open data,[7] ensures that data intermediaries function as trustworthy organisers of data-sharing, and makes it easier for citizens and businesses to donate data when this is intended to be used for societal benefits. It covers both personal and non-personal data in a way compliant with the General Data Protection Regulation.

Also, and since 'data does not flow on rainbows',[8] a few months later—effective from January 2024—the Data Act set new rules on who can access and use data generated by connected devices (vis-a-vis the Internet of Things) and imposes requirements on cloud-computing resources to facilitate data transfers between providers (European Union, 2023).

This breakthrough legislation aims to foster industrial innovation using an amplified Data Economy both within and across economic sectors, creating significant economic benefits and limiting the creation of monopolies in this new digital era. The adopted text establishes clear rules on the permission to access data and the conditions for data migration while trying to ensure that data holders continue to invest in high-quality data generation. It looks out for a fair distribution of the value of data collected, benefiting not only companies but also citizens and public administrations, allowing the latter to access and use data to respond to public emergencies such as pandemics, floods, or wildfires. It also sets provisions to protect businesses from unfair contractual terms in data-sharing and data migration agreements, particularly for SMEs,

[7] 'Open Data' refers to datasets that are freely available for anyone to use, reuse, and redistribute. Is it accessible to everyone without any restrictions, so it can be freely downloaded and used by anyone. As such, it is typically licensed under open licenses, which allow for free use, modification, and sharing, although often with the requirement to attribute the source. These datasets tend to be provided in formats that are easy to use and integrate with other datasets, thus enhancing its usability. Examples of open data include governmental datasets on demographics, environmental data, and public transportation schedules. These datasets can be used for research, innovation, and creating new applications that benefit society. Also, they enhance transparency and accountability, since they allow the public to analyse and understand the data.

[8] This slogan refers to the fact that data services are bound to infrastructure services, as datasets do not live freely suspended on air, and thus the characteristics and prescriptions of the underlying IT systems will have a major impact on the ability to capitalise on data.

promoting the seamless transfer of data between different data holders while maintaining confidentiality.

Similarly, the High-Value Datasets Directive (European Commission, 2022) was published in January 2021, as part of the broader Open Data Directive (European Union, 2019b), to make certain types of data held by public sector bodies available for free reuse in machine-readable formats and via APIs. The purpose, in this case, is to unlock the potential of public sector data to benefit the economic sectors—and the overall society as a whole—by making high-value datasets freely available. These come grouped into 6 thematic categories: geospatial data, Earth observation and environmental monitoring data from satellites, weather and climate data, various statistical datasets collected by public bodies, information about businesses and their ownership structures (especially as it relates to companies and their ownership), and mobility data. Ultimately, these three regulatory frameworks have the purpose of fostering industrial digital innovation, supporting the development of new services and applications, and ultimately creating high-quality jobs. As a nice corollary, this enhanced data accessibility also leads to better decision-making and promotes transparency.

All these recent and innovative regulatory frameworks are expected to support the development of the Common European Data Spaces. This is because the operationalisation of the single data market comes in the form of these data spaces, which are instruments to facilitate data-sharing thanks to a sector-specific common infrastructure and concrete governance frameworks. These drive the real-life pooling, access, and sharing of data, providing cyber-secure and privacy-preserving environments and promoting regimes for transparent and non-discriminatory access rules (vis-a-vis the Data Act) while still enabling data holders to share data against compensation. Along key industries like healthcare, transport, energy, agriculture, the environment and the green deal, finance, tourism, manufacturing, or heritage and culture, these data spaces are intended to hold high-quality data, becoming a common playing ground for the different participants of a given industrial value chain, fostering innovation, and levelling the playing field for SMEs, who would otherwise struggle with the necessary investments and market arbitration.

How to Build the Single Market for Data: A Coherent Orchestration of Programmes and Projects

Having described the various elements that make up the European Data Strategy, designed to generate an uptake of cloud and data, and having insisted on the interconnected and synergetic nature of these two pillars, a remaining critical topic is how to coherently piece them together, so stakeholders can leverage them practically and holistically, leading to impact. The ultimate goal is to deliver a European paradigm where data is protected as it is decentralised while boosting data-sharing in a controlled environment to create a single data market. In this sense, the NIST SP 500–332 architecture (NIST, 2020) can prove useful to conceptualise the data exchange process across different domain layers, allowing us to gain further insight into its foundational elements, as well as to draw a landscape of the different forces involved (Fig. 6.4).

The business domain layer allows organisations to analyse and prescribe how integrating different datasets or the deployment of algorithms (or other forms of computational models) adds value to their business models. We described novel data-based and data-driven business models

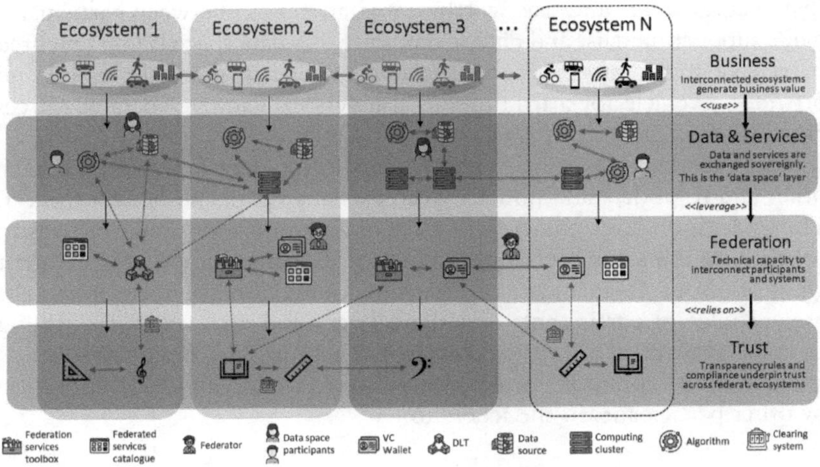

Fig. 6.4 Description of data ecosystems

in the section above, which consequently predicate the need to pursue large quantities of data as raw ingredients. This increased data demand is a fitting scenario for the emergence of markets for digital goods, whereby organisations can also opportunely commercialise (some of) their preexisting assets.

The 'data spaces layer' is where different actors can recurrently capitalise on datasets, algorithms, and/or data models and artefacts that right now remain isolated. For this to happen, at least three elements need to concur: (i) an amicable meeting of market forces so both demand and supply can benefit from the interaction, (ii) a coordinated symbiosis of organisational frameworks so this exchange can happen according to expectations of its participants, including on the variables of time and quality of the exchange, and other service level agreements, and (iii)—finally—technological and semantic matchmaking around these data assets.

Different European organisations have been working for several years towards supporting the development of data spaces, with further advances coming to fruition recently around the deliverables of the Data Spaces Support Centre, an ambitious Coordination and Support Action[9] project from the *Digital Europe Programme*. This provides a formal definition for a data space as 'a distributed system defined by a governance framework that enables secure and trustworthy data transactions between participants while supporting trust and data sovereignty'. 'A data space is implemented by one or more infrastructures and enables one or more use cases' and provides a vehicle for a fruitful and seamless exchange of data resources between business participants.

The Federation layer helps participants in the data spaces to find each other and to understand how they can exchange data and benefit from it. The Federation layer comes with a set of common tools and practices to orchestrate the steps preceding the actual exchange of datasets or other types of resources' metadata or files. The foundational element lies in the user profiles of participants and the services and assets they are willing to make available within the ecosystem. These profiles ought to follow a (standardised) common format, thus allowing querying and verification by other participants in the federation.

[9] Coordinated and Support Action.

Besides this, the federative layer will also typically come with a catalogue, which allows searching for providers and their service offerings. Also, a marketplace is normally offered, with functionalities including the definition of digital offerings and the management of their lifecycle and monetisation, as well as the capabilities to negotiate and sign agreements, including generating the legally binding consent and provisioning of the signed contract. Additionally, after the actual transaction has taken place, there ought to be options to check logs, permitting audits to audit that the data asset usage policies have taken effect, on top of mechanisms to detect and stop fraudulent behaviours, or simply revoke previously signed contracts.

Finally, the Trust layer allows benefits to be appropriated concretely by the participants in the data sharing. It is where participants can find different and alternative routes to satisfy their data-driven business needs, including across varying forms of technological models.

For this to occur, a minimum set of agreements across participants is needed, detailing how to operate symbiotically in a coherent manner. These pacts and conventions relate to the governance of said ecosystems, which—naturally—tend to be specific to the different scenarios concocted. Yet, we find that generating a common semantic corpus provides an overarching measurement of 'trust' that allows comparing, assessing, and even composing these varying sets of domain-based agreements. This is because all these data-driven ecosystem-specific rules and agreements can be expressed using common vocabulary and grammar. This creates unification across the different digital ecosystems, being broad and deep enough to cover those horizontal elements that any data space shall be built upon, yet still allowing domain extensions for particularities.

Thus, developing the aforementioned foundational semantic model is the cornerstone of a distributed and federal 'power-of-the-many' type of ecosystem since its rules will be expressed according to said model. Moreover, building a 'digital version of a language' also enables the automatic validation of said rules, at least to a certain degree of complexity.[10]

[10] I.e. for those rules that can be translated into processes that confer veracity.

Advancing European Digital Sovereignty: A Methodology for Building Data Spaces

As can be seen from the previous analysis, whereas the EU Data Strategy provides a vision for building a single market for data based on a decentralised paradigm, and whereas it has offered the necessary tools to that effect, the actual delivery of that vision and its actuation by market actors is complex and requires trust to emerge from concrete technological and regulatory tools.

We now describe a step-by-step methodology for building data-driven use cases following the data space paradigm. Data spaces offer a unique and distinctive value proposition in the sense of use cases built around them being able to leverage datasets and other pooled data resources that are sourced directly from (various) participants. The interconnected nature of this relationship implies a different approach to that of traditional data-transformation scenarios and—as such—requires a modification to common Data Science methodological approaches (Fig. 6.5).

1. Identification of Business Opportunities

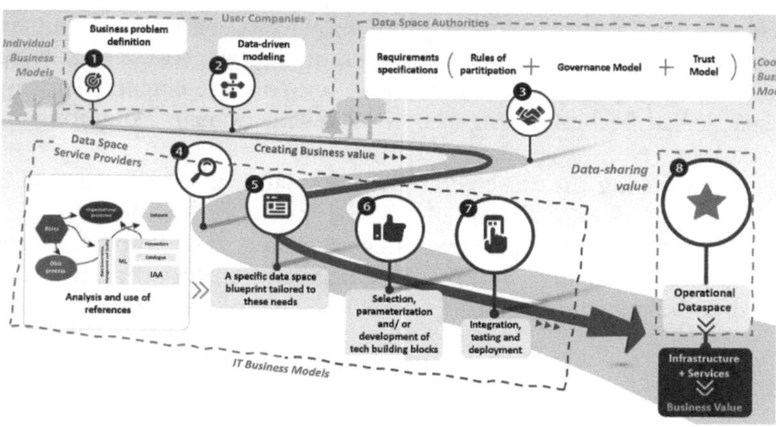

Fig. 6.5 From business definition from building an operational dataspace

The first step in this methodology is the identification of data-driven opportunities within a particular domain or context. We identify that a purposeful and sustainable sharing of data resources ought to lead to the resolution of problems that would otherwise be impossible or inefficient when tackled individually. The aim is thus to bring together different kinds of participants within the value chain of a particular industry around some common needs. These can be of a regulatory or competitive nature (i.e. driven by a third party) or simply motivated by unlocking win-win business opportunities based on collaboration. Ideally, the use case should be centred around data-sharing and the creation of joint value for its participants, not around satisfying very specific information needs, which are likely to be solved more easily by way of ad-hoc agreements.

2. Data-Driven Modelling

Step 2 seeks to understand those data resources required to solve the business problem previously presented, as well as the transformation pipeline to be exercised on the datasets and possibly the technological tools to employ in the process. This stage prescribes the types of data needed, their volumes and formats, their quality and semantics, the means to access them, and their availability and update frequency. Ideally, it conceptualises a data modelling scenario encompassing a significant (but not excessive) number of participants who ought to have a committed interest in establishing a fruitful and sustainable data-sharing ecosystem. The definition of this scenario should also reflect on the specific application domain, the challenges to be addressed, the expected benefits, the main barriers to overcome, as well as the users and roles involved.

3. Specification of Requirements

This step encapsulates the innovative nature of data spaces because it is the first to revolve around collaborative business models. It aims to define a common way for participants to operate together within the limits of the use case just defined, bounding them to adopt specific roles covering the functional requirements set in Step 2. Thus, agreements made at this point will dictate the interactions between participants, establishing data flows, the services offered, as well as the potential secondary uses given to the data exchanged. It is worth noting that all of these prescriptions shall later be transferred into adequate technical requirements, but at this stage, only the rules for participation are being set, which include both the trust and governance models for all the data resources involved.

Likewise, at this stage, a study of the applicable regulations should be taken into consideration, establishing those rules and norms to be upheld and possibly prescribing different industrial standards to be followed that may include cybersecurity perspectives as well as other safeguards specifically addressing information privacy, auditability, and compliance. A detailed definition of requirements for the use case should also culminate with a transversal holistic feasibility analysis, ensuring that the conditions prescribed indeed incentivise a sustainable involvement over time of the different critical stakeholders, truly maximising its chances for viability.

4. Using a Reference Architecture Model

After the aforementioned foundational business and functional analysis is completed, it is time to start considering the technological and systems domain. This is because sector-specific data spaces are all likely to be different according to the specificities of each industry and the varying purposes and shapes of the use cases built around them. There are nonetheless certain commonalities to them all, and this is why using a reference architecture model can help speed up the design and setting-up process, building upon best practices.

5. Data Space Blueprint

These architectural models require further adaptation to a more concrete design for the specific requirements of the use case(s) defined in Step 3. Having a more detailed architectural document allows one to define the ecosystem operatively. This includes the selection and development of necessary components for the inception of the data space and an incremental development approach, progressively adapting/enriching the system as new participants emerge with new scenarios.

6. Selection, Development, and/or Parametrisation of Technical Elements

This is a purely technological step, where the components of the detailed architectural blueprint get developed or (if already available) selected and further parameterised as required by the needs of the use case(s). It should be noted that, when following a given architectural model, it can be common that this may prescribe elements core to the specificities of said model, and this will, in turn, require that said artefacts behave in a given way. To ensure this, certification is a common mechanism that can also be employed.

7. Integration of Participants and Validation of the Use Case

Once the aforementioned subsystems and components are developed, the final stage across the technology domain involves integrating participants within the data space, as well as performing the final validation and commissioning tests for the use case and the foundational systems. However, it should be noted that the integration of various and different IT systems can often be a laborious task, especially if the footprint of software components to synchronise with is large.

Additionally, it is expected that the data space authority (who plays the role of ecosystem orchestrator, performing the basic management of participants) will also require some level of support for the installation and maintenance of those essential technical services, guaranteeing an effective and trusted operation within the ecosystem, as well as dealing with malfunctions that may occur. In this sense, certification of the final ensemble is recommended (to be completed by an entity authorised by the governing body of the reference architecture model), as this will increase confidence in this kind of innovative multiparty system.

8. Data Space Operation

When it comes to cooperation across various parties, the running of the use case shall be governed by the data space authority, who, on top of marketing the initiative, will also define schemes for bilateral or multilateral policies and be ready to intermediate in potential disputes. At all times, decisions should follow the previously approved functional framework of rules and procedures. On top of this, the governing authority may also play (or subcontract) the role of the system operator, tackling day-to-day activities such as registering/unsubscribing participants, upgrading components, or solving technical incidents.

At this point, there is a functioning data space whereby participants can appropriately reutilise the aforementioned datasets, algorithms, data models and any other technical artefacts of interest. These participants can be further split into two groups:

- Data users who aim to access new datasets and resources, or maybe want to access them more simply or conveniently or aim to trust these resources and trace their origins.[11]
- Data providers (preexisting or new ones) who want to enhance sales and distribution channels and thus monetise resources more easily.

What is also new here is that resources are not living under the same monolithic system, but rather drive value by way of being interconnected. Because of this, these resources do not necessarily have to leave their 'premises', and an additional layer of privacy is attained without compromising the effectiveness of the digital modelling.

This is precisely the vision confirmed within the European Strategy for Data, which is based on fundamental rights and values, including data protection. The European model unlocks new value from distributed data resources by exploiting networks of interconnected digital assets. By definition, this model takes sovereignty and user control into consideration from the start by way of controlling access to the services where the assets live. Additionally, and with the operator also typically being in charge of generating usage and other statistical reports, as well as managing necessary changes to admit new use cases, this symbiotic linkage between data and infrastructure services becomes a useful factor in optimising efficiency and allowing end-user flexibility.

Because the system is a distributed one by design, there are enhanced requirements, including trusting that participants are who they claim to be (for data providers), that users will behave according to the guidelines prescribed on the agreed-upon contracts and guidelines, and (for data users) that the providers will ensure the assets have the quality and

[11] This is critical when building complex data-transformation chains, or for auditing and regulatory purposes.

features described, and that using them complies with the appropriate rules, especially across the new and innovative regulatory framework. At last, users also strive to find a data space ecosystem satisfying their data product demands in a flexible, dynamic, and frictionless manner, avoiding onerous lock-in effects that hinder their ability to advance their data-driven digital efforts.

A positive consequence is that within this paradigm, stakeholders in the data space can include the public sector as a guarantor of trust and compliance and contribute to the development of norms, standards, and attestations of conformity/certification. At last, open-source communities also play a relevant role since—still lacking a coherent and stable operational framework at the onset of these new tech environments—systems can be composed and piloted by way of smaller functional pieces, which are often available openly.

Also related is the concept of 'interoperability', in the sense of having different participants and systems cooperating and building complex value chains. For this, there is already a sturdy skeleton in the European Interoperability Framework (EIF), conceived originally for public services' digital applications, and which prescribes four different dimensions for interoperability: legal, organisational, semantic, and technical. These can indeed be considered foundational as they provide basic and orthogonal attributes that we also leverage across our model for interconnected data resources and capabilities, which we, however, structure around those rules and arrangements that help satisfy our participants' needs.

Together, these four layers encompass the different sets of rules, agreements, guidelines, and agreed-upon etiquettes necessary to correctly govern the design and operations of a data space. As such, they are all integral to the European paradigm of a Sovereign Data Economy; however, it should be noted that it is the governance layer that encloses soft-skills dimensions, arguably making it the most challenging one. This is also the case with Trust, which is why we had previously defined Trust as the value proposition of this European digital construct, an innovative paradigm upon which to build large-scale distributed data networks to reshape the current digital landscape.

Conclusion: From the Data Strategy to AI Innovation through a Data Union

Data has been an integral part of the digital economy since its very beginnings. However, it has primarily been in the last two decades that the Data Economy has taken on a life of its own, which has prompted European leaders to inspire and stimulate governmental and privately driven interventions around it, with the hope to regain some of its previously lost momentum as well as push forward new digitally based corporate innovations. The chapter has analysed the importance of data for innovation while also underlining the difficulties in extracting value and presenting two paradigms: one centralised—with possible costs for privacy, and another one decentralised—requiring more data governance and trust building, but more in tune with the European human-centric and privacy-enhancing vision of the digital transformation, and more in line with the objective of digital sovereignty. A key building block in the European Strategy is the data space paradigm as a tool facilitating and governing the interconnection of different and distributed participants across the various realms involved.

The European Data Strategy, while it has a single market logic, also promotes the European way by incentivising data protection and European values and principles, building upon decentralised and egalitarian logic instead of hierarchy by dominant players. It uses a series of tools in terms of funding for data infrastructures and the building of legislative frameworks conducive to building trust and data sharing and emphasises data spaces as a vehicle for data sharing. Data spaces are not per se the answer to new digital products but rather a foundation upon which to access datasets, models and also computing resources that are otherwise scarcely available and thus difficult and costly to capitalise on. They can be thought of as marketplaces where to find the basic ingredients necessary to drive data-driven applications. A methodology has been proposed to develop data spaces more effectively and to deliver the vision of the Data Strategy.

Going forward, building data spaces will be relevant for Artificial Intelligence (AI). The intense processing of extremely vast amounts of datasets (primarily text corpora or media files) is at the heart of AI development, with algorithms improving through training with data. This strenuous effort is also why, despite the modern popularity of this type of application, there are only a handful of companies that have achieved major success so far because of the enormous costs of computing power required to train AI models. This is the basis for the 2025 Data Union strategy proposed by the European Commission. It proposes to complete the single market for data, notably through practical tools like model contract clauses and a helpdesk for SMEs. It also enhances access to high-quality, curated data for developing and training AI models and seeks to streamline and modernise data laws.

In this sense, data spaces become powerful enablers and catalysers for modern AI success. One could argue that the future of AI is pegged not to applications conducting general human-like behaviour but rather to those that are domain-specific. In much the same way that humans are not all equally talented at specific tasks, it would require specific training for these AI algorithms to become proficient at concrete value-added tasks. This specificity would establish the next frontier of digital productivity, the same that started in the 1970s with the computing revolution we alluded to at the beginning of this chapter, and why often this AI-driven future is known as the 4th Industrial Revolution. For this to happen, contextual and well-curated data is the most promising avenue.

Data spaces have the potential to enhance Europe's competitiveness in AI by training models with high-quality, well-governed data (Spanish Presidency of the Council of the EU, 2023), which can not only be more effective (less prone to 'hallucinations') but also environmentally friendlier (requiring lower training efforts as the statistically curated data counter-balances unnecessarily high and often superfluous volumes). Also, and quite remarkably, the resulting products are more inclined to be respectful of intellectual property law as well as other legal and ethical concerns. In 2025, five years after the data strategy was proposed, the Commission announced that it aimed to become the AI continent. Data will be critical for this ambition, and even if a single market for data remains a far-fetched reality, specialised data spaces may play a great part in supporting EU efforts for the efficient deployment of Artificial Intelligence.

Overall, the EU's unique blend of social welfare, economic integration, and sustainable industrial policies differentiates it from other actors. These features of fair redistribution, a levelled playing field, integrative systems, common market rules, the breaking of siloes, and digital enablers for industrial innovation, are also foundational principles of the data space paradigm, which is a distinctive European invention.

Bibliography

Abdulla, A., Janiszewska-Kiewra, E., & Podlesny, J. (2021). *Data ecosystems made simple*. https://www.mckinsey.com/capabilities/mckinsey-digital/our-insights/tech-forward/data-ecosystems-made-simple

Albrecht, J. P. (2016). How the GDPR will change the world. *European Data Protection Law Review, 2*, 287–289.

Annata. (2023, November 29). *From data silos to integrated intelligence: Harnessing analytics in truck & bus businesses*. https://annata.net/harnessing-analytics-in-truck-bus-businesses/

Assur, N., & Rowshankish, K. (2022, January). *The data-driven enterprise of 2025*. https://www.mckinsey.com/~/media/mckinsey/business%20functions/mckinsey%20analytics/our%20insights/the%20data%20driven%20enterprise%20of%202025/the-data-driven-enterprise-of-2025-final.pdf

Boissay, F., Ehlers, T., Gambacorta, L., & Shin, H. S. (2021, October). *Bank for international settlements: Big techs in finance: On the new nexus between data privacy and competition*. https://www.bis.org/publ/work970.pdf

Botin, A. (2022, January). *Data is the new oxygen*. https://www.linkedin.com/pulse/data-new-oxygen-part-4-ana-bot%C3%ADn-/

Bradford, A. (2020). *The Brussels effect: How the European Union rules the world*. Oxford University Press.

Iron Brands. (2024). *How does Google analytics collect data?* https://www.simpleanalytics.com/blog/how-does-google-analytics-collect-data#how-does-google-analytics-collect-data

Chander, A., & Sun, H. (2023). *Data sovereignty—from the digital silk road to the return of the state*. Oxford University Press.

Cole, M., & Salis, F. (2024, May 17). *Evolving view of data in the application of competition law*. https://globalcompetitionreview.com/guide/data-antitrust-guide/first-edition/article/evolving-view-of-data-in-the-application-of-competition-law

Dunne, B., & Gopinatha, A. (2021). *Unleash the power of AI in retail*. https://www.accenture.com/us-en/insights/retail/data-driven-ai-retail

European Commission. (2020). *A European strategy for data*. Retrieved from Shaping Europe's Digital Future: https://digital-strategy.ec.europa.eu/en/policies/strategy-data

European Commission. (2020a). *Towards a next generation cloud for Europe*. https://digital-strategy.ec.europa.eu/en/news/towards-next-generation-cloud-europe

European Commission. (2021, May 9). *Results of the European data market study 2021–2023*. Retrieved from Shaping Europe's Digital Future: https://digital-strategy.ec.europa.eu/en/library/results-european-data-market-study-2021-2023

European Commission. (2022, December 21). *Commission implementing regulation (EU) of 21.12.2022 laying down a list of specific high-value datasets and the arrangements for their publication and re-use*. https://eur-lex.europa.eu/legal-content/EN/TXT/?uri=PI_COM:C(2022)9562

European Commission. (2023). *Call for proposals: Funds for data sets in European Data Space for innovation*. https://home-affairs.ec.europa.eu/news/call-proposals-funds-data-sets-european-data-space-innovation-2023-03-30_en

European Commission. (2024a). *Data Act*. Retrieved from Shaping Europe's Digital Future: https://digital-strategy.ec.europa.eu/en/policies/data-act

European Commission. (2024b). *Approved IPCEI next generation cloud infrastructure and services*. https://competition-policy.ec.europa.eu/state-aid/ipcei/approved-ipceis/cloud_en

European Commission. (2024c). *Simpl: Cloud-to-edge federations empowering EU data spaces*. https://digital-strategy.ec.europa.eu/en/policies/simpl

European Union. (2019b). *Directive (EU) 2019/1024 of the European Parliament and of the Council of 20 June 2019 on open data and the re-use of public sector information*. https://eur-lex.europa.eu/eli/dir/2019/1024/oj

European Union. (2019a). *Regulation (EU) 2019/881 of the European Parliament and of the Council of 17 April 2019 on ENISA (the European Union Agency for Cybersecurity) and on information and communications technology cybersecurity certification and repealing Regulation (EU) No 52*. https://eur-lex.europa.eu/eli/reg/2019/881/oj

European Union. (2022). *Regulation (EU) 2022/868 of the European Parliament and of the Council of 30 May 2022 on European data governance and amending regulation (EU) 2018/1724*. https://eur-lex.europa.eu/eli/reg/2022/868/oj

European Union. (2023). *Regulation (EU) 2023/2854 of the European Parliament and of the Council of 13 December 2023 on harmonised rules on fair access to and use of data and amending Regulation (EU) 2017/2394 and Directive (EU) 2020/1828*. https://eur-lex.europa.eu/eli/reg/2023/2854/oj

European Union. (2024). *The Digital Europe Programme*. https://digital-strategy.ec.europa.eu/en/activities/digital-programme

Ferro, E., & Pizzamiglio, A. (2023). *New business models for data-driven services. Discussion paper*. https://data.europa.eu/sites/default/files/report/New%20Business%20Models%20for%20Data-Driven%20Services_ENG.pdf

Furman, J. (2019, March). *Report of the digital competition expert panel: Unlocking digital*. https://assets.publishing.service.gov.uk/government/uploads/system/uploads/attachment_data/file/785547/unlocking_digital_competition_furman_review_web.pdf

FutureCIO. (2024). *Data and security concerns hinder AI adoption, study finds*. https://futurecio.tech/data-and-security-concerns-hinder-ai-adoption-study-finds

Gartner. (2024). *Data ecosystems to support all your data workloads*. https://www.gartner.com/en/data-analytics/topics/data-ecosystem

Harvard Digital Innovation and Transformation. (2020). *Coca cola leverages data analytics to drive innovation*. https://d3.harvard.edu/platform-digit/submission/coca-cola-leverages-data-analytics-to-drive-innovation/

Helwig, N., & Sinkkonen, V. (2022). Strategic autonomy and the EU as a global actor: The evolution, debate, and theory of a contested term. *European Foreign Affairs Review, 27*(Special Issue), 1–20.

Hummel, P., Braun, M., Tretter, M., & Dabrock, P. (2021). Data sovereignty: A review. *Big Data & Society, 9*.

IDC & the Lisbon Council. (2024). *European data market study 2021–2023*. European Commission.

Manyika, J., Chui, M., Bughin, J., Dobbs, R., Bisson, P., & Marrs, A. (2023). *Disruptive technologies: Advances that will transform life, business, and the global economy*. https://www.mckinsey.com/capabilities/mckinsey-digital/our-insights/disruptive-technologies

Mc Mahon, M. (2021). *Margrethe vestager explains the EU's position in the global battle for data*. https://www.euronews.com/2021/05/07/margrethe-vestager-explains-the-eu-s-position-in-the-global-battle-for-data

Michel, C. (2021). *Digital sovereingty is central to European strategic autonomy—speech by President Charles Michel at "masters of digital 2021" online event*. https://www.consilium.europa.eu/en/press/press-releases/2021/02/03/speech-by-president-charles-michel-at-the-digitaleurope-masters-of-digital-online-event/

Netflix. (2024). *How netflix's recommendations system works*. https://help.netflix.com/en/node/100639

NIST. (2020). *NIST cloud federation reference architecture, NIST SP 500–332*. https://www.nist.gov/publications/nist-cloud-federation-reference-architecture

O'Reilly, T. (2021, February). *Data is the new sand*. https://www.theinformation.com/articles/data-is-the-new-sand

Page, M., & Cecconi, G. (2023). *European data spaces and the role of data.Europa.Eu*. Publications Office of the European Union.

Parsons, M. (2017, November). *The Era of data is disruption*. https://www.linkedin.com/pulse/era-data-disruption-mike-parsons/

Patel, N. (2024). *How uber uses data to improve their service and create the new wave of mobility*. https://neilpatel.com/blog/how-uber-uses-data/

Pezuela, C., & Alonso, D. (2023). *Data spaces: Roadmap and future programmes*. https://european-big-data-value-forum.eu/wp-content/uploads/2023/11/01.-EBDVF-2023-Future-of-Data-Spaces-Summary-vF.pdf

Red Hat. (2024). *What is high performance computing (HPC)?* https://www.redhat.com/en/topics/high-performance-computing/what-is-high-performance-computing

Schäfer, J. (2023, November 2). *Data-based business models—opportunities and successful implementation.* https://konfuzio.com/en/data-based-business-models/

Somers, J. (2018, December 28). *How the artificial-intelligence program alphazero mastered its games.* https://www.newyorker.com/science/elements/how-the-artificial-intelligence-program-alphazero-mastered-its-games

Spanish Presidency of the Council of the EU. (2023, November). *The trinity of trusted cloud, data and AI as gateway to EU's competitiveness.* https://portal.mineco.gob.es/RecursosNoticia/mineco/prensa/noticias/2023/The%20trinity%20of%20trusted%20cloud%20data%20and%20AI%20as%20gateway%20

Stobierski, T. (2021). *Business insights: 5 key elements of a data ecosystem.* https://online.hbs.edu/blog/post/data-ecosystem

University of Sheffield. (2024). *Clive humby.* https://www.sheffield.ac.uk/cs/people/academic-visitors/clive-humby#:~:text=In%202006%2C%20he%20coined%20the,useful%20to%20drive%20business%20innovation

Wikipedia. (2024). *Data.* https://en.wikipedia.org/wiki/Data_(computer_science)

CHAPTER 7

The Evolution of Digital Identity in the European Union—From eIDAS to the EU Digital Identity Wallet

Goran Zeković

Introduction

Identity verification has been a key concern of human civilisation—census records collecting citizens' information were found as far back as the Babylonian empire, 3800 BC—and it has become a critical need in the digital space, with electronic authentication and digital signature being considered the base components of the European Union (EU) Digital Single Market, and with key issues including the fight against identity

Disclaimer: The author is an official of the European Commission. The information and views set out in this chapter are those of the author and do not necessarily reflect the official opinion of the Institution.

G. Zeković (✉)
European Commission, Brussels, Belgium
e-mail: goran.zekovic@ec.europa.eu

T. Kleiner and A. Garcia Rodriguez (eds.), *The Making of a Global Digital Rulebook*, https://doi.org/10.1007/978-981-95-9226-5_7

theft and fake identities, together with the need for privacy protection against the risks of a police state (UNDP, 2023) or of surveillance capitalism (Zuboff, 2019).

In the EU, digital identity encompasses the systems and technologies that validate and authenticate the identity of natural and legal persons in online environments. Over the years, the EU has progressively aimed to harmonise digital identity verification processes across member states, seeking to enhance interoperability, increase security, and improve user convenience. Digital identity in the EU has become a foundation of the Digital Single Market, a policy initiative aimed at ensuring access to online activities like e-commerce, banking, and public services across national borders with minimal friction.

This chapter aims to provide insights into the genesis of this policy and to outline some of the difficulties that had to be overcome in that process. Notably, providing identity is one of the core functions of a sovereign state, making the European Union's (EU) attempt to offer a unified digital identity particularly significant (and challenging) in terms of EU integration, with national interests having to be accommodated. Another challenge came from private alternatives and incumbent solutions that could compete with an EU electronic identity.

The chapter shows that the EU policy for digital identity reflects the EU vision for digital sovereignty, creating a trusted, secure digital space where European values such as privacy, data protection, and democratic accountability are upheld while reducing reliance on foreign technology providers, building technological capabilities, and fostering innovation within Europe. By developing a trusted, European-wide digital identity system, the EU reduces reliance on non-EU digital providers, ensuring that personal data and identity management remain within European legal and ethical standards. The approach not only streamlines processes but also strengthens data protection standards, thus supporting the EU's broader strategy of promoting digitalisation while safeguarding individual rights and boosting economic growth.

At the heart of the EU's digital identity framework is the eIDAS regulation,[1] adopted in 2014 (Regulation (EU) 910/2014, 2014) and amended in 2024 (Regulation (EU) 2024/1183, 2024).

This regulatory framework was a pivotal step towards enhancing the reliability and security of electronic transactions and trust services, setting a clear path for the digital integration of Europe. eIDAS primarily aims to ensure people and businesses can use their own national electronic identification (eID) schemes to access online public services in other EU countries where eIDs are available. It also regulates multiple trust services encompassing electronic signatures, electronic seals, and electronic time stamps, thus fostering trust and security in online transactions.

Building upon the solid foundation laid by the 2014 eIDAS regulation, in June 2021, the European Commission took a significant step forward with the proposal for the EU Digital Identity Wallet. The proposal has led to the 2024 eIDAS regulation revision, aimed at providing a more integrated, user-friendly digital identity solution for all EU citizens based on a digital wallet. As a result, the envisioned digital wallet will, from 2026, enable individuals to identify and authenticate online, but also to store and manage their identity credentials on their personal devices, facilitating easy and secure access to a wide range of online services across the Union.

That transition towards the EU Digital Identity Wallet represents an evolution from a standardised regulatory framework to a practical, accessible tool which addresses the needs of digital citizens. The wallet is designed to be interoperable across all EU countries, ensuring that digital identities and credentials issued by any member state will be recognised EU-wide. That not only promises to enhance the usability and accessibility of digital identities but also aims to bolster the trust and security

[1] The Electronic Signatures Directive (Dir.1999/93/EC) was the first EU initiative addressing trust services, requiring in all Member States for electronic signatures to be recognised as equivalent to hand-written signatures. It had narrower scope than 2014 eIDAS regulation and allowed each Member State to take its own approach towards implementation.

framework established by eIDAS, ultimately making digital interactions within the EU more seamless and secure.

By providing an alternative to national and private solutions, the move from eIDAS to the EU Digital Identity Wallet is therefore an interesting illustration of how a more sovereign EU solution is emerging, which provides an alternative to national and private solutions.

The Foundation of Digital Identity—2014 eIDAS Regulation

Historically, digital identity was first introduced by computer scientist Fernando Corbat, who used usernames and passwords to protect files while working at the Massachusetts Institute of Technology (MIT) in the 1960s (Walker, 2024). To verify identity, though, physical documents have traditionally been relied upon: national governments issue passports, driver's licences, national identity cards, etc. To open a bank account, for instance, one had to show a physical document until recently. For digital identity to be used for legal transactions, etc. It has therefore been necessary to establish some verification mechanisms and standards. In the EU, this has also led to the need to organise identification across borders to facilitate that national electronic ID be used throughout the Single Market.

Purpose

Standing for Electronic Identification, Authentication, and Trust Services, eIDAS was established to create a standardised set of rules for electronic identification and trust services across all EU member states. The purpose of eIDAS was to provide a clear, consistent framework for secure electronic interactions across the EU. Its aim was to enable interoperability between national electronic identity schemes—thus not to create a European electronic identity. By standardising the mechanisms for electronic identification and trust services, eIDAS aims to foster digital single-market growth, enhance cross-border business operations, and improve the interaction between businesses, citizens, and public authorities.

Digital identities and trust services are integral components of the digital ecosystem, each serving distinct purposes. A digital identity is essentially a collection of electronic credentials that represent an individual or entity in the digital realm. This identity includes various pieces of information such as usernames, passwords, and biometric data. The primary function of a digital identity is to authenticate and verify the identity of users or entities when they access online services or systems. It ensures that the person or entity is indeed who they claim to be. Digital identities often comprise personal information, digital certificates, and authentication mechanisms like passwords or biometric data, which are used for logging into systems and accessing services.

On the other hand, trust services are a set of electronic services designed to ensure the security and integrity of electronic transactions. The main objective of trust services is to provide a secure and trustworthy environment for electronic transactions, ensuring data integrity, authenticity, and non-repudiation. Trust services involve the use of digital certificates, cryptographic keys, and secure protocols to validate and protect electronic transactions. They are commonly used in legal, financial, and business transactions to ensure that the data exchanged is secure and trustworthy. In short, while digital identities focus on verifying who you are, trust services are concerned with ensuring that your electronic transactions are secure and reliable.

Different Models of Electronic Identity Schemes

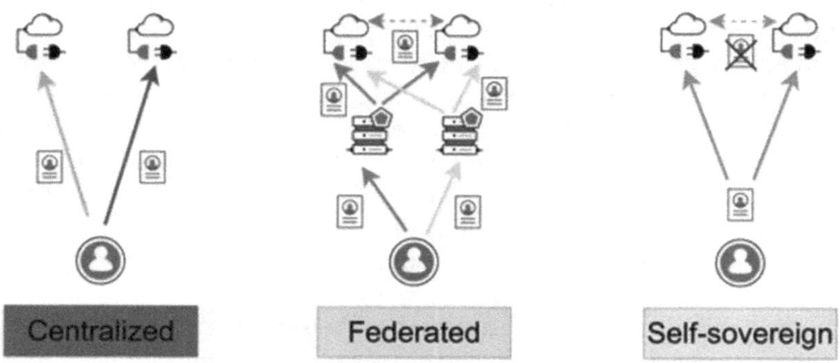

Centralised identities: Entities such as administrators manage centralised identities at the system level (e.g., active directory). As a result, the user's identity is determined by these entities and can only be deleted through them. Reliance on a centralised entity frequently leads to a lack of interoperability. The main reason is due to the fact that the user's identity cannot be transferred without further ado, and it must be recreated for another service provider;

Federated identities: aims to break down the hierarchies based on a single authority by providing a central login solution (IdP) to enable the users to share their identities with different SPs using only one registered credential at the IdP. This solution can solve the problem of password fatigue by providing a Single Sign-On experience and interoperability, but still, the problem of tracking users across multiple SPs remains unsolved. Indeed, it is possible for the IdP to aggregate information from numerous SPs to generate user profiles, which might cause several privacy issues;

Self-sovereign identities are the next and most recent stage of digital identity management that aims to solve the privacy issues in the previous models by giving the users back control of their own data. The main idea is to shift the control from the centres of the network to the edge of the network to enable direct interaction. (Sharif, et al., 2022)

The eIDAS regulation of 2014 provides the legal basis for mutual recognition of national electronic identification (eID) schemes across member states. This ensures that a natural person or legal person identified electronically in one country is recognised across all EU countries. Under eIDAS, trust services include electronic signatures, electronic seals, time stamps, electronic delivery services, and website authentication certificates. These services are essential for ensuring the integrity and security of electronic transactions and data. Additionally, eIDAS sets out the conditions under which member states and the private sector must operate, including data protection requirements and the obligation to provide a certain level of service. The regulation also establishes the legal effects of trust services, ensuring their reliability and acceptance across the EU.[2]

The eIDAS regulation does not harmonise national European digital identities (eIDs) but enables their mutual recognition through a notification process (Regulation (EU) 2024/1183, 2024). Most importantly, the model of eIDAS corresponds to a federated model designed to support interoperability. Implementation of the eIDAS Regulation required member states to recognise and accept eID means and trust services from other EU countries. Each state was tasked with establishing a national framework aligned with eIDAS specifications, involving significant collaboration between national and European authorities to ensure compliance and interoperability.

Results and Shortcomings

The 2014 eIDAS regulation has played a key role in transforming the digital landscape of the European Union by establishing a framework for electronic identification and trust services. While it has brought numerous benefits to the Digital Single Market, enhancing the way individuals and businesses interact across borders, it has also faced challenges that have affected its harmonisation and adoption.

The 2014 eIDAS regulation has been particularly successful in several areas. It has significantly increased the level of trust in electronic transactions across the EU. This regulatory consistency has not only safeguarded data integrity and privacy but also enhanced the security landscape, reducing incidents of fraud and increasing the reliability of electronic interactions. By facilitating mutual recognition of electronic identities,

[2] Qualified Electronic Signatures (QES) have the same legal effect as hand-written signatures in EU Member States. This means that a QES cannot be denied legal effect or admissibility as evidence in legal proceedings solely because it is in electronic form. Other forms of electronic signatures (Simple or Advanced) are also recognised but may not have the same legal presumptions as QES. However, they cannot be denied legal effect solely for being electronic. Trust services (e.g., electronic signatures, electronic seals, and time stamps) that meet the qualified status in one EU Member State must be recognised as legally valid and enforceable across all other Member States.

eIDAS has enabled individuals and businesses to use their own notified national electronic identities to access services across member states. This has been instrumental in promoting digital mobility, allowing EU citizens and businesses to interact and transact across borders with ease, further integrating the internal market. Additionally, the regulation has supported the digital economy by making it easier for companies to operate across borders with the assurance that their electronic transactions are secure and legally recognised. This has not only streamlined operations but also opened new opportunities for businesses to expand their services across the EU. Furthermore, the eIDAS framework has set a precedent that other regions are looking to follow, potentially leading to more interoperable digital identity systems worldwide. This may result in smoother transactions and a more connected global digital economy.

Despite these successes, the 2014 eIDAS regulation has suffered from several key limitations (PWC; DLA Piper, 2021). There has been a low uptake of eID, with slow adoption, fragmented national systems, and limited use in the private sector. Interoperability issues have also been a challenge, as technical standards and the user-friendliness of trust services needed improvement. The absence of a pan-European digital identity and digital wallet has been another significant limitation. Additionally, the processes involved have been complex, with burdensome notification requirements and legal uncertainties, particularly for trust service providers. The regulation has also been less relevant for the private sector, not being well-suited for online transactions and private businesses. Finally, there has been low awareness and trust among citizens, who lack knowledge and confidence in eID and trust services.

The EU Digital Identity Wallet—Concept and Development

Whereas the eIDAS was focused on the interoperability of national electronic identities, the EU Digital Identity Wallet offered a very different approach and put forward for the first time the prospect of an EU identity, coupled with the convenience of an electronic wallet, moving towards a self-sovereign model.

From the COVID Certificate to the Wallet

The first-ever digital wallet is widely accepted to have been created by Coca-Cola in 1997 in Helsinki, enabling consumers to make purchases at a vending machine via text message. In 2011, Google was the first to introduce a wallet on a smartphone, while Apple introduced its wallet app in 2014 (Fry, 2024). At that time, the EU was introducing the eIDAS and not pursuing a route towards a European electronic identity but merely trying to support interoperability between national schemes. Innovative thinking came, however, from a radical experience during the COVID-19 pandemic.

Starting in spring 2020, the COVID-19 pandemic had a deep impact on the development of digital solutions across Europe. During the pandemic, the EU Digital COVID Certificate was introduced to facilitate safe and free movement within the EU. This certificate, which provided proof of vaccination, a negative test result, or recovery from COVID-19, became a crucial tool for travel and public health management (European Commission, 2021a, 2021b). It was widely adopted, with over 2.3 billion certificates issued, and it set a standard for digital health certification (European Commission, 2021c).

The certificate was introduced to a so-called triangle of trust, whereby a QR code is produced and read through a standard and authenticated process; thanks to cryptographic public keys that are provided by an EU Trust Anchor. This guarantees a reliable governance structure and trust in the public keys. This architecture, and the convenience of an app and common standard for the whole of the Union and beyond, led to rapid and vast adoption. The success of the EU Digital COVID Certificate demonstrated the potential of digital solutions in managing public health crises and highlighted the importance of secure, interoperable digital systems. This experience accelerated the push for the EU Digital Identity Wallet, which aims to provide a secure way for EU citizens to access both public and private services online.

The pandemic underscored the need for robust digital infrastructure to support remote access to services, digital financial inclusion, and secure identity verification. The EU Digital Identity Wallet was seen as a step towards enhancing digital transformation, ensuring that citizens can safely and conveniently access a wide range of services online. The European Commission on 23 June 2021 proposed the EU Digital Identity Wallet, making a significant step towards achieving an integrated Digital Single

Market, reducing administrative burdens, fostering trust in digital transactions, and enhancing service accessibility. The 2024 eIDAS Regulation introducing the EU Digital Identity Wallet was voted on by the European Parliament on February 29, 2024, and was published in the Official Journal of the European Union on April 30, 2024. The EU Digital Identity Wallet is expected to be publicly available by the end of 2026.

The EU Digital Identity Wallet (Regulation (EU) 910/2014, 2014) has emerged against a complex backdrop of digital transformation within the European Union. This initiative was part of a broader strategy to enhance the digital autonomy of EU citizens and increase their participation in the digital economy (COM(2021) 118 final, 2021). The European Commission, under the Digital Europe programme, aims to foster a single digital market where citizens can interact seamlessly with public administrations and businesses across member states.

The genesis of this proposal can be traced to the growing necessity for secure, reliable digital identity solutions that can keep pace with the rapid digitalisation of services. The COVID-19 pandemic further underscored the importance of digital tools, with a surge in remote activities demanding robust digital identity systems. Furthermore, the EU's ambitions to lead in regulatory frameworks for technology saw digital identity as a crucial area for innovation and regulation.

Ecosystem and Objectives

The ecosystem of the EU Digital Identity Wallet has involved multiple stakeholders, each with their own interests and influence over the policy outcome. Primarily, the European Commission has played a pivotal role in drafting and promoting the Regulation, supported by the European Parliament and the Council of the European Union. These institutions were crucial in shaping the legislative framework and ensuring that it aligns with broader EU policies on digital transformation and civil rights.

National governments were key stakeholders, as they were responsible for implementing the wallet at the member state's level. Their concerns have often revolved around issues of national sovereignty, the technical feasibility of integrating existing digital identity systems with the new wallet, and the financial implications of deployment.

Both large technology firms and startups have had vested interests in the development of the Digital Identity Wallet. For them, it represented both a potential market and a regulatory framework that could shape their business operations in the EU.

Finally, there were non-governmental organisations (NGOs), advocacy groups, and think tanks concerned with digital rights, privacy, and data protection. Civil society actors were particularly focused on how the wallet would handle personal data and on the safeguards against misuse.

The EU Digital Identity Wallet aims to fulfil several key objectives. First, it seeks to create a unified digital identity framework, establishing a standardised electronic identification system that is accepted across all member states. This will ensure that electronic identities and credentials issued by any member state are recognised throughout the EU, facilitating seamless cross-border access to online services regardless of the user's location.

Another important objective is user empowerment. The wallet will provide EU citizens with full control over their electronic identities, enabling them to choose what data to share and with whom. This aligns with the goal of implementing robust security measures to protect sensitive personal data and uphold privacy rights in line with the General Data Protection Regulation (GDPR).

Additionally, the wallet aims to integrate both public and private services, allowing citizens and businesses to use it for various purposes, including accessing government services, online banking, education, and healthcare. This comprehensive approach is designed to enhance the convenience and security of digital interactions across the EU.

Initial Proposal and Subsequent Modifications

This section provides a comprehensive comparison between the Commission's eIDAS Regulation proposal from June 2021 and the finally adopted amended eIDAS Regulation from April 2024. It delves into the positions taken during the negotiation process, referencing published and documented stances.

After the European Parliament and the Council of the EU approved their negotiating positions on the proposal in March 2023 and December 2022, respectively, they reached a provisional agreement on the creation of a pan-European digital identity framework in November 2023. Numerous key issues have emerged as focal points in the debate over the Digital Identity Wallet proposal and notably: privacy, interplay with national solutions, technical issues, scope of trust services and costs.

As a result, the landscape of forces was particularly complex for the EU Digital Identity Wallet discussions.

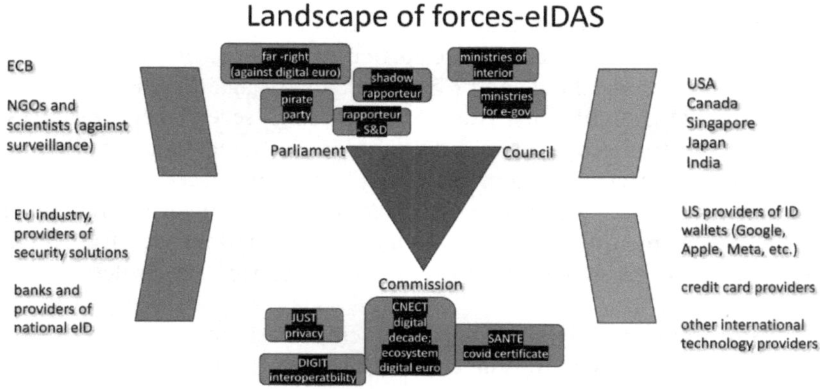

Privacy and data protection were major concerns, with ongoing debates about how personal data will be managed, accessed, and protected. Critics argued that centralising digital identities could make citizens' data more susceptible to breaches and misuse. Some NGOs urged the Commission to rethink the technical requirements for the European eID out of fear that it would allow backdoors for law enforcement and offer no meaningful redress in cases of fraud or identity theft (EpicenterWorks, 2024). The example of international partners was also relevant, as in countries like India, Singapore or Japan, governments had developed certain solutions for electronic identity; they could be a source of inspiration but also opportunities to create common solutions through bigger innovation ecosystems. A specific controversy was linked to the expected use of the identity Wallet to deploy digital euros. The project supported by the European Central Bank was assessed with great scepticism by far-right parties and by conspiracy theorists and libertarian activists alike (e.g. Schickler, 2023).

The European Data Protection Supervisor, in its formal comments on eIDAS, raised concerns about the introduction of a persistent and unique identifier in Article 11a of the Commission's proposal (EDPS, 2021). The final adopted version of Article 11a referred, instead, to identity matching, and Article 12 referred to privacy and security by design. The final version also included additional measures to enhance cybersecurity and privacy. A privacy dashboard was introduced in Article 5a, allowing users to track all transactions executed through the wallet and manage their data more transparently. Privacy-preserving technologies, such as zero-knowledge proofs, were integrated into the wallet to further protect user data.

Interplay with national solutions was also an important issue. A number of Member States had deployed national eID solutions, sometimes around private actors like banks (It's me in Belgium) or national infrastructures (X-road in Estonia). Therefore, security considerations were significant at the national levels. In its general approach, the Council asked that Member States designate public and private bodies accredited to certify the Wallet as provided in the Cybersecurity Act (Council, 2022). Similarly, the Council considered that the initial proposal regarding Assurance levels— the degree of confidence that the person claiming a particular identity is in fact the person to which the identity was assigned— should be changed to accommodate the situation experienced by Member States, and also asked for a specific provision on the on-boarding of users to be added to Article 6a (Council, 2022).

It was decided by the co-legislators that the wallet is voluntary but that it does not replace existing identification and authentication means but complements them (EPRS, 2024). The agreement on the voluntary nature of the Digital Identity Wallet was a significant breakthrough, which was crucial in relieving fears about mandatory adoption. This was achieved by ensuring that the wallet would complement without replacing existing national electronic identification systems. In other words, the compromise found was that an EU identity would have to be accepted everywhere in the Union, but it would not cancel out a national electronic identity, allowing multiple eID for a given individual. In the same vein, the early proposal included basic governance structures to oversee the digital identity framework. However, the need for a more robust governance model became apparent as the vision evolved. The final version introduced a new chapter on governance, establishing the European Digital Identity Cooperation Group (EPRS, 2024). This group was tasked with facilitating cross-border coordination and ensuring a harmonised approach to digital identity management across the EU. In terms of time given for implementation of wallets, the initial proposal required Member States to issue the Digital Identity Wallet within 12 months of the regulation's entry into force. However, as discussions progressed, it became clear that more time was needed to implement such a comprehensive system effectively. The timeline was extended to 24 months, providing Member States with the necessary time to develop and deploy the new system before the end of 2026.

Technical issues were another important aspect in the discussions of the identity Wallet proposal. Some stakeholders, like Mozilla, expressed concern that if QWACs (Qualified Website Authentication Certificates) become the new standard website certificates, they would reduce the safety of the internet (Dullaert et al., 2024). In the adopted legislation, after Parliament's intervention, Web browsers are required to recognise QWACs, so that users can verify the identity of persons or legal entities behind a website, but in case of substantiated security concerns, Web browsers are still allowed to take precautionary measures related to these certificates (EPRS, 2024). Technical challenges also concerned the need to ensure the interoperability of the Digital Identity Wallet across all EU member states. This required the development of a common architecture and reference framework that could seamlessly integrate with diverse national identity systems, which vary widely among member states in terms of technology and the extent of digitisation.

Another key agreement was on the technical standards for interoperability. By agreeing on a common set of technical protocols and standards, the project overcame one of its largest challenges. This consensus was supported by technical trials and pilot projects that demonstrated the feasibility of a pan-European digital identity framework. The open process enabled the industry to reassure itself that services would not be compromised. The concept of electronic attestations of attributes was introduced in the initial proposal, allowing for the verification of various attributes linked to an individual's identity. The final version added detailed requirements for qualified electronic attestations of attributes and their verification against authentic sources. A minimum list of attributes that Member States must ensure can be verified by electronic means was established.

Finally, discussions involved elements linked to the scope of the proposal and to costs. The proposal aimed to extend the scope of trust services to include more types of electronic certificates and services. As the framework was refined, the definition of trust services was further clarified and expanded. The final version included the issuance and validation of certificates for electronic signatures, seals, and website authentication (ex: see article 45). New requirements for non-qualified trust service providers were introduced to manage risks and notify security breaches. The proposal included the idea of electronic archiving services to ensure the long-term preservation of electronic documents. The final version added specific requirements for qualified electronic archiving services, establishing legal effects and ensuring the integrity and authenticity of archived documents. In the initial proposal, the concept of electronic ledgers was introduced to provide a secure and tamper-proof record of transactions. The final version then added detailed requirements for qualified electronic ledgers, ensuring the uniqueness, authenticity, and correct sequencing of data entries. Legal effects and requirements for qualified electronic ledgers were established to promote trust and innovation. The expansion of the scope was applauded by some organisations that had lobbied for it (EUROCROWD, 2023).

While the initial proposal did not specify penalties for non-compliance, the final version introduced penalties for infringements by qualified and non-qualified trust service providers. Administrative fines and enforcement mechanisms were established to ensure compliance with the regulation. A related issue was the financial burden of developing and maintaining the EU Digital Identity Wallet, particularly regarding who will bear these costs—EU institutions, member states, or individual users. The banking sector feared significant costs (Dullaert et al., 2024). The consensus found was that European Digital Identity Wallets can be provided either by the Member State itself or by a private-sector provider, that the wallet is voluntary and free of charge for individuals, while the possibility of charging a fee for business for issuing a trusted service was retained (EPRS, 2024).

The negotiation process over the EU Digital Identity Wallet has been a dynamic interplay of various strategies employed by the involved stakeholders. It reflected the complexities of EU policymaking, where multiple interests must be balanced in the pursuit of innovative and forward-looking digital policies A key aspect of these negotiations was the extensive use of the working groups, formed within the umbrella of the eIDAS Expert Group and consisted of experts from member states, which facilitated specialised discussions on different facets of the digital wallet, such as data security, user interface, and cross-border compatibility. eIDAS Expert Group provided recommendations that shaped a common Toolbox for a coordinated approach towards a European Union Digital Identity Framework. Stakeholder meetings and public consultations also played a crucial role, offering a platform for feedback and helping to ensure that the wallet would be user-centric and privacy-respecting. Thus, in July 2020, the European Commission launched a public consultation on the revision of the eIDAS Regulation. This consultation aimed to gather views from a broad range of stakeholders and citizens to evaluate the existing regulation and consider the impacts of potential revisions. Alongside the public consultation, the Commission conducted targeted consultations with selected groups of stakeholders, aimed to gather detailed data and evidence on specific elements of the proposed revisions. This dual approach helped to refine the proposal and address the nuanced needs and concerns of all parties involved.

Technical Architecture and Functionalities

The eIDAS Regulation is designed to be technologically neutral. This means it does not favour any specific technical solution for electronic identification (eID) implementation. Instead, it establishes a framework that allows for the interoperability of national eID schemes among EU member states, ensuring that various technologies can be used if they meet the regulatory criteria.

The technical architecture of the EU Digital Identity Wallet (EUDI Wallet, 2024) is designed to offer maximum interoperability, security, and user control. It includes several key components. First, the decentralised identity framework ensures secure storage and management of digital credentials. This framework is crucial for maintaining the integrity and security of users' digital identities.

Additionally, the interoperability layer consists of a set of standards and protocols that facilitate seamless communication between national, cross-border, and private digital identity systems. This layer is essential for ensuring that the wallet can function smoothly across different jurisdictions and systems.

Authentication mechanisms are another critical component, employing multi-factor authentication methods to verify user identities. These methods enhance the security of the wallet by requiring multiple forms of verification before granting access.

Finally, data encryption and privacy controls are implemented to protect data both in transit and at rest. Strong encryption standards ensure that sensitive information remains secure, while privacy controls allow users to determine their data-sharing preferences, giving them greater control over their personal information.

The EU Digital Wallet offers a range of main functionalities designed to enhance digital interactions across the EU. One of its primary features is identification and authentication, allowing users to prove their identity online for accessing various digital services. This ensures that users can securely and conveniently verify their identities when needed.

Another key functionality is the storage and sharing of digital credentials. The wallet enables users to securely store and share various credentials, such as driver's licences, academic certificates, and health records. This feature simplifies the management of important documents and ensures they are readily accessible when required.

Cross-border recognition is also a significant aspect of the EU Digital Wallet. Users can utilise their digital credentials across all EU member states without the need for additional verification requirements. This facilitates seamless interactions and transactions across borders, promoting greater mobility and integration within the EU.

The wallet also supports the creation of legally recognised electronic signatures for contracts and documents. This functionality allows users to sign documents electronically, ensuring that their signatures are legally binding and recognised across the EU.

Finally, the EU Digital Wallet enables integration with public and private service providers, such as airlines, hotels, and educational institutions. This integration allows users to access a wide range of services using their digital wallet, enhancing convenience, and streamlining various processes.

Large-Scale Pilots

Large-scale pilots are extensive testing and implementation projects designed to evaluate new technologies, systems, or processes in real-world conditions before they are widely deployed. These pilots typically involve multiple stakeholders, including government bodies, private companies, and research institutions, and cover various sectors such as energy, healthcare, transportation, and digital services.

For example, in the context of the EU, large-scale pilots have been used to test and refine the Digital Identity Wallet. These pilots involve real-world trials to ensure the wallet's interoperability, security, and user-friendliness across different member states and sectors. They help identify potential issues and gather feedback to improve the system before its full-scale implementation.

Currently, there are four main Large-Scale Pilots for the EU Digital Identity Wallet, each focusing on different use cases and sectors. These pilots are testing the wallet in everyday scenarios such as payments, travel, education, and healthcare. The pilots are designed to gather feedback and insights on the wallet's usability, technical performance, and user experience, which will be crucial for its successful implementation (European Commission, 2024).

These Large-Scale Pilots are not only testing the technical specifications of the wallet but also exploring its potential to integrate with various public and private services.

Improvements and Benefits for Citizens—Comparisons with 2014 eIDAS

The EU Digital Identity Wallet represents significant advancements and improvements over the eIDAS regulation. In terms of interoperability, while eIDAS achieved significant interoperability between national eID schemes, the Digital Identity Wallet goes further by ensuring universal acceptance of electronic identities and credentials across borders, including private-sector services. Each EU member state is now obliged to issue at least one EU Digital Identity Wallet, a requirement that did not exist under the 2014 eIDAS regulation.

Regarding user control, eIDAS provided limited control over the data shared via national eIDs. In contrast, the Digital Identity Wallet allows users to choose which data to share and with whom, providing full transparency and optional GDPR certification. This enhancement gives users greater autonomy over their personal information.

In terms of privacy and security, eIDAS placed a strong emphasis on data protection. The Digital Identity Wallet builds on this by introducing enhanced encryption and authentication measures, further improving data privacy and security. Additionally, mandatory EUDI Wallet certification ensures a high standard of protection.

Finally, the Digital Identity Wallet moves towards a decentralised identity model, giving users direct control over their identities. This is a significant shift from the centralised eID systems managed by member states under eIDAS.

These advancements make the EU Digital Identity Wallet a significant improvement over eIDAS, expanding the framework's applicability and providing more flexibility for users.

The EU Digital Identity Wallet offers numerous benefits for both citizens and businesses. For citizens, it simplifies access to public and private services, reducing the need for multiple physical documents. It also provides full control over which data to share, enhancing transparency and privacy. The seamless recognition of digital credentials across all member states aids travellers, students, and expatriates, promoting cross-border mobility. Improved security is another key benefit, with robust encryption and authentication mechanisms protecting sensitive data from unauthorised access. Additionally, the wallet is integrated with various sectors, including healthcare, finance, education, and transportation, enhancing service integration.

For businesses, the EU Digital Identity Wallet reduces administrative burdens by simplifying on-boarding and verification processes. This leads to reduced administrative overhead. The legal recognition of electronic signatures and seals improves trust in electronic transactions, providing legal certainty. Businesses can also expand their market reach, as access to a unified electronic identity framework enables them to reach new customers across borders. Streamlined identity verification processes lead to quicker on-boarding and enhanced customer satisfaction, improving the overall customer experience. Furthermore, the wallet facilitates the development of new digital services and business models, fostering innovation in the digital economy.

The anticipated benefits for citizens and businesses are numerous, ranging from simplified access to services to reduced administrative burdens. However, realising the full potential of this initiative will require concerted efforts in implementation, technological development, and public adoption. The EU Digital Identity Wallet has the potential to revolutionise the way electronic identities are managed and utilised.

Trust Services

Trust services under the eIDAS regulation are essential components that ensure the security, integrity, and reliability of electronic transactions and data across the EU. These services include electronic signatures, electronic seals, time stamps, electronic delivery services, and website authentication certificates.

Electronic signatures are used to sign documents digitally, providing the same legal standing as handwritten signatures. For example, a business contract signed electronically using a qualified electronic signature under eIDAS is legally binding across all EU member states.

Electronic seals serve a similar purpose for legal entities, ensuring the authenticity and integrity of documents. A company might use an electronic seal to certify the origin and integrity of an invoice sent to a client.

Time stamps provide proof that a set of data existed at a specific time. This is particularly useful in legal and financial transactions where the timing of document creation or submission is critical. For instance, a time-stamped digital contract can be proven when the agreement is finalised.

Electronic delivery services ensure the secure transmission of electronic documents and data between parties. These services are often used in legal proceedings to send sensitive documents securely and with proof of delivery.

Website authentication certificates help verify the authenticity of websites, ensuring that users are interacting with legitimate sites. This is crucial for online banking, e-commerce, and other services where secure communication is essential.

In real life, these trust services facilitate a wide range of activities. For example, a citizen might use their national eID to access government services online, such as filing taxes or applying for social benefits. Businesses can streamline their operations by using electronic signatures and seals to sign contracts and certify documents, reducing the need for physical paperwork and speeding up transactions.

Conclusion

The 2024 revision of the eIDAS regulation, often referred to as eIDAS 2.0, introduces several significant changes to trust services to enhance their functionality, security, and interoperability across the EU. It is marked progress in the direction of EU integration and of a digital Union, where any EU citizen can benefit from an EU identity in electronic format.

One of the primary changes is the refinement of rules for qualified trust service providers (QTSPs), particularly concerning identity verification for individuals and businesses receiving qualified certificates. This ensures clearer and more harmonised regulations across the EU. Additionally, eIDAS 2.0 expands the list of trust services to include new qualified trust services such as electronic archiving services, electronic ledgers, and the management of remote electronic signatures and seal creation devices.[2] These new services aim to address the evolving needs of digital transactions and provide more comprehensive solutions for secure electronic interactions.

The updated regulation also introduces stricter security requirements and enhanced encryption standards to further protect data and ensure the integrity of electronic transactions. This includes mandatory certification for the European Digital Identity Wallet, ensuring that all digital identity solutions meet high security and privacy standards. The rich debates and controversies in reaching this result, and the compromises that were found—and notably the possibility of multiple electronic identities and the primacy of governments in assigning them—as well as the emerging ecosystem involved in deploying the wallet, offer an interesting insight in the ability and strategy of the EU to increase its powers. The privacy-enhancing vision of the eID Wallet, as well as its interesting features to include anyone in the digital transformation and to spur new innovations for the public sector and beyond, are a testimony of the human-centric approach of the EU and were critical in gaining momentum for the technology solution offered. It remains to be seen whether the EU wallet will gain traction or whether its voluntary nature will make it less prominent than purely national or private wallets.

Bibliography

Council of the European Union. (2022). *Proposal for a regulation of the European parliament and of the council amending regulation (EU) No 910/2014 as regards establishing a framework for a European digital identity—general approach; doc. 14959/22*. https://data.consilium.europa.eu/doc/document/ST-14959-2022-INIT/en

Dullaert, I., Keren W., Emrys S., & Aaron M. (2024, June). *The European digital identity wallet: Why it matters and to whom*. Caribou Digital Publishing. www.cariboudigital.net/wp-content/uploads/2024/06/European-Digital-Identity-Wallet-Brief.pdf

EpicenterWorks. (2024, June 8). *We sound the alarm–severe shortcomings in European eID implementation*. https://epicenter.works/en/content/we-raise-alarm-severe-shortcomings-in-european-eid-implementation

EUDI Wallet. (2024). *European digital identity wallet architecture and reference framework*. https://eu-digital-identity-wallet.github.io/eudi-doc-architecture-and-reference-framework/1.3.0/arf/

Eurocrowd. (2023). *Council and parliament deal on a European digital identity (eID) includes industry demands—European crowdfunding network*. https://www.eurocrowd.org/blog/2023/06/29/council-and-parliament-deal-on-a-european-digital-identity-eid-includes-industry-demands/

European Commission. (2021a). *Communication from the commission to the European Parliament the council, the European economic and social committee and the Committee of the Regions. 2030 digital compass: The European way for the digital decade*. European Commission.

European Commission. (2021b). *EU digital COVID certificate*. https://commission.europa.eu/strategy-and-policy/coronavirus-response/safe-covid-19-vaccines-europeans/eu-digital-covid-certificate_en

European Commission. (2021c). *EU digital COVID certificate: How it works*. https://www.consilium.europa.eu/en/policies/coronavirus-pandemic/eu-digital-covid-certificate/

European Commission. (2024). *EU digital identity wallet pilot implementation*. https://digital-strategy.ec.europa.eu/en/policies/eudi-wallet-implementation

European Data Protection Supervisor. (2021). *Formal comments of the EDPS on the proposal for a regulation of the European parliament and of the council amending regulation (EU) No 910/2014 as regards establishing a framework for a European digital identity*. https://www.edps.europa.eu/system/files/2021-07/21-07-28_formal_comments_2021-0598_d-1609_european_digital_identity_en.pdf

European Parliamentary Research Service. (2024). *Updating the European digital identity framework*. PE 698.772—June 2024. https://www.europarl.europa.eu/thinktank/en/document/EPRS_BRI(2021)698772

European Union. (1999, December 13). *Directive 1999/93/EC of the European parliament and of the council of 13 december 1999 on a community framework for electronic signatures*. https://eur-lex.europa.eu/legal-content/EN/TXT/?uri=celex:31999L0093

European Union. (2014, July 23). *Regulation (EU) 910/2014 of the European parliament and of the council of 23 July 2014 on electronic identification and trust services for electronic transactions in the internal market and repealing Directive 1999/93/EC*. https://eur-lex.europa.eu/eli/reg/2014/910/oj

European Union. (2024, April 11). *Regulation (EU) 2024/1183 of the European parliament and of the council of 11 april 2024 amending regulation (EU) no 910/2014 as regards establishing the European digital identity framework*. https://eur-lex.europa.eu/eli/reg/2024/1183/oj

Fry, J. (2024, April 17). *The rise of digital wallets: A look at the UK's payment revolution*. https://www.techradar.com/pro/the-rise-of-digital-wallets-a-look-at-the-uks-payment-revolution

PWC; DLA Piper. (2021). *Study to support the impact assessment for revision of the eIDAS regulation final report*. Publications Office of the European Union.

Schickler, J. (2023). *Digital Euro conspiracy theories and privacy concerns put EU central bankers in the hot seat*. https://www.coindesk.com/policy/2023/09/11/digital-euro-conspiracy-theories-privacy-concerns-put-eu-central-bankers-in-the-hot-seat/

Sharif, A., Ranzi, M., Carbone, R., Sciarretta, G., Marino, F. A., & Ranise, S. (2022). The eIDAS regulation: A survey of technological trends for European electronic identity schemes. *Applied Sciences, 12*(24), 12679.

UNDP. (2023). *The impact of digital technology on human rights in Europe and Central Asia*. United Nations Development Programme.

Walker, J. (2024). *The history of digital identity*. Obtenido de Business Reporter. https://www.business-reporter.co.uk/technology/the-history-of-digital-identity

Zuboff, S. (2019). *The age of surveillance capitalism: The fight for a human future at the new frontier of power*. Public Affairs.

CHAPTER 8

EU Cybersecurity Policy

Paul Timmers

Introduction

Cybersecurity is one of the most active areas of EU digital policy development. It has become a top-level policy concern, a *Chefsache,* due to the explosive growth of cyber-incidents, rising geopolitical tensions, changing perceptions on national security and defence, and growing concerns about EU strategic autonomy.

This chapter starts with a short history of 20 years of EU cybersecurity policy. It also identifies some of the big themes that played varying roles over the years: national security, economic and societal resilience, strategic autonomy, geopolitical tensions, and, of course, technological developments. The result today is an EU cybersecurity policy that is fairly comprehensive, be it complete or not. Subsequently, a more profound reflection is given on these themes to enable the reader to gain a better understanding of the wider political context. Next, a deeper dive is provided into some of the pieces of the policy puzzle, that is, enablers or conditions for effective (EU) cybersecurity policy, to conclude with perspectives for the future of EU cybersecurity policy, to address gaps

---

P. Timmers (✉)
University of Leuven, Leuven, Belgium
e-mail: paul.timmers@kuleuven.be

T. Kleiner and A. Garcia Rodriguez (eds.), *The Making of a Global Digital Rulebook*, https://doi.org/10.1007/978-981-95-9226-5_8

and realise promising potential, notably in better-integrated policy and stronger linkage to EU sovereignty.

Awakening, Fortifying, and Defending

A Short History of EU Cybersecurity Policy

In 2001, the European Parliament erupted in anger about a shadowy worldwide electronic spy network, Echelon. Allegedly, Americans could tap into much of the internet traffic and listen to private and secret conversations with friends and foes. The European Commission (EC) was urged to clarify matters, to protest, to defend Europe in order to safeguard rights in the booming internet world. Well, the internet was still booming, but soon the dot-com bubble burst (Wikipedia, 2024). Hyped-up valuations of internet start-ups came crashing down, with the Nasdaq losing nearly 77% of its value.

Just like the internet hype got back to reality, the internet did not go away, and the Echelon upheaval fizzled out, but cyber-spying and other threats of cyberspace did not go away. In the years following, Internet stocks recovered, and 'digital' became ever more part of our lives while a steady trickle of cyber-incidents continued heating up the kettle of cybersecurity. Yet, the proverbial frog in the water—us—kept sitting still. Then came the first real cyber-war—Russia attacking Estonia in cyberspace in 2007—another wake-up call. Some governments saw the writing on the wall and started to take cybersecurity very seriously.

For instance, around 2010, experts in the U.S. started to issue warnings about China's activities in cyberspace, such as cyber-surveillance, censorship, theft of intellectual property, and hacking of U.S. companies. Google pulled out of China. Then came the 2013 Snowden revelations. More cyber-espionage, and this time to a shocking extent, especially for friends of the U.S. The European Commission had just tabled its first cybersecurity strategy.

In the EU, even if the European Commission has the right of initiative, the Member States and the European Parliament are the 'co-legislators', that is, they have to give their political agreement. The strategy turned out to be rather uncontested, as were most elements, except for one: the proposed cybersecurity law, the Network and Information Security (NIS) Directive. This ran into opposition from several European countries as they felt that it infringed on their exclusive prerogative—national security. The Directive was ultimately adopted, despite their concerns, be it in a compromise form. The sensitive but moving balance between national security and common European interests continues to play a role up to today, and there has been a significant evolution towards a greater willingness to cooperate in national security-related matters. This is further analysed below.

Wind forward to 2016. UK hospitals shut down, one-third of them being affected by the Wannacry ransomware.[1] On its heels came the NotPetya attack, a lockout from accessing computer systems that disabled Maersk shipping and FedEx logistics, causing damages estimated at over 10 B. In the same year, the 2016 U.S. presidential elections were marred by online mis-and disinformation, allegedly sponsored by Russia. Big tech did little to prevent platforms from being manipulated, the notable case being the abuse of Facebook by Cambridge Analytica. By now, it was more than clear that cybersecurity was a serious matter, with its impact ranging from direct economic, societal, and democratic damages to long-term erosion of jobs, values, and sovereignty.

It became worryingly clear that Europe had little control over those key technologies that were ever more pervasively and ever more critically underpinning the economy and society, from logistics to social media, from telecommunications to cloud services. This feeling of being out of control was exacerbated by the threats of U.S. President Trump to quit NATO if the European countries did not pay up more (Wax, 2024). In 2016, the words 'strategic autonomy' and 'sovereignty' started to float upwards at the European level, mostly originating from much earlier thinking in France.

When sovereignty is at stake, we talk *Chefsache*. Indeed, cybersecurity quickly rose to the top of political and business agendas—at least at summits of world leaders such as the G7 and meetings of CEOs such as the World Economic Forum in Davos. As some politicians said, cybersecurity became the one issue that kept them awake at night. Again, we go into a deeper dive below on strategic autonomy and sovereignty.

Since 2017, there has been a relentless and ever-growing series of cyber-incidents caused by criminals, state actors, and human error. The nature of attacks evolved from 'simple' theft of valuable information

[1] Ransomware is malicious software (malware) that blocks computer access or encrypts data, rendering it unusable until a ransom is paid.

or money to DDOS[2] attacks shutting down parts of the Internet[3] to ICT[4] supply chain and critical infrastructure intrusions[5] to ransomware at a massive scale affecting millions of companies or taking down critical infrastructures.[6] The technological architecture and design of ICTs and digital infrastructures are increasingly a concern. Constantly, we are confronted with errors in software that require urgent patching.[7] There were doubts that 5G security was designed with the security of the core of government in mind. Billions of Internet of Things devices with weak built-in security are in use. Most recently, we have seen hard-to-beat AI-enabled cybercrime and cyber-intrusion. Security agencies are starting to warn about a collapse of current encryption with quantum computing around the corner. Technology itself is becoming increasingly a concern for cybersecurity policy. EU policymakers started some pushback on 'anything flies as far as technology is concerned' with the 2019 EU 5G Recommendation and the 2024 Cyber Resilience Act.

Finally, cyber and physical security and resilience started to get closely intertwined. Cyber-incidents were seen to affect physical networks like pipelines, as in the 2021 Colonial Pipeline attack in the U.S. (Wikipedia, 2024a). Physical incidents were seen to disrupt digital infrastructures, as in the flooding in the Ahrtal in Germany in 2021 that cut off telecoms networks (Timmers, 2024; VDE, 2024) (see also cyber-resilience below).

While many cyber-policy initiatives had been launched from 2012 to 2018, the pace accelerated further, particularly in law development from 2018 to 2024. The reasons were fourfold:

1. Growing geopolitical and geoeconomic concerns and corresponding top-level legitimisation of action;

[2] DDOS = Distributed Denial of Service.

[3] The poster boy is the Mirai botnet of 2016 involving millions of hacked devices.

[4] ICT = Information and Communication Technologies.

[5] SolarWinds in 2020 is a leading example of ICT supply chain intrusion. Volt Typhoon in 2024 is an example of a hidden intrusion in communications infrastructures by China.

[6] For instance, the Colonial pipeline hack in 2021 and the Kaseya hack affecting Swedish supermarkets.

[7] Patching is updating a piece of software to repair a software error (a 'bug') or vulnerability or improve functioning.

2. increasing acceptance of Member States of EU-level action and a degree of easing of national security concerns, which is further discussed below;
3. growing experience with 'Pieces of the policy puzzle' such as legal basis and governance, as also discussed below; and, last but not least,
4. European Commission policy activism is supported by strong leadership at the EC political and administrative (DG) level.

This evolution led public policymakers to cast an ever-wider net. The time of waking up was over. All across the world, and not the least in the EU, ever-stronger cybersecurity policies were put in place to fortify the economy, society, and politics against cyber threats.

In particular, cyber-policy for resilience has massively expanded with much harder legislative and executive order intervention across the world. The attention of cyber-policy to international affairs has also significantly expanded and hardened. Next to inclusive and soft international cooperation—such as EU-CN cyber-diplomacy (Bozhkov, 2020; European Parliament, 2015)—much more effort was put into cooperation with like-minded parties on concrete problems such as supply chain security and international sanctions. There is ever less expectation of fruitful multilateralist cooperation when both democratic and authoritarian states are at the table, such as in the UN.

Experts argue that Europe is de facto at war, namely in a hybrid (cyber and physical) war which operates below the level of overt war, that is,

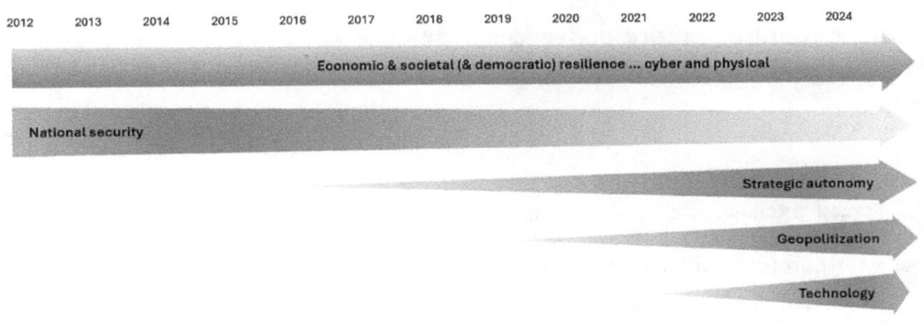

Fig. 8.1 Evolution of the uptake to narratives in relation to cybersecurity

a situation of 'unpeace' (Kello, 2017; Leonard, 2021).[8] We can see the chilling shape of an overt hybrid war in Ukraine. Cybersecurity gets ever more linked to the defensive capabilities and capacities of an EU at war.

A Comprehensive EU Cyber-Policy Package

The result of these last ten years of EU cybersecurity policy development is a large, comprehensive, yet not complete set of policy initiatives, with about 13 initiatives in the first five years followed by an even larger number of about 20 initiatives in the second five years (see Table 8.2 in the Annex).

EU cybersecurity policy can be mapped onto five pillars[9] as shown in Fig. 8.2: cyber-resilience, cybercrime, cyber-industrial/technological, cyber-defence, and cyber-international. The overall framing is provided by the EU Cybersecurity Strategy. A short summary of the main current initiatives as of 2024 is provided in this section, while more information is in 'Annex: A detailed overview of EU cybersecurity policy'.

EU policy is expressed in strategies, soft law, and hard law. Strategies often take the form of broad-ranging policy papers[10] and can also include key speeches by top politicians. Soft laws are European Commission or Council Recommendations.[11] Hard laws are Directives, Regulations, or Decisions.

The first EU cybersecurity strategy was tabled in 2013. This was subsequently updated in 2017 and 2020. The strategy has evolved to reflect three trends: a significant stepping up of cybersecurity as a highly political issue in the economy, society, and democracy; an ever more geopolitical context requiring more active cyber-defence with like-minded partners; and a significant extension of hard-law-based EU cyber-resilience initiatives.

[8] Several intelligence services warned in April 2024 that Russia is 'piloting' sabotage of critical infrastructures in the physical and cyber realms in preparation for preparing for war with Europe (Rathbone et al., 2024).

[9] These pillars were already present in the first EU cybersecurity strategy in 2013 (SWD(2017) 295 final, 2017) (European Commission, 2017).

[10] Presented as European Council Conclusions, European Commission Communications, Council of Ministers Resolutions, European Parliament non-legislative Resolutions, or EP Own Initiative Reports.

[11] Adopted by the Commission or Council.

In *cyber-resilience,* the landmark is the Network and Information Directive (NIS1 in 2016 and significantly updated as NIS2 in 2024). It is based on the internal market legal basis of the Treaty on the Functioning of the European Union (TFEU). It contains obligations for national cyber strategies, EU-wide cooperation of national cyber authorities and expertise centres, and cybersecurity risk management for selected physical and digital service and infrastructure providers. Cyber-resilience initiatives are supported by the EU cybersecurity agency ENISA. This was established in 2004 already and put on stronger footing, financially and in terms of mandate, in 2013 and notably in 2019 by the Cyber Security Act (European Union, 2019).

The Cyber Resilience Act of 2024 imposes stronger cybersecurity for devices that can be connected online. This Act, like the NIS Directive, also refers to the Cybersecurity Act of 2019, which, next to addressing ENISA, also mandates cyber-certification in the internal market. EU-wide cyber-preparedness and cyber-response capability is stepped up by

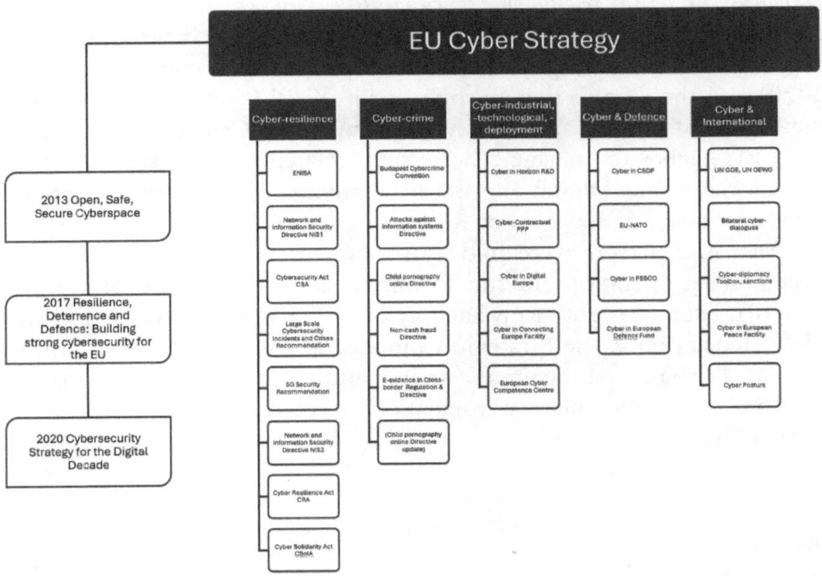

Fig. 8.2 Overview of the EU's cybersecurity policy

means of the Cyber Solidarity Act of 2024. This also includes a European Cybersecurity Alert System to improve the detection, analysis, and response to cyber threats. Finally, the 5G Security Recommendation provides guidance to assess the security of hardware and software in telecoms, that is, part of the ICT supply chain, triggered by concerns about the involvement of the Chinese state in supplier companies.

Cybercrime is the oldest area of legislative action. A Council Directive criminalising attacks against information systems was adopted in 2005 and updated in 2013.[12] Other legislative actions addressed online child exploitation (2011 and updated in 2020), electronic evidence in criminal proceedings (2018), and cybercrime related to crypto-currencies and other non-cash payment fraud (2019). Europol set up the European Cybercrime Centre (EC3) in 2013. As regards data retention, a Directive of 2006 was annulled by the European Court of Justice (EUCJ) in 2014. Since then, data retention has been regulated by Member States individually. The EU and its Member States are also signatories to the Council of Europe Cybercrime Convention.[13]

Industrial and technological capability and capacity in R&D are promoted within Horizon R&D funding.[14] Digital development and deployment are funded by the Digital Europe Programme DEP (since 2020) and the Connecting Europe Facility CEF (since 2016). In 2021, the Bucharest-based European Cyber Competence Centre was established as an EU agency to manage cybersecurity-related financial support of the EU Horizon and Digital Europe programmes and support networked collaboration of national cyber R&D.

Cyber and defence were initially promoted in the context of defensive military operations in the Common Security and Defence Policy (CSDP). Later, this got firmly anchored to the EU's strengthened foreign and defence policy, the Strategic Compass. It has become a top priority due to Russia's war against Ukraine and deeply worrying intrusion by China, affecting military installations directly as well as critical civil infrastructures.

[12] The 2005 Directive was preceded by an EC policy document on combating computer crime in 2000.

[13] Also called the Budapest Convention adopted in 2004.

[14] Currently, the Horizon Europe programme (2021–2027), which was preceded by Horizon 2020 (2014–2020), and before that what were labelled as the EU R&D Framework Programmes (FP7 running from 2007 to 2013).

Cyber and international comprise cyber-diplomacy and cyber-capacity-building with third countries, and more recently, the development of a cyber-diplomacy toolbox which enables the issue of sanctions against state-related actors involved in cyber-attacks, cyber-intrusion, and cyber-espionage. Bringing all together is an international cyber posture doctrine adopted by the Council in 2022.

The Big Picture

Cybersecurity incidents are caused by human error, cyber-criminals, or by states or their proxies, that is, state-sponsored actors. In the big geopolitical picture, cybersecurity is about the stability, security, autonomy, and long-term future of a country, that is, cybersecurity is at the heart of sovereignty. Consequently, cybersecurity policy must concern the means to realise sovereignty, that is, strategic autonomy.

Cybersecurity has become an economy-, society-, and democracy-wide challenge. The costs of cyber-incidents were estimated at over €5.5 trillion in 2020 (European Commission, 2020). A significant number of companies were targeted by cyber-criminals in 2023.[15] Millions of citizens fall victim to cybercrime. Mounting aggregate economic cost, sizeable compared to GDP, is another factor in the big picture.

Rising costs and cyber-incidents do not tell the whole story about the damages: Cyber-incidents also lead to erosion of trust in the digital world, big tech platform providers, and service providers, including the government. While trust erodes, we have all become pervasively dependent on digital technologies. No wonder then those new digital technologies, notably AI, are met by a combination of high expectations of benefits and high levels of mistrust. No wonder, then, that cybersecurity is a core concern in AI regulation such as the EU AI Act. Trust in the large actors in the economy, society, and democracy is, therefore, another factor of the big picture.

Finally, technological development is continuing to race forward, and each next generation seems to bring along new vulnerabilities that are prone to be used by criminals or state actors or where humans trip over. Technology has become a, if not *the*, major factor in geopolitics and in

[15] For instance, in the Netherlands reporting in 2024 stated that 86% of large companies (turnover above 25 million euros), 71% of SMEs, and 55% of self-employed people were targeted by cyber criminals (Monterie, 2024).

our daily lives. Technology is, therefore, yet another factor in the big picture of cybersecurity policy. The next section takes a deeper dive into several of these factors in the chronological order in which they rose to prominence, as depicted in Fig. 8.1.

Economy, Society, Democracy

The primary motivation of EU cybersecurity policy was and continues to be its direct impact on society and economy. Policy actions can address three dimensions of cybersecurity: confidentiality, availability, and integrity of digital information and systems.[16]

Both research data and expert assessments indicate that cyber-incidents cause major economic and societal disruption, even if the cyber-Armageddon predicted by some has not materialised yet. ENISA, in its annual threat reports, (ENISA, 2023) analysed cyber-incidents in detail by revealing their increasing frequency, diversification in nature (ransomware, phishing, etc) and growing impact. ENISA is also projecting forward the cyber threats in the years to come (ENISA, 2022; ENISA, 2024).

In order to prioritise risk prevention and risk response, it is common to use the product of incident probability and incident harm. An illustration of this is given in Fig. 8.3, which is based on ENISA's threat landscape reports (ENISA, 2023).

The focus of countering cyber threats initially was on critical infrastructures, given that they are the underpinning of the economy and society, i.e., in the upper right corner of the diagram. This was the focus of the NIS1 Directive and maintained in NIS2.[17] The ENISA threat reports demonstrated that not only traditional critical infrastructures (energy, transport, etc) were at risk but also public administrations. These were subsequently also included in the scope of NIS2. Moreover, increasingly the dependency of critical infrastructures on their ICT supply chain was exposed through incidents such as the SolarWinds in 2019 and before this time, already in the 5G security discussion, which was a reason to widen the scope of cybersecurity obligations in the 2023 NIS2 Directive and the 2024 Cyber Resilience Act.

[16] Often called the C-I-A of cybersecurity.

[17] Complementary are the Digital Operational Resilience Act (DORA), a Regulation which is comparable to NIS and focused on financial services as well as Recommendations in other critical areas such as energy.

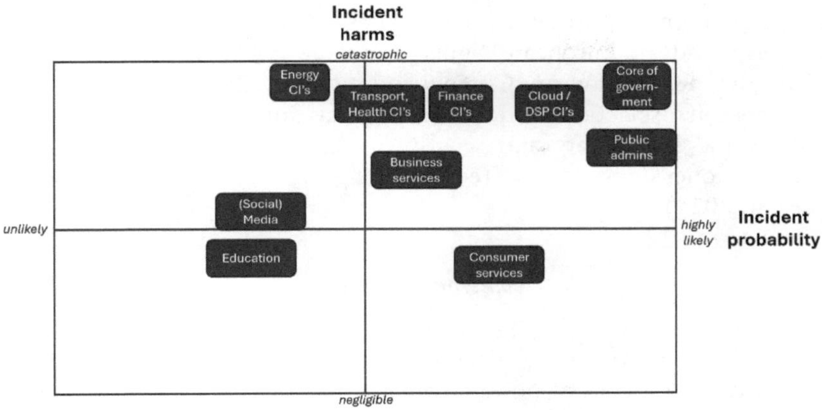

Fig. 8.3 Cyber threat landscape

Concerns about hybrid attacks on critical infrastructures are also on the rise. This can be physical sabotage of telecoms/subsea cables, energy or transport infrastructure, as well as hacking of the information and operations-management IT systems. Threats to democracy through disinformation via online platforms by malicious foreign states have also risen in prominence. Rather than in cybersecurity policy, this, however, was addressed in digital content and platform policy, initially through the voluntary collaboration of big platform companies and, more recently, by legal obligations in the Digital Services Act.

What, then, about democracy and cybersecurity policy? Democracy is, after all, also under attack by digital disinformation, manipulation of elections, and even disruption. Disinformation, for instance, in the 2024 elections in Europe has been analysed by [...]. As regards manipulation, we already mentioned the Cambridge Analytica case. DDoS attacks have been disrupting electoral websites, as reported by ENISA.

EU cybersecurity policy does address the confidentiality and availability dimensions of cybersecurity in relation to democracy by putting relevant digital infrastructures under the NIS2 Directive, but has left the integrity dimension, that is, countering disinformation to other digital policy actions (European Commission, 2024). These include legal obligations for big digital platforms under the Digital Services Act and cooperative or supporting actions such as a Code of Practice for digital platforms and the European Digital Media Observatory.

In the new European Commission, that is, at the political level, the economy, society, and democracy policy lines do get joined up (as well as the sovereignty and security dimensions) viz. the title of the Commissioner-designate for Tech Sovereignty, Security, and Democracy (Leyen, 2024).

National Security

In the EU Treaties jargon, the word 'competencies' is explicitly and extensively used, from the first Articles onwards, and has a special meaning. It concerns the division of powers between the EU level and the national level, that is, the EU Member States (that is, this is an aspect of EU foundational sovereignty). That division of competencies is defined by the Treaties.

A special case is national security, of which the Treaty on the European Union (TEU), Article 4(2), states: "The Union [...] shall respect their essential State functions, including ensuring the territorial integrity of the State, maintaining law and order and safeguarding national security. In particular, national security remains the sole responsibility of each Member State".

This makes cybersecurity, which is closer to national security than many other domains, a challenging case for intervention by EU hard law. Even if, as in other legal acts, one finds exclusion clauses for national security,[18] more than in many other fields, a close link between cybersecurity and national security exists in both the origin (foreign states) and impact (societal destabilisation, espionage) of cyber-disruptions.

National security establishments also felt uneasy about close cooperation at the EU level amongst all Member States since they were at unequal levels of cybersecurity maturity. Moreover, not all Member States were (and are) on the same page as regards relations with foreign states, notably

[18] E.g., a broad exemption in the European Electronic Communications Code which is "without prejudice to [...] actions taken by Member States for public order and public security purposes and for defence"; the e-Privacy Directive of allows Member States to partially restrict its application when "such restriction constitutes a necessary, appropriate and proportionate measure within a democratic society to safeguard national security (i.e., State security)".

Russia and China, affecting their stance on national security and, thereby, in cybersecurity.

No wonder then that in 2013, strong cybersecurity legislation at the EU level (the proposed NIS Directive) was not readily accepted in the Council, notably. However, progress was made when the Commission argued that cooperation could be relatively loose and, moreover, that the legal basis for the NIS Directive properly was Article 114 TFEU, that is, the Internal Market article. This is a powerful legal basis, not only for mutual recognition across the EU of national provisions but also for full harmonisation.[19] The European Commission argued that: (1) cybersecurity is truly an internal market issue given the vital role of network and information systems for the functioning of the internal market, including for cross-border movement of goods, services and people, and "Owing to that transnational nature, substantial disruptions of those systems [...] can affect individual Member States and the Union as a whole"; (2) as a Directive it allows for a degree of national variation in the transposition which could cater for national security concerns; (3) cybersecurity obligations for EU-wide digital infrastructures such as cloud services could be harmonised but more variation could be allowed for territory-related infrastructures such as transport, electricity, health, etc. (as cases of territorial sovereignty); and finally (4) the NIS Directive contained the usual exemption clause "[...] without prejudice to the actions taken by Member States to safeguard their essential State functions, in particular to safeguard national security [...]".

This compromise must be seen in a larger context of evolving EU collaboration in security matters. Trust between EU countries also had to develop. In the early days, 'circles of trust' of countries were imagined that could grow as countries became more competent in cybersecurity. Trust—often on a personal level, such as between personnel of national CSIRTs—would be growing. Cooperation, as circumscribed by the law, could leave room for this. Importantly, ENISA prioritised raising cybersecurity capabilities, such as of CSIRTs in the Member States that were lagging behind, in order to strengthen preparedness and enable wider cooperation in the EU.

[19] Notably in case a uniformly applicable law, that is, a Regulation is proposed, rather than a Directive which still requires transposition into national law which may lead to national variations or gold-plating.

With a dose of realism then, legislators accepted the compromise as regards the mandate as described above. Aware that trust cannot be enforced by law, they also chose to enable rather than oblige countries to collaborate on cyber strategies and operational cyber-incident collaboration. The enabling governance is the NIS Cooperation Group and the NIS CSIRT network (see below for details), with support from ENISA. This accommodating approach turned out to be wise and effective. It prepared the ground for subsequent more extensive and profound collaboration on 5G Security and in NIS2.

However, to some extent, it was also a risky approach as it assumed that time was available to let trust grow. Yet, criminals and malicious states do not wait for the EU and Member States to make up their minds. Indeed, cyber-incidents and damages were growing explosively. Already in 2017, the Commission issued a soft law Recommendation to respond to potentially disastrous and large-scale cyber-attacks. This has been stepped up by hard law with the 2024 Cyber Solidarity Act.

Gradually, insight was growing that 'together is stronger.' In fact, a common and collaborative approach to cybersecurity at the EU level is not at all a zero-sum in terms of sovereignty. That is, more EU sovereignty does not always imply less national sovereignty. Rather, in the case of cybersecurity, there can be a triple-win:

1) Each country is too small to defend itself against cyber-incidents that easily cross from country to country and with far-reaching cross-border impacts. Think of a disruption of the electricity system. Each individual country's sovereignty is strengthened by collaboration, which is the first win.
2) The EU's internal legitimacy towards citizens gets strengthened as strong cyber-defence protects them better, that is a second win.
3) The EU, being stronger in cybersecurity, becomes a stronger and more respected actor internationally, gaining external legitimacy towards third countries, which is the third win (Timmers, When Sovereignty Leads and Cyber Law Follows, 2020).

Internal and external legitimacy, as illustrated above, are two key characteristics of sovereignty in general (Biersteker, 2012).

Strategic Autonomy

In the meantime, from 2016 onwards, the debate on strategic autonomy and sovereignty developed in Europe. This was not only fuelled by concerns about China or Russia but also by trans-Atlantic tensions stoked by the just-elected U.S. President Donald Trump, as well as by rising concerns about abuse of dominance, violation of privacy or lack of protection against disinformation and manipulation by big tech platforms.

Strategic autonomy can be defined as the capabilities, capacities and control (3C) to decide and act on essential aspects of our economy, society, and democracy (Timmers, 2022; Timmers, 2022a). In other words, strategic autonomy is a means to safeguard the sovereignty of the state.

Capabilities are what a country has as knowledge and skills. Capacities are how much a country can produce or how many relevant professionals it has. Control is the power or authority a country has over these capabilities and capacities. This operational definition of strategic autonomy allows measurement and assessment. It derives from defence/military, whose task—obviously—is to defend sovereignty and who must take a practical, operational approach. Namely, the army needs to assess and quantify its strength in terms of the amount of materiel, troops, etc., whether it knows what to do, strategically and tactically, on the battlefield, and how much control it has over military operations, production, and logistics.

This operational analysis of strategic autonomy can be applied to many areas. Indeed, during COVID times, the notion of 'health strategic autonomy' expressed the control over and capacity for vaccine and PPE[20] production. Aware of the risk of dependency on foreign countries for critical raw materials, we nowadays talk of 'materials strategic autonomy'. European policymakers tried to develop 'financial strategic autonomy' for more autonomy in non-dollar trade with Iran and the possibility to bypass U.S. sanctions (which resulted in the INSTEX instrument in 2019). Several BRICS countries similarly seek to pursue financial strategic autonomy to decouple from U.S.-controlled global financial systems.

Digital strategic autonomy can be broken up into semiconductor strategic autonomy, quantum strategic autonomy, cloud strategic

[20] PPE means personal protective equipment such as face masks.

autonomy, etc. Doing so, digital strategic autonomy can focus on measurable and operational matters such as how many cloud companies are in the EU and under EU control, how many quantum specialists have the EU, how many of the leading-edge AI patents originate in Europe, how much control does EU democracy have over critical information flows in digital infrastructures such as 5G, etc.? Similarly, digital strategic autonomy can be articulated for cross-cutting issues. Therefore, it makes sense to talk of cybersecurity strategic autonomy.

Digital strategic autonomy defined in this way is what many authors describe as digital sovereignty or technological sovereignty (Floridi, 2020).[21] Some authors analyse the intent behind 'safeguarding strategic sovereignty', such as safeguarding values through a rights-based approach, enabling the market to deliver, supreme dominance of state or party, or centralised institutional power (Fratini et al., 2024; Floridi, 2020). This is useful as it focuses the debate on rivalling systems in international relations (Bradford, 2023).

Let's get rid of a misunderstanding here, namely, aspiring strategic autonomy does not at all mean going for autarky or self-sufficiency. For instance, a small country such as Estonia realises its strategic autonomy by relying upon partnerships with the rest of the EU, the U.S., and NATO. These provide strong—though not absolute—safeguards for its sovereignty. Sure, Estonia has to accept trade-offs as it does not have absolute control. But its citizens feel that they have a reasonable say about their own future. By implication, strategic autonomy is not about protectionism or creating national—or European!—champions. It may be that strategic autonomy policy in certain cases leads to economic nationalism, but there may also be a 'right' way to do economic nationalism (Rodrik, 2023) (and, by the way, what is wrong about having European champions?).

How can we link cybersecurity policy to sovereignty? Sovereignty concerns three "assets" that need to be governed by (Bickerton et al., 2022): (1) power, which is called foundational sovereignty; (2) physical and digital assets, which is called territorial sovereignty; and (3) the institutional organisation of economy, society, and democracy, which is called institutional sovereignty.

[21] A term such as digital sovereignty may be somewhat confusing as is about both means and ends.

EU policy for cyber-resilience pays attention to territorial sovereignty, such as identifying critical territorial assets in the NIS Directive. It also addresses institutional sovereignty, especially where its Directives and Regulations require competent authorities in the Member States, cooperation within the EU, and some centralised governance. EU cybersecurity policy addresses foundational sovereignty to a limited extent only. This is limited because the Treaties limit the mandate of the EU, where cybersecurity gets close to matters of national security (see also the national security section below). It can be argued that some Treaty changes may create a triple-win for Member States and the EU in terms of sovereignty (see below), yet the Treaties are not likely to change any time soon. This is also limited because of the power of foreign digital companies that provide the larger part of cybersecurity solutions in Europe. By buying their solutions, Europe improves its resilience but reduces its autonomous control.

In conclusion, EU cybersecurity policy is only, to a limited extent, explicitly linked to strategic autonomy, digital sovereignty, or sovereignty. That these notions are mentioned to a limited extent only in cybersecurity policy documents is also shown in Table 8.1.

Geopolitics

The early motivation to develop EU cybersecurity policy was straightforward: cyber-incidents were on the rise, while our dependency on 'digital' was getting ever larger. A defensive and reactive motivation. A secondary motivation was industrial-economic: cybersecurity products and services could become an interesting market for European suppliers (Timmers, 2018). Surely, there was also an international intention in early EU cybersecurity policy, namely 'preserving open, free and secure cyberspace'. This phrase was often accompanied by reference to 'European core values of human dignity, freedom, democracy, equality, the rule of law and the respect for fundamental rights'.[22]

Soon, however, geopolitical motivations came more strongly into play. Evidence was increasing that China was active in highly damaging forms of cyber-espionage, including theft of intellectual property. Russia's war

[22] In hindsight one may wonder whether linking the word European to these values was wise. It suggests 'us' versus 'them'. An inclusive (and non-evangelising) phrasing might be more conducive to cooperation.

Table 8.1 Sovereignty or strategic autonomy in EU cyber-policy until 2024

Policy	*Year*	*Quotes on sovereignty or strategic autonomy*
Cybersecurity strategy	2013	None
Cyber security act	2019	None
Cybersecurity strategy	2017	*Strategic autonomy (not 'open' strategic autonomy)*: The approach set out in this joint communication will make the EU better placed to face these threats. It would build greater resilience and strategic autonomy, boosting capabilities in terms of technology and skills, as well as helping to build a strong single market. Strong cyber-resilience [...] requires a more comprehensive, cross-policy approach to building cyber-resilience and strategic autonomy, with a strong single market, major advances in the EU'S technological capability, and far greater numbers of skilled experts. Those member states with more advanced cybersecurity capabilities and willing to pull them together could consider [..] to include cyber-defence within the framework of a "permanent structured cooperation" (PESCO). This could be underpinned by the work set out above to encourage EU industrial capacities and strategic autonomy. The EU'S international cybersecurity policy is designed to address the continuously evolving challenge of promoting global cyber stability, as well as contributing to Europe's strategic autonomy in cyberspace.
Cybersecurity strategy	2020	*'Technological' sovereignty, interpreted as R&I, no mention of strategic autonomy*: This strategy aims to ensure a global and open internet with strong guardrails to address the risks to the security and fundamental rights and freedoms of people in Europe. Following the progress achieved under the previous strategies, it contains concrete proposals for deploying three principal instruments—Regulatory, investment, and policy instruments—To address three areas of EU action—(1) resilience, technological sovereignty, and leadership, (2) building operational capacity to prevent, deter and respond, and (3) advancing a global and open cyberspace. Cybersecurity industrial, technology and research competence Centre, and network of coordination Centres (CCCN). The CCCN should play a key role, with input from industry and academic communities, in developing the EU'S technological sovereignty in cybersecurity.

(continued)

Table 8.1 (continued)

Policy	*Year*	*Quotes on sovereignty or strategic autonomy*
NIS2 directive	2022	None
Cyber Defence policy	2022	*Defence 'technological sovereignty'*: "The EU needs to take on more responsibility for its own security.[…] to succeed in this, the EU must ensure its technological and digital sovereignty in the cyber field. And "all the EU instruments including DEP, horizon Europe and EDF […] to increase technological sovereignty" and "space […] key asset for technological sovereignty". A technology roadmap was promised for 2023 but not yet delivered.
Cybersecurity posture	2022	*Cyber and international, cyber and defence*: […] investing in innovation and making better use of civilian technology is key to enhancing our technological sovereignty. Strategic compass will enhance the EU'S strategic autonomy.
State of the Union of President Von der Leyen	2020	None
	2021	Tech sovereignty, leadership in cybersecurity
	2022	European sovereignty fund (has not materialised)
	2023	European sovereignty and access to key technologies
Cyber resilience act	2023	None
Cyber solidarity act	2024	*Cyber-resilience*: Focus on threat cooperation. Recital 23: Cyber hubs [..]contributing to union's technological sovereignty, its open strategic autonomy, competitiveness, and resilience and to the development of union capabilities; recital 30: European cybersecurity alert system should enhance the union's technological sovereignty and open strategic autonomy recital 70: (R&I) […] contributes to increasing the resilience of member states and the open strategic autonomy of the union, art 2: This regulation pursues the general objectives of reinforcing the competitive position of industry and service sectors in the union across the digital economy, including microenterprises and small-and medium-sized enterprises as well as start-ups, and of contributing to the union's technological sovereignty and open strategic autonomy

against Georgia and its annexation of Crimea in 2014 were accompanied by intense cyber-attacks. In the meantime, evidence grew of Russia's intentions to destabilise the West. Intelligence services pointed with urgency to such geopolitical challenges. In the U.S., the debate about China started to intensify and became more widely shared with allies.

European policymakers had, in their dialogue on cybersecurity with China, to square interest in collaboration on economic and research issues with growing concerns about suppression of free speech, censorship, and persecution of opposition and cultural minorities. They started to realise that open collaboration[23] sits uneasily with theft of the very intellectual property that should have been the foundation of European future jobs and wealth.

Technology

One might think that all threats to the economy, society or democracy must by now have been addressed by cybersecurity policies, but unfortunately, this is not the case. Firstly, many digital technologies are involved in any application, and each of them can have and most likely has vulnerabilities. Moreover, humans also nearly always come into play and are usually the weakest link in the chain, being naïve, gullible, or malicious. Applications also usually involve a chain of organisations, and each of these can have process, procedure, and management weaknesses that can be exploited.

Complicating matters is that 'digital' is now so widespread that the impact of cyber-incidents tends to spill over from one organisation to another or from one sector to another. A hack of the electricity system can disable nearly all the economy. A hack of a city management system can disable elevators and traffic lights such that people can no longer reach the hospital. A hack of a bank can create mass psychological panic and lead to a bank run, etc.

Cybersecurity is a whole-of-x challenge, where 'x' is technology, economy, society, and democracy. EU cybersecurity policy, however, does not yet take a corresponding holistic approach. Yet, this can well be imagined, building on key technologies lists as established by the EC and others and by systematic analysis (e.g., Timmers & Dezeure, 2021).

Another challenge related to these technologies is that many of them are dominated by foreign firms, notably some of the most critical ones: cloud,[24] platforms, and AI. The related value-added cybersecurity is increasingly in the hands of these firms as they have scooped up many

[23] The EU's Horizon 2020 R&D funding programme was 'open to the world'.

[24] U.S. cloud companies control about 75% of the EU market (Timmers, 2022)

smaller cybersecurity companies, including from Europe (Timmers & Dezeure, 2021). This poses, from a strategic autonomy perspective, a control challenge. A way forward would be a stronger industrial policy for cybersecurity, including proactive risk capital investment, notably for scaling-up companies. The latter has also been put forward, more generally, by authoritative analysis of the (lack of) functioning of the internal market (Letta, 2024). Other policy instruments can act as guardrails for, or monitor, Horizon R&D projects as regards their downstream foreign shareholding. This would complement the EU Foreign Direct Investment screening instrument (European Commission, 2020a).

The EU economic security policy is another important broad policy to reduce foreign dependencies on key technologies (European Commission, 2023; European Commission, 2024a). Cybersecurity is on the list of critical technologies, but the focus appears to be limited to cyber-intrusion detection and does not include Cloud.[25] Reducing foreign control requires a comprehensive policy approach to cybersecurity.

New initiatives do not necessarily need to be of a regulatory nature, but they should work back-to-back with current legislation. Cybersecurity policy must be about more than law.

As a more general point, the underlying logic is that technological and social constructions are closely related (Berger & Luckmann, 1966; Timmers, 2022a). Social constructs include values, norms, laws, procedures, cooperation, organisations, authorities, etc. Technology is related to many more social constructs than law, and therefore, law alone may be incomplete as an answer to challenges. Moreover, technological constructs are emerging that have no counterpart in law, such as autonomous AI for cyber-defence and permissionless distributed blockchain for ICT supply chain security; for these laws may be inadequate.

Digital and hybrid technologies on the horizon will have to be addressed from this perspective of integrated policy and 'beyond law'. Examples are autonomous AI, quantum computing, blockchain, virtual reality (metaverse), and human enhancement such as brain implants and the Internet.[26]

[25] Despite cloud initiatives such as GAIA-X.

[26] Soldiers (and politicians…) of the future may be hacked, see e.g., (Matthews et al., 2024)

Pieces of the Policy Puzzle

Cybersecurity policy is not only about the big picture but also about the 'small picture' of policy components that need to be put together. Next to legal obligations as a component, other components also deserve attention as essential for successful cybersecurity policy and are hard to deal with: awareness, skills, policy resourcing, and policy implementation. This section discusses these components.

As observed above, many individual cyber-policy actions have been proposed and adopted at the EU level. While it may seem remarkable that EU Member States accepted all of these, the main reasons were mentioned before, including the build-up of trust between Member States, the growing understanding that often national security was best alleviated by win-win EU cooperation, and the pragmatic approach of the European Commission and the External Action Service. The European Parliament, as co-legislator, has always been accommodating, constructive, and even leading as regards cybersecurity policy. For MEPs, cybersecurity, generally, transcends party lines. Several influential MEPs have a strong background in (cyber) security and are aware of the digital and geopolitical threats.

Legal Basis

As Table 8.2 below shows, several legal bases underpin EU cybersecurity policy interventions, such as Art. 114 TFEU—Internal Market, Art. 172/173 TFEU—Industry, Art. 182/183—Research, Art. 82/83—Crime & Justice, Art. 172—trans-European Networks, Art. 173—Industry. Some of these can establish funding programmes and funding priorities (work programmes). While funding is important, these legal bases otherwise are mostly about coordination and voluntary action and cannot be used to impose hard cybersecurity requirements. The Justice & Crime and the Internal Market legal bases, however, provide solid ground to impose hard cybersecurity requirements and are, therefore, strong legal bases. Yet, cybersecurity policy always has to carefully balance the desire for impactful interventions derived from a strong legal basis with the limitations in mandate where national security comes into play.

Let's assume that in the future, cybersecurity policy may have to be more integrated and more closely related to building strategic autonomy and safeguarding sovereignty. What is then the scope to call upon other legal bases or to combine several of them? For instance, what about the Solidarity Clause, Art. 222 TFEU? Although this Clause is referred to by the recitals of the Cyber Solidarity Act, it has been chosen to base this Act itself on the industrial legal basis. One might argue that it does so rightly, as Art. 222 is more suited for an acute crisis than for a structural approach to a continuous situation of cyber threats.

What, then, about a legal basis to address more explicitly and coherently cybersecurity strategic autonomy for EU sovereignty? One approach is to combine several instruments under one policy flag. This is certainly feasible and is the approach taken so far in other areas, such as the EU Chips Act, the Critical Raw Materials Act, and the Economic Security Package.

Nevertheless, this raises still leaves questions. Firstly, how to handle cybersecurity policy and the distribution of sovereignty in the EU? Secondly, isn't there a direct legal basis for EU sovereignty provided by the Treaties? As for the first question, it was argued before that addressing cybersecurity jointly at the EU level can deliver a triple-win for sovereignty. Unfortunately, however, and answering the second question, sovereignty is not referred to in the Treaties (remarkably, as they are profoundly about the division of sovereignty). Treaty change is unlikely at this moment in time (Timmers, 2020).

Awareness

Public and political awareness of cybersecurity is essential for realising an ambitious cyber-protection agenda. At first glance, it seems that there has been no lack of attention. In the early days, cybersecurity was yet another issue to deal with. But the wake-up calls described above lifted cybersecurity above the mass of other public policy issues.

At closer inspection, however, sustained awareness in daily life or in the workplace is lacking while cyber threats continue evolving. Organisational behaviour theory would say that this is understandable, as cybersecurity is a hygiene factor rather than a motivating factor (Herzberg et al., 1959). Moreover, cyber-incidents may be considered 'someone else's problem' as long as cyber-insurance covers the damages. There may, however, come an end to this as damages are becoming too large and too widespread.

There is public policy action to keep awareness alive and up to date, such as the annual Cybersecurity Awareness Month, organised by ENISA and many national initiatives. However, these are single, even if important, actions rather than an action programme. These risks leave vulnerabilities in place or do not address emerging vulnerabilities. EU-wide comparative benchmarking could be envisaged here as a case of an open method of coordination with which the EC has much experience. In addition, since ENISA also produces a forward-looking perspective on cyber threats, could this spur an EU-level forward-looking awareness-raising plan?

Lack of a comprehensive, continuous awareness action is also the case in other areas of EU policy. Possibly, stepping up public awareness is considered neither a matter of law[27] nor a matter of EU competence. In the wider picture of strengthening the EU, this may be a mistake as it may weaken the acceptance and, thereby, the effective implementation of the law—think of awareness of personal data protection and acceptance of the GDRP or awareness to consciously choose responsible AI and the effectiveness of the EU AI Act. Giving this a positive turn, sustained and evolving awareness building on cybersecurity is likely a way to enhance the EU's democratic legitimacy in law-making.

Skills

From awareness, we move on to the cybersecurity skills of citizens, SMEs, C-level managers, politicians, policymakers, professionals in any sector, and finally, as cybersecurity professionals. The EU has signalled early on a huge gap in terms of cybersecurity professionals.[28] This gap continues to persist (European Commission, 2024b) and hampers the growth of European cybersecurity companies and the protection of the economy and society. EU policy does make efforts to address this gap, notably through actions supported by Digital Europe funding as well as the COVID-19 Resilience and Recovery Fund (RRF). The Digital Europe programme has successfully been put in place as a new funding facility, positioned in between the Horizon Europe R&D programme and the Connecting Europe Facility infrastructure deployment programme. Whether it has

[27] Although this could be argued to fall under an EU-level duty of care, see e.g., (Hofmann, 2020)

[28] In 2022, the shortage of cybersecurity professionals in the European Union ranged between 260,000 and 500,000 (Digital Europe program call Cybersecurity Skills Academy).

good perspectives to be maintained under the next Multi-Annual Financial Framework remains to be seen. The RRF, on the other hand, was a one-off facility. The EC will have to consider in its next term how to continue supporting cyber-skills development.

EU policy has also paid much attention to promoting women in cybersecurity and increasing the cyber-skills of politicians through desktop cyber-exercises. Finally, the EU actively contributes to increasing cyber-skills internationally (cyber-capacity building, see the next section).

Still, does the gap close? This is not clear, as regular monitoring is missing. Indications are, however, that skills shortages will be chronic. Out-of-the-box thinking is therefore called for, which may include support for intra-EU mobility of cyber-professionals and a programme to step up AI for cybersecurity skills.

Resources

Each element of EU cybersecurity policy requires people and financial support. Costs can be offset against economic benefits, that is, notably, a reduction in the cost of cyber-incidents, which in the NIS2 impact assessment is estimated at 11.3 B€. EC studies estimated that the benefits would far outweigh the cost increase (European Commission, 2020). Compliance costs include increased ICT security spending, ranging from a few to 22%, depending on the sector. Other studies, though, estimate significantly higher compliance costs.[29] These reports do not address who benefits from such increased ICT security spending. For instance, increased cybersecurity spending could benefit the European cybersecurity industry and provide it with a launchpad for global exports.

Authorities will also have to increase personnel for oversight, compliance monitoring, etc., while staffing costs of European authorities (EC, ENISA, EC3) would additionally (but probably to a limited extent) increase in order for market and incident studies and standardisation support. The question is whether a more ambitious staff increase would make EU cybersecurity policy more effective. Surely, when the road forward is more integrated policy (as suggested below) and stronger European cooperation, this may initially require stepping up resources

[29] For instance—without also estimating benefits—estimating NIS2 compliance costs for businesses at over 30 B€, see (Frontier Economics, 2023)

at the European level. This is likely a contentious point in resource negotiations with the Member States, but not addressing it would be ducking the hard reality of cybersecurity. The ground for this needs to be prepared in the coming years in view of the next MFF. It will be instructive to compare the combined resources of cybersecurity authorities in the EU and Member States with the US.

From time to time, policy documents highlighted the need to provide substantial funding for building cyber-industrial capacity as part of EU strategic autonomy in key technologies (technological sovereignty), notably the announced European Sovereignty Fund. This, however, has not materialised. One simple reason may have been that the MFF no longer had enough funding available. This hurdle also hampers stepping up investment in the defence technology and industrial base (EDTIB). The MFF constraints are a highly political issue that the EC will have to address in several priority areas, cyber included.

Implementation and Governance

Even if many EU policy measures are on the table, what ultimately matters most is how they are being implemented. In that respect, the NIS2 Directive will be an instructive case. NIS1 showed that implementation was too fragmented, which was caused by its lack of harmonisation. For instance, under NIS1, some countries registered not even major hospitals as operators of essential services (OES), whereas others registered thousands of hospitals. Some Member States identify waterworks as OESs when they serve more than 10,000 consumers, while other Member States have a threshold of 500,000 consumers (European Commission, 2020). It was concluded that harmonised legislation would be essential. Other crucial aspects of implementation mentioned above are implementation capabilities (i.e., skills) and implementation capacity (i.e., resources).

The EU cyber-laws and policies have put in place extensive governance. As an example of what the NIS Directive entails, see Fig. 8.4.[30]

Over the years, trust in and experience with joint EU cyber-governance have been growing for the reasons mentioned above. Positive examples are joint CSIRT response to cross-border cyber-incidents such as WannaCry (ENISA, 2017) and Log4j (ENISA, 2022a), an impressive list

[30] Diagram: source author; created with Mistral LLM and draw.io; also referenced in forthcoming CERRE report on resilience and security in telecoms.

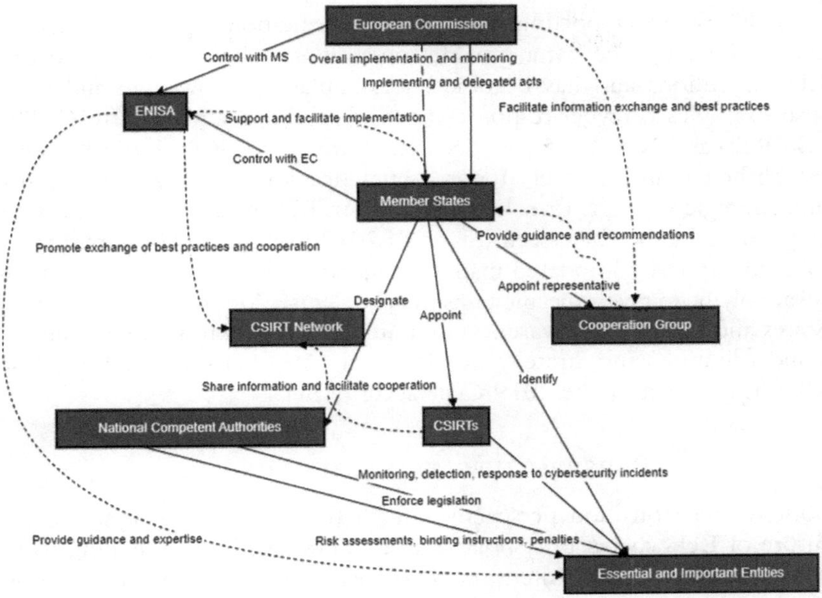

Fig. 8.4 Main elements of NIS2 Governance

of joint strategic publications by the NIS Cooperation Group (European Commission, 2024c), and joint work on cyber-sanctions by the Council (Council of the European Union, 2022a). At the same time, threats are increasing continent-wide, and the need is felt to further step up governance for joint preparedness and response, an example of which is the Cyber Solidarity Act.

This does not mean, however, that a degree of integration has been achieved such that in the future, further EU cybersecurity action will be readily accepted. As argued above and shown in Fig. 8.1, national security and sovereignty concerns continue to keep Member States apart. An example is the unresolved, sensitive debate about the highest levels of security requirements in the European Cybersecurity Certification Scheme for Cloud Services (EUCS) (Kroet, 2024). Furthermore, the differences of view on geopolitical issues and international relations will likely continue to divide the Member States (see 'war' below), which will hamper agreements such as on active cyber-defence.

A key role in supporting practical implementation is played by ENISA and CERT-EU. The latter provides operational cybersecurity support to EU institutions and has become an exemplar of knowledge and practical examples of cyber-response, next to several Member State CERTs (CSIRTs) and National Cyber Security Centres (NCSCs). ENISA is well-established as an EU-level support to practical knowledge and experience and strategic support. Its role is anchored in EU law and was significantly stepped up by the Cybersecurity Act of 2017 from its 2004 establishment Decision and 2013 updated mandate Decision. Furthermore, ENISA has invariably been given specific tasks in cyber legislation to support Member States and industry in awareness building, exercises, knowledge building, standardisation, and strategy development. An evaluation of ENISA in 2024 is foreseen by the 2019 Cybersecurity Act.

Perspectives and Conclusions

Some conclusions and perspectives from the preceding analysis on the future of EU cybersecurity policy can be drawn without intending to be complete. Rather, the intention is to focus here on some of the most challenging issues ahead that may require new approaches to both policy development and policy content.

War

Unsettling as it is, war is looming on the horizon for the EU. An ever-increasing number of intrusions and attacks can, at best, be interpreted as creating a situation of 'unpeace' that is just below the level of war, while some observers rather state that we are already in a hybrid war (with Russia). NATO has also been urging stepped-up war preparedness, as have politicians in several countries. EU cyber-policy is stepping up preparedness for significant, large-scale disruption, such as through the 2017 EC Recommendation on large-scale incidents (European Commission, 2017a), NIS2, the Cyber Solidarity Act, various actions on undersea cables, and the cyber-diplomacy toolbox.

The time may have come to be explicit and make war preparedness part of EU cyber-collaboration. This does not require new legislation but rather priority-setting in various forms of EU collaboration, from NIS Cooperation Group and CSIRT Network to sectorial regulators such as BEREC for telecoms, ACER for energy, etc. This will certainly require political leadership at the EU level and in Member States.

However, common EU-level active cyber-defence would be a significant stepping up from the current EU's cyber posture as formulated by 2022 Council Conclusions (Council of the European Union, 2022). These only 'encourage' Member States to develop proactive measures to protect, detect, defend, and deter against cyber-attacks, and 'possibly' in support of other Member States and the EU. Unanimity on EU-level cooperation, which is needed as this concerns external security, is hard to imagine given the divided views on posture vis-à-vis Russia's aggression against Ukraine and China's military intentions.

A Cybersecurity Emergency Mechanism will be set up under the Cyber Solidarity Act to provide technical and human resources support in case of a large-scale incident. This, however, does not yet include a Cybersecurity Emergency Response Fund, which has been called for several times, such as by the EC in its 2017 Strategy as well as by the Council in its EU Cyber Posture Conclusions.

Cyber-International Relations

The EU's international dimension of cybersecurity has been developing along two axes: (1) international engagement as part of the cybersecurity internal policies, that is, policies that are based on internally oriented interventions such as internal market-based or internal security and (2) as a cybersecurity dimension of external policies, that is, the common security and defence and the foreign policy of the EU. For instance, in the context of ICT supply chain management (NIS2, DORA, CRA), the EC is actively working with counterparts in the U.S. to develop common approaches to supply chain certification and monitoring (such as a standardised Software Bill of Materials or SBOM). This is an example of the internationalisation of internal policies. It would be too far-stretched, however, to conclude that there is as much of a Brussels effect on EU cybersecurity laws as on EU personal data protection law (GDPR) (Bradford, 2020; Bradford, 2023).

Likewise, the EC pursues cybersecurity in bilateral ICT dialogues such as with South Korea, Japan, India and others. The EC also supports European and international standardisation, and cybersecurity standardisation linked to EU legislation figures prominently. The 2024 standardisation plan says, "Develop European standards and European standardisation deliverables corresponding to essential cybersecurity specifications as set out by the Cyber Resilience Act and notably concerning: (i) security specifications relating to the properties of products with digital elements and vulnerability handling specifications; (ii) methodologies concerning assurance levels relating to products with digital elements as referred to above; (iii) evaluation methodologies for evaluating cybersecurity risks associated with products with digital elements" (European Commission, 2024d).

These important actions show increased engagement of governments compared to the past. That 5G security became an issue can partially be attributed to a lack of early government insight into the development of 5G architectures and standards. One can hope that history will not repeat itself in 6G (Timmers, 2020a), although there is still no clear plan (i.e., EU cybersecurity policy) to prevent this. The situation is similarly concerning for IoT, where industry-led standardisation, even more than in 5G, is led by Chinese vendors.

Conversely, prominent examples of cybersecurity within international or external policies are the engagements in the UN First Committee[31] on security under the wings of the UN Office for Disarmament Affairs in the Governmental Group of Experts and in the Open-Ended Working Group on the security of and in the use of information and communications technologies. These two seek to establish international agreement on norms for responsible behaviour of states in cyberspace. Furthermore, derived from the UN's work as confidence-building measures and also as an independent element of the EU's international cyberpolicy is the support to cyber-capacity building in third countries. Such work is financed under the European Peace Facility (for instance, with Moldova) or the Global Gateway. Increasingly, coordination is put in place between cyber-international and digital-international, such as in the Digital for Development Hubs. Likewise, in digital diplomacy supported by the EEAS, a network of Member States' digital ambassadors is to work back-to-back with their cyber ambassadors.

Cyber also figures in trade and investment-related instruments such as foreign direct investment scrutiny. Finally, cyber is prominent in dual-use and export control regulation under the Wassenaar agreement.

[31] Cyber issues also are addressed in the broader economic and social development digital agenda in the UN Second Committee and with a cybercrime, human rights, or digital divide focus on the UN Third Committee. To be mentioned is also the work in UN agencies such as ITU. This is a very brief and incomplete indication only of work at UN level.

However, as in other digital areas, internal-external synergies appear to remain underexploited compared to the approach of China. In line with its dual-circulation approach and loyalty to historical materialism, China has taken a clear export perspective with its massive Belt and Road infrastructure investment initiative. Its industry, in turn, benefits from massive promotion and regulation of domestic cybersecurity commercial activity. China has also significantly stepped up its activity in international standardisation and norms development. Moreover, China has long had a pro-domestic policy to address technology chokepoints, which includes the acquisition of intellectual property through M&A, technology transfer, and import substitution (Murphy, 2022).

The Coming Cyber-AI-Quantum Era

There are numerous analyses on the interplay of AI and cybersecurity (ENISA, 2024a), which can manifest itself in three ways:

1. Cybersecurity vulnerability of AI systems, for instance, manipulating the training data or the algorithm
2. AI for strengthening cyber-resilience and cyber-defence, for instance, massive data monitoring and analysis to detect suspicious behaviour
3. AI for misuse in cybercrime, cyber-attacks, and cyber-espionage, for instance, AI for deepfakes or rapidly producing phishing campaigns.

As for EU policy, in principle, point 1 is addressed by the EU AI Act and, if applicable, NIS (critical providers) and CRA/CSA (cybersecurity certification of devices with embedded AI). Point 2 is the topic of much research as well as an integral part of the CyberShield in the Cyber Solidarity Act. Point 3 can, in principle, be addressed by the DSA (AI and misinformation in platforms), as well as by guidance and standards linked to EU cybersecurity laws such as NIS. An open question is how large the impact of AI is going to be. If cyber-attacks explode due to AI misuse, it may be felt that additional cooperation needs to be set up. Tracking developments is of utmost importance.

Quantum technologies are still an emerging area, one-day hyped-up, the other day declared to be sci-fi. As for AI, there are three areas of interest or concern (G. Rodriguez, 2023; Pupillo et al., 2023):

1. Cybersecurity vulnerability of quantum systems, especially those that rely on a complex configuration of components
2. Quantum technology to strengthen cyber-resilience and cyber-defence, notably quantum communications for secure quantum key distribution (QKD)
3. Quantum technology to break cyber-protection, especially quantum computing to break traditional encryption.

For EU policy, this domain is still in the early days. The first point is still speculative, as larger quantum systems do not yet exist, and hardly any study has been done into their possible cyber vulnerabilities. As for the second point, the EU supports R&D in secure quantum communications, including the use of satellites and the European Quantum Communication Infrastructure (EuroQCI) Initiative (European Commission, 2024e). The third point is the greatest concern, and action is urged to be taken already today. Encrypted information can stay relevant for many years, and foreign governments are suspected of hoarding today's information awaiting the moment of arrival of a powerful quantum computer, even if this may still be several years away, The EC issued a Recommendation to prepare for quantum computing by deploying post-quantum encryption (PQC) (European Commission, 2024f). These are encryption algorithms that are robust against quantum computing. To be prepared today, encryption should be architected such that current classical encryption can be swapped for PQC. International standardisation of PQC is already underway, notably driven by the U.S. standards agency NIST. There is no EU leadership in quantum standardisation, even though EU researchers and industry actively contribute.

Towards Cyber-Industrial Policy Driven by Strategic Autonomy

One may wonder how strongly EU cybersecurity policy and law are linked to strategic autonomy concerns. Table 8.1 gives an overview. The conclusion must be drawn that the linkages are made in words but less in action. The main driver of action continues to be cyber-resilience and combating cybercrime rather than strategic autonomy. Only some elements of industrial policy for cybersecurity that reinforce all three aspects of strategic autonomy—capabilities, capacities, and control—are in place.

The reasons for this relatively weak approach are several. Firstly, there is an immediate need to strengthen cyber-resilience. Any solution, independent of its origin, is, in principle, welcome as long as it delivers. In this thinking, resilience has priority over autonomy. Secondly, solutions are increasingly linked to or integrated into the larger IT environments, that is, cloud platforms. The cloud market is dominated by a handful of US big tech providers. Moreover, U.S. capital (including big tech) has acquired and absorbed many smaller European cybersecurity companies. There are far fewer large European cybersecurity companies than foreign ones.

Thirdly, there has been limited effort to put in place a systematic approach to combine EU industrial, market access, standardisation, competition, public procurement, trade and foreign policies. 'Systematic' here means ensuring that all policy actions are mutually reinforcing, meaning, for instance, that market access policy also benefits the European cybersecurity industry. As a case in point, there is no systematic industrial investment programme that assists European cybersecurity companies to benefit from NIS2 or CRA. In conclusion, EU cybersecurity policy is, at best, a follower of EU strategic autonomy.

Other industrial and trade policies are, in this respect, much clearer about strategic autonomy. Examples are Galileo,[32] the Critical Raw Materials Act (CRMA), and the economic security policy package (European Commission, 2023).

What would be needed to address strategic autonomy in EU cybersecurity as an objective at the same level as other objectives? Above all, be proactive rather than reactive. Then, it needs an inventory of where strategic autonomy matters and to define which capabilities, capacities, and levels of control would be needed to safeguard sovereignty. Inspiration can come from the CRMA and the economic security package. We would need to measure the current state of play in terms of the 3Cs. We would then also have to prioritise, that is, identify which gaps are of greatest concern. Next, we must understand which strategic approaches exist to address gaps. That is, as tempting as it may seem, it is not a matter of gap-filling by throwing money at the problem, but rather to consider which approach is long-term sustainable, also politically.

[32] In 2018, in the context of Brexit, the UK was refused industrial participation in Galileo as otherwise there would be for the EU a "loss of strategic autonomy".

Four approaches can be pursued: complete independence, that is, autarky; sharing with like-minded countries; stable interdependencies with non-like-minded countries or making these countries dependent in a stable way (weaponisation); pursuing global solutions that transcend sovereignty. Combinations of these are also possible. Finally, we can compose the policy package, utilising in principle all instruments from the policy toolbox and from all policy areas (industrial, labour, market access, competition, trade, foreign, etc.).

Let's apply this to cybersecurity and take the example of cloud services. We then need to:

(a) Identify where control (and capability, capacity) matters of cybersecurity in the cloud, e.g., for the core of government or critical infrastructures such as telecoms
(b) Monitor the market for the cloud in these areas, such as the origin of suppliers and market share
(c) Conduct an informed political debate on strategic approaches. Example conclusions could be that autarky is neither feasible nor desirable but that mutual dependency on partners that are long-term like-minded is acceptable while also pursuing global solutions. That is, cybersecurity as part of cloud platforms of U.S. providers would be acceptable, provided the U.S. government stays a like-minded partner and, in parallel, global solutions are promoted, such as quantum-secure cloud.
(d) Propose a policy package consisting of investment in value-added cybersecurity in cloud services; public procurement guidance; multilateral agreement on the security of the cloud and its related supply chain, including standardisation and certification, which will then be part of market access such as NIS, bilateral trade agreements (e.g., EU-U.S.) and international cooperation (e.g., Global Gateway); promoting a multilateral or even global platform for the next-generation quantum-secure cloud; a back-to-back programme to support EU SMEs to benefit from this policy; and using the policy to set priorities in EU Horizon Europe and IPCEI[33] R&D and deployment.

[33] Important Project of Common European Interest. Related is the IPCEI CIS (next-generation Cloud Infrastructure and Services).

Consequently, such 'smart policy' does not put the emphasis on new legislation. That would be myopic, underrating the potential of public policy. Moreover, it offers plenty of opportunities for public-private cooperation.

Conclusions

Cybersecurity policy will likely stay for many years unfinished, an "Unvollendete". Firstly, implementation matters: the large number of cyber-policy initiatives has led to concerns about implementation in terms of clarity, administrative burden, and resources needed. The Council has also stressed the need to now turn attention to implementation and that "significant human, financial and operational resources [are] required from society, businesses and governments" in 2024 Conclusions on the Future of Cybersecurity (Council of the European Union, 2024). In terms of clarity, i.e., navigating the implementation of the various laws, European Commission Recommendations could provide helpful guidance (Timmers et al., 2024).

Secondly, the evolving nature of digital technologies, political and social behaviour, and human ingenuity will continue to lead to new vulnerabilities. This would already be a sufficient reason to continue developing cybersecurity policy. In addition, while acknowledging that EU cybersecurity policy is already extensive and well-developed, it is still incomplete and leaves potential untapped. Specifically, EU policy does not yet fully address the need to increase EU cybersecurity strategic autonomy.

Finally, it is essential to continue being proactive in this domain for sustainable protection and resilience of our economy, society, and democracy. Above all, for EU sovereignty, it is imperative to strengthen cyber capabilities and capacities across the EU and under the control of the EU and long-term, like-minded, trusted partners. Safeguarding sovereignty brings the freedom of political decision-making and the freedom to act, respect for our values, advancement of our knowledge and skills, socially acceptable transformation of jobs, sustainable build-up of industrial capacity and the creation of wealth.

Table 8.2 EU Cybersecurity Policy Initiatives until the end of 2024

Initiative	*Description*	*Legal basis*[34]	*Adoption Date*
Budapest convention	Council of Europe Cybercrime Convention	82 Crime	2001
ENISA regulation	Establishing European Network and Information Security Agency	114 Internal market	2004
Council framework decision on attacks against information systems	Combating cybercrime	82 Crime	2005
Combating the sexual abuse and sexual exploitation of children and child pornography	Directive	82, 83 Crime	2011
Directive on attacks against information systems (cybercrime directive)	Combating cybercrime	83 Crime	2013
Cybersecurity strategy	Overall comprehensive cybersecurity strategy	–	2013
Connecting Europe facility	Regulation deployment funding, including cybersecurity	172 Industry	2013
Horizon 2020 Programme	Council Decision R&D funding, including cybersecurity	182 R&D	2014
cPPP: Contractual public-private partnership on cybersecurity	Collaboration between EU and industry, EC decision	182 R&D	2016
NIS1 directive: Security of network and information systems	National plans, EU cooperation, risk management for critical sectors	114 Internal market	2016
Cybersecurity strategy update	Overall cybersecurity strategy, update	–	2017

[34] Article numbers refer to Treaty on Functioning of the European Union (TFEU) unless Treaty on European Union (TEU) is specified.

Initiative	*Description*	*Legal basis*	*Adoption Date*
Coordinated response to large scale cybersecurity incidents	'Blueprint' recommendation	292 Other	2017
Cyber diplomacy toolbox	Council conclusions	–	2017
Permanent structured cooperation (PESCO) in security and defence	Cybersecurity projects in PESCO (est. by Council Decision 2017)	46 TEU CSDP	2018
Non-cash fraud	Directive on fraud with digital/virtual/ crypto currencies	83 Crime	2019
Cybersecurity of 5G networks	European Commission recommendation	292 Other	2019
CSA: Cybersecurity act	Strengthen EU cyber security agency (ENISA), certification	114 Internal market	2019
Cybersecurity strategy update	Overall cybersecurity strategy in digital decade	–	2020
Horizon Europe Programme	Council decision R&D funding, including cybersecurity	182 R&D	2021
Digital Europe Programme	Regulation innovation funding, including cybersecurity	173 Industry	2021
Connecting Europe facility	Regulation deployment funding, including cybersecurity	172 Industry	2021
European Defence fund	Regulation defence funding, including cybersecurity	173, 182 Industry, R&D	2021
European peace facility	Council decision, including cyber-capacity-building projects	28, 30 TUE CFSP 41,42 TEU CSDP[35]	2021
Global gateway	Political initiative drawing on other programmes for funding	–	2021

(continued)

35 CFSP is Common Foreign and Security Policy, CSDP is Common Security and Defence Policy.

Table 8.2 (continued)

Initiative	*Description*	*Legal basis*	*Adoption Date*
ECCC: EU cybersecurity competence Centre and network	Coordinate cybersecurity research and innovation	173 Industry	2021
DORA: Digital operational resilience act	Cyber requirements for financial institutions	114 Internal market	2022
NIS2 directive	Strengthened NIS rules, expanded scope	114 Internal market	2022
Cyber posture	Council conclusions on cyber and international relations	–	2022
Cross-border access to electronic evidence (e-evidence)	Regulation Directive	82 53, 62	2023
CRA: Cyber resilience act	EU-wide cybersecurity rules for connected products	114 Internal market	2024
Cyber solidarity act	Coordinated EU response to cyber-attacks	173 Industry	2024
Prevent and combat child sexual abuse	CSAM[36] regulation (proposal)	114 Internal market	(open)
EUCS European cybersecurity certification scheme for cloud services	Implementing act of art. 48(2) of cyber security act	114 Internal market	(open)

[36] CSAM: Child Sexual Abuse Material.

Annex: A Detailed Overview of EU Cybersecurity Policy

EU cybersecurity policy can be mapped in a five-pillar structure shown above in Fig. 8.2, which is expanded in Table 8.2 in this Annex with the date and legal basis (if applicable) of policy initiatives.[37] In Fig. 8.2, the initiatives have been ordered, with the more recent ones at the bottom. The diagram, though already rather well-filled, does not show linkages to important related digital and economic policy, such as the EC's annual standardisation programme, the Economic Security Package, various defence and security policy initiatives such as the Strategic Compass, and international and bilateral cooperation such as the Trans-Atlantic Technology Partnership.

Cybersecurity Strategies

Three documents, resp. 2013, 2017 and 2020, presented the evolving EU cybersecurity strategy. They are all policy documents issued jointly by the EC and the EEAS.

The first EU cybersecurity strategy was the joint Communication of 2013 on 'Open, Safe, Secure Cyberspace'. It was constructed around that five-pillar approach. It was largely intentional and soft-law-based, except for the hard-law proposal of the NIS Directive. It set a broad framework but did not yet raise cybersecurity as a top-level political issue.

The strategy was updated in 2017 with the joint Communication on 'Resilience, Deterrence and Defence: Building strong cybersecurity for the EU'. This drew attention to the society-wide relevance of cybersecurity, for the first time referring to strategic autonomy as well as to potential large-scale incidents.

In 2020, the strategy was again renewed and strengthened under the heading 'Cybersecurity Strategy for the Digital Decade'. As the title shows, it was framed within the overall Digital Decade policy. It set the scene for much further-reaching internal policy, preparing the ground for NIS2, CRA, and the Cyber Solidarity Act. It stated, "This strategy aims to ensure a global and open Internet with strong guardrails to address the risks to the security and fundamental rights and freedoms of people in Europe. It also puts more emphasis on external policy, that

[37] A detailed overview of EU cyber legislation can also be found in (Rupp, 2024)

is, international cyber-policy. Following the progress achieved under the previous strategies, it contained concrete proposals for deploying three principal instruments—regulatory, investment and policy instruments—to address three areas of EU action—(1) resilience, technological sovereignty and leadership, (2) building operational capacity to prevent, deter and respond, and (3) advancing global and open cyberspace".

The increasingly tense geopolitical situation created further pressure, leading to strong support at the highest political level for EU policy and Member State-level action. The war of Russia against Ukraine and the massive deployment of cyber-attacks, as well as highly disturbing criminal or state-sponsored cyber-attacks such as Colonial Oil and Solarwinds, helped to create common trans-Atlantic ground and to give impetus to joint EU-US work on ICT supply chain security and incident-management.

The Council adopted important resolutions on cyber-response, the international cyber posture of the EU (Council of the European Union, 2022), following earlier Conclusions on cyber-diplomacy.[38] The EP also was ever more engaged, for instance, on the position of cyber-attacks on one country and the invocation of the EU Solidarity Clause, Art. 222 TFEU. This all catalysed strategic thinking and legitimised the move forward with actions such as the 5G Security Recommendation and a raft of legislative proposals.

Cyber-Resilience

The EU Cybersecurity Act defines cybersecurity as "the activities necessary to protect network and information systems, the users of such systems, and other persons affected by cyber threats" (Regulation (EU) 2019/881, 2019). The terminology of the NIS1 Directive is the security of network and information systems, which means "the ability of network and information systems to resist, at a given level of confidence, any action that compromises the availability, authenticity, integrity or confidentiality of stored or transmitted or processed data or the related services offered by, or accessible via, those network and information systems". The revised Network and Information Security (NIS2) Directive, the main cyber-law

[38] For a number of Council documents see also the EEAS website on cybersecurity (EEAS, 2023).

applicable to critical digital infrastructures, also refers to the CSA definition. A legislative definition of cyber-resilience is not available in EU law, though the simplest would be to refer to 'cyber-incidents' in the 2022 EU Critical Entities Resilience Directive (CER) of resilience as "a critical entity's ability to prevent, protect against, respond to, resist, mitigate, absorb, accommodate and recover from an incident" (Directive (EU) 2022/2557, 2022). The CER Directive concerns physical security for resilience.

The main law addressing cyber-resilience is the NIS Directive (NIS1 and NIS2). This addresses three main pillars: national strategies, authorities and CSIRTs; EU-wide cooperation between Member States and with the EU level; and risk management and reporting obligations on critical providers (operators of essential services and digital service providers). The risk management yardstick is whether efforts have been undertaken according to best efforts and to the state of the art, where standards and ENISA guidance can make this yardstick more measurable. NIS2 adds to the second pillar: vulnerability sharing at the EU level and crisis cooperation (EU-CyCLONe), coordinated security risk assessments of critical supply chains, and certification (building on the CA), and is much more explicit to supervision and enforcement in relation to the third pillar (where the providers concerned are now distinguished into essential and important entities).

In addition, and supportive of the NIS Directives is cyber-resilience addressed by the Cybersecurity Act (CSA), which both establishes the approach to cybersecurity certification (without mentioning specific areas for certification) and provides a stronger basis for ENISA. ENISA, as the EU's cybersecurity agency, has seen its resources grow from about 75 in 2017 to 115 in 2025 (forecast). The more recent Cyber Resilience Act (CRA) imposes secure ICT development and certification requirements on (potentially) connected products.

All these cyber-resilience laws are based on the internal market Article 114 of the Treaty on the Functioning of the European Union (TFEU). Therefore, their basic justification is the economic interest of the free flow of people, goods, services and capital across the EU. It is important to understand this legal basis. For instance, at the early stages of the NIS1 negotiation, some discussion was held on whether Article 222 on solidarity between Member States would be a better legal basis. However, there are several arguments against this, such as that the systemic impact of cybersecurity incidents is the erosion of trust in the internal market and that Article 222, by definition, is reactive, whereas cybersecurity requires a preventative approach such as by market regulation.

The Cyber Solidarity Act (CSOLA) sets up a European cybersecurity alert system, a cyber emergency mechanism with a cybersecurity reserve as a pool of private companies offering support upon request, and a cybersecurity incident review mechanism. An implementing act of the CSOLA is on managed security services, which assist in risk management and can consist of, for example, incident handling, penetration testing, security audits, and consulting related to technical support. This law enables the establishment of European certification schemes for managed security services. Interestingly, the CSOLA is based on Article 173 TFEU, Industry, which is a rather weak legal basis.

Cyber-Industrial and Technological Capabilities

In 2013, extensive consultations were held with industry and researchers to develop a research and innovation agenda for cybersecurity. The outcomes were anchored in the EU's general Horizon 2020 research programme. Subsequently, it was considered from 2015 onwards to step up investment in European R&D&I in this field, which could be achieved by a threefold leveraging of private co-funding (rather than the usual twofold). An agreement was reached in 2016 with a newly established industry association, ECSO, on a so-called contractual private-public-partnership (IP), which is based on a commitment by industry to at least triple EU funding and a commitment by the European Commission to closely involve industry in EU research planning.

Subsequently, European Commission funding increased through Horizon (part of "Civil Security for Society", with a total budget of 1.3 B€), Digital Europe (about 1.6 B€ over 7 years), Connecting Europe Facility, and the Recovery Facility (numbers not available). In 2021, the European Commission decided to devolve funding management and networked collaboration in cybersecurity R&D to the European Cyber Competence Centre, an agency established in Bucharest, essentially managing a network of cyber competence centres in the Member States (Regulation (EU) 2021/887, 2021).

Cybercrime

Cybercrime legislation preceded cyber-resilience legislation in the EU but has since taken more of a backseat. Already in 2005, a Council Framework Decision 2005/222/JHA was agreed on attacks against information systems (2005), which harmonised national laws and criminalised illegal access, system interference, and data interference across EU member states. In 2013, this was followed by an EU Directive on attacks against information systems with further harmonisation. Other legislation related to but not exclusively focused on cyber is a 2011 Directive combatting online child pornography and a 2017 Directive against terrorism, including cyberterrorism, as well as anti-money laundering legislation (AML-5 of 2018), which got extended with measures against suspicious transfer of crypto assets (Council of the European Union, 2023).

Importantly, the EU bases itself on the 2004 Budapest Convention on Cybercrime, an international law instrument of the Council of Europe. While some 68 countries have signed up for this under pressure from China and Russia, who argued that they had not been part of the design of the Budapest Convention, discussion on a UN Treaty on Cybercrime has been initiated. Progress is difficult given that these authoritarian states want to have state security going above all, which democratic states see as a danger to human rights (United Nations, 2024).

Europol's Cybercrime Centre (EC3) has established itself in the EU and internationally as an important actor. It has only grown modestly from a staffing level of around 80 in 2017 to (forecast) 110 in 2025 (Europol, 2024). A contentious issue that continues to surface in the debate is the extent to which law enforcement should be able to bypass encryption (Bijlagen.nos.nl, 2024; Europol, 2024a).

Cyber and Defence

The 2013 cybersecurity strategy did not yet articulate a comprehensive nor forceful approach to cybersecurity and defence—i.e. at the EU level, the Common Defence and Security Policy, as well as relations with NATO and other international partners. Missing from the approach were strong links to defence R&D, defence procurement and defence deployment. All measures were promotional. This has changed with Russia's war against Ukraine and increased cyber-espionage, notably from China, targeting military and defence.

In 2022, the European Commission and European External Action Service (EEAS) adopted a joint cyber-defence policy (European Commission & EEAS, 2022). This included strengthening cyber-defence industrial capacity as part of the European Defence Technological Industrial Base (EDTIB), on which, subsequently, further policy has been developed. A joint EU-NATO task force assessed the cyber vulnerability of critical infrastructures, including undersea cables, in 2013. The EU now actively supports, amongst others from the Peace Facility, the build-up of cyber-capacity in neighbouring countries, also with an interest in reducing the EU's vulnerability in cyberspace. Cyber has become a theme in the Permanent Structured Cooperation (PESCO), the intergovernmental collaboration on defence projects, cyber as a topic in the new European Defence Fund, cyber as a theme in the Strategic Compass, the strategy for security and defence adopted in 2022, as well as in the Coordinated Annual Review on Defence (CARD) (European Defence Agency, 2024).

Cyber and defence recently have been rising to the top due to the open hybrid warfare that Russia is waging against Ukraine and a series of incidents that point to preparation for society-wide disruption by adversary countries (sabotage of subsea cables, deep intrusion of state-sponsored malware (Lyons, 2024), various forms of hybrid attacks (Rathbone et al., 2024). Actions include closer cooperation of EU and NATO, such as a task force on critical infrastructures and including cybersecurity within growing EU defence funding. Nevertheless, while the interest in cyber in the defence domain has risen significantly, cyber still only represents 3% of total military funding in the Member States.

International Cyberspace

International cyberspace activities in the 2013 EU strategy centred around 'preserving an open, free and secure cyberspace' (later, the words 'global' and 'stable' were added (e.g., Council of the European Union, 2022). At that time, cybersecurity was only coming up and still needed to be 'mainstreamed' in EU external relations and the EU Common Foreign and Security Policy (CFSP). Cyber capacity-building in third countries was the other priority. Winding forward, the framework for a joint EU diplomatic response to malicious cyber activities (the "cyber-diplomacy toolbox") was already much more concrete, even though it has been activated only a few times since.

The strategy in the 2017 'Resilience, Deterrence and Defence' Communication could also refer to concrete work ongoing in the UN on norms for responsible state behaviour, applicability of international law (Tiik, 2020), and a range of emerging bilateral cyber dialogues. The EU's position in these has always been to stress human rights and multilateralism, if not global approaches, and consequently engaged strongly in these UN processes on cybersecurity as conducted in the UN Governmental Group of Experts (UN GGE), running until 2022, and currently in the UN Open-Ended Working Group on ICT Security (UN OEWG). At the time, EU values were also put upfront, though this terminology may have shifted more towards 'fundamental values' and shared values. As mentioned above, civil-military collaboration started to step up, also internationally (EU-NATO).

Subsequently, the 2020 EU's Cybersecurity Strategy for the Digital Decade expressed worries about multilateralism and the risk of disruption of the public core of the internet, and started to interweave the international dimension more with defending against cyber-attacks. Interestingly, international standardisation also got a place. The EU also expressed opposition to a new UN-level cybercrime treaty given that the Budapest Convention on Cybercrime is already well-established—nevertheless, the UN is now negotiating this for a new global treaty. One of the signals that the EU and like-minded partners appear to have to concede internationally is some ground to China, Russia and non-aligned countries.

The Council upped the ante, driven by increased geopolitical tensions and the war against Ukraine, by adopting 2022 Conclusions on cyber posture (Council of the European Union, 2022). The wording also shows the concern about the erosion of international law and rules-based international order. Perhaps a reason is also that coordination in cyber matters had moved in the Council to the Horizontal Working Party, even if individual internal market-based (Art 114 TFEU) or industry-based (Art 173 TFEU) files such as NIS2, CRA, and CSOLA continued to be negotiated in the Telecommunications Council Working Party.

Bibliography

Berger, P. L., & Luckmann, T. (1966). *The social construction of reality*. Doubleday.

Bickerton, C., Brack, N., Coman, R., & Crespy, A. (2022, June). Conflicts of sovereignty in contemporary Europe: A framework of analysis. *Comparative European. Politics, 20*(3), 257–274.

Biersteker, T. (2012). State, sovereignty and territory. In I. W. Carlsnaes, T. Risse, & B. A. Simmons (Eds.), *Handbook of international relations*. SAGE Publications Ltd.

Bijlagen.nos.nl. (2024, May 1). *Joint Statement of Scientists and Researchers on EU's New Proposal for the Child Sexual Abuse Regulation,* The Mayan 2, 2024. Retrieved from https://bijlagen.nos.nl/artikel-20171517/Open_Letter_CSA_v2.pdf

Bozhkov, N. (2020, March 9). *China's cyber diplomacy: A primer*. EU Cyber Direct. https://eucyberdirect.eu/research/chinas-cyber-diplomacy-a-primer

Bradford, A. (2020). *The Brussels effect: How the European Union rules the world*. Oxford University Press.

Bradford, A. (2023). *Digital empires: The global Battle to regulate technology*. Oxford University Press.

Council of the European Union. (2022, May 23). *Cyber posture: Council approves conclusions*. https://www.consilium.europa.eu/en/press/press-releases/2022/05/23/cyber-posture-council-approves-conclusions/

Council of the European Union. (2022a, May 16). *Cyber-attacks: Council extends sanctions regime until 18 May 2025*. https://www.consilium.europa.eu/en/press/press-releases/2022/05/16/cyber-attacks-council-extends-sanctions-regime-until-18-may-2025/

Council of the European Union. (2023, May 13). *Anti-money laundering: Council adopts rules which will make crypto-asset transfers traceable*. https://www.consilium.europa.eu/en/press/press-releases/2023/05/16/anti-money-laundering-council-adopts-rules-which-will-make-crypto-asset-transfers-traceable/

Council of the European Union. (2024, June 5). *Council approval of conclusions on the future of cybersecurity*. https://ccb.belgium.be/en/news/council-approval-conclusions-future-cybersecurity

EEAS. (2023, February 12). *Cybersecurity*. https://www.eeas.europa.eu/eeas/cybersecurity_en

ENISA. (2017, May 15). *WannaCry ransomware: First ever case of cyber cooperation at EU level*. https://www.enisa.europa.eu/news/enisa-news/wannacry-ransomware-first-ever-case-of-cyber-cooperation-at-eu-level

ENISA. (2022, November 11). *Cybersecurity threats fast-forward 2030: Fasten your Security-Belt before the ride!* Press Release. https://www.enisa.europa.eu/news/cybersecurity-threats-fast-forward-2030

ENISA. (2022a, January 21). *Log4j Vulnerability—Update from the CSIRTs Network*. https://www.enisa.europa.eu/news/enisa-news/log4j-vulnerability-update-from-the-csirts-network

ENISA. (2023, October 19). *ENISA threat landscape 2023, report/study*. https://www.enisa.europa.eu/publications/enisa-threat-landscape-2023

ENISA. (2024, March 27). *Foresight cybersecurity threats for 2030—Update 2024*. https://www.enisa.europa.eu/publications/foresight-cybersecurity-threats-for-2030-update-2024.

ENISA. (2024a). *Artificial Intelligence (AI)*. https://www.enisa.europa.eu/topics/iot-and-smart-infrastructures/artificial_intelligence

European Commission. (2017, September 14). *Commission staff working document assessment of the EU 2013 cybersecurity strategy*. https://data.consilium.europa.eu/doc/document/ST-12210-2017-INIT/en/pdf

European Commission. (2017a, September 13). *Commission recommendation on coordinated response to large scale cybersecurity incidents and crises and its annex ('blueprint for coordinated response')*. https://eur-lex.europa.eu/eli/reco/2017/1584/oj

European Commission. (2020, December 16). *Impact assessment proposal for directive on measures for high common level of cybersecurity across the union*. Shaping Europe's Digital Future. https://digital-strategy.ec.europa.eu/en/library/impact-assessment-proposal-directive-measures-high-common-level-cybersecurity-across-union

European Commission. (2020a). *FDI screening|DG TRADE*. https://trade.ec.europa.eu/access-to-markets/en/content/fdi-screening

European Commission. (2023, June 20). *An EU approach to enhance economic security*. https://ec.europa.eu/commission/presscorner/detail/en/IP_23_3358

European Commission. (2024, September 24). *Online platforms report on measures to protect European election integrity under the code of practice on disinformation*. https://digital-strategy.ec.europa.eu/en/news/online-platforms-report-measures-protect-european-election-integrity-under-code-practice

European Commission. (2024a, January 26). *New tools to reinforce the EU'S economic security—European Commission*. https://commission.europa.eu/news/new-tools-reinforce-eus-economic-security-2024-01-24_en

European Commission. (2024b, May 22). *Eurobarometer survey confirms EU must reinforce cybersecurity*. Shaping Europe's Digital Future. https://digital-strategy.ec.europa.eu/en/news/eurobarometer-survey-confirms-eu-must-reinforce-cybersecurity-skills

European Commission. (2024c, April 30). *NIS cooperation group|shaping Europe's digital future*. https://digital-strategy.ec.europa.eu/en/policies/nis-cooperation-group

European Commission. (2024d, February 2). *Commission publishes its annual union work programme on European standardisation for 2024*. https://single-market-economy.ec.europa.eu/news/commission-publishes-its-annual-union-work-programme-european-standardisation-2024-2024-02-02_en

European Commission. (2024e, April 23). *The European quantum communication infrastructure (EuroQCI) initiative*. Shaping Europe's Digital Future. https://digital-strategy.ec.europa.eu/en/policies/european-quantum-communication-infrastructure-euroqci

European Commission. (2024f, April 11). *Commission publishes recommendation on post-quantum cryptography*. Shaping Europe's Digital Future. https://digital-strategy.ec.europa.eu/en/news/commission-publishes-recommendation-post-quantum-cryptography

European Commission & EEAS. (2022, November 10). *Cyber Defence: EU boosts action against cyber threats*. Shaping Europe's Digital Future. https://digital-strategy.ec.europa.eu/en/news/cyber-defence-eu-boosts-action-against-cyber-threats

European Defence Agency. (2024, April 27). *Coordinated Annual Review on Defence (CARD)*. https://eda.europa.eu/what-we-do/EU-defence-initiatives/coordinated-annual-review-on-defence-(card)

European Parliament. (2015, June 29). *Cyber diplomacy: EU dialogue with third countries*. Think Tank. https://www.europarl.europa.eu/thinktank/en/document/EPRS_BRI(2015)564374.

European Union. (2019). *Regulation (EU) 2019/881 of the European Parliament and of the council of 17 April 2019 on ENISA (the European Union Agency for cybersecurity) and on information and communications technology cybersecurity certification and repealing regulation (EU) no 52*. https://eur-lex.europa.eu/eli/reg/2019/881/oj

European Union. (2021). *Regulation (EU) 2021/887 of the European Parliament and of the council of 20 may 2021 establishing the European cybersecurity industrial, technology and research competence Centre and the network of National Coordination Centres*. https://eur-lex.europa.eu/eli/reg/2021/887/oj

European Union. (2022). *Directive (EU) 2022/2557 of the European Parliament and of the council of 14 December 2022 on the resilience of critical entities and repealing council directive 2008/114/EC*. https://eur-lex.europa.eu/eli/dir/2022/2557/oj

Europol. (2024). *Programming document*. https://www.europol.europa.eu/publications-events/publications/europol-programming-document

Europol. (2024a). *Joint declaration of the European police chiefs on E2EE: European police chiefs call for industry and government to take action against end-to-end encryption roll out*. https://www.europol.europa.eu/media-press/newsroom/news/european-police-chiefs-call-for-industry-and-governments-to-take-action-against-end-to-end-encryption-roll-out

Floridi, L. (2020, September). The fight for digital sovereignty: What it is, and why it matters, especially for the EU. *Philosophy & Technology, 33*(3), 369–378.

Fratini, S., Hine, E., Novelli, C., Roberts, H., & Floridi, L. (2024, April 21). *Digital sovereignty: A descriptive analysis and a critical evaluation of existing models*. SSRN Scholarly Paper.

Frontier Economics. (2023). *Assessing-the-economic-cost-of-Eu-initiatives-on-cybersecurity*. https://www.frontier-economics.com/media/izyk5rgz/assessing-the-economic-cost-of-eu-initiatives-on-cybersecurity.pdf

Herzberg, F., Mausner, B., & Snyderman, B. (1959). *The motivation to work*. John Wiley.

Hofmann, H. C. (2020). *Between discretion and proportionality: The duty of care in EU judicial review*. SSRN Scholarly Paper.

Kello, L. (2017). *The virtual weapon and international order*. Yale University Press.

Kroet, C. (2024, September 27). *Cyber certificate debate to land on plate of incoming commission*. Euronews. https://www.euronews.com/next/2024/09/27/cyber-certificate-debate-to-land-on-plate-of-incoming-tech-commissioner

Leonard, M. (2021). *The age of Unpeace: How connectivity causes conflict*. Bantam Press.

Letta, E. (2024). *Much more than a market—Speed, security, solidarity. Empowering the SIngle market to deliver a sustainable future and prosperity for all EU citizens*. European Commission.

Leyen, U. (2024, September 17). *Commissioners-designate (2024–2029) Mission letters—European Commission*. https://commission.europa.eu/document/3b537594-9264-4249-a912-5b102b7b49a3_en

Lyons, J. (2024, March 20). *Five eyes issue another China volt typhoon warning*. https://www.theregister.com/2024/03/20/five_eyes_volt_typhoon/

Matthews, L. J., Lee, M., De Bruhl, B. F., Elinoff, D., & Eusebi, C. A. (2024, January 2). *Plagues, cyborgs, and Supersoldiers: The human domain of war*. RAND Corporation. https://www.rand.org/pubs/research_reports/RRA2520-1.html

Monterie, A. (2024, April 23). *Ondanks verfijndere cyberaanvallen weinig besef van risico's*. Computable.nl: https://www.computable.nl/2024/04/23/ondanks-verfijndere-cyberaanvallen-weinig-besef-van-risicos/

Murphy, B. (2022, May). *Chokepoints—China's self-identified strategic technology import dependencies*. Center for Security and Emerging Technology. https://cset.georgetown.edu/publication/chokepoints/

Pupillo, L., Ferreira, A., Lipiainen, V., & Polito, C. (2023, December 6). CEPS. https://www.ceps.eu/ceps-publications/quantum-technologies-and-cybersecurity/

Rathbone, J. P., Jones, S., & Milme, R. (2024, May 5). *Russia plotting sabotage across Europe, intelligence agencies warn*. Financial Times. https://www.ft.com/content/c88509f9-c9bd-46f4-8a5c-9b2bdd3c3dd3

Rodriguez, A. G. (2023, July 17). *A quantum cybersecurity agenda for Europe: Governing the transition to post-quantum cryptography*. European Policy Centre. https://www.epc.eu/en/Publications/A-quantum-cybersecurity-agenda-for-Europe~526b9c

Rodrik, D. (2023, November 7). *Doing economic nationalism the right way|by Dani Rodrik*. Project Syndicate: https://www.project-syndicate.org/commentary/east-asian-model-vindicates-economic-nationalism-by-dani-rodrik-2023-11

Rupp, C. (2024, June 27). https://www.interface-eu.org/publications/navigating-the-eu-cybersecurity-policy-ecosystem.

Tiik, E. (2020, March 4). *International law in cyberspace: Mind the gap. EU Cyber Direct*. https://eucyberdirect.eu/research/international-law-in-cyberspace-mind-the-gap

Timmers, P. (2018, September 2). The European Union's cybersecurity industrial policy. *Journal of Cyber Policy, 2*(2), 363–384.

Timmers, P. (2020, October 13). *When sovereignty leads and cyber law follows*. https://directionsblog.eu/when-sovereignty-leads-and-cyber-law-follows/

Timmers, P. (2020a, January 24). There will be no global 6G unless we resolve sovereignty concerns in 5G governance. *Nature. Electronics, 3*(1), 10–12.

Timmers, P. (2022, December 12). *Digital industrial policy for Europe*. CERRE. https://cerre.eu/publications/digital-industrial-policy-for-europe/

Timmers, P. (2022a). *The technological construction of sovereignty*. Springer.

Timmers, P. (2024). Telecoms resilience and security. In R. Feasey, A. de Streel, P. Alexiadis, M. Bourreau, M. Cave, I. Godlovitch, et al. (Eds.), *The future of European telecommunications: In-depth analysis* (pp. 118–165). CERRE.

Timmers, P., & Dezeure, F. (2021). *Strategic autonomy and cybersecurity in The Netherlands|cyber security council*. Cyber Security Council. https://www.cybersecuritycouncil.nl/documents/reports/2021/02/17/report-strategic-autonomy-and-cybersecurity-in-the-netherlands

Timmers, P., Punter, M., & Stolwijk, C. (2024). *Cybersecurity and digital sovereignty—Bridging the gaps*. TNO.

United Nations. (2024, February 25). *Global cybercrime treaty: A delicate balance between security and human rights*. UN News. https://news.un.org/en/interview/2024/02/1146772

VDE. (2024, February 5). *Mehr Resilienz für die Strom- und Kommunikationsnetze in Deutschland*. VDE. https://www.vde.com/de/etg/arbeitsgebiete/v2/mehr-resilienz-fuer-die-strom%2D%2Dund-kommunikationsnetze-in-deutschland

Wax, E. (2024, January 10). *Trump vowed he'd 'never' help Europe if it's attacked, top EU official says*. Politico. https://www.politico.eu/article/donald-trump-vow-never-help-europe-attack-thierry-breton/

Wikipedia. (2024). *Dot-com bubble*. https://en.wikipedia.org/wiki/Dot-com_bubble.

Wikipedia. (2024a). *Colonial pipeline ransomware attack*. https://en.wikipedia.org/wiki/Colonial_Pipeline_ransomware_attack

CHAPTER 9

Media Policy in the Digital Space

Anna Herold and Sabina Tsakova

Introduction

The media environment has been rapidly evolving in the last ten years. With digital technologies, media services can be increasingly accessed across borders and through various means, while competition in the digital media space is becoming more and more international (COM(2022) 457 final, 2022). Today, consumption of media content takes place increasingly online, on a variety of devices that people use daily, including when travelling. This is particularly true for the younger generations, who shy away from the traditional television sets (COM(2016) 287 final, 2016c). Streaming services by big US players dominate entertainment, while non-EU video-sharing platforms and

Disclaimer: The information and views set out in this chapter are those by the authors and do not necessarily reflect the official opinion of the European Commission.

A. Herold (✉) · S. Tsakova
European Commission, Brussels, Belgium
e-mail: Anna.herold@ec.europa.eu

S. Tsakova
e-mail: Sabina.tsakova@ec.europa.eu

T. Kleiner and A. Garcia Rodriguez (eds.), *The Making of a Global Digital Rulebook*, https://doi.org/10.1007/978-981-95-9226-5_9

social media are the main sources of news, often polarised and not credible at times. At the same time, online platforms act as gateways for access to media content as a core of their business models without properly remunerating content creators.

These digital developments pose unprecedented challenges to the European media sector: the need to protect audiences, particularly the young ones, on all distribution channels and platforms, as well as the imperative to foster independent and competitive European media, which are crucial for Europe's democracies, cultures, and economies. All this required a response by the European Union, as a global actor with a strong media industry evolving in a fast-changing media and geopolitical landscape dominated by US digital players. This response included efforts to modernise the legal framework, tailored previously mostly to broadcasting media, as already flagged in 2015 by the Digital Single Market (DSM) Strategy (COM(2015) 192 final, 2015).

Some argue that the EU had been initially timid back in the early 2000s in tackling the media field and proposing a policy approach at the EU level. This reflected, in their opinion, the rather cautious European stance, whereby media regulation should remain the responsibility of Member States (de la Noue, 2023, pp. 5,6). Regulating media at the EU level is characterised by a continued struggle between Member States' interests in governing their media environments and the aims of implementing a single market for media content and services (Broughton Micova, From the Television without Frontiers Directive to the Audiovisual Media Services Directive, 2023). This has, however, changed in the last years through soft law as well as hard law. As this chapter will attempt to demonstrate, the digital revolution, exacerbated by geopolitical events with a profound impact on Europe's democracies, and a clearer confrontation between the interests of EU actors (e.g. copyright holders and publishers) and those of international digital platforms facilitated the emergence of some EU digital sovereignty and allowed the European Union to establish an ambitious and modern internal market framework for media services.

As part of its DSM Strategy back in 2015, the European Commission proposed to revise or modernise two directives that are crucial to Europe's media industry and content creators: the Audiovisual Media Services Directive (AVMSD) and the DSM Copyright Directive (Broughton Micova et al., 2018). Already at the time, digital platforms had caused a watershed moment not only for markets and businesses but also for media. The global internet giants were seen as disruptive because of their control over digital markets, including media content distribution, and their expansive and innovative strategies (Enli et al., 2019).

Then followed the period of the COVID-19 pandemic, which had a notable impact on the EU media industry. While the production of content and cinemas was hit hard, on-demand (streaming) players managed to expand their audiences during this period, potentially accelerating the shift away from traditional broadcasting. Moreover, one could observe a progressive convergence between broadcast and on-demand services, with the so-called FAST channels as an example of quickly developing digital media services (Dillon, 2023).

Last but not least, geopolitical events, in particular, the outbreak of Russia's war of aggression against Ukraine, with the corresponding wave of disinformation and information manipulation through the media, especially online, and worrying developments in the digital media environment across the European Union where access to independent and impartial media content is increasingly questioned, prompted yet another response in the form of a new legal instrument that complemented the EU media law acquis: the recently adopted European Media Freedom Act.

Considering this, this chapter will focus on the European Union's policies in recent years that aim to render digital actors more responsible when they are active in the media environment or deal with media content. The idea is to describe how a common approach for media is required to bring digital actors to the same or comparable regulatory standard in Europe through the adoption of various legislative acts. Starting from the revised AVMSD and the DSM Copyright Directive and culminating in the recently adopted European Media Freedom Act (EMFA) (Regulation (EU) 2024/1083, 2024), this chapter will describe some of the new rules most pertinent in the digital media environment and their potential to further European integration in the field of media policy.

The Revised Audiovisual Media Services Directive: Caring for Audiences Where They Are

The Context

The Television without Frontiers Directive, adopted in 1989 and revised on two occasions, was subject to a further important revision in 2018. Notably, the revised AVMSD extended the scope of the rules to video-sharing platforms, such as YouTube or Facebook, and provided additional rules for on-demand media service providers, such as Netflix or Amazon.

As stressed in the 2016 Commission proposal for a revised AVMSD, the audiovisual media landscape was changing at a rapid pace due to the ever-increasing convergence between television and services distributed via the internet. Consumers increasingly access on-demand content via smart or connected television sets and portable devices. Young consumers tend to watch videos, including user-generated content, on the internet, and new business models are emerging. Broadcasters are extending their activities online, and new players offering audiovisual media content via the internet (both on-demand providers and video-sharing platforms) are getting stronger and competing for the same audiences. At the same time, the Commission pointed out that television broadcasting, video-on-demand and user-generated content were subject to different rules and varying levels of protection for consumers (COM(2016) 287 final, 2016a). The impact assessment accompanying the Commission proposal referred specifically to the insufficient protection of the most vulnerable consumers—minors—and the lack of a level playing field among market players as reasons for the reform. In response, as already made clear in the DSM strategy, the scope of the European audiovisual media rules had to be broadened to encompass new services and players not covered under the Directive so far.

The revised AVMSD aspires to reflect the new media and platform environment (Ranaivoson et al., 2021). In particular, the objective of creating a level playing field with digital players and protecting cultural diversity in light of the presence of big US streamers contributed to a revision of the Directive (Idiz et al., 2021). At the same time, the policy goals of broadening audiovisual regulation at the EU level were not welcomed by everyone: already back in 2007, when the Television without Frontiers Directive was revised, there was fear that it could prevent growth (Valcke & Stevens, 2007); that same concern was voiced during the negotiations of the 2018 revision, with some arguing it could hurt innovation (Idiz et al., 2021). Several years later, these claims do not seem to have been founded, as we can observe from the growth of the digital audiovisual market (SWD(2023) 150 final, 2023, pp. 13, 14, 21).

Strengthening the Promotion of European Works by On-Demand Providers

As regards the promotion of European works, video-on-demand services (streamers) were required to promote European works already under the 2007 AVMSD: this was nonetheless only a general obligation according to which these services were to promote 'where practicable and by appropriate means, the production of and access to European works'.[1]

With the 2018 revision of the Directive, requirements on the promotion of European works for on-demand services were significantly strengthened (Idiz et al., 2021). Under Article 13(1) of AVMSD, on-demand services are now subject to more stringent and specific obligations whereby they need to ensure at least a 30% share of European content (European works) in their catalogues and give good visibility (prominence) to European content in their offers. To take account of the need to innovate in the media sector, the new rules include a mandatory exemption for companies with a low turnover or low audiences. Member States may also decide to waive such obligations where they would be impracticable or unjustified, given the nature or theme of the on-demand service. To foster a consistent approach on how to calculate the 30% share in the on-demand catalogues and how to apply the exemptions, the Commission issued guidelines in July 2020 (2020/C 223/03, 2020).

Overall, strengthening the promotion of European works on on-demand services was seen by the Commission as a way to ensure a broader and more diverse offer for Europeans. It is also seen as having the potential for positively impacting cultural diversity and bringing more opportunities for European creators (European Commission, 2018).

In transposing Article 13(1), most Member States have chosen to implement the general quota of 'at least 30%', with notably France raising

[1] 'Such promotion could relate, *inter alia*, to the financial contribution made by such services to the production and rights acquisition of European works or to the share and/or prominence of European works in the catalogue of programmes offered by the on-demand audiovisual media service' (Directive 2007/65/EC, article 3i).

that threshold to 60% and adding a sub-quota for production in the original language. Regarding the latter, a handful of countries have done the same, such as Italy and Portugal, who have also added other types of sub-quotas. The obligation to ensure the prominence of European works on video-on-demand services has been transposed verbatim in many countries, with no particular obligation regarding the means to do so. Some have, however, chosen to further specify how such prominence should be achieved, be it through the use of an attractive visual presentation—appearing on the platforms' homepages directly or being highlighted from other content in dedicated sections—or through search tools or promotional campaigns (Lacourt et al., 2023, p. 10; SWD(2023) 150 final, 2023, art. 13,16,17; SWD(2024) 149 final, 2024). As regards the effectiveness of prominence obligations, a test carried out in the context of the study commissioned by the Commission, focusing on a sample of on-demand services, found that, on average, 40% of services included dedicated sections on their homepages for European works or works from the targeted country, while 49% of the services analysed offered the option to filter the works present in their catalogue by country or region (SWD(2023) 150 final, 2023).

In addition to the quotas of European works and the prominence obligation, the co-legislators agreed on other provisions allowing for the promotion of European works in the form of financial contributions under Article 13(2) of the revised AVMSD. Where Member States require media service providers under their jurisdiction to contribute financially to the production of European works, either via direct investment in content or contribution to national funds, they may also require media service providers targeting audiences in their territories but established in other EU Member States to make such financial contributions, provided that they are proportionate and non-discriminatory. Such financial contributions shall be based only on the revenues earned in the targeted EU Member States. If the Member State where the provider is established imposes such a financial contribution, it shall take into account any financial contributions imposed by targeted EU Member States.

The impact of the new rules is already felt on the ground: while US works take the lion's share with 49% of works in video-on-demand catalogues, citizens appear to have access to more European works. The share of such works in video-on-demand catalogues reached 32% in 2022 (Grece, 2022). According to an independent study commissioned by the Commission, European works represented, on average, 35% of catalogues in a selection of 21 Member States and Norway across the entire sample of services in 2023 (SWD(2023) 150 final, 2023).

At the same time, some argue that an increase in the supply of European works does not necessarily lead to exposure diversity, given the online context characterised by user autonomy (Idiz et al., 2021). There also seems to be an increased focus on the obligations to invest in local (national) content more than in European content, partly defying some of the intended aims, notably to foster co-productions and content that can travel well across borders (SWD(2023) 150 final, 2023).

While Europe may have been the precursor on this matter, it seems that international partners, such as Canada, have taken inspiration from some of the AVMSD provisions, again intending to encourage strong and sustainable media actors in the digital world. Most recently, the Online Streaming Act imposed obligations, among others, on video-on-demand and social media services to promote Canadian content and to invest in the production of such content (Government of Canada, 2023a, 2023b). In contrast to Canada, the EU has not gone as far as regards the obligations on video-sharing platforms or other social media services, neither regarding the promotion nor the investments in content.

Better Protecting Minors in On-Demand Services

Given the spreading use of digital services, other than television channels, and their consumption by young people, it was key for the revised AVMSD to consider aligning the rules for the protection of minors by on-demand services with the standards already applicable to television broadcasting services in this area (Portela Trigo, 2017).

Previously, Article 12 of the 2010 AVMSD required the Member States to take appropriate measures to ensure that on-demand services which *might seriously impair* the physical, mental or moral development of minors are only made available in such a way as to ensure that minors will not normally hear or see such on-demand services. No restrictions were applied to potentially harmful programmes provided in on-demand services. In contrast, broadcasters could not include seriously harmful programmes (e.g. pornography and strong violence) but could include potentially harmful programmes (e.g. erotic content and mild violence) provided measures were put in place to prevent children from hearing or seeing them (Article 27). This appeared to be no longer justified, given the evolving consumption trends of minors and the consequent need to level up consumer protection and address the potential competitive disadvantage among market players (Directive 2010/13/EU, 2010, p. 9).

Since 2018, the rules regarding on-demand services have been aligned with the standards for television broadcasting: Article 6a now requires Member States to take measures to ensure that any audiovisual media service, regardless of whether programmes are broadcast by television broadcasters or provided by on-demand providers, that *'may impair the physical, mental or moral development of minors is only made available in such a way as to ensure that minors will not normally hear or see it'*. Moreover, it is specified that measures to be taken may include selecting the time of the broadcast, age verification tools or other technical measures. These measures need to be proportionate to the potential harm of the programme. As for the most harmful content, such as gratuitous violence and pornography, it is subject to the strictest measures. Recital 20 provides examples of encryption and effective parental controls as such strict measures.

Moreover, all media service providers, including both broadcasters and streamers, are required to provide sufficient information to viewers about content which may impair the physical, mental, or moral development of minors. Recital 19 specifies that it could be done, for example, through a system of content descriptors, an acoustic warning, a visual symbol or any other means describing the nature of the content.

According to a Commission report, while watersheds continue to be the main tool used for protecting minors in the linear environment, content rating, age verification, and parental control are used in most Member States to prevent children from accessing harmful content on on-demand services. Most Member States have foreseen new systems to describe the potentially harmful nature of the content of audiovisual media services (content descriptors) in line with the new rules in the AVMSD. Those systems are mainly based on visual symbols and acoustic warnings indicating the types of violent content (for instance, violence, sex, fear, alcohol, and drug abuse). In some Member States, visual symbols must be displayed throughout the programme or at least at the start of the programme. In a few Member States, acoustic warnings must precede the programme. In several Member States, the work to implement the rules on content descriptors is still ongoing (European Commission, 2024a, 2024b). This shows that the new rules have proved useful in practice, but more work to consistently protect minors on streamers' services across the EU is needed.

Protecting Viewers on Video-Sharing Platforms

This section will explain the reasons behind the inclusion of video-sharing platforms—services without editorial responsibility (Directive 2010/13/EU, 2010, Article 1(1)b)—within the scope of the AVMSD as a novel approach in a media-regulatory instrument before looking at the content of the new rules.

Already back in 2007, some academics were asking themselves why such actors were forgotten in the debate and considered that there was a certain gap in the legislation (Valcke & Stevens, 2007). The previous—2007—revision was criticised for not having dealt with all the relevant services: while the AVMSD scope was extended then to on-demand services, it was considered insufficient to address the issues raised by several services and activities, such as multimedia services (converging text-based and audiovisual media), distribution activities, user-generated content, and participatory media (Valcke et al., 2008). Many changes occurred following the revision of the AVMSD in 2007, when such platforms were in their infancy. The importance of video-sharing platforms in the audiovisual landscape has grown rapidly over the last 15 years (Broughton Micova, 2023). Nowadays, video-sharing platforms host profitable and managed channels and offer increasingly influential and profitable content, arguably similar to traditional television programmes (Barata, 2018).

These trends and challenges are also reflected in Recitals 45 to 47 of the revised AVMSD, which explain, among others, that video-sharing platforms are increasingly used to access audiovisual media content, in particular by minors, and that they typically determine the organisation of the content, including by automated means or algorithms. The revised Directive brings video-sharing platforms, such as YouTube, into its scope through Articles 28a and 28b. As agreed by the co-legislators, in 2020, the Commission issued guidelines on the definition of video-sharing platform services (2020/C 223/03, 2020). The guidelines clarify the conditions under which "hybrid" services such as social media (for example, X.com), where the provision of videos and programmes is not the principal purpose of the service but still constitutes an "essential functionality" thereof, are covered by the new rules.

To close the loop regarding the online protection of viewers, in particular the young ones, Article 28b requires Member States to ensure that video-sharing platforms protect minors from harmful content and the general public from incitement to violence or hatred (Directive 2010/13/EU, 2010, Article 28b). Member States must also ensure that such platforms protect the general public from content; the dissemination of which constitutes an activity that is a criminal offence under Union law—notably offences concerning child pornography, provocation to commit a terrorist offence, and offences concerning racism and xenophobia. Video-sharing platforms are also subject to comparable advertising standards as those applicable to audiovisual media service providers, e.g. restrictions for certain types of advertising (e.g. for tobacco products, medicinal products/treatments available only on prescription, advertising alcohol to minors, encouraging behaviour prejudicial to health or safety) (Directive 2010/13/EU, 2010, Article 9).

It is for national media regulatory authorities to verify that video-sharing platforms have adopted appropriate measures. These include, first and foremost, revising their terms and conditions to include the regulated categories of content and enforcing them accordingly. Other measures include appropriate flagging and reporting for users regarding content available on the platform, and functionality for users to declare the inclusion of commercial communications in their videos. As regards the protection of minors, such measures include implementing age verification or parental control systems regarding harmful content for minors, as well as content rating mechanisms. It is also specified that the most harmful content shall be subject to the strictest access control measures. The measures also comprise providing media literacy tools for viewers and raising awareness of them.

The inter-institutional negotiations reveal that both co-legislators—the European Parliament and the Council—agreed on the principle of having such services regulated at the EU level. Co-legislators extended the obligations on video-sharing platforms proposed by the Commission, notably about audiovisual commercial communications but also regarding the protection of users from content that constitutes a criminal offence (Woods, 2018). As regards the means of protection, it seems that co-legislators were overall satisfied with the list of measures proposed by the Commission.

Some have criticised the rules on video-sharing platforms, notably because they would allegedly place into the hands of private parties the regulation of freedom of expression (Barata, 2018). Others put forward that these provisions are to be considered as a simple extension of media regulation and have the potential to improve social media governance (Kuklis, 2021). Others still consider that the AVMSD's approach that focuses on accountability for measures by video-sharing platforms and encourages regulatory cooperation should allow building on existing transnational mechanisms, but argue that it seems unlikely to fill information gaps (Kostovska & Broughton Micova, 2013).

In conclusion, we put forward that the revised AVMSD was much needed to ensure that EU media content regulation is adapted to the advanced convergence of audiovisual media services and content and current technological developments. The aims of the Directive—notably to ensure a high degree of protection of consumers and level the playing field among the different services competing for the same audiences—have enabled further European integration by setting certain minimum standards on key services widely watched by viewers today (Götz & Gramsch, 2021).

The Digital Single Market Copyright Directive: Ensuring Fairness for Creators and creative industries

The Context

There was a long ride before the adoption of the Directive on Copyright in the Digital Single Market in April 2019. Having as its leitmotiv the need to 'modernise' EU copyright rules, in place since the 2001 Copyright in the Information Society Directive, the Digital Single Market (DSM) Copyright Directive tackled several key issues for citizens, creators, and creative industries (Valais, 2016). In particular, rapid technological developments continued to transform the way creative works, including media content, are created, produced, distributed, and exploited. New business models and new actors in media content distribution continue to emerge. Updating the rules at the EU level seemed key, given the importance of digital players giving access to copyright-protected content across the European Union.

Recognising the importance of online players in enabling news access, the DSM Copyright Directive introduced a new right for press publishers to be remunerated for the use of newspapers and magazines by online service providers (Article 15). It also introduced new rules which reinforce the position of rightsholders, such as music and film producers, as well as collecting societies acting on their behalf, to negotiate and be remunerated for the online exploitation of their content by user-uploaded content platforms (Article 17). This section will focus on those two provisions—the publishers' right and the so-called "value gap" provision—which aim to level the playing field between press publishers and rightsholders on the one hand and certain online players, in particular, platforms that provide access to their content.

Articles 15 and 17 were certainly among the most controversial provisions discussed during the negotiation of the Directive (Furgal et al., 2020). The copyright directive is regarded as one of the most lobbied pieces of legislation in the EU in recent years (Thaidigsmann, 2019), with claims that Google alone would have spent 30 million euros in lobbying efforts and with strong confrontations between various stakeholders (e.g. Corporate Europe Observatory, 2018). The confrontation was particularly clear between copyright holders and publishers on the one hand and the online actors benefiting from this content for their economic activities. However, the lobbying efforts involved also various other stakeholders, including artists, as well as content providers. The landscape of forces shows this influence of a diversity of stakeholders, providing a non-exhaustive illustration of such forces.

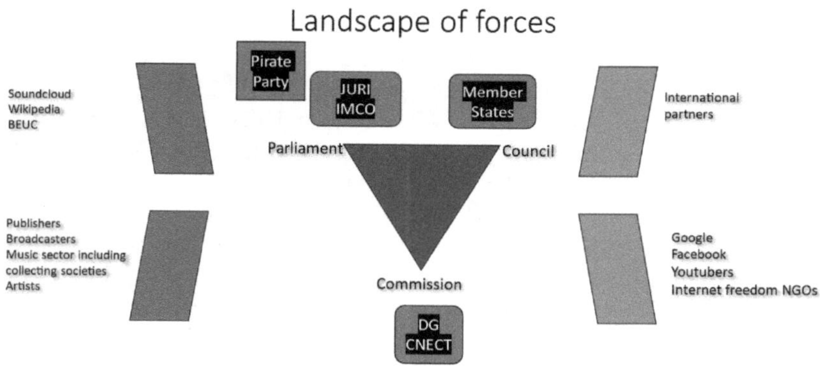

The following sub-sections will describe those new rules and explain the main controversies around those articles and their effects observed so far, including on other jurisdictions. Most interestingly, Max Heermann argues that the success of the EU institutions in adopting the new copyright rules against intense lobbying by online platforms was supported by invoking notions of "digital sovereignty" and by delegitimising heterogeneous lobbying coalitions (Heermann, 2023).

Protecting the Online Uses of Press Publications

Back in 2016, when the Commission proposal was adopted (COM(2016) 593 final, 2016b), the decreasing revenues of publishers and the increased use of news online, in particular through online services or platforms, coupled with advertising competition between publishers and such online players, revealed the need to strengthen the press publishers' bargaining position towards digital intermediaries. The DSM Copyright Directive provided some answers to this by enhancing the protection for publishers' content and their revenues online, but not without several criticisms. Some academics considered that pressing market failures in the online press had to be addressed and made the case in favour of a publisher right (Höppner, 2018). Others argued that a publisher's right was not an appropriate solution to counter the evolution of market realities and the consumption of online news (e.g. Geiger et al., 2017). They considered that such a new, retroactive rule[2] would have an impact on freedom of expression and the freedom of the internet (an intense public debate labelled the new right as a "link tax"), preventing users from freely sharing news online or affecting smaller market players. Still, the EU legislature believed that some answers had to be given to the market developments to help the sector with the challenges it was facing, enhance its sustainability and ultimately foster the availability of reliable information online (Directive (EU) 2019/790, 2019, Recital 55). This led to amending the Commission proposal substantially, nonetheless always to help European publishers by enabling them ultimately to compete with online intermediaries and platforms also for advertising.

According to Article 15(1) of the DSM Copyright Directive, publishers are provided with the rights to reproduce and make available to the public for the online use of their press publications by information society service providers. The concept of "publisher" includes news publishers or news agencies only where they are established in a Member State and have

[2] To note that Article 15, as adopted, and in contrast to the Commission proposal, does not apply to press publications first published before 6 June 2019.

their registered office, central administration or principal place of business within the Union.

At the same time, the new rules guarantee that there would be no impact on the users' ability to share and access information online, a key criticism raised against the proposal during the inter-institutional negotiations (as flagged above). Recital 55 specifies that the right covers only online uses of press publications by information society service providers. Private or non-commercial uses of press publications by individual users are explicitly excluded from the scope. Acts of hyperlinking are explicitly excluded from the scope of the protection, as well as so-called "snippets" (very short extracts) and individual words.

The term of the rights, which was also considered controversial at the time of the Commission proposal (20 years), was reduced to two years from the date of the publication and has no retroactive application. It is also worth noting that the new provision includes a rule whereby Member States shall provide that authors of works incorporated in a press publication receive an appropriate share of the revenues that press publishers receive for the use of their press publications by information society service providers.

More generally, the new rules were narrowed down significantly in the negotiations, which helped them also to go through after the intense legislative process (Furgal et al., 2020).

Regarding the impact of the new regime on the market, already before its transposition into national laws of Member States, licensing deals have been concluded between publishers and digital intermediaries. Further agreements followed, for example, Google reported to have agreements in place covering over 1,500 publications across 15 Member States (Google, 2023). Overall, it is yet too early to measure the overall impact Article 15 has had at the EU level. The review of the DSM Directive taking place no sooner than June 2026 may provide further insights into the impact of this new rule.

Besides its effects in the EU, the adoption of Article 15 inspired or enabled other fora to consider initiatives going in the same direction, i.e. to help counterbalance the relationship between publishers and digital intermediaries, notably due to the loss of advertising revenue for the former. Australia adopted the News Media Bargaining Code in February 2021 (Government of Australia, 2021). This mandatory code of conduct governs the commercial relationships between Australian news businesses and "designated" digital platforms that benefit from a significant bargaining power imbalance. Following the introduction of the code, Google and Facebook (now Meta) have reached voluntary commercial agreements with a significant number of news media organisations (Government of Australia, 2021). Canada followed with the Online News Act in 2023 (Government of Canada, 2023a), which aims to ensure that dominant platforms compensate news businesses when their content is made available on their services. It encourages platforms to reach voluntary commercial agreements with a range of news businesses, and in the absence of such agreements, the Act provides for a mandatory bargaining process (Government of Canada, 2023a). The law is portrayed as "intended to help Canadian news organisations reach fair commercial agreements with the largest online platforms, such as search engines and social media sites" (Government of Canada, 2024).

Addressing the Value Gap

Article 17 of the DSM Copyright Directive aims to solve what has been labelled as a 'value gap' between certain online services giving access to user-uploaded content and rightsholders: in practice, the latter faced difficulties when seeking to monetise and control the distribution of their content online, and there was a growing concern about the sharing of the value generated by online content distribution (Madiega, 2019). This is certainly one of the provisions which has given rise to intense scholarly debate due to its complexity and controversies throughout the adoption and beyond. Some call this provision "the knottiest of Gordian knots", a complex provision within a complex piece of legislation (Hyland & Perry, 2023). Others see it as a provision which, instead of enhancing copyright protection for rightsholders, would level down this protection and allow platforms to escape from liability (Gautier, 2020).

Given the complexity of this provision and the difficulty of finding a compromise which would also take into account the views of the various stakeholders (including rightsholders from the various sectors, users, and platforms), the co-legislators agreed to an obligation for the Commission to issue Guidance on the application of Article 17.[3] The Guidance

[3] See Article 17(10), which requires the Commission to issue guidance on the application of Article 17, regarding the cooperation between online content-sharing service providers and rightsholders.

adopted in June 2021 (European Commission 2021, COM/2021/288 final) aimed to support Member States in their transposition of this article as well as to assist market players when implementing it in practice. Finally, following the adoption of the Directive, Poland submitted a request for annulment of Article 17 before the Court of Justice but has not succeeded in its endeavour (Republic of Poland v European Parliament and Council of the European Union, 2022).

Article 17 applies to online content-sharing service providers, which are defined as a provider of an information society service whose main purpose is to store and give the public access to a large amount of copyright-protected works or other protected subject matter uploaded by its users, which it organises and promotes for profit-making purposes (Directive (EU) 2019/790, 2019, Article 2.6) The definition excludes several services, such as not-for-profit online encyclopaedias (Directive (EU) 2019/790, 2019, Article 17.6).

The EU legislature considered that, because in recent years the functioning of the online content market has gained in complexity and that content-sharing services providing access to a large amount of copyright-protected content have become a main source of access to content online, it was necessary to provide for a specific liability mechanism in respect of the providers of those services to foster the development of a fair licensing market between rightsholders and those service providers. Article 17(1) is clear in this respect when it states that authorisation has to be obtained by an online content-sharing service provider which is considered to perform an act of communication to the public or an act of making available to the public when it gives the public access to copyright-protected works or other protected subject matter uploaded by its users. In such cases, Article 14 of the E-commerce Directive setting out a limitation of liability for certain online players is not applicable.

If an authorisation has not been obtained by the service provider, then Article 17(4) kicks in.[4] The online service will need in that case to demonstrate that it made best efforts (i) to obtain an authorisation and (ii) to ensure, by high industry standards of professional diligence, the unavailability of specific works and other protected subject matter for which the rightsholders have provided the service providers with the relevant and

[4] For example, some rightsholders notably from the audiovisual industry were not keen to give authorisation for the use of their content as they want to retain control over this dissemination.

necessary information; and (iii) in any event that it acted expeditiously, upon receiving a sufficiently substantiated notice from the rightsholders to disable access to, or to remove from their websites, the notified works or other protected subject matter, and did their best to prevent their future uploads by point (ii).[5]

One important aspect which was intensely debated during the negotiations concerned the impact of the new provision on users of online services (Furgal et al., 2020). Article 17(7) is clear on the fact that the cooperation between online content-sharing service providers and rightsholders should not result in the prevention of the availability of works or other protected subject matter uploaded by users who do not infringe copyright and related rights, including where such works or other protected subject matter are covered by an exception or limitation. That provision lists those exceptions and limitations on which users in each Member State must be able to rely. The CJEU, in the context of the Polish challenge of the article, was clear that this paragraph prescribes a specific result to be achieved and is not only a best-effort obligation (Republic of Poland v European Parliament and Council of the European Union, 2022, paragraph 78).

As is the case with such complex provisions with potential impacts on several stakeholders, Article 17 did not escape, even in its final version, from certain criticisms at the time of adoption (e.g. some Member States even voted against and a few abstained) (Hirche, 2019). Nonetheless, several years later, some consider that the predicted negative impacts of Article 17 on freedom of expression and other user rights have not materialised, with any overblocking of content being only marginal (Keller, 2024). While licensing agreements have been concluded by platforms, it is still too early to reflect on the full impact Article 17 has had on solving the value gap. The DSM Directive review mentioned earlier may provide an opportunity to understand how this article has performed in practice.

[5] An exception was made for new online services available for less than 3 years with an annual turnover below 10 million euros, which did not have to comply with the second condition—see Article 17(6).

The European Media Freedom Act: Safeguarding Free and Independent Media Online

The path to the adoption of the European Media Freedom Act (EMFA) (Regulation (EU) 2024/1083, 2024) was certainly not a walk in the park. But what was considered initially by some as impossible to achieve, in the end, became a rather unique and strong instrument advancing the internal market for media and protecting EU values of media freedom and pluralism in an increasingly digital media environment. This section will first provide a brief overview of the context leading to the adoption of the European Media Freedom Act proposal by the Commission in 2022. It will also discuss specifically several provisions relevant to media content in the digital environment.

The Context

The debate over the extent of regulation of media at the EU level has been the source of many academic debates. As a sector where the economic aspects are underpinned by cultural ones, the media sector holds a special place, as media companies are not like other market players (Leyen, 2021). Media play a role in safeguarding freedom of expression and enabling people to exercise their right to seek and receive information (Council of Europe, 2013). Member States have traditionally held the primary responsibility for safeguarding media freedom and pluralism. Nonetheless, the political and academic debate has been revolving over the need for a coordinated approach at the EU level (Brogi et al., 2023). Several attempts to regulate at the EU level some of the conditions for the functioning of the media in the internal market were unsuccessful in the late 1990s and the beginning of the 2000s. Instead, a soft law approach was followed in the form of risk assessments. In 2013, the European Centre for Media Pluralism and Freedom (ECMPF) conducted a pilot test implementation of the Media Pluralism Monitor Tool (MPM). The MPM, applied regularly since then, has been key to identifying potential risks to media pluralism in the European Union and providing support to policy and rulemaking processes.

It was only in 2021, in the context of the State of the Union speech, that the President of the Commission announced the preparation of a European Media Freedom Act (EMFA). The moment was ripe for such an initiative, given the worrying trends concerning media pluralism and media freedom at the national level—notably the ones identified in the context of the rule of law reports of the Commission—but also, more generally, the risks to fundamental rights and the rise of disinformation.

Academics note that the EMFA is an ambitious project, giving more control power to the EU (de la Noue, 2023). During the inter-institutional negotiations, some Member States had raised doubts about the use of Article 114 TFEU as the legal basis of the EMFA Regulation. Underpinning such considerations were also doubts about the regulation of certain aspects of media policy at the EU level.

This chapter will not analyse such discussions on the division of competencies at the Member State and EU level—nonetheless, it is important to note a certain evolution in the Union's media policy aimed at further integration by setting certain principles at the EU level. This integration is particularly felt when it comes to objectives related to the relationship between media and digital actors. Already back in 2011, the Council of Europe's Committee of Ministers made a Recommendation in which it referred to the variety of online intermediaries and platforms as being 'essential' for digital media's outreach and access to media by people (Council of Europe, 2013). In 2022, the Council of Europe underlined the heavy dependence of media on platforms. In this light, the EMFA could not avoid looking at how to bring media in line with the digital realities and equip them—and media users—with certain tools given future sustainability and better access to media diversity online, ultimately furthering the level playing field with digital players.

In this context, this chapter will focus on EMFA's provisions which are of relevance in the digital environment. First, it will explain the safeguards that EMFA put in place to ensure the free provision of media content on online platforms (Regulation (EU) 2024/1083, 2024, Article 18). Secondly, it will focus on guarantees provided by EMFA to users of devices or digital interfaces which give access to their media offers (Regulation (EU) 2024/1083, 2024, Article 18, Article 20). Thirdly, it will shed light on the new provisions for online audience measurement (Regulation (EU) 2024/1083, 2024, Article 24). Lastly, it will briefly explain the new framework for the assessment of media market concentrations and their relevance for online platforms (Regulation (EU) 2024/1083, 2024, Article 23).

Safeguards for Media Content on Very Large Online Platforms

Before diving into the discussion on Article 17 of the Commission proposal (now Article 18 of the Regulation), a side note on the Digital Services Act ('DSA') adopted in 2022 (Regulation (EU) 2022/2065, 2022) is in order. The reference to the new digital rulebook is needed to give some context regarding the discussions on the moderation of media content that took place before the adoption of the EMFA proposal.

The DSA requires online platforms, when moderating content, to pay due consideration to the impact on media freedom and pluralism that results from the implementation of their terms of service.[6] Article 14(4) of the DSA states that Providers of intermediary services shall act in a diligent, objective, and proportionate manner in applying and enforcing the restrictions referred to in paragraph 1, with due regard to the rights and legitimate interests of all parties involved, including the fundamental rights of the recipients of the service, such as the freedom of expression, freedom and pluralism of the media, and other fundamental rights and freedoms as enshrined in the Charter (Regulation (EU) 2022/2065, 2022, Recital 47). This provision appears to be the result of a compromise found between the co-legislators, where heated discussions took place due to certain proposals, such as a so-called 'media exemption' (which was ultimately not agreed upon) (Bujis, 2022). These debates were based on the one hand on the premise that media content has a special value and is time-sensitive, meaning that a content piece taken down for several hours has a real implication for freedom of expression and freedom of information; on the other hand, it was argued that a possible media exemption might bear risks of spreading disinformation online.

With Article 18 of EMFA, the objective of the Commission was to give more reassurance to media complying with journalistic standards and using very large online platforms for the distribution of their content. The underlying idea was to provide media that are subject to regulatory requirements or self- or co-regulatory mechanisms and that are editorially independent with some safeguards that their content will not be removed without prior information. Moreover, if the content were to be removed,

[6] Moreover, under Article 34 (b) of the DSA, VLOPs are required to assess systemic risks, notably any actual or foreseeable negative effects for the exercise of fundamental rights, in particular freedom of expression and information, including freedom and pluralism of the media, enshrined in Article 11 of the Charter.

the media have the advantage of a priority treatment of their complaints and the possibility to engage in a dialogue with very large online platforms in case of frequent restrictions or suspensions.

Article 18 became quite quickly one of the most discussed provisions of the proposal, with opposing views both inside the Council and among parliamentary groups in the Parliament. For some, in particular, those attached to the 'internet freedom' (Regulation (EU) 2024/1083, 2024), the disinformation community and online platforms themselves, it was important to keep the status quo and avoid providing further safeguards to media beyond the general rules applicable under the DSA. Others, in particular media freedom proponents, media regulators and media players themselves, considered that even stronger safeguards than those provided by the proposal are needed to ensure media pluralism in the digital realm and curb the platforms' reliance on terms and conditions (European Parliament, 2023).

Ultimately, the proposal of the Commission was reinforced in several aspects: first, the conditions for the self-declaration by media were strengthened—to ensure that only media that are editorially independent, transparent on their ownership and subject to regulatory requirements or self- or co-regulatory mechanism can rely on the new rules. Also, an opinion-making role was given to the newly created Board for Media Services in the case of repeated restrictions or suspensions of the content posted by media. Moreover, and perhaps more importantly, the safeguards for the reputable media service providers were reinforced by (i) providing them with the possibility not only to be informed before any suspension of their content but also before any restriction of visibility, as well as (ii) by requiring that very large online platforms provide the media with a possibility to reply within 24 hours, or a shorter period in the context of a crisis as referred to in the DSA (Bertuzzi, 2023). During that period, the content would remain online. This does not capture any content, however—the co-legislators agreed that this would not apply as regards illegal content on very large online platforms but also when it comes to the compliance of such platforms with their obligations to mitigate systemic risks under the DSA or the protection of minors under Article 28b of the AVMSD.

The impact of that provision—applicable as of August 2025—remains to be seen. Nonetheless, the EU's determination to tackle this topic certainly had the aim of bringing more balance to the relationship between media and platforms. It is also a question of principle so that platforms not only mitigate systemic risks but also take a proactive approach to keep legal media content online for the benefit of their users.

Guarantees for Users of Devices or User Interfaces Giving Access to Media Offers

Another topic of key importance for the sustainability of the media sector is the right to customise the media offering. Article 20 of EMFA is meant to facilitate access to European media services by users who should be able 'to change, at any time, in a simple, easily accessible and user-friendly manner, the configuration, including default settings, of a device, such as a remote control, or of a user interface controlling or managing access to and the use of media services providing programmes' (Recital 57). In practice, what this right implies for manufacturers, developers, and importers of such devices or user interfaces is to put in place a functionality allowing users to customise their devices and user interfaces, giving access to media offerings and thereby not only relying on pre-defined or pre-installed applications, for example, on smart television sets.

The safeguard provided in Article 20 was meant to ensure that consumers can choose the content they want to watch or listen to according to their preferences and not only according to default settings (which are often the result of commercial agreements for content prioritisation) (Regulation (EU) 2024/1083, 2024, Recital 57). In this way, not only the freedom of users to access the broadest possible variety of media content is preserved, but also the continuous availability and findability of European media offers are facilitated to the benefit of greater media pluralism in a digital environment.

Increasing the Transparency in Measuring Audience Shares

Audience measurement, which consists of collection, interpretation or processing of information about the use of media content, including content shared by users on online platforms—that are primarily used to access such content—has a profound impact on advertising strategies and the related revenues for media. Media service providers rely on audience measurement to assess the performance of their content and make sure that their media and advertising activities are fairly remunerated (Ognjanov & Mitic, 2019).

In the offline world, audience measurement methodologies were often developed and agreed upon by industry standards within self-regulatory organisations like the Joint Industry Committees (Ognjanov & Mitic, 2019). With the proliferation of online platforms, audience measurement systems have also developed outside self-regulatory approaches. The latter tend to be used by certain online players, including online platforms, that self-measure or provide their proprietary audience measurement systems to the market without abiding by the commonly agreed industry standards or best practices.

Hence, one of the EMFA's objectives was to ensure more transparency in the market to ensure that, notably, platforms, as any other provider of audience measurement systems, abide by certain principles to foster the ability for media and advertisers to make informed choices.[7] In addition to being transparent to media on the methodologies used by their audience measurement systems (an obligation that has been featured in the Commission proposal already), the inter-institutional negotiations led to an additional obligation for proprietary audience measurement—for example, systems used by certain online platforms, some of which are main ways for consumption of media content today and compete with the media whose content they distribute—to provide to media, upon their request, with information on audience measurement results relating to their media content and media services (Regulation (EU) 2024/1083, 2024, Article 24.2).

Overall, the provisions on audience measurement are meant to ensure transparency in the media market, which is key considering the impact such measurement has on the media's revenues and potential for growth. Indirectly, those provisions are meant to bring about a more level playing field among actors who compete for advertising revenues, where audience measurement providers are also intermediaries involved in content distribution.

[7] Under Article 24(1) of EMFA, providers of audience measurement systems are required to "ensure that their audience measurement systems and the methodology used by their audience measurement systems comply with the principles of transparency, impartiality, inclusiveness, proportionality, non-discrimination, comparability and verifiability".

Assessing Media Market Concentrations in the Digital Era

Articles 22 and 23 of EMFA set out a minimum harmonisation framework for the assessment of certain media market concentrations from a media pluralism perspective. Concretely, this entails that Member States (through their media regulators) should assess media market concentrations that could have a significant impact on media pluralism and editorial independence (see Article 22(1)). The text specifies that this assessment is distinct from any relevant competition assessment.

These provisions will, in the future, ensure that a media pluralism test is conducted by Member States for certain key media market concentrations. In this way, the likely impact of EMFA is to avert certain instances of risk to media pluralism, for example, through the adoption of commitments from the companies involved in such a transaction, also considering the criterion of economic sustainability in the absence of the merger. The Board for Media Services (composed of national media regulators) will have an important role to play by assisting its members through opinion-making, where a concentration is likely to affect the functioning of the internal market.

During the negotiations, the notion of media market concentration evolved to capture not only a concentration involving at least one media service provider (as in the Commission proposal) but also a concentration involving at least one provider of an online platform providing access to media content. This amendment was suggested by the European Parliament to ensure that this rule would also capture the impacts that online platforms could have on media pluralism, which was seen as ensuring that EMFA would be future-proof. Awaiting evidence that these provisions show their impact on the ground, certain academics commended EMFA's provisions in this area, noting, however, that there is still room for improvement in how EU regulations tackle the issues of dependence on and the power of platforms amidst the rising trend of media concentration (Helberger et al., 2024).

Conclusion

This chapter has shown how active the European Union has been in the last ten years in regulating the increasingly digital media information space. Stepping up its efforts in this area has been a priority, highlighting increasing digital sovereignty. It was the result of the fast paced trends in the digital environment, with a strong position taken by several global online platforms in various key areas for citizens, including enabling access to media content. More generally, it was also a consequence of worrying developments in Europe's information space and democracies, such as the rise of disinformation. The EU has been tireless in providing workable solutions—often consisting of guidance and minimum harmonisation and coordination of national approaches, including via the EU network of national regulators—always navigating between the Member States' interest in the sensitive field of media policy and the imperative to provide pan-EU answers to increasingly digital and thus transnational challenges to media freedom and pluralism. Injecting a certain degree of level playing field through regulation has been necessary and has also set an example for other jurisdictions. This move was also key from a geopolitical point of view: to show the world that strong media and creative industries are not left alone in Europe, in particular in a world of evolving consumption trends and growing disinformation. More generally, such regulation could not be done only on a country-by-country basis: regulating the information space in a more globalised manner has been the proper way forward and, hopefully, will also be a successful one.

References

Barata, J. (2018, October 24). *The new audiovisual media services directive: turning video hosting platforms into private media regulatory bodies*. Retrieved from Center for Internet and Society: https://cyberlaw.stanford.edu/blog/2018/10/new-audiovisual-media-services-directive-turning-video-hosting-platforms-private-media/

Bertuzzi, L. (2023, October 26). *First compromises and tension points emerge in EU's media law negotiations*. Retrieved from Euractiv: https://www.euractiv.com/section/media/news/first-compromises-and-tension-points-emerge-in-eus-media-law-negotiations/

Brogi, E., Borges, D., Carlini, R., Nenadic, I., Bleyer-Simon, K., Kermer, J., Reviglio, U., Trevisan, M., & Verza, S. (2023, July). *The European media freedom act: Media freedom, freedom of expression and pluralism*. Retrieved from European Parliament: https://www.europarl.europa.eu/RegData/etudes/STUD/2023/747930/IPOL_STU(2023)747930_EN.pdf

Broughton Micova, S. (2023). From the television without frontiers directive to the audiovisual media services directive. In H. Ranaivoson, S. Broughton Micova & T. Raats (Eds.), *European audiovisual policy in transition*. Routledge.

Broughton Micova, S., Hempel, F., & Jacques, S. (2018). Protecting Europe's content production from US giants. *Journal of Media Law, 10*(2).

Bujis, D. (2022). *The digital services act and the implications for news media and journalistic content (Part 1).* Retrieved from DSA Observatory: https://dsa-observatory.eu/2022/09/29/digital-services-act-implications-for-news-media-journalistic-content-part-1/

Corporate Europe Observatory. (2018, December 10). *Copyright directive: How competing big business lobbies drowned out critical voices.* Retrieved from https://corporateeurope.org/en/2018/12/copyright-directive-how-competing-big-business-lobbies-drowned-out-critical-voices

Council of Europe. (2013). *Recommendation CM/Rec(2011)7 on a new notion of media.* Retrieved from https://edoc.coe.int/en/media/8019-recommendation-cmrec20117-on-a-new-notion-of-media.html

de la Noue, C. (2023). *Protection of media pluralism: towards a virtuous and efficient legal framework at the European Union level?* Retrieved from https://www.cnam.ie/wp-content/uploads/2023/07/CnaM_Trinity-essay-2023_Claire-de-Villiers-de-la-Noue_.pdf

Dillon, D. (2023). *FAST in Europe: Growth opportunities and market trends.* Retrieved from https://www.newscaststudio.com/2024/02/27/free-ad-supported-television-trends-europe/

Enli, G., Raats, T., Sivertsen, T., & Donders, K. (2019). Media policy for private media in the age of digital platforms. *European Journal of Communication, 34*(4).

European Commission. (2015). *Communication from the commission to the European Parliament, the Council, the EESC and the committee of regions.* Retrieved from https://eur-lex.europa.eu/legal-content/EN/TXT/?uri=celex%3A52015DC0192

European Commission. (2016a). *Proposal for a directive of the European Parliament and of the Council amending directive 2010/13/EU on the coordination of certain provisions laid down by law, regulation or administrative action in Member States concerning the provision of audiovisual m.* Retrieved from https://eur-lex.europa.eu/legal-content/EN/HIS/?uri=COM%3A2016%3A287%3AFIN

European Commission. (2016b). *Proposal for a directive of the European Parliament and of the Council amending directive 2010/13/EU on the coordination of certain provisions laid down by law, regulation or administrative action in Member States concerning the provision of audiovisual m.* Retrieved from https://eur-lex.europa.eu/legal-content/EN/TXT/?uri=COM%3A2016%3A287%3AFIN

European Commission. (2016c). *Proposal for a directive of the European Parliament and of the Council on copyright in the digital single market.* Retrieved from https://eur-lex.europa.eu/legal-content/EN/TXT/?uri=CELEX%3A52016PC0593

European Commission. (2018, June 7). *Digital single market: updated audiovisual rules*. Retrieved from Press Corner: https://ec.europa.eu/commission/presscorner/detail/en/memo_18_4093

European Commission. (2020). *Communication from the commission guidelines pursuant to article 13(7) of the audiovisual media services directive on the calculation of the share of European works in on-demand catalogues and on the definition of low audience and low turnover 2020/C 223/*. Retrieved from https://eur-lex.europa.eu/legal-content/EN/TXT/?toc=OJ%3AC%3A2020%3A223%3ATOC&uri=uriserv%3AOJ.C_.2020.223.01.0010.01.ENG

European Commission. (2021). *Communication from the commission to the European parliament and the council, guidance on article 17 of directive 2019/790 on copyright in the digital single market COM/2021/288 final*. Retrieved from https://eur-lex.europa.eu/legal-content/EN/ALL/?uri=COM:2021:288:FIN

European Commission. (2022). *Proposal for a regulation of the European Parliament and of the Council establishing a common framework for media services in the internal market (European Media Freedom Act) and amending Directive 2010/13/EU*. Retrieved from https://eur-lex.europa.eu/legal-content/EN/TXT/?uri=CELEX%3A52022PC0457

European Commission. (2023, May 17). *The European media industry outlook*. Retrieved from https://digital-strategy.ec.europa.eu/en/library/european-media-industry-outlook

European Commission. (2024a). *Commission staff working document detailed reporting on the application of Articles 13, 16 and 17 of directive 2010/13/EU as amended by directive (EU) 2018/1808 for 2020–2021*. Retrieved from https://data.consilium.europa.eu/doc/document/ST-11676-2024-ADD-1/en/pdf

European Commission. (2024b). *Application reports and reports on European works*. Retrieved from Shaping Europe's Digital Future: https://digital-strategy.ec.europa.eu/en/policies/avmsd-reports

European Parliament. (2023). *REPORT on the proposal for a regulation of the European Parliament and of the Council establishing a common framework for media services in the internal market (European Media Freedom Act)*. Obtenido de https://www.europarl.europa.eu/doceo/document/A-9-2023-0264_EN.html#_section1

European Union. (2007). *Directive 2007/65/EC of the European Parliament and of the Council of 11.12.2007 amending Council Directive 89/552/EEC on the coordination of certain provisions laid down by law, regulation or administrative action in Member States concerning the pursuit*. Retrieved from https://eur-lex.europa.eu/legal-content/EN/TXT/?uri=celex%3A32007L0065

European Union. (2010). *Directive 2010/13/EU of the European Parliament and of the Council of 10 March 2010 on the coordination of certain provisions laid down by law, regulation or administrative action in Member States concerning the provision of audiovisual media services*. Retrieved from https://eur-lex.europa.eu/eli/dir/2010/13/oj

European Union. (2019). *Directive (EU) 2019/790 of the European Parliament and of the Council of 17 April 2019 on copyright and related rights in the Digital Single Market and amending Directives 96/9/EC and 2001/29/EC*. Retrieved from https://eur-lex.europa.eu/eli/dir/2019/790/oj

European Union. (2022). *Regulation (EU) 2022/2065 of the European Parliament and of the Council of 19 October 2022 on a single market for digital services and amending directive 2000/31/EC (Digital Services Act)*. Retrieved from https://eur-lex.europa.eu/eli/reg/2022/2065/oj

European Union. (2024). *Regulation (EU) 2024/1083 of the European Parliament and of the Council of 11 April 2024 establishing a common framework for media services in the internal market and amending directive 2010/13/EU (European Media Freedom Act)*. Retrieved from https://eur-lex.europa.eu/legal-content/EN/TXT/?uri=CELEX%3A32024R1083

Furgal, U., Kretsschmer, M., & Thomas, A. (2020). *Memes and parasites: A discourse analysis of the copyright in the digital single market directive*. Retrieved from CREATe Working Paper 2020/10: https://papers.ssrn.com/sol3/papers.cfm?abstract_id=3712007

Götz, C., & Gramsch, M. (2021, June 24). *In brief: Media law and regulation in European Union*. Retrieved from Simmons & SImmons: https://www.lexology.com/library/detail.aspx?g=98b9cbeb-5f49-468e-9eb3-6094fdbf24f1

Gautier, P.-Y. (2020). *Why internet services which provide access to copyright infringing works should not be immune to liability*. Retrieved from WIPO Knowledge Repository: https://tind.wipo.int/record/46275

Geiger, C., Bulayenko, O., & Frosio, G. (2017). The introduction of a neighbouring right for press publisher at EU Level: The unneeded (and unwanted) reform. *European Intellectual Property Review 202, 39*(4).

Google. (2023). *Google licenses content from news publishers under the EU Copyright Directive*. Retrieved from Google: https://blog.google/around-the-globe/google-europe/google-licenses-content-from-news-publishers-under-the-eu-copyright-directive/#:~:text=While%20Member%20States%20continue%20to,1%2C500%20publications%20across%2015%20countries.

Government of Australia. (2021). *Treasury laws amendment (news media and digital platforms mandatory bargaining code) Act 2021*. Retrieved from Federal Register of Legislation: https://www.legislation.gov.au/C2021A00021/latest/text

Government of Canada. (2023). *Online streaming act*. Retrieved from https://www.canada.ca/en/canadian-heritage/services/modernization-broadcasting-act.html

Government of Canada. (2023a). *Online news act*. Retrieved from https://laws.justice.gc.ca/eng/acts/O-9.3/page-1.html

Government of Canada. (2024). *Implementing the online news act*. Retrieved from https://crtc.gc.ca/eng/industr/info.htm

Grece, C. (2022, December). *Film and TV content in TVOD, SVOD and FOD catalogues 2022 Edition*. Retrieved from European Audiovisual Observatory: https://rm.coe.int/vod-catalogues-2022-film-and-tv-content-2022-edition-c-grece/1680a9b5d7

Höppner, T. (2018). EU Copyright reform: The case for a publisher's right. *Intellectual Property Quarterly, 1*, 1–21.

Heermann, M. (2023). Undermining lobbying coalitions: The interest group politics of EU copyright reform. *Journal of European Public Policy, 31*(8), 2287–2315.

Helberger, N., de Vreese, C., Ausloos, J., & Seipp, T. J. (2024, November). Between the cracks: Blind spots in regulating media concentration and platform dependence in the EU. *Internet Policy Review, 13*(4).

Hirche, T. (2019). *Council lets copyright reform pass—the die is cast*. Retrieved from IGEL: https://ancillarycopyright.eu/news/2019-04-16/council-lets-copyright-reform-pass-die-cast.html

Hyland, M., & Perry, T. (2023). *The knottiest of Gordian knots: Article 17 of the Copyright Directive*. Retrieved from European Intellectual Property Review: https://arrow.tudublin.ie/buschacart/59/

Idiz, D., Irion, K., Ebbers, J. J., & Vliegenthart, R. (2021). European audiovisual media policy in the age of global video on demand services: A case study of Netflix in the Netherlands. *JDMP, 12*(3), 425–449.

Keller, P. (2024, June 7). *Article 17—five years later*. Retrieved from Kluwer Copyright Blog: https://copyrightblog.kluweriplaw.com/2024/06/07/article-17-five-years-later/

Kostovska, I., & Broughton Micova, S. (2013). Video-sharing platforms under the AVMSD: Building on transnational collaboration and co-regulation. In H. Ranaivoson, T. Raats, & S. Broughton Micova (Eds.), *European audiovisual policy in transition* (pp. 93–111). Routledge.

Kuklis, L. (2021). Video-sharing platforms in AVMSD—A new kind of content regulation. In P. Parcu & E. Brogi (Eds.), *Research handbook on EU media law and policy*. Elgar Publishing.

Lacourt, A., Munch, E., & Radel-Cormann, J. (2023). *AVMSDigest*. Strasbourg: European Audiovisual Observatory.

Leyen, U. (2021). *2021 state of the union address by president von der Leyen*. Retrieved from https://ec.europa.eu/commission/presscorner/detail/en/SPEECH_21_4701

Madiega, T. (2019, June). *Copyright in the digital single market. Briefing*. Retrieved from European Parliament: https://www.europarl.europa.eu/RegData/etudes/BRIE/2016/593564/EPRS_BRI(2016)593564_EN.pdf

Ognjanov, G., & Mitic, S. (2019). TV audience measurement in Europe: Do advertisers really know what they are paying for? *Journal of Emerging Trends in Marketing and Management, 1*(1).

Portela Trigo, M. (2017). *The protection of minors in the European Union audiovisual media services directive: A forward-looking analysis of the proposals by the European Commission and Parliament*. Ghent University.

Ranaivoson, H. R., Broughton Micova, S., Dewaele, S., & Donders, K. (2021, February). *Transposing the audiovisual media services directive: Where to go?*. Retrieved from https://researchportal.vub.be/en/publications/policy-brief-43-transposing-the-audiovisual-media-services-direct

Republic of Poland v European Parliament and Council of the European Union, Case C-401/19 (European Court of Justice (Grand Chamber) April 26, 2022).

Thaidigsmann, M. (2019, March 27). *A closer look at Europe's disputed copyright rules*. Retrieved from In House Legal-EU: https://inhouse-legal.eu/public-policy-regulations/eu-copyright-law/

Valais, S. (2016). *European Commission: New proposals for the modernisation of EU copyright rules in the digital single market*. Retrieved from IRIS Merlin: https://merlin.obs.coe.int/article/7684

Valcke, P., & Stevens, D. (2007). Graduated regulation of 'regulatable' content and the European audiovisual media services directive one small step for the industry and one giant leap for the legislator? *Telematics and Informatics, 24*, 285–302.

Valcke, P., Stevens, D., Werkers, E., & Lievens, E. (2008). Audiovisual media services in the EU: Next generation approach or old wine in new barrels? *Communications & Strategies, 71*, 103.

Woods, L. (2018, May 18). *Revision of audiovisual media services directive—video-sharing platforms*. Retrieved from EU Law Analysis: https://eulawanalysis.blogspot.com/2018/05/revision-of-audiovisual-media-services.html

CHAPTER 10

Regulating Big Tech: Tracing the Trajectory of Platform Regulation in the Age of AI

Cornelia Kutterer and Giovanni De Gregorio

Introduction

The entering into force of the Digital Markets Act (DMA) (Regulation (EU) 2022/1925, 2022a) and the Digital Services Act (DSA) (Regulation (EU) 2022/2065, 2022b) has defined a constitutional revolution in the European approach to digital services. While the DMA aims to curb anti-competitive practices by major tech companies, promoting fairer competition by preventing these 'gatekeepers' from leveraging their power to disadvantage rivals and potentially offering growth opportunities for smaller entities (Savin, 2018), the DSA focuses on enhancing users' safety while protecting fundamental rights, particularly by mandating procedural obligations and rules on systemic risk assessment, also involving algorithmic decision-making. Together, these

C. Kutterer (✉)
MIAI (Chair Legal and Regulatory Implications of AI), University of Grenoble, Grenoble, France
e-mail: kutterercornelia@uclawsf.edu

G. De Gregorio
Católica Global School of Law, Lisbon, Portugal
e-mail: gdegregorio@ucp.pt

T. Kleiner and A. Garcia Rodriguez (eds.), *The Making of a Global Digital Rulebook*, https://doi.org/10.1007/978-981-95-9226-5_10

acts underscore the EU's strategic intent to create a safer, more competitive digital environment based on the protection of fundamental rights and democratic values.

Nonetheless, from a broader perspective, these steps are part of a larger path of transformation that started at the advent of the Internet when platforms were not yet in the game. The 'platformisation' of the digital economy started in the 2000s and was mainly the result of a neoliberal approach to digital technologies with the adoption of the 1996 Communication Decency Act in the United States and the approach initiated by the 2000 e-Commerce Directive in the European Union (European Union, 2000). Both opened new possibilities for business models, as underlined by the growing, even if not immediate, reliance on advertising business models.

This regulatory framework has contributed to leading the transformation of the Internet from a static medium for disseminating information to an interactive Internet with more digital services. Providers developed platforms for external use, with user activity enhancing the platform's value through network effects. This new 'Web 2.0' (O'Reilly, 2007, p. 17) leveraged connectivity, sharing, and collaboration and started to transcend traditional boundaries and jurisdictions, making regulation a nuanced and complex matter (Le Borgne-Baschmidt et al., 2008, p. 302). This era was also starting to underline the crucial role of data as platforms grew in value through the extensive collection of user-generated content. This wealth of data not only improved the functionality of these platforms but also introduced regulatory challenges, particularly in areas like data protection, copyright, intermediary liability, and competition (Lessig, 2000).

During this period, the term 'platform' transitioned from a purely technical term to a broader concept. It evolved to signify not merely a basis for delivering applications but a foundational layer that facilitates a wide array of services and interactions (Zodi, 2022). Gillespie (2010), for example, linked today's meaning of 'platform' specifically to the acquisition of YouTube by Google. Gillespie emphasised the role of large corporations in shaping the regulatory environment and the public's perception of platforms, emphasising platforms as spaces for user-generated content, interaction, and network effects. Benkler (2007) argued that the social and cultural changes of this networked information society offer significant opportunities for enhancing individual freedom and societal well-being. However, these positive outcomes, he argued in foresight, are not guaranteed and depend on the legal and policy choices made in response to the challenges posed by the transition from an industrial information economy to a networked information environment.

Those developments were underpinned by the rapid adoption of different technologies, including cloud computing in the 2010s, which reshaped the platform ecosystem and transformed business models and roles across various industries (Millard, 2021), and VoIP, which enabled voice communications over IP networks and seamlessly integrated with various devices (Stone, 2023). From there, the evolution of AI systems can be considered another enabling technology for online platforms developing increasingly sophisticated services with a broader impact on fundamental rights and democracy, thus leading towards articulated regulatory solutions.

This chapter retraces the processes and dynamics that enabled the EU to enrich its strategy to regulate online platforms and to embrace a more constitutional perspective, starting with rights rather than trying to complete a single market. By focusing on the different policy approaches, it examines how the strategy of the EU, focused on protecting fundamental rights and democratic values in the digital age, has been shaped by a myriad of adjunct policies, political concepts, and digital developments, as well as institutional and external influences from expert knowledge and interest groups. The chapter then examines the DSA and the DMA as critical steps of this process and concludes with an outlook on the rapidly changing platform ecosystem in the age of AI.

The First Steps: The Barroso Commission(s)

Since Ursula von der Leyen assumed office in 2019, the EU's efforts to regulate digital markets have significantly accelerated. However, the drive to focus on platforms had already been building like a gathering storm from the mid-2010s. Online platforms rose to prominence in both social and economic spheres under the Barroso I and Barroso II Commission (2004–2009 and 2010–2014). The introduction of 'platforms' as a concept in information technology circles has been seen largely as a net positive and a contributor to the European internal market reaching businesses and consumers across its borders and as a positive impact on freedom of expression. For a time, the Arab Spring was celebrated as an example of the positive impact of these platforms, but this perception was ultimately short-lived (Hintz, 2012; Robinson & Merrow, 2020).

Meanwhile, acquisitions of core and emerging technologies played a crucial role in achieving market leadership of big tech during this period. Google acquired YouTube in 2006, DoubleClick in 2007, Waze in 2013 and DeepMind Technologies in 2014 (Muse, 2024a). Meta (aka Facebook) acquired Instagram in 2012 and WhatsApp in 2014 (Muse, 2024b); Microsoft acquired Skype in 2011 and Mojang in 2014 (Muse, 2024c). Apple acquired core technologies such as Siri in 2010 (Muse, 2024d). The acquisition of online advertising company DoubleClick by Google in 2007 may have been the first that raised significant privacy concerns, making it more than a mere competition case (Euractiv, 2008b). Concerns were raised by leading consumer organisations on both sides of the Atlantic, but contrary to today (Meta Platforms Inc and Others v Bundeskartellamt, 2023), the interplay between competition and privacy protections was largely ignored (Euractiv, 2008a).

During the same period, several high-profile scandals underscored the urgent need for improved online privacy and child safety measures. Facebook faced intense scrutiny over predators using the platform to target minors, prompting enhanced security protocols while also dealing with the fallout from its Beacon programme that shared users' activities without consent (Newcomb, 2018). YouTube struggled with exposing children to inappropriate content, leading to calls for stricter age restrictions and better content moderation (BBC News, 2017). The Apple App Store was criticised for unauthorised in-app purchases by children, resulting in legal action and stricter parental controls (Dredge, 2014). Google's Street View data collection scandal in 2010, where personal data from unencrypted Wi-Fi networks was inadvertently collected, raised significant privacy concerns (Kiss, 2010). Snapchat's 2013 data breach exposed millions of users, including teenagers, highlighting security flaws (CBS News, 2014).

Meanwhile, the social networking site Ask.FM was linked to multiple teen suicides due to cyberbullying, which brought attention to the platform's inadequate moderation and reporting tools (Pappas, 2015). These incidents spotlighted significant vulnerabilities in online platforms and drove the push for stronger regulatory frameworks to moderate content, protect user privacy, ensure child safety and improve cybersecurity while also addressing emerging competition issues in the tech stack, at least through sectoral approaches. Early attempts to address these concerns were fragmented, with policies on privacy, safety, and market regulations developing as parallel endeavours, largely ignorant of each other's implications and interconnections.

Existing data protection instruments were no longer considered sufficient, particularly in the context of the rapidly emerging platform economy. These frameworks were established before the advent of digital platforms that now dominate the economy, driving new forms of interaction, commerce, and data collection at an unprecedented scale. The explosive growth of platforms, along with related developments such as Big Data and the Internet of Things (IoT), highlighted the inadequacy of existing regulations to address the unique challenges posed by these digital ecosystems. Consequently, both the EU and the Council of Europe undertook the preparation of new or updated ('modernised') data protection instruments to better regulate this evolving landscape (Korff & Georges, 2019). The General Data Protection Regulation (GDPR) emerged as a dominant priority during the two Barroso Commissions, shaping much of the legislative agenda.

With similar sentiments and in the aftermaths of the Snowden revelation (Greenwald, 2013; BBC News, 2013), a proposal for a 'Schengen Cloud', i.e., an integrated network and electronic communication system exclusive to Europe, was discussed (but never saw the light of the day) (Pollmann, 2014). The concept envisioned Germany, France, and other European nations to manage their networks independently, without reliance on the United States as an intermediary. This marked one of the earliest efforts that addressed market regulation and privacy policies simultaneously, aiming to curtail the growing dominance of US cloud providers by addressing both market concentration and the need for robust protection of European personal data. The idea was revived in August 2013 when Thierry Breton, then CEO of EU cloud provider Atos (and France's former Minister of Economy, Finance and Industry) proposed 'a kind of Schengen for data' (Cate et al., 2015). An Office of the United States Trade Representative (USTR) report made clear that the US government regards the 'Schengen cloud' argument as a front for naked protectionism by the EU: 'The United States and the EU share common interests in protecting their citizens' privacy, but the draconian approach proposed by DTAG and others appears to be a means of providing a protectionist advantage to EU-based ICT suppliers' (Office of the United States Trade Representative, 2014).

While cloud services were just beginning to attract regulatory attention, the telecommunications sector had long been subject to ex-ante market regulations, which were now facing new challenges. During that period, the Commission aimed to address pressures for telecom providers from over-the-top (OTT) services and a decrease in classic communication services like SMS and phone calls with the Digital Agenda for Europe, which was published in May 2010 (COM(2010)245 final, 2010). The economic challenges faced by telecom providers were primarily examined through the lens of net neutrality from 2010 to 2013, with the hope of identifying new revenue streams. During this period, EU institutions conducted an intensive evaluation of the practices and behaviours of both market players and users (Gadringer, 2020). This entrenched battle between primarily EU-headquartered telecom providers and platform providers marks the beginning of rising concerns about the dominance of an industry that is largely non-European.

Despite these rising concerns about non-European industry dominance, the full regulatory implications had not yet come into focus within competition policy. While Joaquín Almunia, who served as the Competition Commissioner from 2010 to 2014, emphasised enforcement continuity and focused on state aid and private damages actions, he did not yet explicitly address the emerging platform ecosystem in his priorities. Almunia nevertheless initiated investigations into Google's business practices that would eventually lead to significant antitrust cases under his successor, Margrethe Vestager.

The investigation began in November 2010, when Almunia announced that the European Commission was formally investigating allegations that Google had abused its dominant position in the search engine market. The trigger for this investigation was a series of complaints from competitors, including Foundem, back in 2006, a UK-based price-comparison website, which accused Google of favouring its own services in search results while demoting those of competitors. Almunia's decision to launch the investigation was driven by growing concerns over Google's increasing influence on the digital market in Europe and the potential harm to consumers and innovation due to anti-competitive practices.

Almunia aimed to determine whether Google was leveraging its dominant position in search to stifle competition, particularly in vertical search markets such as shopping, travel, and local search. As the investigation progressed, the scope widened, and by 2013, the focus had expanded to include concerns about Google's advertising practices and its Android mobile operating system. Almunia initially sought to reach a settlement with Google, allowing the company to propose voluntary changes to address the Commission's concerns. However, these settlement efforts faced significant opposition from Google's competitors and other stakeholders, who argued that the proposed remedies were insufficient, which ultimately led to their collapse (Manthorpe, 2017). By the time Almunia's term ended in November 2014, no final resolution had been reached, leaving the complex and high-stakes cases to be inherited by Margrethe Vestager, who would take a more aggressive stance in her handling of the Google investigations.

While competition issues remained unresolved, parallel efforts were underway to address broader digital challenges, with a growing emphasis on online safety. In the first Digital Agenda (COM(2010)245 final), led by Vice President Kroes, the Commission focused on creating a vibrant digital single market, interoperability and standards, trust and security, fast internet access, and ICT benefits for society. Two notable action points that emerged were illegal content online and self-regulation among European and global service providers, especially regarding the use of their services by minors. This led to the CEO coalition 'Making Internet a Better Place for Children' on 1 December 2011, and on 2 May 2012, to a 'new strategy for safer internet and better internet content for children and teenagers' (Livingstone et al., 2012). The Commission introduced a detailed strategy to implement these goals, involving collaboration with industry, civil society, and governments to protect children from online risks and foster a safer, more positive digital environment. While no hard law was introduced, we observe a soft emerging push for greater responsibilities of platforms. In retrospect, these early attempts at addressing digital challenges would prove to be largely inconsequential, overshadowed by the mounting complexities of the digital landscape.

The Acceleration: The Juncker Commission

The Juncker Commission began its tenure in 2014 with a commitment to leverage digital transformation to revitalise the European economy, which was still grappling with the aftermath of the financial and European debt crises. Heightened scrutiny of platforms concerning their privacy commitments did not immediately result in legislation specifically targeting these platforms. However, the GDPR—proposed in 2012 and progressing through the legislative process amid the Snowden revelations—was significantly influenced by 'social networking and online activities'. Their activities and scandals were major political drivers for reforming the 1995 Data Protection Directive (Sloot et al., 2019).

In Juncker's political guidelines, the word platform is still absent (Juncker, 2014). Less than a year later, the Commission's communication on 'A Digital Single Market Strategy for Europe', published on 6 May 2015, finally committed to assessing the role of platforms. The strategy's core legislative initiatives, however, were still focused on improving the existing acquis with a focus on access to digital goods and services across Europe. A second pillar aimed at creating a conducive environment for digital network competition and personal data protection, involving reforms in telecommunications, cybersecurity, and audiovisual media services. A third pillar sought to maximise the growth potential of the European digital economy by encouraging digital transformation across industries, stimulating investment, ensuring access to data and capital, and fostering data protection and the free movement of data, including the development of a European cloud.

The Commission kicked off a public consultation in September 2015 focusing on the social and economic role of online platforms; transparency, e.g. in search results; terms of use; ratings and reviews; the use of information by platforms; the relation between platforms and their suppliers; the conditions of switching between comparable services offered by platforms; and the role of online intermediaries including ways to tackle illegal content on the Internet (European Commission, 2015). While platforms were considered to serve 'multilateral market gateways' for industry that create value by enabling interaction between multiple groups of economic actors, concerns that platform owners will also shift a major part of value creation outside their business sphere have been acknowledged in the 2016 paper on the Digitalisation of European Industry (COM(2016) 180 final, 2016b).

The Commission's strategy towards digital platforms shifted only gradually. In its May 2016 Communication on Online Platforms (SWD(2017) 500 final, 2017b), the Commission identified two specific issues for further investigation: safeguarding a fair and innovation-friendly business environment and ensuring that illegal content online is timely and effectively removed, with proper checks and balances, from online platforms.

The European Commission's competition enforcement team continued to deal with competition cases involving online platforms by strictly applying existing rules, defending the resilience of competition law and its ability to cope with new market circumstances and the requirements of the new digital economy and society (Cini & Czulno, 2022). In 2017, Vestager fined Google €2.42 billion for favouring its own comparison-shopping service in search results over those of competitors (Google shopping case, European Commission, 2017a) (Google and Alphabet v European Commission, 2017). In 2018, she imposed a record €4.34 billion fine on Google for abusing its dominance in the mobile operating system market with Android (Google Android case) (Google and Alphabet v European Commission, 2018), and in 2019, she fined Google €1.49 billion for anti-competitive practices in its online advertising business, specifically for imposing restrictive clauses in contracts with third-party websites, preventing Google's rivals from placing their search ads on these websites (Commission Decision C(2019) 2173, 2019).

While these decisions highlighted the European Commission's increasingly firm stance on regulating major tech companies, the framework for future actions against digital giants remained uncertain. In 2018, Competition Commissioner Vestager stated that: 'the fact is, the competition rules are designed to adapt. The principles they set out are valid for every market, for the ones we know today and the ones we'll see in the future. And that's why dealing with digital markets isn't really about new rules. It's about deepening our understanding of how those markets work' (Cini & Czulno, 2022).

Between 2014 and 2019, additional high-profile acquisitions continued to make headlines, including Microsoft's acquisition of LinkedIn in 2016 and GitHub in 2018. While Google, Amazon, Meta, Apple, and Microsoft ('GAFAM') acquired hundreds of companies during this period, the European (and US) competition authorities had not prohibited a single concentration and only investigated a small fraction despite rhetoric on prohibitions of so-called killer acquisitions, more scrutiny, and possible break-up (Witt, 2022).

Developments concerning network neutrality also evolved in parallel. As the internet 'became more about content than communication', telecom providers began advocating for a tiered-lane approach to net neutrality to secure continued income (notably supported by Digital Commissioner Günther Oettinger). The discussion led to the Telecom

Single Market Directive in 2015[1] and the BEREC guidelines in 2016 (Gadringer, 2020), positioning telecom providers and cloud/content providers, primarily from the United States, on opposing sides of yet another policy debate (Beckedahl, 2015). The reform of the EU telecommunication framework was at the forefront of the level playing field discussion (Savin, 2018), often illustrated with striking photoshopped slides showing football fields tilted to one side. More importantly, the sector-specific ex-ante telecommunication rules served as a blueprint for ex-ante competition regulation in the platform economy.[2] The pursuit of a 'level playing field' became the guiding principle in the EU's strategy for regulating platforms.

> The concept of a **'level playing field'**, central to the EU's approach to regulating internet platforms, involves a delicate balancing act between imposing identical rules on all players and carefully considering potential pitfalls of an overly rigid application of the 'level playing field' concept and unintended consequences on overall market dynamics.

Politically, a more influential France (Elysee, 2017) following the 2016 Brexit vote, along with Germany, increased pressure on the Commission to act on platforms. On 20 March 2017, Germany published its influential Digital Platforms White Paper (Bunderministerium für Wirtschaft & Energie, 2017). The White Paper proposed several policy measures promoting digital platforms through fair competition while also ensuring the protection of individual rights and data sovereignty.

In tandem, German and French economic ministers Peter Altmaier and Bruno Le Maire publicly called for ex-ante regulation in an open letter to the European Commission. In the Mid-Term Review of the Digital Single Market Strategy (COM(2017) 0228 final, 2017c), the European

[1] The EU adopted net neutrality rules as part of the Telecoms Single Market (TSM) regulation, which was approved by the European Parliament on October 27, 2015. The regulation came into effect on April 30, 2016, establishing strong net neutrality protections across the EU, ensuring that internet service providers treat all online traffic equally without discrimination, restriction, or interference (Regulation (EU) 2015/2120)

[2] The EECC was adopted by the European Parliament and the Council on December 11, 2018. It was published in the Official Journal of the European Union on December 17, 2018, and entered into force on December 20, 2018. Member States were required to transpose the EECC into national law by December 21, 2020.

Commission declared its intention to develop legislative measures to tackle the problems of unfair contractual terms and trading practices found in platform-to-business (P2B) relationships. Caught in a market-correcting governance mindset, the Juncker Commission still significantly fell short of implementing a broad regulatory approach for online platforms (Hoeffler & Morand, 2023), not least due to opposition still voiced by competition authorities in Member States and within the Commission, particularly by Commissioner Vestager (The Antitrust Source, 2016).

Although the e-commerce Directive (Directive 2000/31/EC, European Union (2000)) faced criticism from the outset by copyright holders for its perceived failure to protect copyrighted content and prevent the spread of illegal content, the Commission resisted opening it for review for many years. This reluctance was partly due to the complexity of the issues involved and the fear of weakening the country-of-origin principle, which aims to prevent fragmentation of the Digital Single Market. However, the proliferation of harms related to content management and the distribution of illegal content amplified the negative perceptions increasingly associated with digital platforms.

The 2016 Brussels terrorist attacks in the heart of the European Union highlighted the critical role of platforms in disseminating hate speech and terrorist content, bringing this issue to the forefront of the agenda (European Commission, 2016a). In the same year, significant political developments, including Donald Trump's election as president of the United States (Fujiwara et al., 2021) and the Brexit referendum (Polanski, 2017), brought further scrutiny to platforms and their influence over election outcomes and the moral minefield between upholding freedom of expression and preventing harm caused by misinformation. Their involvement, especially through controversial practices like Cambridge Analytica's microtargeting campaigns (Bakir, 2020), intensified scrutiny on social media platforms. Yet, during the third evaluation of the ECD in 2016–2017, the Commission reaffirmed that the principles and rules of the ECD were robust (de Streel & Husovec, 2020).

Nonetheless, it recognised the growing significance of online platforms and the emerging risks of fragmentation in the Digital Single Market (European Commission, 2020). This observation prompted a three-pronged strategy: (i) updating sector-specific legislation to address particular issues; (ii) providing additional guidance on the ambiguous aspects of the e-commerce Directive, especially concerning notice-and-takedown procedures and the use of voluntary preventive measures; and

(iii) promoting coordinated EU-wide co-regulation and self-regulation for especially harmful illegal materials, leading to a patchwork of vertical content-related platform initiatives (Frosio, 2017). These included the Directive against Child Exploitation (Directive 2011/93/EU, European Union, 2011), the Terrorism Directive (Directive (EU) 2017/541, European Union (2017)), reforms to EU copyright rules (Directive (EU) 2019/790, European Union (2019)) and the updated Audiovisual Media Services Directive (AVMSD) (Directive (EU) 2018/1808, European Union (2018). Complementary non-legislative tools included, e.g., the Code of Conduct on Countering Illegal Hate Speech Online (European Commission, 2019), the EU Internet Forum's efforts against terrorist propaganda (EUIF, 2024), and the revised Memorandum of Understanding on the sale of counterfeit goods (European Commission, 2016c).

Notably, the AVMSD defined first-time video-sharing platforms as services that provide programmes and user-generated videos without editorial responsibility, organising content through algorithms or other automatic means (Savin, 2018). This designation legally recognises platforms based on three aspects: user content, lack of editorial control, and algorithmic content management. Despite this, the directive treats these platforms as media service providers. Similarly, the 2019/790 Copyright Directive was largely influenced by the rise of platforms and addressed new technologies, business models, and actors.

It focuses on 'content-sharing service providers' with three characteristics: they host and provide access to copyright-protected content uploaded by users for profit and impose extra obligations on larger platforms, generating over €10 million in revenue. The directive outlines two main responsibilities: obtaining licences for transmitted works and adhering to the notice-and-takedown procedures established by the e-commerce Directive to avoid liability for unauthorised communications of protected content (Quintais & Schwemer, 2022).

By 2017, the Commission adopted a Communication to tackle illegal content online and enhance the responsibility of online platforms. This Communication provided guidance and did not, as such, change the applicable legal framework or contain legally binding rules; it primarily aimed at guiding online platforms on the ways in which they can live up to their responsibility as regards tackling the illegal content they host. It also aimed at mainstreaming good procedural practices across different forms of illegal content to promote closer cooperation between platforms and competent authorities.

On 1 March 2018, the Commission adopted an additional recommendation on measures to effectively tackle illegal content online (C(2018) 1177), thereby continuously pushing online platforms and, in particular, social media to do more. Following the Communication and in view of the European election in 2019, the Code of Practice on Disinformation was established in October 2018 (European Commission, 2022). It was developed by the European Commission in collaboration with online platforms, advertisers, and other industry stakeholders to combat the spread of disinformation and fake news.

Content moderation rules also began to be implemented at the national level, with several countries introducing regulations and guidelines to hold online platforms accountable for the content shared on their sites,[3] threatening a fragmentation of the single European market in the process. The Commission thus finally announced the evaluation of the necessity for further measures, including potential legislative actions to strengthen the existing framework.

However, the Commission still maintained that collectively, these efforts create a robust framework for regulating online platforms, protecting users, and balancing content moderation with freedom of expression within the EU. The European Commission resisted reopening the e-Commerce Directive for a long time due to the complexity of the rapidly evolving digital landscape and the diverging interests among EU member states, each with its own legal traditions and economic priorities.

Balancing the need for regulation with the desire to foster innovation added to the challenge, as there were concerns that new regulations could stifle the growth of European digital companies. Legal and institutional inertia further complicated the process, as the e-Commerce Directive served as the foundational legal framework for online services across the EU, making substantial changes daunting. Additionally, intense lobbying from Big Tech companies, who feared stricter regulations, and the fragmentation of regulatory approaches among member states created further obstacles. The Commission's attention was fragmented across various regulatory initiatives, such as the General Data Protection Regulation (GDPR) and the Digital Single Market strategy, diluting its focus and

[3] Such as the German Netzdurchführungsgesetz.

political capital. Crucially, these efforts remained disconnected from the emerging debate around ex-ante regulation of platforms, which presented a distinct and complex set of challenges.

As the Juncker Commission took office, the clamour for regulating Big Tech and the so-called 'GAFA(M)'[4] companies reached a crescendo, yet the regulatory roadmap remained stubbornly unclear. The digital policy landscape was a patchwork of competing priorities, with divergent approaches to cloud computing vying for attention alongside increasingly vocal, yet disjointed, calls for ex-ante regulation of digital platforms. Meanwhile, a robust Directorate-General for Competition (DG Comp) remained firmly rooted in traditional competition theories, resisting the push for more proactive measures.

Despite growing concerns that conventional competition rules were proving insufficient—offering too little, too late—their impact on policy remained limited. The calls for stronger regulatory frameworks were met with resistance, as the Commission struggled to reconcile these emerging demands with established legal and economic principles. This period was characterised by a tension between the urgent need for new regulatory approaches and the inertia of existing institutional frameworks, leaving the regulatory landscape for Big Tech in a state of flux.

In 2019, at the end of the Juncker Commission, the adoption of the Platform to Business (P2B) Regulation marked the sole milestone in developing distinct platform law. It targeted platforms and intermediaries of goods and services to level the playing field for businesses. The initial steps towards 'light' ex-ante regulation have unfolded against a backdrop of various EU member states revising their competition laws to address growing dependencies, underscoring the increasing importance of national rules. Simultaneously, at the EU level, there has been a vigorous debate within competition law regarding whether antitrust enforcement should also encompass 'fairness', including the protection of less efficient competitors (Bania, 2020). The P2B Regulation was the first attempt to introduce horizontal and competition-based regulation adapted to the platform economy. However, despite these efforts, the regulation fell short of fully addressing the complexities of digital market dynamics.

[4] Google (Alphabet), Amazon, Apple, Facebook (Meta), and Microsoft.

The Consolidation: The Von der Leyen Commission

The introduction of lighter regulatory approaches failed to meet the expectations of key stakeholders, including France and Germany, incumbent European telecom providers, and civil society groups. Their ongoing campaigns gained further momentum due to significant changes in the economic and geopolitical climate, such as the policy shifts in the United States and the impact of the COVID-19 pandemic (Hoeffler & Merand, 2023). Upon taking the helm of the European Commission in late 2019, Ursula von der Leyen highlighted 'A Europe Fit for the Digital Age' as a cornerstone of her presidency. Following this, Margrethe Vestager, previously the Competition Commissioner under the Juncker Commission, broadened her portfolio to encompass both competition policy and broader aspects of the digital economy and society, the latter in tandem with Commissioner Breton.

The notion of EU digital sovereignty has become the EU's strategic interest and was declared by the German Presidency of the EU Council to be a 'leitmotiv of European digital policy' (Andriychuk, 2021). Referencing the principles of the single market, the Commission indicated that further regulatory measures might be necessary. These additional regulations would aim to enhance market contestability and fairness, foster innovation, facilitate market entry, and safeguard public interests that surpass strictly economic or competitive considerations.

In February 2020, the European Commission unveiled its Digital Strategy, followed in March by the introduction of a new industrial policy aimed at supporting the EU's dual transition towards a green and digital economy while advocating for 'open strategic autonomy'. The concept of open strategic autonomy, distinct yet related to digital sovereignty, has been the subject of intense discussion as strategic autonomy has expanded beyond its origins in defence and national security. It now encompasses broader geopolitical and market concerns aimed at protecting the EU from potentially exploitative practices by foreign states and companies. The emphasis on strategic autonomy has inherently fostered an environment conducive to the development of more robust regulatory tools aimed at governing digital platforms, particularly those originating from non-EU countries. This focus on strategic autonomy reflects the EU's broader ambition to assert greater control over its digital ecosystem, reducing reliance on external entities and ensuring that European values, standards, and interests are upheld.

By prioritising strategic autonomy, the EU has laid the groundwork for a more assertive regulatory stance to curb the dominance of foreign tech giants, protect European consumers, and promote fair competition, thereby reinforcing the EU's sovereignty in the digital sphere (Michels et al., 2023). The Commission's Digital Strategy sought to translate the broad goals of the Digital Single Market (DSM) into specific initiatives aimed at cultivating a 'fair and competitive digital economy'. By December 2020, the European Commission acknowledged that competition policy alone was insufficient to address all systemic challenges arising within the platform economy.

Digital sovereignty has been a key concern under the Juncker Commission to ensure control over its digital infrastructure, data, and technology, ensuring independence from external influences. The concept has further evolved to **open strategic autonomy** by promoting self-reliance in critical technologies while remaining engaged in global trade and cooperation, balancing independence. Both concepts have laid the foundation for a more assertive regulatory stance to curb the dominance of foreign tech giants.

The proposed New Competition Tool (NCT) was one of three measures, alongside vigorous enforcement of EU competition laws and potential ex-ante regulation for digital gatekeepers, to address gaps in existing competition rules, allowing for timely interventions against structural competition problems in various markets and to complement existing rules by addressing issues like monopolisation by non-dominant companies and ineffective enforcement against dominant companies (Carugati, 2020). This tool would allow the Commission to directly address certain market structures or failures without the need to demonstrate violations of current competition laws.

Initially, there was uncertainty regarding how these initiatives would interact with existing digital market regulations, such as the telecommunication framework and competition laws, as the Commission also proposed a New Competition Tool (NCT) designed to tackle structural competition challenges not only in digital markets but across all sectors. The development of the DMA and the interplay between Commissioners Margrethe Vestager and Thierry Breton underscore the internal complexities and strategic positioning within the Commission in relation to competition and competitiveness, respectively, industrial policy. Their divergent approaches, reflected in a separate NCT and a broad Digital Services Act comprising content and market regulation, reflected the political dynamics of the EU's regulatory agenda.

The European Commission and its various Directorates-General sought insights from numerous influential experts, including the three Special Advisers, Heike Schweitzer, Jacques Crémer, and Yves-Alexandre de Montjoye (Cremer et al., 2019), in addition to public consultation (European Commission, 2020). There was a consensus among most contributions that the legislation should enforce both prohibitions and obligations for gatekeeper platforms, with remedies primarily procedural in nature (Cini & Czulno, 2022). Only parts of the NCT concept were ultimately incorporated into the DMA; the market regulatory part separated from the DSA.

This decision to separate these proposals proved to be a wise move, allowing for a more focused and effective regulatory approach in each area. Competition lawyers specialising in online platforms were relatively unfamiliar with the ex-ante regulations traditionally applied in the telecom sector, which may have contributed to their reduced influence during the political and legislative process. The discussions surrounding the DSA largely took place in a separate 'bubble', with limited interaction between stakeholders involved in the DSA and those focused on the DMA and market regulation. Even within companies, there was often a disconnect between teams handling different aspects of these regulations, leading to a fragmented approach to addressing the broader regulatory landscape.

The draft DMA was adopted on December 15, 2020, and finally adopted during the 2022 French presidency of the Council on September 14, 2022.

> Between the Juncker and von der Leyen Commissions, the EU's **ex-ante regulation** of digital platforms evolved through several key policy options:
>
> Maintaining the Status Quo: Initially, existing competition laws and sector-specific regulations were used reactively.
>
> Targeted Ex-Ante Regulation: Discussions began on proactive rules for large platforms with significant market power.
>
> Soft Law and Self-Regulation: Options included guidelines and self-regulation, though these were seen as less effective.

> Sector-Specific Regulation: Ex-ante rules were considered for specific sectors like telecoms, where market dominance was a concern.

The Digital Markets Act

The DMA targets major technology companies, imposing specific prohibitions and obligations to promote contestability and fairness within the digital economy. It specifically focuses on large digital platforms that provide Core-Platform Services (CPS), play a significant role in the digital economy, and maintain a sustained and durable market position. The DMA aims at specific online services that act as critical gateways connecting large numbers of users and businesses (i.e. gatekeepers). These include online intermediation services, search engines, social networks, video-sharing platforms, messenger services (specifically, number-independent interpersonal communication services), operating systems, web browsers, virtual assistants, cloud computing services, and online advertising services. Extreme economies of scale, strong network effects, the ability to connect numerous business users with many end users due to their multi-sided nature, significant dependence by both business users and end users, lock-in effects, limited multi-homing by end users for the same purpose, vertical integration, and data-driven advantages are listed by the DMA as common characteristics of these 'core-platform services' (Akman, 2022).

The designation involves meeting three qualitative criteria: size, gateway, and durability. The size criterion refers to having a significant impact on the internal market, typically indicated by an EU-wide turnover of EUR 7.5 billion or a market valuation of EUR 75 billion, and providing the same core-platform service in three EU Member States. The gateway criterion involves providing a service that is an important gateway for business users to reach end users, with at least 45 million monthly active end users and 10,000 annual active business users. The durability criterion is met by holding, or soon holding, an entrenched and durable position, evidenced by meeting the gateway criterion in each of the last three financial years. As in the case of the DSA, Apple (challenging the App Store, iOS, and Safari), ByteDance (challenging TikTok) (TikTok, 2024), and Meta (challenging Facebook Marketplace and Facebook Messenger). Designated by the Commission have brought legal challenges concerning some of their services due to potential business impacts.

Gatekeepers must adhere to the obligations detailed in Articles 5, 6, and 7 of the DMA for each CPS specified in the relevant designation decision. These articles outline specific business practices identified by EU legislators as problematic ('the don'ts') as well as the expected behaviours ('the dos') for gatekeepers in relation to their CPS. Many of the obligations in the DMA originated from ongoing or concluded antitrust cases (de Streel et al., 2024).

The DMA identifies limits and obligations. Among the limitations, gatekeepers cannot self-preference their own products or services in rankings; require that users utilise a gatekeeper's other services as a condition of accessing a core-platform service; prevent business users from using differential pricing terms and conditions on their own websites or other platforms; track users' digital activities for advertising, absent explicit permission. At the same time, gatekeepers are obliged to allow users to change default settings or uninstall any software apps, unless necessary for the operating system to function; to install third-party apps or app stores that do not endanger their devices or operating systems; to communicate between business users and end users; to provide business users with real-time access to their platform-related data. Finally, the DMA provides an obligation to inform about concentrations and to disclose profiling techniques through an independent audit.

The DMA does not foresee tools such as codes of conduct. Unlike the DSA or the GDPR, it does not introduce co-regulatory measures to implement certain areas, thus making it harder for the Commission (and third parties) to monitor compliance. The effectiveness of the DMA will ultimately depend on its ability to achieve the necessary balances both in theory and in practice. This, in turn, hinges on the extent to which the DMA can enhance the enforcement of competition laws in digital markets (Akman, 2022).

Enforcement has followed the trend towards centralisation. The processes of investigation, monitoring, and enforcement are within the European Commission, allowing only minimal participation from Member States. The Digital Markets Advisory Committee consists of Member State representatives acting in an advisory capacity, enabling three or more Member States to propose a market investigation to the Commission. This configuration predominantly assigns an advisory role to Member States. The DMA also establishes specific timelines to circumvent delays and stagnation, reflecting insights gained from experiences with the GDPR (Vergnolle, 2021). Observers (e.g. Geradin, 2021) have pointed out that this centralised model of regulation marks a departure from the norm in EU digital and economic policy.

The question remains whether the Commission will allocate sufficient resources to independently handle the DMA's extensive responsibilities and whether it will negatively impact competition control in Member States, as some Member States have articulated (BMWK, 2024). Should any non-compliance be detected, it has the authority to enforce these rules by levying penalties of up to 20% of global turnover.[5] Additionally, the Commission may impose behavioural and structural remedies, including the potential breakup of gatekeepers.[6] However, the DMA does not prescribe specific methods for gatekeepers to ensure compliance or concrete outcomes (Akman, 2022). Instead, it allows them the flexibility to devise compliance solutions that are both necessary and proportionate. Within a short time following the applicability of these new rules, the Commission initiated proceedings against, e.g., Alphabet, Apple, and Meta due to concerns that these gatekeepers are not fully complying with their obligations under the DMA (European Commission, 2024c).

Those concerns relate to Apple's and Alphabet's app store obligations relating to current charges when app developers direct consumers to external offers, Alphabet's favouring its own vertical search services, and Apple's restricting user choice through the design of its web browser choice screen. Many of the rules embedded in the DMA have their roots in past competition cases, reflecting the EU's experience in dealing with the market dominance of large digital platforms through antitrust enforcement.

Over the years, the European Commission has tackled various high-profile cases involving major tech companies, often addressing issues like abuse of dominance, anti-competitive practices, and unfair trading conditions. These cases highlighted the limitations of traditional competition law when dealing with fast-evolving digital markets, where harm to competition could occur rapidly and with widespread impact. Drawing on these experiences, the DMA was crafted to proactively address and

[5] DMA, Art 30.

[6] Ibid, Art 18.

prevent the types of market distortions that had previously been dealt with on a case-by-case basis. By codifying certain practices as inherently problematic, such as self-preferencing or imposing unfair terms on business users, the DMA seeks to create clear, ex-ante rules that prevent anti-competitive behaviours before they can take root.

This shift from reactive enforcement to proactive regulation marks a significant evolution in the EU's approach, ensuring that the lessons learned from past competition cases inform a more robust and effective regulatory framework for overseeing digital platforms. The Meta 'pay or consent' model for EU users differs from traditional antitrust cases in several key ways, particularly in its focus on data privacy and user consent rather than solely on market dominance or anti-competitive practices (European Commission, 2024c) and exemplifies the innovative approach. Since the applicability of the DMA, additional players have also been designated as gatekeepers (European Commission, 2024c) demonstrating the EU's commitment to closely monitoring and regulating dominant digital platforms. This expansion reflects the dynamic nature of the digital market and the EU's proactive stance in ensuring that competition remains fair and that consumers are protected. As the DMA continues to evolve, it is likely that more platforms will come under its scrutiny, further solidifying the EU's regulatory framework in the digital economy.

The Digital Services Act

The Digital Services Act (DSA) was adopted against the backdrop of sector-specific legislation, such as the reform of the Directive on copyright, the Regulation for terrorist content, and the AVSMD, as well as soft law instruments such as the Commission's Recommendation on measures to effectively tackle illegal content online, as well as national legislative measures to address illegal online content, the European Commission adopted the draft DSA on the same day as the DMA (on December 15, 2022) and adopted on 29 September 2022.

The rapid evolution of the digital economy has changed significantly with the rise of social media, online marketplaces, and other digital platforms that did not exist when the original rules were created. Yet, in the absence of an updated directive for over 20 years, many of the rules governing online platforms were developed through case law. The European Court of Justice (ECJ) played a crucial role in interpreting the e-Commerce Directive, considering new technological developments and business models. For example, the ECJ dealt with cases related to the liability of online platforms, content moderation, and the responsibilities of intermediaries.

These rulings gradually filled some of the regulatory gaps but were often reactive and specific to individual cases, resulting in a fragmented and occasionally inconsistent regulatory landscape. However, they provided valuable guidance when the process of revising the framework eventually began. Ultimately, revising the e-Commerce Directive involved navigating several difficult value tensions. On the one hand, there was a need to protect fundamental rights, such as freedom of expression and the right to conduct a business. (Schwemer, 2022). On the other hand, there was growing concern about illegal content, online harm, and the market power of large digital platforms. Accordingly, the revision process also had to contend with the differing interests of various stakeholders, including member states, digital platforms, civil society, and traditional industries. Some stakeholders advocated for stronger regulations to protect intellectual property rights, while others feared that overly restrictive rules could stifle innovation and harm smaller businesses (European Commission, 2020).

Nonetheless, the liability rules from the e-Commerce Directive was kept with minimal changes. Indicating that the Commission intends to keep the foundational principles of the liability regime for hosting providers intact (Buiten, 2021). Consequently, online platforms remain fundamentally not responsible for third-party content. Based on the framework of the e-Commerce Directive, the liability for digital intermediaries is still based on their knowledge of specific illegality, and they do not have a special obligation to monitor the content their users upload (Senftleben & Angelopoulos, 2021), but the DSA introduces comprehensive and tiered procedural obligations, which increase with the size and prevalence of the service (Wilman, 2023).

The DSA focuses on managing information flow, outlining how content is promoted, contested, and removed (Savin, 2021). It establishes procedural standards for all online platforms, with more stringent requirements for very large online platforms (VLOPs) and very large search engines (VLOSEs), whose designation by the European Commission led to complaints currently under the review of the European General

Court as in the case of Zalando and Amazon.[7] In other words, without regulating content, it requires platforms to comply with procedural safeguards, thus making the process of content moderation more transparent and accountable. These obligations lead online platforms towards a bureaucracy of online content, which designs the 'administrativisation' of content moderation. The procedural rules on the notice-and-takedown or the statements of reasons are just two primary examples of how the Union is trying to require online platforms to be more transparent and accountable.

Moreover, specific rules are introduced for VLOPs, which, as other online platforms, are also bound by the general obligation to conduct their activities of content moderation in a diligent, objective and proportionate manner, particularly considering the fundamental rights of users as enshrined in the European Charter.[8] This focus on fundamental rights is a critical change in terms of accountability, particularly recognising the role of online platforms in balancing conflicting constitutional interests.

When it comes to their specific obligations, VLOPs are mandated to annually identify, analyse, and assess systemic risks stemming from their services' design, functionality, and usage. These evaluations prioritise several key areas, including the presence of illegal content and behaviours (e.g., hate speech, copyright infringements, bullying, child abuse material, unsafe products, etc.), potential impacts on fundamental rights, and specific issues such as civic discourse, electoral processes, public security, gender-based violence, public health, and minors' welfare. Mitigation measures may encompass adjustments to amplification and moderation tools, modifications to content and advertising regulations, bolstering trust and safety resources, refining incident documentation and management, and implementing protective measures for vulnerable user groups. These efforts must account for diverse local contexts across languages and countries.

Furthermore, VLOPs are obligated to finance independent audits to verify compliance with all due diligence obligations. In case of unfavourable audit findings, VLOPs must consider operational recommendations provided by auditors. Any non-implementation of these recommendations must be duly justified in an implementation report,

[7] Case T-348/23; Case T-367/23.

[8] DSA, Art. 14(4).

alongside self-assessments, mitigation strategies, and audit results. These reports are submitted to the European Commission and made publicly available in a redacted format. They are complemented by codes of conduct that companies may develop as a risk mitigation effort, as could be the case for the Strengthened Code of Practice on Disinformation. In addition, the DSA defines other obligations for VLOPs concerning crisis protocols, recommender systems, advertising transparency, and data access for oversight and research purposes.

The DSA's enforcement model introduces a more intricate framework of entities alongside the Commission, creating a complex network of duties (Hoboken & Zeybek, 2023). For very large online platforms, the Commission has direct supervisory and punitive authority, including the ability to impose fines up to 6% of a provider's global turnover for severe violations. In this role, the Commission acts as the primary regulator, with the Board serving an advisory role and the Member States being less involved in major cases.

While some see this model as potentially increasing efficiency and speed, akin to competition law practices, others worry about the risks of centralisation and the exclusion of Member States from significant cases. Over the last months, the DSA has been vigorously implemented, with the European Commission launching multiple investigations into major digital platforms, including AliExpress, TikTok, Facebook, and Instagram. These probes have targeted a variety of compliance issues ranging from inadequate risk assessments to improper handling of data scraping and advertising archives (Husovec, 2024b). Specific cases have spotlighted TikTok for its addictive algorithm features and Meta for potential mismanagement in political content and disinformation.

Alongside these enforcement actions, the Commission has issued guidance on elections, consulted on delegated acts concerning transparency and data access, and faced several legal challenges in courts regarding advertising archives and platform obligations. These developments underscore a dynamic period of regulatory activity aimed at enhancing the transparency and accountability of digital services across Europe (Husovec, 2024a). Notably, platforms like Facebook, Snapchat, TikTok, YouTube, and Google have been specifically asked to outline how they plan to address electoral integrity risks. This move reflects a broader effort by the Commission to ensure robust compliance with the DSA, marking a significant step in regulating online platforms' responsibilities and their impact on public discourse and safety.

The Way Forward for DMA and DSA

Both the DMA and the DSA underline how the transition from an adversarial model of enforcement to a more collaborative regulatory dialogue presents its own unique set of challenges. First of all, with the return of Donald Trump in the White House, the US administration is aggressively opposing EU enforcement of the DMA and DSA, threatening to take trade counter-measures, issuing visa bans to individuals—including the former European Commissioner Thierry Breton—and attacking the DSA in particular as being a censorship instrument. The ability of the Union to effectively implement its sovereign laws is therefore under constant test. Secondly, as the European Commission engages in frequent, sometimes weekly or monthly meetings with major digital gatekeepers, it allocates substantial time and resources to establish and maintain these relationships. However, this intense focus can inadvertently leave little room for developing similarly robust relationships with smaller competitors. Interpersonal dynamics are critical in advocacy, and the lack of meaningful engagement with these smaller entities might hinder their ability to voice concerns and participate effectively in the regulatory process. This imbalance could potentially impact the fairness and effectiveness of regulatory outcomes, as smaller competitors may not have the same opportunities to influence discussions and decisions that directly affect their market environment.[9] This could be observed in the workshops that the Commission held in March 2024, where gatekeepers and the enforcers were sitting side by side, demonstrating a collegial atmosphere while third parties were in the audience and allowed to ask questions (European Commission, 2024e).

Next to resource and jurisdictional challenges, the speed of enforcement actions will be crucial. The digital economy moves at a rapid pace, and regulatory interventions that come too late may have limited effect or may address problems that have already evolved. The challenge will be to make the enforcement process agile enough to respond quickly to emerging issues while still ensuring due process and thorough investigation.

Lastly, there's the challenge of regulatory coherence. With the DSA and DMA interacting with existing regulations like the GDPR, as well

[9] Conversation with a smaller competitor engaged with enforcement of the DMA.

as with national laws, ensuring a consistent and complementary enforcement approach across different legal instruments and jurisdictions will be essential. The success of the EU's new regulatory framework will depend largely on how effectively these enforcement challenges are addressed in practice.

This framework is also relevant for the next steps of the European Commission in the regulation of artificial intelligence. As will be explained in the next section, the intricate framework of obligations and enforcement defined by the new wave of EU regulation, primarily the DSA and the DMA, will require further coordination, particularly in the case of the Artificial Intelligence Act introducing horizontal rules for AI systems.

Platform Regulation in the Age of AI: Challenges for Von der Leyen's Second Commission

While current platform regulation primarily addresses established technologies like social media and search engines, the rapid evolution of the digital ecosystem necessitates forward-thinking approaches to emerging technologies. The DMA and DSA, while groundbreaking, may require further evolution to effectively govern emerging technological paradigms. Regulators must strike a delicate balance between addressing current issues and maintaining the flexibility to adapt to future technological developments.

The political discourse in view of the priorities of the second Von der Leyen's Commission focuses—beyond the Letta and Draghi reports as the foundations for political priorities—on enforcement of the new EU digital acquis, which includes but is not limited to sui generis platform regulations. However, 2023 has significantly shifted the attention to the increasing platformisation of the AI ecosystem, which already impacts the discourse of the DMA enforcement, the DSA enforcement and the broader sovereignty discourse (Mugge, 2024). Neither the DMA nor the DSA, however, addresses the platformisation of the AI ecosystem, or AI for that matter.

As AI technology rapidly advances, concerns about the dominance of large players in digital markets are growing (European Commission; CMA; US Department of Justice; US Federal Trade Commission, 2024). Microsoft's deal with Inflection, where the company hired most of the startup's staff and licensed its technology, is under the spotlight. Although it allegedly bypassed traditional merger review processes, the

EU is now considering the implications of such quasi-acquisitions. The UK's CMA, following the FTC's lead, has begun enquiries into AI-related partnerships involving major tech firms like Microsoft (CMA, 2024).

The Commission might not treat these partnerships as formal mergers due to the lack of control, yet it is exploring the antitrust implications of exclusivity clauses and other competitive restrictions within these deals. One other aspect is that cloud providers play a crucial role in AI development by offering scalable infrastructure, extensive storage capacity, and access to specialised hardware like GPUs and TPUs, which are essential for training and deploying AI models. The main bottlenecks and entry barriers in artificial intelligence revolve around critical inputs: data, computing power, and talent. Consequently, the potential designation of cloud computing providers as gatekeepers under the DMA could gain importance in the future. However, the Commission has not yet designated any cloud providers, likely due to concerns that such a decision could be challenged in court, given the potential weaknesses in the DMA's framework for this designation (Bania & Geradin, 2024).

Contrarily, a competitive chatbot market could potentially displace a monopolistic search engine market, potentially rendering DMA rules for search engines unnecessary (Martens, 2023). The Commission, hence, could monitor the interplay between search and answer engines, particularly when both are offered together on the same page. If substitution occurs, it could boost competition from dedicated chatbots. However, if the services are complementary, it might reinforce the market position of established search engines, maintaining their dominance driven by network effects (Martens, 2023).

The AI ecosystem is increasingly shifting towards platformisation, where generative AI is offered not just as standalone products but as comprehensive platforms. Just as OTT platforms evolved to include features such as chat and video conferencing within broader productivity suites, AI agents are transitioning from isolated applications to integral components of multiple products (Kutterer, 2024). OpenAI exemplifies this trend by developing large foundational models like GPT-4 and DALL-E, which serve as versatile bases for numerous applications (Yasar et al., 2023).

Models are directly accessible via APIs, leading to a new range of services yet to be categorised under the new platform acquis. While some generative AI applications might indirectly fall under the DMA, such as preventing gatekeepers from using business user data to compete and from tying services together, it wasn't designed with AI in mind and may not adequately cover generative AI systems or platforms. Yasar et al. (2023) argues that unfair practices are emerging that would undermine market contestability, highlighting the need for explicit DMA coverage of generative AI. He argues that generative AI services exhibit gatekeeper characteristics such as significant computing power, early mover advantages, and extensive data resources and integration. The generative AI market is dominated by a few companies (OpenAI, Google, Microsoft, Meta) with significant advantages in computing power and data resources, specialised hardware, vertical integration, network effects, and early mover status. Without regulation, these advantages may lead to entrenched positions in generative AI (Nylen & Bass, 2023), as seen in other digital markets.

On 17 May 2024, the High-Level Group of the DMA additionally announced a special focus on generative AI so that AI development aligns with the DMA and other regulatory frameworks, preserving market contestability and innovation incentives. Key areas of focus include cloud infrastructure, data access, standardisation, and interoperability. Additionally, the group will assess the influence of incumbent companies on innovative startups and address risks related to fundamental rights, consumer protection, intellectual property, cybersecurity, and disinformation. Ongoing cross-regulatory discussions will aim to ensure a consistent approach across the DMA and other legal instruments. The High-Level Group's efforts will include monitoring AI policy developments and interactions with the DMA, exchanging enforcement experiences and regulatory expertise regarding AI and the DMA, and developing effective cooperation to ensure a consistent regulatory approach across the DMA and other legal frameworks (High-Level Group for the Digital Markets Act, 2024).

Several civil society groups have equally urged regulators to address concentration in AI. The group also proposes several solutions that the Commission can use to address these high levels of concentration and control, including by making reforms to the EU's merger control regime to facilitate investigations of AI partnerships and minority investments that potentially fall outside of the scope of the existing merger regulation, and which can have a significant impact on competition in the market. Additionally, the group proposes introducing a legal presumption against acquisitions by dominant firms—for example, gatekeepers designated under the DMA. Acquisitions by this subset of firms would be presumed to be illegal under the EU's merger control regime (Open Markets Institute, 2024).

Whether this can be done within the DMA is unclear. Article 12(1) empowers the European Commission to enhance the obligations specified in Articles 5 and 6 of the DMA through delegated acts (Article 49). The specific parameters and limitations of this delegation are outlined in Article 12(2) of the DMA, which clearly defines the permissible updates through the procedure of Article 12 of the DMA. This procedure is intended to refine or expand upon existing obligations and cannot be used for broader amendments, such as introducing new obligations or removing existing ones. For significant changes, the legislative process must follow the ordinary legislative procedure (Article 294 TFEU). Whether this flexibility in the DMA is sufficient to ensure the legislation remains adaptable and relevant amid evolving digital market dynamics and new market realities remains to be seen.

The advent of AI technologies makes it necessary to undertake certain re-evaluations in view of a further shifting information asymmetry and considerations that go beyond the individual as the protégé and concern risks to democratic structures and foundations. Algorithmic recommender systems, which dictate the content users encounter, have already blurred the lines of responsibility and control. Additionally, a recent ECHR court decision, which has faced substantial criticism from Husovec (Husovec et al., 2024), warrants further consideration. Moreover, the DSA does not cover all digital services in its scope; further reflections are needed to consider the value chain in AI so as to avoid gaps in the approach to accountability and liability. AI models which are trained on content, i.e., extensive training datasets, can reflect undesirable elements of their training data in their outputs. The distribution chain for models has evolved into a complex value chain, presenting intricate governance challenges related to content moderation (Hao et al., 2023) and the applicability of the DSA, as well as other EU laws such as the AI Act, GDPR, and broader liability regulations.

AI is already considered in the DSA in recommender systems, in a special task force of the CoP on disinformation that is now adapted to generative AI, and in guidelines for VLOPS and VLOSEs on election integrity (European Commission, 2024b). Regarding the integration of general-purpose AI into search and recommender systems, the Commission requested more information from certain VLOPs and VLOSEs on 14 March 2024 (European Commission, 2024f). In addition, generative

AI is recognised as a potential systemic risk, and there are draft guidelines for providers of VLOPs and VLOSEs on the Mitigation of Systemic Risks for Electoral Processes (European Commission, 2024d).

Lemoine & Vermeulen (2024) assesses to what extent different generative applications could fall within the scope of the DSA (Lemoine & Vermeulen, 2024). The question of whether generative AI products fall under the DSA is challenging to assess in the abstract and requires an analysis on a product level. Lemoine and Vermeulen conclude that generative AI applications that are self-standing products could be covered by the DSA as intermediaries if they are considered 'online search engines' or 'hosting' services. This is not new; the distinction between a feature and a service has previously caused uncertainty in the application of the DSA.

Google Bard and OpenAI's new version of ChatGPT or its premium service, ChatGPT Plus, might be considered online search engines. A standalone GPAI model accessible through an API could only be considered a hosting service regarding the input data, as far as it is memorised, but not the output data or training data. It is thus important to keep in mind that there is content that is always illegal to possess or process, such as sexual child abuse image material or content that is only illegal when made publicly available, such as illegal hate speech. A similar debate (Hendrix, 2023) is currently happening in the United States, with some arguing that it is like a search and others arguing that ChatGPT should not benefit from the exemption (Ariyaratne, 2023).

AI model marketplaces such as GitHub or HuggingFace present other complex platform governance challenges due to their dual nature as content containers and tools. These platforms are at the early stages of developing new norms for model access and incentivising the integration of safety systems and thus pose complex questions like those faced by social media platforms in terms of content moderation. Gorwa and Veale (2024) recommend new developing practices such as licensing, access restrictions, automated content moderation, and open policy development to respond to moderation demands.

As new service types emerge, existing policies must be reconsidered and adapted, as the convergence of technologies and the rapid pace of innovation increasingly blur traditional categorisations and challenge the clear delineation of applicable rules. This dynamic environment demands a flexible and forward-thinking regulatory approach that can keep pace with these changes and effectively address the complexities of the evolving digital landscape.

Conclusions

The development of the DMA and DSA marks a significant shift in the regulation of digital markets, aiming to curb anti-competitive practices and enhance user safety and platform transparency. These regulations target primarily large tech companies, or 'gatekeepers', ensuring they do not abuse their dominant positions to stifle innovation and competition while maintaining a safer and more transparent online environment for users.

The EU's approach to platform regulation stands in stark contrast to those adopted by other major global players. While the EU has pursued a proactive and comprehensive regulatory framework with the DSA and DMA, the United States has largely maintained a more hands-off approach, relying on existing antitrust laws and Section 230 of the Communications Decency Act. This divergence reflects fundamental differences in regulatory philosophy and the balance between innovation and consumer protection. Meanwhile, China has taken a third path, implementing stringent controls over digital platforms, often intertwining economic regulation with political considerations. These differing approaches have created a complex global landscape for digital platforms, with the EU positioning itself as a regulatory trendsetter.

The novelty of these regulations, in terms of both substance and procedure, introduces a considerable degree of uncertainty that will need to be navigated over time. As these new rules are implemented and enforced, their real-world impact and the practicalities of enforcement will unfold while requiring ongoing adaptation and refinement to keep pace with technological advancements. Academia and legal experts are meticulously analysing the laws, the steps the Commission is taking, as well as the already emerging case law.[10] This scholarly attention underscores the complexity and significance of both regulations, as stakeholders from diverse groups, including competitors, civil society, and regulated entities, evaluate their effectiveness in shaping a fair and safe digital market.

[10] Multiple books have already been published on both the DSA and the DMA. Valuable contributions and ongoing observations can for example be found at: e.g. Geradin, The Platform Law Blog (2024)

European platform regulation has thus emerged as a substantial sui generis domain of European tech policy, gradually recognising and responding to the complexities introduced by digital platforms within the technological, economic, societal, and legal ecosystem. Over a period of two decades, this evolution has led to the development of this dedicated legal domain centred on the markets these platforms operate in and the content they distribute, intersecting with both vertical and horizontal legal domains such as data protection, copyright, consumer protection, competition, and contract law. The regulation of online platforms has been shaped by a myriad of political, industrial, and digital developments, as well as internal factors within the European Commission and external influences from expert knowledge and interest groups. Only the combination of these factors can explain the driving forces behind regulations in the platform economy.

If the enforcement mechanisms laid out in the DSA and DMA manage to avoid some of the delays and inertia seen in the GDPR's cross-border enforcement system, they are not without criticism (Vergnolle, 2021). The centralisation of enforcement power in the European Commission for the DMA and DSA presents several issues. The Commission faces a heavy enforcement burden, requiring extensive data analysis and an expanded skill set, including technical expertise. This centralisation also challenges the traditional separation of powers within the EU, with the Commission taking on increasing roles typically associated with legislative and judicial bodies, such as issuing non-compliance decisions, further substantive adaptation of laws through delegated acts and imposing fines. The risks that the Commission could overstep its competencies by going further have been widely discussed in the context of risk mitigations (Husovec, 2024b). This dual role poses long-term democratic risks, as it undermines the balance of power essential for preventing abuse. The new Commission presents an opportunity to address these concerns through organisational adaptations, such as consolidating the enforcement units under a dedicated Commissioner.

In conclusion, the DMA and DSA set a foundation for regulating digital markets, even if the questions about their role in the age of generative AI are still relevant. This European approach could become a benchmark for global digital regulation, emphasising consumer protection, fairness, and transparency in the digital economy. The success of these regulations will depend on effective enforcement, especially in front of a US challenge, continuous adaptation, and the integration of emerging technologies like AI into their regulatory scope.[11]

References

Akman, P. (2022). Regulating Competition in Digital Platform Markets: A Critical Assessment of the Framework and Approach of the EU Digital Markets Act. *European Law Review, 85*.

Andriychuk, O. (2021). *Shaping the New Modality of the Digital Markets: The Impact of the DSA/DMA Proposals on Inter-Platform Competition*. https://strathprints.strath.ac.uk/77300/1/Andriychuk_WCLER_2021_Shaping_the_new_modality_of_the_digital_markets.pdf.

Ariyaratne, H. (2023, May 17). *ChatGPT and Intermediary Liability: Why Section 230 Does Not and Should Not Protect Generative Algorithms*. https://papers.ssrn.com/sol3/papers.cfm?abstract_id=4422583

Bakir, V. (2020, September 3). Psychological Operations in Digital Political Campaigns: Assessing Cambridge Analytica's Psychographic Profiling and Targeting. *Frontiers in Communication*.

Bania, K. (2020). The Platform-to-Business Regulation: Taming the "Big Tech" Beast? *Article l Concurrences, 2*, 52–64.

Bania, K., & Geradin, D. (2024). The Regulation of Cloud Computing: Why the European Union Failed to Get It Right. *Information & Communications Technology Law, 33*(1), 99–113.

BBC News. (2013, August 20). *Edward Snowden: Timeline*. BBC News. https://www.bbc.com/news/world-us-canada-23768248

BBC News. (2017, November 25). *Predatory Comments Prompt YouTube Ad Suspension*. BBC News. https://www.bbc.com/news/technology-42110068

Beckedahl, M. (2015, March 6). *Günther Oettinger: Netzneutralität tötet, Befürworter sind Taliban-artig*. Netzpolitik: https://netzpolitik.org/2015/guenther-oettinger-netzneutralitaet-toetet-befuerworter-sind-taliban-artig/

Benkler, Y. (2007, May). The Wealth of Networks: How Social Production Transforms Markets and Freedom. *Journal of Media Economics, 20*(2), 161–165.

BMWK. (2024). *Strengthening the Digital Markets Act and Its Enforcement*. https://www.bmwk.de/Redaktion/DE/Downloads/M-O/non-paper-friends-of-an-effective-digital-markets-act.pdf?__blob=publicationFile&v=4

[11] In the preparation of this article, we utilised Artificial Intelligence tools to assist with the analysis of existing literature and the enhancement of language clarity. The literature analysis was supported by AI tools such as Elicit for mining key information from PDFs.

Buiten, M. (2021, June 21). *The Digital Services Act: From Intermediary Liability to Platform Regulation*. SSRN. https://papers.ssrn.com/sol3/papers.cfm?abstract_id=3876328

Bunderministerium für Wirtschaft und Energie. (2017). *Weissbuch Digitale Plattformen: Digitale Ordnungspolitik für Wachstum, Innovation, Wettbewerb und Teilhabe*. https://www.de.digital/DIGITAL/Redaktion/DE/Publikation/weissbuch.pdf?__blob=publicationFile&v=1

Carugati, C. (2020, December 2). *The New Competition Tool: An Analysis of the Policy Options and Institutional Set-Up*. SSRN. https://papers.ssrn.com/sol3/papers.cfm?abstract_id=3737996

Cate, F. H., Kuner, C., Millard, C., Svantesson, D. B., & Lynskey, O. (2015). Internet Balkanization Gathers Pace: Is Privacy the Real Driver? *Articles by Maurer Faculty, 2629*.

CBS News. (2014, January 2). *Millions Affected In Snapchat Security Breach*. CBS News. https://www.cbsnews.com/sacramento/news/snapchat-suffers-security-breach/

Cini, M., & Czulno, P. (2022). Digital Single Market and the EU Competition Regime: An Explanation of Policy Change. *Journal of European Integration, 44*(1), 41–57.

CMA. (2024, July 16). *Microsoft Corporation's Hiring of Certain Former Employees of Inflexion and Its Entry into Associated Arrangements with Infection*. UK Competition & Markets Authority. https://assets.publishing.service.gov.uk/media/66964b6fce1fd0da7b59260c/Commencement_notice.pdf

Commission Decision C. (2019). 2173, AT.40411 (March 20, 2019).

Cremer, J., de Montjoye, Y.-A., & Schweitzer, H. (2019). *Competition Policy for the Digital Era*. Publications Office of the European Union.

de Streel, A., & Husovec, M. (2020). *The e-Commerce Directive is the Cornerstone of the Internal Market*. European Parliament.

de Streel, A., Cremer, J., Heidhues, P., Dinielli, D., Kimmelman, G., Monti, G., Podszun, R., Schnitzer, M., & Scott Morton, F. M. (2024, January 5). *Enforcing the Digital Markets Act: Institutional Choices, Compliance, and Antitrust*. SSRN. https://papers.ssrn.com/sol3/papers.cfm?abstract_id=4314848

Dredge, S. (2014, January 17). *Who is Responsible for Kids and In-App Purchases: Apple, Developers or Parents?* The Guardian. https://www.theguardian.com/technology/2014/jan/17/kids-in-app-purchases-apps-parents

Elysee. (2017, September 26). *President Macron Gives a Speech on a New Initiative for Europe*. https://www.elysee.fr/en/emmanuel-macron/2017/09/26/president-macron-gives-speech-on-new-initiative-for-europe

EUIF. (2024, October 24). *European Union Internet Forum*. https://home-affairs.ec.europa.eu/networks/european-union-internet-forum_en

Euractiv. (2008a, March 12). *EU Gives Green Light to Google/DoubleClick Merger*. Euractiv. https://www.euractiv.com/section/competition/news/eu-gives-green-light-to-google-doubleclick-merger/

Euractiv. (2008b, January 14). *Google-DoubleClick Merger Brings EU into Uncharted Territory*. Euractiv. https://www.euractiv.com/section/competition/news/google-doubleclick-merger-brings-eu-into-uncharted-territory/

European Commission. (2010, May 19). *Communication from the Commission to the European Parliament, the Council, the European Economic and Social Committee and the Committee of the Regions A Digital Agenda for Europe*. https://eur-lex.europa.eu/legal-content/en/ALL/?uri=celex%3A52010DC0245

European Commission. (2015). *Public Consultation on the Regulatory Environment for Platforms, Online Intermediaries, Data and Cloud Computing and the Collaborative Economy*. https://digital-strategy.ec.europa.eu/en/consultations/public-consultation-regulatory-environment-platforms-online-intermediaries-data-and-cloud-computing

European Commission. (2016a, April 17). *Belgium: After the Attacks, Several Initiatives to Combat Hate Speech*. https://migrant-integration.ec.europa.eu/news/belgium-after-attacks-several-initiatives-combat-hate-speech_en

European Commission. (2016b, April 19). *Communication from the Commission to the European Parliament, the Council, the European Economic and Social Committee and the Committee of the Regions—Digitising European Industry Reaping the Full Benefits of a Digital Single Market*. https://eur-lex.europa.eu/legal-content/EN/TXT/?uri=CELEX%3A52016DC0180

European Commission. (2016c). *Memorandum of Understanding on the Sale of Counterfeit Goods on the Internet*. https://single-market-economy.ec.europa.eu/industry/strategy/intellectual-property/enforcement-intellectual-property-rights/memorandum-understanding-sale-counterfeit-goods-internet_en#:~:text=The%20Memorandum%20of%20understanding%20on%20the%20sale%20of,of

European Commission. (2017a, June 17). *Antitrust: Commission Fines Google €2.42 Billion for Abusing its Dominance as a Search Engine by Giving an Illegal Advantage to Own Comparison Shopping Service*. Press Corner. https://ec.europa.eu/commission/presscorner/detail/en/ip_17_1784

European Commission. (2017b, September 13). *Commission Staff Working Document Impact Assessment Accompanying the Document Proposal for a Regulation of the European Parliament and of the Council on ENISA, the "EU Cybersecurity Agency", and Repealing Regulation (EU) 526/2013, and on Information and C*. https://eur-lex.europa.eu/legal-content/EN/TXT/?uri=CELEX:52017SC0500

European Commission. (2017c). *Communication from the Commission to the European Parliament, the Council, the European Economic and Social*

Committee and the Committee of the Regions on the Mid-Term Review on the implementation of the Digital Single Market Strategy A Connected Digital S. Obtenido de. https://eur-lex.europa.eu/legal-content/EN/TXT/?uri=COM:2017:228:FIN

European Commission. (2018). *Commission Recommendation on Measures to Effectively Tackle Illegal Content Online*. https://digital-strategy.ec.europa.eu/en/library/commission-recommendation-measures-effectively-tackle-illegal-content-online

European Commission. (2019). *The EU Code of Conduct on Countering Illegal Hate Speech Online*. https://commission.europa.eu/strategy-and-policy/policies/justice-and-fundamental-rights/combatting-discrimination/racism-and-xenophobia/eu-code-conduct-countering-illegal-hate-speech-online_en

European Commission, Shaping Europe's Digital Future. (2020, 19 February). https://commission.europa.eu/system/files/2020-02/communication-shaping-europes-digital-future-feb2020_en_4.pdf

European Commission. (2022, June 16). *2018 Code of Practice on Disinformation*. https://digital-strategy.ec.europa.eu/en/library/2018-code-practice-disinformation

European Commission. (2024b). *Commission Guidelines for Providers of Very Large Online Platforms and Very Large Online Search Engines on the Mitigation of Systemic Risks for Electoral Processes Pursuant to Article 35(3) of Regulation (EU) 2022/2065*. https://digital-strategy.ec.europa.eu/en/library/guidelines-providers-vlops-and-vloses-mitigation-systemic-risks-electoral-processes

European Commission. (2024c, March 25). *Commission Opens Non-Compliance Investigations Against Alphabet, Apple and Meta Under the Digital Markets Act*. Press Corner. https://digital-markets-act.ec.europa.eu/commission-opens-non-compliance-investigations-against-alphabet-apple-and-meta-under-digital-markets-2024-03-25_en

European Commission. (2024d, March 14). *Commission Sends Requests for Information on Generative AI risks to 6 Very Large Online Platforms and 2 Very Large Online Search Engines under the Digital Services Act*. Press Room. https://digital-strategy.ec.europa.eu/en/news/commission-sends-requests-information-generative-ai-risks-6-very-large-online-platforms-and-2-very

European Commission. (2024e). *DMA Stakeholders Workshops*. https://digital-markets-act.ec.europa.eu/events/workshops_en

European Commission. (2024f). *Guidelines for Providers of Very Large Online Platforms and Very Large Online Search Engines on the Mitigation of Systemic Risks for Electoral Processes*. https://ec.europa.eu/newsroom/dae/redirection/document/102290

European Commission; CMA; US Department of Justice; US Federal Trade Commission. (2024, July 23). *Joint Statement on Competition in Generative*

AI Foundation Models and AI Products. https://competition-policy.ec.europa.eu/document/download/79948846-4605-4c3a-94a6-044e344acc33_en?filename=20240723_competition_in_generative_AI_joint_statement_COMP-CMA-DOJ-FTC.pdf

European Union. (2000). *Directive 2000/31/EC of the European Parliament and of the Council of 8 June 2000 on Certain Legal Aspects of Information Society Services, in Particular Electronic Commerce, in the Internal Market ('Directive on electronic commerce')*. https://eur-lex.europa.eu/legal-content/EN/TXT/?uri=CELEX%3A32000L0031

European Union. (2011). *Directive 2011/93/EU of the European Parliament and of the Council of 13 December 2011 on Combating the Sexual Abuse and Sexual Exploitation of Children and Child Pornography and Replacing Council Framework Decision 2004/68/JHA*. https://eur-lex.europa.eu/eli/dir/2011/93/oj.

European Union. (2015). *Regulation (EU) 2015/2120 of the European Parliament and of the Council of 25 November 2015 Laying Down Measures Concerning Open Internet Access and Amending Directive 2002/22/EC on Universal Service and Users' Rights Relating to Electronic Communications*. https://eur-lex.europa.eu/eli/reg/2015/2120/oj

European Union. (2017). *Directive (EU) 2017/541 of the European Parliament and of the Council of 15 March 2017 on Combating Terrorism and Replacing Council Framework Decision 2002/475/JHA and Amending Council Decision 2005/671/JHA*. https://eur-lex.europa.eu/eli/dir/2017/541/oj

European Union. (2018). *Directive (EU) 2018/1808 of the European Parliament and of the Council of 14 November 2018 amending Directive 2010/13/EU on the Coordination of Certain Provisions Laid Down by Law, Regulation or Administrative Action in the Member States Concerning the Provision*. https://eur-lex.europa.eu/eli/dir/2018/1808/oj

European Union. (2019). *Directive (EU) 2019/790 of the European Parliament and of the Council of 17 April 2019 on Copyright and Related Rights in the Digital Single Market and Amending Directives 96/9/EC and 2001/29/EC (Text with EEA relevance.)*. Obtenido de. https://eur-lex.europa.eu/eli/dir/2019/790/oj

European Union. (2022a, September 14). *Regulation (EU) 2022/1925 of the European Parliament and of the Council of 14 September 2022 on Contestable and Fair Markets in the Digital Sector and Amending Directives (EU) 2019/1937 and (EU) 2020/1828 (Digital Markets Act)*. https://eur-lex.europa.eu/eli/reg/2022/1925/oj

European Union. (2022b, October 19). *Regulation (EU) 2022/2065 of the European Parliament and of the Council of 19 October 2022 on a Single Market For Digital Services and Amending Directive 2000/31/EC (Digital Services Act)*. https://eur-lex.europa.eu/eli/reg/2022/2065/oj

Frosio, G. (2017, March 1). From Horizontal to Vertical: An Intermediary Liability Earthquake in Europe. *Oxford Journal of Intellectual Property Law and Practice, 565*(12).

Fujiwara, T., Muller, K., & Schwarz, C. (2021). The Effect of Social Media in Elections: Evidence from the United States. *National Bureau of Economic Research, Working Paper* (28859). https://www.nber.org/system/files/working_papers/w28849/w28849.pdf

Gadringer, S. (2020). Network Neutrality in the European Union: A Communications Policy Process Analysis. *Internet Histories, 4*(2), 178–195.

Geradin, D. (2021, April 7). DMA Proposal: Should There be a Greater Role for the Member States? *The Platform Law Blog*.

Geradin, D. (2024). *The Platform Law Blog*. https://theplatformlaw.blog/author/dgeradin/

Gillespie, T. (2010). The Politics of 'Platforms'. *New Media & Society, 12*(3).

Google and Alphabet v European Commission, T-612/17 (Judgment of the General Court June 27, 2017).

Google and Alphabet v European Commission, T-604/18 (Judgment of the General Court in Case July 18, 2018).

Gorwa, R., & Veale, M. (2024). Moderating Model Marketplaces: Platform Governance Puzzles for AI Intermediaries. *Law Innovation and Technology, 16*(2). https://arxiv.org/abs/2311.12573

Greenwald, G. (2013, June 6). *NSA Collects Phone Records of Millions of Verizon Customers Daily*. The Guardian. https://www.theguardian.com/world/2013/jun/06/nsa-phone-records-verizon-court-order

Hao, S., Kumar, P., Laszlo, S., Poddar, S., Radharapu, B., & Shelby, R. (2023). *Safety and Fairness for Content Moderation in Generative Models*. CVPR Workshop Paper/arXiv: https://arxiv.org/abs/2306.06135

Hendrix, J. (2023, March 23). *Generative AI, Section 230 and Liability: Assessing the Questions*. Tech Policy Press. https://www.techpolicy.press/generative-ai-section-230-and-liability-assessing-the-questions/

High-Level Group for the Digital Markets Act. (2024, March 22). *High-Level Group for the Digital Markets Act Public Statement on Artificial Intelligence*. European Commission: https://digital-markets-act.ec.europa.eu/high-level-group-digital-markets-act-public-statement-artificial-intelligence-2024-05-22_en

Hintz, A. (2012). Challenges to Freedom of Expression in the Digital World: Lessons from WikiLeaks and the Arab Spring. *ESSACHESS Journal for Communication Studies, 5*(1).

Hoboken, J., & Zeybek, B. (2023, August). *The Enforcement Aspects of the DSA and its Relation to Existing Regulatory Oversight in the EU*. https://dsa-observatory.eu/2022/02/04/the-enforcement-aspects-of-the-dsa-and-its-relation-to-existing-regulatory-oversight

Hoeffler, C., & Merand, F. (2023, December 22). Digital Sovereignty, Economic Ideas, and the Struggle Over the Digital Markets Act as a Political-Cultural Approach. *Journal of European Public Policy*, *31*(8), 2121–2146.

Husovec, M. (2024a). *Tech Notes: IT/IP & Digital Services Act*. https://husovec.eu/2024/05/the-dsa-newsletter-5/

Husovec, M. (2024b). *The Digital Service Act's Red Line: What the Commission Can and Cannot Do About Disinformation*. SSRN. https://papers.ssrn.com/sol3/papers.cfm?abstract_id=4689926

Husovec, M., Grote, T., Mazhar, Y., Mikhail, C., Kumar, S., Sinha, K. P., & Sreenath, S. (2024). Grand Confusion After Sanchez v. France: Seven Reasons for Concern about Strasbourg: Jurisprudence on Intermediaries. *Maastricht Journal of European and Comparative Law*, *31*(3), 385–411.

Juncker, J.-C. (2014, July 15). *A New Start for Europe: My Agenda for Jobs, Growth, Fairness and Democratic Change*. European Commission: https://commission.europa.eu/document/download/ad3f4ceb-aed8-4cc5-b6bb-4c60f448a5f2_en?filename=juncker-political-guidelines-speech_en.pdf

Kiss, J. (2010, May 15). *Google Admits to Collecting Wi-Fi data Through Street View Cars*. The Guardian. https://www.theguardian.com/technology/2010/may/15/google-admits-storing-private-data

Korff, D., & Georges, M. (2019, July 30). The Data Protection Officer Handbook. *The Data Protection Officer Handbook*.

Kutterer, C. (2024, February 27). *What If You Move on from Your AI Companion? Data Portability Rights in the Era of Autonomous Agents*. https://ai-regulation.com/what-if-you-move-on-from-your-ai-companion-data-portability-rights-in-the-era-of-autonomous-ai-agents/

Le Borgne-Baschmidt, F., Girieud, S., Leiba, M., de Munck, S., Limonard, S., Poel, M., Kool, L., Helberger, N., Guibault, L., Janssen, E., Eijk, N., & Swart, E. (2008). *User-Created-Content: Supporting a Participative Information Society*. IDATE.

Lemoine, L., & Vermeulen, M. (2024, October 9). *Assessing the Extent to Which Generative Artificial Intelligence (AI) Falls Within the Scope of the EU's Digital Services Act: an Initial Analysis*. https://papers.ssrn.com/sol3/papers.cfm?abstract_id=4702422

Lessig, L. (2000, January 1). *Code is Law: On Liberty in Cyberspace*. Harvard Magazine: https://www.harvardmagazine.com/2000/01/code-is-law-html

Livingstone, S., Olafsson, K., O'Neill, B., & Donoso, V. (2012). *Towards a Better Internet for Children: Findings and Recommendations from EU Kids Online to Inform the CEO Coalition*. The London School of Economics and Political Science.

Manthorpe, R. (2017, June 16). *Google Could be Fined $1bn by the European Commission as its Antitrust Case Comes to an End*. Wired. https://www.wired.com/story/timeline-googles-marathon-anti-trust-case-with-the-eu/

Martens, B. (2023, July 18). What Should Be Done About Google's Quasi-Monopoly in Search? Mandatory Data Sharing Versus AI-Driven Technological Competition. *TILEC Discussion Paper,* (12).

Meta Platforms Inc and Others v Bundeskartellamt, C-252/21 (Court (Grand Chamber) July 4, 2023).

Michels, J. D., Millard, C., & Walden, I. (2023, October 31). On Cloud Sovereignty: Should European Policy Favour European Clouds? *Queen Mary Law Research Paper,* (412).

Millard, C. (2021). *Cloud Computing Law* (2nd ed.). Oxford Academic Books.

Mugge, D. (2024). EU AI Sovereignty: For Whom, to What End, and to Whose Benefit? *Journal of European Public Policy, 31*(8), 2200–2225.

Muse, T. (2024a, September 9). *List of Key & Recent Acquisitions by Facebook.* HistoryOasis. https://www.historyoasis.com/post/facebook-meta-acquisitions-mergers

Muse, T. (2024b, September 9). *List of Key Acquisitions by Microsoft.* HistoryOasis. https://www.historyoasis.com/post/microsoft-acquisitions-mergers

Muse, T. (2024c, September 9). *List of Major Acquisitions by Apple.* HistoryOasis. https://www.historyoasis.com/post/apples-acquisitions-mergers-over-the-years

Muse, T. (2024d, September 9). *List of Major Acquisitions of Google.* HistoryOasis. https://www.historyoasis.com/post/google-alphabet-acquisitions

Newcomb, A. (2018, March 24). *A Timeline of Facebook's Privacy Issues—and Its Responses.* NBC News. https://www.nbcnews.com/tech/social-media/timeline-facebook-s-privacy-issues-its-responses-n859651

Nylen, L., & Bass, D. (2023, March 25). *Microsoft Threatens Data Restrictions In Rival AI Search.* Bloomberg. https://finance.yahoo.com/news/microsoft-threatens-restrict-data-rival-002746878.html?guccounter=1

Office of the United States Trade Representative. (2014). *2014 Section 1377 Review on Compliance with Telecommunications Trade Agreements.* https://www.ustr.gov/sites/default/files/2013-14%20-1377Report-final.pdf

Open Markets Institute. (2024, March 14). *Open Markets & Partner Civil Society Organisations Urge EU Regulators to Address Concentration in AI.* Open Markets. https://www.openmarketsinstitute.org/publications/submission-ec-ai-concentration

O'Reilly, T. (2007). What is Web 2.0: Design Patterns and Business Models for the Next Generation of Software. *Communications & Strategies,* (1).

Pappas, S. (2015, June 23). *Social Media Cyber Bullying Linked to Teen Depression.* Scientific American. https://www.scientificamerican.com/article/social-media-cyber-bullying-linked-to-teen-depression/

Polanski, V. (2017). *Impact of Social Media on the Outcome of the EU Referendum*. EU Referendum Analysis 2016. https://www.referendumanalysis.uk/eu-referendum-analysis-2016/section-7-social-media/impact-of-social-media-on-the-outcome-of-the-eu-referendum/#:~:text=Our%20large-scale%20social%20media%20data%20analysis%20shows%20that,active%20supporters%20across%20alm

Pollmann, M. (2014, September 11). *Privacy, Security & The Geography of Data Protection*. Dark Reading. https://www.darkreading.com/cloud-security/privacy-security-the-geography-of-data-protection

Quintais, J., & Schwemer, S. F. (2022, January 28). The Interplay Between the Digital Services Act and Sector Regulation: How Special is Copyright? *European Journal of Risk Regulation*, *13*(2), 191–217.

Robinson, K., & Merrow, W. (2020, December 3). *The Arab Spring at Ten Years: What's the Legacy of the Uprisings?* Council on Foreign Relations. https://www.cfr.org/article/arab-spring-ten-years-whats-legacy-uprisings

Savin, A. (2018). Regulating Internet Platforms in the EU—The Emergence of the 'Level Playing Field'. *Computer Law and Security Review*, *34*(6).

Savin, A. (2021, February 16). The EU Digital Services Act: Towards a More Responsible Internet. *Journal of Internet Law*, (21–04).

Schwemer, S. F. (2022). Digital Services Act: A Reform of the e-Commerce Directive and Much More. In A. Savin (Eds.), *Research Handbook on EU Internet Law*.

Senftleben, M., & Angelopoulos, C. (2021, January 4). *The Odyssey of the Prohibition on General Monitoring Obligations on the Way to the Digital Services Act: Between Article 15 of the E-Commerce Directive and Article 17 of the Directive on Copyright in the Digital Single Market*. SSRN. https://papers.ssrn.com/sol3/papers.cfm?abstract_id=3717022

Sloot, B., Hoofnagle, C. J., & Borgesius, F. Z. (2019). The European Union General Data Protection Regulation: What It Is and What It Means. *Information & Communications Technology Law*, *28*(1), 65–98.

Stone, K. (2023, January 10). *The History of VoIP and Internet Telephony: From the 1920s to Present Day*. GetVoIP. https://getvoip.com/blog/history-of-voip/

The Antitrust Source. (2016, June). *Interview with Andreas Mundt, President of the German Bundeskartellamt (Federal Cartel Office)*. https://www.bundeskartellamt.de/SharedDocs/Publikation/EN/Interviews/the_antitrust_source%20-%20An_interview_with_Andreas_mundt.pdf?__blob=publicationFile&v=3

TikTok. (2024). *Appealing our 'Gatekeeper' Designation Under the Digital Markets Act*. Newsroom. https://newsroom.tiktok.com/en-eu/appealing-our-gatekeeper-designation-under-the-digital-markets-act

Tsuji, K., & De Beaurepaire, C. (2023, April 25). *EU Eyes New Rules for Generative AI this Year: Vestager*. Nikkei Asia. https://asia.nikkei.com/Editor-s-Picks/Interview/EU-eyes-new-rules-for-generative-AI-this-year-Vestager

Vergnolle, S. (2021, September 3). *Enforcement of the DSA and the DMA: What Did We Learn from the GDPR?* Vergassungsblog. https://verfassungsblog.de/power-dsa-dma-10/

Wilman, F. (2023, January 9). *The Digital Services Act (DSA)—An Overview*. SSRN. https://papers.ssrn.com/sol3/papers.cfm?abstract_id=4304586

Witt, A. C. (25 de January de 2022). Platform Regulation in Europe—Per Se Rules to the Rescue? *Journal of Competition Law & Economics, 18*(3), 670–708.

Yasar, A. G., Chong, A., Dong, E., Gilbert, T. K., Hladikova, S., Maio, R., Mougan, C., Shen, X., Singh, S., Stoica, A. A., Thais, S., & Zilka, M. (2023, July 7). *AI and the EU Digital Markets Act: Addressing the Risks of Bigness in Generative AI*. ICML'23 Workshop Generative AI + Law (GenLaw). https://arxiv.org/abs/2308.02033

Zodi, Z. (2022). Characteristics of the European Platform Regulation: Platform Law and User Protection. *Public Governance, Administration and Finances Law Review, 7*(1), 91–108.

CHAPTER 11

Governing the Internet's Technical Future

Esteve Sanz

Introduction

It is not possible to appreciate EU digital policies without looking at the Internet, how the EU has positioned itself towards the multistakeholder model of Internet governance, and how it can influence the next stages of technological development. In that context, it is worth recalling that the fathers of the Internet, who were academics, were clearly inspired by universalistic objectives and wanted the Internet to be for everyone and to benefit humanity (Berners-Lee & Fischetti, 1999). This original design was, however, somehow lost in the development of the mobile Internet, with different operating systems developing walled gardens and regions around the globe, like China or Russia, erecting barriers to shield their citizens from global interactions. Some have argued that the EU's vision for the future of the Internet, embodied in the Declaration on Digital

Disclaimer: The author is an official of the European Commission. The information and views set out in this chapter are those of the author and do not necessarily reflect the official opinion of the Institution.

E. Sanz (✉)
European Commission, Brussels, Belgium
e-mail: Esteve.sanz@ec.europa.eu

T. Kleiner and A. Garcia Rodriguez (eds.), *The Making of a Global Digital Rulebook*, https://doi.org/10.1007/978-981-95-9226-5_11

Rights and Principles, is an attempt to go back to this original design of the Internet (Viola & De Biase, 2023). Investigating future developments at a time when new technologies are revisiting the technological building blocks of the Internet offers the opportunity to deepen this question and to ask whether EU digital sovereignty can be a chance to protect the Internet.

This chapter delves into the intricate challenges of governing the Internet's evolving technical landscape in the era of Web 4.0, highlighting the necessity of safeguarding the future potential of its technical architecture. It briefly explores the technological advancements that define this new era, evaluates how they test the limits of existing governance frameworks and discusses the efforts led by the EU to foster global consensus on the future of Internet governance. By reflecting on several initiatives, the chapter will finally underscore the importance of maintaining the Internet's foundational principles while adapting to the demands of its continuous evolution.

The Global and Multi-stakeholder Model of Internet Governance

When considering the Internet as a whole, it is useful to differentiate, albeit somewhat superficially, between three layers: technical, content, and connectivity. The technical layer of the Internet, the standards and protocols that interconnect global networks of devices, has evolved relatively stably and with few issues, focussing on core features that ensure global interoperability and smooth functioning (Castells, 2001). In contrast, the platform or content layer, encompassing major technology companies and service providers, has faced challenges related to market power and content regulation, among others (Regulation (EU) 2022/2065, 2022a). Meanwhile, the connectivity or telecommunications layer, despite advances such as satellite communications and enhanced broadband speeds, continues to grapple with the digital divide and the lack of universal access to the Internet (Joint Research Centre, 2023). Innovations in connectivity have not sufficiently bridged global disparities in Internet access, highlighting the need for more equitable solutions.

As a result, the two layers, telecommunications and platforms, are increasingly the object of regulation and direct government intervention, while the technical layer has maintained the collaborative approach that is foundational to the global, distributed character of the Internet. Indeed, over the past five decades, the technical layer of the Internet has evolved from a network of government laboratory connections into a foundational global infrastructure (Degezelle, 2022; The Internet Society, 2020). This transformation has been shaped by key organisations: the Internet Engineering Task Force (IETF), which develops and promotes voluntary Internet standards; the Internet Corporation for Assigned Names and Numbers (ICANN), which manages the DNS to ensure domain stability and security; and the World Wide Web Consortium (W3C), which creates standards to ensure long-term growth for the Web (Internet Governance Forum, 2024). Additionally, the Internet Governance Forum (IGF), established by the United Nations in 2006 following the Tunis Agenda, serves as a vital platform for multi-stakeholder dialogue on public policy issues related to the Internet (ICANN, 2024a).

These organisations exemplify a commitment to open, consensus-based, and bottom-up governance, contributing to the Internet's transformation into a dynamic network that connects the vast majority of the world's population. They are the key parts of the multi-stakeholder model of Internet governance (ICANN, 2024b). In this broader ecosystem of governance, as depicted in Fig. 11.1, stakeholders from around the world—including the European Commission (EC), European Union Member States (EUMS), European civil society, companies, and the technical community—collaborate across distinct but interdependent layers to ensure policies are not only informed but actively shaped by diverse voices. In this model, stakeholders don't merely offer input before decisions; they play a pivotal role in achieving a collective consensus that drives the Internet's evolution.

If the technical architecture of the Internet were to be centralised and subjected to overarching control and regulation, it would fundamentally alter the nature of the global network (Drake & Kleinwächter, 2016). This shift away from an open technical and governance architecture, which is built on globally accepted, consensus-driven standards like the end-to-end principle and modular protocols such as TCP/IP, would compromise the interoperability that underpins global connectivity.

Centralised control would introduce rigidities that hinder global interconnections and innovation and limit adaptability—features essential for the internet's evolution and responsiveness to new demands. Moreover, the global diffusion of these foundational internet protocols—a unique achievement unlikely to be repeated on such a scale due to today's

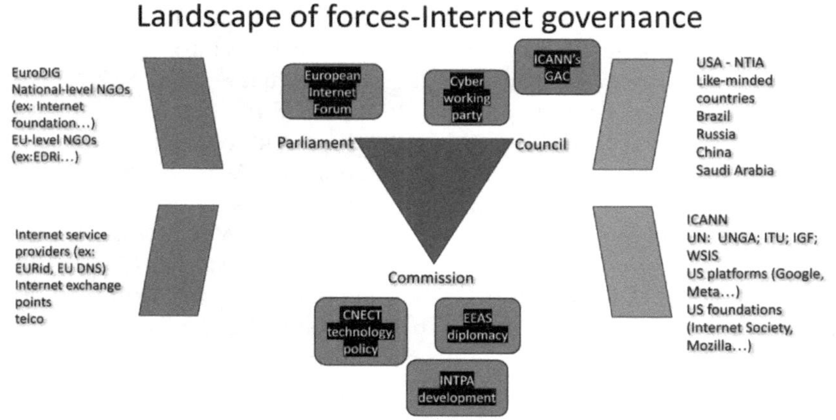

Fig. 11.1 Landscape of forces: the Embodied Internet: Technological Advancements Driving Web 4.0

complex geopolitical landscape—would face significant barriers. Fragmentation in adoption would be inevitable, as illustrated by Russia's "Sovereign Internet Law", which seeks to facilitate, albeit unsuccessfully, Russia's partition from the global internet by establishing a national Domain Name System (DNS) and tightly regulating internet access (Epifanova, 2020). Such measures showcase how centralisation risks fragmenting the global internet, stifling the open environment needed for innovation, broad-based access, and socio-economic development.

In global discussions on the future of digital governance, issues specific to telecommunications networks and platform layers are often bundled into proposals that, in reality, aim to alter the governance of the internet's core technical architecture. A notable example is the constant push by Russia in the UN-based discussions on the Global Digital Compact, the International Telecommunications Union (ITU), the Open-ended Working Group on Security in the Use of Information and Communications Technologies or the Cybercrime Convention to assert control over internet content and surveillance by embedding such measures within the technical layer—achieving state control but at the cost of severing connections to the global, interoperable internet.

This Russian approach, which conflates the three layers of the internet for essentially political reasons, is often framed as necessary to "bridge the digital divide", presenting it as beneficial for developing nations. However, during the recent negotiations on the Global Digital Compact, many developing countries have recognised and rejected this framing, choosing not to align with Russia's vision. China, despite its severe internal restrictions, continues to benefit from and support the need for a global internet, as its economic growth and technological advancement have heavily depended on participation in a globally interconnected network. In fact, China's aim is more aligned with influencing and potentially leading a more top-down technical architecture of the future global internet, which is reflected in its consistent and indiscriminate push for new internet standardisation proposals, including within ITU. In contrast, Russia's approach seeks to advance a model of technical internet control through the UN that essentially emphasises state sovereignty over a globally unified internet. Both approaches, however, risk weakening the open, resilient structure that has allowed the Internet to flourish on a global scale.

To safeguard the evolution and future potential of the internet's global technical architecture, it is essential to address the distinct challenges faced by each of its layers while preserving the integrity and decentralised nature of its foundational structure. The European Union, recognising the shifting political dynamics—particularly in the United States—has increasingly taken the lead in opposing both Russian and Chinese efforts to centralise internet governance and technical standards within the United Nations framework. Furthermore, the EU has proactively sought new partnerships with the developing world and led reflections on governance structures that can support the Internet's future. As rapid technological advancements drive change in telecommunications and application layers, necessitating regulatory responses, it is critical to strengthen the open, consensus-driven model of the technical layer, ensuring it adapts to support future innovation.

A key risk is that multistakeholder institutions, in striving to maintain the current internet, may overlook the need to accommodate and anticipate emerging technologies that will reshape their technical infrastructure. This role could be taken by other institutions, thus de facto fragmenting the internet as we know it. For the EU and developing countries alike, preserving an open, globally connected internet is essential not only for digital innovation but also to enable economies of scale and growth across digital sectors, which other regions of the world have already experienced (Denardis, 2020).

The landscape of forces shows, therefore, that Internet governance has a certain complexity with a number of actors that represent corporate or national interests, without this being always transparent. EU governments operate through forums that participate in multistakeholder processes, including the Council of the EU, where they discuss views on Internet Governance between experts and diplomats and through the ICANN Governmental Advisory Committee (GAC).

The GAC constitutes the voice of Governments and Intergovernmental Organizations (IGOs) in ICANN's multistakeholder structure and provides advice to ICANN on issues of public policy, especially where there may be an interaction between ICANN's activities or policies and national laws or international agreements. The Parliament does not have a strong role, given the absence of legislation governing the multistakeholder Internet governance model, but Members of Parliament are nevertheless active and participate in the Internet Governance Forum and organise activities in associations regrouping some of them, like the European Internet Forum.

The presence and influence of U.S. entities are quite significant, either because of the strong role of the U.S. government (notably the National Telecommunications and Information Administration) or because of the many companies and NGOs involved in the technical, content, and networking layers of the Internet. International actors are also significant, given the global nature of the Internet, but there are different positioning between countries like Russia, China, and the United States and like-minded countries, whereas other countries like Brazil or Saudi Arabia may have international clout and influence too. By contrast, European actors are mostly those involved with the infrastructures of the Internet (telco, exchange points, Internet service providers), and there is less of a presence in terms of platforms and content, reflecting European industrial weaknesses. The EU is, however, supporting the UN agencies and structures like EuroDIG, an open multi-stakeholder platform to exchange views about the Internet and how it is governed.

Many stakeholders, including the EC (European Commission, 2023), view the evolution of the Internet´s core infrastructure as facilitating the convergence of physical and digital spaces. That´s what´s generally known as Web 4.0. The evolution from Web 1.0 to Web 3.0 reflects a profound shift in the Internet's structure and user interaction (Berners-Lee, 1998).

Web 1.0, from the early 1990s to 2004, was a static phase focussed on one-way information sharing, with users passively consuming content managed solely by webmasters. Web 2.0 introduced interactivity and user-generated content, transforming the internet into a collaborative space with blogs, social media, and wikis (Solanki & Dongaonkar, 2016). Now, Web 3.0, as defined by the EC in a recent communication, is marked by "openness, decentralisation, and users' full empowerment" to control their data, manage identities, and participate in web governance. This phase integrates semantic web capabilities to link data across platforms and employs decentralised technologies to support peer-to-peer transactions, transparency, and data democracy along entire value chains (Rudman, 2015).

The Internet of the future would no longer be an Internet disassociated from the body and the territory via a simple screen. In contrast, it would facilitate the seamless integration of real and virtual spaces, where technology enhances physical presence, augments human capabilities, and enables AI agents to perform routine tasks across digital and physical environments. While keeping the TCP/IP protocol at its technological core, the network of networks would turn into some sort of human-computer-object-space hybrid. This integration would make digital interactions more intuitive and embodied, allowing individuals to interact with virtual environments through direct sensory experiences. This future Internet would, in turn, give rise to transformative applications in telemedicine, remote work, education, entertainment, socialisation, political participation and many other areas of social life, fundamentally reshaping our daily interactions and connectivity.

To fully realise the potential of a hybrid digital-physical Internet, advancements in foundational technologies are essential, enabling seamless integration across digital and physical realms. There is a widespread consensus that key foundational technologies—such as artificial intelligence (AI), quantum computing, edge and cloud computing, next generation connectivity and blockchain among others—will be pivotal in creating a secure, adaptive infrastructure if the internet's core is to be deeply integrated into the physical realm. Recently, a very significant development has been the acceleration of agentic AI: systems that do not merely generate content, but access tools, exchange information, coordinate with other agents, and act across digital and physical environments through emerging protocols and standards.

Moreover, more upper-layer technologies like the Internet of Things (IoT), brain-computer interfaces, and Extended Reality (XR) are so transformative that their widespread adoption could also drive profound changes in the Internet's technical architecture. All of them are the object of research, development and even standardisation tracks in IETF and other organisations, including ITU. Balancing these innovations with adaptable governance structures will be crucial to sustaining an inclusive internet that remains resilient and capable of evolving with emerging technologies:

- AI is becoming the organising layer of Web 4.0. It already leverages machine learning algorithms to analyse vast amounts of data, enhancing our ability to understand user behaviours, preferences, and patterns while creating efficiencies in multiple realms that are yet to be discovered. More importantly, the rapid development of agentic AI suggests that future internet interactions will increasingly involve autonomous or semi-autonomous agents acting on behalf of users, organisations, devices and services. Emerging agent-to-agent and agent-to-tool protocols point towards a new interoperability challenge: AI systems will need to communicate securely, exchange content, discover capabilities, negotiate tasks and coordinate across heterogeneous environments without becoming locked into proprietary silos. Developing modular AI interactions—where internet-connected objects can independently function while also interacting harmoniously within a broader physical network—will be crucial for realising an integrated digital-physical environment (European Commission, 2024b). As physical AI and world models develop, AI will also increasingly learn from simulated and real-world interactions, allowing systems to respond with greater nuance, adaptability, and precision.
- Edge and Cloud Computing are crucial in managing the vast data flows from digital interactions, which, with Web 4.0, will include an exponential amount of new physical interactions to be codified. Edge computing processes data close to its source, optimising response times in applications such as autonomous vehicles and IoT devices, while cloud computing offers scalable resources necessary for processing and storing extensive data across consumer and enterprise applications. These technologies are essential for the robust data infrastructure required in Web 4.0 (European Commission, 2024a).

- Blockchain technology offers a secure, decentralised method for recording transactions and managing data, essential for applications demanding high transparency and security, such as supply chain management and secure medical records. As Web 4.0 evolves, blockchain could play a critical role in enhancing data integrity and trust across digital transactions that also occur in the physical world (European Commission, 2024c).
- Quantum Technologies promises to transcend traditional computing limitations by solving complex problems that current technologies cannot tackle efficiently. The integration of quantum computing into the Internet and Web 4.0 (Quantum Internet) could revolutionise fields such as cryptography and system optimisation, offering new levels of efficiency and security that will expand complex interconnectivity between devices and the broader physical world (European Commission, 2024d).
- Brain-computer interfaces (BCI) enhance human–computer interaction by enabling direct communication pathways between the brain and external devices. This technology not only augments human capabilities but also offers the potential to restore them, particularly benefiting individuals with disabilities. BCIs could become integral to personalising user interactions in Web 4.0 by translating neural activities directly into digital commands (14).
- The Internet of Things (IoT) and Next Generation Connectivity expand Internet connectivity into everyday objects, making them "smart" and capable of autonomous performance. Enhanced by next-generation technologies like 5G, IoT facilitates a more interconnected and automated environment, crucial for the responsive, integrated systems envisioned in Web 4.0 (COM(2021)118 final, 2021).
- Extended Reality (XR), encompassing Virtual Reality (VR) and Augmented Reality (AR), blends digital information with the real world to create immersive environments. For example, in educational settings, XR provides interactive experiences that transport students to historical sites or allow them to simulate complex scientific processes in real time. For XR to serve as a foundational element of Web 4.0, it must embrace open standards and interoperability to integrate into the broader technical framework of the Internet. This integration will help unify currently fragmented investment and innovation ecosystems. However, XR also needs to overcome

challenges such as enhancing tactile feedback for more realistic experiences and reducing latency to ensure seamless interactions (European Commission, 2024f).

As we envision the transition into Web 4.0, the collective advancement of key technologies will fundamentally redefine the technical architecture of the Internet. This transformation promises to not only enhance our interactions with digital technologies but also to drive them towards greater integration, security, and responsiveness. The merging of digital and physical realms will transform the Internet into a more immersive and interactive extension of our environment, where actions in one sphere can directly affect the other.

While the potential of this transformation is vast, the extent and impact remain speculative. The Internet is already a vast, multifaceted technology that continues to reshape societies and economies in unforeseen ways. The advent of powerful new technologies suggests an even greater expansion of its capabilities and applications. This has triggered a different range of predictions about its concrete future integration with our physical bodies and environments. Such advancements could revolutionise services across sectors, including education and healthcare, particularly in developing countries, by enhancing how we experience presence and interaction, including with Artificial Intelligence systems. The lack of embodied presence would no longer be the central shortcoming of the Internet (Dreyfus, 2008).

However, these advancements also bring substantial risks to core values like privacy, freedom, and inclusivity. As digital and physical realms become increasingly integrated through Web 4.0, the potential for new vulnerabilities emerges. In the upcoming section, we will tackle the critical governance challenges posed by these technological shifts. An evolved multi-stakeholder model will be crucial to navigate these complexities, ensuring that Web 4.0 not only enhances user experiences but also preserves the foundational principles that have fuelled the Internet's growth and success.

Governance Challenges of the Future Internet

As we move towards the era of Web 4.0, the integration of transformative technologies like Extended Reality (XR), Artificial Intelligence (AI), and Brain-Computer Interfaces (BCI) is reshaping the interaction between digital and physical worlds, promising to significantly enhance user experiences. However, this deep integration raises complex governance challenges (Denardis, 2020), especially as these potent experiences become intricately woven into users' daily lives and potentially even their biological functions.

- Openness and interoperability: A crucial governance objective is ensuring that these technologies are open and interoperable, allowing them to enhance the Internet's infrastructure rather than creating fragmented, isolated networked spaces. This is particularly evident in XR, where private sector initiatives may limit openness as major tech companies strive to dominate or control their ecosystems. Additionally, state-designed systems may inherently carry sovereign principles that restrict global applicability. Multi-stakeholder organisations face the challenge of fostering openness amidst varied incentives between private and public entities. This challenge is especially urgent for agentic AI: proprietary agent-to-agent and agent-to-tool standards could reproduce mobile-style walled gardens at a deeper infrastructural level, while open and secure standards could reinforce the Internet's distributed architecture.
- Inclusivity and access: Technological advancements should not widen the digital divide but rather aim to bridge it. The significant investments required to incorporate and upgrade technological infrastructures pose adoption challenges for developing countries. Moreover, standard-setting organisations, often dominated by actors from developed nations, typically design protocols suited to higher connectivity environments. It is essential that these technologies are also viable under conditions of limited or no broadband access, ensuring that innovations are accessible and beneficial to all segments of society, including underserved and marginalised communities.
- Security vulnerabilities: The increasing complexity and interconnectivity of systems mean that vulnerabilities in one area can have widespread repercussions across the network. Strong security protocols are vital to protect against sophisticated cyber threats exacerbated by the expansion of IoT and other technologies. The development of a quantum internet represents a crucial frontier in security; its evolution must be managed under a consensus-based, multi-stakeholder framework to prevent potential conflicts in cyber security.

- Environmental impact: The growing digital infrastructure, from energy consumption to electronic waste, presents significant environmental challenges. Multi-stakeholder organisations governing the foundational internet architecture must integrate sustainable practices into their operations and standard-setting processes. This includes developing codes of conduct and certification systems that signal adherence to environmentally respectful practices.
- Privacy and surveillance: An Internet that pervades every aspect of life raises significant privacy concerns. The ubiquitous connectivity of even mundane objects like doors or the proliferation of surveillance cameras can lead to substantial privacy invasions. Governance frameworks need to robustly protect personal privacy without stifling the benefits of technological advancements. It is crucial for civil society organisations to amplify their role in multi-stakeholder discussions, advocating for stringent privacy protections and acting as intermediaries with the broader society. The same concern applies to agentic and physical AI systems, which may require continuous contextual, spatial and behavioural data to operate effectively, thereby making the governance of consent, data minimisation, purpose limitation and auditability even more central.
- Knowledge asymmetries and stakeholder engagement: The sophistication of emerging technologies necessitates the inclusion of a broader range of stakeholders in governance discussions. There is a need for experts, particularly from the private sector and academia, to effectively communicate technical implications to non-experts. This communication must occur without vested interests overshadowing the need for broad understanding and equitable decision-making.

Addressing these governance challenges is imperative as we advance towards a more integrated, immersive Internet. The multi-stakeholder model must evolve to accommodate these changes, ensuring that the future Internet remains a resilient, inclusive, empowering, and democratically governed space.

The European Union's Strategic Role in Shaping Internet Governance for Web 4.0

As we delve into the future governance of the Internet, the EU demonstrates a nuanced approach to its regulatory and participatory roles. While the EU has implemented rigorous regulations for the platform and telecommunications layers—evident in measures such as the Digital Services Act (DSA) and the Digital Markets Act (DMA)—it preserves the integrity of the technical layer by supporting the multi-stakeholder model of internet governance. This approach ensures that while the EU addresses market power and consumer protection within its jurisdiction, the fundamental architecture of the Internet remains under the stewardship of global, consensus-driven entities.

In understanding the landscape of forces shaping the EU's approach to Internet governance, it's essential to view this landscape within the broader, complex ecosystem of global Internet governance. Key EU stakeholders strongly agree that the multistakeholder model and an open internet rooted in human rights should guide the EU's international positions, helping the EU to grow its influence on the global stage. This unified stance, which includes a strong consensus within EUMS participating in Council discussions, is proven to be essential in countering approaches by nations like Russia, which seek to control the internet's core technical architecture under the guise of bridging the digital divide—a strategy that, if unchecked, could fragment the global Internet.

The EC actively consults with stakeholders, including civil society and industry representatives, through groups like the High-Level Internet Governance Group to ensure that the EU's policies reflect a diverse range of perspectives. In standards-setting discussions, the EU emphasises multistakeholder forums as legitimate spaces to advance internet technologies, though it continues working to boost EU companies' participation, as they currently hold less influence than their Chinese and American counterparts. Additionally, civil society groups increasingly call on the EU to play a more assertive role in defending the open internet and supporting anti-censorship technologies globally in the face of growing digital authoritarian practices. Together, these actors underscore the EU's commitment to a governance model that prioritises human rights, consensus-building, and resilience amid emerging global challenges.

Building on its cohesive internal stance, the EU has undertaken numerous international initiatives to promote an open, human-centric internet, notably in Africa. With DG INTPA (International Partnerships) and the EEAS (European External Action Service) now contributing to internet governance alongside DG CNECT, which maintains a leadership role in this field, the EU has mobilised its Delegations and leveraged Global Gateway funding to support open internet infrastructure in developing regions. This expanded role, including annual delegations of Members of the European Parliament to the Internet Governance Forum, has fostered critical alliances with policymakers worldwide, reinforcing the EU's commitment to digital rights and inclusivity. Through these efforts, the EU has been crucial in resisting centralised governance models advanced by Russia and China while promoting a multistakeholder governance model that is responsive to emerging technologies and developed in partnership with countries across the Global South (European Commission, 2022b).

The EU took the opportunity to shape global governance at the World Summit on the Information Society (WSIS+20) in late 2025. Originally launched by the United Nations in 2003 and 2005, WSIS aimed to bridge the global digital divide and foster a people-centred information society. One of its key achievements was establishing the Internet Governance Forum (IGF) as a legitimate space for collaborative Internet policy discussions among governments, civil society, and the private sector, thus establishing a de facto global consensus on the overall Internet governance ecosystem.

The WSIS+20 summit delivered an outcome document that provided both stability and continuity, and perspectives to protect the future of the Internet in front of new developments. Central to the preparation of the summit was the negotiation of the Global Digital Compact, which finally includes an unprecedented reaffirmation of the multistakeholder model, aligning global actors around open, decentralised internet governance and isolating Russia's state-controlled vision. This renewed commitment also opened new attention to pressing digital divide issues and evolving governance structures to accommodate new technologies. (European Commission, 2022b).

The WSIS+20 has been considered a highly significant, stabilising success—in particular given its context (Vahtre, 2026). Its main value was to confirm that an open, free, global, interoperable, reliable and secure Internet remains a global consensus project, at least on paper. First, the mere fact of reaching consensus on a common text in a situation of U.S. withdrawal from multilateral instances, and reservations from both autocratic and developing countries, is a real and welcome achievement. Second, the WSIS vision from 2005 was reaffirmed and updated through a of a human-centric and human rights-based understanding of digital transformation, anchored in international law. An important achievement was to make the Internet Governance Forum (IGF) a permanent institution, thus consolidating it as the central legitimating forum of the multistakeholder model of internet governance. This provides continuity for global internet governance discussions and strengthens the institutional space through which governments, the technical community, civil society, academia and the private sector can address emerging digital challenges impacting the internet, without moving towards a state-centric or fragmented governance model. Also significant was the establishment of a forward looking implementation process through action and objective-oriented roadmaps, whcih can help organise UN digital policymaking round existing frameworks, avoid duplication and give practive effect to the WSIS outcome. Taken together with the permanent institutionalisation of the IGF, this reates a stronger basis for the kind of multistakeholder governance labs promoted by the EU: practical spaces within the IGF ecosystem to anticipate and address emerging technology challenges affecting the openness, interoperability and integrity of the internet. These elements closely reflected priorities set out in the Line-to-Take decided by the Council of the European Union for WSIS+20 (Payne & McDonald, 2026).

Indeed, as the digital landscape continues to evolve with the advent of technologies like AI, the EU acknowledges its pivotal role in shaping the discourse around the future of the internet in the context of WSIS+20. The EU is actively participating in initiatives that prepare for the complexities of future digital environments, as evidenced by its involvement in multiple pilot projects exploring the potential of the transition to Web 4.0. These projects aim to assess and develop the necessary infrastructures and governance frameworks that anticipate the needs and challenges of more immersive and pervasive digital experiences.

The Declaration on Digital Rights and Principles is invoked as guiding the future direction of these emerging technologies (European Commission, 2022b). To this end, the European Commission and the European Council, as part of its efforts to lead on internet governance, convened a global multi-stakeholder discussion in Brussels in order to find solutions to advance the multi-stakeholder model with a proactive and anticipatory approach, ensuring that it remains relevant and effective in managing the complexities of emerging digital technologies (European Commission, 2024e).

This highlights the attempt of the EU to chart its own course in the digital space and to develop its digital sovereignty in line with the values it promotes. As such, the EU is positioning itself as a guarantor of the values that initially shaped the internet. This approach is, interestingly, different from what other regions are deploying to maintain or expand their influence in global internet governance. While the United States builds on the existing multistakeholder model, China is building alliances with countries to change these institutions and to shift power towards governments and their proxies, like the decision bodies of the United Nations. The EU, by adopting a principles-driven, inclusive and consultative approach—in line with the model of digital sovereignty it has developed—is staying true to the way the Internet has developed.

This commitment is crucial as the EU continues to navigate the complexities introduced by emerging technologies that could reshape the internet's infrastructure. By maintaining a clear distinction between the need for regulatory intervention at the platform and telecommunications layers and advocating for an ever-improved and evolved consensus-based approach at the technical layer, the EU helps ensure that the future internet remains a robust, inclusive, and dynamic space.

Conclusion

The EU's strategic engagement in global internet governance reflects its vision of an open, resilient, and human-centred internet. Amid evolving geopolitical dynamics, including a less assertive stance from the new U.S. administration, the EU is taking greater responsibility in defending the open internet. This role is both politically and economically significant: a global, open internet reduces geopolitical tensions, upholds human rights, and ensures companies from Europe and developing countries can benefit from the same opportunities as U.S. and Chinese firms had.

The EU aims to promote a model of internet governance where technology operates within a resilient, sustainable, and trusted framework. This approach reinforces the internet's foundational principles of openness and interoperability, protecting it from undue influence by state actors and large private interests. By advancing standards and regulations that support a multistakeholder model, and by promoting anticipatory spaces such as multistakeholder governance labs within the IGF ecosystem, the EU seeks to safeguard an internet that is accessible and beneficial to all, promoting democratic values and reducing the risk of digital fragmentation.

The follow up to the WSIS+20 offers a crucial platform for the EU to rally international support for this vision, building on the Global Digital Compact's affirmation of the multistakeholder model. The stakes are high, as the technologies and governance challenges identified in this chapter are of major magnitude. The blurring of the digital and physical realms, accelerated by agentic AI, virtual worlds and physical AI, creates significant opportunities but also major vulnerabilities in terms of security and rights. As technological advancements reshape the digital landscape, the EU will continue advocating for a governance model that balances innovation with democratic principles, ensuring a fair, inclusive, and resilient global internet that supports peace and development worldwide.

Bibliography

Berners-Lee, T. (1998). *The World Wide Web: A very short personal history*. Retrieved from https://www.w3.org/People/Berners-Lee/ShortHistory.html

Berners-Lee, T., & Fischetti, M. (1999). *Weaving the web: The original design and ultimate destiny of the World Wide Web by its inventor*. Harper Collins Publishers.

Castells, M. (2001). *The internet galaxy*. Oxford University Press.

Degezelle, W. (2022, June). *"The Open Internet as cornerstone of digitalisation," provides a comprehensive overview of the fundamental principles of the open internet and the multi-stakeholder model of internet governance*. Retrieved from https://fpi.ec.europa.eu/document/download/442ade63-f1ee-4a33-a270-a70600fa8348_en?filename=The%20Open%20Internet%20as%20cornerstone%20of%20digitalisation%20DIGITAL.pdf

Denardis, L. (2020). *The internet in everything: Freedom and security in a world with no off switch*. Yale University Press.

Drake, W., & Kleinwächter, V. C. (2016). *Future of the internet initiative white paper, internet fragmentation: An overview*. World Economic Forum.

Dreyfus, H. L. (2008). *On the internet: Thinking in action* (2nd ed.). Routledge.

Epifanova, A. (2020). *Deciphering Russia's "sovereign internet law"*. Retrieved from DGAP: https://dgap.org/en/research/publications/deciphering-russias-sovereign-internet-law

European Commission. (2021). *Communication from the Commission to the European Parliament, the Council, the European Economic and Social Committee and the Committee of the Regions: Digital Compass: The European way for the Digital Decade*. Retrieved from https://eur-lex.europa.eu/legal-content/en/TXT/?uri=CELEX%3A52021DC0118

European Commission. (2022a). *Regulation (EU) 2022/2065 of the European Parliament and of the Council of 19 October 2022 on a Single Market For Digital Services and amending Directive 2000/31/EC (Digital Services Act)*. Retrieved from https://eur-lex.europa.eu/eli/reg/2022/2065/oj

European Commission. (2022b). *Declaration on European Digital Rights and Principles*. Retrieved from https://digital-strategy.ec.europa.eu/en/policies/digital-principles.

European Commission. (2023). *Towards the next technological transition: Commission presents EU strategy to lead in Web 4.0 and virtual worlds*. Retrieved from https://digital-strategy.ec.europa.eu/en/news/towards-next-technological-transition-commission-presents-eu-strategy-lead-web-40-and-virtual

European Commission. (2024a). *Cloud computing*. Retrieved from https://digital-strategy.ec.europa.eu/en/policies/cloud-computing

European Commission. (2024b). *European approach to artificial intelligence*. Retrieved from https://digital-strategy.ec.europa.eu/en/policies/european-approach-artificial-intelligence

European Commission. (2024c). *Blockchain strategy*. Retrieved from https://digital-strategy.ec.europa.eu/en/policies/blockchain-strategy

European Commission. (2024d). *Quantum technologies*. Retrieved from https://defence-industry-space.ec.europa.eu/eu-space/research-development-and-innovation/quantum-technologies_en

European Commission. (2024e). *Pilot project in the space of the metaverse: Virtual world and transition to Web 4.0*. Retrieved from https://digital-strategy.ec.europa.eu/en/funding/pilot-project-space-metaverse-virtual-world-and-transition-web-40

European Commission. (2024f). *Web 4*. Retrieved from https://ec.europa.eu/commission/presscorner/detail/en/ip_23_3718

ICANN. (2024a). *Home*. Retrieved from www.icann.org

ICANN. (2024b). *The multistakeholder model of internet governance*. Retrieved from https://itp.cdn.icann.org/en/files/government-engagement-ge/multistakeholder-model-internet-governance-fact-sheet-05-09-2024-en.pdf

Internet Governance Forum. (2024). *Home*. Retrieved from https://www.intgovforum.org

Joint Research Centre. (2023, July 3). *Next generation virtual worlds*. Retrieved from JRC Publications Repository: https://joint-research-centre.ec.europa.eu/jrc-news-and-updates/next-generation-virtual-worlds-opportunities-challenges-and-policy-implications-2023-07-03_en

Payne, R., & McDonald, E. (2026, January 6). *Twenty years on: What WSIS+20 means for international digital governance*. Tech Policy Press. Retrieved from https://www.techpolicy.press/twenty-years-on-what-wsis20-means-for-international-digital-governance/

Rudman, R. (2015). Web 3.0: Governance, risks and safeguards. *Journal of Applied Business Research (JABR), 31*(3), 1037–1056.

Solanki, M. R., & Dongaonkar, A. (2016). A journey of human comfort: Web 1.0 to Web 4.0. *International Journal of Research and Scientific Innovation (IJRSI), 3*(9), 124–134.

The Internet Society. (2020, September). *The internet way of networking defining the critical properties of the internet*. Retrieved from https://www.internetsociety.org/wp-content/uploads/2020/09/IWN-IIAT-Defining-the-critical-properties-of-the-Internet.pdf

The Internet Society. (2022). *Who makes the internet work: The internet ecosystem*. Retrieved from https://www.internetsociety.org/internet/who-makes-it-work/

Vahtre, M. (2026, January). *WSIS+20: Why a "small" agreement still matters for our digital future*. Estonian Internet Foundation. Retrieved from: https://www.internet.ee/eif/news-archive/wsis-20-why-a-small-agreement-still-matters-for-our-digital-future

Viola, R., & De Biase, L. (2023). *Il codice del futuro, la carta europea dei diritti digitali e il senso dell'innovazione*. Il Sole 24 Ore.

CHAPTER 12

The EU Needs Semiconductor Supply Security to Achieve Digital Sovereignty

Alicia García-Herrero and Gary Ng

Introduction

The European Union (EU) is always a frontrunner in formulating regulations within its large single market. While the EU may have advanced in many areas, including data protection, it is facing growing challenges in the digital space as the service providers and component producers are outside of the block. In particular, the EU's massive reliance on semiconductor imports can be an Achilles heel as the component is critical in future megatrends ranging from cloud computing to tech adoption in core sectors, such as automobile and artificial intelligence. To safeguard digital sovereignty, the EU must learn from the past and navigate

A. García-Herrero (✉)
Bruegel, Brussels, Belgium
e-mail: alicia.garcia-herrero@bruegel.org

Hong Kong University of Science and Technology, Hong Kong, Hong Kong

G. Ng
Natixis, Paris, France
e-mail: gary.ng@natixis.com

Central European Institute of Asian Studies, Bratislava, Slovakia

T. Kleiner and A. Garcia Rodriguez (eds.), *The Making of a Global Digital Rulebook*, https://doi.org/10.1007/978-981-95-9226-5_12

the future in an increasingly geopolitically shaped world with constructive industrial policies.

In this chapter, we aim to offer a roadmap for the EU's strategy to enhance its semiconductor industry with the general goal of enhancing its digital sovereignty. We first set the stage in explaining the relevance of semiconductors in digital sovereignty under the EU context. Second, we analyse the past episodes and the present position of Europe in the global chip supply chains with a specific focus on the EU. Third, we further look at the EU Chip Act against the backdrop of the evolving geopolitical environment and the rise of industrial policies. Lastly, we examine the case of China, a competitor to the EU with different value propositions and strong state support for years. Comparing the EU Chip Act to China's model and understanding U.S.-led geopolitical evolution should provide the EU with the soil for policy recommendations regarding the best strategies to reposition itself in the modern semiconductor supply chains and uphold digital sovereignty.

Relevance of Semiconductors in Digital Sovereignty

Greater Focus on Digital Sovereignty

After the shocks from the COVID-19 pandemic and the Russian invasion of Ukraine, supply chain security has become a key objective for the EU to facilitate digital and green transition. For the former, a key focus is on enhancing digital sovereignty. The concept refers to the EU's ability to act independently in the digital economy and reduce excessive critical foreign dependencies. From Artificial Intelligence to the Internet of Things, most sectors worldwide are indispensable from digitalisation. The difference is that the EU is not in the driving seat of such innovation, which is not the case in the previous technological revolutions. Such dependence may look dominated by digital services, but there is a crucial hardware aspect that is required to enable these technologies, namely semiconductors.

Semiconductor Is an Enabler of Digitalisation, but with Risks in Supply Security

Semiconductors have always been important, but they have drawn greater attention after the shortage and supply chain disruptions surrounding the COVID-19 pandemic. The Ukraine–Russia war has further amplified the fear of economic and supply chain security in energy and various raw materials, especially in Europe. Geopolitical uncertainties, lockdowns affecting China's production and ports, and the growing logistical uncertainties due to extreme weather have also prompted governments to rethink chip supply. The idea was first advocated by the US that more local production can avoid potential supply chain disruptions, but more countries have followed the same policy directions. The EU is equally aware of the risks of the current chip supply setup for European industrial capacity and digital sovereignty.

In the past few decades, the development in the semiconductor industry has been following Moore's law, meaning the number of transistors on a single chip would double every two years at minimal costs. With fierce competition and heavy capital expenditure, chip production has consolidated with horizontal integration. Different steps of chip manufacturing, such as design, fabrication, assembling, and testing, may no longer be completed by the same firm. It indicates that semiconductors have become a more globalised product, and each step is held in the hands of different firms. With lower costs and better productivity, much of the activities have also shifted to Asia. From the security perspective, it implies a potential concentration risk at Asia's geographical and corporate levels.

While Asia may not necessarily be the next geopolitical flash point, tensions are rising from the Taiwan Straits to the South China Sea, showing it is sensible to prepare for diversification to at least manage, if not avoid, all risks. It brings the question of whether the EU can achieve digital sovereignty without local semiconductor production under the more intense geopolitical climate in the event of a sudden supply shock or blockade faced by key chip exporters. If the answer is negative, the EU needs to invest more to build the capacity, at least at a more comfortable supply level, to meet part of the demand.

Beyond the regulatory and legislative framework, domestic chip production is a prerequisite for the EU to achieve digital sovereignty, which is also a weakness at the moment. The EU should learn from the experience of other countries with similar ideas in supply chain security in semiconductors and extend its scope to the pursuit of digital sovereignty.

Past and Present: Europe's Chipmaking History and the Current Position

The Failed State-Led Approach in the 1950s–1970s

While the US seems to hold the key to modern semiconductor technologies, Europe can be traced back to the birthplace when German physicist Karl Ferdinand Braun invented the rectifier in 1874. Since then, a breakthrough came from the invention of the point-contact transistor in 1947 by research scientists John Bardeen and Walter Brattain at Bell Laboratories in the US, ultimately leading to the success of Fairchild Semiconductor and Intel. In contrast, European semiconductor development was stalled.

In the 1950s, there was a strong call for government intervention and industrial policies in Europe after World War II to narrow the income and technological gap with the US, leading to nationalisation and excessive government intervention, mainly through subsidies. Starting from the UK, the government expanded state control of the economy with large-scale nationalisation with priority in sectors such as aviation, nuclear, and computers. In France, the government also began to use nationalisation and economic planning to promote industrial development. De Gaulle, who came to power again in 1958, was determined to propel France into the forefront of industrial power with his "Plan Calcul", but the cultivation of the local computer industry was not on the radar until the rise of IBM computers in the 1960s.

Conversely, West Germany saw an economic growth miracle stemming from the non-intervention policy and privatisation strategy. However, West Germany was prohibited from developing defence-related industries due to post-war restrictions, including computers. Although Siemens achieved great results in ultra-pure silicon processes, Germany's semiconductor industry made limited progress.

The failure of industrial policies can be attributed to the ineffective allocation of resources, as subsidies were deployed to resist deindustrialisation and support declining heavy industries, especially in the government's inability to pick winners. Other factors include the fragmentation of markets and producers, different regulations across Europe, etc. With the ineffectiveness and the poor economic result, most governments changed their approach in the late 1960s.

In 1968, the UK merged and established International Computers Limited (ICL) by merging a few key computer manufacturers in the country as the government supported R&D investment and made preferential pronouncement of products. Despite the greater government support, the timing was too late as the investment was mainly in mainframes while personal computers from IBM were on the rise. By the same token, France merged a few key firms and divisions to form Sescosem in 1968 and 1969, which was controlled by the Thomson group. In the 1970s, French President d'Estaing began to reduce government intervention to encourage new startups.

During the period, the industrial development in Europe also had a strong national flavour. A typical case is that British Prime Minister Harold Wilson proposed market and technology integration to European countries, but the idea was firmly opposed by French President Charles de Gaulle. The political reality made the corporation's involvement in manufacturing, technology, and innovation very complex.

Dawn from European Integration, Free Markets, and Constrictive Policies in the 1980s–2000s

After adopting a market-driven approach with less friction in cooperation with other countries, the development of the semiconductor industry saw significant improvement compared to the previous era. The goal of European countries switched towards improving the business environment for all enterprises, allowing free competition, and advocating European integration. Barriers to cross-border trade and investment were removed, state-controlled industries such as electricity and telecommunications were partially privatised, and the government's ability to protect local enterprises was also weakened.

With the past episodes of poor experiences and lessons, more countries were forced to rethink their industrial policies. As Margaret Thatcher took office in 1979, the UK began the neoliberal development stage. The privatisation of enterprises and the introduction of foreign capital increased the vitality of British enterprises. In the 1980s, several innovative companies in the field of information technology were born in an area around the University of Cambridge, which was later known as the "Silicon Swamp". It includes Acorn Computer Company, which is now part of ARM.

The combination of policy changes has caused the UK to voluntarily give up its independence in semiconductor manufacturing and eventually focus on software services. As the UK sold most local computer producers, the country relied on supply from the US, Japan, and Germany. ARM also gave up the production of processor chips and transformed into a processor IP licensing service provider.

However, the situation was more complicated in France as the wave of privatisation did not start until 1986. Under the left-wing agenda of President Mitterrand, France nationalised five of the biggest companies, including Thomson Semiconductors, in 1982. With strong government support, the firm was able to acquire Mostek in the US at the cost of a difficult debt situation. In 1987, a joint venture was established with Italy's SGS Microelettronica, later renamed ST Microelectronics.

Unlike the past era, Germany experienced an economic slowdown and high unemployment in the aftermath of the East–West Germany merger and two oil crises. The strong inertia in traditional manufacturing industries has also led to difficulties in transitioning towards information technology and biotechnology.

Despite the wave of privatisation, we should not undermine the role of government in the transition and innovation. The government-led closer integration on all fronts is one of the key factors driving the more rapid development in the semiconductor industry. To improve the competitiveness of European industries, several major countries have launched two measures. One is the European Strategic Plan for Research in Information Technology (ESPRIT) to replicate Japan's success in the field of microelectronics, including "Research on Advanced Communications in Europe" (RACE) and "Basic Research on European Industrial Technology" (BRITE). The other is a single market plan to establish an integrated market and remove obstacles to the cross-border flow of goods, capital, and people.

In 1985, French President Mitterrand proposed the establishment of a European research coordination agency, later known as "Eureka" (Eureka Plan). In 1988, the Eureka Project launched the Joint Semiconductor Submicron Silicon Initiative (JESSI). Participants in the plan included Germany, France, Italy, the Netherlands, and Belgium. The main project leaders started with the three largest electronics groups in Europe at the time—Philips, Siemens, and SGS Microelettronica, bringing together a total of 50 companies, universities and research institutes. Despite the pullout of Philips in 1990 to cut losses in its computer division, there was a significant result in DRAM chips, contributing to revenue in the next decade. The approach became a role model for plans, such as Microelectronics. Development for European Applications (MEDEA) for 1997–2000.

The Grand Shift Towards Asia from the 1980s

As Europe attempted to compete with the US, Asia became the centre of gravity in semiconductor production. After semiconductors originated and developed in the US in the 1950s, the global production centre shifted to Japan in the 1970s due to strong policy support. With Japan's bubble economy burst and the introduction of the US–Japan semiconductor trade agreement in 1986, including raising the domestic market share for foreign firms to 20% within five years, there was a second transfer towards South Korea and Taiwan thanks to favourable industrial policies in the late 1980s and onwards. Since then, lower costs have been a driver of semiconductor production in China in the 2000s and 2010s. The trend is now halted or diverted due to geopolitical tensions and friend-shoring.

Where Does Europe Stand Now?

The problem for the EU is that the chip production capacity is low, with a hefty reliance on the US for design and on Asia for fabrication. As semiconductors become more important globally and an integral part of more products, the EU has also seen an increase in direct consumption over the past decade. The global demand increased by 78% between 2012 and 2023, and the European market[1] also grew slower by 67% (Garcia Herrero & Ng, 2021a). While Europe's share of global consumption looks small, the number does not suggest the actual importance of semiconductors to the region (Fig. 12.1).

Europe consumed 9% of global semiconductors in 2022, similar to 9% in production. While there is no mismatch between the share of production and consumption, there is indeed an underlying imbalance in demand and supply. Due to how the global supply chains are established

[1] Although the definition of Europe includes countries in Africa, Russia, and the Middle East, the EU and the UK make 99% due to their role in manufacturing. The other countries form a small part of the demand due to the economic size and the role of supply chains in importing final goods.

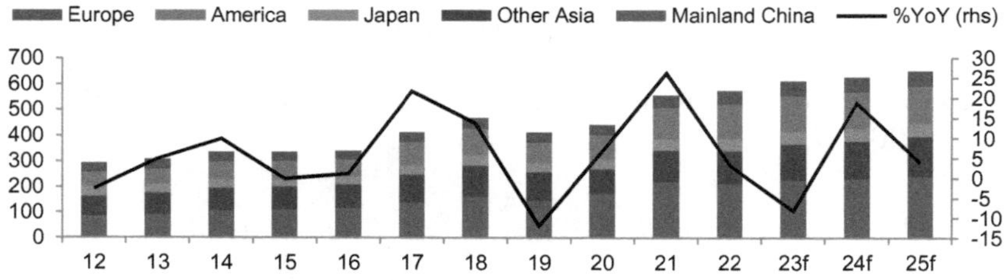

Fig. 12.1 Demand for semiconductors by region (USD billion) (*Source* Natixis, SEMI, IDC, Bloomberg, WIND)

in reducing manufacturing costs, China has become the biggest consumer of chips, thanks to the international trade setup and its role in assembling electronics products, forming 44% of the total in 2023. China imports a huge amount of advanced chips as it has not mastered the technologies. While China also imports lithography machines to produce mature chips, the EU is importing more of such products to feed its supply chains, including demand for the important automobile industry. The EU also has indirect exposure to chips through final goods from China and the rest of the world (Fig. 12.2).

On the supply side, the modern semiconductor supply chain is as complex as globalised, requiring input from various countries and for various production stages. As measured by corporate revenue, Europe

Fig. 12.2 Global market share of demand and supply of semiconductors (%, 2022) (N.B. Included foundries. Supply estimated by revenue. *Source* Natixis, Financial Statements, TrendForce, IC Insights, Bloomberg)

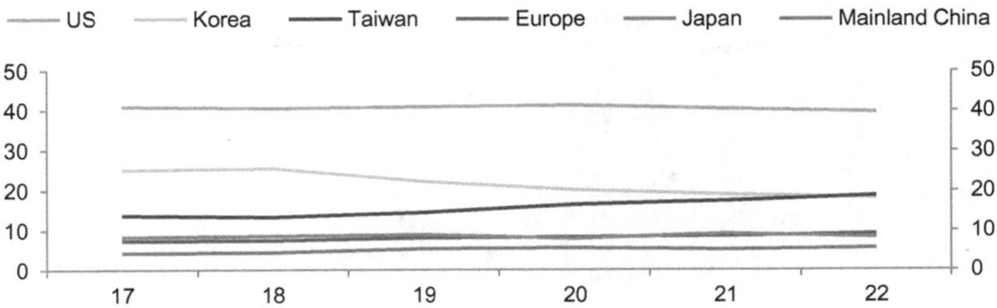

Fig. 12.3 Global market share of the semiconductors' supply chain (%) (N.B. Included foundries. Estimated by revenue. *Source* Natixis, Financial Statements, TrendForce, IC Insights, Gartner, Bloomberg)

forms around 10% of the global market share, with little change in recent years (Fig. 12.3).

Fabrication is the process of chipmaking starting with a silicon wafer through deposition, photoresist coating, lithography, etching, ion implantation, and packaging. The supply chain moved from the US to Asia (mostly Japan, and later South Korea and Taiwan for fabrication, but with the US still dominating the design). The EU developed a niche focus on industrial and automotive applications, with 10% of the global production of chips. So far, Europe cannot make cutting-edge chips and plays a small role in chip design. It accounts for only 2% of the market for chip design outside of integrated device manufacturers (IDMs), companies that both design and produce chips. For outsourced semiconductor assembly and test (OSAT), the presence of Europe is also very limited due to the much lower cost in Asia (Fig. 12.4).

Still, Europe is a very significant upstream of the semiconductor ecosystem. One of the most critical and complex steps in chipmaking is lithography, a system where light is projected through a blueprint of the pattern to be printed. The step determines the manufacturing process of the chip and the performance of the device. Deep ultraviolet (DUV) machines are the mainstream technology for making chips above 38 nm, mainly produced by Nikon and Canon from Japan and ASML from the Netherlands. The availability of extreme ultraviolet (EUV) has taken the game to the next level. ASML is the only producer of state-of-the-art EUV lithography equipment that can produce chips below 7 nm (Garcia Herrero & Ng, 2021b) (Fig. 12.5).

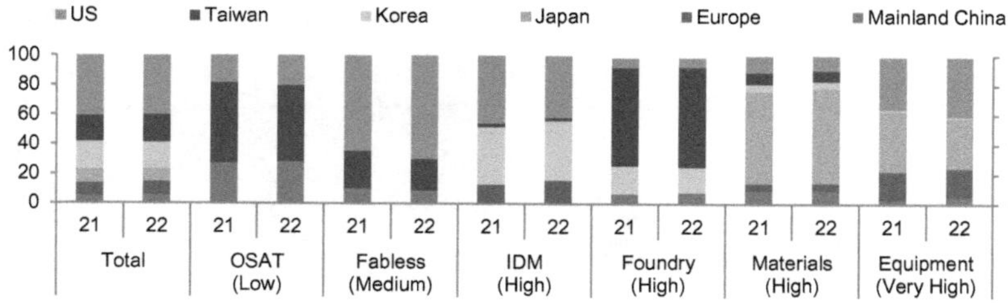

Fig. 12.4 Global market share of supply by sub-sector (%) in semiconductors (N.B. Included foundries. Estimated by revenue. *Source* Natixis, Financial Statements, TrendForce, IC Insights, Bloomberg)

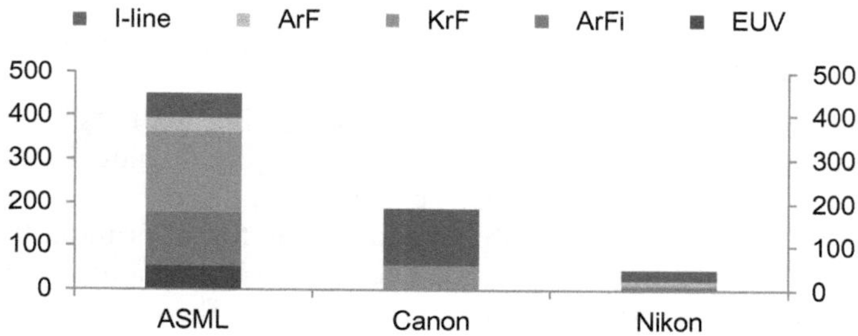

Fig. 12.5 Sales of lithography equipment by company and type (number of units, 2023) (*Source* Natixis, Financial Statements, Bloomberg)

As such, the Netherlands has almost a monopoly in the high-end market with European-centric supply chains behind its lithography machines. Europe is also present in high-end design, with the IMEC in Belgium considered the most important research institute. However, Europe's production capacity is very limited in the rest of the chip supply chain.

The Rise of Industrial Policy for Chip Security: The EU Chip Act

Relevance of Chips for Tech Hegemony

Looking beyond the rapidly globalised world after the Cold War and following China's assertion into the World Trade Organization (WTO), a key factor in the development of semiconductors is geopolitics. Semiconductors have become the new oil in manufacturing in a form that is more digital and integrated into supply chains, especially under a green transition. For existing leaders, especially the US, maintaining the tech hegemony and the tech edges versus China is critical both for economic and national security, as chips are used for dual technology. It comes as China moves up the ladder in the production of chips, while it takes a more confrontative approach to economic and foreign policies, while the West has also adopted a more protectionist stance across many issues.

With trust across big powers waning, the endgame is that chips have become increasingly stuck amid geopolitical tensions. Losing access or growing imbalance in production in China can be problematic when there are more mutual trade restrictions. Without chip production, achieving security and other policy objectives may not be feasible, even though such goals and definitions can vary across different countries. The combination of the trends has intensified the competition between China and the West on the geopolitical fronts and, more importantly, on semiconductors.

US Containment on China Through Export Controls and Industrial Policies

Since the trade war that started in 2018, the barrage of arrows shooting from the US to China has been more targeted. Unlike the comprehensive product coverage solely on trade, the focus is narrowed to China's tech sectors. It began with the crackdown on Huawei for its 5G technologies in May 2019. The restrictions were strengthened by including foreign firms using U.S. tech and extended to the semiconductor industry after Huawei's fabless unit HiSilicon and Semiconductor Manufacturing International Corporation (SMIC) were hit in 2020.

In October 2022, the CHIPS and Science Act and the chip ban took tech scrutiny further. First, it no longer targets a single firm and type of tech but a range of Chinese firms and more fields, such as artificial intelligence, supercomputers, software, and memory chips. Second, the benchmark of being included in the chip ban is lower. Firms are given a short time to identify the end users of their products upon request from the US. Third, U.S. persons are banned from supporting China's chipmakers. It will be hard for foreign firms to do business with China, dampening China's ability to integrate global tech.

Beyond export control, the US is also using industrial policies through subsidies to expand production capacity and attract foreign chip makers to establish their presence locally. The recipients include major chipmakers, such as Intel, TSMC, Samsung, Micron, and Global Foundries. While there is no clear rule right now, the CHIPS Act generally prohibits funding recipients from expanding semiconductor manufacturing in China. It is reported that Samsung and SK Hynix may have received a permanent waiver to keep important tools for their plants in China. However, it is also reported that other chipmakers may have only secured one-year waivers. In October 2024, the US also finalised rules to restrict U.S. investment in China in high-tech sectors, including AI, semiconductors, and quantum technology.

Taiwan Is a Geopolitical Flashpoint but a Key Partner

Another point of concern is the uncertainties in Taiwan, the biggest chipmaker, especially in advanced chips. Taiwan's large share in the global production of semiconductors, basically in a duopoly with South Korea, should protect Taiwan from potential aggression by China due to its very complex international interests. At the same time, the growing concentration of high-end chip production has spiked concerns for many countries regarding the excessive reliance on semiconductor imports from the island. The major worry is that any military conflict in the Taiwan Strait can lead to a blockade and loss of access to chips temporarily or permanently, as in more intense international relations (Fig. 12.6).

As a result, Taiwan has switched its economic relations with the world from trade to investment. With the support of government subsidies, TSMC is now building more plants and sharing the know-how with many countries, with the US and Japan being the frontrunners. However, such relationships also come with challenges. The Japan example shows that not only is fast and consistent government support essential to building chipmaking facilities from scratch, but the cultural norm is also crucial in smoothening the transition of skills from Taiwan to other plants. The

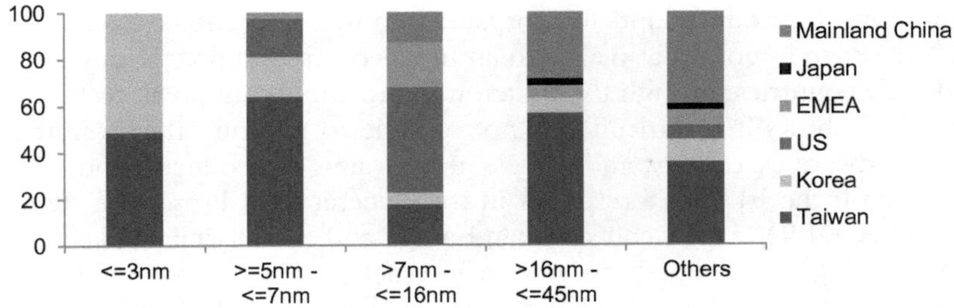

Fig. 12.6 Global: share of fabrication capacity of foundries by location and node process (%, 2022) (*Source* Natixis, SEMI, Bloomberg)

construction of TSMC's plant in Japan (JASM) started in April 2022, which was later than the Arizona plant in the US at the end of 2021. JASM not only has a smooth construction progress, but it also schedules mass production this year as scheduled, surpassing the Arizona plant, which has been postponed to 2025. It takes a much longer time for TSMC to adapt to the U.S. culture, which still eventually leads to good yield.

Whether the expansion overseas of Taiwan's chip producers, especially TSMC, will reduce the "silicon shield" effect is obviously an open question. One could argue that the previous position was untenable as Taiwan has other types of risk, such as droughts and earthquakes. A strategy of expanding plants through friend-shoring might finally offer Taiwan more support from allies than concentrating its production in one single spot in the world.

Looking ahead, the future of the growing adoption of artificial intelligence (AI), the Internet of Things (IoT), and data centres will only drive demand for chips further in quantity and performance, especially for advanced chips. Europe will not be absent from the trend on the demand side, but its dependence on external producers will increase without local production. It means the EU may see growing dependence on Taiwan and South Korea, mostly in high-end chips, and China in legacy chips.

Unlike the EU, the US focusses less on digital sovereignty but has stepped up industrial policies to secure domestic chip production and impose rules on imports of different materials and parts, such as the China-related activities of the subsidy recipients. With the CHIPS and Science Act introduced in August 2022, the US has incentivised overseas chip firms to produce in its territory and imposed restrictions. Even if the US needs to import, it also aims to ensure its overseas supply chains are in friendly countries through the Inflation Reduction Act in green tech. The example shows it is difficult and not sensible to rely on other countries for hardware excessively, and the US at least aims to produce some.

Even if the EU is a forerunner in the General Data Protection Regulation (GDPR) in data collection and usage and the Digital Markets Act in ensuring fair competition among internet giants, the main development has happened in the regulatory space. The European Chips Act was indeed enforced in September 2023, but progress is limited compared to that of the US and other fast-moving peers, such as Japan. The US has already attracted chipmakers, such as Taiwan Semiconductor Manufacturing Company (TSMC) and Samsung, to set up factories with subsidies and loans. Japan started later but reached the goal earlier than the US through a fully operating Kumamoto plant in February 2024.

The EU in the Crossfire of the Chip War

Although Europe is not a big producer of chips, it is hit by the chip war indirectly due to its dominant role in lithography equipment. As the US is taking more steps to restrict China's chipmaking capability to 16 nm or below, there is also a broader move to align other countries to act together with the US. While ASML was unable to ship extreme ultraviolet (EUV) lithography machines to China for long time, there were fewer restrictions on the less advanced deep ultraviolet (DUV) systems. A major policy deficiency is that China can produce chips at 16 nm with Argon Fluoride immersion (ArFi) DUV machines, but at a higher cost and possibly also a lower yield. The US cannot act alone, and the nods from the Netherlands and Japan are more crucial than ever as they are leading in DUV production.

As a result, Japan added 23 chip-manufacturing items requiring export approvals in July 2023. Dutch firms need to apply for a license to export certain advanced semiconductor manufacturing equipment outside of the EU since September 2023. The Dutch government also withdrew permits for ASML to export its equipment to China due to fears it may be used for military purposes in February 2024.

In the past few decades, high competition and capex have led to industry consolidation in fabrication. The breakthrough in lithography equipment has also become a game-changer for chip-making. As such, there are two bottlenecks in the upgraded part of the semiconductor supply chain in the hands of Taiwan Semiconductor Manufacturing Company (TSMC) from Taiwan and ASML from the Netherlands.

The success of TSMC and ASML always goes hand in hand. As a foundry, TSMC has a high dependence on extreme ultraviolet (EUV) lithography equipment. ASML is the sole provider of EUV machines, and TSMC is one of the biggest clients and the first firm putting the technology into practice, which is then used by Samsung and Intel. In other words, the duo holds the key for 7 nm chips or below made for new-generation technologies, such as artificial intelligence (AI), data centres, advanced driving assistance systems (ADAS), high-performance computing, 5G communications, and smartphones.

ASML is the sole provider of EUV machines and has now reached the milestone of the 100th EUV equipment shipment. Such technology is at the core of recent semiconductor manufacturing, pushing the boundary of Moore's Law. The company also expects the delivery of high-NA EUV machines in 2023 to further facilitate chip production below 2 nm. However, such advanced equipment is not accessible to all due to the high cost and complexity of design and production.

The high efficiency in TSMC and the limited supply of the EUV mean a high entry barrier for newcomers. On the one hand, the competition in acquiring the machines and the pivot towards Asia are shown by the fact that Taiwan, China, and Korea together made up 81% of lithography equipment purchases in 2023. On the other hand, it is difficult for firms to replicate the success without access to EUV unless there is a revolution of current technologies, especially with tougher geopolitical tides.

For Europe, it poses two questions for its indirect involvement in the chip war. First, it will need to keep its tech edge in advanced equipment to be relevant in the chipmaking industry, especially given the low participation in other steps. Second, geopolitics is a reason to ramp up some production in advanced chips for security. It ultimately depends on how Europe views the concepts of de-risking, whether it should be produced by European firms domestically or foreign firms investing in Europe can also do the job. Either way, having greater capacity domestically is positive in maintaining economic security and helps achieve digital sovereignty.

EU Chips Act

To maintain existing tech edges and further ensure chip supply security, the EU has introduced its own Chip Act, especially after the massive investment by. The European Chips Act promises €43 billion in "policy-driven investment" up to 2030 through three pillars, including the Chips for Europe Initiative, a framework to ensure supply security and a coordination mechanism for monitoring and crisis response (Regulation (EU) 2023/1781, 2023). The Act complements the existing Important Project of Common European Interest (IPECI), which encourages bringing large-scale projects together from different Member States for a single EU goal. In this case, it is about microelectronics. The bloc aims to restore chip manufacturing and reach 20% of the global market value by 2030 (European Commission, 2024).

Within the Act, the first pillar focusses on R&D and innovation to ensure Europe has the technological capacity for semiconductors, including research and talent. It includes €11 billion in funding, mainly supported by €5 billion under the Multiannual Financial Framework (MFF) and €3.3 billion under Horizon Europe and Digital Europe. The remaining gap will be filled by €1.8 billion under Key Digital Technologies (KDT) Joint Undertaking and €1 billion from Quantum Technologies Flagship under Horizon Europe. In addition, a €2 billion Chip fund will be utilised to help start-ups and small and medium enterprises (SMEs), including funding from the European Investment Bank (EIB) group.

The second pillar aims to maintain supply security by introducing a new state-aid exemption allowing EU countries to finance the construction of foundries. Key initiatives will include attracting leading global chipmakers to establish their presence and bring their supply chains to Europe, such as TSMC, Samsung, and Intel. Industrial subsidies under this pillar will account for most of the headline number funded by member states' budgets.

The third pillar introduces the new emergency measures for monitoring and identifying potential supply chain risks and shortages, including joint procurement of chips by the European Commission. It includes a new European Semiconductor Board (ESB) for governance with representatives of Member States.

Although the Act looks well covered in domestic funding, incentives to attract foreign chipmakers and emergency responses, there are challenges as the old models and experience of industrial policies may not be fully transferable to modern days with a new competitive and geopolitical environment. The upsides are that the EU should strengthen its semiconductor manufacturing capacity to cater to its demand and support innovation and talent in forming a more resilient ecosystem. However, there are also critics of how effective the subsidies and industrial policy would be, as it was not the first time that a strong government-led approach failed in Europe.

Regarding the usage of funding and targets, there is a debate about whether the money should be used for building advanced or matured nodes (Garcia Herrero & Poitiers, 2022). As almost every major country in the world has been announcing subsidies, it is possible to see an overcapacity in semiconductors, especially in the matured nodes. Advanced chips are indeed important in competing for the new demand, but matured chips are often still being used in many products. To complement this, the CHIPS Act 2.0. was proposed in June 2026, aiming to stimulate European demand and industrial uptake for European chips, reinforcing support for the whole semiconductor value chain, from raw materials and design to packaging; and not only for the most advanced chips.

As China may be restricted in developing towards the high-end tech curve, it is likely to see greater investment and capacity accumulation in matured nodes, which form close to 70% of the market (Garcia Herrero & Ng, 2023). This has sparked concerns from the US in real actions with tariffs and the EU in potentially investigating China's subsidisation of legacy chips. Under this scenario, Europe will need to think seriously about its strategy in what kind of chips and under what magnitude it wants its industrial policies to target to achieve security and digital sovereignty (Fig. 12.7).

Another problem is funding for the size of investment and to what degree state aid should be used. While the investment size in the EU Chip Act is smaller than that of China and the US, especially when considering a large part of the money comes from the existing budget, it still marks a turning point for Europe's industrial policy. The EU has strong state-aid rules intended to prevent subsidy races within the block. The exemption is now made for a sector as critical as semiconductors, as it is essential to have some autonomy in production to achieve other policy goals and reduce geopolitical risks.

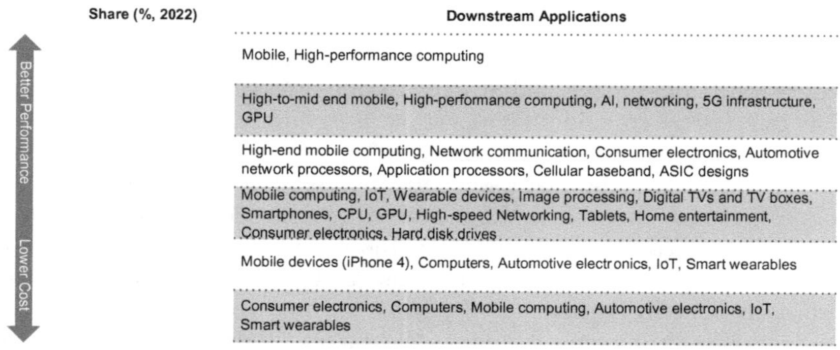

Fig. 12.7 Global: fabrication capacity of foundries by process node and applications (*Source* Natixis, TSMC, SEMI, Bloomberg)

In this regard, balancing the role of state aid and the existing principle of equity within the block remains a difficult task. Focussing purely on advanced chips can be a solution to allowing state aid through the first-of-a-kind concept. A gatekeeper mechanism through the Directorate-General for Competition is also possible, with clear clauses allowing such subsidies with challenges such as Important Projects of Common European Interest (IPCEI) on research and not on established production.

Beyond the rule of state aid, the role of EU Member States is another important point in assessing industrial policies. Compared to the past, it is more important than ever for the EU to act as a single bloc in terms of its relative economic size to the US and China. The historical experience shows that a fragmented Europe with competition in industrial policies does not necessarily bring the best outcome, which is a result of resource misallocation and the underutilisation of the comparative advantages of different countries or EU member states under the current scenario.

While countries could have gone solo in providing subsidies, they ultimately need to work with other EU member states as the supply chains are more integrated than before, with clusters in different sectors. For example, the automobile industry in Germany is deeply integrated with central and eastern European countries. The ability of the EU to produce car chips in another country within the bloc will enhance the supply chain security as a whole.

It looks like some flexibility with limits designed based on EU principles would fit the EU's economic and political reality the most. Historically, Germany and others have used regional aid, but the maximum amounts were capped with clauses, such as limiting the usage to investment or a certain percentage of eligible costs. In the recent plant by European Semiconductor Manufacturing Company (ESMC), an affiliated entity of TSMC, Germany was allowed to subsidise its Dresden facility by EUR 5 billion.

Indeed, there is a growing trend that EU member states would act with solidarity on economic and other issues. The joint purchasing of vaccines during COVID was an example, and the security of chip supply shares the same underlying principle in common interests among Member States. The CHIP act is a good start and a breakthrough, but more is needed in how the bloc would contribute more collectively to develop supply chain security semiconductors to accelerate decision-making, including the potential change to Qualified Majority Decisions for critical issues (European Semiconductor Industry Association, 2024).

The Case of China: Different Ways in State Support and Results

The Quest for Self-Sufficiency

The shortcut for China to achieve self-sufficiency lies in the strong state-led effort to boost its capability through subsidies. The interlaced relationship lies in the fact that China is the most important market due to rising domestic consumption, and its role is the world's exporter of electronics. However, the targeted approach to building national champions has caused worries in other economies about unfair competition and unequal access to state support, which will put them at a disadvantage.

With the growing domestic market, China's purchase of chipmaking equipment has ballooned between 2014 and 2023. Regarding market share, China is the biggest equipment buyer, forming 34% of the total in 2023, up from 12% in 2015. With the growing domestic market, China's purchase of chipmaking equipment has increased eight-fold between 2014 and 2023. Regarding market share, China is the biggest equipment buyer, forming 34% of the total in 2023, up from 12% in 2015 (Garcia Herrero & Ng, 2023). As a result, China's fabrication capacity has increased from 19% in 2017 to 26% in 2023 (Garcia Herrero & Ng, 2022b) (Figs. 12.8 and 12.9).

For China, there are still at least two problems. Most capacity is from foreign investors, such as Taiwan and South Korea. There is a risk of foreign investors retreating from China if they need to meet any potential regulatory requirements in the future. In addition, China is still very reliant on foreign equipment to produce chips despite being the most prominent global buyer. In 2022, the US will be the biggest source of chipmaking equipment to China, supplying more than half of the total. China's domestic share grew from 7% in 2017 to 14% in 2022, but it remains a relatively small share, mostly not in critical equipment.

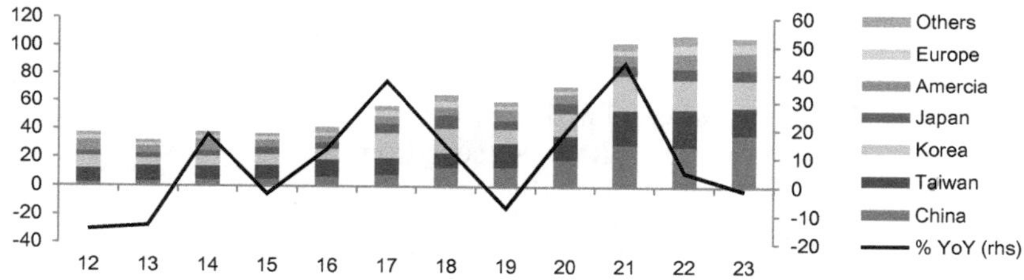

Fig. 12.8 Purchase of semiconductor equipment (USD billion) (*Source* Natixis, Semiconductor Equipment Association of Japan, WIND)

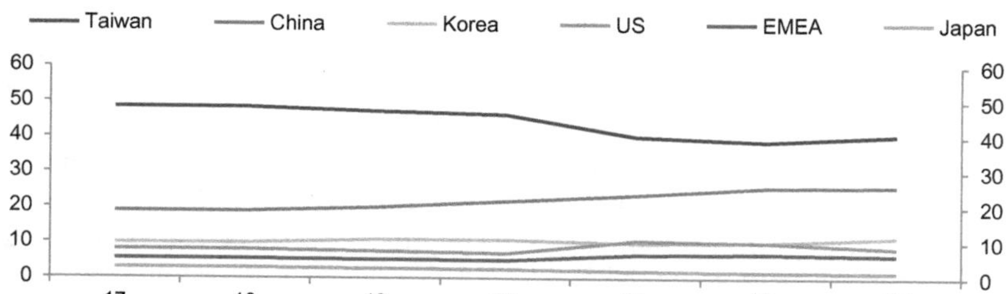

Fig. 12.9 Global: share of fabrication capacity of foundries (%) (*Source* Natixis, SEMI, Bloomberg)

The Approach by China

The Chinese government has mapped its "China Manufacturing 2025" goal and emphasised its strategy to achieve self-reliance in 2015. Following the US–China trade war, the Chinese government launched the "China Standards 2035" in 2020, a 15-year blueprint covering global technology areas such as artificial intelligence (AI), telecommunications networks, and data flows that define the next decade. It has further identified semiconductor manufacturing capability as a strategic technology priority, requiring a whole-of-society effort to "achieve technological self-reliance in the 14th Five-Year Plan released in 2021. China has stepped up its industrial policy throughout the decade to grow its technological capabilities. Further ambition is seen in several policies, the revised State Secrecy Law, and the forced pronouncement shift from foreign to Chinese firms.

Looking back, China's pursuit of self-reliance and the lack of comparative neutrality for foreign firms have become a starting point for the global industrial policy race. China may not have used the wording of digital sovereignty, as in the EU case. However, they share similarities in China expanding its reach from physical supply chain security to the digital space, including semiconductors and regulations. Of course, the rationales behind and the definition of security significantly differ. The EU aims to ringfence the risks to economic security. China targets geopolitical influence and domestic social stability, especially considering the broader state control over the internet platforms and tech sectors from 2021.

China's industrial policy on semiconductors can come from the central and local government levels. Among all, the most apparent direct support comes from the China Integrated Circuit Industry Investment Fund, also known as the Big Fund. The program has two phases of five years, each with Big Fund I (2014–2019) and Big Fund II (2019–2024), with the respective amounts of $21 billion (or RMB 139 billion) and $35 billion (or RMB 204 billion).

A vital characteristic of the Big Fund is the involvement of government capital beyond the Ministry of Finance and China Development Bank, one of the three policy banks (Fig. 12.10). It also includes government-funded investment companies and state-owned enterprises with limited semiconductor industry linkages, such as China National Tobacco Corporation. The investor composition draws the difference between China and many Western countries, such as the EU, in the ability and strength to mobilize state capital to build national champions. Beyond the national level, local governments have created at least 15 funds, a total of $25 billion, to support chip production (Semiconductor Industry Association, 2021). The OECD has estimated that all funds may have contributed up to $150 billion to support the Chinese semiconductor industry from 2014 to 2020 (OECD, 2019).

There are also other types of government support through grants, tax incentives, and low-interest loans for an amount estimated to be around $50 billion (Semiconductor Industry Association, 2019). Tax breaks were introduced to encourage the production of higher-end semiconductors. Firms that have operated for more than 15 years were exempted from corporate income tax for up to 10 years if they manage to produce 28 nm chips or below. Producers of chips from 65 to 28 nm were exempted from corporate income tax for five years and could get a 50 per cent discount on the corporate rate for the next five years. The effective tax rate of Chinese semiconductor firms is only 9% in 2022, lower than that of their global peers (Fig. 12.11). Companies can also deduct from their taxable income 200% of their research and development (R&D) costs.

Additional financial support comes in the form of borrowing at below-market rates; banks were encouraged to support the sector. Chinese semiconductor firms also enjoy a lower interest rate of 2.6% in 2022, which is lower than the asset-weighted interest rate of 4.2% in 2022. The

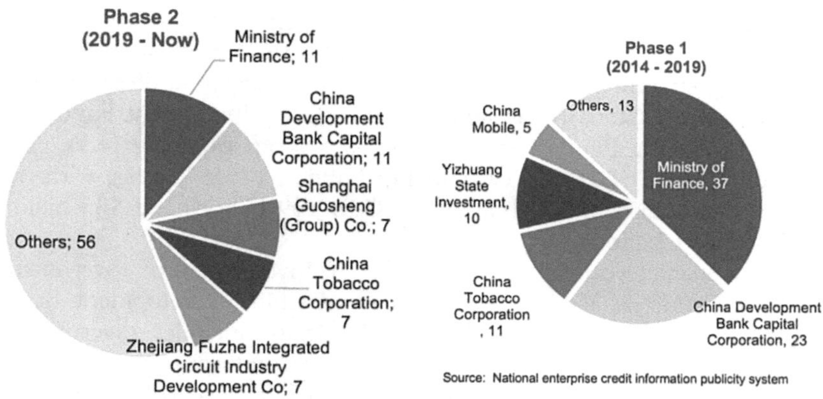

Fig. 12.10 Composition of China's integrated circuit industry investment fund (%)

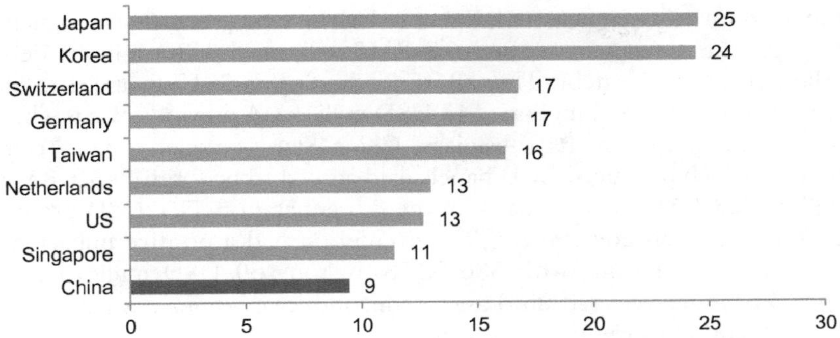

Fig. 12.11 Effective tax rate for semiconductor firms (%, 2022) (N.B. Top 200 listed semiconductor firms. Companies without sufficient data excluded. *Source* Natixis, Bloomberg)

government also supports semiconductor producers in raising equity on the Shanghai Stock Exchange (SSE) Science and Technology Innovation Board (STAR Market), established in 2019. Using SMIC as an example, its valuation is way higher for its debut IPO in the onshore market versus Hong Kong, meaning the flagship Chinese chipmaker can get access to more liquidity from investors (Fig. 12.12).

The exemption of the loan is also apparent in the technological or semiconductor industry, with strong support from the local government. On 22nd Jan 2018, BOE Technology, covering display devices, smart systems, and healthcare services, signed the "Debt Waiver Agreement of the Investment Framework on the 8.5 New Semiconductor Panel" with

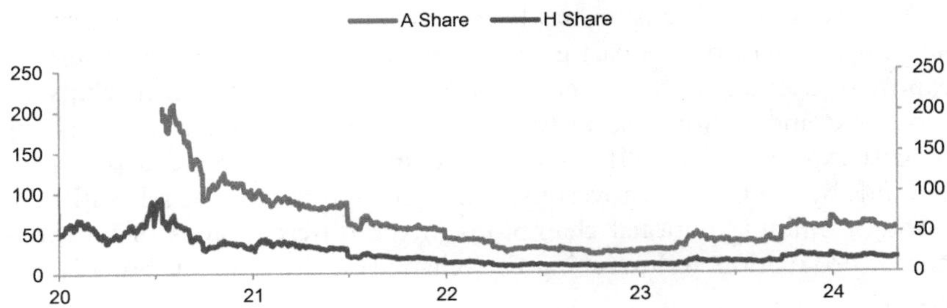

Fig. 12.12 SMIC price to earning ratio (%). (*Source* Bloomberg)

the Fuzhou government and Fuzhou Urban Construction Investment Group. The agreement offered 6.3 RMB billion (1 USD billion) debt relief, 10.6% of the debt. Thus, BOE Technology's 2017 financial result gains about 900 RMB million (143 USD million). A previous case is when TCL announced that its subsidiary, China Star Optoelectronics Technology, which produced LCD panels, had agreed to be forgiven 5.1 RMB billion (0.8 USD billion) loans on the 8.5 generation TFT-LCD project by the Shenzhen government. The exemption had a positive impact on 2013 financial results, with 380 RMB million (60 USD million) gain and 27% of debt cleared up. Lastly, semiconductor companies have been offered land at below-market prices.

Assessment of China's Strategy of State Support

Before the recent global subsidies race, it was clear that China provided more support to its chip industry than any other economy (García-Herrero & Weil, 2022a). Some of the largest Chinese chipmakers, including Semiconductor Manufacturing International Corporation (SMIC), Tsinghua Unigroup, Hua Hong Semiconductor, and Jiangsu Changjiang Electronics Tech Co (JCET), and Tsinghua Unigroup have received enormous government support versus peers.

The result is that China has grown its chipmaking capacity. Since 2012, the sales of China's semiconductor industry in fabrication, design, and OSAT grew 6 times from $27 billion (RMB 216 billion) to $150 billion (RMB 1201 billion) in 2023 (Garcia Herrero & Ng, 2022). While foreign firms may have contributed to the capability through direct ownership or joint ventures, it is apparent that China has developed skills in chipmaking (Fig. 12.13).

Still, geopolitical tension has become the most significant uncertainty derailing China from its past growth model in semiconductors. The U.S. export restrictions have fuelled China's fear of losing access to chips for economic and national security reasons, especially as electronics is the biggest export category. It has triggered an even more rapid deployment of funds by the Chinese government into the industry to be self-sufficient through building national champions in the different steps of semiconductor production and reducing the reliance on the US and, broadly, the West.

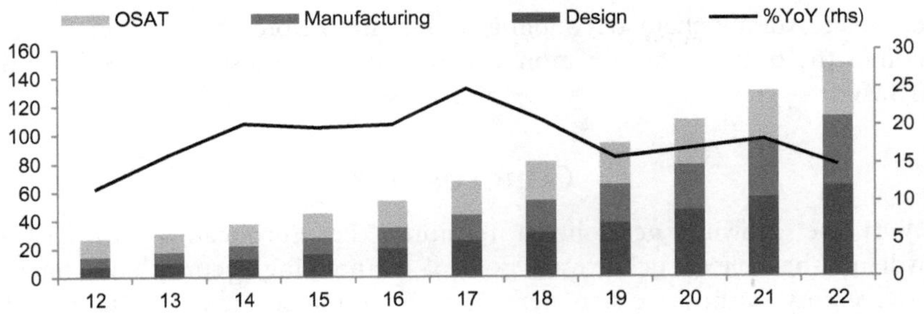

Fig. 12.13 China: sales in the integrated circuit industry (USD billion) (*Source* Natixis, WIND)

China has achieved its objective in the last part of the chipmaking cycle, which is assembling and testing. However, this is the least value-added and carries the smallest strategic importance compared to other procedures. China has gradually built its ability to produce standard semiconductors, especially for memory chips, but it is still far from the highest end of the nano race. Furthermore, export restrictions on software design or manufacturing equipment, imposed by the US and some like-minded countries (such as the Netherlands), are making it even more complicated than it already was for China to move up the ladder.

Given the massive investment through subsidies, China's industrial policy of developing an advanced chip industry has yielded mixed results. External reliance on semiconductors, especially high-end chips, continues unabated. One reason for this could be the increasingly limited role of the private sector as the state exerts greater control over the industry over time. Companies receiving such large amounts of funds have not been able to absorb them and have become over-leveraged, leading to defaults in the case of several large companies.

This development is not unusual in highly competitive sectors where money cannot buy upgrades, especially in industries like semiconductors with high specialisation and concentration. In addition, the US has leverage over several key bottlenecks in production, and it is strengthening export controls on China. This means China will face more difficulties securing the mass production of high-end chips due to the more difficult access to equipment and software as well as talent shortages. China has made some progress but has yet to achieve the specific objectives and timeline for becoming self-reliant and bypassing technological barriers. A complete supply-chain decoupling seems impossible unless China overcomes the bottlenecks and monopolies of companies such as ASML and TSMC.

Conclusions

With the growing geopolitical tensions, the European Union (EU) will not be able to achieve its goal of maintaining security and digital sovereignty without a stronger focus on semiconductors. The EU is heavily reliant on imports, with 92% of global manufacturing capacity located in Asia, and the US leading high-level chip design. Such dependence can be a more important issue than ever, as advanced semiconductors are almost a prerequisite for artificial intelligence (AI) development, leading to problems for competitiveness and supply chain resilience. The heavy concentration of manufacturing capacity in Taiwan may also face disruption from natural disasters and geopolitical risks from China.

We argue that the EU should consider producing some chips domestically as a safety net and climb the supply chain participation ladder by R&D, especially in design, meaning industrial policy is necessary. In this regard, China's policies to reduce its external dependence on semiconductors were introduced before the US, and therefore, more lessons can be drawn about their effectiveness. The lesson is that China's policies have been very costly in terms of capital deployed and not always successful. However, given the strategic importance of the sector and the increasingly harsh U.S. tech containment, China's industrial policy may have served the purpose. While it is too early to tell, China's direction of progress is clear. One key concern, though, is the still relatively small role of market forces, which also implies that China's lessons might not be fully applicable to Europe.

The comparison with the world will help analyse the current EU measures, namely the Chips Act introduced in September 2023. While such a policy is much needed, given the strategic importance of semiconductors, we argue that improvements are necessary. First, the chip industrial policy should have a clearer mission, including the distribution of responsibilities at the EU and national level to avoid excessive competition among member states through subsidies, thereby increasing the cost of the localisation strategy.

Second, the objective should not only be chip production in the EU but also to increase our participation in the value chain, especially at the highest end of the value added. This will be easier said than done, as the current EU policies include less fresh money than the US and China. Given the flurry of subsidies, importing chips is likely to be much cheaper than producing them with excessively large and unaffordable subsidies. This means that the EU Commission will need to be very selective about which areas to subsidise, and those should be R&D and design, while producing enough strategic reserves for supply chain resilience.

Third, the EU must avoid a race to the bottom due to competition among member states by replicating the Airbus model, meaning a vertically integrated chipmaking ecosystem through creating design and production clusters while keeping it open to foreign technologies. The openness aspect is particularly important as the modern semiconductor supply chain is one of the most global and complex sectors, which means that no country or region can be completely self-sufficient. The EU would also benefit from attracting more investment from the highest end chip producers in South Korea and Taiwan, similar to what the US and Japan have in recent years.

Finally, the production of semiconductors requires access to critical raw materials that the EU lacks now. Given that the supply chain of critical raw materials is clearly dominated by China, Europe's vulnerabilities are even larger in chip production, which is a final product. To mitigate the negative impact of such an important bottleneck, the EU should step up its collaboration with countries like Australia and Indonesia, with abundant resources in critical raw materials. Unfortunately, the EU's negotiations with these countries for mega trade and investment deals are stalled. More targeted deals would be needed to respond more quickly.

As the world is decoupling to some extent, it is impossible to return to the old days fully. Subsidising the semiconductor industry to build local production capacity and technological capability seems sensible for the EU's digital sovereignty and green transition. The best industrial policy for the EU is one that moves from only focusing on production (building fabs) to the highest end part of the supply chain (design and R&D), but still producing some strategic stocks in Europe in the light of potential disruptions either in the Taiwan straits or elsewhere. Collaboration with producers of critical raw materials but also with producers of advanced chips will be necessary to achieve this goal with happen at the EU level (with the Airbus example in mind) and not at the national level to increase efficiencies by making full use of the single market.

Bibliography

European Commission. (2024). *European Chips Act: The Chips for Europe Initiative.* Retrieved from Shaping Europe's digital future: https://digital-strategy.ec.europa.eu/en/factpages/european-chips-act-chips-europe-initiative

European Semiconductor Industry Association. (2024). *Towards a more competitive semiconductor industry in Europe.* Retrieved from European Semiconductor Industry Association: https://www.eusemiconductors.eu/sites/default/files/ESIA_Key%20Recommendations%202024-2029_digital_final_0.pdf

European Union. (2023). *Regulation (EU) 2023/1781 of the European Parliament and of the Council of 13 September 2023 establishing a framework of measures for strengthening Europe's semiconductor ecosystem and amending Regulation (EU) 2021/694 (Chips Act).* Retrieved from Official Journal of the European Union. Accessed 5 May 2024. https://eur-lex.europa.eu/legal-content/EN/TXT/PDF/?uri=CELEX:32023R1781

Garcia Herrero, A., & Ng, G. (2021a). *Asia-driven pent-up demand of semiconductors is not temporary.* Retrieved from Natixis Research: https://research.natixis.com/Site/en/publication/C2fCpXQ6yL6QAPQCy6oADQ%3D%3D?from=share

Garcia Herrero, A., & Ng, G. (2021b). *The duo in the semiconductor bottleneck.* Retrieved from Natixis Research: https://research.natixis.com/Site/en/publication/Tyu-jOhLQUpLhwf_FbpSVw%3D%3D?from=share

Garcia Herrero, A., & Weil, P. (2022a). *Lessons for Europe from China's quest for semiconductor self-reliance.* Retrieved from Bruegel: https://www.bruegel.org/policy-brief/lessons-europe-chinas-quest-semiconductor-self-reliance

Garcia Herrero, A., & Ng, G. (2022b). *The latest U.S. chip ban is a game changer for Asia and the world.* Retrieved from Natixis Research: https://research.natixis.com/Site/en/publication/WxpaL6jtW2ucy5CLZoClDA%3D%3D?from=share

Garcia Herrero, A., & Ng, G. (2023). *U.S.-led chip ban heralds a turning point for China and Asia's semiconductor industry.* Retrieved from Asia Thematic Research Semiconductors, Natixis Research: https://research.natixis.com/Site/en/publication/xGTiD7wHBiUhY-qWCpz9aA%3D%3D?from=share

Garcia Herrero, A., & Poitiers, N. (2022, October 17). *Europe's promised semiconductor subsidies need to be better targeted.* Retrieved from Bruegel: https://www.bruegel.org/blog-post/europes-promised-semiconductor-subsidies-need-be-better-targeted

OECD. (2019). *Measuring distortions in international markets: The semiconductor value chain* (OECD Trade Policy Papers 234). Retrieved from OECD: https://www.oecd-ilibrary.org/trade/measuring-distortions-in-international-markets_8fe4491d-en

Semiconductor Industry Association. (2019). *Chipping in: The U.S. semiconductor industry workforce and how federal incentives will increase domestic jobs*. Retrieved from https://www.semiconductors.org/wp-content/uploads/2021/05/SIA-Impact_May2021-FINAL-May-19-2021_2.pdf

Semiconductor Industry Association. (2021). *Taking stock of China's semiconductor industry*. Retrieved from https://www.semiconductors.org/wp-content/uploads/2021/07/Taking-Stock-of-China%E2%80%99s-Semiconductor-Industry_final.pdf

CHAPTER 13

Genesis and Evolution of the EU Approach to Artificial Intelligence

Andrea Renda

Introduction

Among the many subjects addressed by the EU over the past years to promote a lawful, sustainable, and innovative digital ecosystem, Artificial Intelligence (AI) stands out as possibly the most far-reaching, multi-faceted, ever-evolving, and, as a result, hard to handle. In this field, EU institutions have gone through a long and winding road since 2017, charting a substantially different path compared to other parts of the world, including the United States and China. At the time of writing, the AI Act is still not fully in force, and it is difficult to predict how challenging the implementation of this piece of legislation will be. At the same time, the new von der Leyen Commission is taking steps to boost AI innovation in Europe, and has entrusted the new Executive Vice President Henna Virkkunen with the preparation of a new EU Cloud and AI Development Act. In her confirmation hearing at the European Parliament, Virkkunen also stated her intention to transform Europe into an "AI continent".

A. Renda (✉)
Centre for European Policy Studies (CEPS), Brussels, Belgium
e-mail: Andrea.renda@ceps.eu

T. Kleiner and A. Garcia Rodriguez (eds.), *The Making of a Global Digital Rulebook*, https://doi.org/10.1007/978-981-95-9226-5_13

In order to illustrate how Europe developed its approach to AI policy and innovation, it is useful to break down the past decade into different phases: a first, confused phase triggered by a rather awkward first move of the European Parliament; a listening phase in which the Commission refocussed its approach; the legislation phase started with the adoption of the proposed AI Act in April 2021; and a reflexive phase in which lawmakers had to cope with the need to update the text of the Act ahead of its adoption, and at the same time, realised that Europe is falling behind in the development of this general-purpose technology, for which sovereignty becomes increasingly an imperative.

2015–2018—Spotlight on AI

When the European Parliament started working on a resolution on "Civil law rules for robotics" in 2015, Artificial Intelligence (AI) was certainly not hitting the headlines. There was no generative AI, no deepfakes spreading on the Web, and even search engines and smartphones were not as fraught with AI as they are today. No expert in neural networks had won the Nobel Prize for Physics or Chemistry.[1] Very few civil society organisations have had an epiphany on the possible opportunities and challenges that AI would create for society and the economy. The halls of Congress in the United States had not yet seen heated debates on whether frontier AI systems should be regulated, as they may be as dangerous as nuclear weapons. Civil society organisations had just started paying attention to AI, and software developers were slowly waking up to the need for ethical principles in a domain traditionally focussed on "making things work" or even "moving fast and breaking things" rather than on ethical alignment.[2]

That awareness of AI's potential risks and opportunities was very limited should not come as a surprise. It was only in 2012 that the yearly edition of the ImageNet Large-Scale Visual Recognition Challenge showed the world a specific approach to AI development, known

[1] The reference is to Geoffrey Hinton and Demis Hassabis, who were awarded the Nobel Prize for Physics and Chemistry, respectively, in 2024.

[2] The expression "move fast and break things" is attributed to Mark Zuckerberg, was adopted at Facebook until 2014 and become a slogan for companies inspired by agile management practices and principles.

as convolutional neural networks, that could lead to promisingly accurate results. The scientific community was becoming more confident in the potential of machine learning techniques after two decades of "AI winter", a period in which research had not shown the expected progress, and incentives to continue investment had cooled down significantly. A period of "AI summer" followed suit, with error rates in image recognition plummeting year on year and the learning-based approach to AI gradually flanking and surpassing rule-based systems in terms of accuracy and reliability.

The success of machine learning was difficult to predict, at least in the "winter years", which were also partly a pre-Internet age. It was indeed also due to the massive digitalisation of data, as well as the availability of an end-to-end architecture that would support its diffusion (i.e. the Internet), that an approach to AI once downplayed as inefficient and too expensive could become the poster child of the AI summer. The boom that followed was hence deeply related to the evolution of the Internet and to the rise of what scholars have called the "attention economy", or the age of "competition for eyeballs". The accumulation of massive swaths of user-generated data in the hands of a few tech giant companies led their performance to gradually decouple from that of the rest of the economy. Google started implementing increasingly sophisticated machine learning solutions in its search engine (e.g. the auto-complete function). Microsoft started experimenting with conversational bots (e.g. the Tay bot released on, and rapidly withdrawn from, Twitter already in 2016). Amazon started using AI in its recommendation engine, keeping end users on its marketplace and nudging them to buy more. Facebook famously relied on AI to profile customers and designed its algorithms to maximise user engagement.[3]

Governments were also starting to realise the potential of AI, though here, the associated risks became almost immediately evident. Since 2012, Californian police authorities have been piloting a crime-prediction system called PredPol that used relatively simple statistical inference based on available crime data per neighbourhood; the system, however, ended up sending police squads always to the same ghettos, eventually

[3] In 2018, the risks associated with these practices were exposed to public opinion. See, for example Zuboff (2019).

amplifying pre-existing biases in the data.[4] In the United States, ProPublica unveiled in 2016 the discrimination potential of the Correctional Offender Management Profiling for Alternative Sanctions (COMPAS) algorithm used to assess the likelihood of recidivism and thus determine who, among convicted individuals in jail, should be given parole. China started testing social credit scoring systems in some of its provinces in 2017.[5] In Europe, early experiments with risk prediction models included the "Risk-Based Verification" system used *ex-lege* in the UK by local authorities to determine an individual's eligibility for housing and council tax benefits; the *System Risico Indicative* (SyRI) model used in the Netherlands to determine the risk of fraud for social security/welfare; and profiling or credit scoring systems such as the one tested in the Danish city of Gladsaxe as part of the country's "ghetto plan" in January 2018 to detect children in vulnerable circumstances at an early stage. Other systems were used in law enforcement, as well as in the judiciary, often with rather disappointing results given the recurrence of bias.

These and several other developments were starting to wake up the public opinion on the risks associated with an unregulated diffusion of AI solutions in the market. The gradual awakening of software developers to responsible practices led, in 2017, to the adoption of the 23 "Asilomar principles", which later became a key reference for the debate on responsible AI development (Future of Life Institute, 2017). At the international level, the Montréal Declaration on Responsible AI was adopted in the same year in the context of the G-7 and outlined several principles that would become the basis for future legislation around the world, including the need for AI's orientation towards human well-being, the principle of human autonomy, the promotion of social equity and fairness, the respect for privacy, the need for explainability and transparency of AI systems, and the principle of accountability of developers and users for impacts caused by AI (Université de Montréal, 2013). Following this development, tech

[4] The system would then be shut down in 2022.

[5] The system can be traced back to the 1990s. In December 2017, the National Development and Reform Commission and People's Bank of China selected "model cities" that demonstrated the steps needed to make a functional and efficient implementation of the Social Credit System. Among them are Hangzhou, Nanjing, Xiamen, Chengdu, Suzhou, Suqian, Huizhou, Wenzhou, Weihai, Weifang, Yiwu, and Rongcheng. These pilots were deemed successful in their handling of "blacklists and 'redlists'", their creation of "credit sharing platforms", and their "data-sharing efforts with the other cities".

giants such as Google and Microsoft adopted their ethical principles on AI in 2018.

Against this background, the European Parliament's, 2017 Resolution on Civil Law Rules for Robotics raised concerns among commentators and scholars. By announcing the advent of advanced AI systems and evoking dystopian metaphors such as Prague's Golem and Mary Shelley's Frankenstein, the Resolution proposed, i.e. to introduce electronic personhood for "smart autonomous robots". A proposal that would eventually attribute legal rights and duties to these artefacts rather than to the humans who decide to deploy them. An open letter was sent to the European Parliament by 156 experts, including Nobel laureates, arguing that it would be ethically and legally misguided to attribute legal personality to machines. Experts highlighted the risks associated with blurring the lines between humans and machines and emphasised that machines, no matter how advanced, lack consciousness, emotions, and moral reasoning. They added that the concept of electronic personhood was problematic in terms of responsibility, as it would potentially exempt designers, developers, and users from accountability (contrary to the approach adopted, i.e. by the Asilomar principles and the Montréal Declaration).

The 2017 Resolution on Civil Law Rules for Robotics called on the European Commission to take several actions related to AI and robotics (P8_TA(2017)0051, 2017). These included the development of a comprehensive legal framework that would address "liability, ethics, and accountability" for actions taken by AI systems and autonomous robots, adding specific concerns for data protection and privacy; the adoption of Ethical Guidelines on AI; the possible creation of a European Agency for robotics and AI; the promotion of innovation in the AI and robotics domain; the assessment of prospective impacts on employment and possible "job displacement due to automation".

The 2017 Resolution marked the beginning of a long and winding road for EU institutions, which reached an important milestone with the adoption of the final text of an Artificial Intelligence Act in August 2024. After the adoption of the Resolution, the European Council of October 2017 reiterated the urgency of addressing AI "while at the same time ensuring a high level of data protection, digital rights and ethical standards". The Council hence invited "the Commission to put forward a European approach to artificial intelligence", which eventually saw the light with the Communication on "AI for Europe" in April 2018 (COM(2018) 237 final, 2018). In the Communication, the European

Commission presented a strategy aimed at boosting the EU's technological and industrial capacity and AI uptake across the economy, both by the private and public sectors; preparing for socio-economic changes brought about by AI; and ensuring an appropriate ethical and legal framework, based on the Union's values and in line with the Charter of Fundamental Rights of the EU.

Since then, EU institutions started a long and tortuous path in which they showcased their ability to act as "learning systems", able to develop sophisticated knowledge on the opportunities and risks of AI and adapt and update such knowledge as the technology evolves. While the European Commission's work on robotics certainly pre-dates the European Parliament Resolution and the Council conclusions, these two documents can be seen as the first of a long series of policy steps, which would lead the European Union to become a pioneer in the regulation of AI.

2018–2020—The European Commission's "Listening Phase"

While the European Commission was considering its first policy steps, some EU Member States started adopting their AI strategies. Notably, in France, the national AI strategy was based on the 2018 report of the so-called "Mission Villani" and proposed i.e. a policy framework on predictive algorithms that made humans responsible at each stage of the reasoning process, as well as a clarification of applicable liability rules in fields such as healthcare (Villani, 2018). Other countries (e.g. Germany) were clearer in their rejection of additional rules on civil liability for AI.[6] Overall, developments in Member States gave the impression that, in the absence of action at the EU level, the landscape of AI regulation would rapidly become very fragmented. Meanwhile, non-EU countries like Singapore were adopting very flexible self-regulatory approaches to AI, starting with Singapore's Model Governance Framework launched already in 2019 (Renda et al., 2021).

[6] The Bundestag had set up a committee of inquiry on AI, tasked with examining questions of liability and responsibility for AI. In the context of healthcare, the committee has recommended introducing a common certification for AI medicinal products and assessing whether there are liability gaps not covered by the general rules (Deutscher Bundestag, 2018, 2019).

The European Commission decided to put itself in listening mode by adopting two main initiatives, as anticipated in the "AI for Europe" 2017 Communication. First, the launch of an AI Alliance platform, which would rapidly gather thousands of participants engaged in a wide variety of discussion threads. Second, the establishment of a High-Level Expert Group (HLEG) on AI, tasked with the definition of ethical guidelines and the formulation of policy recommendations to bolster the EU's competitiveness in this domain. The HLEG was composed of 52 experts, some of whom were independent academics, and others represented stakeholders from industry and civil society. The group (of which the author of this chapter was a member) delivered two main outputs. The most influential and important of them was the Ethics Guidelines for Trustworthy AI, released in April 2019 and coupled one year later with an online, open-sourced Assessment List for Trustworthy AI (ALTAI), which garnered a lot of interest among stakeholders.

A brief account of the work of the HLEG for the Ethics Guidelines is important to understand how the EU's approach to AI evolved. Importantly, the HLEG decided to depart from its initial, relatively narrowly defined mandate of drafting ethical principles for AI and broadened its scope to embrace "trustworthy AI", a term that is now commonly used in the international jargon on AI policy and was at the time relatively new.[7] In the HLEG's interpretation, to be trustworthy, an AI system needs to be at once legally compliant, ethically aligned, and socio-technically robust. The Guidelines then broke down the second and third pillars of trustworthiness by identifying four main ethical principles (respect for human autonomy, transparency, fairness, and explicability). Even more importantly, such principles were further translated into seven requirements of trustworthy AI, which ended up forming the basis for subsequent legislative initiatives. They included human agency and oversight, technical robustness and safety, privacy and data governance, transparency, diversity, non-discrimination and fairness, the orientation of the AI system towards societal and environmental well-being, and the accountability of the AI system.

The seven requirements proved to be a very important feature of the Ethics Guidelines. Until then, public institutions, businesses, and research associations had adopted largely aspirational documents aimed

[7] IBM was using the term "Trusted AI" at the time.

at raising awareness and triggering spontaneous uptake rather than being effectively monitored and enforced. The Ethics Guidelines were the first step towards the formalisation of a complete regulatory framework for AI. Being the product of an independent expert group, they had to be converted into a legislative text, and this happened gradually, with the support of a large-scale debate with the AI Alliance, as well as the launch in December 2018 of a Coordinated Action Plan between the EU and Member States.[8]

The release of the Ethics Guidelines on Trustworthy AI in April 2019 and the first steps of the decade-long Coordinated Plan with Member States provided important inputs to the new European Commission, led by Ursula von der Leyen, which started its mandate at the end of 2019. Despite initial announcements by von der Leyen, who would have wanted a binding initiative on AI already within 100 days of her first presidential mandate, the European Commission decided to adopt a non-binding White Paper on AI, which saw the light in February 2020 (COM(2020) 65 final, 2020). The White Paper reiterated the Commission's commitment to going beyond the formulation of ethical principles and legal rules on AI. The White Paper posits that, to succeed in this domain, the EU should ensure the emergence of both an "ecosystem of trust" based on legislation and standards and an "ecosystem of excellence" along the entire value chain, encompassing research and innovation and the uptake of AI-based solutions in the market, particularly by SMEs. As will be recalled later in this chapter, the two ecosystems have unfortunately evolved at different speeds since then, with the excellence one still lagging.

The White Paper laid the foundations for the ambitious legislative initiative in the domain of AI von der Leyen had evoked in her inaugural speech, yet not before an additional round of stakeholder consultation and a comprehensive impact study, which lined up existing evidence of risks and harms caused by AI use with a specific focus on fundamental rights and safety (Renda et al., 2021). What emerged from that study was that AI uptake in private and public entities, despite the undeniable potential benefits to society and the economy, was capable of weakening virtually all fundamental rights rather than being only a possible source of

[8] The Action Plan contemplated 70 joint actions for closer and more efficient cooperation between Member States, and the Commission in key areas, such as research, investment, market uptake, skills and talent, data and international cooperation.

discrimination. The impact study also led to a first assessment of the costs associated with the introduction of a conformity assessment system for high-risk AI systems, at a time when most of the contours of the future legislative initiative were still far from properly defined, and an assessment of the possible cost of setting up an AI agency.

2021—Taking Legislative Measures on Trustworthy AI

The proposal for an AI Act finally saw the light on 21 April 2021, immediately attracting the world's attention as the first-ever comprehensive proposal to regulate Artificial Intelligence, an endeavour that, per se, most commentators deemed challenging, futile, or even preposterous. Finalising the text required taking very important decisions, which still shape the debate on AI around the world today.

A Broad Definition of AI

The European Commission proposed a broad definition of AI. Article 3, point 1 of the proposal defined AI as "software that is developed with one or more of the techniques and approaches listed in Annex I and can, for a given set of human-defined objectives, generate outputs such as content, predictions, recommendations, or decisions influencing the environments they interact with". Annex I then indicated specific techniques and methods such as machine learning approaches, logic- and knowledge-based approaches, and statistical approaches. The advantage of specifying the techniques that would correspond to the definition in Article 3(1) was that annexes could be modified more swiftly and frequently. Modifying the main text would require reopening the whole ordinary legislative procedure and thus achieving consensus between all co-legislators (the European Commission, the European Parliament, and the Council). Hence, the European Commission was trying to preserve the adaptive, future-proof nature of the AI Act, knowing that the fast evolution of the subject would require adjustments to the list of techniques over time. In addition, the European Commission partly relied on the definition that had been adopted by the HLEG already in 2018, though not calibrated for regulatory purposes. It also opted for such a definition to nurture Europe's ambition to set a global standard, as a similarly broad and technology-neutral definition was being given to AI systems by the OECD network of AI experts (OECD, 2024).

The decision to adopt a broad definition of AI was heavily criticised by some stakeholders, who saw the risk of over-regulation and complained that the remit of the AI Act would even reach ordinary software such as spreadsheets and word processors. Both arguments, that of over-regulation of AI and the risk of regulating non-AI products, were, however, flawed. As a matter of fact, the broad definition was already narrowed down by the specification of techniques under Annex I. Moreover, as will be explained below, the Commission's proposal for an AI Act adopted a rather strict risk-based approach, which aimed at capturing a small minority of AI systems on the market and subjecting only those to regulatory requirements akin to the ones identified by the HLEG. This meant that, however broad the definition, the AI systems that would end up being regulated remained a tiny minority compared to the unregulated ones.

Regulating AI Applications, Not AI per se. The Genesis of a Refined Risk-Based Approach

Another very important feature of the Commission proposal was that only specific AI applications, not the adoption of AI techniques and methods in and of themselves, were subject to regulatory requirements. This was inspired by the massive reflection that preceded the proposal, which clarified that not all uses of AI would generate similar levels of risk for fundamental rights and safety. The European Commission, therefore, decided to single out specific use cases as particularly risky and to subject them to regulation. Initially, the guesstimate used by the Commission was that between 5 and 10% of the AI systems circulating on the market should be subject to regulatory requirements. This led the Commission to discard the initial option of identifying entire sectors (e.g. health, government, education) that would be considered as areas AI could particularly hamper fundamental rights of safety. Choosing entire sectors would have had the advantage of allowing more flexibility and gradually adjusting the scope of the AI Act to the evolution of use cases within those sectors; at the same time, it carried the risk of disproportionately regulating certain uses, conflating them with others that created more evident risk (e.g. human-mediated X-ray scanning as compared to triage in hospitals).

Importantly, until the very end of the preparation of the Commission proposal, the approach adopted by the AI Act was "binary", i.e. aimed at identifying high-risk applications and low or no-risk applications, which would not be subject to regulatory requirements. However, several stakeholders, including prominent academics and the German Data Ethics Commission, had already flagged the need for a more refined approach, which would lead to a 4- or 5-tier classification based on the degree of riskiness of AI applications. Such an approach had the very important added feature of enabling the European Commission to single out applications that were to be considered unacceptably risky and, as such, to prohibit their introduction in the EU market. Until then, the idea of creating "redlines" or a list of prohibited applications was not contemplated in the debate on the AI Act. Another important opportunity offered by adopting a multi-tier risk classification was the possibility of identifying a category of AI systems that would only warrant transparency requirements, as they could potentially generate confusion as to the human or non-human nature of the user interface.

Eventually, the text of the proposed AI Act featured a four-tier risk classification, with applications being classified as "unacceptably risky", "high risk", "limited risk" (later relabelled as transparency risk), and "low or no risk". Unacceptably risky applications (Article 5) included AI systems considered "a clear threat to the safety, livelihoods, and rights of people", particularly systems or applications that manipulate human behaviour to circumvent users' free will and systems that allow "social scoring" by governments. High-risk cases included safety–critical applications for large-scale assets, such as critical infrastructure; applications susceptible to generating discriminatory results in delicate sectors, such as education and the workplace; and an array of public sector applications, including essential services, law enforcement, migration, asylum and border control management, and the administration of justice and democratic processes. A third category, of limited risk, triggered only transparency requirements, such as the obligation for providers of AI systems, such as chatbots, to make users aware that they are interacting with a machine, so they can make an informed decision to continue or step back.[9] Finally, a "low or no risk" category, presented as encompassing

[9] Transparency obligations were mandatory for AI systems that interact with humans, detect emotions determine association with (social) categories based on biometric data, and generate or manipulate content ("deep fakes").

the majority of AI systems, was defined as possibly subject to voluntary codes of conduct.

High-risk AI applications were subject to regulatory requirements that largely echoed the seven requirements specified by the HLEG (except for the orientation towards societal and environmental well-being) and thus touched on data management and quality, documentation and traceability, transparency, human oversight, accuracy, and robustness.

A Focus on AI "Providers", Anchored in Product Safety Legislation

A key feature of the proposed AI Act was the almost exclusive focus on AI providers as the entities in charge of ensuring compliance with the regulatory requirements. AI providers were defined as natural or legal persons, public authorities, agencies, or other bodies that develop an AI system or that have an AI system developed "with a view to placing it on the market or putting it into service under its own name or trademark, whether for payment or free of charge". These are, in other words, the entities at the end of the value chain who take responsibility to place the AI system into the market or put it into service so that it interacts with the external environment. This predominant focus in the AI Act is the direct consequence of the Act's emphasis on concrete applications and use cases rather than on AI as a technology. At the same time, it placed the responsibility on one of many possible entities that populate the increasingly complex life cycle of an AI system: as such, it implicitly relies on an approach adopted particularly in consumer law, according to which concentrating the responsibility for securing compliance on downstream providers and giving the latter possible redress in case of negligent conduct during upstream phases allows for more effective monitoring and enforcement, as well as protection of end users. Another underlying assumption is that providers have all the information that is necessary to carry out conformity assessment.

The focus on providers also echoed a feature of product safety legislation, under which manufacturers are responsible for carrying out conformity assessments of their products ahead of placing them on the market. In this case, given the nature of the systems at hand, providers were also given enhanced responsibility to monitor the behaviour of the system after it has been placed on the market (or put into service) and periodically repeat their assessment. Yet, the reference to product safety legislation, ever-present in the AI Act, found a limit in the fact that many (indeed, most) AI systems are not embedded in a product that is already subject to that legislation. Accordingly, while for products already subject to "CE marking" regulations, the scrutiny of compliance with the AI Act was integrated with the already-foreseen conformity assessment procedure to be carried out by a notified body, for all other cases (with one exception, i.e. the use of remote biometric identification) the European Commission clarified that providers could comply by simply carrying out "internal checks" regarding the conformity of the product. For the vast majority of high-risk AI systems, this possibly implied a highly reduced compliance cost and administrative burden, a feature that very few stakeholders highlighted in the aftermath of the presentation of the proposal.

A Minimalistic Yet Ground-Breaking Legislative Proposal

The European Commission's first attempt at AI regulation was cautious and proportionate, if not minimalistic, despite complaints by most business stakeholders, who saw a looming risk of over-regulation of a technology that many considered to be still in its infancy. Echoes of the "better safe than sorry" approach rooted in the EU precautionary principle and often contrasted (though often with a degree of exaggeration) with the United States' greater orientation towards innovation were everywhere in commentaries, position papers, and blog posts. Yet, there was little trace of over-regulation in the proposal. On the contrary, the AI Act stood out as the first-ever proposed legislation to build a framework for banning specific uses of AI and the introduction of concrete regulatory requirements for a family of techniques and use cases that continuously evolve, promoting lawmakers to lay the foundations for a continuously learning policy framework.

If anything, other problems loomed over the proposed AI Act. Besides regulatory humility, only a few other elements of the proposal were fully consistent with the need for adaptive regulation. Besides the broad definition of AI and the introduction of provisions for regulatory sandboxes at the national level, the choice to place all lists in Annexes potentially created the space for a periodic update without having to reopen the whole ordinary legislative procedure. On the other hand, this choice was not accompanied by the proposed creation of a sufficiently powerful and capable institution, which would then oversee the constant knowledge update backing the designation of prohibited, high-risk, and limited-risk applications. The debate on the possible creation of an AI agency, which started already in the European Parliament in 2017, had been further nurtured by an ad hoc report in the IMCO Committee of the European Parliament (Del Blanco report). Yet, the European Commission ended up proposing the creation of an AI Board, composed of one representative per Member State, in what appeared to be a mere coordination mechanism, insufficient to ensure concrete and responsive monitoring of such a complex and ever-evolving subject matter.

The lack of sufficient institutionalisation at the EU level was coupled with a monitoring and implementation system at the national level, where Member States have the task to designate a competent authority. Here, too, approaches have diverged significantly, with some countries choosing data protection authorities as competent for the AI Act, whereas other countries have created ad hoc institutions (e.g. Spain) or even tried to establish frameworks for cooperation between regulators with complementary expertise (along the example of the UK Digital Regulatory Cooperation Forum). Securing suitable implementation and enforcement is of the essence, even more so given the Act's reliance on "internal checks" by AI providers, as well as the significant informational asymmetry existing between regulated entities and regulators in this domain. The risk is to provoke a "Volkswagen scandal on steroids", to echo a well-known case in which co-regulation based on conformity assessment has led to massive avoidance of compliance.

Moreover, it must be recalled that in addition to being risk-based and thus only applicable to specific applications, the AI Act proposal was not all-encompassing. To the contrary, besides not applying to military uses, the original proposal also shied away from covering AI systems used by large online platforms and search engines, which were already subject to another ground-breaking piece of legislation (the Digital Services Act). As will be explained below, this clear division of labour between the two overarching pieces of legislation would wane during the Ordinary Legislative Procedure, particularly as a result of the many amendments proposed by the European Parliament to the text.

2022–2024—Course Corrections and U-Turns

The aftermath of the presentation of the Commission's proposal for an AI Act was as hectic as the preparation phase. Around the world, governments and experts saw the EU approach either as a North Star (e.g. Brazil, initially Korea) or as an excessively cumbersome body of rules requiring significant capacity for implementation. But when the European Parliament started working on its first reading of the Act, things started to change. Key highlights of the early work of the Parliament include the creation of a dedicated Special Committee on Artificial Intelligence in a Digital Age (AIDA) and the drafting of a joint report of the two leading committees in the Parliament, the one for Internal Market and Consumer Protection (IMCO) and the one for Civil Liberties, Justice and Home Affairs (LIBE). The joint report was particularly important, as it marked a decisive U-turn from the Parliament's approach in the 2017 Resolution on Civil Law Rules for Robotics.

More specifically, in June 2022, the draft joint IMCO-LIBE report carried the following statement: "The concept of decision autonomy for machines is at its core in conflict with fundamental notions of our societies, such as human dignity, autonomy, and the rights to private life and the protection of personal data ... [The AI Act] should reconcile the potential benefits to society offered by AI with the primacy of humans over machines". In other words, attributing rights and duties to machines was eventually seen as the wrong approach to AI, where a human-centric approach implies that the ultimate responsibility for deploying or not an AI system to perform a specific task is, and should always be, human.

A full account of the changes proposed by the two co-legislators to the text of the Act, resulting in thousands of proposed amendments, would transcend the purposes of this chapter. That said, it is worth mentioning some of the most contested aspects on which convergence between the three institutions has been challenging. On the definition of AI, the Council has consistently advocated the adoption of a narrower approach focussed on machine learning, whereas the Parliament overall favoured an even broader definition than the one originally introduced by the Commission. Eventually, the final text of the AI Act presented a broad definition, very aligned with the ones adopted in the United States and at the OECD level.

The Parliamentary debate gradually extended the list of prohibited AI uses and high-risk applications, substantially extending the original scope of the AI Act and gradually overlapping with the Digital Services Act (DSA). The "redlines" started including the use of remote biometric identification in public places, the practice of predictive policing, and algorithms to predict recidivism. High-risk applications welcomed creditworthiness assessments, access to public benefits, triage in healthcare, eligibility for life insurance, emergency response, AI used in political campaigns, deepfakes, and recommender systems used by prominent social media (thereby, the overlap with the DSA). Eventually, in the final trialogue, the list of redlines was more affected than the high-risk one by such expansionist attempts.

Other changes occurred during 2022 and 2023 and significantly changed the scope and text of the AI Act. The debate in the European Parliament led to an expansive interpretation of the notion of harm, which, from a pure focus on individual harm, also started encompassing harm to society and the environment, and psychological harm. This also led to a reconciliation between the original requirements of trustworthy AI specified by the HLEG (which included societal and environmental well-being) and the text of the AI Act. The need for more effective enforcement triggered a discussion that ranged from providing the European Commission with additional powers to initiate proceedings to the need for private enforcement and a bigger, more powerful, and inclusive AI Office. The provisions on regulatory sandboxes, originally specified at the purely national level, were gradually coordinated to ensure mutual learning among national competent authorities. The European Parliament obtained, especially for providers that are bodies governed by public law or private entities providing public services, the introduction of an obligation to perform a Fundamental Rights Impact Assessment before placing high-risk AI systems on the market.[10]

But the most important deviation from the original proposal came at the end of 2022 when Rapporteurs in the European Parliament started to realise that the text of the AI Act did not place sufficient emphasis on the cooperation between upstream designers and developers of AI systems that were becoming increasingly versatile and foundational, and those downstream deployers that used such systems for a specific purpose becoming subject to the AI Act as providers, whenever their applications fell under the lists of prohibited high- or limited-risk applications. The reckoning was shocking for some of them, as scholarly papers gradually

[10] Such Impact Assessment would contain a description of (i) the deployer's processes, and time of use of the high-risk AI system in line with its intended purpose; (ii) the categories of natural persons and groups likely to be affected; (iii) specific risks of harm likely to have an impact on these categories; (iv) the implementation of human oversight measures foreseen for the AI system in question; and (v) measures to be taken in the case of the materialisation of those risks, including arrangements for internal governance and complaint mechanisms.

shed light on the fact that the AI value chain was becoming increasingly complex and heterogeneous and certainly more and more concentrated in the hands of a few companies providing powerful general-purpose AI systems (GPAIS) (Renda & Engler, 2022).

This *impasse*, initially addressed by adding provisions on cooperation along the value chain in the main text but without altering the foundations of the Act and its focus on providers, became unsustainable with the release of OpenAI's ChatGPT in November 2022 and the ensuing flurry of new generative AI models that started populating the market in 2023. As the market was quickly reorganising around a fistful of powerful GenAI developers and a massive crowd of downstream deployers only accessing GenAI functionalities through Application Programming Interfaces, it became clear that the AI Act's prevalent focus on providers was partly missing the mark. This led Rapporteurs in the European Parliament to decide not to adopt any final text in February 2023 and to start working on new provisions, which would account for stricter scrutiny of GPAIS.[11]

This move marked a significant deviation from the original commitment not to regulate AI but only its concrete applications. EU lawmakers were gradually opening the door to a parallel system of enforcement, centralised at the EU level, and targeting AI systems that are not placed on the market for a specific purpose but constitute the basis for a variety of possible applications, given their versatility. The need to lay the foundations for such a new *corpus* of rules brought with it significant novelties also in terms of enforcement. Centralising the scrutiny and regulation of GPAIS at the EU level would have implied either the creation of an independent AI Agency or an internal service of the European Commission in charge of implementing the rules.

Eventually, the latter option prevailed. The AI Act sets up an AI Office as a service internal to the European Commission, DG CONNECT, to be endowed with dozens of new experts with competence in computer

[11] A General Purpose AI (GPAI) system is defined as an AI system that displays significant generality and is capable of competently performing a wide range of distinct tasks regardless of the way the model was originally released on the market. These AI systems can be integrated into a variety of downstream systems or applications. GPAI models are also often referred to as Foundation Models. They have purposefully been designed to perform a wide range of tasks and to easily adapt to new situations. To this end, they are trained on very broad sets of unlabelled data and can be used for many different tasks without much fine-tuning (Regulation (EU) 2024/1689, 2024).

science and AI. At the time of writing, the AI Office is still being set up, but its mandate is already clear and broad, spanning from overseeing the application of the EU's AI Act and ensuring compliance with its provisions to providing guidance to businesses and public organisations on best practices for AI development and deployment; tracking the development and impact of AI technologies across the EU, including assessing risks and benefits; advocating for trustworthy AI practices that align with EU values; working with member states, industry stakeholders, and international partners to harmonise AI standards and regulations; and promoting research and innovation to advance safe and beneficial AI technologies in Europe.

When it comes to regulatory scrutiny, the AI Office focusses, in particular, on GPAIS. In general, GPAIS are obliged to maintain the technical documentation of their model, including training and testing processes, along with results of evaluations; maintain documentation for other AI providers that plan to integrate with the GPAI, including details of specifications and limitations; establish a policy for complying with EU copyright law; and publish a detailed summary of the content used for training the AI model. When they pose "systemic risk" (proxied with cumulative compute power, and possibly with the number of end users, registered businesses using the model, and the number of tokens and parameters used in the model), GPAIS are subject to additional measures such as model evaluation, risk assessment and mitigation, incident reporting, and meeting sufficient cybersecurity levels. One of the first steps taken by the AI Office was the launch of consultation and an expert group for the drafting of a Code of Practice that will detail the AI Act rules for providers of general-purpose AI models and general-purpose AI models with systemic risks.

The final version of the AI Act, on which a political agreement was finally found in December 2023, was published in the Official Journal of the EU only in August 2024. Its entry into force will take place gradually: bans on unacceptably risky AI applications will take effect 6 months after publication; rules on GPAIS will apply 12 months after publication; and the rest will only become binding 24 months after publication in the Official Journal. Regardless of the merits of the text, a problem that was flagged by some commentators is that the text, as approved, bears very little resemblance with the original proposal presented by the European Commission and that, contrary to that proposal, the new text was never subject to stakeholder consultation or an *ex-ante* impact assessment.

As a result, the proportionality assessment performed for the original proposal, which, as explained, featured a rather minimalistic scope, cannot be extended by analogy to the final text of the Act, which appears potentially much more impactful and possibly also costlier for regulated entities.

Conclusions

Despite the adoption of the AI Act, much still needs to be done at the EU level to complete the vision of promoting trustworthy AI in Europe. Several developments are expected in the coming years.

With its text now finalised, the AI Act needs to be implemented, and this will be far from trivial. Even if the standardisation mandate conferred to CEN-CENELEC will successfully shed light on the conformity assessment procedure, much of the implementation will require interpretive guidance and cooperation with sectoral regulators, as main risks and related mitigation measures typically depend on the specifics of the use case. Delays in providing the required standards prompted the Commission to propose delaying the application of some provisions of the AI Act in the Digital Omnibus. The AI Office will still need to deliver clarification and streamlining of the relationship between the rules contained in the Act, AI-related rules contained in the Digital Services Act, the Cyber Resilience Act, and other legislative measures, and sector-specific rules such as the Medical Devices Regulation. Meanwhile, the subject matter will continue to evolve. The approach of the Trump administration to consolidate its technological leadership by largely eliminating regulation—notably repealing the Executive Order of the Biden administration and its governance structure—became an enduring challenge to the Commission's regulatory path.

The AI Act may lead to the deployment of more trustworthy AI systems in Europe, at least for specific use cases considered particularly risky (though measures related to GPAIS may lead to a more extensive impact). This will certainly contribute to the creation of what the European Commission defined back in 2021 as an "ecosystem of trust", which will need to be complemented with guidance and standards, as well as a world-class monitoring and enforcement that is going to prove problematic at best, due to the significant informational asymmetry existing between the developers of powerful GPAIS and the AI Office.

A degree of cooperation with other AI Safety Institutes at the international level (in the UK, Canada, Japan, Singapore, and Korea), despite their narrower scope of action, may come to the rescue, and the activation of a dedicated regime for access to GPAIS by "vetted researchers" along the lines of Article 40 of the DSA (Regulation (EU) 2022/2065, 2022), and as already considered in some of the iterations of the text almost through to its finalisation. This could become a way to strengthen civil society's ability to reign in as an additional source of accountability for AI giants that appear to have unmatched power in today's market.

What remains to be seen is whether the AI Act will still be a relevant piece of legislation or will have incurred obsolescence just as occurred to its draft version when ChatGPT entered the market at the end of 2022. As the AI world departs from the transformer models to embrace new approaches, it is far from clear what the market will look like when the AI Act finally enters into force in its entirety. The hope is that the current structure and scope of the Act will prove resilient to these changes, but only time will tell.

Two final comments are in order in what tried to be an accurate, yet far from exhaustive, account of eight years of AI debate in the European Union. First, in the international landscape of AI governance, the AI Act stands out as a much more assertive attempt to place rules on AI than what is being done in legal systems such as the United States and, to some extent, also China and India. On whether it is possible to remain agile while firmly regulating AI, the jury is still out. To be sure, the finalisation of the text, over three years after the Commission's proposal, marks a milestone on a much longer road towards successful implementation at a time when the dominant mood in the EU is oriented towards streamlining and simplifying legislation.

Second, while the ecosystem of trust has made substantial inroads with the adoption of the AI Act (together with the DSA and the possible future adoption of the proposed rules on liability in the AI Age), much remains to be done on the so-called "ecosystem of excellence". There, evidence suggests that Europe only attracts 6% of total AI-related venture capital and relies on four main AI hubs, which do not cooperate when it comes to research and innovation (Balland & Renda, 2023). This is a pity as available data show that Europe trains more leading AI-focussed graduates than the United States (and slightly less than China), yet most of them end up in the United States, attracted by a larger and more dynamic market, as well as higher salaries.

Building the ecosystem of excellence would require capitalising on Europe's world-class supercomputing infrastructure, promoting the availability of data, ensuring talent retention, and pooling resources by fostering cooperation between leading AI centres in Europe—possibly including those in the UK. To progress on the ecosystem of excellence, in January 2024, the European Commission proposed an AI Innovation Package containing several measures: an amendment of the EuroHPC Regulation to set up AI Factories, a new pillar for the EU's supercomputers Joint Undertaking activities, an EU AI Start-Up and Innovation Communication outlining financial support measures, education, training, skilling and reskilling activities, measures to promote venture capital, measures to promote data spaces, and the launch of the "GenAI4EU" initiative, devoted to industrial and public sector use cases for generative AI (European Commission, 2024b). The AI Continent Action Plan was delivered in 2025 to consolidate these efforts and intensify investments in so-called AI Factories and AI Gigafactories.

These measures, taken altogether, may still come too late for Europe to catch up with other world powers on AI development. Meanwhile, the Draghi report on the future of European competitiveness (2024) proposes a path to simplification as well as much bolder industrial policy measures aimed at developing EU-wide vertical AI use cases in several sectors of the economy to promote the uptake of AI in those parts of the economy that need revamping and a productivity boost. What is true is that artificial intelligence will remain high on the political agenda in the upcoming years to help Europe progress in completing the ecosystem of excellence and catch up with other world powers in this key technological domain, which is poised to dramatically impact the European economy, society, and global geopolitics in the decades to come.

References

Balland, P.-A., & Renda, A. (2023). *Forge ahead or fall behind: Why we need a United Europe of Artificial Intelligence*. Retrieved from CEPS https://www.ceps.eu/ceps-publications/forge-ahead-or-fall-behind/

Deutscher Bundestag. (2018). *Einsetzung einer Enquete-Kommission Künstliche Intelligenz – Gesellschaftliche Verantwortung und wirtschaftliche, soziale und ökologische Potenziale*. Retrieved from https://dserver.bundestag.de/btd/19/029/1902978.pdf

Deutscher Bundestag. (2019, December 18). *Projektgruppe KI und Gesundheit: Zusammenfassung der vorläufigen Ergebnisse*. Retrieved from https://www.bundestag.de/resource/blob/672950/fed938366dcf1b3f79c2ff177e0f86f5/PG-3-Projektgruppenbericht-data.pdf

Draghi, M. (2024). *The future of European competitiveness: A competitiveness strategy for Europe*. European Commission.

European Commission. (2018, April 25). *Communication from the Commission to the European Parliament, the European Council, the Council, the European Economic and Social Committee and the Committee of the Regions, Artificial Intelligence for Europe*. Retrieved from https://eur-lex.europa.eu/legal-content/EN/TXT/?uri=COM%3A2018%3A237%3AFIN

European Commission. (2020). *White paper on artificial intelligence—A European approach to excellence and trust*. Retrieved from https://commission.europa.eu/document/download/d2ec4039-c5be-423a-81ef-b9e44e79825b_en?filename=commission-white-paper-artificial-intelligence-feb2020_en.pdf

European Commission. (2022). *Proposal for a regulation of the European Parliament and of the Council on horizontal cybersecurity requirements for products with digital elements and amending Regulation (EU) 2019/1020*. Retrieved from EUR-Lex https://eur-lex.europa.eu/legal-content/EN/TXT/?uri=celex%3A52022PC0454

European Commission. (2024a). *AI factories*. Retrieved from Shaping Europe's Digital Future https://digital-strategy.ec.europa.eu/en/policies/ai-factories#:~:text=This%20package%20is%20designed%20to,the%20creation%20of%20AI%20Factories

European Commission. (2024b, January 24). *Commission launches AI innovation package to support Artificial Intelligence startups and SMEs*. Retrieved from Press Corner https://ec.europa.eu/commission/presscorner/detail/en/ip_24_383

European Parliament. (2017, February 16). *Civil law rules on robotics, European Parliament resolution of 16 February 2017 with recommendations to the Commission on Civil Law Rules on Robotics (2015/2103(INL)*. Retrieved from https://www.europarl.europa.eu/doceo/document/TA-8-2017-0051_EN.html#title1

European Union. (2022, October 19). *Regulation (EU) 2022/2065 of the European Parliament and of the Council of 19 October 2022 on a single market for digital services and amending directive 2000/31/EC (Digital Services Act)*. Retrieved from https://eur-lex.europa.eu/eli/reg/2022/2065/oj

European Union. (2024). *Regulation (EU) 2024/1689 of the European Parliament and of the Council of 13 June 2024 laying down harmonised rules on artificial intelligence and amending Regulations [...] (Artificial Intelligence Act)*. Retrieved from EUR-Lex https://eur-lex.europa.eu/eli/reg/2024/1689/oj

Future of Life Institute. (2017). *Asilomar AI principles*. Retrieved from Future of Life Institute https://futureoflife.org/open-letter/ai-principles/

OECD. (2024). *Explanatory memorandum on the updated OECD definition of an AI system*. Retrieved from https://www.oecd-ilibrary.org/science-and-technology/explanatory-memorandum-on-the-updated-oecd-definition-of-an-ai-system_623da898-en

Renda, A., & Engler, A. (2022). *Reconciling the AI value chain with the EU's Artificial Intelligence Act*. Retrieved from CEPS https://www.ceps.eu/ceps-publications/reconciling-the-ai-value-chain-with-the-eus-artificial-intelligence-act/

Renda, A., Arroyo, J., Fanni, R., Laurer, M., Sipiczki, A., Yeung, T., & de Pierrefeu, G. (2021). *Study to support an impact assessment of regulatory requirements for artificial intelligence in Europe*. Publications Office of the European Union.

Université de Montréal. (2013). *Montréal declaration of responsible AI*. Retrieved from https://montrealdeclaration-responsibleai.com/

Villani, C. (2018). *Rapport de Cédric Villani: donner un sens à l'intelligence artificielle (IA)*. Retrieved from Ministère de l'Enseignement Supérieur et de la Recherche https://www.enseignementsup-recherche.gouv.fr/fr/rapport-de-cedric-villani-donner-un-sens-l-intelligence-artificielle-ia-49194

Zuboff, S. (2019). *The age of surveillance capitalism: The fight for a human future at the new frontier of power*. Public Affairs.

CHAPTER 14

Outer Space Governance

Ludwig Moeller, Sara Dalledonne, and Lucas Bersegol

Introduction

Space is an integral part of the digital economy. Satellite communications, Earth observation (EO) meteorology, and satellite navigation provide essential space applications and services. Space technology is increasingly woven into the fabric of the information age as part of 5G/6G mobile networks, data for weather forecasts and climate change monitoring, positioning, and timing services.

Today, space stands at the beginning of a new age, only comparable to that of the internet about 25 years ago. The space industry is experiencing unprecedented momentum, which has remarkably grown over the last decade, reaching 1000 active space companies in 2022 compared to 600 in 2012 and attracting a substantial influx of both public and private capital. Space is a major opportunity for a European internal market, well beyond the perimeter of the space economy, with the value of space-based services for the wider economy forecasted to reach more than 7 trillion dollars by 2040 (ESPI & BCG, 2023). For example, the agriculture industry can use satellite solutions to unlock value through farming

L. Moeller (✉) · S. Dalledonne · L. Bersegol
European Space Policy Institute (ESPI), Vienna, Austria
e-mail: hermann.ludwig.moeller@espi.eu

T. Kleiner and A. Garcia Rodriguez (eds.), *The Making of a Global Digital Rulebook*, https://doi.org/10.1007/978-981-95-9226-5_14

automation and improved data-driven decision-making.[1] Similarly, Global Navigation Satellite System (GNSS) solutions are a core enabler of modern finance networks, performing a timing and synchronisation function, particularly relevant, given the high volume of transactions and the level of security required. Beyond economic factors, space profoundly impacts society and positively influences the lives of people on Earth, for example, directly contributing to achieving the Sustainable Development Goals (SDGs), acting as a core enabler of net zero climate change ambitions, and supporting the energy transition.

This chapter aims to investigate the central role of space in Europe's Digital Decade targets, where space will be part of Europe's digital sovereignty and data strategy, from satellite constellations providing connectivity and AI-enabled geoinformation services to data centres in space, leveraging optical and quantum technologies, all as part of a low Earthorbit-based economy, including commercial space stations. Space technology has the unique ability to serve various sectoral policies and play a central role in socioeconomic sustainability and growth, in particular as a technological tool for digital transformation.

After a brief introduction, this chapter focuses on the role of space in digital policies, including an analysis of how EU digital policies consider space solutions as useful tools to tackle challenges and respond to digital and data policy objectives. Section "Space in Europe and Beyond" provides an overview of the European space domain, including all the major stakeholders dealing at the crossroad between space and digital, as well as an overview of the most significant factors providing space governance disruption in the coming years. These factors include a speedily expanding space sector in terms of actors, activities, and economy; a disruptive technological context favoured by the verticalisation of the space sector; an increasing congestion in space, and a more challenging operational space environment, as well as aspects related to the growing geopolitical tensions and security concerns, extending into the space environment.

While relevant space actors have always been national governments, cheaper launches and manufacturing have facilitated actions in outer space by private companies. The role of space agencies is shifting as space also

[1] Particularly, precision fertilisation has the potential to improve average local yields and generate cost savings on crops.

becomes a policy function of governments. In addition, space is increasingly supporting public sector policies, including in energy, transport, security, and agriculture, as well as business strategies in markets like telecommunications and geointelligence, automotive, financial services, and pharmaceuticals.

Section "Key Governance Challenges for European Decision Makers" expands on key governance challenges for European decision makers, including issues and concerns related to autonomy and freedom of action, competitiveness and market, industrial policy, safety and sustainability, and security and stability. Finally, section "The Way Forward: Europe as a Space Power" aims to investigate the fitness of the current European space governance in the context of the unfolding and shifting global space landscape. It concludes that Europe will need a mix of new policy initiatives, diplomatic strategies, and commercial actions to assert its leadership and influence in the space sector, thereby securing its international position and role in the broader context of Europe's digital sovereignty.

Europe has achieved significant milestones in space, with a range of state-of-the-art space capabilities like EO and the EU Copernicus programme that enable unique socioeconomic benefits, supporting and increasingly transforming many other policy domains and industrial sectors. However, Europe lags behind prominent space powers in several critical areas, such as human space exploration, space situational awareness, and space control. What is more, that gap is widening, and Europe risks losing further ground vis-à-vis former peers and emerging powers, such as India, accelerating the use of space nationally and as a tool of diplomacy. The recent European launcher crisis provided a poignant illustration of the inherent risk of losing strategic capabilities. The consolidation of the European space programme—as reflected in the EU Regulation for the Space Programme, the negotiations for the next Multiannual Financial Framework (MFF), as well as the new IRIS^2 Programme, shows the willingness of European stakeholders to respond to the global space race. However, in achieving these objectives, not only will Europe be confronted with internal challenges, but equally important, with international ones (ESPI, 2022a, 2022b). Indeed, space is becoming geopolitical, a means to project progress and power (ESPI, 2023a, 2023b, 2023c, 2023d, 2023e).

In the 2040 timeline, decisive European space initiatives as an element of a digital Europe can help capture 25% of the estimated global value of space for the broader digital economy. This would involve a reinforcement and expansion of its competitive advantage in meteorology, EO, and satellite navigation. Europe would also have the capacity to cultivate secure connectivity solutions to support the development of private actors and their commercial solutions. Europe would assume its global leading role while leveraging space data and services for sustainability on Earth, aligned with net zero objectives and respective initiatives. Finally, Europe would have enhanced capabilities thanks to concerted efforts in the development of innovative applications and dual-use solutions for security and defence, notably in areas such as emergency communications, protection of critical infrastructure and their increased resilience, and crisis response.

As these advancements unfold, they intersect with the broader context of the space sector and policy frameworks, in particular space exploration—a field where Europe must assert its influence. Revolution Space, today symbolised by industrial actors such as SpaceX, is still at an early development stage (ESA, 2023), and space remains a vast opportunity, one that Europe can seize if it acts swiftly and aligns its endeavours with wider European policy objectives for prosperity, peace, and future generations (ESPI, 2023a).

The Role of Space in the European Digital Agenda

Transformative technologies impact our daily lives. They are all pervasive across sectors of the economy. A world without e-commerce is hard to imagine today. The disruptive impact of AI may bring the biggest systemic changes nations and people will face in the digital age. Such disruptive transformation has far-reaching economic, societal, and geopolitical repercussions.

The space sector is rapidly evolving, with satellite communication and connectivity applications playing a central role in Europe and globally. Space is increasingly becoming part of the broader digital infrastructure, with satellite communication services integrated into terrestrial networks, serving solutions across various industry and market verticals.

Several EU digital policies consider space solutions as a useful tool to tackle challenges and respond to digital and data policy objectives.[2] The use of a range of solutions, embedding the space-based component,

[2] The policy analysis includes policies released in the last 10 years.

is consistent with the Commission's recent commitment to developing adequate frameworks so that "all market players benefiting from the digital transformation (…) make a fair and proportionate contribution to the costs of public goods, services and infrastructures" (European Commission, 2022). The EU Action Plan to digitalise the energy system of 2022 considers that "Copernicus, EO component of the Union Space Programme and Destination Earth, provides environmental data that enable, for example, better siting and operation of renewable energy generation" (COM(2022) 552 final, 2022a) (Fig. 14.1).

The Digital Compass of 2021, which aims to achieve gigabit connectivity all over Europe by 2030, clearly outlines space as a means to achieve this policy goal. It outlines that "this ambition can be reached with any technology mix, the focus should be on the more sustainable next-generation fixed, mobile and satellite connectivity, with Very High-Capacity Networks" (COM(2021) 118 final, 2021).

The European strategy for data of 2020 aims to position the EU as a leader in a data-driven society. Satellites are integral to this strategy, underlining that "the EU will also contribute data and infrastructure from the Copernicus EO programme to underpinning the European data spaces where relevant. At the same time, enhancing the Copernicus ecosystem through the application of European digital technological solutions will

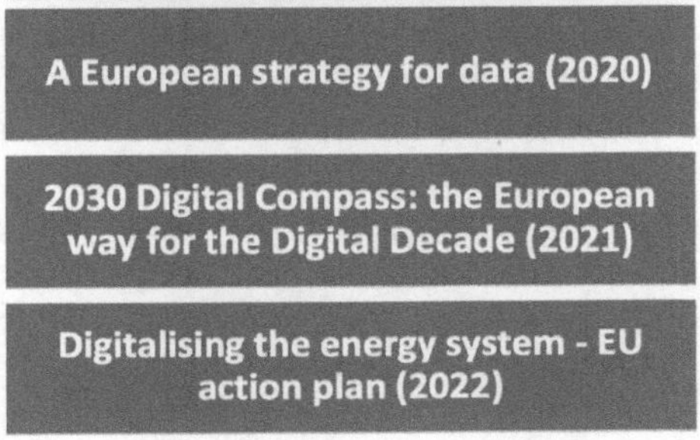

Fig. 14.1 Post-2015 digital policies that mention space

offer new innovation opportunities to the data spaces' constituency, both public and private". The strategy also aims to invest in a High Impact Project, which aims at developing common European data spaces and interconnecting cloud infrastructures (COM(2020) 66 final, 2020).

The Digital Single Market Strategy for Europe of 2015, which seeks to improve access to online goods and services while fostering the growth of the European Digital Economy, highlights that "Europe needs a more harmonised copyright regime which provides incentives to create and invest while allowing transmission and consumption of content across borders, building on our rich cultural diversity. [...] The Commission will review the satellite and cable directive to assess the need to enlarge its scope to broadcasters' online transmissions and the need to tackle further measures to ensure enhanced cross-border access to broadcasters' services in Europe" (SWD(2015) 100 final, 2015).

Beyond the European digital agenda, space can provide solutions to address unprecedented challenges for Europe and the world, including societal ones. Space is instrumental not only in monitoring the climate crisis but also in offering solutions for the mitigation and adaptation of future-proof sustainable societies, notably in the gaps and challenges identified by the Intergovernmental Panel on Climate Change (IPCC). Today, European satellites, particularly through programmes like Copernicus, play a crucial role in assessing over half of the 50 essential climate variables—parameters critically contributing to understanding our planet's climate. Additionally, satellite capabilities, as enabled by the EU's Copernicus, Galileo, and European Geostationary Navigation Overlay Service (EGNOS) programmes, can enhance food security through smart and precise agriculture, revolutionising farming productivity and resilience.

Next to climate change-related risks and natural disasters, geopolitical confrontation and warfare, including technological vulnerabilities, are among the top future risks. Space assets enable managing and decisively acting upon natural and anthropogenic crises, supporting European disaster management, civil protection, and law enforcement agencies, as well as national defence stakeholders in pursuing their strategic missions. Space-based capabilities have long been crucial enabling pillars of national and allied security and defence portfolios, as also recognised by the EU Strategic Compass for Security and Defence.

Overall, space plays a crucial role in the EU's path to digital sovereignty. However, despite relevant synergies between the two sectors, the majority of EU digital policies do not mention space solutions. Space infrastructure, especially Copernicus, is identified as a key component in the creation of European data spaces, the growth of the digital economy, and achieving connectivity. GOVSATCOM, EU Space Surveillance and Tracking (SST), and EGNOS are not mentioned at all.

Space in Europe and Beyond

The beginning of space affairs goes back a long way, during World War II, with the development of launching capabilities (e.g. Germany, the United States), already demonstrating at that time the dual nature of rocket technology. Soon after, the advancements made in the space sector significantly shifted towards the projection of (soft) power to a new frontier space. In 1957, the Union of Soviet Socialist Republics launched Sputnik, the first satellite to orbit Earth, sending out audio beeps. This was followed by a succession of space endeavours as part of the global space race, also reflected by the creation of national and transnational space agencies (e.g. NASA, 1958; CNES, 1961; DLR, 1965; ISRO, 1969, ESA, 1975).

Space is marked by a diverse range of space domains, each characterised by distinct dynamics in both policy frameworks and implementation strategies, as well as varying relationships between national governments and other institutional or commercial entities. For instance, space capabilities that contribute to defence, security, or strategic activities are deeply intertwined with national sovereignty concerns. Due to their critical role in ensuring nations' security and strategic autonomy, these domains require significant governmental involvement. In contrast, other domains such as EO, satellite broadcasting, and broad space-based internet services appear to be more commercially driven, primarily catering to civilian needs. It is through the development of the private sector, with the support of policy, that wider market forces have largely guided the development of these domains, also demonstrating a robust path forward for future advancements. The challenges stemming from the ambition of becoming a leading stakeholder in the space ecosystem, together with enhanced global competition, have paved the way towards a more integrated European approach regarding the development of space affairs and programmes.

Europe is one of the most experienced actors in the international space arena and operates highly regarded space programmes. Through its different constituents, Europe has mastered a wide array of capabilities that address the whole range of space activities, including telecommunications and operational EO, navigation, and space sciences.

An Evolving European Space Governance

The European space governance architecture is constituted by the so-called Governance Triangle, which is composed of the Member States, the EU, and the European Space Agency (ESA). Each member state has a governance structure and participates in several organisations engaged in space matters (Fig. 14.2).

European Union

The founding treaties of the European Communities did not comprise specifications regarding competencies in space matters, and Member States traditionally had exclusive autonomy on space affairs, acting at national, multilateral, and intergovernmental levels (mostly ESA). Solid foundations for EU competencies in space activities have been created by the Lisbon Treaty. Indeed, following the entry into force of the Treaty in 2009, space was included as one of the policies pursued by the EU, albeit as an area of shared responsibilities (transversal intervention area) (2007/C 306/01, 2007).

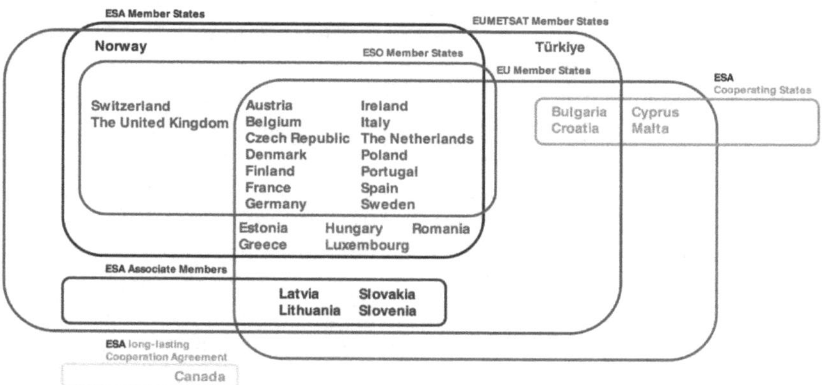

Fig. 14.2 European space Governance

Article 2(2) of the Treaty on the Functioning of the European Union (TFEU, 2007) provides for the shared competencies concept between the EU and its Member States and avoids the applicability of the principle of preemption. It restricts the extent of the EU's capability to establish the European space programme. Article 4(3) TFEU (2007) states that in areas such as space, "the Union shall have the competence to carry out activities, in particular, to define and implement programmes; however, the exercise of that competence [by the Union] shall not result in Member States being prevented from exercising theirs".

Unlike what usually happens in matters of shared competence, space matters are covered by a sui generis competence, parallel and symmetrical with respect to the State, as it leaves Member States authority to implement their own domestic legislation in the realm, even after the exercise of powers by EU institutions. In this regard, Article 189(1) TFEU (2007) confers to the EU the mandate to develop and implement a European space policy. It associates the development of such a policy with the EU's goal to pursue "technical and scientific progress, industrial competitiveness and the implementation of its policies". Then, Article 189(2) TFEU (2007) provides the legal basis for adopting a European space programme and explicitly excludes that such acts may provide for harmonisation of the laws and regulations of the Member States (European Union, 2016).

Building on its long-lasting expertise, the EU introduced its ambition to create a unified EU Space Programme in 2018. After more than 2 years of trilateral interinstitutional negotiations at the EU level (among the Commission, European Parliament, and the Council of the European Union), the Parliament and the Council of the EU finalised Regulation (EU) 2021/696 establishing the Space Programme of the Union for 2021–2027 and the EU Agency for the Space Programme (EUSPA) in 2021.

The single space programme grouped together the existing flagship programmes Galileo/EGNOS and Copernicus, as well as two new programme components: GOVSATCOM and Space Situation Awareness (SSA). The regulation led to the establishment of the EU SST Partnership, which is currently composed of 15 EU Member States. The development of the European constellation IRIS^2 (Infrastructure for Resilience, Interconnectivity and Security by Satellite), the EU's new flagship satellite programme, is expected to increase space references in digital policies, most likely due to its wide scope of commercial and security purposes.

Unlike Galileo and Copernicus, IRIS² would operate within an existing market and rely on a public–private partnership. This double challenge entails providing secure EU communications services while enabling the industry to leverage commercial offerings. The EU assigns various responsibilities for the EU Space Programme mostly to three institutions: the European Commission and EUSPA. Other main stakeholders related to space affairs are the Council of the EU, the European Parliament, the European External Action Service (EEAS), the European Defence Agency (EDA), and the EU Satellite Centre (SatCen).

At the European Commission level, the Directorate-General for Defence Industry and Space (DG DEFIS) oversees space affairs, grouping them with the defence industry. The establishment of an EU Commissioner for Defence could reshape the space portfolio; e.g. space may either remain associated with the defence industry or shift focus to commercialisation. DG DEFIS is responsible for the development and implementation of EU policy on defence industry and space, and it aims to consolidate all EU space-related activities into one "EU Space programme." Other DGs dealing with space but from a more user-oriented perspective include the Directorate-General for European Civil Protection and Humanitarian Aid Operations (DG ECHO), Directorate-General for Climate Action (DG CLIMA), and Directorate-General for Communications Networks, Content and Technology (DG CONNECT).

EUSPA aims to bridge space services with user needs to maximise the benefits of the EU Space Programme investment for both users and the economic growth and competitiveness of the EU. As a result, EUSPA manages the Galileo and EGNOS programmes, develops markets for Copernicus services and data, coordinates user-related aspects of the GOVSATCOM programme, and works to ensure the increasing contribution of space to the EU market.

The EEAS is the EU's diplomatic service, which defines and implements an effective and coherent Common Foreign and Security Policy (CFSP). The EEAS works in cooperation with Member States, the Council of the EU, the European Commission, and the European Parliament. Within the EEAS, space affairs fall under the responsibility of the Deputy Secretary General (CSDP) and crisis response (DSG-DEF), under the Secretariat General of the EEAS. EEAS is headed by the EU's High Representative / Vice President (HR/VP), who is also the head of EDA and the head of the Foreign Affairs Council (FAC) configuration at the Council. EEAS is responsible for representing the EU and its Member

States in several international forums related to space, including the UN Committee for Peaceful Uses of Outer Space (UN COPUOS).

From a budgetary perspective, the EU Space Programme's budget falls under the MFF,[3] while another important financial instrument of the EU Space Programme is Horizon Europe, the research and innovation funding programme established in April 2021.[4] This space component aims to fulfil the R&I needs of the EU Space Programme, and its implementation is overseen by the Executive Agency HaDEA. Meanwhile, EUSPA manages more specific domains, such as the European Global Navigation Satellite System (EGNSS) and Copernicus downstream applications, as well as the Galileo PRS service application.

European Space Agency

ESA is an international organisation established in 1975 as a result of a "merger" between two previously existing organisations, the European Space Research Organisation (ESRO) and the European Launcher Development Organisation (ELDO).

Under the ESA Convention, the purpose of ESA is "to provide for and to promote, for exclusively peaceful purposes, cooperation among European States in space research and technology and their space applications, with a view to their being used for scientific purposes and for operational space applications systems" (ESA, 1975, Article 2). On the policy level, this mandate is to be undertaken through an elaboration of a long-term European space policy by recommending objectives to its 23 Member States,[5] and by concerting policies of Member States. Under the ESA Convention, only two organs within the ESA governance framework are explicitly defined: the Council and the Director General.

Article 189(3) of the TFEU strengthens the European Space Agency's (ESA) role by advocating for the EU to "establish appropriate relations with the ESA". This recognises ESA's distinct technical expertise and its involvement in developing and implementing the EU Space Programme.

[3] The MFF for the 2020–2027 period, earmarking €14.8 billion in current prices.

[4] Under Cluster 4, titled "Digital, Industry and Space", Horizon Europe has a €14.9 billion budget until 2027, with a portion dedicated to space projects in alignment with the current MFF.

[5] Slovenia signed the Accession Agreement to the ESA Convention on 18 June 2024. Upon ratification, Slovenia will become the 23rd ESA Member State.

The Framework Agreement between the European Commission and ESA in 2004 laid the foundation for EU–ESA relations. The ESA Convention, Article II, defines its purpose as "elaborating and implementing a long-term European space policy [...] by concerting the policies of its Member States".

ESA's Agenda 2025 (ESA, 2021a, 2021b), introduced in 2021, sets five primary goals for the future, including fortifying the ESA-EU relationship, further emphasised by the recent Financial Framework Partnership Agreement (FFPA) signed in the same year (ESA, 2021a). The FFPA establishes the roles and responsibilities of the Commission, EUSPA, and ESA regarding the EU Space Programme, including cost distribution and coordination mechanisms for the European space initiative and to prevent duplication of efforts. Additionally, it allows ESA members outside the EU, such as Norway, Switzerland, and the United Kingdom, to participate in certain EU space programmes.

Besides public actors, the European private space sector also plays an important role in implementing policy objectives operationally across a wide array of space domains. For instance, Europe is marked by a strong presence of leading multinational satellite manufacturers with companies such as Airbus Defence and Space, Thales Alenia Space, and OHB SE, mostly developing satellites for various applications (e.g. EO, Satcom, PNT). Through its launcher segment, Europe also regained autonomous access to space, represented, among others, by companies like Arianespace, with the capability to operate from European-owned spaceports (e.g. Guiana Space Centre). Additionally, Europe plays a well-established role in the space economy thanks to world-leading satellite operators and manufacturers, as well as organisations such as ESA and EUMETSAT. Finally, Europe is investing in the development of impactful downstream applications, particularly emphasised in EO and satnav areas (e.g. Copernicus Programme, EGNOS, EGNSS).

Overall, considering both institutional and private elements of the space domain, EU space governance is complex, with various internal and external organisations setting and influencing commercial and programmatic priorities and policies. Strategic choices are necessary, particularly in areas most closely related to European sovereignty, while also acknowledging that a challenge persists in balancing national sovereignty with more global and collective European actions. This is particularly exacerbated by the fact that space is becoming geopolitical, a means to project progress and power (ESPI, 2023a, 2023b, 2023c, 2023d, 2023e).

However, the EU has the opportunity to play a pivotal role in fostering cooperation and Member States' funding, hence ensuring that both governmental and commercially driven domains contribute to cohesive political values and objectives. Lastly, space is increasingly part of international engagement and considered a tool for diplomacy in a multi-polar world, with new leading actors like China and emerging stakeholders like India. It has become a contested domain and is subject to increased global competition. It is an element of industrial competitiveness.

Factors of Disruption

The space sector is undergoing profound transformations that have repercussions on the positioning of Europe in the international space scene. In this context, various trends are affecting specific space domains and activities (ESPI, 2020).

A speedily expanding space sector in terms of actors, activities, and economy

In recent years, one of the most noticeable trends is the significant increase in the number of entities, both public and private, involved in space activities. Regarding the public sector's involvement, recent years have seen the emergence of numerous new spacefaring nations,[6] and the establishment of several new space agencies. This has expanded the participation in space activities from a select few countries to a much wider group of both developed and developing nations, each with diverse capabilities. For instance, the number of countries that have launched their first satellite has more than doubled, increasing from 50 in 2008 to 110 in 2023 (Krebs, 2024).

As a result of this growing engagement by both developing and established space actors, the number of orbital launches has witnessed an appreciable acceleration in the last few years, setting new records every year. In 2023, 221 orbital launches were conducted, doubling the ~100 launches in 2019. The number of spacecraft placed into orbit, especially after 2019, is also remarkable. Between 2014 and 2019, this number steadily increased from 298 to 490 spacecraft. However, 2020 marked

[6] i.e. countries that have developed access to space capabilities, or more likely, launched their first satellites).

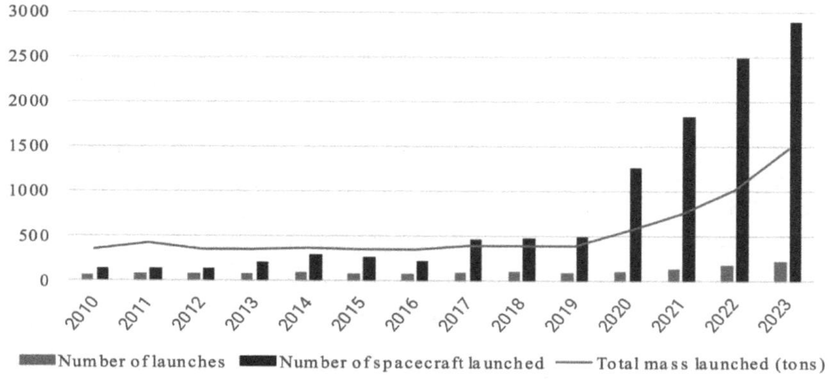

Fig. 14.3 Evolution of launch activity 2010–2013 (*Source* ESPI)

a turning point with 1266 spacecraft launched.[7] By 2023, this number skyrocketed to 2889, almost ten times the number in 2014(Fig. 14.3).[8]

In line with the growth predictions of the sector, the number of operating satellites is expected to continue to increase dramatically (e.g. AGI, 2020; Euroconsult, 2024), with tens of thousands of new satellites expected to be launched in the coming years. The impact of these new public and commercial endeavours is potentially enormous. SpaceX has been instrumental in the notable surge of US space launches from 2020 to 2023, conducting 80% of all launches. The deployment of the Starlink satellite constellation significantly contributes to a boost in launches, with Starlink missions accounting for 62% of SpaceX's launch activities during this period.[9]

In addition, the worldwide intensification of space efforts reflects new sectoral dynamics, encompassing the evolving role of public actors from owners to anchor customers and enablers, alongside a wider ranging approach to space. A more prominent role is played by private actors, pursuing the eventual goal of conducting space business independently

[7] The are 1843 in 2021, 2491 in 2022.

[8] ESPI launch database.

[9] ESPI launch database.

from governments. This commercially driven approach to space is characterised by ambitious undertakings to capture space markets through innovative schemes and business models, often focussing on cost-reduction efforts to disrupt existing markets or tap into new mass markets.

Recent public policies, notably in the United States, have spurred the emergence of this NewSpace phenomenon, introducing new public procurement schemes enabling and optimising industrial organisation and leading to an improvement in cost-effectiveness. Agencies have started readjusting their roles and adapting their industrial policy and procurement to foster the emergence of private endeavours and investments. The new approach takes the shape of numerous types of public–private partnerships, leading to shared costs and risks and to the transfer of control of key programmes. One of the most prominent examples is NASA's management of human spaceflight, awarding contracts to Boeing and SpaceX to develop manned capsules to transport cargo and astronauts to the International Space Station (ISS). NASA's involvement was a key enabler for SpaceX's development, not only to develop the Falcon-9 launcher but also to subsequently develop the Starlink satellite constellation, in turn attracting significant investment (i.e. ~$10 billion) from the private sector like Google (Fig. 14.4).

In Europe, the shift in industry relations appeared with the development of Ariane 6, granting more room to manoeuvre, autonomy, and responsibility to the industry to both develop and design the rocket.

The increase in space actors and activities has been accompanied by a consistent increase in global funding, both from public and private entities. Public investments continue to represent the bulk of funding in space activities, at a level of about 85% globally. National governments primarily fund space activities through procurement and grant mechanisms to public agencies, research institutes, universities, and the private sector. This funding supports a variety of objectives, including national security and defence objectives, socio-economic goals, and national prestige (OECD, 2024). In Europe, governments continue to be the main source of funding for space, contributing around 80% of total public investment in space, with about 60% allocated to ESA. Over the past few years, private funding has also grown tremendously, "with unprecedented private capital flows in the space sector from angel and venture capital investments" (OECD, 2019). Various promising markets have been identified for business ventures, including, e.g. global connectivity and geoinformation services.

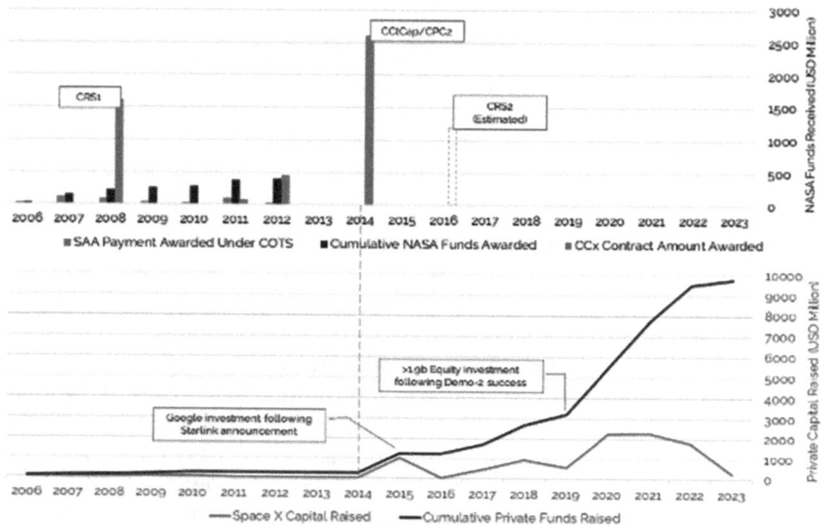

Fig. 14.4 SpaceX institutional support through space act agreements (SAA) in COTS, NASA commercial crew contracts and private capital raising in million $ (*Source* ESPI)

A disruptive technological context, favoured by the verticalisation of the space sector

The structural changes of the "enlarged" space sector are also associated with a more disruptive technological framework. This transformation is driven by diverse technological factors affecting all aspects of the space systems value chain, from production and operation to service provision and application potential.

Breakthroughs in hardware and spacecraft design have shifted the production paradigm towards affordable and miniaturised space systems, while preserving and expanding capabilities and unlocking new services and application areas.

Another notable trend is the emergence of spacecraft mass production, resembling automotive manufacturing on assembly lines, with greatly improved manufacturing output. Moreover, reusable spacecraft technology greatly contributes to lowering financial and capital barriers to entry into space activities.

Furthermore, the specificities of space technologies compared to technologies of other industrial sectors are diminishing. Although some space system technologies are endemic to the space sector (e.g. propulsion systems), advancements in the space sector are also largely driven by universal technological developments. In recent years, some of these new concepts have been increasingly integrated into space, adding to the emergence of new services and their applications. For example, advancements in the EO segment have linked space with big data (Soille et al., 2019).

Additionally, automation, AI, and machine learning are increasingly vital for handling large data volumes, processing complex calculations, or executing time-consuming processes across various scientific sectors, industrial fields, and public policies. The globally growing demand for enhanced connectivity, including greater data volume, availability (spatial and temporal), and speed, creates new avenues of opportunities for the satellite industry. Within machine-to-machine communication, namely the Internet of Things (IoT) trend, innovative small satellite start-ups are emerging to address this growing demand (ESA, 2018). Moreover, there are potential prospects for the space sector to adopt additional concepts such as quantum and cloud computing.

The integration of space systems with terrestrial digital systems is deepening and expanding across various sectors and policy domains. This expansion is reshaping established practices regarding ground segments, the integration of space with terrestrial or aerial communication networks, and the use of local or open sources of data, mostly of a geospatial nature. Hence, a growing demand for capable ground segments is foreseen, in particular, to achieve and sustain current plans for future LEO, geostationary orbit (GEO), or hybrid satellite systems.[10]

Besides synergic and enabling functions in the broader telecommunications sector, the future of connectivity brings about a confrontation between space and terrestrial (fibre or wireless) systems. Indeed, non-space companies, including large ICT companies, are entering the space sector to expand their activities and build on cross-fertilisation effects between ICT and space applications. In parallel, the space sector is undergoing verticalisation across multiple domains, including agriculture, aviation, maritime, and more.

[10] For instance, in EO applications, the integration of space data with terrestrial sources is becoming more pervasive and provides additional added-value for different purposes ranging from climate monitoring to international treaty verification mechanisms.

An increasing congestion and a more challenging operational space environment

As recognised by the UN Secretary-General in "Our Common Agenda", while space assets have "transformed the way we live and outer space systems are vital for understanding and solving global problems" (United Nations Secretary General Report, 2020), the outer space environment is confronted by new risks to security, safety, and sustainability. The International Telecommunications Union (ITU) states have registered radio frequencies for the launch of over 1 million satellites by 2029, compared to less than 10,000 satellites on our planet at the moment. Increased activities in space are not distributed evenly across all orbital regimes traditionally utilised for space missions (ESPI, 2023a, 2024a). The continuing increase in launch activity and orbital traffic further amplifies operational hazards with more risks of collisions and interference. The increase in spaceflight has been producing a more complex and dynamic orbital traffic, both in terms of operational space objects as well as space debris.

However, operational satellites account for a very small fraction of the total population of objects currently in orbit. Active satellites share space with "space debris", including inactive satellites and rocket bodies, as well as countless fragments of various sizes, nature, and origin. Space debris has increased even more steeply than the number of operating satellites over the past decade. This increase is largely due to a few orbital explosions and collisions, such as the Chinese ASAT kinetic test on the decommissioned weather satellite Feng Yun 1C in 2007 and the collision between the Russian Cosmos 2251 satellite and the American Iridium 33 satellite in 2009. These incidents alone boosted the space debris population by 40%.

The crowded space environment naturally creates risks for space operations (e.g. collision and interference hazards). Catastrophic collisions can lead to costly mission terminations, significant financial losses, and the creation of more debris, perpetuating the cycle of collisions. Although the congestion of the space environment is affecting space activities broadly, the LEO orbit is particularly affected by increasing physical congestion (ESPI, 2023b).

Space safety and sustainability concerns have become widely recognised issues in policymaking, and the available evidence signals a continuation of this trend in the foreseeable future. Measures to mitigate the creation of new space debris and collision risks between space objects have been completed or are underway (e.g. UN Guidelines for the Long-term Sustainability of Outer Space Activities (UNOOSA, 2019), the ESA Zero Debris Charter (ESA, 2022), and Space Sustainability Rating (Space Sustainability Rating, 2024).

Growing geopolitical tensions extending into the space environment

The Russian war on Ukraine has demonstrated the value of space for security and defence, reshaping the perception of space's role in national security. This change may lead to one of the most significant developments in Europe's space sector, where public funding in space for security and defence is much lower than in the United States. Currently, about 50% of global space funding originates from the security and defence sector.

Rising tensions and changes in the balance of power are reviving a new era of great power competition that extends into outer space. This is primarily reflected in the expansion of military space activities. The relevance of space for military operations, including in space, has been increasingly recognised by major space powers over the past few years. Space capabilities now routinely support the conduct of military ground, sea, and air operations. Services provided by space infrastructures are also increasingly integrated into a number of safety and security applications, including those used by the armed forces or for national security purposes. In parallel, threats have multiplied. Space assets have become potential military targets. Major space powers have invested in the elaboration of means to physically disrupt others' space capabilities. Several anti-satellite (ASAT) technologies have been developed and tested in actual conditions over the last few years, including China (2007), the United States (2008), and India (2019). Beyond "Kinetic kill", Rendezvous and Proximity Operations (RPO) technologies are other means of impairing a spacecraft. Similarly, cyber threats to space systems are also rapidly increasing (ESPI, 2023c), and progress has been made in research on directed-energy weapons.

Facing the multiplicity of such new threats does not rely solely on technical countermeasures but includes the elaboration of various deterrence strategies, political alliances, or attempts to agree internationally on some "rules of the game" for space operations. Many nations are already reconsidering their postures and doctrines regarding space. Countries like the

United States, Japan, and France are realigning space within their military organisation.

Key Governance Challenges for European Decision-Makers

The unfolding transformations of the global space sector, combined with the sizable dependence of societies on the continuing utilisation of services provided through space, are translating into key governance challenges for European decision-makers (ESPI, 2020).

Autonomy and Freedom of Action Issues

While Europe today still possesses the broad majority of the industrial capabilities needed to develop space programmes, it lags behind prominent space powers in several critical areas, such as human space exploration. What is more, that gap is widening, and Europe now even risks losing further ground vis-à-vis former peers, which are accelerating the use of space in their countries.

It is important to highlight, however, that the most worrisome aspect is not Europe's reliance on final products or systems but rather on the foundations associated with basic technologies (Moeller, 2023a, 2023b, 2023c). European stakeholders still need to externally source many components and raw, advanced materials, as well as some critical digital technologies and building blocks, like monitoring and control software, cloud services, that are not available within European boundaries. This most notably includes EEE components, software, advanced materials, equipment, processes, and modelling tools.

Due to the complex tangle of relationships, institutions, and multi-level sharing of competencies, Europe as a whole lack the fundamental features defining autonomy over space matters. Specifically, the interplay between national, intergovernmental, and communitarian frameworks is still a source of institutional misalignment, often harming Europe's ability to develop a clear and coherent strategy for the future and to act decisively.

What is first and foremost at stake is Europe's political sovereignty over space matters, its ability to develop the full benefit of space, and its declared objective to assert itself as a global player and partner. The extensive benefits offered by the space sector are inseparable and can only be fully realised through a cohesive, at-scale, and globally competitive

European space industry. In this context, while national ambitions do play an important role in the development of space capabilities, they are most effective when aligned with broader European policy objectives, including digital policies. This alignment is particularly crucial for reinforcing and strengthening collective European sovereignty, which is absolutely vital for protecting Europe's interests and ensuring its independence in critical areas.

The importance of a unified approach becomes even more apparent at the EU level. A coordinated European policy framework can indeed leverage transnational advantages such as resources, expertise, and market size. This upscaling not only enhances global competitiveness but also ensures that Europe as a whole can set its own strategic directions, standards, and policies.

Europe's lack of autonomous capacities may, in fact, impact its freedom of action and digital sovereignty and ultimately restrict its ability to decide when and under what conditions to develop and deploy its space programme. In addition, by maintaining the status quo, Europe may not fully enjoy the autonomy to freely choose its partners, remaining at the mercy of external forces and accepting a higher level of vulnerability (Moeller, 2023a).

Competitiveness and Market Issues

Most of the trends presented in section "Space in Europe and Beyond" are bound to exercise a significant impact on the international competitiveness of Europe and the European space sector, posing a number of new challenges or magnifying already existing ones. The expansion of globally operational space actors and activities has fostered a growth in the number of competitors. Europe is already faced with strong international competition, but new competitors are arising due to the greater involvement of the private sector in space activities and the rise of new "spacefaring" nations bringing new ambitions into space.

The growth in competition is premised on the more aggressive space strategy pursued by all major space powers, which are now increasingly emphasising the importance of international space markets and hence directly or indirectly challenging Europe's leading positions, particularly in the commercial launch market and in the satellite manufacturing market.[11]

Another major challenge for the competitiveness of the European space industry is the changing competition dynamics brought about by the combination of new private entrants with the adoption of innovative industrial approaches and disruptive market solutions (e.g. integrated services, lower prices, reduced lead times, lower complexity, or higher performance among other value proposition features) (Vernile, 2018). Such new entrants challenge the traditional approach adopted for space programmes with new processes, business models, and solutions. Consequently, well-established European industry players must adapt their strategy to compete and sustain. Moreover, the limited availability of risk capital funds hinders ventures seeking to commercialise their innovative technologies, including digital and space synergies. The scarcity of scale-up funding in Europe is a critical shortfall, often leading to talent and companies migrating to the United States, where the financing landscape is currently more favourable (de Concini & Toth, 2019).

Another major challenge for the competitiveness of the European space industry is the disruption of traditional business models and markets brought about by the unfolding technological evolution and the uncertain

[11] For instance, looking at the launch service market, Europe has historically had a principal competitor in Russia, with most of the market shares disputed between Ariane and Proton launchers. However, over the past few years, the commercial launch market has experienced an abrupt change in the main competitors. The most visible and structural change is the abrupt advent of SpaceX, which in the span of a couple of years has imposed itself as the dominant player on the commercial launch market. Thanks to its large backlog of U.S. institutional payloads and the significant support received from the U.S. government through the COTS programme, the company has been able to pursue an aggressive penetration pricing strategy in the commercial market, thereby surpassing established launch providers. Moreover, significant development programmes are currently underway in all major spacefaring nations, including the United States, Europe, China, India, and Japan. The next few years will be thus characterised by a larger offer of launch vehicles. As major development efforts are progressing towards operational readiness, offering increased flexibility and promising cost reductions, competitive pressures are expected to further stiffen. In Europe, the past year has been characterized by a launcher crisis. Initially planned for its maiden flight in 2020, the intended successor to the Ariane 5 launcher. Furthermore, the Vega-C rocket, which is expected to return to service with a launch in November, had been temporarily grounded following a launch failure in December 2022. Complicating the situation, Russia's invasion of Ukraine in February 2022 deteriorated international relations with Roscosmos, Russia's space agency, leading to the discontinuation of the Soyuz rocket for Western launches.

changes in the demand conditions in commercial space markets. The most evident case in point is the global telecommunication sector, which has traditionally been instrumental in sustaining the entire European space industry but whose profound transformation from GEO to LEO solutions is now having uncertain ripple effects along the entire value chain. Besides uncertain market evolutions, the expansion of institutional captive markets poses another key challenge to the competitiveness of the European space industry. Worldwide, the space market cannot be considered an open business, and the open commercial market represents just a fraction of the total. In fact, the volume of orders in these captive institutional markets produces a distortion of competition as it allows competitors to generate larger scale production in their home markets, allowing them to offer lower prices in export markets.

Industrial Policy Issues

Public actors in all the major space countries heavily support their space industry sector through specific national policies and regulations to limit foreign competition and sustain the competitiveness of national industries. These policies include industrial and procurement policies making use of anchor tenancy arrangements, policies that "prescribe" the use of specific space-based services, export control regulations, trade policies, and economic diplomacy. Besides generating distortions to the competition terms, the preference granted by most institutional customers to national suppliers contributes to creating challenging asymmetries in terms of market access.

A major challenge is posed by the increasingly active involvement of governments in regulatory affairs. Government policy, laws, and regulations can restrict the penetration of space markets by European industries or generate extraterritorial effects, putting European space companies at a competitive disadvantage. As an example, the United States stated the willingness to "prioritise regulatory reforms that will unshackle American industry and ensure we remain the leading global provider of space services and technology".[12]

Besides securing an institutional domestic market for their space industries, foreign competitors are also increasingly adopting aggressive market

[12] In February 2018, the re-established U.S. National Space Council adopted a second Space Policy Directive on "Streamlining Regulations on Commercial Use of Space".

penetration strategies to support the competitiveness of their industry by favouring space exports. Together with price dumping and unfair price competition through national subsidies, trade policy and economic diplomacy have become important instruments that major countries have turned to in order to support and expand the positions of their national space industry worldwide. These tools have been particularly important for those countries seeking to circumvent export control restrictions, as in the case of China, or those countries seeking to compensate for the limited domestic demand, as in the case of Japan.

The competition challenge posed by the emergence of private actors is further amplified by supporting measures put in place by all major space actors to stimulate the consolidation of this new dynamic. This includes creating business-friendly space regulations,[13] incentivising private ventures through competitions, prizes, and awards (e.g. NASA Lunar Lander Challenge), and promoting mechanisms to connect actors in the space economy and nurture spin-in/spin-off innovations.

European institutions have also been proactive in fostering space entrepreneurship and private investment trends in Europe. Their efforts are now yielding the first concrete results, with various success stories emerging across Europe. Notwithstanding, Europe is lagging in its capacity to trigger and embrace private business leadership. Investment power is still small compared with the United States and China.

The landscape of space sector support mechanisms is fragmented, making it challenging for entrepreneurs to navigate through the different funding options. European market fragmentation and lower demand affect the potential viability of business models. Overall, there appear to be two missing elements in the European approach to support New Space: creating a sustainable market for space-based services (i.e. promoting a "demand-pull" approach) and exploring new procurement approaches such as anchor tenancies or "innovation partnerships" to address the lack of a market (ESPI, 2024b).

To conclude, these support measures constitute an inherent challenge for European upstream and downstream space providers and satellite operators, including those heavily dependent on digital technologies like image processing and fusion.

[13] E.g., the United States Space Act in 2015.

Safety and Sustainability Issues

As seen in "Space in Europe and Beyond", the space operating environment is changing, marked by a rapidly growing traffic of active satellites and debris and by the emergence of new concepts such as megaconstellations, CubeSats, and on-orbit services. A congested space environment naturally amplifies the number of risks for space operations, in particular concerning collision and interference hazards. In this context, the adequacy of current solutions to monitor space, detect hazards, and prevent them, as well as the suitability of current regimes governing space activities, proves to be very limited (ESPI, 2023b).

Today, the prevention of risks of collision and other space safety and sustainability issues consists of a complex set of laws, regulations, standards, and other binding and non-binding rules followed in different ways by international players. Among the tools to prevent the escalation of collision risks, the principal one has been the definition and implementation of a set of principles outlining how space systems should be designed, operated, and disposed of to mitigate their impact on the space environment, in particular regarding the generation of space debris. Even though some fundamental principles have been consensually adopted in international frameworks, the enforcement of these principles is left to the goodwill of governments, agencies, and private companies, raising the inevitable question of the level of compliance.

Additionally, the physical availability of orbits and near-Earth space environment is an essential space resource, while the protection of operating satellites from collisions requires the capability to properly detect, evaluate, and respond to collision risks. However, reduced orbit availability and uncertainties about potential collision risks jeopardise the long-term sustainability of European space investments. The United States possesses world-leading capabilities, while Russia and China are considered autonomous players in this domain. In Europe, the development and enhancement of national and European SST capabilities is also progressing, being one of the pillars of SSA and contributing to the goal of improved protection of European space assets (Hrozensky & Dvoracek, 2019). Improved global SSA capabilities are a prerequisite to a future Space Traffic Management (STM) system. However, the current level of cooperation on SSA/STM-related issues remains rather limited, inevitably confronting Europe with a number of challenges to properly detect, evaluate, and respond to collision risks (EU SST, 2024).

Furthermore, the international community is witnessing growing pressures for access and utilisation of the electromagnetic spectrum for various means of telecommunications, including those enabled by space systems. Demand for access to spectrum is rapidly growing due to emerging spectrum-hungry connectivity concepts of terrestrial operators, such as the awaited 5G mobile networks, leading to shortages and intense competition despite optimisation efforts of spectrum usage. This reduced availability of spectrum could potentially lead to the unavailability of this precious resource, hence jeopardising European space activities (e.g. ESPI, 2023a, 2024a).

Security and Stability Issues

In the past years, a major shift has taken place in the importance given to military space operations. In particular, this evolution has taken place at three levels.

First, at the strategic and doctrinal level, major space powers have increasingly addressed space as an operational warfighting domain alongside land, sea, air, and cyber. This has led to more assertive postures considering the conduct of operations directly in orbit and the publication of military strategies dedicated to the space domain in many countries (the United States, the United Kingdom, France, Australia, Luxembourg, etc.). In parallel, some countries, especially the United States and other Western countries, are increasingly willing to establish international alliances in space in order to defend common interests and values in the face of potential adversaries (namely China and Russia).

Secondly, at the organisational level, many advanced spacefaring nations have been restructuring their military apparatus in order to better integrate space; this has especially taken the form of the creation of entities devoted to military space issues (space forces, space commands). These entities usually have two main objectives: support the good integration of space solutions with other branches of the military and ensure the protection of space assets in orbit against potential threats to make sure that they can continue providing their services. A few examples include the creation of the U.S. Space Force in December 2019, the establishment of a Defence Space Command in Australia in 2022, or, earlier, the foundation of the PLA Strategic Support Force in China in 2015. In Europe, as well, the trend has taken shape, with a few countries having created their own military entities dedicated to space, among which are France (2019), Italy (2020), Germany (2021), and the United Kingdom (2021).

Finally, at the capability level, an increasing number of nations are investing in military space systems, either by developing them themselves or by acquiring capacities. For instance, in January 2023, Poland bought two very high-resolution satellites from Airbus, with their ground segment and associated services, for defence purposes. In addition, a smaller set of states is also actively developing, testing, and, in some cases, fielding counter-space capabilities. These anti-satellite systems can be destructive[14] or non-destructive.[15] The latter capability is attracting increasing interest as it does not create any debris and, therefore, does not put at risk the space assets of the attacker. Moreover, the use of non-destructive systems may be more difficult to attribute, and they usually rely on dual-use technology, which means that they can be developed under the cover of civil programmes. Cyber-attacks are also a threat on the rise; in recent years, such attacks on both terrestrial and space systems have become ever more frequent, and the war in Ukraine has illustrated their use in an operational context. For instance, the conflict started with a cyberattack against the KA-SAT satellite, which disrupted its civil service, such as monitoring of energy networks, and impacted Ukrainian military forces that were relying on it (ESPI, 2022a).

The EU and its Member States have become aware of the increasing role played by space in the security and defence area and are willing to invest more in this dimension of the space sector. Among EU initiatives on defence (e.g. Permanent Structured Cooperation, European Defence Fund), several projects are addressing space specifically and contributing to the development of space solutions for security and defence. Moreover, to frame its future activities in the field, the EU released in March 2023 its first EU Space Strategy for Security and Defence, which calls for and proposes measures for a more collaborative approach to these questions to better protect the EU's and Member States' assets and interests in orbit (ESPI, 2024b).

[14] With four tests having been conducted since 2007 by China, the United States, India and Russia.

[15] E.g., lasers to blind other satellites, technologies for rendezvous and proximity operations with cooperative and non-cooperative objects tested in orbit.

The Way Forward: Europe as a Space Power

European space initiatives are a crucial element of European digital sovereignty and Europe's Digital Decade targets, with space helping to capture approximately 25% of the estimated global value of space for the broader digital economy. However, to this day, Europe lacks full autonomous capacity across the whole spectrum of space capabilities and activities, preventing it from being a space power. When commenting on the release of the EU 2022 Strategic Compass for a stronger EU security and defence in the next decade, for instance, Josep Borrell, the High Representative of the European Union for Foreign Affairs and Security Policy, asserted that Europe holds the status of a "significant space power" thanks to its substantial market share in the global space industry and European success stories like Galileo and Copernicus (European Council, 2022).

Still, to achieve and maintain its status, Europe will have to take appropriate measures, such as advancing its capacity edge through the sustained development of its hard capacities and their integration into European and national infrastructures, policies, and strategies. This level of autonomy would allow Europe to operate its space programme independently, without the necessity of seeking permission from anyone. Conversely, becoming a space power would also enhance industry and programmatic security, ensuring mission independence when necessary.[16] It would allow Europe to grasp the invaluable benefit of space, unfolding its impact in a number of strategic domains, including prosperity, wealth, peace, security, climate action, sustainability, society, and empowerment for future generations (Moeller, 2023b).

Developing and maintaining autonomous capacities across the entire spectrum of activities is the task of the decade. Europe has all the prerequisites to develop into a full space power by bringing together, federating, and developing the excellence of its European, national, and industrial capabilities. However, considering the numerous challenges that must be overcome, Europe's path towards space power status will be a complex process.

Europe, together with its EU Member States, can secure and extend Europe's competitive edge in several satellite applications, including meteorology, EO, and satellite navigation. They can also better develop

[16] E.g., in case of an impending natural disaster or a war.

secure connectivity solutions, including optical and quantum technologies and direct-to-device solutions as part of a geoinformation system, also ensuring that European private actors have the capability to build commercial solutions. In addition, space data and services could be better leveraged for sustainability on Earth towards net-zero, including support to smart cities, energy transition, Green Deal, and climate action. New breakthrough applications and dual-use solutions could also be developed for security and defence objectives (e.g. emergency communications and crisis response). In this context, space technology is a key enabler of Europe's digital transformation, guaranteeing an impactful digital sovereignty and extending into other critical areas.

In the future, the European Union will need a more politically oriented profile to attain such status, requiring a revisiting of the overarching policy drivers of the European approach to space, including strengthening the integration and recognition of space into the broader digital agenda. European space policy faces a double-sided challenge: stimulating a more competitive economic dimension and industrial transformation while developing the largely neglected security dimension and demanding a deeper advancement of the political dimension of the European project. The amount of investment needed to assert itself as a full-fledged space power is within reach in the context of Europe's economic strength, especially given that the average GDP share of space investment in Europe is about one-fifth of that of the United States. Recovering unity of vision and action will be the key tool to fully attain Europe's space power potential, supported by a doubling of investment in space by 2040 (0.15% GDP) (ESPI, 2023a).

In addition to scaling up existing state-of-the-art programmes, the policy impact could also include the provision of political direction to economic actors, going beyond economics as the sole driver for Europe's ambitions in space. To date, European space policy and programme action is mostly concerned with space capabilities, such as satellites and launchers, and less so with the policy impact of space. This includes how to integrate space into other policy domains of governments, political programmes, parliamentary actions, and policy directions for the development of space for the wider economy. It will entail the alignment of space policy with strategies across other sectors (mostly digital but also green, security and defence, energy, mobility, and health) and designing space policy in support of business strategies beyond the space industry.

Lastly, diplomacy will play an important role moving forward in ensuring the development of space programmes.

The EU's recent successes (e.g. EO capability) and challenges (e.g. launchers) demonstrate the benefits of collective action in creating ground-breaking innovations but also the underlying need for greater alignment, coordination, and coherence. Strengthening the EU's role in space is essential to securing its position as a global leader, also in the digital economy and in pursuing European digital sovereignty and Europe's Digital Decade targets.

References

AGI. (2020). *107,000 Planned Satellites by 2029*. Retrieved from https://www.youtube.com/watch?v=oWB7ZySDHg8

de Concini, A., & Toth, J. (2019). *The future of the European space sector. How to leverage Europe's technological leadership and boost investment for space ventures*. Retrieved from European Investment Bank. https://www.eib.org/en/publications/the-future-of-the-european-space-sector-report

ESA. (1975). *ESA convention*. Retrieved from https://www.esa.int/About_Us/Law_at_ESA/ESA_Convention

ESA. (2018). *Space-enabled Internet of Things shown in Berlin*. Retrieved from https://www.esa.int/Applications/Connectivity_and_Secure_Communications/Space-enabled_Internet_of_Things_shown_in_Berlin

ESA. (2021). *Agenda 2025*. Retrieved from https://www.esa.int/About_Us/ESA_Publications/Agenda_2025

ESA. (2021a, June 22). *The financial framework partnership agreement*. Retrieved from https://vision.esa.int/the-financial-framework-partnership-agreement/

ESA. (2022). *The Zero Debris charter*. Retrieved from https://www.esa.int/Space_Safety/Clean_Space/The_Zero_Debris_Charter

ESA. (2023, March). *Report of the high-level advisory group on human and robotic space exploration for Europe: Revolution Europe*. Retrieved from https://esamultimedia.esa.int/docs/corporate/h-lag_brochure.pdf

ESPI & BCG. (2023, November). *More than a space programme: The value of space exploration to empower the future of Europe*. Retrieved from https://www.espi.or.at/wp-content/uploads/2023/11/231115-More-than-a-Space-Programme.pdf

ESPI. (2020, November 11). *European space strategy in a global context*. Retrieved from https://www.espi.or.at/reports/european-space-strategy-in-a-global-context/

ESPI. (2022a, December 22). *IRIS2: The new (material) girl on the block.* Retrieved from https://www.espi.or.at/briefs/iris2-the-new-material-girl-on-the-block/

ESPI. (2022b, October 10). *The war in Ukraine from a space cybersecurity perspective.* Retrieved from ESPI: https://www.espi.or.at/reports/new-espi-short-report%e2%80%95the-war-in-ukraine-from-a-space-cybersecurity-perspective/

ESPI. (2023a, October 1). *Europe as a space power.* Retrieved from https://www.espi.or.at/briefs/europe-as-a-space-power/

ESPI. (2023b). *ESPI2040: Space for prosperity, peace and future generations.* Retrieved from https://www.espi.or.at/espi-2040/

ESPI. (12 de October de 2023c). *Space spectrum management: Foundations for an informed policy discussion towards WRC-23 and beyond.* Obtenido de https://www.espi.or.at/reports/space-spectrum-management-foundations-for-an-informed-policy-discussion-towards-wrc-23-and-beyond/

ESPI. (23 de September de 2023d). *Space safety and sustainability momentum.* Obtenido de https://www.espi.or.at/reports/space-safety-and-sustainability-momentum/

ESPI. (2023e, November 3). *Space, cyber and defence: Navigating interdisciplinary challenges.* Retrieved from https://www.espi.or.at/reports/space-cyber-and-defence-navigating-interdisciplinary-challenges/

ESPI. (2024a, March 21). *From WRC-23 to the next cycle: How to make everyone happy? (Hint: You Can't).* Retrieved from https://www.espi.or.at/briefs/from-wrc-23-to-the-next-cycle-how-to-make-everyone-happy-hint-you-cant/

ESPI. (2024b). *Ventura capital financing gap: Towards a European space investment fund?* Retrieved from ESPI https://www.espi.or.at/wp-content/uploads/2024/04/05.04_Final_Perspective_Interactive.pdf

ESPI. (2024c, February 29). *What's next for Europe in multilateral engagement on space security? The UN OEWG and its success(ORS).* Retrieved from ESPI https://www.espi.or.at/reports/whats-next-for-europe-in-multilateral-engagement-on-space-security/

EU SST. (2024). *What is EU SST?* Retrieved from https://www.eusst.eu/

Euroconsult. (2024). *Satellites to be built & launched, 27th edition.* Retrieved from https://digital-platform.euroconsult-ec.com/product/satellites-to-be-built-launched/?_amc-currency=USD

European Commission. (2015, May 6). *Commission staff working document a digital single market strategy for Europe—Analysis and evidence accompanying the document communication from the commission to the European Parliament, the Council, the European Economic and Social Committee and the.* Retrieved from https://eur-lex.europa.eu/legal-content/EN/TXT/?uri=CELEX%3A52015SC0100

European Commission. (2020, February 19). *Communication from the Commission to the European Parliament, the Council, the European Economic and Social Committee and the Committee of the Regions: A European strategy for data*. Retrieved from https://eur-lex.europa.eu/legal-content/EN/TXT/?qid=1582551099377&uri=CELEX%3A52020DC0066

European Commission. (2021). *Communication from the Commission to the European Parliament the Council, the European Economic and Social Committee and the Committee of the Regions. 2030 Digital Compass: The European way for the Digital Decade*. European Commission.

European Commission. (2022a, December 15). *European declaration on digital rights and principles*. Retrieved from https://digital-strategy.ec.europa.eu/en/library/european-declaration-digital-rights-and-principles#:~:text=The%20Declaration%20on%20Digital%20Rights%20and%20Principles%20presents%20the%20EU%27s,version%20of%20the%20Declaration%20available

European Commission. (2022b, October 18). *Communication from the Commission to the European Parliament, the Council, the European Economic and Social Committee and the Committee of the Regions: Digitalising the energy system - EU action plan*. Retrieved from https://eur-lex.europa.eu/legal-content/EN/TXT/?uri=CELEX%3A52022DC0552&qid=1666369684560

European Council. (2022, March 21). *A strategic compass for a stronger EU security and defence in the next decade*. Retrieved from https://www.consilium.europa.eu/en/press/press-releases/2022/03/21/a-strategic-compass-for-a-stronger-eu-security-and-defence-in-the-next-decade/

European Union. (2007). *Treaty of Lisbon amending the Treaty on European Union and the Treaty establishing the European Community, signed at Lisbon*. Retrieved from December 13, 2007, from https://eur-lex.europa.eu/legal-content/EN/TXT/?uri=CELEX:12007L/TXT

European Union. (2016). *Treaty on the functioning of the European Union*. Retrieved from https://eur-lex.europa.eu/EN/legal-content/summary/treaty-on-the-functioning-of-the-european-union.html

Hrozensky, T., & Dvoracek, M. (2019, June). European SST landscape: Current status and challenges on the way ahead. *Journal of Space Safety Engineering, 6*(2), 122–129.

Krebs, G. D. (2024). *Gunter's space page*. Retrieved from https://space.skyrocket.de/index.html

Moeller, H. L. (2023). *July 2023 Director's perspective*. Retrieved from https://www.espi.or.at/news/july-2023-directors-perspective/

Moeller, H. L. (2023a). *January 2023 Director's 'perspective'*. Retrieved from ESPI https://www.espi.or.at/news/january-2022-directors-perspective/

Moeller, H. L. (2023b). *Perspectives: Much more than a space programme—Give European ambition a chance*. Retrieved from https://www.espi.or.at/wp-content/uploads/2023/04/ESPI-Perspectives-March-2023.pdf

OECD. (2019, July 5). *The space economy in figures*. Retrieved from https://www.oecd.org/en/publications/the-space-economy-in-figures_c5996201-en.html

OECD. (2024, March 6). *Bridging the financing gap in the European Space Sector: Alternative funding pathways in tightening markets*. Retrieved from https://www.espi.or.at/reports/bridging-the-financing-gap-in-the-european-space-sector-alternative-funding-pathways-in-tightening-markets/

Soille, P., Loekken, S., & Albani, S. (Eds.). (2019). Turning data into insights. In *Proceedings of 20019 big data from space (BiDS'19)*. Joint Research Centre.

Space Sustainability Rating. (2024). *Home*. Retrieved from https://spacesustainabilityrating.org/the-rating/

United Nations Secretary General Report. (2020). *Our common agenda*. Retrieved from https://www.un.org/en/content/common-agenda-report/

UNOOSA. (2019). *'The guidelines for the long-term sustainability of outer space activities (LTS guidelines)*. Retrieved from https://spacesustainability.unoosa.org/content/the_guidelines

Vernile, A. (2018). *Executive summary—The rise of private actors in the space sector*. Retrieved from ESPI https://www.espi.or.at/reports/executive-summary-the-rise-of-private-actors-in-the-space-sector/

CHAPTER 15

Quantum Technologies: Paving the Way Towards "Smart Competition" in the EU

Andrea G. Rodríguez

> If quantum mechanics hasn't profoundly shocked you, you haven't understood it yet
>
> Niels Bohr, Danish quantum physicist

Introduction

In 1959, Richard Feynman outlined in a famous lecture how the application of quantum mechanical principles would unlock a new wave of technological innovation. In "Plenty of Room at the Bottom" (Feynman, 1959) overviewed the principles that would configure the birth of nanotechnology but also offered important insights that would influence future developments in what is today the field of quantum technologies. Feynman, a California Institute of Technology professor who participated in the Manhattan Project, was already a renowned scientist. A few years

A. G. Rodríguez (✉)
Centre for European Policy Studies (CEPS), Brussels, Belgium
e-mail: andrea.rodriguez@ceps.eu

T. Kleiner and A. Garcia Rodriguez (eds.), *The Making of a Global Digital Rulebook*, https://doi.org/10.1007/978-981-95-9226-5_15

later, he would become a Nobel Prize laureate for his contribution to quantum physics.

The origins of quantum theory date back to the beginning of the twentieth century and are closely related to the city of Brussels. In 1927, the most renowned scientists of the time, like Albert Einstein, Edwin Schrödinger and Marie and Pierre Curie, met at the Solvay Library to discuss the future of the field in the light of theoretical advancements that challenged the traditional understanding of physics.

These discoveries demonstrated that, at the subatomic level, observations were not deterministic but probabilistic (Institut international de physique Solvay, 1928) and paved the way to what was later known as the First Quantum Revolution, which saw the emergence of the first wave of quantum technologies. These technological advancements were based on the behaviour of many quantum particles (Jaeger, 2018). Thanks to this new way of looking at things, scientists were able to develop lasers or transistors that dramatically impacted fields like medicine, communications or any form of digital innovation.

The Second Quantum Revolution, in which we are now embedded, differs from that one in that applications and technological advancements depend on manipulating "the states of single quantum particles" (Jaeger, 2018, p. 18) instead of the lot, a feat that enables a leap in fields like computation, communications or sensing.

In perspective, the technological innovations that followed the first quantum revolution at the beginning of the century have been fundamental in shaping contemporary digital societies. Modern quantum technologies will have a similar transformative effect.

In addition to that, quantum technologies have practical applications that influence national security. The combination of quantum computing and machine learning will pave the way to advanced artificial intelligence, and universal quantum computers are already known to compromise some types of widely used encryption (G. Rodríguez, 2023).

These parallel processes, one on the side of opportunity and the other on the side of risk, have facilitated the emergence of a technology hype in quantum technologies (Smith III, 2020). This *hype* is critical in understanding their securitisation. Narratives around quantum technologies transform the actions affecting innovation. Scholars have long argued the performativity of security (e.g. Buzan, 1998; Balzacq, 2019; Csernatoni & Martins, 2023; Waever, 1995) that can lead to the take up of urgent political measures, such as policy and investments, to mitigate the perceived threats.

In the European Union, the process of securitisation of quantum technologies relates to the internal political dynamics affecting the identity of the EU as an economic union with increased political character. In this sense, securitisation and digital sovereignty, as this chapter argues, are driving factors of the EU's interest in quantum technologies. The announcement of a European Quantum Act (Virkkunen, 2024) follows this path.

At the EU level, quantum policy materialises in two ways. On the one hand, EU member states are fuelled by the availability of resources after the COVID-19 pandemic. After the pandemic, the EU put at the disposal of member states to reboot the economy €712 billion to invest in reform and economic transformation projects. To unlock the funds, member states had to prove that at least 20% of the funds would be used for the digital transformation (European Commission, 2024). This availability of resources is what arguably convinced some member states to launch their quantum programmes.

On the other hand, at the EU level, there has been a cumulative historical process that peaks with the publication of the 2023 Economic Security Strategy. This process, paired with events at the geopolitical scale, is fundamental to understanding how quantum technologies have found a way into the security narrative in the EU. This chapter investigates (1) the relationship between Europe's digital sovereignty and access to quantum technologies, (2) the historical approach of the EU to the development of quantum technologies and (3) EU capacities and capabilities in quantum.

An Overview of Quantum Technologies

Quantum technologies leverage quantum mechanics to create new applications. Despite accelerated investments in quantum technologies, development does not come without challenges. For example, quantum systems are vulnerable to noise and need to be fault-tolerant to mitigate decoherence, a characteristic due to which the system loses its quantum effect through its interaction with the environment (Bacciagaluppi, 2020). From the applications' side, quantum technologies can be packed up into three big technological clusters: quantum computing, quantum communications and quantum sensing.

Quantum Computing

Digital data is stored in *bits*, binary digital units that assume either a 1 or 0 state. Quantum bits (*qubits*) differ from classical bits in different ways. First, they don't have a binary (0; 1) value. They are in a superposition state, which means that they are both in 0 and 1 state at the same time. Only when the scientist "reads" it can the state be known.

On top of that, two or more *qubits* can be liaised and influence each other even if each of them is on different sides of the universe (Jaeger, 2018). This property is called "entanglement". Combined, the natural superposition of states of quantum bits and entanglement allows for the parallelisation of operations, increasing computational power.

Quantum computing is still in an experimental state. Yet, quantum machines are already in use to improve optimisation problems and, in combination with high-performance computers (HPC), to help solve problems efficiently that supercomputers could not solve before or could with a lot of effort. As technology and industry mature, quantum computers will play an important role in upgrading processes and speeding discoveries in chemistry or material sciences.

In the field of medicine, for example, quantum computing can help "disrupt, manipulate, and ultimately control live organisms at the molecular level" (Allende Lopez & Da Silva, 2019, p. 51). This has a direct effect on the speed and precision at which diseases are detected and treated. Similarly, quantum computers will be used to understand the properties of current materials and synthesise new ones, combining the most promising features. Novel materials will open the door to improvements in a wide variety of sectors, from the aerospace industry to telecommunications (Matz, 2024).

Quantum Communications

Quantum communications use quantum mechanics to create ultra-secure networks. Using technologies like quantum key distribution (QKD) and quantum repeaters, these networks enable information sharing in quantum states between different points of connection (nodes). Because of the properties of quantum bits, data shared in QKD networks can't be either copied or stored away, unlike in classical networks, which prevents information theft.

Moreover, because any disturbance can be felt by the network at the risk of interference, communication can be stopped. This offers a new leap in cybersecurity. Terrestrial QKD segments rely on fibre optic networks, which means that their expansion will go hand in hand with increasing capacity networks. Limitations in entanglement technology and qubits' sensitivity to noise limit the extent of quantum networks (approx. 200 km), making necessary the use of repeaters, trusted nodes and space links.

Quantum Sensing

Quantum sensors are the most mature technological field in quantum technologies, which leverage quantum mechanical properties to enhance precision and sensitivity. Quantum sensors can enhance detection and tracking across domains, which favours the creation of applications also for security and defence, from the identification of submarines to increased efficacy of early warning systems (Spencer, 2023). Moreover, quantum gyroscopes or applications like the quantum compass allow guidance in GPS-denied areas (Dunning & Angus, 2023).

Quantum Technologies and EU Sovereignty

The importance of ensuring access to technological innovation is a topic widely studied in international relations literature and has a tight relationship with debates around strategic autonomy. From the strategic studies community, Barry Buzan argues that the development and deployment of new technologies have an impact on military advantage (Buzan, 1987). Moreover, he adds, technological innovation affects the security dilemma, a structural feature of international relations by which states engage in a constant loop of actions and reactions.

Changes in the level of technological innovation oblige states to react either by acquiring foreign technology or by developing their own to maintain an adequate level of security. "Even if states are only interested in maintaining the status quo, they will be driven to introduce new weapons in response to advances in the general level of technology" (Reppy, 1990, p. 102).

Though most classical authors explored the advantage provided by nuclear weapons in a military context (e.g. Herz, 1950; Waltz, 1981), contemporary authors have focused on the impact of artificial intelligence in international relations (e.g. Hudson, 1991; Csernatoni, 2019). However, mentions of the effect of quantum technologies in the strategic landscape are more limited.

From a liberal perspective, Der Derian and Alexander Wendt (2020) argue that the development of emerging technologies with great economic, security and social repercussions, such as AI and quantum, impacts the distribution of power and knowledge. The staggering cost of investing in quantum technologies is not for every country's budget, which is creating a fragmented geography of who and where technology is developed.

While global powers like the U.S. and China invest billions, middle powers like Canada, Japan and Singapore build their quantum programmes "pursuing comparative advantages through collaborative research and development projects [...] clearly in pursuit of a step change through quantum technology that might well register as an increase in geopolitical status" (Der Derian & Wendt, 2020, p. 3).

The European Union and its member states have been increasingly paying attention to quantum technologies, increasing available funds for research but also supporting initiatives to ensure the availability of talent and mitigate supply chain dependencies. This exceptional interest puts the EU and member states second in public investment in quantum technologies, only behind China (G. Rodriguez, 2024).

Quantum technologies are fundamental to realise Europe's strategic autonomy ambitions (see Chapter 4). Strategic autonomy, a term that was born out of military lingo, has evolved to include concerns regarding the bloc's "economic and technological dependency and its ability to shape global norms and policies" (Helwig & Sinkkonen, 2022, p. 7).

In a global context, security, interlinked with reducing strategic dependencies, goes beyond the imperative of innovation (Buzan, 1987). It is closely intertwined with the network of exchanges that tie together the EU economy with other countries at different levels. As Drezner, Farrell and Newman argue (2021), global economic networks form structures subject to coercive action. Physical goods and infrastructure, services, information and financial flows can be instrumental in geopolitical competition.

Control over quantum components and devices, raw materials or even quantum professionals can be a source of strategic competition. The opportunities for the weaponisation of network infrastructure affect how countries intervene and invest and how companies develop their products and services. Consequently, the concept of access to quantum technologies comes closer to the idea of control of critical network segments, what the authors call "hubs" (Drezner et al., 2021), nodes in that network of interconnection that are more relevant than others, such as quantum chips or dilution refrigerators.

Historical Engagement of the EU and the Quantum Technologies Community

Quantum technologies offer great economic opportunities but also create new challenges that affect sovereignty. Access or denial to quantum applications can compromise EU competitiveness in both mature and emerging industrial sectors. Similarly, in a moment in which quantum supply chains are in the process of configuration, thus favouring the accumulation of critical components and devices in a few hands, a lack of action can create problems in the long run. Paired with global geopolitics, supply chain vulnerabilities and asymmetric investment in innovation can position Europe in an unwanted position of dependence.

For that reason, individual member states and the EU itself have launched different initiatives to harness the economic potential of quantum technologies and to protect them from unwanted security implications. This engagement can be divided into three phases: inception, consolidation and strategic awakening.

Inception Phase (2016–2018)

The year 2016 was officially a kick-off of structured engagement in quantum technologies. The topic was not at all foreign to Europe. European scientists were the protagonists of the first quantum revolution, and European universities have a long tradition in quantum science. The European Commission had already invested cumulatively €550 million in 2016, and European authors were at the forefront of the publication of high-impact academic research in quantum physics (Mlynek et al., 2017).

However, investment in quantum technologies lacked strategic direction. This was precisely what the 2016 Quantum Manifesto, signed by 3400 members of academia and the industry, called upon: strategic investments in quantum technologies to achieve well-defined goals. Following the example of other unique initiatives in areas like neuroscience, the

Manifesto called for the establishment of a flagship programme for quantum technologies.

While the Quantum Flagship was officially born three years later, this inception period is mostly characterised by the scientific approach to quantum technologies and the opportunities lying in a nascent quantum industry. During this phase, efforts were based on boosting basic research and innovation and demonstrating scientific and engineering advancements in the three core quantum technology areas (computers, communications and sensors). Scientists and academics were the ones pushing for the establishment of new initiatives, which rendered mentions of the strategic value of quantum technology scarce. In fact, they were mostly made in the field of cryptography, and the overall tone echoed the search for scientific leadership, not geopolitical competition.

Consolidation Phase (2019–2021)

The Quantum Flagship was presented in October 2018 to make Europe "a worldwide knowledge-based industry and technological leader" in quantum technologies (EU Quantum Flagship, 2018, p. 3). It pledged €1 billion for the period 2019–2029 and pursued the creation of a favourable innovation ecosystem that would attract investment and be capable of creating disruptive applications.

The Flagship was organised around five scientific pillars (computing, simulations, sensing & metrology, basic science, and communications) following the recommendations of the high-level steering committee (Mlynek, et al., 2017) formed by academics and some industrial players. The Flagship would aim to fund disruptive projects with a potential market approach, create a quantum workforce and increase awareness.

The first strategic research agenda was published in the spring of 2020, highlighting three aspects of each technological pillar: socio-economic challenges, R&I challenges and the proposal of a roadmap with scientific and engineering goals. The Agenda also dedicated space to reflect on potential use cases and international cooperation, but strategic considerations remained marginal.

Though the document discussed nascent strategic issues such as supply chains and infrastructure, it was mostly focused on warnings about production needs and the identification of critical suppliers (EU Quantum

Flagship, 2020, p. 83). Mentions of geopolitical rivalries, the risks of over-dependence and the fact that critical supply chain areas might be placed outside of Europe were not an area of concern.

However, some events of geopolitical importance during the first years of the Flagship added pressure for European initiatives in quantum technologies to recognise that their impact would be well beyond the economy increasingly. In 2019, Google published a paper claiming quantum supremacy (Arute et al., 2019). In the paper, the team of scientists described how they were able to run an operation that would have taken a classical computer 10,000 years in less than 3 minutes and a half using a quantum processor. In parallel, papers showing how to break widely used cryptography systems started to proliferate (e.g. Bhatia & Ramkumar, 2020; Mengoni et al., 2020).

On top of that, several policy documents in the U.S. (e.g. U.S. Congress, 2018; U.S. National Science & Technology Council, 2018; U.S. National Quantum Coordination Office, 2020) and in China (NDRC, 2016; NDRC, 2021) demonstrated a change of tone in matters related to quantum technologies, underlying their strategic importance for peace and security and long-term prosperity.

This change was reflected in some EU member states that released new programmes for the development of quantum technologies much more centred on their strategic relevance for digital sovereignty rather than on advancing basic science and engineering. The Netherlands pledged €615 million in 2019 (QDNL, 2019), and Germany unveiled €2 billion in support for quantum technologies in its post-pandemic economic stimulus package strategy (BMBF, 2020). During this phase, EU member states took the reins to lead strategically in quantum technologies as the EU implemented a research agenda that did not reflect the geopolitical dynamics already affecting quantum technologies.

Third Phase: Strategic Awakening (2021—)

The addition of the surname "industrial" in the next Quantum Flagship's strategic research agenda (2022) indicated a shift towards industrial policy and that things were at stake with the development of quantum technologies, much more than remaining at the scientific top of quantum research, particularly in the areas of economic and national security Table 15.1.

The COVID-19 pandemic had brought to light the vulnerabilities of a global trade system based on interdependence, and, as the case of the semiconductor crisis showed, the European Union could afford not to prepare a backup plan for quantum. The new agenda reduced the pillars from 5 to 4, shifting basic research for industry-driven initiatives that increased Europe's position in nascent quantum markets, including efforts on standardisation.

During this phase, CEN-CENELEC created a dedicated working group for quantum technologies (JTC22), and three EU countries released quantum strategies. France published its strategy in 2021, committing €1,05 billion (Government of France, 2021), Denmark in 2023 in two parts with €150 million (June and September) and Ireland (Government of Ireland, 2023).

The meaning of technological disruption, intimately linked with uncertainty and indeterminacy (Smith III, 2020), changed from a positive understanding of "new commercial opportunities" (Quantum Manifesto, 2016, p.7) to embrace the ability to "enable and transform" socio-economic realities (European Commission, 2023), and so the word "quantum" started to appear more frequently in policies beyond the spectrum of the Quantum Flagship.

The EU Digital Compass reflected on the opportunities of quantum technologies and proposed that by 2025, Europe should "have its first computer with quantum acceleration [...] and to be at the cutting edge of quantum capabilities by 2030" (COM(2021) 118 final, 2021, p. 8). The 2022 Strategic Compass argued the value of quantum computing for security and defence, particularly in the area of cyber security (EEAS, 2022, pp. 45, 47) Fig. 15.1. The EU Chips Act included an explicit mention of the need to establish pilot lines for quantum chips in Europe (Regulation (EU) 2023/1781, art. 5) and other sectoral documents (e.g. C(2024) 2329 final) started to propose actions concerning quantum technologies and their cyber and industrial challenges.

In this context, Fig. 15.2 shows that the field of quantum-related policy is developing fast and that despite the many initiatives taking shape at the heart of the European Commission, the role of national actors is very significant. Member states have occupied the vacuum of the European Union in coordinating investments and launching programmes of strategic relevance for both national and economic security.

The landscape of forces, moreover, shows that while there is diversity when it comes to actors (EU-international; public-private), some of them have already consolidated their authority and position, which shows that

Quantum cybersecurity

Cryptography is an essential aspect of cybersecurity. Using encryption algorithms, communications happen online safely and securely. Cryptography has five primary functions CITATION Lel21 \l 3082 (Lele, 2021): ensuring that intended parties can read the message ("key exchange"), ensuring that the message has been sent ("non-repudiation"), ensuring that only those for whom the message is can read it ("confidentiality"), ensuring that those parties are verified ("authentication"), and ensuring that the message remains unchanged ("integrity").

Modern cryptography is based on problems that advanced supercomputers cannot solve, such as factorisation. For that reason, once a sufficiently developed quantum computer is made available, some widely used encryption algorithms will be affected. This is a problem well-known since the mid-90s (e.g. Shor 1994; Grover, 1996), but only with the renewed interest in quantum computing as a science and the technological breakthroughs showing progression governments have started to act to find cryptographic alternatives to it

Fig. 15.1 Note on quantum and risks to encryption

the EU will have a tough time reclaiming space in an area deeply marked by security considerations.

Furthermore, the important dimension of quantum technology policy shows a certain degree of imbalance between the EU and other regions due to the limited presence of large industrial players, whereas in the U.S. or China, the tendency is to concentrate infrastructure and power in a few large actors, hyperscalers, focusing on this emerging market where customers are scarce.

In 2023, the publication of the European Economic Security Strategy (EESS) was the culmination of a period of strategic reflection on the vulnerabilities of the European economy and the maturity of the ideas around digital sovereignty and digital sovereignty. The EESS described a series of actions needed to guarantee Europe's security, including in the economic aspect, in a moment in which interconnectedness can be a source of weakness, not only of strength.

The EESS described priorities across three axes: promote, protect and partner. Quantum technologies, as well as other emerging technologies like AI, (C(2023) 6689 final, 2023) are important drivers of competitiveness and security that are subject to several systemic risks that span from

Table 15.1 Comparison of national quantum strategies in selected countries until April 2025 (G. Rodríguez, 2024)

Country	*National strategy*	*Public funding (€)*	*Years*
China	14th five-year plan 2021*	~13,8 billion	2021–2025
United States	National Quantum Initiative, 2018	3,4 billion	2019–2023
UK	National Quantum Strategy, 2023	2,91 billion	2023–2033
Germany	Economic Stimulus Package, 2020	2 billion	2021–2025
France	France National Quantum Strategy, 2021	1,05 billion	2021–2025
Netherlands	National Agenda for Quantum Technology, 2019	615 million	2021–2028
Denmark	Danish Strategy for Quantum Technology, 2023 (June/Sept)	150 million	2024–2027
Ireland	Quantum 2030, 2023	Budget not disclosed	2023–2030
Spain	National Quantum Strategy, 2025	808 million	2025–2030
Finland	Finland's Quantum Technology Strategy, 2025	Budget not disclosed	2025–2035

*China's strategic focus on Quantum technology dates back several years. However, accurate estimates of the investments in quantum are difficult to make due to lacking information and unreliability. McKinsey (2023) evaluates ~$15 billion in governmental investments as a part of the 14th Five Year Plan (2021), which mentions quantum as an essential technology for China's digital sovereignty

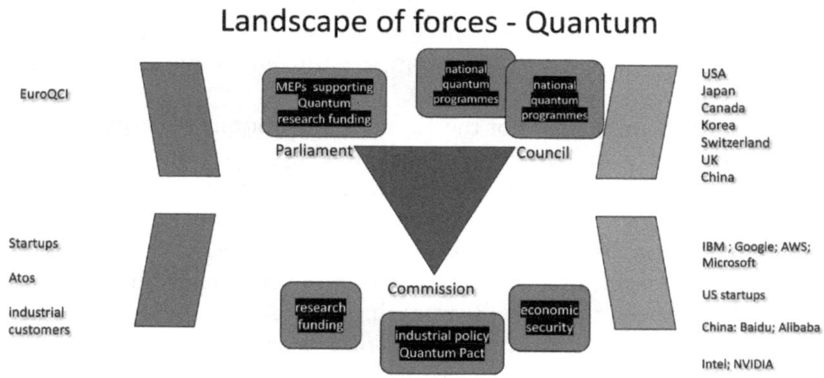

Fig. 15.2 Landscape of forces

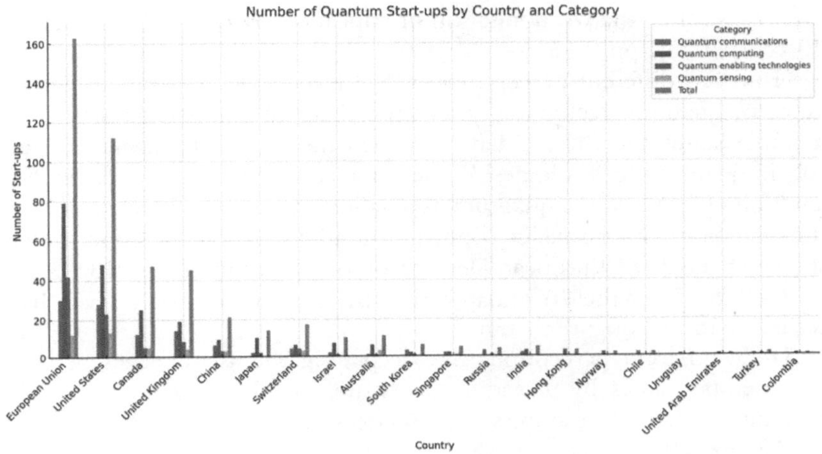

Fig. 15.3 Number of start-ups per technology segment (data from November 2024). Source: Quantum Infinity Airtable Dashboard

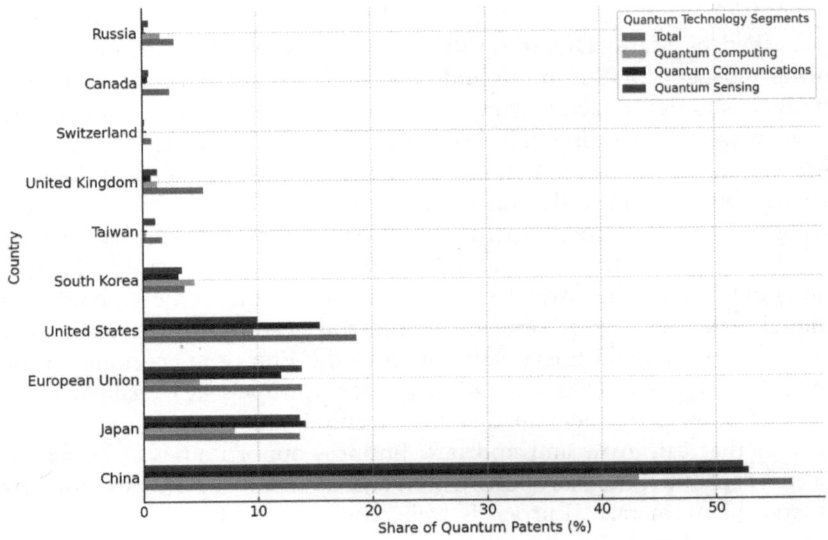

Fig. 15.4 Quantum Technology Patent Share (2000–2022)

supply chains to the weaponisation of critical dependencies (JOIN(2023) 20 final, 2023a, pp. 4, 5).

However, different perceptions of EU leaders of the strategic importance of quantum technologies and the share of competencies between member states and the EU have impeded the EU from having a bigger role in quantum technologies. While some countries, such as the Netherlands and Germany, see quantum as a national priority, it barely shows on the agenda of other smaller countries, despite the political commitment shown in the 2023 European Declaration on Quantum Technologies. Up to April 2025, of the 26 signatories of the Declaration, only seven have realised national quantum strategies.

These different perceptions risk deepening the asymmetries between EU member states by providing a first-mover advantage to those who accumulate critical resources and services, investment and talent (G. Rodríguez, 2024).

European Capacities in Quantum Technologies

Innovation in quantum technologies is key to competitiveness. As a report published by Mario Draghi on the matter finds, declining demographics make it urgent for Europe to find new ways to increase productivity and mitigate strategic dependencies. Digital technologies will be key in finding new ways of addressing this issue, but far behind techno-optimism in which deep technologies become Deus ex machina at the end of the play, saving Europe from a demographic, climate and economic catastrophe, Draghi warns that more structural and comprehensive reform is needed.

The word "quantum" is mentioned 59 times in the report. For Draghi, quantum computing "will have a foundational role in next-generation digital ecosystems with large economic and security implications" and could "contribute with to €850 billion to the European economy in the next 15–30 years" (Draghi, 2024, p. 80). Europe's key challenge will be to sustain investment in quantum technologies to create a dynamic market that can grow and find new business opportunities at home. As Sect 3 explained, the European Union and its member states are not new in the quantum race. Europe is well positioned to become a leader in quantum technologies.

Out of the existing 472 registered quantum technology start-ups (data from October 2024), 163 are in the European Union (Fig. 15.3). Germany, the Netherlands, France and Spain are the four countries with the most quantum technology start-ups (41, 37, 26 and 10, respectively). Of these 163 start-ups, almost half of them (48.47%) are quantum computing start-ups and about 26% focus on quantum enabling technologies.

However, the ability of European Union countries to create and dynamise the nascent industrial ecosystem does not necessarily reflect leadership in important metrics such as intellectual property. Figure 15.3 illustrates the global distribution of quantum technology patents until 2022, representing various countries and ordering information by technological quantum sub-field. China's dominance is striking, with 56,6% of total quantum technology patents with significant leverage across all segments (43.2% in quantum computing, 52,8% in quantum communications and 52.3% in quantum sensing). This advantageous position demonstrates Chinese ambitions and its ability to sustain long-term investments with political direction Fig. 15.4.

In the European Union, however, the number of patents has multiplied in the last decade, showing an above-average share of patent applications, which shows the high expectations for the economic opportunities of quantum technologies (Douarche et al., 2023). Europe is advancing faster in the field of quantum communications, with companies like Nokia or Deutsche Telekom having the strongest portfolios (QuIC, 2024, p. 24). Part of the success in quantum communications can be delegated to the EUROQCI programme, which aims to create a quantum internet network in the EU to secure communications.

However, in European territory, U.S. companies like IBM, Microsoft and Google are still filling the most patents in fields like quantum computing (QuIC, 2024, p.25), which demonstrates the attractiveness of the European market for these companies in search of quantum talent and investment.

While patents are good indicators of a level of capacity for innovation, there are other important metrics to consider, such as access to quantum talent. Professionals with relevant knowledge in the fields of quantum physics and engineering are scarce, and even though the number of universities offering quantum technology-related programmes is growing, it will be hard to keep up with the needs of the companies. Still, the European Union has the highest concentration of quantum talent, followed by India and China (McKinsey Digital, 2024). This number reflects the focus on the need to develop talent in the numerous Quantum Flagship initiatives, as well as talent being a priority for member states (e.g. Netherlands, Spain).

Conclusions

This chapter has argued the importance of securing access to quantum technologies, emphasising the potential of these innovations to both empower and challenge the EU's position on the global stage. The development of quantum technologies is closely tied to geopolitical competition. Several countries, including EU member states and the European Union, are competing for funding and talent in the race to develop technologically significant capabilities. All in all, advancements in standardisation, implementation of quantum solutions and the creation of industry-relevant use cases will characterise the new phase of development of quantum technologies, with applications leaving the lab and being deployed in a real environment. Only then these innovations will be able to show their true strategic value.

Though the European Union pioneered the first quantum revolution, during this second wave, it has taken several years to catch up on the necessary degree of awareness to bridge vulnerability gaps and advance strategically towards common goals beyond research and innovation. The numerous national quantum strategies released by member states show that EU countries individually are already thinking in strategic terms when it comes to quantum technologies without taking into consideration the big European picture as a whole.

While this political fragmentation has arguably helped the EU become the second-largest investor in quantum technologies and amass talent and start-ups, it is precisely the pulse for securitisation the one that can truly thwart the ability of the EU to enact new strategies and impose necessary fixes to ensure Europe has enough capacity as quantum technology keeps developing.

The European Economic Security Strategy presents a unique opportunity to engage smaller actors that have not yet entered the quantum race, as well as to find common objectives and identify limits in cooperation in quantum technologies inside the Union. Thanks to this, the European Commission adopted in the summer of 2025 the Quantum Europe Strategy, promising action to eliminate market fragmentation, accelerate startup scaling, secure tech supply chains and accelerate quantum adoption. As technology *hype* and security narratives keep driving investment and attention to quantum technologies, learning where the red lines lie will be fundamental to ensuring the EU's coordinating role serves as a catalyser for strategic innovation.

In a moment in which technology, economic prosperity and national security are as interlinked as ever, the EU has the chance to lead in this emerging domain. However, it will take bold moves to ensure that companies can scale in Europe and dedication to foster their leadership position in some critical areas of quantum value chains while acting internationally to mitigate potential risks of supply.

There is an opportunity for the EU to act in areas like interoperability and standards, fostering system modularity to improve supply chain resilience and the participation of as many actors as possible. This aspect—targeted investments, standards, interoperable interfaces and a good command of the supply chain and European actors—can become in itself a new strategy for Europe. *Smart competition* will be a key aspect to develop in the years to come for the European Union to become the place for quantum innovation and growth. All in all, whether the EU succeeds as a global leader in quantum technologies will be a mix of strategic genius, consensus with national leadership, smart competition and diplomacy. And unlike other technological revolutions, this time, the EU has truly a chance.

Bibliography

Allende Lopez, M., & Da Silva, M. (2019). *Quantum technologies: Digital transformation, social impact, and cross-sector disruption*. Inter-American Development Bank.

Arute, F., Arya, K., Babbush, R., Bacon, D., Bardin, J. C., & Barends, R. D. (2019). Quantum supremacy using a programmable superconducting processor. *Nature, 574*(779), 505–510.

Bacciagaluppi, G. (2020, April 21). *The Role of Decoherence in Quantum Mechanics*. Standford Encyclopedia of Philosophy https://plato.stanford.edu/entries/qm-decoherence/

Bazacq, T. (2019). Securitization theory: Past, present, and future. *Polity, 51*(2), 331–348.

Bhatia, V., & Ramkumar, K. (2020). An efficient quantum computing technique for cracking RSA using Shor's Algorithm. *IEEE 5th International Conference on Computing Communication and Automation (ICCCA)*, 89–94.

Buzan, B. (1987). *An introduction to strategic studies: Military Technology & International Relations*. Palgrave Macmillan.
Buzan, B., Waever, O., & de Wilder, J. (1998). *Security: A new framework for analysis*. Lynne Rienner.
Csernatoni, R. (2019, March). Between rhetoric and practice: Technological efficiency and defence cooperation in the European drone sector. *Critical Military Studies*, 1–25.
Csernatoni, R., & Martins, B. O. (2023). Disruptive Technologies for Security and Defence: Temporality. *Performativity and Imagination. Geopolitics, 93*(3), 849–872.
Danish Government. (2023). *Strategy for quantum technology: Part 1–world-class research and innovation*. Ministry of Higher Education and Science.
Danish Government. (2023a). *National Strategy for quantum technology part 2–commercialisation, security and international cooperation*. Ministry of Industry, Business and Financial Affairs.
Der Derian, J., & Wendt, A. (2020). Quantizing international relations: The case for quantum approaches to international theory and security practice. *Security Dialogue, 51*(5), 1–15.
Douarche, N., Grilli, M., Soltmann, C., Totir, C., & Volkmer, M. (2023). *Quantum computing: Insight report*. European Patent Office.
Draghi, M. (2024). *The future of European competitiveness: A competitiveness strategy for Europe*. European Commission.
Drezner, D. W., Farrell, H., & Newman, A. L. (Eds.). (2021). *The uses and abuses of weaponized interdependence*. Brookings Institution Press.
Dunning, H., & Angus, T. (2023, May 26). *Home College and Campus Science Engineering Health Business Quantum sensor for a future navigation system tested aboard Royal Navy ship*. Imperial College https://www.imperial.ac.uk/news/245114/quantum-sensor-future-navigation-system-tested/
EU Quantum Flagship. (2018, October 29). Press dossier: Kick-off Event. Vienna.
EU Quantum Flagship. (2020). *Strategic research agenda*. European Commission.
EU Quantum Flagship. (2022). *Strategic research and industry agenda*. European Commission.
EU Quantum Flagship. (2024). *Strategic research and industry agenda 2030*. European Commission.
European Commission. (2021). *Communication from the commission to the European Parliament the council, the European economic and social committee and the Committee of the Regions. 2030 digital compass: The European way for the digital decade*. European Commission.

European Commission. (2023, October 3). Commission recommendation on critical technology areas for the EU'S economic security for further risk assessment with member states.

European Commission. (2023a). Joint communication to the European Parliament, the European council, and the council on "European economic security strategy".

European Commission. (2023b, December 6). *European Declaration on Quantum Technologies*. Shaping Europe's Digital Future https://digital-strategy.ec.europa.eu/en/library/european-declaration-quantum-technologies

European Commission. (2024). *Recommendation on a coordinated implementation roadmap for the transition to post-quantum cryptography*. European Commission.

European External Action Service. (2022). *A strategic compass for security and Defence for a European Union that protects its citizens, values and interests and contributes to international peace and security*. European External Action Service.

European Union. (2023). *Regulation (EU) 2023/1781 of the European Parliament and the council establishing a framework of measures for strengthening Europe's semiconductor ecosystem and amending regulation (EU) 2021/694 (chips act)*. Official Journal of the European Union.

Federal Ministry of Education and Research (BMBF). (2020). *Economic Stimulus Package* https://www.bundesregierung.de/breg-en/search/corona-steuerhilfegesetz-1760128

Feynman, R. (1959). *Plenty of room at the bottom*. American Physical Society.

Rodriguez, A. G. (2023). *A quantum cybersecurity agenda for Europe: Governing the transition to post-quantum cryptography*. European Policy Centre.

Rodriguez, A. G. (2024). *Finland in the race for quantum advantage: Policy recommendations for a national quantum strategy*. The Finnish Innovation Fund.

Government of France. (2021). Stratégie nationale sur les technologies quantiques.

Government of Ireland. (2023). *Quantum 2030 a National Quantum Technologies Strategy for Ireland*. Department of Further and Higher Education, Research, Innovation and Science.

Grover, L. K. (1996). A fast quantum mechanical algorithm for database search. *Proceedings, 28th Annual ACM Symposium on the Theory of Computing (STOC)*, 212–219.

Helwig, N., & Sinkkonen, V. (2022, April). Strategic autonomy and the EU as a global actor: The evolution, debate, and theory of a contested term. *European Foreign Affairs Review, 27*.

Herz, H. J. (1950). Idealist internationalism and the security dilemma. *World Politics, 2*(2), 157–180.

Hudson, V. (1991). *Artificial intelligence and international politics*. Westview Press.

Institut international de physique Solvay. (1928). *Electrons et photons: rapports et discussions du cinquième Conseil de physique tenu à Bruxelles du 24 au 29 octobre 1927*. Gauthier-Villars et cie.

Jaeger, L. (2018). *The second quantum revolution: From entanglement to quantum computing adn other super-technologies*. Springer.

Lele, A. (2021). *Quantum technologies and military strategy*. Springer.

Matz, M. (2024, July 17). *A new approach to accelerate the discovery of quantum materials*. Berkeley Lab: https://newscenter.lbl.gov/2024/07/17/a-new-approach-to-accelerate-the-discovery-of-quantum-materials/

McKinsey Digital. (2024). *Quantum Technology Monitor*. https://www.mckinsey.com/~/media/mckinsey/business%20functions/mckinsey%20digital/our%20insights/quantum%20technology%20sees%20record%20investments%20progress%20on%20talent%20gap/quantum-technology-monitor-april-2023.pdf

Mengoni, R., Ottavani, D., & Iorio, P. (2020). Breaking RSA security with a low noise D-wave 2000Q quantum Annealer: Computational times, limitations and prospects. *arXiv*. https://arxiv.org/abs/2005.02268

Mlynek, J., Blatt, R., Buzek, V., Calarco, T., Delsing, P., Giacobino, E., & Cavaliere, F. (2017). *Quantum technologies flagship final report*. European Commission High-Level Steering Committee.

National Development and Reform Commission (NDRC). (2016). *The 13th five year plan for Economic and Social Development of the people's Republic of China*. https://en.ndrc.gov.cn/policies/202105/P020210527785800103339.pdf

Quantum Delta Nederland. (2019). *National Agenda for Quantum Technology*. https://qutech.nl/wp-content/uploads/2019/09/NAQT-2019-EN.pdf

Quantum Manifesto. (2016). *Quantum manifesto: A new era of technology*. Futurium: https://ec.europa.eu/futurium/en/content/quantum-manifesto-quantum-technologies.html

QuIC. (2024). *A portrait of the global patent landscape in quantum technologies*. European Quantum Industry Consortium.

Reppy, J. (1990). The technological imperative in strategic thought. *Journal of Peace Research, 27*(1), 101–106.

Shor, P. W. (1994). Polynomial-time algorithms for prime factorization and discrete logarithms on a quantum computer. *Proceedings of the 35th Annual Symposium on Foundations of Computer Science.*

Smith, F. L., III. (2020). Quantum technology hype and national security. *Security Dialogue, 1*(19), 499–516.

Spencer, J. (2023, October 3). *Quantum sensing: Enhancing situational awareness in Defence & Military operations*. Karve International: https://www.karveinternational.com/insights/quantum-sensing-enhancing-situational-awareness-in-defence-military-operations

The 14th Five Year Plan for Economic and Social Development and Long-range objectives through the year 2035 of the People's Republic of China. (2021). *Obtenido de National Development and Reform Commission*: https://en.ndrc.gov.cn/policies/202203/P020220315511326748336.pdf

U.S. Congress. (2018). *National Quantum Initiative Act*. Library of U.S. Congress: https://www.congress.gov/bill/115th-congress/house-bill/6227

U.S. Congress. (2023). *National Quantum Initiative Reauthorization Act*. U.S. Library of Congress: https://www.congress.gov/bill/118th-congress/house-bill/6213

U.S. National Quantum Coordination Office. (2020). *Quantum Frontiers: Report on community input to the nation's strategy for quantum information science*. Executive Office of the President of the United States.

U.S. National Science & Technology Council. (2018). *National Strategic Overview for quantum information science*. Executive Office of the President of the United States.

Virkkunen, H. (2024, November 12). *Confirmation hearing of Henna Maria VIRKKUNEN, Commissioner-designate, Tech Sovereignty, Security and Democracy*. European Parliament: https://multimedia.europarl.europa.eu/en/webstreaming/cult-juri-itre-afco-libe-sede-imco-committee-meeting_20241112-1830-COMMITTEE-CONFIRMATION-HEARING-B

Waever, O. (1995). Securitization and Desecuritization. In R. D. Lipschutz (Ed.), *On security* (pp. 46–86). Columbia University Press.

Waltz, N. K. (1981). The spread of nuclear weapons: More may be better. *The Adelphi Papers, 21*(171).

Xin, L., & Wei, C. (2023). Economic impacts of quantum computing: Strategies for integrating quantum technologies into business models. *Eigenpub Review of Science and Technology, 7*(1).

CHAPTER 16

The Evolution of the Digital Global Gateway

Chloe Teevan

Introduction

The EU Global Gateway (GG) is a strategic initiative to foster investments in hard and soft infrastructure in partner countries. Under the Commission political guidelines, 2024–2029, Global Gateway is the third pillar of an emerging economic foreign policy (Leyen, 2024). It aims to bring together EU geopolitical aims, the growing European focus on competitiveness and the EU's commitment to working with international partners to achieve the Sustainable Development Goals (SDGs).

It was born from the sense that despite the EU having significant combined investment, trade and development cooperation in many parts of the Global South, the EU and its member states were less effective than others (notably China) in using this economic leverage to support diplomatic goals. Further, the initiative aims to address the investment needs and development agenda of EU partner countries and regions while promoting an ambitious, interest-driven economic agenda that engages the European and partner countries' private sectors.

C. Teevan (✉)
European Centre for Development Policy Management (ECDPM), Maastricht, Netherlands
e-mail: cte@ecdpm.org

T. Kleiner and A. Garcia Rodriguez (eds.), *The Making of a Global Digital Rulebook*, https://doi.org/10.1007/978-981-95-9226-5_16

This agenda can be seen as an integral part of the EU's pursuit of "open strategic autonomy," indicating a concern for European economic security, together with a continued belief in economic openness and international cooperation (Council of the European Union, 2022a). It also integrates sustainability and security criteria that aim to further European values and demonstrate Europe's added value vis-a-vis competitors. GG seeks to mobilise up to €300 billion from public and private resources by 2027, including the EU budget, member states, development and export finance institutions, the European Investment Bank (EIB), the European Bank for Reconstruction and Development (EBRD) and private sector investments (Bilal & Teevan, 2024).

The digital pillar of the Global Gateway (GG) initiative focuses on investments in hard and soft infrastructure, supporting an enabling environment in partner countries to attract private sector investments and providing digital economy packages to specific countries. It is a vital dimension of the European Union's (EU) efforts to build technological influence beyond its borders. First and foremost, the GG emphasises hard infrastructure, and the European Commission lays out the aim to invest in "submarine and terrestrial fibre-optic cables, space-based secure communication systems as well as cloud and data infrastructures," with a focus on underserved regions and with a strong emphasis on sustainability. Alongside this, wider digital economy packages are being agreed upon with a select number of partner countries, including Colombia, Kenya, Nigeria and the Philippines. The initiative aims to integrate compliance with EU standards and protocols for network security and resilience, cybersecurity, interoperability and an open, plural and secure internet. It also aims to strengthen and support personal data protection, trustworthy artificial intelligence (AI), and fair and open digital markets (JOIN(2021) 30 final).

Yet, while the digital GG combines some interesting elements and could be a key element of the EU's pursuit of digital sovereignty, there are still a number of vital ingredients that are missing if the GG is to achieve its strategic and developmental aims. In the first section, I explore the challenge that the digital GG seeks to address—both in terms of European strategic aims and in terms of global sustainable development. I then look at the key actors driving GG and what role they might play in actually implementing the Global Gateway. Finally, I analyse some of the problems faced in actually implementing the Global Gateway and make a number of proposals about how it can become a meaningful pillar of a meaningful and open vision of European digital sovereignty.

The Challenge

The Global Gateway is presented as the EU's offer to developing and emerging economies, developed in the aftermath of COVID-19 and with a clear desire to offer an alternative to China in developing and emerging markets. A recently leaked memo from DG International Partnerships (DG INTPA) makes clear the shift that Global Gateway is looking to affect: "…in today's world, Emerging markets and Developing Economies are geopolitical and geoeconomic players that should be invested in. The EU cannot take its position for granted. We must avoid any sense of complacency and recognise that our economic security and competitiveness are inextricably linked to global dynamics. A global investment strategy is needed to complement the EU's industrial strategy and the European Green Deal" (European Commission, 2024a). Global Gateway is thus explicitly developed as an element of the emerging agenda on open strategic autonomy.

In the digital sphere, the EU is particularly conscious that despite its strong track record as a regulatory power, in the past, it has not been aggressive in working closely with developing and emerging economies on digital topics. The absence of a more concerted effort by the EU and like-minded partners opened the door for Chinese companies to become the dominant actor in digital infrastructure across the developing world and for China to build direct and indirect influence in terms of digital development and governance choices, and implicitly or explicitly to influence multilateral institutions and processes. In the face of US big tech and its approach to data extractivism, China has actively promoted its vision of state-centric digital sovereignty and data localisation to a sometimes-receptive audience that felt powerless to reign in these powerful multinational forces.

Thus, the digital GG comes in the context of growing anxiety about Europe's own digital sovereignty, including a growing sense of the need to promote a better economic and governance model globally. It aims to present an alternative European model for digital sovereignty, anchored in the European approach to human-centric digital governance as developed in the EU's Digital Compass and in the European Declaration on Digital Rights and Principles. Although the term is often poorly defined, it can be seen as bringing together civil and political rights, with elements of a developmental agenda rooted in economic and social rights (Muscat, 2024). It also clearly makes the link with what is undoubtedly the EU's greatest international success: the "Brussels effect," notably in the area of data protection, where its General Data Protection Regulation (GDPR) has been widely copied by countries across the world, including many in Africa, Asia and Latin America (Bradford, 2020).

Indeed, the GG comes alongside efforts to build a common European approach to digital diplomacy and to improve the EU's standing at multilateral fora. Council Conclusions in July 2022 and June 2023 aimed to begin to lay out a common European vision for its digital diplomacy (Council of the European Union, 2022b; Council of the European Union, 2023), while the EU has also begun to develop a much more concerted approach to institutions such as the ITU and opened a delegation in San Francisco to engage more meaningfully with industry leaders (European Union External Action Service, 2022). In 2025, the International Digital Strategy for the EU laid out a more comprehensive framing of the EU's digital diplomacy, together with packaging the EU's external offer in terms of technologies and regulatory approaches as the 'Tech Business Offer' (EC & HRVP, 2025).

With the GG, the EU thus hopes to offer an alternative to China that responds to a clear demand for hard and soft infrastructure from partner countries across the Global South, particularly in Africa. For example, internet use stood at 66% in Asia-Pacific, 69% in the Arab states and just 37% in sub-Saharan Africa in 2023. This contrasts with 87% in the Americas and 91% in Europe. These figures reflect major regional differences in access to both fixed and mobile broadband (ITU, 2023). Meanwhile, in 2017, a major G20 initiative on infrastructure estimated that the global funding gap for infrastructure was expected to be US$15 trillion by 2040, including around 60% in developing and emerging economies (Global Infrastructure Hub, 2017).

Over the past twenty years, Chinese companies such as Huawei and ZTE have responded to this real gap by providing affordable infrastructure, together with accessible financing for developing countries. For example, Chinese companies are responsible for building approximately 70% of 4G infrastructure in Africa, according to figures compiled by Arnold (Arnold, 2024). Quite simply, few others were providing a competitive price tag and the kind of financing necessary for developing countries to build this kind of infrastructure. This has undoubtedly played a role in extending China's influence, although some researchers have questioned whether China had any kind of master strategy, suggesting that China and its companies were rather opportunistic in their approach to digital development. The Digital Silk Road is clearly a catch-all that covers quite a haphazard array of projects in practice, but the thinking behind it has certainly allowed China to extend its influence in the digital sphere (Hillman, 2021). Further, Gagliardone argues that China's state-centred model, which is seen to prioritise local government priorities, has real appeal with African governments (Gagliardone, 2021).

The EU wants to offer an alternative, linking with its own standards and emphasising security, with the EU's own cybersecurity and 5G toolboxes serving as tools to guide investments under Global Gateway. Further, the EU clearly links Global Gateway to its vision of the Open Internet "given its role as a key driver of innovation, socio-political, economic, and cultural development," in clear contrast with the Chinese approach (European Commission, 2021).

The Global Gateway Communication also expresses a clear desire to influence the regulatory environments and governance conversations in partner countries, including through furthering the trend towards adoption of regulations modelled on the EU's General Data Protection Regulation (GDPR) and open and competitive markets. It also aims to support European industry players who complain that they have faced an unfair regulatory environment in many partner countries until now that has made it impossible for them to compete. Infrastructure is one of the few digital sectors where the EU has industry leaders. Recent statistics suggest that Ericsson and Nokia collectively accounted for about 28% of global telecom equipment sales in 2023 (Pongratz, 2024). Through support to the regulatory environment in partner countries and a focus on safe, secure and resilient connectivity, the EU hopes to ensure that its funding for digital connectivity does not finance Chinese infrastructure giants. At the same time, member states have raised the need for the GG to open up opportunities for a wider cross-section of the European digital economy, notably small and medium enterprises. There is also a strong interest in understanding how GG can support the private sector in partner countries.

The main instruments for implementing the GG are development cooperation instruments, which complicate the EU's efforts to build a comprehensive approach. This is because within the EU's multiannual financial framework, most of the external resources available fall under the Neighbourhood Development and International Cooperation Instrument-Global Europe (NDICI-GE), which was already agreed in advance of the GG's launch. 93% of funds under this instrument must qualify as Overseas Development Aid according to the criteria for ODA of the Development Assistance Committee of the Organisation for Economic Cooperation and Development (OECD) (Regulation (EU) 2021/947). This means that in most cases, GG projects must have a clear development cooperation rationale and limit the geographies where most EU funds can be used. Efforts are ongoing to expand the Global Gateway to include other kinds of funding, notably by creating linkages between member state development finance institutions and export credit agencies. Furthermore, the Commission's proposals for the next MFF should include a wider range of external financing instruments, allowing the Commission to play a more important role in trade facilitation with low- and middle-income countries. Yet, the new MFF will only come into force in 2028.

The digital Global Gateway is not a perfect strategy that has been thoroughly developed in advance but will need to be perfected as it is developed. The first step has simply been to step up the EU's global engagement in the area of digital cooperation and to begin to develop projects with real scale. A real challenge has been to get the EU institutions and EU member states to begin to work together to act on this question. Yet, given the strategic motivations underlying the Global Gateway, this chapter argues that going forward, the EU will need to integrate the digital Global Gateway as part of a much more comprehensive political dialogue with partner countries.

Digital Global Gateway in Practice: A Quick Introduction

In practice, the EU is looking to build undersea cables, satellite connectivity, fibre backbones and data centres in various parts of the world. The International Digital Strategy also laid out other areas where the EU hopes to step up its activity, including digital public infrastructure, artificial intelligence and other areas (EC & HRVP, 2025). It also entails a variety of large "Team Europe Initiatives" bringing together the European Commission, EU member states, their development agencies and development banks. These focus on supporting various aspects of digital transformation across the world, including digital governance and regulation, digital health, innovation and e-governance, amongst other issues. They aim to use some combination of development cooperation, technical assistance and investments.

The EllaLink Cable with Latin America, which provides connectivity for educational and research institutions, is something of a model for the kinds of large infrastructure projects that the GG hopes to spearhead. This cable will be extended to the rest of Latin America and is being paired with a wider programme under the EU-Latin America-Caribbean (LAC) digital alliance, which also includes a regional Copernicus Strategy with the launch of two data centres in Panama and Chile and the launch of an EU-LAC Digital Accelerator to support collaboration between companies, SMEs and start-ups in the two regions (European Commission, 2023a).

Global Gateway also includes the Medusa Cable, which is set to become the largest submarine high-capacity optical-fibre cable initiative in the Mediterranean (European Commission, 2024d), plans for a cable connecting Europe with Japan via the Arctic (European Commission, 2023b), the EU-Central Asia Digital Bridge (European Commission, 2024c), the EurAfrica Gateway Cable, connecting the EU with Africa along the Atlantic Ocean coast and a planned network of fibre backbones in Africa, which would connect multiple under-connected regions of the continent. This includes, for example, plans to construct 10,000 km of regional fibre-optic backbone across six countries in Central and Southern Africa (Democratic Republic of Congo, Zambia, Zimbabwe, Malawi and Mozambique). The Digital Investment Facility, created as part of the EU's Data Governance in Africa Flagship was set up to begin to develop bankable data infrastructure projects in various sub-regions of Africa.

The Actors: Who Is Responsible for GG?

While various actors within the EEAS and DG Connect have long advocated for a more developed connectivity strategy, visible in the 2018 Strategy EU-Asia Connectivity Strategy (European Commission, 2018), the Global Gateway only became a reality after Ursula von der Leyen took office and the idea was championed from the very top of the Commission. It responds to Council Conclusions on Connectivity in which EU member states called for such a strategy (Council of the European Union,

2021), and has been consistently championed by the Commission President, who launched the Global Gateway Forum in November 2023 and raised GG in many of her public appearances with partner country officials (European Commission, 2023c, 2023d).

In practice, within the Commission, the leadership of the GG rests with DG International Partnerships, which is responsible for much of the EU's external action budget together with DGs MENA and DG ENEST and thus has the budget to actually drive the initiative. However, there are tensions between the very geopolitical vision for GG that is espoused by the European Commission and the more traditional development agenda that DG INTPA (previously DG Development) has been responsible for. As already mentioned above, the resources that DG INTPA and the other geographical DGs manage, which are the principal resources available to support the achievement of the GG, fall under the NDICI-GE, which is a development aid instrument. While the Commission highlights that GG will aid the achievement of the Sustainable Development Goals (SDGs) and respond to real demand from partner countries, many members of the international development community object to what they see as "selling out international cooperation" (Concord, 2024).

For digital investments, DG Connect has a vital role in providing strategic vision and technical knowledge to colleagues in DGs INTPA MENA and ENEST. DG Trade also has a role to play as the European Commission works towards integrating trade facilitation tools into the Global Gateway. This role should grow through the establishment of a larger trade budget, enabling the EU to provide Export Credits to better facilitate investments by European companies beyond those under the development budget. The EU External Action Service (EEAS) also has a role in the overarching strategic steering of GG, and it chairs the Working Party of Foreign Relations Counsellors (RELEX), which oversees the GG for the Council.

Member states will be vital if the digital pillar of Global Gateway is to really get off the ground. They play a formal governance role through the GG Board and on an ongoing basis through RELEX. However, they have also played an essential role in developing the agenda for digital cooperation on the ground in partner countries. Indeed, a number of member states, including Germany, France, Belgium and Luxembourg, have already been active in digital cooperation for many years and have driven the expansion of the EU's digital role through the digital development hub (D4D Hub), which brings together 16 EU member states with an interest in digital cooperation as of November 2024. The focus of the majority of member states has not been on hard infrastructure but rather on other areas, including governance, skills and innovation.

The success of the digital GG will require the full buy-in of member states and their financial institutions, and yet it has been difficult to bring them fully on board for a variety of reasons. Member states have a real role to play in financing the GG, but also in bringing their political and diplomatic weight to bear in the strategic steering of the initiative and in developing networks on the ground. They are a key conduit to the European private sector, which is first and foremost the private sector of the 27 EU member states. They also bring expertise and networks that could strengthen the initiative. The decisions of the member states will also be vital in deciding the future shape and size of the next EU MFF, which could have a major influence on the future of the GG. However, as we will see in the final section, member states have struggled to see how the GG can support their interests and how they, in turn, can shape it.

Ultimately, the Global Gateway will depend on the ability of European businesses to find opportunities for investment and to navigate complex business environments. The Business Advisory Group of the Global Gateway provides the private sector with a forum to provide input into the development of the initiative, but many private sector actors continue to raise doubts about the real opportunities provided by the GG. As colleagues and I have argued elsewhere, bringing the European private sector on board will require strengthening the in-house expertise within EU delegations, and tailoring future financial instruments to the needs of the private sector (Bilal & Teevan, 2023; Bilal et al., 2024). A number of EU Delegations already have experts dedicated to leading their digital cooperation in partner countries, and they can often work together with in-country experts working for member state development agencies such as GIZ and Expertise France. However, the hiring and upskilling of these experts will need to be scaled up, including developing a clear mandate for these experts to develop deep ecosystem expertise and play a real role in directing European investments to key partner countries. We will touch on the financing issues in the next section.

Teething Problems and the Way Forward

While the digital Global Gateway has laid out an impressive array of projects, it initially lacked any clear overarching strategy and was planned in a somewhat hodgepodge manner. This is not so surprising for a new initiative, and as already noted, the Digital Silk Road did not appear to have any great masterplan at the outset either. Yet having a clearer strategy might help bring the 27 member states and their private sectors along. Secondly, the Global Gateway should be more smoothly integrated into the evolving domestic conversation about competitiveness and technology sovereignty that has ramped up in the aftermath of the Draghi Report. GG flagships should be better integrated into a wider political and industrial dialogue with partner countries, particularly in the Global South. Thirdly, there needs to be a strong focus on the impact of these projects, building on local digital ecosystems to ensure they have meaningful outcomes and do not simply produce white elephants. Finally, the speed of implementation is currently gruellingly slow, and the financial instruments available are ill-suited to the aims of the GG. The effectiveness and speed of implementation will need to be greatly increased if the Global Gateway hopes to have any chance of putting the EU on the map as an international digital actor.

A Strategic Framing

If Global Gateway is to really shift relations with countries in the Global South and have an influence on regulatory and governance choices, there is a need to have a clearer political strategy, including much more overt policy dialogue with key partner countries. The way GG was initially rolled out is still very closely related to old ways of doing development cooperation rather than a truly comprehensive approach bringing together digital and cyber diplomacy, trade, investment policy and development cooperation. The 2025 International Digital Strategy began to address this point by bringing together digital diplomacy, with a more strategic framing of the European offer as the "Tech Business Offer". Yet, there is still a need for further conciliation between policy areas, notably with regard to digital trade.

The EU has also stepped up its digital diplomacy with a wide range of partner countries, for instance re-committing to the Trade and Technology Council with India, launching a digital dialogue with Morocco and holding bilateral digital investment events with a variety of digital partners in late 2025 and early 2026, from Vietnam to Nigeria. This increased focus on political dialogue is necessary to make the "digital economy packages" announced under the GG meaningful. These were initially announced for Nigeria, Kenya, Brazil, Columbia and the Philippines, and at first appeared to be more of a hobbling together of various unrelated projects rather than truly representing comprehensive packages developed in response to a meaningful analysis of partner countries' needs (EU Delegation to Colombia, 2023; European Commission, 2022, 2023e, 2024b). An increased focus on political dialogue and private sector engagement hints at a real shift in approach. At the regional level, the EU-LAC Digital Alliance was built on existing cooperation around the first EllaLink cable, and is coupling the extension of the cable with ongoing dialogue, technical assistance and selected development programmes.

Going forward, a crosscutting team bringing together the EEAS, DG Connect, DG INTPA and the other regional DGs, DG Trade and DG Just could provide steering for the digital GG. Greater attention should be paid to the political framing of digital partnerships, and further country and regional packages should be developed as part of a meaningful sectoral dialogue that accompanies hard and soft infrastructure and technical assistance. This would necessarily involve a reflection on the external dimension of EU internal policies and would thus be closely connected with the EU's evolving competitiveness agenda.

European Competitiveness and Technology Sovereignty

Despite the rhetoric of Ursula von der Leyen's "geopolitical commission," there remains a disconnect between many domestic policy agendas and their international dimension. This applies both to the host of new laws regulating platforms and AI, but is also true of the discussion around competitiveness, where defensive policies aimed at countering China have tended to dominate the conversation around the external dimension of the EU's emerging industrial strategy. If the EU hopes to use the Global Gateway to increase its connectivity with the rest of the world, but also to build its influence in the area of digital regulation and governance, it needs to bring partners on board with an open and inclusive vision of "technology sovereignty."

The current geoeconomic context has led to a strong focus on economic security and competitiveness, coupling defensive and offensive policies to alternatively protect and stimulate European industry, but thus far, Global Gateway has been an afterthought for most European leaders. Moving forward, it will be important to integrate Europe's partners into some of the EU's more proactive economic and industrial policies as the new European Commission aspires to a more ambitious agenda of "technology sovereignty" during the second von der Leyen term (von der Leyen, 2024). The Draghi report hints at a more ambitious approach to partners around energy and critical raw materials, but it is essential that the EU also begins a more proactive dialogue with partner countries around digital and emerging technologies as part of its emerging "economic foreign policy" (Draghi, 2024). During a time of growing economic nationalism, Europe will need to consider how it brings partners along with its emerging vision of technology sovereignty.

At the same time, the EU has embraced the idea of the externalisation of EU regulations via market mechanisms in what has come to be known as the "Brussels effect" and is now also actively promoting the adoption of data protection regulation styled on GDPR in partner countries in Africa and elsewhere. Yet many new policies and laws do not really integrate consideration of their external impacts in a meaningful way, even though the EU hopes that they will be as influential as GDPR. There is an assumption in Brussels that the "Brussels Effect" will necessarily cause the world to follow Brussels when it comes to various regulatory choices. A more meaningful analysis of the potential impacts of the Digital Services Act or AI Act on the EU's partners in its neighbourhood, Africa and further afield might be worthwhile.

Understanding Context: An Ecosystem Approach

There is a need to avoid building white elephant prestige projects that do not actually drive economic growth and human development. In many developing countries, the issue is not simply a question of lack of infrastructure alone but also a question of accessibility and affordability. Thus, cables and data centres need to be part of a wider approach rooted in an understanding of local digital ecosystems.

The EU and member states have launched informal D4D Hubs, bringing together officials and experts from the EU and member state agencies in Brazil, Columbia, Nigeria, Kenya, Tanzania and a variety of other countries globally, showing that a bottom-up approach is gradually emerging. Yet very few EU delegations have real digital experts at present, and in many cases, the digital focal points are also responsible for other policy areas.

Going forward, the EU will need to further develop its expertise in delegations and should be supported by more member state officials and experts. "Digital economy packages" should be developed by in-country experts in EU delegations, who develop a strong understanding of the local context and develop programmes in close coordination with local authorities and innovation ecosystems. These experts should also act as focal points to help connect the European private sector to opportunities on the ground.

As my colleagues and I have written elsewhere, truly developing a bottom-up ecosystem approach to partner countries would also require better coordination amongst European actors and with partners from the UN, World Bank and like-minded countries. This might be done through the use of country-led financing platforms to allow for better sharing of information and coordination around opportunities (Bilal et al., 2024).

Overcoming Financing Challenges

There have been big pledges regarding expected investment levels under the Global Gateway, which aims to raise €300 billion during the current budgetary cycle, 2021–2027. The EU initially needs to be seen to begin to deliver investments or lose credibility. Yet, the instruments that the EU currently has available to finance these investments are development cooperation instruments that are often slow and do not necessarily allow for the kind of financing actually required by the private sector. It simply does not have the range of instruments and the flexibility to implement a truly strategic approach to the GG.

There is growing agreement that a more varied toolbox will be necessary to spur increased investment, including in digital infrastructure. For example, conversations are ongoing around how EU member state export credit agencies that support exports might better support digital transformation, including not only hard infrastructure, but also digital public infrastructure and digital services (Klasen & Meyer, 2026), as well as how they can work better with development finance institutions so as to bring together domestic economic interests with the SDGs. DG INTPA is in the process of launching a Digital Leap Fund, which aims to support equity investments in digital infrastructure.

Conversations are also underway about how to overhaul the EU's external action budget within the next MFF so as to integrate a more varied array of external action instruments and make current instruments more fit for purpose. This does not mean scrapping the development budget but rather complementing it with a more varied set of instruments. For example, there is growing discussion around the need for a European export credit facility to complement the development tools currently available (Schlogl et al., 2023). Yet, the ambitions of the next MFF will depend on the negotiations between the EU institutions, and ultimately, the size and composition of the MFF will be vital in terms of carrying out the ambitions of the GG.

Conclusion

The Digital Global Gateway is an important part of developing a wider toolbox to influence the direction of global digital development and, by extension, the evolution of global digital governance. The EU ultimately hopes to put forward and promote its own vision of digital sovereignty based on democratic values and human rights. Much has been done to begin to lay the groundwork for future digital cooperation with countries around the world. Yet, this chapter has argued that the Global Gateway is still very much in need of clear political direction in order to give it shape, as well as personnel and tools to ensure effective implementation.

Bibliography

Arnold, S. (2024). Africa's roads to digital development: Paving the way for Chinese structural power in the ICT sector? *Review of International Political Economy, 31*(4), 1148–1172.

Bilal, S., & Teevan, C. (2023, November 27). The Global Gateway at two: Implementing EU strategic ambitions. *ECDPM*. https://ecdpm.org/work/global-gateway-two-implementing-eu-strategic-ambitions

Bilal, S., & Teevan, C. (2024, June). Global Gateway: Where now and where to next? *ECDPM*. https://ecdpm.org/work/global-gateway-where-now-and-where-next

Bilal, S., Teevan, C., & Tilmes, K. (2024, June). Financing Inclusive Digital Transformation under the EU Global Gateway. *ECDPM*: https://ecdpm.org/work/financing-inclusive-digital-transformation-under-eu-global-gateway.

Bradford, A. (2020). *The Brussels effect: How the European Union rules the world.* Oxford University Press.

Concord. (2024, April 22). *A sell-out of international cooperation': DG INTPA turns its back on commitments to put human development at the centre of its international cooperation in leaked briefing.* https://concordeurope.org/2024/04/22/a-sell-out-of-international-cooperation-dg-intpa-turns-its-back-on-commitments-to-put-human-development-at-the-centre-of-its-international-cooperation-in-leaked-briefing/

Council of the European Union. (2021, July 21). *A globally connected Europe—Council conclusions.* https://data.consilium.europa.eu/doc/document/ST-10629-2021-INIT/en/pdf

Council of the European Union. (2022a, March 29). *Council conclusions on the EU's economic and financial strategic autonomy: One year after the commission's communication.* https://data.consilium.europa.eu/doc/document/ST-6301-2022-INIT/en/pdf.

Council of the European Union. (2022b, July 18). *Council conclusions on EU digital diplomacy.* https://data.consilium.europa.eu/doc/document/ST-11406-2022-INIT/en/pdf.

Council of the European Union. (2023, June 26). *Council conclusions on EU digital diplomacy—Council conclusions approved by the council at its meeting on 26* June 2023. https://data.consilium.europa.eu/doc/document/ST-11088-2023-INIT/en/pdf

Draghi, M. (2024). *The future of European competitiveness—A competitiveness strategy for Europe.* https://commission.europa.eu/topics/strengthening-european-competitiveness/eu-competitiveness-looking-ahead_en.

EU Delegation to Colombia. (2023, March 15). The European Union launches the Digital Economy Package to strengthen its partnership with Colombia in the sector. https://www.eeas.europa.eu/delegations/colombia/european-union-launches-digital-economy-package-strengthen-its-partnership-colombia-sector_en?s=160.

European Commission. (2018, September 19). Joint communication to the European Parliament, the council, the European economic and social committee, the Committee of the Regions and the European Investment Bank. Connecting Europe and Asia—Building blocks for an EU Strategy. https://www.eeas.europa.eu/sites/default/files/joint_communication_-_connecting_europe_and_asia_-_building_blocks_for_an_eu_strategy_2018-09-19.pdf

European Commission. (2021, December 1). *Joint Communication to the European Parliament, the Council, the European Economic and Social Committee, the Committee of the Regions and the European Investment Bank. The Global Gateway.* https://eur-lex.europa.eu/legal-content/EN/TXT/?uri=CELEX%3A52021JC0030

European Commission. (2022, February 23). *H.E. Prof. Yemi Osinbajo, vice president of the Federal Republic of Nigeria, and H.E. Margrethe Vestager, executive vice-president of the European Commission, met in Abuja on 13* February 2022. https://ec.europa.eu/commission/presscorner/detail/en/STATEMENT_22_1023

European Commission. (2023a, July 17). *Joint Declaration on a Digital Alliance European Union—Latin America and Caribbean.* https://international-partnerships.ec.europa.eu/document/download/15512057-a80d-4428-bf34-24608adfb0e4_en?filename=EU-Latin_America_and_Caribbean__Joint_Declaration_on_a_Digital_Alliance.pdf

European Commission. (2023b, July 13). EU and Japan boost strategic cooperation on digital and on critical raw materials supply chains. https://ec.europa.eu/commission/presscorner/detail/en/ip_23_3831.

European Commission. (2023c, October 25). Opening speech by President von der Leyen at the Global Gateway Forum. https://neighbourhood-enlargement.ec.europa.eu/news/opening-speech-president-von-der-leyen-global-gateway-forum-2023-10-25_en.

European Commission. (2023d, February 8). Press statement by president von der Leyen following the meeting with Spanish prime minister Sánchez and Mauritanian president Mohamed Ould El-Ghazouani. Retrieved from Press Corner: https://ec.europa.eu/commission/presscorner/detail/en/statement_24_703

European Commission. (2023e, October 3). Global Gateway*: EU launches Digital Economy Package for Kenya to boost connectivity, skills and inclusive governance.* Retrieved from News: https://international-partnerships.ec.europa.eu/news-and-events/news/global-gateway-eu-launches-digital-economy-package-kenya-boost-connectivity-skills-and-inclusive-2023-10-05_en

European Commission. (2024a). Briefing book—Policy field: International partnerships. https://www.politico.eu/wp-content/uploads/2024/04/18/draft-IntPa-briefing-for-next-Com-April-2024-1-cleaned.pdf.

European Commission. (2024b, February). Digital Economy Package Philippines. https://international-partnerships.ec.europa.eu/document/download/9fad4b92-bf39-4515-b1a9-28f55ace1484_en?filename=EU-Philippines-digital-economy-package.pdf&prefLang=fr.

European Commission. (2024c). EU—Central Asia digital connectivity. https://capacity4dev.europa.eu/resources/team-europe-tracker/partner-countries/middle-east-asia-and-pacific/eu-central-asia-digital-connectivity_en.

European Commission. (2024d, October 25). EU and EIB's support helps accelerate the MEDUSA high-speed digital connection under the Mediterranean Sea. https://neighbourhood-enlargement.ec.europa.eu/news/eu-and-eibs-support-helps-accelerate-medusa-high-speed-digital-connection-under-mediterranean-sea-2023-10-25_en.

European Union. (2021). *Regulation (EU) 2021/947 of the European Parliament and of the council of 9 June 2021 establishing the Neighbourhood, development and international cooperation instrument—Global Europe, amending and repealing decision no 466/2014/EU of the European Parl.* https://eur-lex.europa.eu/eli/reg/2021/947/oj.

European Commission and High Representative of the Union for Foreign Affairs and Security Policy. (2025). *Joint Communication to the European Parliament and the Council. An International Digital Strategy for the European Union.* https://digital-strategy.ec.europa.eu/en/library/joint-communication-international-digital-strategy-eu

European Union External Action Service. (2022, September 1). US/Digital: *EU opens new Office in San Francisco to reinforce its Digital Diplomacy.* Retrieved from Press Room: https://www.eeas.europa.eu/eeas/usdigital-eu-opens-new-office-san-francisco-reinforce-its-digital-diplomacy_en

Gagliardone, I. (2021). *China, Africa, and the future of the internet.* Zed.

Global Infrastructure Hub. (2017). Global infrastructure outlook: Infrastructure investment needs 50 countries, 7 sectors to 2040. https://cdn.gihub.org/outlook/live/methodology/Global+Infrastructure+Outlook+-+July+2017.pdf.

Hillman, J. E. (2021). *The digital silk road: China's quest to wire the world and win the future.* Harper Business.

ITU. (2023). Measuring Digital Development—Facts and figures 2023. https://www.itu.int/hub/publication/d-ind-ict_mdd-2023-1/

Klasen, A. & Meyer, H. (2026). Public export finance for digital transformation. *ECDPM*. https://ecdpm.org/work/public-export-finance-digital-transformation

Leyen, U. (2024). *Europe's choice: Political guidelines for the next European Commission 2024–2029.*. Retrieved from European Commission: https://commission.europa.eu/document/download/e6cd4328-673c-4e7a-8683-f63ffb2cf648_en?filename=Political%20Guidelines%202024-2029_EN.pdf

Muscat, S. (2024, November 27). *The EU needs a clear pitch for its 'human-centric' approach to digital transformation.* ECDPM.

Pongratz, S. (2024, March 13). Worldwide telecom equipment market slumps in 2023. Retrieved from Dell'Oro Group: https://www.delloro.com/worldwide-telecom-equipment-market-slumps-in-2023/

Schlogl, L., Pfaffenbichler, D., & Raza, W. (2023, March 31). Aligning European export credit agencies with EU policy goal. Retrieved from European Parliament Think Tank: https://www.europarl.europa.eu/thinktank/en/document/EXPO_IDA(2023)702590

CHAPTER 17

EU and US Data Economies in the Age of Competition for Digital Power—From Borderless Data Flows to Strategic Autonomy

Kristo Lehtonen and Stefan Lindström

Introduction

The relationship between the European Union and the United States has long been a cornerstone of the global security and economic order, marked by deep economic ties and shared democratic values. In the early 2000s, this partnership thrived in an era of globalisation and technological integration, where the free flow of data across borders was celebrated as a driver of innovation, economic growth and closer international collaboration. Landmark data exchange agreements, such as the EU-US Safe Harbor Agreement, symbolised a mutual commitment to borderless data

K. Lehtonen (✉)
The Finnish Innovation Fund (Sitra), Helsinki, Finland
e-mail: Kristo.lehtonen@sitra.fi

S. Lindström
Finnish Ministry of Foreign Affairs, New Delhi, India
e-mail: stefan.lindstrom@gov.fi

T. Kleiner and A. Garcia Rodriguez (eds.), *The Making of a Global Digital Rulebook*, https://doi.org/10.1007/978-981-95-9226-5_17

flows while maintaining fundamental rights, such as privacy and data protection.

However, as the digital landscape evolved, so did the challenges underpinning this once-unquestioned collaboration. The early enthusiasm for borderless internet and data flows has given way to security concerns, trade wars and competing regimes for regulating the concentration of digital. Increasing concerns over data privacy and growing economic competition began to strain the EU-US relationship. The invalidation of Safe Harbor, followed by the introduction of the General Data Protection Regulation (GDPR), marked a significant shift in the EU's approach to data governance, reflecting a growing desire to assert more control in the digital realm. The open hostility of the Trump administration towards EU digital legislation has created further rift and a dangerous risk of de-coupling.

The shift in strategic autonomy represents more than just a regulatory adjustment; it signals a broader reorientation of EU-US relations in the context of a changing global landscape. As the European Union increasingly seeks to reduce its dependency on foreign technologies and assert control over its digital infrastructure, it is also redefining its role on the global stage, balancing cooperation with the United States against the need for independence and self-reliance. Moreover, China's growing role on the global stage significantly impacts the EU-US relations.

Traditional approaches to trade and industrial policy focused on market liberalisation, deregulation and international free trade in order to drive economic growth. New strategies are emerging, characterised by greater government intervention as well as subsidies to drive strategic investments and support key industries.

In this chapter, we will explore the concept of strategic autonomy in application to EU-US relations and examine the question of borderless data flows as an example of the evolution of the transatlantic relationship. Section 2 provides an overview of the concept of strategic autonomy. In it, we argue that we are witnessing a new wave of thinking of strategic autonomy in the EU.

Section 3 uncovers the topic of data flows as an example of how the EU-US relationship has changed over the years, providing examples and analysing key events and policies that have shaped this transition. By understanding this trajectory, we can gain insight into the future of the EU-US partnership in data relations and the broader implications for global governance in an increasingly digital world.

Strategic Autonomy Entering Centre Stage in the Transatlantic Relationship

The Concept of Strategic Autonomy in the Transatlantic Relationship

In the technology context, both the EU and the US seek to reduce their dependence on foreign technologies, in particular, related to so-called critical technologies, which are pivotal to the future of economic development and national security. These include artificial intelligence or quantum technologies. Moreover, both actors aim to assert control in the digital sphere. For the EU-US relations, it represents a delicate balancing act between independence, interdependence and cooperation. EU-US relations have gone through different phases that can be paired with the development of the different waves of strategic autonomy thinking in the EU, in which the Union has been increasingly recognising a set of actions to ensure that Europe has sufficient leeway in a world characterised by interdependence.

The concepts of "economic security", "digital sovereignty" and "strategic autonomy" are all used in this context and are mistaken to mean the same thing. The diagram below depicts their relations (Diagram 17.1).

In this text, the concept "strategic autonomy" is defined as a state's (e.g. the European Union's) ability to defend and promote its values and pursue its national interests without being overly reliant on foreign actors.[1]

"Digital sovereignty" is related to the digital aspects of strategic autonomy. It can be defined as control for data, software, standards, processes, hardware, services and infrastructure.[2]

"Economic security" is related to the economic aspects of strategic autonomy. It can be defined as the "promotion of state's economic base and

[1] For the evolution of the term "strategic autonomy" see, e.g., Helwig & Sinkkonen (2022).

[2] Digital sovereignty as a concept can be defined as control (i.e. the de facto ability to influence) for: data (the raw material used by the critical technologies), software (e.g. AI algorithms or coronavirus app), standards (e.g. 5G standards and standard essential patents), processes (e.g. ability to access own data from a smart device after purchase or ability to transfer operations from one cloud computing provider to another), hardware (e.g. mobile phones), services (e.g. social media platforms such as Tik Tok) and infrastructure (such as 5G networks or smart cities). See, e.g., Floridi (2020).

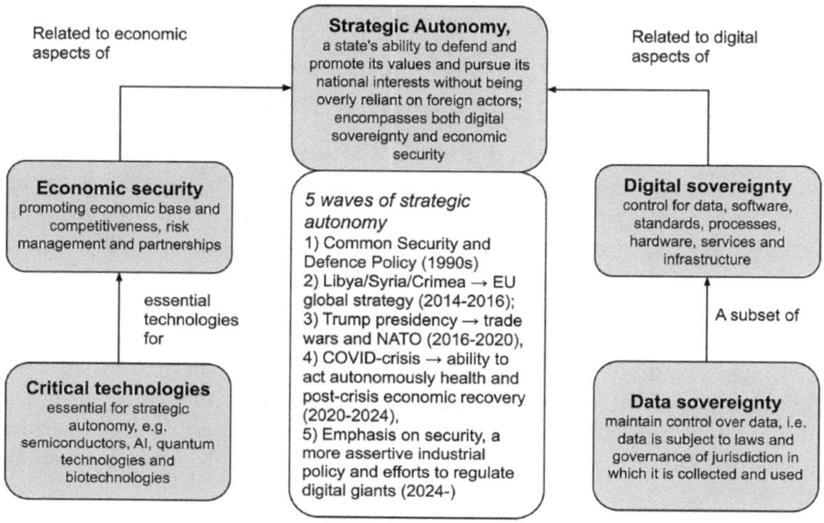

Diagram 17.1 Concept of "Strategic autonomy" in relation to other related concepts

competitiveness, risk management and beneficial partnerships". In January 2024, the European Commission proposed new initiatives to strengthen European economic security,[3] following the European Economic Security Strategy from June 2023 (JOIN(2023) 20 final, 2023).

"Critical technologies" are technologies that are essential for achieving strategic autonomy or economic security. They include technologies such as AI, semiconductors, 5G and 6G, quantum technologies, high-performance computing, space technologies and biotechnologies (Alanko et al., 2023). The European Commission identified ten critical technology areas for the EU's economic security in October 2023.[4]

[3] Economic security has been defined as "a common framework for achieving economic security by promoting the EU's economic base and competitiveness; protecting against risks; and partnering with the broadest possible range of countries to address shared concerns and interests" (European Commission, 2024).

[4] The list includes: Advanced Semiconductor Technologies, AI, Quantum technologies, Biotechnologies, 6G, Advanced sensing technologies, Space, Energy, Robotics and Advanced materials/manufacturing/recycling technologies (European Commission, 2023a).

Data serves as the essential raw material for critical technologies. The concept of "data sovereignty" is used in this context. It refers to the ability to maintain control over data, i.e. data is subject to laws and governance of the jurisdiction in which it is collected and used (Chander & Sun, 2023).

Several waves of strategic autonomy can be identified, all connected to the EU-US relationship. We use classification for the four first waves from Helwig and Sinkkonen (Helwig & Sinkkonen, 2022) and introduce a fifth wave, which we argue began in 2024.

The first wave of strategic autonomy can be traced to the end of the 1990s with the creation of the Common Security and Defence Policy, which focused on strengthening European military capability in the event of US disengagement from Europe. In the 1990s, following the Cold War, the US and the EU sought to strengthen economic ties (U.S. Department of State, 1998). Moreover, in 1995, the New Transatlantic Agenda was signed to foster closer cooperation between the US and the EU (U.S. Department of State, 1997). Lastly, in 2007, the Transatlantic Economic Council was created as a forum for economic dialogue between the EU and the US (U.S. Department of State, 2024).

The second wave in the 2010s was a reaction to the wars in Libya, Syria and Crimea (Ukraine). As a result, the 2016 EU global strategy talked explicitly about strategic autonomy as the basis for "Europe's ability to promote peace and security within and beyond its borders". In 2013 started the negotiations for the Transatlantic Trade and Investment Partnership (TTIP) during President Obama's administration. TTIP aimed to promote trade as a traditional trade liberalisation programme by fostering international integration for mutual benefit. However, TTIP faced challenges and ultimately failed. President Trump's opposition to TTIP played a significant role in its demise. Additionally, political resistance from Germany and France contributed to the failure (Welfens & Hanrahan, 2022, p. 1). The failure of TTIP also meant the failure of EU-US cooperation to jointly contribute to industrial and technological standards. With the rise of the Chinese economy, the fear was that Chinese interests might increasingly dominate global rule-setting and standards in the coming decades.[5]

[5] The development of the International Telecommunication Union (ITU) is a prominent example of this risk being realized. See: Schaefer & Pletka (2022).

Donald Trump's presidency marked the third wave of discussion about strategic autonomy in the EU with Trump's threats not to protect NATO members who did not invest sufficiently in defence, as well as the trade wars that Trump initiated. During the Trump Presidency, the EU-US trade relations deteriorated significantly, leading to the imposition of tariffs and counter-tariffs in 2018.[6] President Trump's decision to freeze the TTIP negotiations and impose tariffs was a clear message to the EU that the US under President Trump had stopped seeing the EU as a valuable, strategic partner. Instead, President Trump saw that the EU was "set up to take advantage of the United States" (Galindo, 2018).

The fourth wave came with COVID-19. In particular, in the fourth wave, the discussion became much more connected to the EU's ability to act autonomously in health and post-crisis economic recovery. This led to the deepening of the debates around strategic autonomy in a moment in which EU-US relations were at an all-time low because of the disagreements under the Trump term. This is fundamental to understanding current developments and the establishment of the EU-US Trade and Technology Council (TTC). The Trade and Technology Council was first proposed in the summer of 2020 by EU's Trade Commissioner Phil Hogan to "reset the relationship between the EU and the US" (Ministère de l'Économie et des Finances, 2019). TTC did not materialise as the Trump administration showed little interest in strengthening trade with the EU (Palmer & Moens, 2020). Following the election of President Biden and against the backdrop of the COVID-19 pandemic's rupturing effect on global supply chains, the Biden administration started to re-engage in EU-US trade relations (Welfens & Hanrahan, 2022, pp. 2, 3). The first meeting of TTC took place in September 2021 in Pittsburgh, US, followed by five meetings until April 2024.[7]

We are at present witnessing the fifth wave of strategic autonomy marked by a renewed emphasis on security, a more assertive industrial policy, data governance and efforts to regulate digital giants. The fifth wave began before President Trump's re-election in November 2024,

[6] In March 2018 US imposed 25% tariffs on steel and 10% tariff on aluminum. The EU countered with "rebalancing measures", i.e. counter-tariffs, targeting up to 6,4 billion euros worth of goods starting in June 2018 (European Parliament, 2018).

[7] Since the inaugural meeting the TTC has convened in May 2022 in Paris, in December 2022 in Maryland, in May 2023 in Luleå, in January 2024 in Washington D.C. and in April 2024 in Leuven.

but has accelerated markedly since then. A related topic is the growing awareness of the threat posed by China, specifically by the US and increasingly by Europe. The EU has produced a set of strategic documents that illustrate the shift towards digital sovereignty as a guiding principle for cooperation.

The Strategic Agenda 2024–2029 by the European Council is organised around three pillars: (1) a free and democratic Europe, (2) a strong and secure Europe as well as (3) a prosperous and competitive Europe. The first pillar underscores core values, such as human dignity, democracy and the rule of law, as guiding principles for the EU, both internally and externally. The second pillar focuses on enhancing the EU's strategic role in a more confrontational global landscape, emphasising defence readiness, support for Ukraine and improved crisis response. The third pillar aims to bolster economic security by reducing dependencies, diversifying strategic supply chains and advancing key technologies such as artificial intelligence, net-zero technologies and semiconductors, supported by an "ambitious" trade policy (European Council, 2024).

Ursula von der Leyen's political guidelines for the next European Commission 2024–2029 emphasised the risks posed by dependencies and vulnerable supply chains, citing examples such as medical shortages during the pandemic, "Putin's energy blackmail" and "China's monopoly on raw materials essential for batteries or chips". The guidelines advocate for a "new approach to competition policy" that supports the scaling up of European companies in global markets. A central initiative is the "Clean Industrial Deal", aimed at promoting policies that enable the EU to simultaneously decarbonise and industrialise its economy (Leyen, 2024).

Lastly, the Draghi report (2024) echoes the emphasis on decarbonisation as a driver of economic growth. It proposes a new industrial strategy for Europe aimed at increasing investment rates and closing the innovation gap with the United States. The strategy seeks to foster the emergence of larger companies within the European Single Market, capable of competing with US digital giants (Draghi, 2024).

The fifth wave of strategic autonomy has driven a broader shift in the EU-US agenda. While both sides continue to view China as a central strategic challenge, President Trump's re-election in November 2024 has made the transatlantic relationship more transactional and less institutionalised. The EU–US Trade and Technology Council, which had served as a key forum for cooperation on trade and technology, has effectively fallen dormant. In April 2025, the Trump administration imposed sweeping reciprocal tariffs, including on the EU, before turning in mid-2025 to negotiations with the European Commission, which culminated in a trade agreement in August 2025 (European Commission, 2025). In Von der Leyen's political guidelines, the President describes the current historical phase as an "age of geostrategic rivalries", marked by the "more aggressive posture and unfair economic competition from China" that reflects "a shift from cooperation to competition" with China (Leyen, 2024, p. 25). The US, having made a strategic pivot towards China in 2011,[8] has moved away from its traditional "Europe-first" policy, prioritising Asia instead. The Trump administration has explicitly reasserted an "America First" approach to foreign and trade policy (The White House, 2025). Since Trump's return, the EU has had to respond not only to the long-term rise of China, but also to a more demanding and unpredictable United States. Washington has intensified pressure on Europe to assume greater responsibility for its own defence. At the 2024 Munich Security Conference, Senator J.D. Vance and the candidate for Vice-President of the United States urged the EU to take greater responsibility for its own security, reaffirming the US's growing focus on China.[9]

The second Trump administration has intensified the fifth wave of strategic autonomy, with EU data legislation—particularly measures affecting US digital giants and social media platforms—heightening the likelihood of retaliatory actions. This escalation raises the prospects of increased tariffs and trade conflicts.[10]

Moreover, without a strategic approach to critical technologies, the EU risks missing out on the next wave of innovation that can bring value to the European economy, but also pose new security risks. The fear is that falling behind in next-generation innovation will lead to the EU becoming too dependent on technologies controlled by other countries, such as China and the US. The EU is already highly dependent on the US and China in digital products and services in general, as pointed out

[8] President Obama announced the strategic pivot towards China in 2011 (Blackwill, 2024).

[9] Vance said that while he does not advocate for the U.S. to pull out of NATO, he believes Europe needs to step up its defense capabilities, as relying heavily on U.S. support is no longer sustainable, at a time when the US is focusing more on threats from China (Vance, 2024).

[10] Vice-President elect JD Vance said recently that US could drop support for NATO if Europe tries to regulate Elon Musk's platforms (Kilander 2024, September 17).

by research (Timmers, 2023, pp. 105–115) and objective measurements such as the Digital Dependency Index.[11]

Critical technologies represent the potential choking points in the supply, and in the absence of sufficient domestic capabilities, the EU faces the risk of supply chain shortages or price surges (JOIN(2023) 20 final, 2023). As an example, during the COVID-19 pandemic and the subsequent supply chain crisis, European car manufacturers were faced with involuntary production stoppages due to the lack of microchips produced in the EU (ACEA, 2021). The emphasis on different aspects of strategic autonomy is likely to enhance resilience and supply chain security—and it could boost investments—but it may also lead to increased political and geopolitical instability (Aaronson, 2019, pp. 541–577).

"Strategic autonomy" serves as an overarching concept that integrates economic, digital and traditional security concerns within political discourse. In the next sections, we will provide a more in-depth analysis of the elements of fifth wave of strategic autonomy that impacts the transatlantic agenda: the battle to regulate digital giants, industrial policy, trade policy and the challenge of the rise of China.

The Battle to Regulate Digital Giants

Digital data has become the most important raw material of our era, leading to intensified competition for digital power—a megatrend that profoundly influences EU-US relations (Dufva & Rekola, 2023). This is evident in both regions' political discourse and efforts to regulate major tech companies. For instance, in his 2023 State of the Union address, President Biden urged Congress to regulate "Big Tech" (The White House, 2023).

[11] The Digital Dependence Index (DDI) measures the dependence level on different technology sectors (e.g. hardware and software) of 23 countries. Categories are "low sensitivity" (= autonomy very high) with DDI index < = 0.25; "high sensitivity" (= domestic supply delivers majority of digital tech) with 0.25 < DDI < = 0.5; "low vulnerability" (= global markets supply majority in digital tech) with 0.5 < DDI < = 0.75; high vulnerability (= autonomy very low, foreign digital technology is in a dominant position) with DDI > 0.75. DDI index sub-indices include Hardware, Software and IPR. Major EU countries such as Germany (DDI index 0.82), France (DDI 0.84) and Italy (0.86) demonstrate high vulnerability, whereas the US (DDI 0.47) has the best score and, hence, lowest vulnerability out of any of the 23 countries included in the index. URL: https://digitaldependence.eu/en/.

Digital giants are very large companies that have a strong economic position and a large user base.[12] These companies have emerged as dominant forces in the modern data economy, primarily due to their capacity to amass vast amounts of data. Consequently, a significant portion of the economic benefits, as reflected in aggregate market value, has been accrued by digital giants based in the United States and China. Most notable digital giants—that are seen as national champions for their respective countries—include Alphabet, Meta, Amazon, Apple and Microsoft in the US, and Alibaba, Baidu and Tencent in China.

The US government has started several antitrust investigations against the digital giants. For example, in August 2024, a judge in the US District of Columbia ruled against Google, stating that by spending billions of dollars to secure exclusive agreements with developers, carriers and equipment makers to be the default search engine, Google has violated antitrust law. The legal procedures are likely to continue for years, but the genie is out of the bottle (US District of Columbia. v. Google LLC, 2024).

The polarised US Congress has thus far been unable to pass new legislation on this matter comparable to the data legislation from the EU. A notable, recent exception to this trend is the legislation that mandated ByteDance, the parent company of TikTok, to divest its ownership of the popular social media platform or face a ban in the United States (Maheshwari & McCabe, 2024).

Legislatures in both the EU and the US have realised that the internet cannot be unregulated anymore and that the self-regulation by the companies has not worked. The Cambridge Analytica Scandal would not have been possible without a corporate culture at Facebook (later rebranded as Meta) that prioritised profits over data protection and privacy. This culture was exemplified by the motto of Facebook's founder, Mark Zuckerberg: move fast and break things (Härkönen et al., 2022).

In the European Union, Google has received the largest recorded fines in the history of competition law due to repeated misuse of its dominant market position, culminating in fines exceeding 8 billion euros

[12] In comparison, the European Commission defines a "gatekeeper" as companies that meet 3 criteria: (1) a strong economic position, significant impact on the internal market and are active in multiple EU countries; (2) a strong intermediation position, meaning that they link a large user base to a large number of businesses; (3) an entrenched and durable position in the market, meaning that their position has been stable over time (European Commission, 2024c).

since 2017 (European Commission, 2017; European Commission, 2018; European Commission, 2019). Despite these record-breaking penalties, further instances of wrongdoing have persisted (Bräutigam, et al., 2022).

The EU currently lacks digital giants comparable to those in the US and China. While factors such as a fragmented single market and limited risk capital are often cited, the reasons remain debated (Alanko et al., 2023). However, the EU has excelled in regulating digital giants, with legislative innovations like gatekeeper rules and regulating data at the source, which we will cover in the next section. Some argue that the EU's data legislation has hindered the emergence of digital giants, but this claim is unfounded. The internet was unregulated for years, yet no digital giants arose in the EU. In fact, EU data legislation, such as the Digital Markets Act (DMA), largely responded to the misconduct of existing digital giants and has been welcomed by major European companies such as Spotify and those in the gaming industry (e.g. Spotify, 2024).

Data Legislation Impacts Different Parts of the Value Chain

Modern data economies often naturally exhibit a "winner-takes-it-all" nature, leading to the consolidation of market power among a few dominant players. While historical evidence shows that such markets can remain competitive, this typically requires legislative intervention. Markets prone to oligopoly often need regulation to complement competition law and enhance market efficiency. The telecom sector provides a successful example: despite a limited number of operators in most markets, competition remains strong, enabling customers to switch providers while retaining their number and data. This outcome was made possible through legislation that complements competition law.[13]

Different legislation impacts different parts of the value chain. The EU's Data Act is an example of legislation whose impact is particularly strong in the first phase of the value chain, i.e. the data collection phase. An example could be a smart sensor, like a smart ring, that gathers heart rate data.

After data collection, the service provider processes the data, such as a smart ring developer offering an accompanying app. An example of legislation whose impact is particularly strong in this phase of the value chain is GDPR.

[13] For examples and details how legislation allowed telecom and finance markets to remain competitive, see, for example: Raunio (2020)

The third phase involves data monetisation and usage. The smart ring manufacturer uses the data to provide services to customers. The service provider is regulated under the EU's Digital Services Act, among other legislation (Diagram 17.2).

These regulations—Data Act, GDPR and DSA—function as "ex-ante", meaning that they prevent unlawful behaviour from the outset. This contrasts with competition law, which operates "ex-post", addressing violations after they occur. Initially, the EU considered amending existing competition law to better address issues in the data economy. Another option considered was a "new competition tool", which would have allowed the European Commission to address structural barriers to competition. Ultimately, the EU opted for a third approach, introducing the Digital Markets Act (DMA), which has been called a hybrid between traditional competition law and ex-ante regulation (Ibañez Colomo, 2023, pp. 124–127).

In the example of the smart ring company, the data is not used solely by the company. The app is likely downloaded from an app store, typically controlled by a digital giant, and operates on a mobile phone's operating system, possibly sharing data with the giant's other apps. If the digital giant holds a dominant market position in a relevant geographical or product market, competition law can be applied. DMA complements competition law in the EU. Competition cases can take years to resolve,

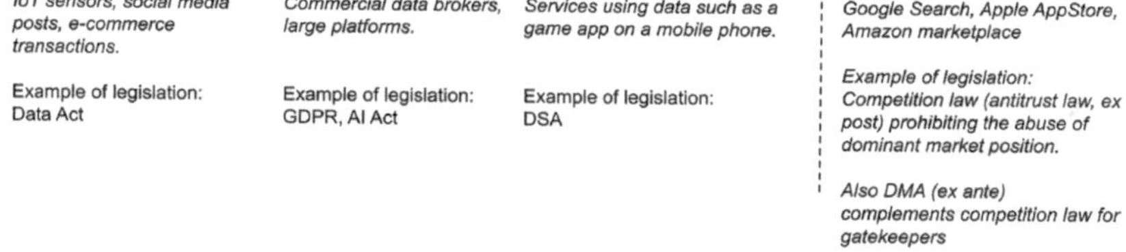

Diagram 17.2 Impact of legislation in the value chain from data generation to usage

and even record fines have failed to effectively deter unlawful behaviour, underscoring the need for legislation like the DMA.

In conclusion, the EU has demonstrated an ability to regulate digital giants effectively, a feat the US has yet to achieve. The EU has introduced legislative innovations, such as the Data Act, targeting the early stages of the value chain, as well as DMA, a hybrid legislation that draws on the best practices from sectors such as telecom and finance and effectively complements traditional competition law, which has proven too slow and ineffective in controlling the power of digital giants.

The Brussels Effect

EU's data legislation exemplifies the so-called Brussels Effect, a term coined by Anu Bradford (Bradford, 2020) to explain the influence of European regulation in shaping laws outside of the EU. An example of the Brussels Effect is GDPR, which influenced similar legislation outside the EU. The Californian Consumer Privacy Law, introduced in 2018, was modelled in part after GDPR (Moubayed, 2023). Similarly, GDPR influenced the Chinese equivalent, the Personal Information Protection Law (Zhu, 2014).

The EU is not the continent of origin for digital giants (e.g. GAFAM), but it remains "the primary source of the rules that govern those technologies". At the same time, "the American market-driven regulatory model is fading in its normative appeal and global influence". This shift is exemplified by the growing support within US domestic political discourse for increased regulation to curb the power of digital giants (Bradford, 2023, pp. 361–362).

The US is aware of the effects of European regulation, in particular of the fact that EU's new data legislation, i.e. DSA and Data Act for example, could, in the absence of US legislation, "be setting de facto global rules or standards", as was noted in the US Congressional Research Service report shortly after introduction of the new legislative proposals by the European Commission (Congressional Research Service., 2021, p. 14). Despite the criticism suggesting that "judges do not win games", particularly with regard to the abundance of new legislation in the data economy within the European Union, it remains an indisputable fact that the EU has demonstrated its capacity to enact legislation and inspire rule-setting beyond its own borders. The US has recently taxed European legislation as going against freedom of speech or being targeted at harming American companies, and invoking trade instruments as a threat to the enforcement of EU legislation.

It is noteworthy that China has also increased its efforts to regulate the data economy and is, in some cases, going further in its regulation, such as in the area of regulating algorithms. China, however, lacks the EU's ability to inspire and influence other countries—in particular democratic nations—with its legislation. There is no Chinese equivalent of the Brussels effect. This is understandable since China's state-driven approach to data legislation infringes on fundamental rights and contributes to the oppression of minorities through surveillance (Bradford, 2023, p. 365).

The unwillingness to regulate within the US Congress is widely recognised and means that significant legislation is unlikely to emerge from the United States in the foreseeable future. The five legislative attempts based on the House Antitrust Subcommittee's October 2020 report (Merger Filing Fee Modernisation Act, Augmenting Compatibility and Competition by Enabling Service Switching (ACCESS) Act, American Choice and Innovation Online Act, Ending Platform Monopolies Act and the Platform Competition and Opportunity Act) have practically gone nowhere (US House of Representatives, 2020).

The necessary condition for a major piece of legislation is that a single political party was to control all three branches of government—the Presidency, the Senate, and the House of Representatives—while also securing the 60-seat supermajority in the Senate necessary to overcome filibusters. While it is pursuing a deregulation agenda, an alternative perspective may also be proposed: Has the United States effectively outsourced regulatory issues to the EU?

From Traditional Industrial Policy to Strategic Autonomy

Traditional approaches to industrial policy often focused on market liberalisation and deregulation, emphasising the role of free markets in driving economic growth. However, new approaches to industrial policies and strategies are emerging in response to several geopolitical and economic shifts. Major trading blocs are moving away from the traditional market economy to what can be described as strategic capitalism.

Industrial policies are today more characterised by greater government intervention and coordination, with an emphasis on strategic investments, targeted support for key industries and the promotion of sustainable and inclusive growth (Moraes & Wigell, 2020).

Concepts such as strategic autonomy and economic security reflect a re-evaluation of traditional economic paradigms and a recognition of the need for more proactive and assertive policies to address contemporary challenges (Calleja Mediano et al., 2024). Security considerations have started to influence or take over trade policy.

The key drivers of this new kind of globalisation are the US-China relationship, Chinese economic and political developments and activities in general, the emergence of new critical technologies, the evolving green transition as well as Russian aggression activities, including the war in Ukraine. The paradigm of great power competition shades everything. These external changes drive internal changes and strategies (Allen, 2024; Rudd, 2024; Sanger, 2024).

These new industrial strategies form a broad approach to strengthening the competitiveness, innovation and sustainability of national industries. State-supported activities include investing in critical technologies such as artificial intelligence, robotics and biotechnology, moving towards low-carbon and resource-efficient production, applying circular economy principles and developing environmentally friendly production methods. Another vital element of the new strategy is to upgrade the training and skills of workers to meet modern requirements (Moraes & Wigell, 2020).

Industrial strategies are the key factor in today's geopolitical struggle and a pillar of national security. During the Biden presidency, the United States enacted the Inflation Reduction Act (IRA) (Stokes, 2024). It represented the most extensive use of tax subsidies in the history of the US to mobilise private capital to achieve a policy objective—in this case, to accelerate the energy transition. The IRA (U.S. Government, 2022), together with the Infrastructure Investment and Jobs Act (IIJA) (U.S. Government, 2022a) and the CHIPS semiconductor law passed around the same time (U.S. Government, 2022b).

The CHIPS Act, or "Creating Helpful Incentives to Produce Semiconductors for America Act", was designed to promote the domestic semiconductor industry. The legislation was proposed in response to the global semiconductor shortage in general and the United States in particular. The three legislative packages are estimated to have both immediate and significant long-term impacts on the economy. At the same time, national security objectives such as resilience will be strengthened (Shivakumar & Wessne, 2022).

The implementation of the IRA, was at the time a large signal of investment in clean energy projects worldwide.

Since President Trump's re-election, however, both IRA and CHIPS Act have come under pressure and are being supplanted by more traditional forms of tariff protectionism. Nevertheless, the reindustrialisation push is here to stay. The EU is forced to react or become increasingly uncompetitive. It is possible for the US and the EU to also find common ground in selected areas, even in industrial policy, as the common worry for both regions is China.

Present Challenge: China and Geopolitics

Over the past decade, Asia's strategic importance has surged, becoming a global economic engine and a centre of high-tech production. Semiconductors illustrate this shift, with Asia's booming markets driven by a growing middle class and China's ambitions for global leadership (Khanna, 2019; Seong et al., 2023). This rise in technological competition, particularly between the US and China, has introduced new geopolitical dynamics and concerns over "weaponised interdependence", where global supply chains and networks, once seen as stabilising, are now viewed as vulnerabilities (Drezner et al., 2021).

The US, wary of China's exploitation of global trade and innovation systems, took significant measures during the Trump administration, notably against Huawei, citing national security threats.[14] This can be defined as the emergence of the need for trusted connectivity. This included placing Huawei on the US Commerce Department's entity list, limiting its access to critical technologies (Drezner et al., 2021). Secretary of State Mike Pompeo, under the Trump administration, went so far as to convey to the EU leaders that allowing Huawei to participate in the deployment of the next-generation (5G) networks within the EU could potentially lead to the US restricting the flow of personal data of US citizens to the EU.[15] In response, Huawei criticised the US efforts to ban its participation in 5G tenders as a pretext to ensure the NSA could

[14] The approach adopted by the Trump administration towards Huawei was widely perceived as favouring European telecommunications network manufacturers Nokia and Ericsson, who were likely to benefit from any business opportunities that Huawei might have lost (Floridi, 2020).

[15] According to Reuters, Secretary of State Mike Pompeo stated in a news conference in May 2019: "(There is) a risk we will have to change our behavior in light of the fact that we can't permit data on private citizens or data on national security to go across networks that we don't have confidence (in)" (Brunnstrom, 2019).

continue collecting vast amounts of data, alluding to the Snowden revelations and alleged corporate partnerships between the NSA and technology companies (Drezner et al., 2021).

Meanwhile, China has strategically expanded its global influence through initiatives like the Belt and Road programme, leveraging economic dependencies to secure access to infrastructure and resources (Daniels, 2023). China's growing power, seen as a direct threat to the US, contrasts with Russia's more traditional challenges (Huang et al., 2022). The Biden administration has responded by fostering a new industrial policy aimed at curbing China's influence, emphasising sustainable growth and national security. This technological rivalry poses challenges not only for the US and China but also for third countries navigating the shifting geopolitical and geoeconomic landscape (Alperovitch, 2024).

From the beginning, the Chinese government has set out to control the internet in order to preserve its political power and maintain autocratic rule in China.[16] China's data protection laws, such as the Personal Information Protection Law that went into force in November 2021 and the Data Security Law that went into force in September 2021, have drawn inspiration from EU legislation, including the GDPR, DGA and DSA. These Chinese laws reflect the influence and impact of the EU (Zhao, et al., 2022).

China has adopted a state-driven approach to regulating the data economy and perceives itself as a global leader in data economy regulation, surpassing the EU in this domain in its own mind. The Chinese government recognises that digital giants within China, including Alibaba, Baidu and Tencent, have grown too powerful compared to the state. Consequently, in recent years, China has taken stringent measures against these companies, conducting antitrust investigations and implementing new legislation to prevent the misuse of customer data (Bradford, 2023, p. 8). However, the primary objective of regulatory and law enforcement measures within an autocratic regime such as China is to preserve the authority of the state.

[16] In 2010 the Chinese government released a white paper on internet policy, aiming explicitly at "internet sovereignty", meaning that foreign companies offering services or operating in China had to abide by Chinese laws and be subject to Chinese government's oversight (Wu, 2010).

EU-US Data Relations: An Example of Unwinding Relations

Data flows between the EU and the US were relatively free from regulation and restrictions in the early days of the internet in the 1990s. The world was coming out of the Cold War era. The old Communist regimes, wary of losing control, had sought to limit access to digital information and tightly regulate online spaces. The victorious Western block embraced a more liberal approach. The early internet came with the promise of freedom for individuals and the online platforms as "guardians and amplifiers of those freedoms" (Bradford, 2023, p. 1). The internet and the emergence of platforms did provide many benefits, such as access to information and increased civic engagement. For those reasons, the regulation of online activities was something that was not thought of until the 2010s. In the beginning, the EU adopted a free market approach towards the expansion of the internet, following the US lead. They also brought along misinformation, addictive algorithms and monopolistic market dynamics (Lehtonen, 2022; Siripurapu, 2020).

The EU and the US have the largest bilateral trade and investment relationship and enjoy the most integrated economic relationship in the world (European Commission, 2024b). The US and EU's alliance is marked by shared democratic values (European External Action Service, 2023). At the time of writing, the data flows between the EU and the US are estimated to be the highest in the world, higher than, for example, between the EU and Asia (Meltzer, 2014). Circa 50% of data flows in the US and in Europe are transatlantic transfers (AmChamEU, 2024; U.S. Chamber of Commerce, 2021). This makes cross-border data flows between the EU and the US one of the pillars of the global data economy. The EU and the US also possess enormous rule-setting power: any standards or practices agreed by the EU and the US with regard to data exchange are likely to become a global norm.

Given the staggering volumes of data generated and shared between the EU and the US on a daily basis, technologies, such as artificial intelligence (AI), are needed for its effective processing. Data is considered the most valuable resource in contemporary times (Härkönen et al., 2022), and AI has been recognised as the foremost general-purpose technology of our era (Brynjolfsson & McAfee, 2017). However, emerging technologies like quantum and space technology are also becoming crucial for processing and disseminating data. In EU-US political discourse, data and technology are deeply interconnected.

Text Box 17.1 The Data Flows between the EU and the US in Numbers[17]

Trillion dollar data flows in numbers

149 zettabytes (ZB) of data (149 trillion gigabytes) of data was produced **in the world in 2024**.

Circa **50% of all data flows** in the US and in Europe are transatlantic.

Over 90% of EU-based firms transfer data to and from the United States. **2 times more data flows via transatlantic cables** than over transpacific and intra-Asian routes.

The value of transatlantic data flows estimated to underpin **8.3 trillion euros economic relationship** of trade and investments between the EU and the US. Most data are not traded and hence cannot be easily measured in market statistics. As a reference, the size of EU data economy has been estimated to be over **800 billion euros by 2025**.

Modern data processing technologies cannot be relied on without data flows. For instance, when an EU resident uses services provided by a US-based company, such as ChatGPT by OpenAI, data is exchanged between EU and US servers. In this example, the majority of value-added engineering and data processing is likely occurring in the US, where the large language model (LLM) was trained, and major parts of the service developed.

For multinational companies operating in global markets, seamless data movement across continents is essential for business continuity. Personal data can be transferred from the EU to the US by virtue of an adequacy decision by the European Commission, ensuring an adequate level of data protection.[18] American companies are able to assure through self-regulation that their internal practices provide an adequate level of data protection for EU citizens.

[17] Sources: Statista (2024); AmChamEU (2024); Hamilton and Quinlan (2021); OECD (2023); Eurostat (2024).

[18] For EU-US data transfers the most recent adequacy decision was done in July 2023 (European Commission, 2023b).

There are several notable actors relevant to the EU-US data flows, which are illustrated below (Diagram 17.3).

For years, politics, protectionist policies and security concerns have significantly influenced the ideal of seamless data flows and the vision of the internet as a global, free and open infrastructure grounded in multi-stakeholder governance (Stengg 2024, pp. 39–41). For example, mandatory data localisation has been enforced in various forms in countries such as China, India and Russia (Bradford, 2023; Cory & Dascoli, 2021, p. 234). Similar developments were visible in the US, especially after the 9/11 attacks.[19]

Snowden Revelations Shaking the Foundations of EU-US Data Transfers

The 9/11 attacks led to heightened alertness in the US intelligence community, prompting new powers and methods in the war on terror under President Bush. This, combined with the growing interconnectivity of the internet, resulted in mass surveillance by agencies like the NSA (Ball, 2013; Council of Councils, 2021; Savage, 2013).

For several years, the legal basis for the transfers was based on the EU-US Safe Harbor Agreement, which was signed in 2000. The agreement was struck down in 2015 by the Court of Justice of the European Union (CJEU)—a decision commonly known as "Schrems I", referring to the original case title "Maximillian Schrems vs. Data Protection Commissioner".

Maximilian Schrems, an Austrian privacy activist, had filed a complaint in 2013 against Facebook with the Irish Data Protection Commissioner, the lead data protection authority for Facebook in the EU. Schrems' complaint was triggered by the revelations from Edward Snowden in

[19] E.g. after 9/11 attacks the US authorities started demanding Passenger Name Records (PNR) and later other Advanced Passenger Information (API), which required changes to global flight booking systems such as Amadeus (European Union, 2006). Also Microsoft found itself in difficult situation in 2013 when US prosecutors requested the company to hand over data from company's servers in Ireland for an ongoing drug-trafficking investigation, which was in contrast to EU's rights-driven model. The decision was appealed and later on resulted in the US passing the CLOUD Act, authorizing the US government to enter into bilateral data-sharing agreements with countries with adequate legal protections (Bradford, 2023, p. 222).

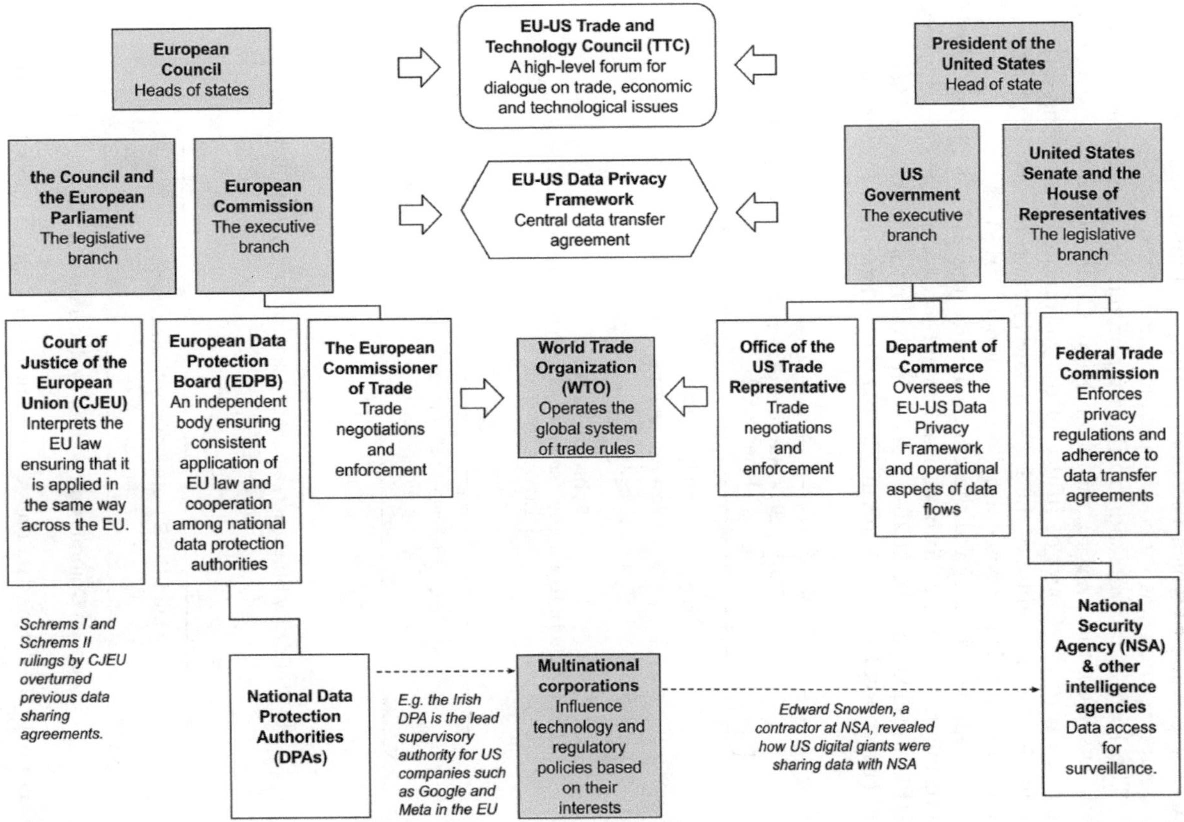

Diagram 17.3 Key players in the EU-US trade and data exchange

2013, according to which Facebook participated in the mass surveillance programme known as PRISM (Diagram 17.4).

The Irish Data Protection Authority rejected the complaint, but Mr. Schrems filed the case to the Irish High Court, which subsequently referred it to the Court of Justice of the European Union. The CJEU's ruling led to the demise of the EU-US Safe Harbor framework (Maximillian Schrems v Data Protection Commissioner, 2015).

In response, the EU and the US established the EU-US Privacy Shield agreement. However, this new arrangement faced a similar fate when the CJEU invalidated it in 2020—a decision commonly known as "Schrems II" (Facebook Ireland v Schrems, 2020). These agreements were followed

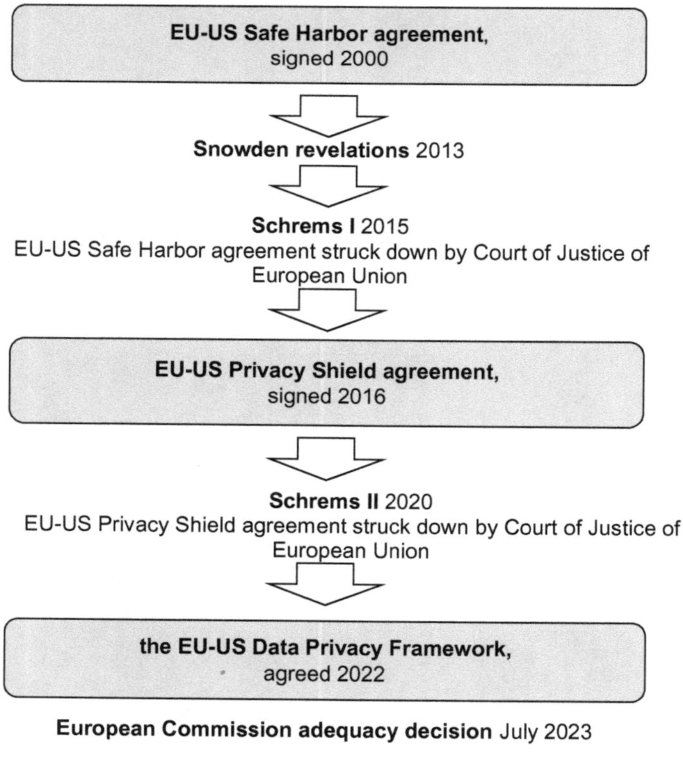

Diagram 17.4 Major data transfer agreements and related impactful events

by the EU-US Data Privacy Framework that was agreed on 25 March 2022.

Text Box 17.2 Snowden Revelations Had a Profound Impact on EU-US Data Flows[20]

Snowden revelations

In 2013, Edward Snowden, an NSA contractor, leaked classified information revealing widespread surveillance of personal data by the NSA, including the PRISM programme, which accessed data from major U.S. tech companies, and the tapping of undersea internet cables. The NSA also monitored mobile phone data on a massive scale, collecting billions of records daily.

One of the most alarming revelations was the NSA's "war on encryption", where the agency circumvented or cracked much of the encryption used in everyday internet activities. NSA maintained a 50-page catalogue, outlining various vulnerabilities and so-called backdoors in the solutions provided by technology companies.

The US Constitution prohibits "unreasonable searches and seizures", which is why mass surveillance targeted non-Americans. Furthermore, non-American individuals who were subjected to surveillance or found themselves on the NSA's "blacklist" had limited access to judicial remedy in the event they felt their rights were violated. This led to a two-tier justice system and left non-Americans, subject to surveillance, with limited legal recourse.

Snowden's disclosures highlighted violations of EU citizens' fundamental rights such as data protection rights, leading ultimately to the invalidation of the EU-US data transfer agreements.

US Bends to EU Demands in the Data Privacy Framework

In the summer of 2023, the EU-US Data Privacy Framework (DPF) was established through legislative actions on both sides of the Atlantic. President Biden issued an Executive Order enhancing safeguards for US signals

[20] Sources: The Washington Post (2013); The New York Times (2013); Spiegel (2013); Senate Committee on Homeland Security & Government Affairs (2022).

intelligence activities (The White House, 2022). The European Commission made an adequacy decision under the EU GDPR, concluding that the US provides an adequate level of protection for personal data transferred from the EU to US companies participating in the DPF (European Commission, 2023b).

Under DPF, the personal data of EU citizens can be transferred to certified US companies committed to the agreed protection measures. These companies must comply with detailed privacy obligations, such as deleting unnecessary data and ensuring continued protection when sharing data with third parties (The Office of the Data Protection Ombudsman of Finland, 2023).

New redress mechanisms were introduced, allowing EU citizens to seek independent resolution if their data is mishandled, including access to their data and correction or deletion of incorrect or unlawfully handled data. The Framework also provides EU citizens whose data would be transferred to participating companies in the US with several new rights, such as to obtain access to their data or obtain correction or deletion of incorrect or unlawfully handled data (The Office of the Data Protection Ombudsman of Finland, 2023).

The DPF is administered by the International Trade Administration (ITA) within the US Department of Commerce. US-based organisations can self-certify their compliance, which must be recertified annually.[21]

The US agreed to implement basic necessity and proportionality checks for data gathering, including for national security and law enforcement purposes. These concessions include creating a Data Protection Review Court (DPRC) to provide EU citizens with an independent mechanism for redress regarding data collection by US intelligence agencies (European Commission, 2023b).

This framework marks a significant shift from past practices, reflecting the EU's refusal to tolerate infringement on the fundamental rights of its citizens, as revealed by the Snowden disclosures. In hindsight, it can be stated that the European Court of Justice played a critical role in enforcing the EU's Charter of Fundamental Rights, unaffected by political pressures to maintain transatlantic relations.

The DPF's influence extended beyond the EU, impacting data transfers with the UK and Switzerland. The UK extension to the EU-US Data

[21] Organizations can also be removed from the list at which point they must cease making claims about participation or compliance (DPF, 2024).

Privacy Framework took effect on 12 October 2023, applying to data transfers from the UK and Gibraltar to organisations participating in the EU-US framework. Switzerland also negotiated its own framework based on the EU-US agreement (DPF, 2024).

Text Box 17.3. Meta Threatening to Leave the EU Market Prior to Data Privacy Framework[22]

Meta threatening to leave the EU

In the 2020s there were reports in the media about Meta allegedly threatening to abandon the European market due to uncertainties surrounding EU-US data transfers and Meta's refusal to ensure that EU citizens' data would not be replicated to the US without proper legal basis.

The situation changed with the introduction of the EU-US Data Privacy Framework (DPF) and the subsequent Adequacy decision by the European Commission. These developments provided the necessary legal safeguards for data transfers between Europe and the US, allowing Meta to continue its services in Europe.

Meta has denied that it ever threatened to leave the EU.

Divergent Approaches to Regulating Data Economy

Diverse jurisdictions are characterised by distinct historical backgrounds, values and traditions, which significantly influence their approaches to regulating the data economy. These differences are illustrated in the diagram below (Diagram 17.5).

The democratic camp comprises the like-minded EU and the US, whose regulatory frameworks for the data economy are rooted in democratic values and principles, such as freedom, human rights and the rule of law.

On the other hand, China and Russia exemplify the authoritarian approach to regulating the data economy, drawing upon traditions and values emphasising security, conformity and obedience. In authoritarian regimes, the state controls the data and, through that, their citizens (Bradford, 2023, p. 8).

[22] Sources: Bloomberg (2022); Meta (2022).

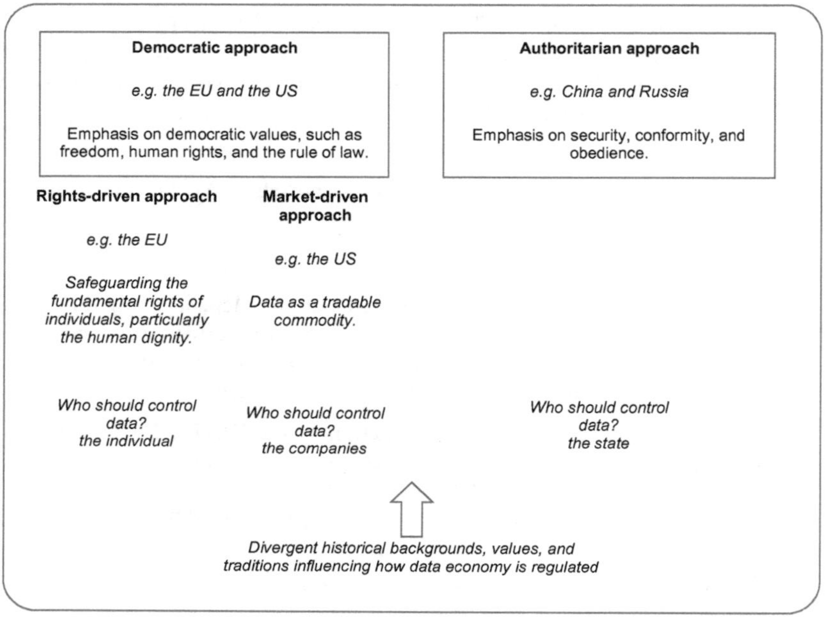

Diagram 17.5 Divergent approaches to regulating data economy

Furthermore, within the democratic camp, a notable distinction can be observed. The EU embraces a rights-driven approach, which places a strong emphasis on safeguarding the fundamental rights of individuals in the data economy, particularly with regard to human dignity. Data legislation in the EU, generally speaking, intends to enhance individuals' control over their data. In contrast, the United States adopts a more market-driven approach, perceiving data primarily as a tradable commodity (Bradford, 2023, p. 9).

The American Market-Driven Approach to Data Legislation

The American market-driven approach stems from the techno-optimist ethos that emerged during the early days of the internet. This model emphasises the principles of free markets, limited government intervention and a deep admiration for technology entrepreneurs, also referred to as the "Californian ideology" (Barbook & Cameron, 1996, p. 35). This approach is further underpinned by a strong commitment to the protection of free speech, as enshrined in the First Amendment of the United States Constitution. In Silicon Valley, the prevailing mission has been to generate profits while simultaneously changing the world. The belief was that the internet cannot be—and, hence, should not be—regulated (Barlow, 1996).

The 26 words of Section 230 of the Communications Decency Act, enacted in 1996, established legal safeguards for online intermediaries, shielding them from potential liability for user-generated content on their platforms. "No provider or user of an interactive computer service shall be treated as the publisher or speaker of any information provided by another information content provider". Consequently, platforms like Facebook were not held to the same legal standards as traditional media outlets, such as the Washington Post, regarding the content uploaded by users (Siripurapu, 2020).

However, there has been a notable shift in the deregulatory sentiment in recent years, first under the administration of Republican President Trump and later under Democratic President Biden. In May 2020, President Trump issued an Executive Order with the aim of curtailing the legal protections provided by Section 230 after Twitter appended fact-check labels to several of his tweets. The executive order states that:

> Section 230 was not intended to allow a handful of companies to grow into titans controlling vital avenues for our national discourse... when they use their power to censor it... (Siripurapu, 2020).

Newer cracks have emerged to the protections offered by Section 230 in the form of newer court cases, including an appeals court decision stating that TikTok's algorithmic recommendations constitute the platform's own speech—instead of third-party speech (Feiner, 2024).

The European Rights-Driven Model to Data Legislation

The European rights-driven model has an in-built belief that technology companies do not respect the fundamental rights of users, which, in turn, necessitates government intervention (Bradford, 2023, p. 7). This can be seen as a political reaction to the misuse of trust and dominant market positions by the gatekeeper platforms in the digital sphere.[23]

In Europe, the level of data protection is higher than, for example, in the United States. Data protection is specifically recognised as a distinct fundamental right for all EU citizens in the EU's Charter of Fundamental Rights. Moreover, compliance with the protection of personal data is subject to control by an independent authority in the EU.[24] EU citizens' personal data (identified or identifiable to a natural person) cannot be transferred outside of the EU under the GDPR without adequate data protection for EU citizens.[25]

The EU has introduced a flurry of significant regulations in recent years, starting with GDPR, which was proposed and entered into force in 2018 and followed by an unprecedented tsunami of data legislation under the EU Data Strategy of 2020. Prime examples of this data legislation are the Data Act and the Digital Services Act (DSA) (Bräutigam, et al., 2022).

[23] This has been called "digital constitutionalism" in the EU which has replaced the "digital liberalism" of the early days of the development of the internet (de Gregorio, 2021).

[24] EU Charter of Fundamental Rights, Article 8, "Protection of personal data". The article reads: "1. Everyone has the right to the protection of personal data concerning him or her. 2. Such data must be processed fairly for specified purposes and on the basis of the consent of the person concerned or some other legitimate basis laid down by law. Everyone has the right of access to data which has been collected concerning him or her, and the right to have it rectified. 3. Compliance with these rules shall be subject to control by an independent authority". Article 7 is about "respect for private and family life" and it encompasses privacy of communications. Article 7 reads in full: "Everyone has the right to respect for his or her private and family life, home and communications". In the EU the concept of "personal data" is often used in this context, whereas in the US the concept of "privacy" is used while the practical use cases are sometimes in the cross-section of the fundamental rights depicted in articles 7 and 8.

[25] General Data Protection Regulation (2016/679), Article 45.1 states: "A transfer of personal data to a third country or an international organization may take place where the Commission has decided that the third country, a territory or one or more specified sectors within that third country, or the international organization in question ensures an adequate level of protection" (Regulation (EU) 2016/679, 2016).

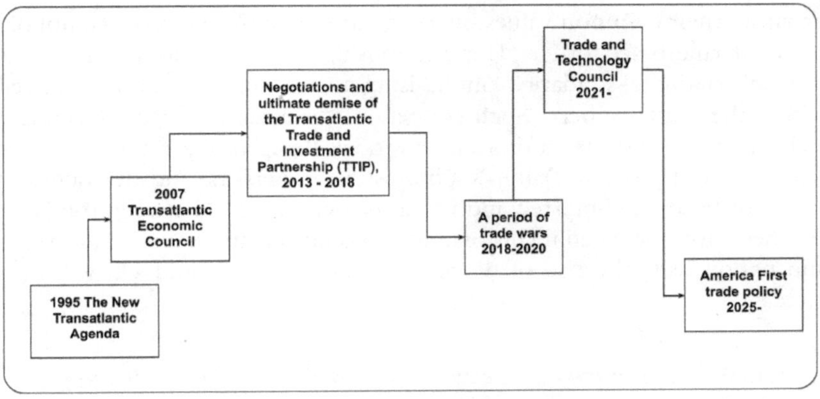

Diagram 17.6 A brief history of the Trade and Technology Council (TTC)

From Trade Wars to the Establishment of the Trade and Technology Council

The EU-US Trade and Technology Council (TTC) has emerged as a key forum to coordinate EU-US trade, economic and technology issues. The diagram below summarises key events leading to the establishment of the TTC (Diagram 17.6).

New developments show that these structures of cooperation have given place to an "America first" agenda, where tech dependency is leveraged for economic domination by the Americans.

Conclusions and Strategic Implications for the Future

Democratic Values as the Cohesive Force for the Transatlantic Data Economy

Despite the prevailing trends that are driving the US and the EU further apart, shared values can bind the EU and the US together as a guiding principle for politicians on both sides of the Atlantic.

As the tension between authoritarian and democratic values escalates, the preservation of democratic values can serve as the cohesive force that draws the EU and the US closer. The EU and the US have the ability to promote their common values by joint action and, in the process, uphold a global rule-based order. The relationship should be founded on the principle of digital solidarity, emphasising mutual support in times of need within the digital sphere. Such cooperation is essential for establishing a viable alternative to the authoritarian model. Reciprocally, if the autocratic temptation of Donald Trump's administration persists, and the values of the West become contested and in-fights increase, e.g. between solidarity and nepotism, between inclusion and exploitation, and between globalists and nationalists, the risk of de-coupling between EU and US will only increase.

Strategic Autonomy at the Expense of the Democratic Alliance Is Shortsighted

Europe's rights-oriented approach to regulating digital power and the US market-driven approach find themselves juxtaposed against the autocratic approach adopted by China. The EU and the US should strive to align their approaches to the greatest extent possible. Such harmonisation would facilitate the free flow of data across the Atlantic and enhance their capacity to shape global standards.

Failing to strengthen the transatlantic relationship may result in Chinese interests exerting increasing influence and potentially dominating global rule-setting and standards in the forthcoming decades. It is imperative to prevent such a scenario at all costs.

Promoting strategic autonomy is also important in the light of the real threat posed by Russia. Dual-use goods play a critical role in ensuring military security. Providing allies, such as Ukraine, with access to necessary technologies is a means of supporting their efforts and strengthening democratic countries' collective security.

Avoiding Trade and Subsidy Wars with a more Coordinated Approach to Industrial Policy

Traditional strategies focused on market liberalisation, deregulation and international free trade are being replaced by increased government intervention and subsidies. This development seems unavoidable but should be controlled.

Coordinated action is urgently required in industrial policy. The tariffs and subsidies pose a significant threat and could potentially trigger a global cycle of harmful trade wars. The US, in particular, must exercise restraint in this regard.

China has effectively exploited the openness of international trade and Western innovation systems to advance its domestic technology development and establish Chinese national champions. Both trade and industrial policies are necessary to contain China's economic influence.

In the EU, competition with subsidies should never occur among EU member states but rather at the EU level and only in response to subsidies outside the EU. The same principle should hold in EU-US relations but is unlikely to be realistic politically, considering the most recent democratic and republican administrations in the US and their current political platforms.

The Brussels Effect in Service of Democratic Values and Effective Competition

The world is currently witnessing a global competition between various approaches to regulating digital giants. The EU has successfully influenced regulations beyond its borders, unlike China. While China's autocratic model may offer short-term efficiency in curbing digital giants' power, enforcement often serves state interests rather than fairness. In contrast, democratic approaches are more sustainable in the long term. The US market-driven model has allowed digital giants to innovate and dominate their markets, but issues like the impact of social media on children highlight the need for stronger safeguards despite challenges in the politically divided US Congress to pass new legislation.

Given this context, the EU should not hesitate to assert its influence and power in safeguarding effective competition and democratic values. This will not be easy in front of US stark opposition, but it could ultimately prove to be the only solution for true digital sovereignty. Through strict enforcement of its new data laws, the EU can promote fair competition, innovation and consumer protection. Ensuring digital giants do not treat fines as mere cost of doing business is crucial. Ultimately, the EU's rights-driven model, when aggressively enforced, will prove to be more sustainable than the US market-driven and Chinese authoritarian models.

Legislation Working at the Source of Data Is Needed

Competition law and gatekeeper regulations, like the Digital Markets Act, are insufficient on their own. Addressing the issue at the point of data generation is essential to prevent monopolistic control over data, ensuring a competitive market and providing consumers with real choices. Relying on competition law and fines after digital giants have accumulated vast amounts of data is often too late.

The EU's Data Act exemplifies horizontal legislation, which works at the source of the problem where data is generated, promoting competition. However, effective enforcement is essential for success, as seen in other sectors like telecom and finance, where market-enhancing legislation requires continuous adaptation and sufficient resources.

As US and Chinese digital giants expand into traditionally European industries, such as automotive, it is crucial that data standards are rooted in democratic values to prevent dominance misuse. While the Data Act is a step forward, additional measures targeting data collection in other sectors may be necessary. This may not require new legislation but will demand proactive efforts from EU companies to establish data-sharing rules before such rules are imposed by digital giants from autocratic nations.

Critical Technologies as a Test Case for EU-US Democratic Alliance

A good testing ground for the democratic alliance is next-generation critical technologies. Without a strategic approach to critical technologies such as AI, semiconductors, biotech, 6G and quantum technologies, coupled with strategic partnerships with like-minded countries, the EU and the US risk losing to China in the competition for the next wave of innovation. This entails implementing new tools like enhanced foreign investment screening, as well as monitoring and assessing investment risks. The US "America first" approach is however undermining this joint effort, and rather pushes the EU towards reducing dependencies from the US as well as from China.

An alternative to the EU efforts to de-couple from China and from the US may exist. Bilateral trade and investment could be pursued, mitigating technical trade barriers, and fostering collaboration on technology policies and regulatory frameworks. It needs, however, to be more operational and to be based on common values between the EU and the US. Ironically, this path may only be possible after the EU has demonstrated its ability to reinforce its digital sovereignty. The alternative is for the EU to become a digital colony of America.

Cyber Arms Race Threatens the Openness of the Internet

There is an urgent need for an international convention to limit the cyber arms race, as unchecked expansion of espionage and surveillance threatens to fragment the internet and create isolated data enclaves. The Snowden revelations highlighted the importance of political oversight and balancing fundamental rights with intelligence gathering, emphasising the need to ban efforts by agencies to undermine encryption. Encryption is essential to internet trust, and creating backdoors, as seen with the NSA and China's practices, erodes this trust and disrupts global supply chains. The EU must avoid placing its companies in a similar position, and restricting intelligence agencies' methods is crucial.

The digital internal market relies on consumer trust, including privacy in online searches and encrypted banking connections. The cyber arms race, driven by major powers like the US, China and Russia, goes beyond espionage and threatens critical infrastructure during conflicts. The increasing frequency of cyber incidents raises the likelihood of a catastrophic event unless action is taken to break this cycle.

State-sponsored cyber activities also target private companies, stealing trade secrets and heightening awareness of vulnerabilities in critical infrastructure. To address these risks, intelligence agencies must reduce bulk data collection and avoid using cyber capabilities for commercial gain. International treaties, similar to nuclear non-proliferation agreements, are needed to safeguard trust in the internet, which underpins not only commerce but also critical infrastructure. Cyberattacks on this trust could be as devastating as nuclear attacks and must be prevented.

The Global Imperative of Ethical AI

AI is the most significant general-purpose technology of modern times, making it essential to address its ethical implications. A global framework is necessary to establish shared principles for the responsible development and use of AI, particularly regarding the collection and use of data, including personal and copyrighted data, and protecting children.

This requires collaboration between governments, industry, researchers and civil society to develop international standards that mitigate risks like bias and discrimination. A unified global ethical framework, supported by the EU and US, would promote trust, accountability and transparency, aligning AI development with democratic values and the collective good.

At Crossroads-Transatlantic Data Economy in the Age of Strategic Autonomy

The EU-US transatlantic relationship stands at a crossroads. The Trump presidency has escalated tariffs on the EU, reigniting trade wars. Simultaneously, the EU faces increasing pressure to bolster its competitiveness through industrial policy, enhance security capabilities and take a more active role in supporting Ukraine—efforts aimed at advancing EU's strategic autonomy.

The data economy and our digital world in general are characterised by a geopolitical order that makes us more interconnected but, at the same time, too discordant to live in genuine peace. In this context, the EU-US transatlantic data economy exhibits both promise and discord, necessitating careful navigation to maintain cooperation and address shared challenges in the digital domain.

The emergence of the next generation of technology presents new opportunities as it transforms value chains and enables the rise of new market participants who have the potential to disrupt the market power of established gatekeepers. It is crucial to bear in mind that the dominance of digital giants, whether based in the US or China, may appear eternal at the peak of their power, but in reality, it is always transient. The next-generation giants can emerge from the European Union as well as the US—and in any case, their emergence from the democratic countries would be preferable to the choice of a few autocratic data giants controlled by their autocratic states imposing their digital power globally.

It takes strong political will to anchor our approach to common values as we steer the EU and the US relationship towards a fairer transatlantic data economy, not succumbing to the forces tearing us apart.

Bibliography

Aaronson, S. A. (2019, October). What are we talking about when we talk about digital protectionism? *World Trade Review, 18*(4), 541–577.

ACEA. (2021, October 17). *Chip shortage: auto industry calls for more EU-made semiconductors*. https://www.acea.auto/message-dg/chip-shortage-auto-industry-calls-for-more-eu-made-semiconductors/

Alanko, K., Peltomäki, A., Aarnio, R., Halenius, L., & Lehtonen, K. (2023). *Ensuring European leadership in the data economy*. Sitra Working Paper.

Allen, B. (2024). *Beijing rules: How China weaponized its economy to confront the world*. Harper Collins.

Alperovitch, D. (2024). *World on the brink: How America can beat China in the race for the twenty-first century*. Public Affaires.

AmChamEU. (2024, March 17). *The transatlantic economy 2024*. https://www.amchameu.eu/publications/transatlantic-economy-2024

Ball, J. (2013, June 8). *NSA's Prism surveillance program: how it works and what it can do*. https://www.theguardian.com/world/2013/jun/08/nsa-prism-server-collection-facebook-google

Barbook, R., & Cameron, A. (1996). The Californian ideology. *Science as Culture, 6*(26), 44–72.

Barlow, J. P. (1996, February 8). *A declaration of the independence of cyberspace*. Electronic Frontier Foundation (EFF). https://www.eff.org/cyberspace-independence

Blackwill, R. D. (2024, August 1). *The rise and fall of the economic pivot to Asia*. https://foreignpolicy.com/2024/08/01/lost-decade-us-economic-pivot-to-asia-defense/

Bloomberg. (2022, July 29). *Meta repeats why it may be forced to pull Facebook from EU*. https://www.bloomberg.com/news/articles/2022-07-29/meta-repeats-threat-it-may-pull-facebook-instagram-from-europe.

Bradford, A. (2020). *The Brussels effect: How the European Union rules the world*. Oxford University Press.

Bradford, A. (2023). *Digital empires: The global Battle to regulate technology*. Oxford University Press.

Bräutigam, T., Cunningham, F., Aholainen, M., Geus, M., Kukorelli, F., & Toivanen, M. (2022, June 7). *EU regulation builds a fairer data economy*. www.sitra.fi/en/publications/eu-regulation-builds-a-fairer-data-economy/.

Brunnstrom, D. (2019). *Pompeo tells Germany: Use Huawei and lose access to our data*. https://www.reuters.com/article/us-usa-germany-idUSKCN1T10HH/

Brynjolfsson, E., & McAfee, A. (2017, July 18). *The business of artificial intelligence*. Harvard business review. https://hbr.org/2017/07/the-business-of-artificial-intelligence

Calleja Mediano, T., Garcia-Salmones, A., Gil Gomez, J., & Rutten, P. (2024, February 28). *Strengthening national security through a more resilient supply chain*. McKinsey insight. https://www.mckinsey.com/industries/aerospace-and-defense/our-insights/strengthening-national-security-through-a-more-resilient-supply-chain

Chander, A., & Sun, H. (2023). *Data sovereignty—From the digital silk road to the return of the state*. Oxford University Press.

Congressional Research Service. (2021, March 25). *EU digital policy and international trade, Report R4673*. https://crsreports.congress.gov/product/pdf/R/R46732

Cory, N., & Dascoli, L. (2021, July). *How barriers to cross-border data flows are spreading globally, what they cost, and how to address them*. Information Technology and Innovation Foundation (ITIF). https://www2.itif.org/2021-data-localization.pdf

Council of Councils. (2021, September 1). *The 9/11 effect and the transformation of global security*. https://www.cfr.org/councilofcouncils/global-memos/911-effect-and-transformation-global-security

Daniels, O. J. (2023, September). *CSET Analyses of China's technology policies and ecosystem: The PRC'S efforts abroad*. Center for Security and Emerging Technology.

de Gregorio, G. (2021). The rise of digital constitutionalism in the European Union. *International Journal of Constitutional Law, 19*(1), 41–70.

DPF. (2024). *Welcome to the data privacy framework (DPF) Programme*. https://www.dataprivacyframework.gov/

Draghi, M. (2024). *The future of European competitiveness—A competitiveness strategy for Europe*. https://commission.europa.eu/topics/strengthening-european-competitiveness/eu-competitiveness-looking-ahead_en

Drezner, D. W., Farrell, H., & Newman, A. L. (Eds.). (2021). *The uses and abuses of weaponized interdependence*. Brookings Institution Press.

Dufva, M., & Rekola, S. (2023). *Megatrends—understanding an era of surprises*. Sitra studies 225. https://media.sitra.fi/app/uploads/2023/03/sitra_megatrends-2023_v3.pdf

European Commission. (2017, July 17). *Antitrust: Commission fines Google €2.42 billion for abusing dominance as search engine by giving illegal advantage to own comparison shopping service—Factsheet*. https://ec.europa.eu/commission/presscorner/detail/en/memo_17_1785

European Commission. (2018). Antitrust: Commission fines Google €4.34 billion for illegal practices regarding Android mobile devices to strengthen dominance of Google's search engine. *European Commission*, Press release 18 July 2018. European Commission

European Commission. (2019). Antitrust: Commission fines Google €1.49 billion for abusive practices in online advertising, *European Commission*, Press release 20 March 2019. European Commission

European Commission. (2021, June 15). *EU-US launch Trade and Technology Council to lead values-based global digital transformation*. https://ec.europa.eu/commission/presscorner/detail/en/IP_21_2990

European Commission. (2023, June 20). *Joint Communication to the European Parliament, the European Council and the Council on "European Economic Security Strategy"*. https://eur-lex.europa.eu/legal-content/EN/TXT/?uri=CELEX%3A52023JC0020&qid=1687525961309

European Commission. (2023a, October 3). *Commission Recommendation of 03 October 2023 on critical technology areas for the EU's economic security for further risk assessment with Member States*. https://defence-industry-space.ec.europa.eu/commission-recommendation-03-october-2023-critical-technology-areas-eus-economic-security-further_en

European Commission. (2023b, July 10). *Adequacy decision for the EU-U.S. Data Privacy Framework*. https://commission.europa.eu/document/fa09cbad-dd7d-4684-ae60-be03fcb0fddf_en

European Commission. (2024, January 24). *Commission proposes new initiatives to strengthen economic security*. https://ec.europa.eu/commission/presscorner/detail/en/IP_24_363

European Commission. (2024a, May 3). *EU-US trade and technology council (2021–2024)*. https://digital-strategy.ec.europa.eu/en/factpages/eu-us-trade-and-technology-council-2021-2024

European Commission. (2024b). *EU trade relations with the United States. Facts, figures and latest developments*. https://policy.trade.ec.europa.eu/eu-trade-relationships-country-and-region/countries-and-regions/united-states_en

European Commission. (2024c). *The Digital Markets Act: ensuring fair and open digital markets*. https://commission.europa.eu/strategy-and-policy/priorities-2019-2024/europe-fit-digital-age/digital-markets-act-ensuring-fair-and-open-digital-markets_en

European Commission. (2025). Joint statement on a United States-European union framework on an agreement on reciprocal, fair and balanced trade. *European Commission*. European Commission

European Council. (2024, July 10). *Strategic agenda 2024–2029*. https://www.consilium.europa.eu/en/european-council/strategic-agenda-2024-2029/

European External Action Service. (2023, October 20). *EU and US together for a more peaceful, safer and fairer world*. https://www.eeas.europa.eu/eeas/eu-and-us-together-more-peaceful-safer-and-fairer-world_en

European Parliament. (2018, June 21). *US tariffs: EU response and fears of a trade war*. https://www.europarl.europa.eu/RegData/etudes/ATAG/2018/623554/EPRS_ATA(2018)623554_EN.pdf

Eurostat. (2024, February). *USA-EU–iIternational trade in goods statistics*. Eurostat Statistics Explained. https://ec.europa.eu/eurostat/statistics-explained/index.php?title=USA-EU_-_international_trade_in_goods_statistics.

European Union. (2006). *Agreement with the USA on the use of Passenger Name Record data*. https://eur-lex.europa.eu/LexUriServ/LexUriServ.do?uri=OJ:C:2006:305E:0250:0254:EN:PDF

European Union. (2016). *Regulation (EU) 2016/679 of the European Parliament and of the Council of 27 April 2016 on the protection of natural persons with regard to the processing of personal data and on the free movement of such data repealing Directive 95/46/EC (GDPR)*. https://eur-lex.europa.eu/legal-content/EN/TXT/?uri=uriserv%3AOJ.L_.2016.119.01.0001.01.ENG&toc=OJ%3AL%3A2016%3A119%3ATOC

Eurostat. (2024, February). *USA-EU–nternational trade in goods statistics*. Eurostat Statistics Explained. https://ec.europa.eu/eurostat/statistics-explained/index.php?title=USA-EU_-_international_trade_in_goods_statistics.

Facebook Ireland v Schrems, Case C-311/18 (European Court of Justice July 16, 2020).

Feiner, L. (2024, August 28). *TikTok must face a lawsuit for recommending the viral 'blackout challenge'*. The Verge. https://www.theverge.com/2024/8/28/24230523/tiktok-blackout-challenge-lawsuit-appeals-court

Floridi, L. (2020). The fight for digital sovereignty: What it is, and why it matters, especially for the EU. *Philosophy & Technology, 33*, 269–378.

Galindo, G. (2018, June 18). *Trump: EU was 'set up to take advantage' of US*. Politico. https://www.politico.eu/article/donald-trump-eu-was-set-up-to-take-advantage-of-us-trade-tariffs-protectionism/

Hamilton, D. S., & Quinlan, J. P. (2021). *The Transatlantic Economy 2021—Annual Survey of Jobs, Trade and Investment between the United States and Europe*. Foreign Policy Institute. https://www.uschamber.com/assets/archived/images/transatlanticeconomy2021_fullreport_lr.pdf. Accessed on 1st September 2024;

Härkönen, T., Vänskä, R., Vahti, J., & Lehtonen, K. (2022). *Tracking Digipower—How data can be used for influencing decision-makers and steering the world*. Sitra Studies 215. https://www.sitra.fi/en/publications/tracking-digipower/.

Helwig, N., & Sinkkonen, V. (2022). Strategic autonomy and the EU as a global actor: The evolution, debate and theory of a contested term. *European Foreign Affairs Review, 27*.

Huang, C., Silver, L., & Clancy, L. (2022, April 28). *China's Partnership With Russia Seen as Serious Problem for the U.S.* Pew Research Center Report. https://www.pewresearch.org/global/2022/04/28/chinas-partnership-with-russia-seen-as-serious-problem-for-the-us/.

Ibañez Colomo, P. (2023). *The new EU competition law*. Hart Publishing.

Khanna, P. (2019). *The future is Asian*. Simon & Schuster.

Kilander, Gustaf (2024, September 17). *JD Vance says US could drop support for NATO if Europe tries to regulate Elon Musk's platforms*. https://www.independent.co.uk/news/world/americas/us-politics/jd-vance-elon-musk-x-twitter-donald-trump-b2614525.html

Lehtonen, K. (2022). *It's in Finland's interest to better understand what Web 3.0 is all about*. https://www.sitra.fi/en/articles/its-in-finlands-interest-to-better-understand-what-web-3-0-is-all-about/

Leyen, U. (2024). *Europe's Choice—Political Guidelines for the Next European Commission 2024–2029*. https://commission.europa.eu/document/download/e6cd4328-673c-4e7a-8683-f63ffb2cf648_en?filename=Political%20Guidelines%202024-2029_EN.pdf

Maheshwari, S., & McCabe, D. (2024, April 23). *Congress passed a bill that could ban tik Tok*. Now Comes the hard part. https://www.nytimes.com/2024/04/23/technology/bytedance-tiktok-ban-bill.html

Maximillian Schrems v Data Protection Commissioner, Case C362/14 (European Court of Justice October 6, 2015).

Meltzer, J. P. (2014, October 21). *Cross-border data flows, the internet and what it means for U.S. and EU trade and investment*. The Brookings Institution. https://www.brookings.edu/articles/cross-border-data-flows-the-internet-and-what-it-means-for-u-s-and-eu-trade-and-investment/

Meta (2022, February 8). *Meta is absolutely not threatening to leave Europe*. Markus Reinisch, Vice President, Public Policy Europe. https://about.fb.com/news/2022/02/meta-is-absolutely-not-threatening-to-leave-europe/.

Ministère de l'Économie et des Finances. (2019, March 6). *Projet de loi relatif à la taxation des grandes entreprises du numérique*. https://src.bna.com/F9D

Moraes, H. C., & Wigell, M. (2020). *The emergence of strategic capitalism: Geoeconomics, corporate statecraft and the repurposing of the global economy* (p. 117). FIIA Working Paper.

Moubayed, D. (2023, March 29). *An introduction to California's consumer privacy act*. Harvard Business Review. https://journals.law.harvard.edu/hblr/2023/03/an-introduction-to-californias-consumer-privacy-act-2/

OECD. (2023, February 2). *Measuring the value of data and data flows*. DSTI/CDEP/GD(2022)1/FINAL. https://one.oecd.org/document/DSTI/CDEP/GD(2022)1/FINAL/en/pdf.

Palmer, D., & Moens, B. (2020, January 13). *EU's tough new trade boss seeks reset with Trump*. https://www.politico.com/news/2020/01/13/european-union-phil-hogan-trump-097392

Raunio, E. (2020, October 1). *The future of the data economy at stake—Lessons from telecom and financial markets*. Sitra publication. https://www.sitra.fi/en/publications/the-future-of-the-european-data-economy-at-stake/

Rudd, K. (2024). *The avoidable war—The dangers of a catastrophic conflict between the US and xi Jinping's China*. Public Affairs.

Sanger, D. E. (2024). *New cold wars: China's rise, Russia's invasion, and America's struggle to defend the west*. Crown.

Savage, C. (2013, August 8). *N.S.A. said to search content of messages to and from U.S.* https://www.nytimes.com/2013/08/08/us/broader-sifting-of-data-abroad-is-seen-by-nsa.html

Schaefer, B. D., & Pletka, D. (2022). *Countering China's growing influence at the international telecommunication Union*. https://www.aei.org/wp-content/uploads/2022/03/Pletka-ITU-edited.pdf?x85095.

Senate Committee on Homeland Security & Government Affairs. (2022, November). *The rising threat of domestic terrorism—A review of the Federal Response to domestic terrorism and the spread of extremist content on social media*. https://www.hsgac.senate.gov/wp-content/uploads/imo/media/doc/221116_HSGACMajorityReport_DomesticTerrorism&SocialMedia.pdf.

Seong, J., Bradley, C., Leung, N., Woetzel, L., Ellingrud, K., Kumra, G., & Wang, P. (2023, September 22). *Asia on the cusp of a new era*. McKinsey Global Institute. https://www.mckinsey.com/mgi/our-research/asia-on-the-cusp-of-a-new-era

Shivakumar, S., & Wessne, C. (2022, June 8). *Semiconductors and National Defense: What Are the Stakes? Center for Strategic and International Studies*. https://www.csis.org/analysis/semiconductors-and-national-defense-what-are-stakes

Siripurapu, A. (2020, December 2). *Trump and section 230: What to know*. Council on Foreign Relations. https://www.cfr.org/in-brief/trump-and-section-230-what-know

Spiegel. (2013, December 29). *Catalog advertises NSA toolbox*. https://www.spiegel.de/international/world/catalog-reveals-nsa-has-back-doors-for-numerous-devices-a-940994.html.

Spotify. (2024, January 24). *The DMA means a better Spotify for artists, creators, and you*. https://newsroom.spotify.com/2024-01-24/the-dma-means-a-better-spotify-for-artists-creators-and-you/

Statista. (2024, November 21). *Volume of data/information created, captured, copied, and consumed worldwide from 2010 to 2023, with forecasts from 2024 to 2028*. https://www.statista.com/statistics/871513/worldwide-data-created/.

Stengg, W. (2024). *Digital policy in the EU—Towards a human-Centred digital transformation*. Edward Elgar Publishing.

Stokes, B. (2024, February). *EU-US relations after the inflation reduction act and the challenges ahead*. European Parliamentary Research Service. https://www.europarl.europa.eu/thinktank/en/document/EPRS_STU(2024)759588

The New York Times. (2013, September 5). *N.S.A. able to foil basic safeguards of privacy on web*. https://www.nytimes.com/2013/09/06/us/nsa-foils-much-internet-encryption.html.

The Office of the Data Protection Ombudsman of Finland. (2023, July 11). *Tiedonsiirto Yhdysvaltoihin helpottuu—Euroopan komissio hyväksyi päätöksen Yhdysvaltojen tietosuojan riittävästä tasosta*. https://tietosuoja.fi/-/tiedonsiirto-yhdysvaltoihin-helpottuu-euroopan-komissio-hyvaksyi-paatoksen-yhdysvaltojen-tietosuojan-riittavasta-tasosta

The Washington Post. (2013, December 31). *Here's what we learned about NSA's spying programs in 2013*. http://www.washingtonpost.com/blogs/the-switch/wp/2013/12/31/heres-what-we-learned-about-the-nsas-spying-programs-in-2013/.

The White House. (2022, October 7). *Executive order on enhancing safeguards for United States signals intelligence activities*. https://www.whitehouse.gov/briefing-room/presidential-actions/2022/10/07/executive-order-on-enhancing-safeguards-for-united-states-signals-intelligence-activities/

The White House. (2023, February 7). *Script and video of president Biden's state of the Union address*. https://www.whitehouse.gov/state-of-the-union-2023/.

The White House. (2025). America first trade policy. *The White House*, January 20. https://www.whitehouse.gov/presidential-actions/2025/01/america-first-trade-policy/?utm_source=chatgpt.com

Timmers, P. (2023). Strategic autonomy for Europe: Strength at home and strong in the world. *Illusion or Realism. Digital Ethics Yearbook*, 105–115.

U.S. Chamber of Commerce. (2021, September 21). *Transatlantic data flows: Moving data with confidence*. https://www.uschamber.com/technology/data-privacy/transatlantic-dataflows

U.S. Department of State. (1997, May 6). *New transatlantic agenda conference—bridging the Atlantic: People-to-people links*. https://1997-2001.state.gov/regions/eur/eu/ntaconfdoc.html

U.S. Department of State. (1998, May 26). *U.S.-EU relations. A fact sheet released by the bureau of European and Canadian affairs*. https://1997-2001.state.gov/regions/eur/eu/fs_980526_useu.html

U.S. Department of State. (2024). *Transatlantic economic council*. https://www.state.gov/transatlantic-economic-council/

U.S. Government. (2022). *Inflation reduction act (IRA)*. https://www.energy.gov/lpo/inflation-reduction-act-2022

U.S. Government. (2022a). *Infrastructure investment and jobs act*. https://www.congress.gov/bill/117th-congress/house-bill/3684

U.S. Government. (2022b). *CHIPS and science act*. https://www.congress.gov/bill/117th-congress/house-bill/4346

US District of Columbia. v. Google LLC, Case No. 20-cv-3010 (APM) (August 14, 2024).

US House of Representatives. (2020). *Jerrold Nadler, chairman, committee on the Judiciary & David N. Ciciline, chairman, subcommittee on antitrust, commercial and administrative law*. https://democrats-judiciary.house.gov/uploadedfiles/competition_in_digital_markets.pdf

Vance, J. (2024, February 18). *Transcript: Senator Vance delivers a 'wake-up call' to Munich security conference*. https://www.vance.senate.gov/press-releases/senator-vance-delivers-a-wake-up-call-to-munich-security-conference/

Welfens, P. J., & Hanrahan, D. (2022, May 18). *The EU-US trade and technology council: Developments, key issues, and policy options*. European Economy and International Economic Relations, Discussion Paper. https://www.researchgate.net/publication/360784821_The_EU-US_Trade_and_Technology_Council_Developments_Key_Issues_and_Policy_Options

Wu, T. (2010). Is internet exceptionalism dead? In B. Szoka & A. Marcus (Eds.), *The next digital decade—Essays on the future of the internet* (p. 179). TechFreedom.

Zhao, M., Zhao, W., Ding, Y., Jinghua, L., Ho, W., & Wang, J. A. (2022, February 17). *China: Between domestic priorities and global rulemaking. Rewiring Globalization, Carnegie Europe*. https://carnegieeurope.eu/2022/02/17/china-between-domestic-priorities-and-global-rulemaking-pub-86377

Zhu, J. (2014, February 14). The personal information protection law: China's version of the GDPR? *Columbia Journal of Transnational Law*. https://www.jtl.columbia.edu/bulletin-blog/the-personal-information-protection-law-chinas-version-of-the-gdpr

CHAPTER 18

EU'S Engagement with the Indo-Pacific: Trade and Technology Council with India and Digital Partnership Agreements with Japan, Republic of Korea and Singapore

Raquel Jorge Ricart

An Assessment of the Evolution of the European Union's Engagement with the Indo-Pacific Region on Digital Policy

The Geostrategic Importance of the Indo-Pacific: Security and Economy

The Indo-Pacific region covers 60 per cent of the world's population (UNFPA, 2024)—approximately 4.3 billion people, and includes the world's most populous countries, namely China and India. It also encompasses over 40% of global GDP (World Bank, 2023). In turn, it also includes three global powers—China, Japan and India—the countries

R. J. Ricart (✉)
Associate Research Fellow, Center for European Policy Studies (CEPS) think tank, Brussels, Belgium
e-mail: raqueljorgericart@gmail.com

T. Kleiner and A. Garcia Rodriguez (eds.), *The Making of a Global Digital Rulebook*, https://doi.org/10.1007/978-981-95-9226-5_18

with some of the most important, intensive high-technology economies—Japan and Republic of Korea—financial hubs—Tokyo, Hong Kong and Singapore—and critical geopolitical areas, including the maritime tensions on the South China Sea, the long-lasting tension between India and Pakistan over the Kashmir region, the Korean peninsula and the debates over the recognition of Taiwan either as an independent country or as part of China (University of Cambridge, 2024).

The return to great power competition in international relations has turned the Indo-Pacific region into a key theatre of engagement and increasing role in global politics, security and economic policymaking. According to some experts (Wilkins, 2019), there are three main alignment blocs in the region: countries that join the US-led alliance networks, the members of the Shanghai Cooperation Organization strategic partnership network and the ASEAN security community.

However, this situation has evolved and currently, there is a robust, large structure of alliances, dialogues and partnerships that serve to influence and structure strategic interactions across the region. Some countries follow a "continuity approach" (Scott, 2021) in the way they relate to their Indo-Pacific neighbours within the region (e.g. Japan, the Republic of Korea and Singapore often establish partnerships among them in similar terms, values and policies, priorities and decision-making processes). Other countries set out various layers of partnerships with different countries. This is the case of India, which is part of the BRICS group jointly with China, Brazil, Russia and South Africa, and is also part of the Quadrilateral Security Dialogue (called "Quad") jointly with Australia, Japan and the United States.

The Indo-Pacific region comprises around 40 economies, although there is no definite number of countries, as there are other subregions in Asia. It encompasses countries ranging from low-income households to high-technology economies, and countries with solid rule of law standards and non-democratic institutions. Beyond this case-by-case analysis, this chapter aims to reinforce the idea that the Indo-Pacific is a geostrategic region in economic and security terms—and increasingly through the lens of "economic security", as stated by the European Union (European Commission, 2023).

This geoeconomic and security importance may be showcased by the fact that some Indo-Pacific countries have released their own internal strategies on the region. This is the case of the Republic of Korea's Strategy for a Free, Peaceful and Prosperous Indo-Pacific Region

(Government of the Republic of Korea, 2022), whose principles are made on the basis of inclusiveness, trust and reciprocity. Their core lines of effort include the building-up of a regional order based on norms and rules, the cooperation to promote the rule of law and human rights, the strengthening of non-proliferation and counter-terrorism efforts across the region, the expansion of comprehensive security cooperation, the establishment of economic security networks, the engagement in "contributive diplomacy" through tailored development cooperation partnerships and the nurturing of certain areas such as cooperation in critical domains of science and technology. Japan has also released its own strategy for a Free and Open Indo-Pacific (Government of Japan, 2024), which acknowledges the importance of shifting the global power balance towards the region while ensuring that this concept is open, inclusive, respects the rule of law, human rights, democratic values and an open, fair global economy.

On the other hand, other countries address the Indo-Pacific region as a strategic area of interest, and at the same time as a competition region vis-à-vis third countries, such as China with the United States. Over time, there has been an increasing awareness of the US-China competition in the Indo-Pacific region. This competition may be seen as a tangible outcome in several ways. As for the influence, the ability of one actor to shape another actor's actions is relative and depends on a partner's shared interests with the United States (versus China) and what the United States can offer the partner (with regard to China). In the Indo-Pacific, in 2020 it was acknowledged by RAND Corporation (Lin et al., 2020) that China had more economic influence and the United States had more diplomatic and military sway, even if partners generally valued economic development over security concerns. Also, areas of influence were country focused.

Further analysis has been developed on the specific impact of their influence. However, there are three main elements where the competition over the region has been put on the spotlight: military presence in key maritime areas such as the South China Sea and military preparedness over potential emergencies or crises; the increasing ownership of technology design, development, deployment and use (where China, India and Japan have leaderships depending on the technology); and the economic relationships through infrastructure, where China is increasingly gaining terrain through its investments, and other actors such as the United States and the European Union are also increasingly cooperating with partners with level-playing field in the region.

The Increasing Policy Approach to the Indo-Pacific Region as a Whole

The first time the European Union acknowledged the Indo-Pacific as a top-priority region was in 2021. The Joint Communication "The EU Strategy for Cooperation in the Indo-Pacific", launched in September 2021 by the High Representative and the European Commission, and tasked by the Council of the European Union's Conclusions from April 2021, points out that the EU and the Indo-Pacific are "natural partner regions". The EU intended to increase its engagement with the region in a principled and long-term manner.

Until then, the EU's engagement with the region had been limited in two ways: geographic scope and the coordination with many particular EU Member States that set out their own bilateral relationships with the region.

First, references to "Indo-Pacific" had been largely missing. The Joint EU-Japan Statement on Sustainable Connectivity and Quality Infrastructure Partnership from September 2019 is the first official EU document (Cunningham, 2021) where the term "Indo-Pacific" is showcased. The EU's engagement had been so far structured through a number of instruments: bilateral Partnership and Cooperation Agreements (PCAs) with some countries, including Malaysia and Thailand, and Partnership Agreements with African, Caribbean, and Pacific (ACP) countries; political dialogues with Pacific island States; and ASEAN, with whom the EU has developed a multifaceted strategic partnership over more than 40 years in political, security, economic, environmental, climate, sociocultural and connectivity issues. Except for ASEAN, the relationship was mostly bilateral with no references to the region as a whole.

Second, France, Germany and the Netherlands had already set out their own approaches to the Indo-Pacific as a region before the EU. Through the Ministry of Defence, France was the first EU Member State to release a policy paper on Indo-Pacific security in 2018, which was translated into a 2019 Strategy led by the Ministry of Foreign Affairs (MFA). Germany's Ministry of Foreign Affairs followed this pathway in September 2020, which launched Policy Guidelines for the Indo-Pacific region. The Netherlands' MFA published similar Guidelines for strengthening Dutch and EU cooperation with partners in Asia in November 2020.

These three countries published a confidential EU non-paper calling for EU's engagement with the Indo-Pacific in October 2020, which was co-sponsored by seven other Member States. This document pushed the debate to the EU level, and the EU Council started discussions in December 2020, which led to the conclusions from April 2021, a few months later, which called for a unified EU strategy in the Indo-Pacific.

The growth of national strategies on the Indo-Pacific by other countries (Japan in 2007, Australia in 2013, the United States in 2017, ASEAN's Outlook on the Indo-Pacific in 2019, New Zealand and India in the same year, and the United Kingdom in 2020) did not get pressure on the EU. The intensification of the United States-China competition, which was showcased in the US Indo-Pacific Strategy during the President Trump's administration, slowed down the decision-making process over the principles, priorities and measures vis-à-vis the Indo-Pacific region, as well as the direct and indirect effects in the relationship with China. The EU had developed a robust multifaceted policy towards China in 2019 with its Joint Communication "EU-China: A Strategic Outlook", by which it defines China as a cooperative partner, negotiating partner, economic competitor and systemic rival.

At the time the EU Council started discussions in December 2020, Joe Biden had been elected President of the United States one month before. The European Commission and High Representative unveiled "The New EU-US Agenda for Global Change" (European Commission, 2020) in December 2020, which called for an increased focus on the Indo-Pacific to help deepen cooperation with like-minded partners in the region.

The combination of these internal and external factors led to the launch of the EU Strategy for Cooperation in the Indo-Pacific in September 2021. It identified seven priority areas: sustainable and inclusive prosperity, green transition, ocean governance, digital governance and partnerships, connectivity, security and defence, and human security. This allowed the EU to come up with a broadened approach to the Indo-Pacific after the EU's Trade Policy Review (COM(2021) 66 final) from February 2021 located Asia-Pacific as the second to last priority area, behind the EU's neighbourhood and Africa—which were flagged as geographic priorities—and the need to improve transatlantic and EU-China relations, and only ahead of South America.

As a conclusion, it remains open the debate on the extent of influence by the EU or its Member States to exert influence in the development of the first-ever strategy for the region, or to limit the development thereof. As it occurs in other policy areas, there are three main avenues. First, the

European Union institutions form a European policy towards the Indo-Pacific, and its Member States support it. Second, national perspectives limit the EU's ability to steer influence in the development of an EU-wide strategy. Third, the EU institutions develop its own approach, tools, funding, capacity-building actions, structures and governance towards the region, and at the same time some Member States follow up with their own national engagement in the region or with selected Indo-Pacific countries.

While this article cannot conclude any specific approach, evidence proves that a few Member States, which were first developing their own national strategies, pushed the European Union institutions to follow a "communitarisation" process to convert the strategic interest in the Indo-Pacific into an EU-wide strategy. This shift from a few Member States towards the European Union triggered the expansion of nationally led strategies on the Indo-Pacific across many other Member States that had never had an approach to the region until then. This example showcases the mixture between intergovernmental and Community methods between Member States and the EU, where the impetus of three countries encouraged the development of an EU policy which, in turn, encouraged other countries in the Union to follow the same path. This also aligns with the "cascade effect" of norms by scholars Martha Finnemore and Kathryn Sikkink (Finnemore & Sikkink, 1998).

The Increasing Policy Importance of Digital Policy with the Indo-Pacific Region: From Connectivity Partnerships, through the Overall EU Strategy, Towards an International Agenda on Digital Policy and Institutionalised Diplomacy

The increasing approach to the Indo-Pacific region did not go in parallel with the maturity of the EU's international agenda on digital policy within the region. The EU had already set out specific areas of collaboration on digital policy in previous years. However, it is important to note that these lines of work were part of larger "connectivity partnerships or strategies". No digital-specific strategies were launched at that time. The reference to partnerships was made at a time when Free Trade Agreements negotiations worldwide were taking longer than expected due to the blockade of the full negotiation due to a particular disagreement on certain area. The use of partnerships has been identified as a faster method to kick-start policy dialogues on selected topics.

In September 2018, the European Commission and the High Representative launched the Joint Communication for a strategy on connecting Europe and Asia. The so-called Connectivity Strategy (JOINT(2018) 31 final) did not focus on digitalisation but located digital connectivity as its second line of action, only after transport and ahead of energy and people-to-people connectivity. Concretely, it alluded to high-capacity network links; universal and affordable access to the Internet; peaceful, secure and open ICT environment; addressing cybersecurity threats; online protection of human rights and freedoms; personal data protection; coherence of regulatory approaches; digital infrastructure investments; and the Digital4Development strategy (European Commission, 2017).

This strategy was materialised for the first time on a bilateral basis with the EU-Japan Partnership on Sustainable Connectivity and Quality Infrastructure (European Commission & Government of Japan, 2019) from September 2019, the EU's first partnership with a non-EU country. It includes the first mention of the Indo-Pacific in an official EU document. Digital connectivity is acknowledged as an enabler of inclusive growth and sustainable development, including through digital and data infrastructure, and policy and regulatory frameworks. Both partners emphasised the need to operationalise the concept of data free flows with trust, or DFFT, as proposed by Japan's Presidency of the G20 in 2019, including the enhancement of trust for data security and privacy. Also, the partnership shows the intention to collaborate on the promotion of international policy discussions on electronic commerce at the WTO, and the need to continue promoting policies in Artificial Intelligence, cloud, quantum computing and blockchain.

The second connectivity agreement was forged with the ASEAN in December 2020. Practical deliverables included the joint importance of due recognition of data protection and cybersecurity, the facilitation of digital economy under the EU-ASEAN Dialogue on ASEAN Digital Index (ADIX) as a policy tool to measure the progress and impacts of digitalisation, the encouragement to implement an EU-ASEAN Statement on Cybersecurity Cooperation, the exploration of opportunities offered by the EU's global satellite navigation system, Galileo, and the EU's Earth Observation Programme, Copernicus and potential cooperation on smart cities.

This was not the first time the EU launched connectivity discussions with countries in the South and East Asian region. The Asia-Europe Meeting (ASEM), an informal platform for dialogue between 30 European and 21 Asian countries, already established the ASEM Pathfinders Group on Connectivity (APGC) in 2016, identified five areas of cooperation in connectivity, including digital in 2018, but no specific results have been outlined so far.

The engagements with ASEAN and Japan were tangible outcomes from the EU's Connectivity Strategy since 2018. However, with the launch of the EU's Strategy for Cooperation in the Indo-Pacific in 2021, the digital area moved from "connectivity partnerships and digital policy" towards "digital governance and partnerships" in the EU's Strategy for Cooperation in the Indo-Pacific, which is in many respects the externalisation of internal EU policies.

Concretely, the strategy locates digital governance and partnerships as the fourth area out of seven priority topics. In particular, the EU aims to enhance its international digital partnerships in the Indo-Pacific region and set up new ones, in line with the Communication 2030 Digital Compass that foresees the 2020 digital decade needs to be pronged into four areas—businesses, skills and people, infrastructure and public services. Also, these digital partnerships were aimed to be underpinned by a toolbox, drawing on regulatory cooperation, capacity building and skills, and investment in international cooperation and research partnerships.

The digital governance and partnerships area is structured in three tracks: digital policy, research and innovation, and education. As for digital policy, several main instruments were proposed are as follows. First, the formalisation of Digital Partnership Agreements (DPAs) with the most advanced cases, to be negotiated with like-minded partners. At an initial stage, the EU proposed to explore the launch of negotiations with Japan, Republic of Korea (ROK) and Singapore. Second, a digital partnership between the EU and India, which was strengthened in May 2021. At the time of this strategy, the EU did not foresee the EU-India Trade and Technology Council (TTC) which has been ongoing since 2022 and follows a similar pattern as the EU-United States TTC. Third, the EU aimed to support the ASEAN Digital Masterplan 2025. Fourth, the EU aimed to continue its engagement in the region to promote convergence between data protection regimes both within and outside the region through "data adequacy decisions".

In the area of research and innovation, the EU's Global Approach to Research and Innovation is the key axis to promote greater levels of reciprocity and level-playing field in academic freedom, research, open science and evidence-based policymaking. The EU aims to strengthen ties with like-minded Indo-Pacific countries under Horizon Europe, whose informal discussions started with Australia, Japan, ROK, New Zealand and Singapore at that time. Also, it aimed to promote cooperation in human capital development, mobility of researchers and scientific cooperation. In the area of education, the EU intended to increase investments in education to at least 10% of the Neighbourhood, Development and International Cooperation Instrument (NDICI)–Global Europe, and to increase Erasmus+ programmes and academic exchanges between students and teachers from both regions.

The multiplicity of initiatives, exploration of partnership agreements and promotion of tangible measures shows that this broadened strategy *in* the Indo-Pacific region has been translated into *deepened, institutionalised, bilateral agreements*. This means that the bilateral approach is still ongoing, but it has been institutionalised through structured, permanent dialogue settings, and with a clear distribution of specific mandates across the Directorate-Generals, actors and agencies of the European Union institutions.

Some exceptions to this bilateral approach, with the goal to "multilateralise" the EU's engagement within the region, are the Joint Declaration by the European Union, Australia, Comoros, India, Japan, Mauritius, New Zealand, the Republic of Korea, Singapore and Sri Lanka on privacy and the protection of personal data (European External Action Service, 2022), which was endorsed at the Ministerial Forum for Cooperation in the Indo-Pacific in Paris in February 2022, and expresses a common vision of a human-centric approach to the digital transformation, where the effective protection of personal data plays a crucial role, and underlines the importance of data free flow with trust as key to harnessing the opportunities of the digital economy.

Also, closer EU's engagement with ASEAN is another example of an attempt to multilateralise this relationship. The ASEAN Digital Ministers Meeting (ADGMIN) was held for the first time in January 2021 and offers a platform for cooperation. Their policy areas are most focused on e-commerce and data management, fintech, online platforms governance and digital development assistance.

If the EU's Strategy for Cooperation in the Indo-Pacific from 2021 was the definite push to institutionalise the regional engagement, including digital policy among others, the institutionalisation of the digital policy engagement as such was triggered in July 2022 with the Council of the European Union's Conclusions on a more concerted approach towards EU's digital diplomacy (European Council, 2022). The institutionalisation of digital diplomacy as a core component and an integral part of the EU external action, closely coordinated with other EU external policies, stressed the importance of counting on an international agenda on digital policy. These conclusions were fast-tracked (European Council, 2023) in June 2023, with new conclusions from the EU Council that called for priority actions to be set out for stronger EU action in global digital affairs. In particular, the 2023 conclusions stressed the need to bring digital diplomacy to the next level by engaging strategically in all the relevant multilateral fora, by incorporating digital diplomacy in the Global Gateway and by strengthening the EU's position as a shaper of the global digital rulebook through enhanced bilateral and regional digital partnerships and alliances.

Institutionalising the EU'S International Agenda on Digital Policy with the Indo-Pacific Region

The highest level of institutionalisation has taken place with the Digital Partnership Agreements (DPAs) with Japan, the Republic of Korea and Singapore, and the EU-India Trade and Technology Council (TTC) until 2024. This chapter assesses these two instruments' governance approaches and the particularities each partnership provides for the EU's engagement in the region.

Digital Partnership Agreements (DPAs)

Digital Partnership Agreements (DPAs) are the first type of instrument that the EU's Strategy for Cooperation in the Indo-Pacific sets out in the digital policy pillar. All currently existing DPAs are foreseen as a flexible cooperation instrument that goes beyond dialogue and information-sharing between the EU and the corresponding country. It aims to deliver concrete, tangible outcomes in line with the EU's Digital Compass, Digital Diplomacy and each country's initiatives.

The governance structure of all DPAs is similar. These partnerships aim to build concrete policy deliverables based on existing cooperation mechanisms. This means that the partnership does not intend to create any new structures, rights or obligations under international or domestic low, or any financial implications on either side. To give a practical case, the DPA with Japan is expected to prepare deliverables building on existing cooperation mechanisms such as the annual bilateral Digital Policy Dialogue, Industrial Dialogue, the EU-Japan Centre for Industrial Cooperation, the EU-Japan Business Round Table, the Cybersecurity Dialogue, the Economic Partnership Agreement Committees and dedicated expert workshops. Also, the DPA with the Republic of Korea aligns this partnership through the bilateral High-Level Policy Dialogue on the Digital Economy, the Free Trade Agreement (FTA) Committees, the ROK-EU Joint Committee, the Joint Committee on Scientific and Technological Cooperation established under the Science and Technology Agreement, and dedicated expert workshops.

While it aims to leverage existing cooperation activities, not to replace them, and should not result in additional bureaucratic burdens or high coordination costs, each DPA does count on a Secretariat, which is responsible for coordinating activities on respective sides, involving all relevant services. The DPA intends to provide both sides with an overarching framework for bilateral cooperation in the digital field. For this to happen, priorities are to be defined and communicated through the Digital Partnership Council, which should be provided with progress reports by the Secretariat to take stock of the progress achieved and provide strategic guidance on the priorities and next steps.

Jointly with these similarities, the DPAs may differ at three levels: EU Member States' engagement, the depth of cooperation in other parallel structures and the prioritisation of digital policy topics.

First, an important element of the DPAs governance is the complementarity between actions at the EU and Member States' levels. The DPA's Joint Statements require endorsement by Member States through the so-called Non-Binding Instrument, through the COREPER, which is responsible for this endorsement process. However, this remains a challenge, considering the different prioritisation and mapping of opportunities and threats that the Indo-Pacific region and the differentiated level of engagement with specific countries pose. Despite these differences among Member States, the fact that Member States have endorsed the

DPA's Joint Statements through COREPER confirms the institutionalisation argument of this chapter, and the idea that there is a mixture of intergovernmental process—three Member States being France, Germany and the Netherlands encouraging the EU to develop a Strategy for the Indo-Pacific—and of Community methods—the EU leading DPA's Joint Statements, while it requires the Member States' endorsement.

Second, the existence of DPAs does not mean that the previous relationship with those respective countries has been strong for a long time. The EU has developed DPAs with Japan, the Republic of Korea and Singapore. However, the EU has Free Trade Agreements (FTAs) with ROK and Singapore, but neither with India (negotiations stage in 2024) nor Japan (with whom the EU relies on the Economic Partnership Agreement and the Strategic Partnership Agreement). The EU also has an FTA in place with New Zealand, but no proposal for a DPA has been made. Also, the EU is negotiating by 2024 a FTA with Indonesia and the Philippines. At the same time, the EU has Science and Technology Agreements (European Commission, 2024b) with India, Japan and ROK, but not with Singapore. A third instrument is the data adequacy decision (European Commission, 2024c) that helps the EU identify whether a non-EU country meets the conditions for personal data to flow from the EU (and Norway, Liechtenstein and Iceland) to that third country without any further safeguard being necessary. In the Indo-Pacific, only Japan, New Zealand and ROK dispose of it.

Third, the DPAs may differ in the priority-setting agenda of topics, calendars, expected deliverables and the stage of technological maturity of these policy developments. As reflected below, some countries with DPAs already had a close engagement on digital policy with the EU before the establishment of this partnership, while others did not.

EU-Japan Digital Partnership Agreement: From Data Free Flows with Trust to an Overarching Digital-Focused Partnership

The EU-Japan relationship in technology dates back to 2009, when both sides signed the Science and Technology Cooperation Agreement, which entered into force in 2011. It matured from the first meeting where both recognised the importance of resolute political will and frequent policy consultations to intensify the cooperation, to the second meeting, which identified key areas of mutual interest—critical raw materials, aeronautics and ICTs—until the third meeting in 2015 which included seven launched coordinated calls, out of which two were on ICTs.

This mechanism was followed by the "Joint Vision" towards a closer relationship in research and innovation, and the new Strategic Partnership in Research and Innovation between the European Commission and the Government of Japan in 2015. This Strategic Partnership in R&I articulated five priority areas: frequent consultation at multiple levels, focusing on thematic cooperation in strategic areas, frameworks that facilitate collaboration, science, technology and innovation (STI) policy exchange, and support activities and public engagement.

However, the overall bilateral partnership was eventually channelled through the Japan-EU Strategic Partnership Agreement (SPA) and the Japan-EU Economic Partnership Agreement (EPA). It was not centred on technology or digital policy, but it was created as the overarching framework for high-level political engagement between both partners with a selected number of identified priority sectors, including digital.

Although digital policy took part in previous discussions, there was still no specific instrument to funnel these policy discussions into tangible outcomes with a centrality of digital policy. The Japanese Presidency of the G20 in 2019 and the Data Free Flows with Trust (DFFT) pitch was one example of closer engagement with the EU.

However, the institutionalisation occurred in May 2022, with the launch of the first-ever Digital Partnership Agreement between the EU and a third country. Acknowledging that both sides are "like-minded partners", the DPA is considered a top-priority instrument that complements the Strategic Partnership Agreement and the Economic Partnership Agreement.

The main goals of the DPA are various: collaborate on the development of tech, specifically in research and innovation; establish mechanisms for collaboration in international groups and organisations; shape digital trade principles and promote regulatory cooperation on key technology enablers for digital trade; implement concrete pilot projects in cutting-edge areas such as Artificial Intelligence and digital identity to drive technology development and standardisation; pursue a common approach to the digital transformation based on democratic principles including defending the open Internet and developing Digital Principles; and share views and best practices, promote regulatory cooperation and develop common principles for rules and standards where appropriate.

Until 2024, the EU-Japan Digital Partnership Council has met twice, in July 2023 and April 2024. Outstanding results from the first meeting were the need to deliver results in the strategic areas of semiconductors, High Performance Computing (HPC) and Quantum technology, 5G/Beyond 5G, Data Free Flow with Trust (DFFT), digital trade principles and resilient digital connectivity, and the need for a constructive dialogue in the areas of platform regulation, data governance and cybersecurity. Specific deliverables included the signature of a Memorandum of Cooperation[1] establishing in-depth cooperation on semiconductor; a Memorandum of Cooperation[2] on submarine cables for secure, resilient and sustainable global connectivity; the launch of a call for proposals for the EuroHPC Joint Undertaking; the exploration of concrete actions for quantum computing infrastructure; and the need to complete the negotiations on a cross-border data flows whose protocol[3] was ultimately signed in 2024. The second meeting, in April 2024, highlighted the negotiations to expand the scope for data adequacy decision to academia and the public sector; the preparation of an Administrative Arrangement on a Public Support Transparency Mechanism in the semiconductor sector, and three main deliverables: a Memorandum of Cooperation on Digital Identities and Trust services, continued collaboration on Common European data spaces and Japan data spaces (including DATA-EX and Ouranos

[1] The MoC includes an early warning mechanism for the semiconductor supply chain; research and development for semiconductors; advanced skills for the semiconductor industry; use cases of semiconductor applications; and subsidy transparency. On the EU side, all collaborative research actions will be funded by the EU's Research & Innovation programme Horizon Europe including the actions launched through the Chips Joint Undertaking.

[2] This Memorandum of Cooperation includes shared recognition of mutual advantages by reducing the latency of communication, increasing redundancies of routes and secure connectivity through cooperation in international submarine cables, as well as the relevance of the routes connecting Japan and the EU via the Arctic. To realise these advantages, this Memorandum of Cooperation expresses a shared intention to explore and facilitate joint and respective support actions, as appropriate, on trans-oceanic submarine cables, such as awareness raising, financial support, demand aggregation and, as appropriate, facilitating relevant administrative processes.

[3] The protocol aims to provide greater legal certainty, ensuring that data flows between the EU and Japan will not be hampered by unjustified data localisation measures, and also ensuring the benefit from the free flow of data according to the EU and Japan's rules on data protection and the digital economy.

Ecosystem), and an administrative arrangement between the EU AI Office and Japan's AI Safety Institute.

EU-Republic of Korea Digital Partnership Agreement: Emerging Topics in Digital Freedoms, Economic Resilience and a First-Ever Digital Trade Agreement

Unlike Japan, the ROK and the EU have had a longer relationship in science and technology policy, as well as in trade. Both have a Free Trade Agreement since 2011 and ratified it in 2015. It went further than any of the EU's previous agreements in lifting trade barriers and was also the EU's first trade deal with an Asian country.

As for technology, in 2006 ROK and the European Union signed the first-ever Agreement on Scientific and Technology Cooperation, which evolved and delved into an ICT-focused approach already in 2014 with the Joint Declaration on Strategic Cooperation in Information Communications Technology and 5G.

The DPA with the Republic of Korea was the second partnership to be set, a few months after the DPA with Japan. In November 2022, the DPA was released as the flexible cooperation instrument for both "trusted and technologically advanced partners". This reference differs from Japan's DPA, which pinpoints "like-minded partners".

The overall political vision of the EU-ROK Digital Partnership Agreement has a greater scope than that of other countries. While the trade and economic dimension is evident (HPC, quantum, cybersecurity, 5G and 6G, digital infrastructure and digital capacity building, AI, digital platform economy, data laws, digital trade, SMEs and start-ups), the joint launch statement explicitly includes two additional elements: digital freedoms and economic security.

The DPA with also acknowledges the importance of "trust" in Data Free Flows with Trust and broadens this approach by referring to the need to operate a consultation mechanism between ROK and the EU to discuss ways to strengthen digital solidarity for the freedom of digital citizens. For instance, the launch statement warns about protecting vulnerable groups and persons with disabilities from digital threats. Also, both sides reinforce the need for mutual economic resilience at bilateral and multilateral levels.

Moreover, the Digital Partnership Council has met twice in June 2023 and March 2024. The first meeting established the ROK-EU Forum for Semiconductor Researchers,[4] created a Quantum Experts Working Group, explored mechanisms to facilitate and enable researchers' access to respective HPC infrastructure and to jointly develop applications, launched a call for proposals on research topics in the fields of Radio Access Networks (RAN) and 6G technology, and exchanged information on platforms governance[5] and on foundational models and generative AI. The second meeting has broadened the scope and aims to expand bilateral cooperation in new areas such as secure digital connectivity infrastructure links, including submarine cables, digital skills and capacity building, and exchange of best practices on digital start-ups.

Similarly, ROK's formalised access to Horizon Europe has been approved to participate in Pillar II, which is the largest collaborative part of the programme and is primarily focused on shared global challenges: climate, energy, digital economy and health.

Beyond these deliverables, another emerging topic where ROK is again a groundbreaking country in the EU's engagement with an Asian country is the negotiations for a Digital Trade Agreement between both sides. The negotiations, launched in October 2023, would represent the first-ever discussion to have a digital trade-focused agreement focused on playing a leading role in setting digital trade rules, countering digital protectionism, complementing the existing preferential trade framework with ROK, and provide consumer trust, predictability and legal certainty vis-à-vis the emergence of unjustified barriers to digital trade.

EU-Singapore Digital Partnership Agreement: Further Indirect Engagement with ASEAN

As with ROK, the EU also has a Free Trade Agreement with Singapore and the EU-Singapore Investment Protection Agreement, which serve as strategic pathfinders towards closer region-to-region connectivity between the EU and ASEAN. Also, similarly to ROK, the EU is negotiating a Digital Trade Agreement since July 2023.

[4] The ROK-EU Forum for Semiconductor Researchers intends to promote research in complementary areas. Research collaboration may be explored under the Chips Joint Undertaking on the EU side, and next-generation semiconductor R&D project on the Korean side.

[5] EU platform legislation (Digital Services Act and Digital Markets Act) on the EU side and the recently adopted "Self-Regulation for Platforms" on the Korean side.

The case of Singapore is particular due to its strong linkage to digital diplomacy. Although it is the first DPA to be launched—in February 2023—it is the first DPA which mentions the EU Council Conclusions on Digital Diplomacy. The EU-Singapore DPA aims to connect relevant internal and external digital initiatives in their cooperation as like-minded partners. Also, Singapore is establishing its own Digital Economy Agreements with third partners. Moreover, the Singapore-EU engagement results in further strengthening of ASEAN. This supports the EU-ASEAN Joint Ministerial Statement on Connectivity from December 2020, and the ASEAN Digital Masterplan to establish a frictionless ASEAN digital market.

However, unlike ROK but closer to Japan, the DPA with Singapore is a purely economic agreement, even technical. No references are made to digital rights or economic security. The main topics are digital trade, digital connectivity including data centres and submarine telecommunications cables, 5G and 6G, DFFTs, cybersecurity, semiconductor supply chain, online platforms, digitalisation in financial sector, trust services, SMEs digital transformation, digital skills, and standards, technical regulations and conformity assessment procedures (STRACAP).

In summary, while the three DPAs are equally focused on the trade dimension of digital policy, there are four main differences. First, the DPA with ROK is the most comprehensive DPA, which goes beyond the trade dimension and adds concerns on digital freedoms and economic security. Second, the innovative negotiation for a Digital Trade Agreement is taking place in ROK and Singapore, but not in Japan. Third, the maturity of the deliverables differs among the three DPAs, as the outcomes with Japan and ROK tend to be much more technologically advanced than in the case of Singapore. Fourth, the DPA with Singapore can be considered the more "multilateral" partnership, as engaging with Singapore leads to further strengthening of ASEAN-EU relations and accomplishes the EU's digital diplomacy goals in the region.

EU-India Trade and Technology Council (TTC): Beyond Digital Policy. The Nexus between Technology, Security and Trade

Unlike the DPAs, which have been established for the first time with Asian countries, the model of a Trade and Technology Council is not a first-of-its-kind instrument in Asia. The EU precedes another TTC with the United States since June 2021.

The particularity of the EU-India TTC is that it goes beyond the purely digital policy scope of the Digital Partnership Agreements. As a Trade and Technology Council, it focuses on the nexus between trade, security and technology policy, which also plugs into clean and green technologies, biotechnology and other technologies such as energy propulsion and raw materials. The potential interest of the EU in launching a TTC with India—unlike DPAs with Japan, Republic of Korea and Singapore—may be related to the increasing geoeconomic role that India plays in the region and worldwide. As stated in the first sub-section, India is a country that partners up with both China (e.g. BRICS) and the United States (e.g. Quad) indistinctively. The TTC has a greater level of institutionalisation and governance structure than the DPAs, referring to the number of Working Groups and the greater coordination that is required on a frequent basis. This strategic interest in India may explain the difference when approaching India through a TTC platform.

The EU is India's second largest trading partner, accounting for €120 billion worth of trade in goods in 2022 or 10.8% of total Indian trade. India is the EU's tenth largest trading partner, accounting for 2% of EU total trade in goods in the same year. However, they do not have a Free Trade Agreement, which is being negotiated by June 2024.

The Trade and Technology Council was announced (European Parliament Research Service, 2024) in April 2022, as a "strategic coordination mechanism will allow both partners to tackle challenges at the nexus of trade, trusted technology and security". While the DPAs are foreseen as "flexible cooperation instruments", the TTC is conceived as a "strategic coordination mechanism". This difference between cooperating and coordinating explains why the TTC calls for political steer and necessary structure to operationalise political decisions, coordinate technical work and report to the political level to ensure implementation and follow-up in the identified areas.

Until 2024, the EU-India TTC has three working groups. The first working group revolves around strategic technologies, digital governance and digital connectivity, with specific discussions on cooperation in quantum and HPC for climate change, natural disasters, healthcare via personalised medicine; trustworthy AI; a Memorandum of Understanding on semiconductors; digital skills; and the need to promote Digital Public Infrastructures. India is a global leader in the development of DPI, where it has put in place an ecosystem for the implementation and adaptation of three critical aspects of DPI, also known as the "India stack": digital identity, digital payments and data-sharing.

The second working group is about green and clean energy technologies, concretely on wastewater management, recycling of batteries for e-vehicles and standards through pre-normative research, and start-ups. The third working group tackles trade, investment and resilient value chains and addresses market access and FDI screening issues.

Other Engagements in the Indo-Pacific

Jointly with these higher-level institutionalised instruments—the flexible cooperation mechanisms of DPAs and the strategic coordination platform of the TTC—the European Union has also launched some initiatives with concrete countries. With ASEAN, the EU-ASEAN Partnership on Sustainable Connectivity aims to support the ASEAN Digital Masterplan 2025.

A specific instrument is the Digital Economy Package (DEP), which the EU has established with some African countries and also with the Philippines in the Indo-Pacific region. Through this Digital Economy Package, the EU aims to support the Philippines in becoming a digital connectivity hub in the region, expand Copernicus in Southeast Asia and tackle disaster risk management and climate change mitigation. Its duration is already set from 2024 to 2028. The Philippines is the first country in the region to benefit from the Copernicus programme. ASEAN Digital Masterplan 2025: EU-ASEAN partnership on sustainable connectivity in the areas of higher education, civil aviation and intellectual property.

Moreover, the EU is also negotiating specific Free Trade Agreements (FTAs) with some Asian countries, as is the case of Indonesia.

The International Dimension of the EU's Engagement in the Indo-Pacific on Digital Policy

The previous examples have proven to be framed from a bilateral perspective, except for the case of Singapore, which aims to strengthen the EU-ASEAN relationship. However, beyond these cases, an interesting policy angle is how these bilateral relationships are capable of "multilateralism", the agenda-setting and influencing decision-making processes in third spaces.

This chapter proposes three levels for the "internationalisation of the bilateral partnership":

(a) "Joint positioning agendas in international organisations": The bilateral partnership agrees on common policy areas of interest to cooperate, coordinate, align or co-create joint agendas to be moved up to the highest levels of decision-making in international organisations.
(b) "Multilateral technology rapprochement": The bilateral partnership works or coordinates to reach out to several countries within and outside the region to agree on common agendas.
(c) "Technology triangles": The bilateral partnership influences individual third countries within the region.

Joint Positioning Agendas in International Organisations

This is the most present, already existing proposal across the EU's instruments of engagement with Indo-Pacific countries. The EU-India Trade and Technology Council's first working group aims to strengthen coordination within the Global Partnership on Artificial Intelligence (GPAI) at the OECD. The EU-Japan Digital Partnership Agreement aims to do the same in similar organisations, including UNESCO. It also looks forward to improving the functioning of the global digital economy on respective bilateral and multilateral work at the G7, G20, OECD and WTO.

However, it is important to distinguish the scope, impact and effects of these lines of cooperation in international organisations. They may be divided into two types of engagement: alignment of approaches in non-mandatory issues and actual coordination in proposals that may lead to binding technical decisions with grounded impact. The alignment of approaches in non-mandatory decisions usually occurs in policy areas revolving around Artificial Intelligence—GPAI at OECD, UNESCO, UN Technology Envoy's Office—or the support for digital freedoms in the United Nations Global Digital Compact negotiations. The reference to GPAI is made by all country cases that have been addressed. Particularly, the ROK and EU aim to coordinate approaches in GPAI to new member candidates. A second example is the Memorandum of Cooperation on Digital Identities and Trust services between the EU and Japan, which was presented at the OECD as a bilateral best practice to facilitate Data Free Flow with Trust.

The actual coordination in proposals that may lead to internationally binding technical decisions is a sensitive matter that requires further coordination across services and political engagement. This is the case of the negotiations of the WTO negotiations under the framework of the Joint Statement Initiative on electronic commerce, which may result in the setting of new rules governing digital trade. The DPAs with Japan and Singapore explicitly set out this priority of joint cooperation, while the DPA with the Republic of Korea has not mentioned it for the time being. A second case is standard settings in international standardisation bodies, which the DPA with Japan also pinpoints.

Multilateral Technology Rapprochement

The bilateral partnership works or coordinates to reach out to several countries within and outside the region to agree on common agendas. This "multilateral technology rapprochement" serves as a means and goal to build political coalitions and alliances. At the same time, it agrees on common agendas that come up with tangible outcomes at the policymaking level.

The multilateral technology rapprochement may be approached with two lenses: long-lasting multilateral meetings whose structure is sustained and structured and the level of coordination is long-term oriented, and ad hoc coalitions which have been created most recently and whose portfolio is made up of outcomes that are expected to be tangible and operationalised in the short run.

As for the long-lasting multilateral meetings, the G7 and the G20 platforms are acknowledged throughout all EU instruments with Japan, India, Korea and Singapore on digital policy. The EU has cooperated with Japan to operationalise the G7 Roadmap for Cooperation on Data Free Flow with Trust and the Action Plan for Promoting the DFFT framework. Also, the EU has contributed to the G7 discussions on generative AI in the Hiroshima AI process, where both also supported the priority of setting up an institutional arrangement for a Partnership to operationalise Data Free Flow with Trust (DFFT). Also, the EU has supported ROK, India and Japan in the promotion of bilateral best practices enabling the use of digital identity, trusted web and the digital identity wallet.

However, the policy focus differs depending on the Indo-Pacific country. While with Japan, the "multilateral technology rapprochement" with third countries is carried out on AI and Data Free Flows with Trust, the expected snowball effect of the engagement with India in third partners is made with Digital Public Infrastructure (DPI). Under the Indian presidency of the G20, the 2023 G20 Leaders' Declaration welcomed the "G20 Framework for Systems of Digital Public Infrastructure", recognising the role of DPI in the delivery of services for the whole of society. The EU has also worked on these areas under its Digital Decade Policy Programme 2030 and its Global Gateway, which focuses on digital technology and infrastructure to promote inclusive growth and sustainable development in developing countries. It is also the case of ROK, which has hosted the 2nd AI Safety Summit in 2024, by which it encourages AI Safety Institutes and AI Offices, part of national governments, to cooperate on technicalities.

Also, there are some windows of opportunity in which the EU has not yet participated but would be of strategic interest. This is the case of the ASEAN-India and the ASEAN-Japan ICT Work Plans, which illustrate the ASEAN's interest in broadening its relevance in the Indo-Pacific region. The closer relationship between the EU and ASEAN should be leveraged towards this multilateral opportunity within the region.

As for the ad hoc coalitions, the European Union is a "norm entrepreneur" in as much as it has triggered the "Joint Declaration by the European Union, Australia, Comoros, India, Japan, Mauritius, New Zealand, the Republic of Korea, Singapore, Sri Lanka on privacy and the protection of personal data", which was endorsed at the Ministerial Forum for Cooperation in the Indo-Pacific in February 2022. This is aligned with the "data adequacy decisions" by the European Union, which has already yielded results and is present in Japan, New Zealand and ROK by 2024.

Moreover, some partners are gaining traction in ad hoc coalitions without the EU's participation. This is another avenue for cooperation to be built. Japan is present in the Quad Initiative or the Blue Dot Network; the latter has led to a project on an undersea fibre optic cable connecting the Republic of Palau to an international cable in Guam. Most importantly, Japan has its own vision of a Free and Open Indo-Pacific (FOIP), which showcases the goal of having common rules of understanding for the digital economy.

Another line of work is the multilateral technology rapprochement with several partners simultaneously. Japan launched with India the Asia-Africa Growth Corridor (AAGC) in its 2017 vision document to ensure physical, people-to-people and institutional connectivity. However, no concrete implementation plans have so far been identified. It is also the case of the Economic Corridor India-Asia-Europe, launched by the G20 India in 2024 with support from members, although there is no news.

Technology Triangles

In technology triangles, the bilateral partnership influences individual third countries within the region. Technology triangles mean that two countries that share a strategic interest in certain assets (security, economic, technological) agree to combine joint resources, diplomatic tools, investments or political negotiations to influence or work with a third country of common strategic interest. It can be divided into two types: triangles that are led by the EU, one of the aforementioned countries, and a targeted country because it is a relevant partner in itself within the region or triangles that partner with a country because the latter has a broader influence in the wider neighbourhood.

A paradigmatic case of the first category is that of Memorandums of Understanding (MoU) on undersea cables with ROK and Japan, respectively. In each of them, both sides go beyond the purely bilateral engagement and aim to cooperate with like-minded countries involved in transoceanic undersea cables, including Arctic connectivity, to join forces with their trusted entities to manufacture, install, operate and maintain submarine cables. It is also the case of the Philippines Digital Economy Package, or the MoUs on semiconductors with India and Japan, as both sides aim to find like-minded partners in the region to avoid a subsidy race and the risk of crowding out private investments that would themselves contribute to our security and resilience.

The second type is represented by the Singapore-EU DPA, which aims to serve as a pathfinder for EU-ASEAN initiatives to enhance region-to-region digital cooperation and connectivity. This supports the EU-ASEAN Joint Ministerial Statement on Connectivity from 2020 and the ASEAN Digital Masterplan to establish a frictionless ASEAN digital market. Similarly, the annual "Industrial Control Systems Cybersecurity Week", which is part of the EU-Japan DPA, includes the ASEAN countries, co-hosted by Japan, the EU and the United States to work towards the compatibility of product security frameworks, notably the upcoming European Cyber Resilience Act and Japan's Internet of Things (IoT) labelling scheme currently under development.

Emerging Policy Challenges in the EU's International Agenda on Digital Policy in the Indo-Pacific Region

In summary, the EU's engagement with the Indo-Pacific region in the digital policy agenda has not followed a linear path. A patchwork of initiatives has helped build the current scenario of strong digital partnerships in the region. It initially started with Connectivity Partnerships, where digital policy was an important element, and in a handful of countries. The push by certain Member States to launch the EU's Strategy for Cooperation in the Indo-Pacific helped institutionalise *regional engagement*, where digital policy was given a top-priority role. Then, the support of EU Member States for a concerted approach to a digital diplomacy playbook was the final stimulus to strengthen the *subject-matter expertise engagement in digital policy*. These two separate driving forces have guided and led to the current scenario of a truly "international agenda of digital policy in the Indo-Pacific" and have also helped increase its geographic scope from a bilateral towards a multilateral basis within the region.

The current scenario of the EU's engagements with the Indo-Pacific region on digital policy is at a growth stage. The next step should be the consolidation of the expected tangible outcomes into grounded results and the maturity of some policy areas to move from information-sharing to actual capacity development and entry into the market.

This chapter assesses a patchwork of emerging policy challenges that this relationship should consider in the coming years.

From Free Trade Agreements to Digital Trade Agreements

The EU has FTAs with Singapore, ROK and New Zealand, and is in 2024 negotiating new FTAs with India, Indonesia and the Philippines. However, an emerging policy topic is the establishment of Digital Trade Agreements (DTAs), which are currently being negotiated with ROK and Singapore. DTAs are expected to unlock new markets that offer a wider choice of better-quality goods and services that can easily be found and procured online, make electronic transactions easier, promote a safe online environment for consumers, ensure consumer and data protection, create legal certainty for businesses and boost trust; improve access to electronic commerce; and facilitate digital trade. This issue has received limited attention from a policy, technical, economic and academic perspective, so it is a topic to delve into to make sure the EU's partnerships are fit for purpose in this realm.

Effective and Impactful Involvement from Member States and Efficient Coordination with the EU Level

The governance structure of DPAs was the core element of this flexible cooperation instrument. In particular, it addresses the need for complementarity between actions at the EU and Member States' levels. It is highlighted that EU Member States should be closely involved in the implementation of the DPAs. However, this remains a challenge, considering the different prioritisation and mapping of opportunities and threats that the Indo-Pacific region and the differentiated level of engagement with particular countries pose. Moreover, while the complementary was searched for in the case of DPAs, no reference is made for the TTC with India, which is an area to explore in the future.

The Policy Mindset Shift Towards Economic Security

The European Commission released the proposal for a Strategy on Economic Security (European Commission, 2023) in 2023 to carry out a thorough assessment of risks in four areas: supply chains, including energy security, risks to the physical and cyber security of critical infrastructure, technology security and technology leakage, and weaponisation of economic dependencies or economic coercion. In particular, the strategy sets out how to mitigate identified risks through a three-pronged approach that is called the "three P's": Promote, Protect and Partner.

Despite this overall approach, economic security does not appear across all of the EU's instruments with the Indo-Pacific. The DPA with Japan does not make any reference to economic security—only supply chain resilience neither does so Singapore. Instead, the DPA with ROK explicitly highlights the need to cooperate in this matter, and the EU-India

TTC continuously addresses the issues revolving around economic security, such as market access or FDI screening. This coincides with the fact that the ROK has its own economic security strategy and approach and has developed a National Strategic Technology Nurture Plan (NSTNP), which sets out similar instruments that the EU's, including dual-use technologies, research security and a list of critical technologies. Additionally, the subsidy race is mentioned across the three DPAs, while it is not in the case of India's TTC.

An additional challenge in the EU's engagement of its economic security approach with third countries is the very involvement of Member States. One of the first deliverables of this proposal is the development with Member States of a framework for assessing risks, including a list of critical technologies with a view to devising appropriate mitigating measures.

Undersea Cables

Undersea cables are an already existing technical topic but an underdressed policy issue that has received limited attention so far. In the last EU-ROK Digital Partnership Council, the European Commission highlighted the importance of cooperation on connectivity. This includes undersea cable connectivity projects through the Arctic to provide trusted data flows and cooperation on secure and resilient connectivity in third countries. In turn, the European Commission has also launched a Recommendation on the Security and Resilience of Submarine Cables (European Commission, 2021b), where the international engagement dimension is also included. The Digital Partnership Council with Japan also highlighted this matter. Likewise, the Singapore-EU DPA also addresses the need to invest in data centres and submarine telecommunications cables for connectivity between the EU and ASEAN.

This is an area of opportunity which requires further policy contrast within the EU at the domestic and European levels to ensure the international dimension is built coherently and effectively.

Establishment of a Three-Pronged Framework on Critical Technologies' Capabilities, Dependencies and Vulnerabilities

In order to ensure that the priority-setting of technologies is efficiently elaborated, it would be of interest to develop jointly between the EU and each bilateral partner three scenarios of technologies where both sides need coordination, cooperation, or there is no need at all. These three scenarios to zoom into the technologies that would allow a region to possess actual economic security are as follows: (1) the EU and its partner already have a competitive edge over certain technology; (2) they have the potential to establish themselves as a frontrunner; or (3) they have to have minimal and critical capacities to at least avoid shocks and disruptions. In this categorisation, the first step is for each stakeholder to identify their own capacities, dependencies and vulnerabilities. The second step is to channel discussions between the European Union and each bilateral partner on this matter to identify sensitive technology areas where their priority-setting should be focused.

Joint Investments

The European Union has launched a toolkit of diverse initiatives revolving around industrial policy for green, digital and defence sectors. In particular, the Strategic Technologies for Europe Platform (STEP) enhances EU industrial competitiveness by focusing on developing critical technologies for a sustainable, competitive future. It tests new strategic measures and strengthens EU industrial policy. STEP focuses on projects in the development and manufacturing stages in three sectors: digital and deep technologies; climate, clean and green technologies; and biotechnologies. The selection of programmes falling within the scope of STEP is made based on two criteria: innovativeness (innovative, emerging, or cutting-edge and demonstrate significant economic potential on development or manufacturing, or spillover effects across Member States) and strategic dependencies (it should contribute to reducing or preventing them).

While each side is funnelling investments to build up its own technological footprint, they might find common areas of technology interest to jointly invest or help the partner with missing capabilities by relying on an external trustworthy partner in a sustained manner instead of reinventing the wheel from scratch. Similar models include the Quad Investors Network or the EU-LAC Digital Accelerator.

Leverage the Global Gateway Projects

So far, the Global Gateway accounts for five projects in the Asian region on digital policy: the Central Asia Digital Connectivity (to enhance access to a secure Internet through trusted satellite connectivity); Connectivity Revolution in Bangladesh (on ICT infrastructure); Digital Transformation and Connectivity Initiative in the Philippines (Copernicus mirror site to all ASEAN countries to provide high-speed Internet capacity); the implementation and upgrading of the critical infrastructure of Thailand's main energy operator; the Electricity Generating Authority of Thailand (EGAT) in Thailand with smart grid technology; and the construction of digital infrastructure including ultrafast broadband in Nusantara, the new capital of Indonesia, with smart urban infrastructure fed with data-rich smart poles and data and application platforms.

The opportunities of the DPAs and the TTC bring new avenues for cooperation with other Indo-Pacific countries through the Global Gateway, either in technology triangles or multilateral technology rapprochement.

Bibliography

Cunningham, G. (2021). *The EU'S strategy for cooperation in the Indo-Pacific*. Sasakawa peace foundation. https://spfusa.org/publications/the-eus-strategy-for-cooperation-in-the-indo-pacific/#_ftn9

European Commission. (2017, May 19). *Digital development: Mainstreaming digital technologies and services into EU development policy*. https://digital-strategy.ec.europa.eu/en/library/digital4development-mainstreaming-digital-technologies-and-services-eu-development-policy

European Commission. (2020, December 2). *EU-US: A new transatlantic agenda for global change*. https://ec.europa.eu/commission/presscorner/detail/en/ip_20_2279

European Commission. (2021b). *Recommendation on the security and resilience of submarine cable infrastructures*. https://digital-strategy.ec.europa.eu/en/library/recommendation-security-and-resilience-submarine-cable-infrastructures

European Commission. (2023, June 20). *An EU approach to enhance economic security*. https://ec.europa.eu/commission/presscorner/detail/en/ip_23_3358

European Commission. (2024b). *Bilateral cooperation: Science and technology agreements with non-EU countries*. https://research-and-innovation.ec.europa.eu/strategy/strategy-2020-2024/europe-world/international-cooperation/bilateral-cooperation-science-and-technology-agreements-non-eu-countries_en

European Commission. (2024c). *Adequacy decisions*. https://commission.europa.eu/law/law-topic/data-protection/international-dimension-data-protection/adequacy-decisions_en

European Commission & Government of Japan. (2019). *The partnership on sustainable connectivity and quality infrastructure between the European Union and Japan*. https://www.eeas.europa.eu/sites/default/files/the_partnership_on_sustainable_connectivity_and_quality_infrastructure_between_the_european_union_and_japan.pdf

European Council. (2022, July 18). *EU digital diplomacy: Council agrees a more concerted European approach to the challenges posed by new digital technologies*. https://www.consilium.europa.eu/en/press/press-releases/2022/07/18/eu-digital-diplomacy-council-agrees-a-more-concerted-european-approach-to-the-challenges-posed-by-new-digital-technologies/

European Council. (2023). *Digital diplomacy: Council sets out priority actions for stronger EU action in global digital affairs*. https://www.consilium.europa.eu/en/press/press-releases/2023/06/26/digital-diplomacy-council-sets-out-priority-actions-for-stronger-eu-action-in-global-digital-affairs/

European External Action Service. (2022, February 23). *Joint declaration on privacy and the protection of personal data*. https://www.eeas.europa.eu/eeas/joint-declaration-privacy-and-protection-personal-data_en

European Parliament Research Service. (2024). *EU-India trade and technology council*. https://www.europarl.europa.eu/RegData/etudes/ATAG/2024/757587/EPRS_ATA(2024)757587_EN.pdf

Finnemore, M., & Sikkink, K. (1998). International norm dynamics and political change. *International Organization, 52*(4), 887–917.

Government of Japan. (2024). *Free and open Indo-Pacific strategy*. https://www.asean.emb-japan.go.jp/files/000352880.pdf

Government of the Republic of Korea. (2022). *Strategy for a free, peaceful and prosperous Indo-Pacific region*. https://www.mofa.go.kr/eng/wpge/m_26382/contents.do

Lin, B., Chase, M. S., Blank, J., Cooper III, C. A., Grossman, D., Harold, S. W., & Orner, P. (2020, November 12). U.S. Versus Chinese powers of persuasion does the United States or China have more influence in the Indo-Pacific region? https://www.rand.org/pubs/research_briefs/RB10137.html

Scott, D. (2021). Indo-Pacific positioning of the United States: Evaluating dis/continuities. In B. J. Cannon & K. Hakata (Eds.), *Indo-Pacific strategies: Navigating geopolitics at the Dawn of a new age*. Routledge.

UNFPA. (2024). *Population trends*. https://asiapacific.unfpa.org/en/topics/population-trends-9#:~:text=Population%20trends-,The%20Asia%20and%20the%20Pacific%20region%20is%20home%20to%2060,populous%20countries%2C%20China%20and%20India

University of Cambridge. (2024). *Indo-Pacific strand*. Centre for geopolitics. https://www.cfg.polis.cam.ac.uk/research/indo-pacific/

Wilkins, T. S. (2019). Evolving security alignments of the Indo-Pacific: The US alliances, the Shanghai cooperation organisation, and ASEAN. *Japan Review, 3*(2), 71–80.

World Bank. (2023). *GDP current US$*. https://data.worldbank.org/indicator/NY.GDP.MKTP.CD

CHAPTER 19

The Unexpected Digital China Challenge for the European Union

Tim Rühlig

Introduction

In the last twenty years, the relations between the European Union (EU) and the People's Republic of China (PRC) have undergone a dramatic change, and digital technology has moved to the very core of it. At the height of cooperation, the EU and the PRC concluded a "comprehensive strategic partnership" in 2003 (European Commission, 2003). In more than sixty dialogues, the EU's willingness to cooperate was inspired by the hope that such collaboration could be transformational and contribute to the economic and political liberalisation of the PRC (European Commission, 2003a). The Europeans seemed to be certain: either the EU could witness China change or the PRC would fail to catch up with the industrialised countries. Only free economies and free societies, it was widely assumed, could generate the necessary innovation to become and remain prosperous.

Ten years later, Europe's hopes started to strip away as China was tightening authoritarian control and strengthening the state-permeated

T. Rühlig (✉)
European Union Institute for Security Studies (EU ISS), Paris, France
e-mail: tim.ruehlig@iss.europa.eu

T. Kleiner and A. Garcia Rodriguez (eds.), *The Making of a Global Digital Rulebook*, https://doi.org/10.1007/978-981-95-9226-5_19

economy instead of further liberalisation. At the heart of European illusion, innovation and digital transformation turned out not to be where China failed, but the PRC became an unexpected innovation powerhouse. In 2019, China was no longer only described as a "partner" and "economic competitor" but, for the first time, also as a "systemic rival" to the EU (European Commission, 2019). Decreasing critical dependencies on Chinese technology and primary goods turned into the defining goal of the EU's China policy, as described by European Commission President Ursula von der Leyen in a speech in March 2023 (European Commission, 2023a). Ever since, such technological "de-risking" has been further spelt out in the European Economic Security Strategy (EESS) that is being steadily implemented in the form of several policy packages (European Commission, 2024).

This chapter focuses on China's evolution into a digital technology innovation powerhouse, explains its importance for the EU and the EU's reaction to it, and carves out future directions of EU responses.

China: Unexpected Innovation Powerhouse

Against most expectations, the People's Republic of China (PRC) has developed into an innovation powerhouse (Allison et al., 2021; Rühlig, 2023). Recent Australian research found that China leads in 37 of 44 critical technologies, as measured by international research output (Wong-Leung et al., 2023). The latest Cyber Power Index prepared by the Belfer Center ranks China second, falling short only of the cyber capabilities of the United States (Voo et al., 2022). The World Intellectual Property Organization's Global Innovation Index paints a slightly different picture: China is placed 11th but still ahead of several industrialised economies, including France (Dutta et al., 2022). These and other similar studies might be unable to grasp the full complexity and degree of China's technological advance. While only approximations, however, all these reports paint a clear picture: the PRC is highly innovative.

China's emergence as a technological power presents the EU with a reality it did not anticipate. At least five distinct features of Western innovation ecosystems that stand in sharp contrast to China were widely assumed to be a guarantee of Western technology leadership. First, open markets in the West contrast with Chinese protectionism, enabling the free flow of information, knowledge and technology, which facilitates innovation. Second, democracies provide freedom that is crucial for creativity. China's oppressive authoritarianism, by contrast, primarily rewards loyalty, while inventiveness is considered secondary. Third, innovation is prized and comes with effective protection of intellectual property (IP) rights and legal certainty as a result of the West's rule of law. China is widely regarded as a culture of copycats with a legal system deeply intertwined with the party-state. Fourth, the PRC's state planning is contrasted with the entrepreneurial individualism of Europe and the US, which has driven many innovative companies. Fifth and finally, the risk-based allocation of resources is believed to create efficient technology ecosystems. In contrast, China's dysfunctional allocation of resources is the result of a lack of functioning capital markets and of Chinese party-state control over the banking sector. In short, for decades, European policymakers ascribed Western digital prowess to the beneficial combination of liberal democracy and free market capitalism.

As a non-democratic, non-free-market state, China was believed to be unable to emulate this success. As recently as 2014, journals such as the *Harvard Business Review* could get away with publishing articles on "Why China Can't Innovate" (Abrami et al., 2014). Granted, numerous studies discussed China's growing power based on the PRC's economic might (Hoge, 2004; Ramo, 2004; Ross & Zhu, 2008). However, the predominant perspective characterised Chinese actors as extractors of economic wealth by mimicking and refining Western technology without innovative breakthroughs.

This interpretation has turned out to be completely false. Today's China is deeply embedded in global technology development and production, as well as shaping the norms and standards that govern disruptive technologies (Rühlig, 2023a). This success goes far beyond catching up with the West. The fundamental "sin" driving the PRC's growth model—the theft of IP—cannot account for why China has overtaken the West in a number of emerging and foundational technologies. If IP theft alone had been the sole characteristic of the China model, the PRC would have run out of steam as China gained technological leadership.

For example, China has overtaken the EU-27 in terms of total R&D expenditure and R&D expenditure per GDP (Figs. 19.1, 19.2). Such massive R&D investment has resulted in a high number of granted patents across technology sectors. When the quality of innovation is measured by the share of top-10% cited articles, China is leading and has overtaken the US.

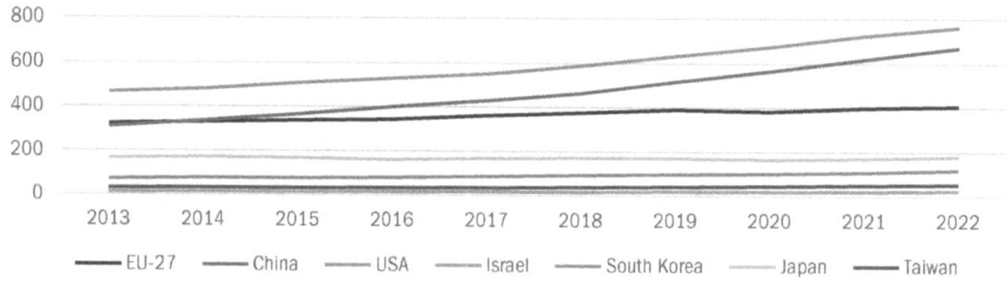

Fig. 19.1 Total gross domestic expenditure on R&D of the EU-27 and selected countries (in PPP converted billion, $US, 2013–2022) (*Source* OECD)

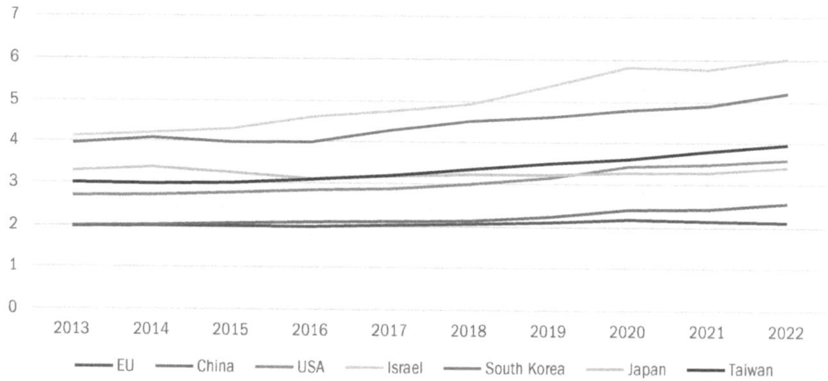

Fig. 19.2 Gross domestic expenditure on R&D per GDP (in %) of the EU-27 and selected countries (2013–2022) (*Source* OECD)

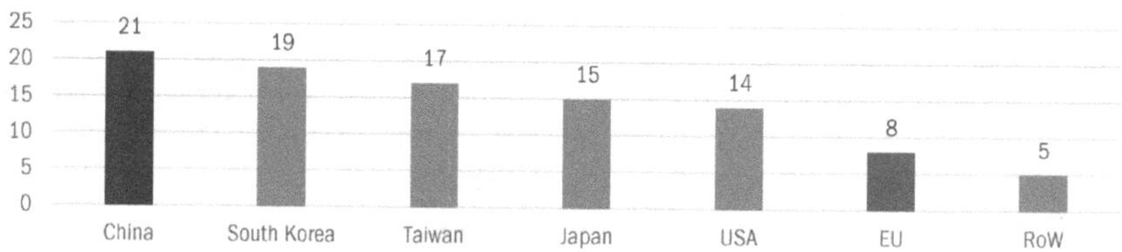

Fig. 19.3 Projected front-end manufacturing market shares in 2032 (in %) (*Source* SIA)

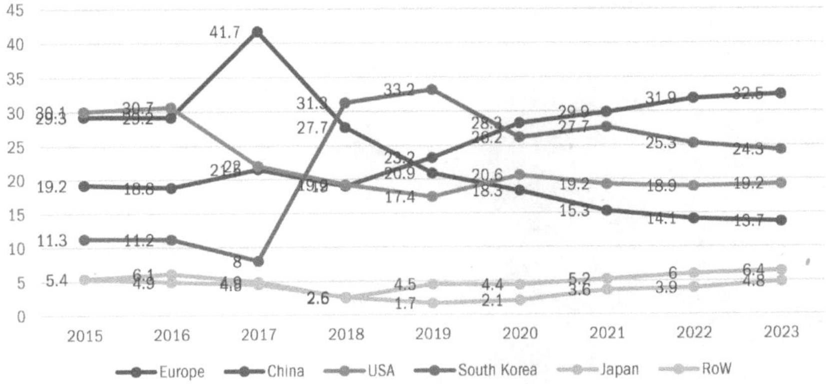

Fig. 19.4 5G patent family (EPO or USPTO granted) share by the headquarters region of 5G owning companies (*Source* LexisNexis)

When global semiconductor market shares are considered, China is projected to be leading by 2032 (Fig. 19.3). Despite all US and allied efforts, Huawei has evolved into and remains the world's leading supplier of Radio Access Network (RAN) technology for wireless infrastructure, followed by Ericsson (Sweden), Nokia (FI) and ZTE (China). South Korean and Japanese vendors follow at a distance. Statistical anomalies in certain years due to technical registration issues aside, Fig. 19.4 illustrates a steady downward trend in Europe's share of 5G patent families. China has taken the lead, followed by South Korea and the United States. A final example is quantum technologies, where China outperforms all other countries (Fig. 19.5). All these figures may overestimate China's innovativeness and novelty of its technology. However, it provides a first indication that China has evolved into a technology powerhouse that is at least on par with the EU but has rather exceeded it.

There is no doubt that China's innovativeness has profited from technology mimicry. IP theft by means of espionage or reverse engineering has contributed to China's technological development. US officials have estimated that China steals intellectual property worth $250 to $600 billion from the United States on an annual basis (Huang, 2019). The wide range of this estimate illustrates how difficult attributions of espionage are.

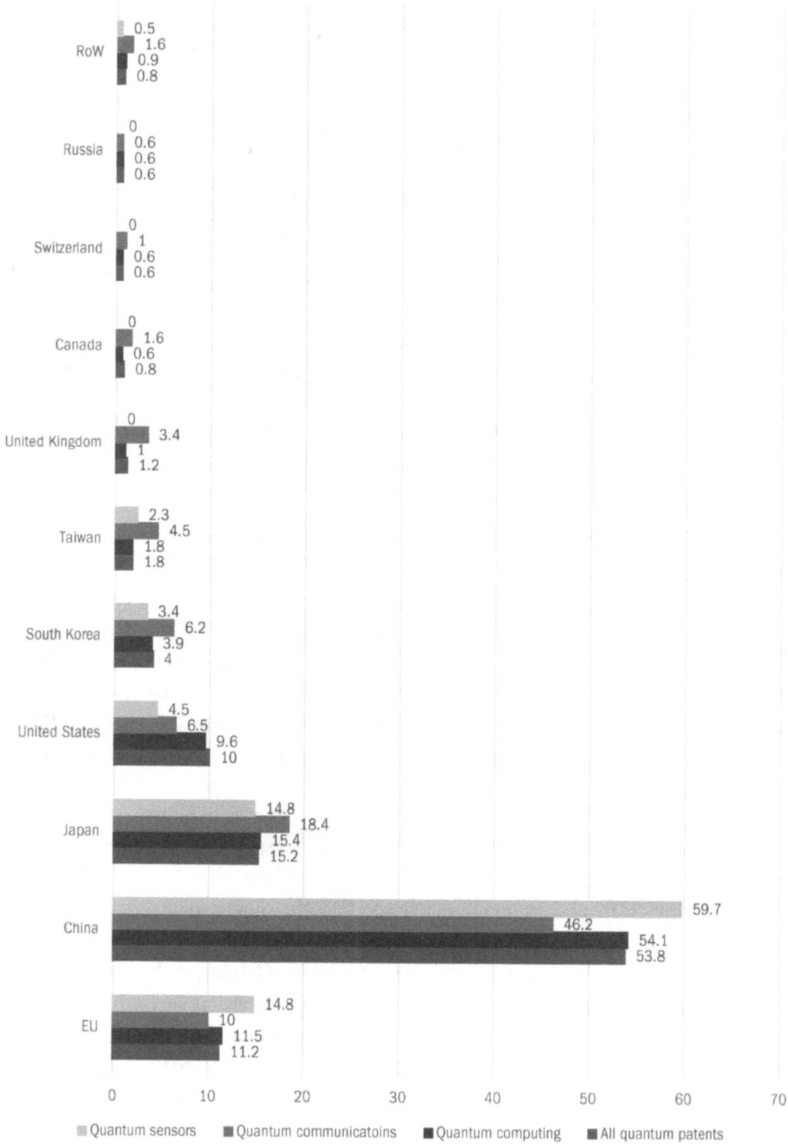

Fig. 19.5 Share of quantum patents by company headquarters, 2000–21 (in %) (*Source* McKinsey)

At first glance, China's prioritisation of digital technology advances has paid off and rather represents a strength of the PRC. However, China remains reliant on foreign inputs for its technological development. The United States and the European Union, among others, have announced their intention to reduce their dependency on the Chinese market in order to "de-risk" (European Commission, 2023a).

The change of policy started with a disillusionment of China's development under paramount leader Xi Jinping. In 2013, the Third Plenum of the Central Committee of the Chinese Communist Party published a communique that was widely interpreted as the beginning of economic liberalisation. After a decade of minimal change, many in the West hoped that Xi Jinping would restart an economic reform agenda. However, political and economic liberalisation as a result of trade—often summarised in the formula "change through trade" —did not become a reality. Quite to the contrary, European leaders started to realise that Xi was tightening the authoritarian grip of control over both the economy and the society. To catch up with Western technological capabilities, China invested in its own innovativeness but also aimed to acquire Western technology leaders. The purchase of German robotics company Kuka turned out to be a sea change in Europe. Then German chancellor Angela Merkel, normally known for her rather cooperative China policy, aimed to prevent the sale and lobbied for the development of a European inbound investment screening mechanism.

Only a few years later, the EU was confronted with the newly elected US President, Donald Trump, who leveraged economic import and export dependencies against both the EU and China. The resultant trade war accelerated the previous Chinese self-reliance policy. Accordingly, China doubled down on indigenous technological development.

Supply chain shortages of medical equipment and semiconductors during the COVID-19 pandemic, energy dependencies from Russian fossil fuels as well as Chinese economic coercion against Lithuania all reminded the EU and its Member States of its supply chain vulnerabilities and that geopolitical tensions could come with enormous economic costs.

When in 2018, Australian and, soon afterwards, US intelligence services warned of inherent security risks of Chinese mobile infrastructure equipment for 5G networks and European countries faced dual pressure: The US administration demanded the replacement of critical Chinese network equipment if Europe wanted to uphold the exchange of sensitive, security-relevant information with its transatlantic partner. China, in turn, threatened economic retaliation if Chinese mobile infrastructure vendors, most prominently Huawei, were to be banned.

Even though the EU Member States aimed for a unitary approach developing with the European Commission in the NIS Cooperation Group the "5G toolbox" to mitigate the existing risks in a consistent manner, the actual implementation differed enormously (see below). The policies of the EU Member States might diverge, but all agree that decoupling from China is not realistic. There is general support for the de-risking agenda, but what de-risking precisely means remains contested. Countries with particularly deep economic ties with China (primarily Germany and the Netherlands), as well as those with deep-rooted support for free trade (e.g. Sweden), tend to advocate a narrower definition of de-risking where threats can be clearly identified. Member States with a long tradition of an ideological conviction that Europe should be as autonomous and strong as possible, primarily France, tend to advocate a broader definition and are willing to support more industrial policy. Countries in geographical proximity to Russia, including Poland and the three Baltic states, are also in favour of broader de-risking but in close alignment with the US as their main security guarantor in NATO. Quite the opposite, the rather hesitant perspective of the Spanish government seems to be partly informed by a rather US-sceptical position.

All these differences aside, the overall EU policy has undergone a shift from cooperative interaction to technological competition, if not rivalry. If announcements of European de-risking are followed through with serious efforts to establish new sources of supply (e.g. by means of free trade agreements), the attractiveness of the Chinese market could suffer. International firms could find themselves operating in alternative markets that are less regulated and more predictable than the Chinese ones. As a consequence, China's porous protectionism could turn out to be too unattractive and scare away international tech companies. In parallel with increased barriers to market entry, the attractiveness of the Chinese market has significantly decreased in light of lowering growth (see above). Western political leaders are limiting export and investment guarantees. Germany's new China Strategy, for example, confirms the "general ceiling for investment guarantees of three billion euros per company and country" (Federal Republic of Germany & Federal Foreign Office, 2023, p. 38). This sends a signal to companies that the risks associated with doing business with China will no longer be socialised.

Ironically, what is currently being discussed as de-risking is, in effect, the end of European taxpayers bearing liability, thereby de-risking Chinese business for European companies.

Western countries, including the EU and its member states, have further enacted laws and regulations that impede liaison between European and Chinese actors. For example, the EU and some of its member states have adopted screening mechanisms to control foreign direct investment (FDI) (Regulation (EU) 2019/452, 2019). While these instruments were designed to be actor-agnostic, Chinese investments were clearly the main target.

Another example is export controls. In October 2022 and 2023, the US adopted a comprehensive and complex set of export controls that require licensing of the export of semiconductor equipment (U.S. Department of Commerce, 2022). In the summer of 2023, the Netherlands and Japan issued complementary regulations that control the export of lithography machinery essential for the production of semiconductors (Government of the Netherlands, 2023). While these export regimes are justified with reference to dual-use export controls, it cannot be denied that they stall Chinese semiconductor capacity at 5 nm logic. While it is certainly the case that these export controls will stimulate the indigenous production of chips within the PRC, lack of access to chipset below 5 nm logic restricts the PRC's chances of developing generative Artificial Intelligence. While China's trailing-edge semiconductor production is likely to flourish, innovation based on cutting-edge semiconductors is likely to be hindered if not completely choked off (Kleinhans & Lee, 2022).

The West is also placing the preferential treatment provided to Chinese actors under increasing scrutiny, not least through the development by the EU of a number of defensive policy tools, such as the anti-dumping and anti-subsidy instruments. Neither instrument is entirely new, but recent amendments have made them more effective.

If the two structural challenges and China's reliance on input from Europe and the US are considered, the growing number of measures restricting technological interaction with the PRC turns out to be a real challenge for the PRC. China's reliance on digital technology is both a strength as it invests in technological advances but also constitutes a severe vulnerability. If it does not master the transformation, the power of the CCP is in question.

Europe's Digital China Challenge and the EU'S De-Risking Policy

As a result of China's efforts to make technological advances, the PRC has a strong position in the supply chains of emerging and foundational technologies (Allison et al., 2021). Today, the EU is highly dependent on Chinese technology. One example is critical inputs for the semiconductor value chain (see Table 19.1).

Such dependencies that exist in a number of critical technology supply chains come with economic, political, security and ideational costs (Creemers et al., 2022). The below-outlined risks underline that the EU and China have moved from an interaction that is primarily shaped by cooperation to a mode of competition, if not outright systemic rivalry.

Table 19.1 EU dependency on non-EU imports in selected products used in the semiconductor value chain, 2021

Segment	*Product*	*EU dependency on foreign imports %*	*Top importer in the EU*	*Share of top importer in total EU imports %*
Raw materials	Germanium oxides and zirconium dioxide	63	China	32
Intermediate goods used in equipment production	Fans of a kind used solely or principally for cooling microprocessors	84	China	48
Intermediate goods used as input for foundries	Lenses, prisms, mirrors and other optical elements	70	China	20
Chips	Light-emitting diodes, incl. Laser diodes	83	China	34
Chips	Photosensitive semiconductor devices, incl. Photovoltaic cells	88	China	78
Chips	E2PROMs (excl. Flash E2PROMs)	73	China	18

source JRC

Many of the conflicts are rooted in different economic, political and ideological systems:

Economically, an uneven playing field favours Chinese tech firms that benefit from preferential treatment and lower data protection and environmental standards. This endangers the EU's digital industrial competitiveness. *Politically*, China is able to leverage political concessions from technologically (over-)dependent third countries, including EU member states. The PRC is also actively engaging with global cyber-governance in an effort to rewrite institutional processes and increase its power. In the *security field*, the inclusion of Chinese digital equipment can come with cyber insecurities that enable espionage and sabotage by a state with which the EU has no security alliance. *Ideationally*, China's technological stronghold calls into question whether the governance principles of the digital technologies that are increasingly penetrating entire societies reflect liberal and democratic values. Among the notable fields of divergent ideational conception between Europe and China are technical standards, data governance and effective protection of the environment.

This is not to argue that the EU should cut all ties with China. Nor is decoupling considered a feasible or desirable option. The ecosystems of emerging and foundational technologies are deeply transnational, and countries are extremely interdependent. The existing technological interdependence is not only a vulnerability of China (see above) but also of the EU. This is why the European Union strives for what is referred to as Open Strategic Autonomy (European Commission, 2021; Joint Research Centre, 2022). Its basic idea is that the EU should avoid dependencies that significantly constrain its ability to act independently due to the leverage of competitors. In the following, this chapter refers to this idea as "digital sovereignty".

This complexity of supply chains contributes to China being simultaneously a partner, competitor and systemic rival of the EU (European Commission, 2021a). While initially, the EU was clear that China plays different roles depending on the policy field, more and more policymakers are acknowledging that the PRC has characteristics of all three roles in all policy fields. These multiple roles indicate that operationalising digital sovereignty in emerging and foundational technologies vis-à-vis China will be highly complex.

Although Open Strategic Autonomy, in the meantime complemented by reference to economic security and technological de-risking, reads well in the abstract, it is difficult to operationalise any of these terms in practice. The European Commission has offered a rather loose approach in its Economic Security Strategy and the resultant first economic security package. Internationally, the EU's Trade and Technology Council (TTC) with the United States is also shaping the agenda, as are ongoing discussions within the G7 revolving around terms such as resilient supply chains, standards-based trade or trustworthiness. However, both conceptually and practically, de-risking remains in the infant stage. Other than US-China trade relations that are decoupling, EU-China trade is rather intensifying—against declared political will.

At an abstract level, digital sovereignty is about enabling or preserving Europe's ability to act in its own best interests. To this end, the EU has begun to identify critical dependencies (SWD(2024) 91 final, 2024a; European Commission, 2021b; European Commission, 2022; Gislev & Grohol, 2018). However, EU actors still need to address divergent risks when aiming for digital sovereignty and economic security. The EU has presented several attempts to operationalise the risks. For example, technological de-risking is broadly divided into the attempt to prevent "technology leakage" and achieve "technology security", understood as access to critical technologies (European Commission, 2024). However, this broad categorisation remains rather abstract and hardly helpful in developing a consistent de-risking policy.

For example, risk assessments in technology fields such as semiconductors, artificial intelligence, biotechnology and quantum computing are yet to yield results. The exercises that the European Commission has launched are illustrative of their complexity, the remaining low ownership of several EU Member States and how difficult proper de-risking is.

A more positive example is the above-mentioned development of a toolbox to mitigate the risks of 5G networks. However, even in 5G, the results diverge enormously. Within Europe, Chinese RAN suppliers have suffered significant losses in market share since the introduction of the EU's 5G toolbox. This, however, does not apply to all EU Member States. While Chinese vendors have lost 92% market share in the Czech Republic, they gained 25% in Ireland.

The remaining market share of Chinese RAN vendors across EU Member States varies enormously from 100% in Cyprus to 0% in the Czech Republic, Denmark, Estonia, Latvia, Lithuania, Luxembourg, Malta, Slovakia, and Sweden.

The Digital Power China (DPC) research consortium has made a different proposal distinguishing four sets of risks. All these risks have, implicitly or explicitly, become the subject of the EU's de-risking efforts in recent months. The four dimensions include:

1. *Risks to the resilience of global supply chains and second and third-order effects:* The global value chains (GVC) of many, if not all, emerging and foundational technologies are characterised by a transnational division of labour. No region is in control of all the production steps and its supplier markets. Thus, to strengthen the security of supply, it might be in Europe's best interests to strengthen the resilience of the GVC in order to reduce second- and third-order negative impacts on European industries in case of supply disruptions. Strategies to strengthen resilience vary greatly between specific GVCs, such as semiconductors, batteries or quantum computing, depending on their individual characteristics.
2. *Risks to national and European security:* Not reducing *strategic dependency* or losing *strategic capacity* might have (in)direct negative impacts on European member states' national security. Of the four dimensions, assessing the potential impact on national security is the one with which policymakers are traditionally the most familiar. However, strategic dependencies in foundational technologies, such as semiconductors, or general-purpose technologies, such as AI, might have an indirect impact on national security. The national security risks that stem from dependence on Chinese mobile network equipment vendors are different from the national security risks to member states that rely heavily on drones, surveillance cameras or AI chips from Chinese vendors. Some of these risks can be mitigated at the technical level, while others come down to the trustworthiness of the technology provider. One example is Europe's increasing dependence on Chinese back-end manufacturing (the last step of semiconductor manufacturing), which could be utilised to compromise a chip or to implement hardware backdoors or kill switches.
3. *Risks to universal values and sustainability:* Strategic dependency or technology cooperation can also conflict with European values. Like the implementation of export restrictions to protect human rights, strategic dependence can also be scrutinised according to the human rights violations that such technology would enable. One

example is the increased scrutiny of Hikvision surveillance cameras in Europe and the company's ban in the US due to its involvement in human rights violations against Uyghurs in China (Griffin, 2022). Thus, reducing dependency on Chinese surveillance cameras could be based on European values rather than solely national security concerns. Similarly, sustainability is of growing concern, and emerging and foundational technologies play an increasingly important role. While both Europe and China emphasise its importance, the priority attributed and approaches to sustainability vary, which has implications far beyond the EU for global goods such as combating climate change.

4. *Risks to European competitiveness:* Europe might invest in strategic capacities or try to reduce strategic dependencies to be able to compete internationally in the long term if a certain technology or market is deemed highly important in the future. Current examples include Europe's investments in quantum computing and photonics. The Dutch government, for example, has invested heavily in the PhotonDelta consortium to strengthen the long-term competitiveness of its domestic photonics ecosystem (Optics.org, 2022). In light of the intensifying US-China technological rivalry, government incentives to support the technological competitiveness of a specific domestic industry or technology provider can also be motivated by maintaining "strategic indispensability"; that is, ensuring that a company continues to play an indispensable role within the GVC in the long term (Tomoshige, 2022). Technological competitiveness, therefore, creates geopolitical leverage.

All four dimensions are not of equal concern to the EU in every emerging and foundational technology. In addition to the four dimensions, geopolitical contextualisation is required to identify the extent to which and in what ways the EU is being challenged. These are not dependencies as such, but a proper risk calculation that considers the criticality of the item under consideration, the degree of reliance on suppliers and whether options exist for substitution, as well as political factors such as security alliances and regime type. The severity of the challenges in the four dimensions and the likelihood that a given dependency might be weaponised are decisive.

The European Commission recognises that a dependency is not necessarily bad in and of itself but that this depends on various factors and that its digital sovereignty can be strengthened if a mutual dependency exists with a trusted international partner. The Commission also recognises that such an approach fundamentally relies on intricate and continuous mapping of important technology ecosystems, as well as a case-by-case assessment of appropriate policy measures.

These four dimensions should help to identify the weaknesses that the EU strives to address in any given foundational or emerging technology. In some cases, tensions exist between the dimensions. The three examples below illustrate the relationships between the dimensions.

Semiconductor front-end manufacturing: Semiconductor front-end manufacturing and the extent to which fabrication plants ("fabs") should be given substantial subsidies are two issues currently receiving considerable attention from EU policymakers. A key element of the proposed EU Chips Act is a new subsidy strategy for "first-of-a-kind" fabs in Europe. The goal is to become less dependent on semiconductor manufacturing in Asia, especially Taiwan and South Korea, which are currently the only places in the world with cutting-edge (5 nanometres, nm) manufacturing capacity (Kleinhans, 2021). The problem is that Europe's strongest semiconductor end-customer industries (industrial applications and medical equipment) predominantly rely upon and will continue to rely on older manufacturing technologies (40 nm, 90 nm or even 180 nm) (ASML, 2022).

Globally, most of the new fab launches by companies such as TSMC, Samsung, Intel and others are on cutting-edge capacity at 10 nm and below. China is already an important location for "trailing-edge" fabs (20–45 nm) and manufacturing on "mature nodes" (>45 nm). Moreover, China has outspent every other region on manufacturing equipment (Kleinhans, 2022). US export restrictions mean that this is almost entirely trailing-edge equipment. China spent over five times more on equipment than Europe in the same timeframe.

What does this mean? In the future, especially for older manufacturing technology, European companies will be more dependent than today on fabs in China, whether operated by Chinese or foreign companies. As there is a shortage of these older fabs globally, this strengthens *supply chain resilience*—giving European companies access to more manufacturing capacity than before. From a *national security* perspective, however, being dependent on a "systemic rival" for chip manufacturing may not be in Europe's best interest. Finally, regarding *technological competitiveness,* these older manufacturing technologies are still important and are being innovated for a variety of chips, from sensors to micro-controllers, power semiconductors and radio frequency applications. In a nutshell, China's investment spree in trailing-edge fabs is good for *global supply chain resilience* but poses very real *national security* and *technological competitiveness challenges* for Europe. This should encourage Europe to invest in its own manufacturing capabilities in these "older" technologies.

Technical standardisation of 5G technology: 5G infrastructure is a critical digital infrastructure that is foundational in a broad range of use cases. Mobile infrastructure is highly standardised and relies mostly on global standards developed by the International Telecommunications Union (ITU) and the Third Generation Partnership Project (3GPP). Whoever sets the technical standards in these institutions defines the technological parameters of the backbone of global critical digital infrastructure. These technical standards have a wide range of implications, not least the network security of the critical digital infrastructure (Rühlig, 2021).

China's influence on the ITU and the 3GPP has grown significantly in recent years. Given the potential national security concerns and the criticality of 5G standardisation, the rapid growth of China's influence in relevant standard-developing organisations should be of concern to the EU.[1] From a national security perspective, China's strength in these institutions could lead Europeans to advocate ignoring the technical standards developed based on Chinese contributions or even withdrawing from these international institutions.

What may sound like a logical solution from a national security perspective misses the very nature of technical standard setting. Technical standards are effective only if they achieve a broad consensus and are accepted by the market. Wireless infrastructure technology is global, and no country can dominate the standard-setting process. From this perspective, neither exclusion nor withdrawal but a strengthening of European

[1] In the ITU-T, the most influential branch of the ITU in standardization, China has the second largest number of members, falling only slightly short of the United States. In the ongoing study period, China holds the most technical leadership positions in the ITU-T study groups, focus groups and work programmes. In 3GPP, China has the highest share of individual members and technical leadership positions in technical specification groups and work programmes. Accordingly, China's share of 5G standard contributions has increased more than that of any other state compared to the previous mobile generation, 4G/LTE. China has also declared the most patent families to be standard essential.

capacities coupled with continuous cooperation is necessary to boost European competitiveness.

In sum, although the national security perspective might suggest an isolation strategy, investment in Europe's own capabilities to better position cooperation is preferable from a technological competitiveness perspective.

Artificial Intelligence for facial recognition: The global market for facial recognition technology is projected to grow from US$5 billion in 2022 to almost US$13 billion by 2027 (Grand View Research, 2023). Facial recognition is alleged to increase security, but it also challenges fundamental values, as it is based on enormous quantities of personal data in capturing the physiognomy of faces. AI algorithms are being trained and refined by collecting sensitive data without the consent of citizens. Surveillance, privacy, algorithmic biases and discrimination coupled with unresolved accuracy issues form the core of values-based concerns. However, facial recognition technology is deemed critical to societal and national security. Facial recognition is integral to many smart city solutions, which are now part of critical infrastructure. The vulnerabilities in facial recognition technology recently demonstrated by two Chinese companies operating in Switzerland provide actors with bad intentions with easy access to critical information, compromising national security (Heubl & Schürer, 2022). Strikingly, Chinese firms have a legal obligation to report vulnerabilities to the PRC government within two days of their detection (Cyberspace Administration of China, 2021).

Some values-based challenges can be mitigated with effective regulation, such as the AI Act, the Digital Markets Act (DMA) and the General Data Protection Regulation (GDPR). However, regulations cannot resolve security vulnerabilities, and Europe does not provide an example of how a sensitive use case of AI, such as facial recognition, can be developed and refined in line with EU norms.

Strikingly, Europe is not technologically competitive in facial recognition. The industrial leader is Hikvision, a Chinese state-owned firm involved in human rights violations in Xinjiang. Until 2021, Hikvision cameras were still being used in the European Parliament building, among many other places in Europe (Kleinhans & Rühlig, 2022; Rollet, 2021).

This case illustrates another facet of the four dimensions of digital sovereignty. Although Europe does not need to be technologically competitive in all fields of emerging and foundational technologies, the challenges to European values and national security dimensions make Europe's lack of technological competitiveness a serious problem.

In response to these risks, the European Union has developed a framework of several risk assessments striving to gain economic security. The European Economic Security Strategy may be the most visible and most recent of these efforts, but the EU has effectively followed this agenda for a few years, even if it used different terminology. For example, the European Commission's DG Connect, in collaboration with the EU Member States in the NIS Cooperation group, have carried out risk assessments on the new mobile infrastructure technology 5G as well as a separate assessment on a related technology called Open RAN (Kleinhans & Rühlig, 2022). For such assessments, concrete measures have been put in place, such as the 5G Toolbox. The above-mentioned European Chips Acts or the European Commission's initiative for a Critical Raw Materials Act are another example of efforts striving to make the EU more resilient and prepared for a situation in which China could weaponise existing dependencies for political purposes.

These initiatives have strengths and weaknesses and address existing challenges better than others. However, what unites them all is a serious attempt to avoid technological decoupling while increasing European resilience at a time of growing geopolitical tensions over digital technology. De-risking is not another word for decoupling. Europe's de-risking policy is about understanding the risks of demarcating where challenges make cooperation with China problematic. Reverse, where the EU does not identify serious risks, it will remain open to cooperation.

The visible shift from cooperative interaction to multi-layered technology de-risking does not imply that the EU has given up on dialogue with China. In fact, both sides have newly installed a High-level Digital Dialogue. In its second edition in 2023, both sides discussed issues around data transfer, ICT standards and AI regulation, among other subjects.

Conclusion and Outlook

The geopolitical contestation over disruptive technologies between the US and the PRC leaves a deep imprint on Europe. Policymakers in the EU are concerned that technological (over)dependencies could constrain the policy choices at their disposal. Europe's reliance on Chinese technologies is a particular subject of concern (European Commission, 2023b).

The digital technological footprint of the PRC is rapidly growing. China's party-state-permeated economy has created favourable conditions for a further increase in the global market share of Chinese technology companies (Rühlig, 2022). This undermines the competitiveness of European firms. The assumption that an authoritarian country such as China is incapable of ground-breaking innovation has turned out to be an illusion (Rühlig, 2023b). On the contrary, China has been able to subtly spread the authoritarian values inscribed in its digital technologies across the globe (Scharre, 2023). This goes against Europe's stated core interests. No European state is in a security alliance with the PRC, and Europe and China could find themselves on opposing sides of an escalating conflict. The friendship between Russia and China may not be as "limitless" as proclaimed (President of Russia, 2022), but China's technological development could pose a direct security threat to Europe if the PRC decided to share parts of its dual-use know-how with Russia. Many fear that the possibility of the PRC leveraging its technological dependencies against Europe could constrain the strategic choices of the EU.

In response, Europe is aiming for a reduction in risk. Several policy instruments have been put in place to this end, such as the EU's investment screening mechanism or the 5G Toolbox. Most prominently, the EU has launched a European Economic Security Strategy (EESS) that it is now implementing. The Commission published the first implementation package in January 2024 (European Commission, 2024). It outlines the next steps, some of which have already begun at the time of writing, such as risk assessments of four critical technologies.

Most of these instruments are reactive and protective in nature. Europe is striving to address its technological weaknesses and reduce its overdependencies on technologies and raw materials that are considered critical. Such de-risking is certainly a necessary process of adaptation to the new geopolitical realities, especially if Europe can successfully differentiate between diverging risk profiles across several emerging and foundational technologies and adopt policy instruments that meet these specific profiles (Rühlig, 2023c).

However, what the current de-risking policies neglect is that it is virtually impossible to reduce strategic dependencies to a degree that provides the economic security and technological sovereignty the EU and the UK are seeking. The cost of such decoupling would be enormous, and for good reason: nobody is realistically willing to pay such a high price. The development and production of most emerging and foundational technologies are based on a highly transnational division of labour. All actors are likely to remain interdependent for the foreseeable future. Technological decoupling is impossible and explicitly not desired.

However, if technological self-reliance is neither feasible nor Europe's goal, Europe will need to remain technologically *indispensable* in order to be a strategic actor in global supply chains. In other words, under conditions of persistent interdependence, Europe can only prevent being constrained by technological dependencies if it pursues two complementary strategies at the same time: reducing strategic dependencies on China where possible and ensuring that it remains technologically indispensable to China. Each technological ecosystem requires a different mix of policies that aims for "autonomy" or "strategic entanglement". However, reverse dependencies on China should be factored into Europe's policies more prominently. Europe will preserve its sovereignty if the PRC leadership considers the cost of going against the EU's and the UK's core interests to be too high.

It might be argued that the logic of interdependence has not prevented Russia from violating international law and attacking Ukraine. Indeed, a high technological and economic cost for China is no guarantee that the PRC will not go against European core interests, which is why Europe must reduce its strategic dependencies on China, as it is currently doing. Studies have demonstrated that the economic costs of decoupling were higher for Russia before the war than they would be for China now (Matthes, 2022). However, in the absence of a feasible decoupling strategy, maintaining a high cost for China is the best of all imperfect policy options to complement—rather than replace—efforts to reduce strategic dependencies. The fact that Russia has acted irrationally is no evidence that China will do the same. The PRC is in the middle of a structural economic transformation, and economic growth is still considered vital for the legitimacy of the rule of the CCP. Security considerations gain importance relative to economic development, but this does not mean that the Chinese leadership does not consider a further deterioration in economic growth to be a threat to its power. In other words, while there is no guarantee, imposing economic and technological costs still has a fair chance of shaping the considerations of the CCP leadership.

Preserving European technological strengths sounds more trivial than it is, as such a policy will require a shift in perspective. It is not weaknesses alone that should be at the centre of our considerations, but also how to preserve technological strengths and maintain technological leadership. It will require more policy-oriented research to understand China's dependencies and how the EU could keep the PRC reliant on its own technological strengths.[2]

The focus of EU-China digital technology interaction has shifted from cooperation to competition. Dialogues between the EU and China are primarily for the purpose of developing guardrails for the existing rivalry that results from China's fundamentally different approaches to politics, economy, values and security. Therefore, a shift back to cooperation between the two sides is rather unlikely.

Bibliography

Abrami, R. M., Kirby, W. C., & McFarlan, F. W. (2014, March). *Why China can't innovate*. Retrieved from Harvard Business Review: https://hbr.org/2014/03/why-china-cant-innovate

Allison, G., Klyman, K., Barbesino, K., & Yen, H. (2021, December 7). *The great tech rivalry: China vs the U.S.* Retrieved from Belfer Center for Science and International Affairs, Harvard Kennedy School: www.belfercenter.org/sites/default/files/pantheon_files/GreatTechRivalry_ChinavsUS_211207.pdf

ASML. (2022, February). *EU chips act: Position paper*. https://www.asml.com/-/media/asml/files/news/2022/asml-position-paper-on-eu-chips-act.pdf?rev=cc4554892d7a4304bee8b056b96e4dee

Creemers, R., Fischione, C., & Rühlig, T. (2022). Getting China's digital technology policy right: Implications for the EU. In T. Rühlig (Ed.), *China's digital power. Assessing the implications for the EU* (pp. 5–19). Digital Power China.

Cyberspace Administration of China. (2021, July 13). *工业和信息化部 国家互联网信息办公室 公安部关于印发网络产品安全漏洞管理规定的通知“*. https://www.cac.gov.cn/2021-07/13/c_1627761607640342.htm

Dutta, S., Lanvin, B., Rivera Leon, L., & Wunsch-Vincent, S. (2022). *Global innovation index 2022: What is the future of innovation-driven growth?* World Intellectual Property Organization.

European Commission. (2003, October 30). *Sixth China-EU summit, joint press statement*. https://www.consilium.europa.eu/uedocs/cms_data/docs/pressdata/en/er/77802.pdf

[2] Tim Rühlig (ed.), "Reverse dependency. Making Europe's digital technological strengths indispensable to China," *Digital Power China*, Berlin: DGAP, accessed 29 August 2024, at https://dgap.org/en/research/publications/reverse-dependency-making-europes-digital technological strenghts.

European Commission. (2003a, September 10). *EU-China: Commission adopts new strategy for a maturing partnership*. https://ec.europa.eu/commission/presscorner/detail/en/ip_03_1231

European Commission. (2019, March 12). *European commission and HR/VP contribution to the European council EU-China—A strategic outlook*. https://commission.europa.eu/system/files/2019-03/communication-eu-china-a-strategic-outlook.pdf

European Commission. (2021, May 5). *Communication from the commission to the European parliament, the council, the European economic and social committee and the committee of the regions. Updating the 2020 new industrial strategy: Building a stronger single market for Europe's recovery*. https://eur-lex.europa.eu/legal-content/EN/TXT/PDF/?uri=CELEX:52021DC0350&from=EN

European Commission. (2021a). *An open, sustainable and assertive trade policy: Open strategic autonomy*. https://trade.ec.europa.eu/doclib/docs/2021/february/tradoc_159434.pdf

European Commission. (2021b). *Commission staff working document: Strategic dependencies and capacities*. https://commission.europa.eu/documents_en?prefLang=es

European Commission. (2022). *Critical raw materials for strategic technologies and sectors in the EU: A foresight study*. https://rmis.jrc.ec.europa.eu/uploads/CRMs_for_Strategic_Technologies_and_Sectors_in_the_EU_2020.pdf

European Commission. (2023a, March 30). *Speech by President von der Leyen on EU-China relations to the mercator institute for China studies and the European policy centre*. https://ec.europa.eu/commission/presscorner/detail/en/speech_23_2063

European Commission. (2023b, June 20). *Joint communication to the European parliament, the European council and the council on "European economic security strategy"*. https://eur-lex.europa.eu/legal-content/EN/TXT/?uri=CELEX%3A52023JC0020&qid=1687525961309

European Commission. (2024, January 24). *Commission proposes new initiatives to strengthen economic security*. https://ec.europa.eu/commission/presscorner/detail/en/ip_24_363

European Union. (2019). *Regulation (EU) 2019/452 of the European parliament and of the council of 19 march 2019 establishing a framework for the screening of foreign direct investments into the union*. https://eur-lex.europa.eu/legal-content/EN/TXT/HTML/?uri=CELEX:32019R0452&qid=1696287250158

Federal Republic of Germany & Federal Foreign Office. (2023, June 20). *Strategy on China of the government of the federal republic of Germany*. https://www.auswaertiges-amt.de/blob/2608580/49d50fecc479304c3da2e2079c55e106/china-strategie-en-data.pdf

Gislev, M., & Grohol, M. (2018). *Report on critical raw materials and the circular economy*. http://publications.europa.eu/resource/cellar/d1be1b43-e18f-11e8-b690-01aa75ed71a1.0001.01/DOC_1

Government of the Netherlands. (2023, June 30). *Government publishes additional export measures for advanced semiconductor manufacturing equipment*. https://www.government.nl/latest/news/2023/06/30/government-publishes-additional-export-measures-for-advanced-semiconductor-manufacturing-equipment

Grand View Research. (2023). *Facial recognition market size, share & trends analysis report by technology (2D, 3D, facial analytics), by application (access control, security & surveillance), by end-use, by region, and segment forecasts, 2023–2030*. https://www.grandviewresearch.com/industry-analysis/facial-recognition-market#:~:text=The%20global%20facial%20recognition%20market,15.4%25%20from%202021%20to%202028

Griffin, J. (2022, May 4). *Report: U.S. may impose sanctions on Hikvision*. https://www.securityinfowatch.com/video-surveillance/article/21266640/report-us-may-impose-sanctions-on-hikvision

Heubl, B., & Schürer, C. (2022, May 19). *Schweizer behörden setzen auf chinesische Sicherheitskameras*. https://www.srf.ch/news/schweiz/sicherheitsmaengel-schweizer-behoerden-setzen-auf-chinesische-sicherheitskameras

Hoge, J. F. (2004). A global power shift in the making: Is the United States ready? *Foreign Affairs, 83*(4), 2–7.

Huang, Y. (2019, October). *China's record of intellectual property rights is getting better and better*. https://foreignpolicy.com/2019/10/16/china-intellectual-property-theft-progress/

Joint Research Centre. (2022, October 10). *Shaping and securing the eu's open strategic autonomy by 2040 and beyond*. https://op.europa.eu/en/publication-detail/-/publication/7e1bcf73-06e2-11ec-b5d3-01aa75ed71a1/language-en

Kleinhans, J.-P. (2021, April 8). *The lack of semiconductor manufacturing in Europe: Why the 2nm fab is a bad investment*. Retrieved from Stiftung Neue Verantwortung: https://www.interface-eu.org/publications/3045

Kleinhans, J.-P. (2022, June 9). *Testimony before the US–China economic and security review commission, US congress, hearing on US–China competition in global supply chains*. Retrieved from Siftung Neue Verantwortung: https://www.uscc.gov/sites/default/files/2022-06/Jan-Peter_Kleinhans_Testimony.pdf

Kleinhans, J.-P., & Lee, J. (2022). *China semiconductor observatory baseline report*. Stiftung Neue Verantwortung.

Kleinhans, J.-P., & Rühlig, T. (2022, August). *The false promise of open ran why open ran does not solve the "5G China challenge"*. Retrieved from Digital Power China: https://dgap.org/system/files/article_pdfs/DPC-Open%20RAN%20-%20FULL%20REPORT%20-%20FINAL.pdf

Matthes, J. (2022). *Gegenseitige Abhängigkeiten im Handel zwischen China, der EU und Deutschland. Eine empirische Faktensammlung*. Retrieved from Institut der Deutschen Wirschaft: https://www.iwkoeln.de/fileadmin/user_upload/Studien/Report/PDF/2022/IW-Report-2022-Gegenseitige-Abhaengigkeiten.pdf

Optics.org. (2022, April 20). *Netherlands group claims €1.1BN for photonic chip scale-up*. https://optics.org/news/13/4/26

President of Russia. (2022, February 4). *Joint statement of the Russian federation and the people's republic of China on the international relations entering a new Era and the global sustainable development*. http://www.en.kremlin.ru/supplement/5770

Ramo, J. C. (2004). *The Beijing consensus: Notes on the new physics of Chinese power*. Foreign Policy Centre.

Rollet, C. (2021, April 29). *EU parliament removes hikvision, citing human rights abuses*. https://ipbm.com/reports/hik-eu

Ross, R. S., & Zhu, F. (2008). *China's ascent: Power, security and the future of international politics*. Cornell University Press.

Rühlig, T. (2021). *China, Europe and the new power competition over technical standards*. Swedish Institute of International Affairs.

Rühlig, T. (2022). *China's digital power: Assessing the implications for the EU*. https://dgap.org/en/research/publications/chinas-digital-power-assessing-implications-eu

Rühlig, T. (2023, October). *No. 5 october 2023 Dr. Tim Rühlig senior research fellow, German council on foreign relations the sources of China's innovativeness why China's "unstoppable" innovation powerhouse might falter*. Retrieved from DGAP Analysis: https://dgap.org/system/files/article_pdfs/DGAP%20Analysis%20No-5_October-2023_16pp.pdf

Rühlig, T. (2023a, June 15). *Transatlantic tech de-risking from China: The case of technical standard-setting*. Retrieved from Testimony before the U.S.-China Economic Security Review Commission. Hearing on "Europe, the United States and Relations with China: Convergence or Divergence?" Panel II: Technology, Standards/Data, and Trade: https://www.uscc.gov/sites/default/files/2023-06/Tim_Ruhlig_Testimony.pdf

Rühlig, T. (2023b). *The roots of China's innovativeness: Why China's unstoppable innovation powerhouse might falter*. DGAP Analysis no. 5.

Rühlig, T. (2023c, January 25). *Europe's strategic technology autonomy from China: Assessing foundational and emerging technologies*. https://dgap.org/en/research/publications/europes-strategic-technology-autonomy-china-assessing-foundational-and

Scharre, P. (2023, May 4). *The dangers of the global spread of China's digital authoritarianism. testimony before the US-China economic and security review commission: Hearing on rule by law: China's increasingly global legal reach*. https://s3.us-east-1.amazonaws.com/files.cnas.org/documents/Paul_Scharre_Testimony.pdf

Tomoshige, H. (2022, September 19). *Japanese semiconductor industrial policy-making in the Twenty-First Century*. https://www.csis.org/blogs/perspectives-innovation/japanese-semiconductor-industrial-policymaking-twenty-first-century

U.S. Department of Commerce. (2022, October 7). *Commerce implements new export controls on advanced computing and semiconductor manufacturing items to the People's Republic of China (PRC)*. https://www.bis.doc.gov/index.php/documents/about-bis/newsroom/press-releases/3158-2022-10-07-bis-press-release-advanced-computing-and-semiconductor-manufacturing-controls-final/file

Voo, J., Hemani, I., & Cassidy, D. (2022). *National cyber power index 2022*. Retrieved from Belfer Center for Science and International Affairs, Harvard Kennedy School: https://www.belfercenter.org/publication/national-cyber-power-index-2022

Wong-Leung, J., Robin, S., & Cave, D. (2023). *ASPI's critical technology tracker the global race for future power*. Retrieved from ASPI: http://ad-aspi.s3.ap-southeast-2.amazonaws.com/2023-03/ASPIs%20Critical%20Technology%20Tracker_0.pdf?VersionId=ndm5v4DRMfpLvu.x69Bi_VUdMVLp07jw

CHAPTER 20

EU Digital Policy in Multilateral Fora

Fabian Delcros

Introduction: Why Does the EU Need to Act Internationally to Realise Its Digital Policy Ambitions?

The European Union (EU) has consistently prioritised international engagement through multilateral fora because it aligns with its foundational principles of cooperation, peace, and shared rules-based governance. The promotion and support of multilateralism are embedded in the EU's constitutional framework. Article 21 of the Treaty on European Union (TEU) outlines the EU's principles and objectives in its external actions, explicitly stating that the Union "shall promote multilateral solutions to common problems, particularly within the framework of

The author is an official of the European Commission. He represents the EU on Digital policy issues in G20, G7 and Trade negotiations and teaches International Digital Policies and regulations at Sciences-Po Paris. The information and views set out in this chapter are those of the author and do not necessarily reflect the official opinion of the Institution.

F. Delcros (✉)
European Commission, Brussels, Belgium
e-mail: Fabian.delcros@ec.europa.eu

T. Kleiner and A. Garcia Rodriguez (eds.), *The Making of a Global Digital Rulebook*, https://doi.org/10.1007/978-981-95-9226-5_20

the United Nations". This commitment reflects the EU's dedication to a rules-based international order, where global challenges are addressed through collective action and cooperation with other international actors.

Multilateralism also allows the EU to amplify its influence by building consensus among a wide range of global actors, ensuring that international rules reflect its values and standards. This approach has been particularly evident in various areas, including trade, climate change, and human rights, where the EU has been at the forefront of promoting a rules-based international order.

The EU began to act internationally on digital policy in the early 2000s, initially focusing on issues like internet governance and digital trade. The EU's international digital policy efforts gained significant momentum with the adoption of the Digital Single Market Strategy in 2015 (COM(2015) 0192 final, 2015). The EU Digital Single Market was officially launched in May 2015 as part of the European Commission's broader strategy to create a unified digital economy across its member states. The strategy involved a comprehensive plan consisting of 16 key initiatives, focusing on three main areas: improving access to digital goods and services, creating an environment where digital networks and services can prosper, and maximising the growth potential of the digital economy. The initiatives aimed to harmonise digital regulations, remove barriers, and foster innovation across the EU.

The establishment of the EU's internal digital market significantly enhanced its international digital policy. The Digital Single Market Strategy does not include provisions for engaging with global partners to shape international digital standards and governance; its implementation has positioned the EU as a normative power in the digital space, allowing it to promote its values of privacy, human rights, and the rule of law on a global scale. The EU's international digital policy aims to extend these values beyond its borders, ensuring that the global digital environment reflects the principles that underpin the internal digital market. This proactive stance in global digital governance not only protects the EU's economic interests but also reinforces its commitment to a fair, open, and secure digital world.

By harmonising digital regulations across its 27 member states, the EU has created a unified market that attracts global businesses and sets a high standard for digital governance. This market power has enabled the EU to influence international digital norms and standards, as companies outside the EU had to comply with EU regulations to maintain access to the 440 million consumers' European market. Consequently, the EU's internal digital market legislative framework has not only given the EU Institutions (notably the EU Commission) the competence to act internationally on behalf of the EU in digital policy but also has served as a benchmark for global digital governance, compelling the EU to actively participate in shaping international rules and standards.

In recent years, the EU has increasingly recognised that its internal market alone is not sufficient to achieve its digital ambitions. The global nature of the digital economy means that the EU must build alliances with like-minded countries and engage in international negotiations to shape the rules that will govern digital technologies worldwide. This is evident in the EU's active participation in international bodies like the World Trade Organization (WTO), the OECD, and the United Nations, as well as in its bilateral digital partnerships with countries like Japan and Canada.

Moreover, the geopolitical landscape has shifted, with digital technology becoming a new arena for competition between global powers. The EU faces challenges from both the United States, where tech giants dominate the global market, and China, which has pursued a state-driven model of digital governance.

The International Competition to Shape the Global Digital Space

Governments are vying to influence and shape the future of cyberspace. In recent years, three main groups of countries have sought to assert their regulatory models and values to influence potential international digital standards. As detailed by Professor Anu Bradford in her book "Digital Empires (Bradford, 2023), the digital policies of the European Union (EU), the United States (US), and China have played pivotal roles in shaping the global cyberspace and technology landscape. As they participate in international multilateral forums such as the World Trade Organization (WTO), G20, and G7, their respective approaches share some commonalities but primarily reflect diverse perspectives on digital governance, privacy, security, and economic interests.

The European Union champions a comprehensive and rights-based approach to digital policy. Prioritising the protection of individuals' privacy and the encouragement of digital innovation, the EU has been a leader in crafting regulations protecting personal data, notably the

General Data Protection Regulation (GDPR) (Regulation (EU) 2016/679, 2016). Additionally, recent efforts have extended to regulations encompassing all data, both personal and non-personal, through Acts such as the Digital Services (Regulation (EU) 2022/2065, 2022) and Market (Regulation (EU) 2022/1925, 2022a) Acts, as well as the AI Act (European Parliament, 2024). Leveraging its first-mover advantage, the EU has been promoting international governance frameworks that align with its values, advocating for a multistakeholder model that incorporates input from governments, businesses, and civil society.

On the flip side, the United States, renowned for its technology-driven economy (and where Congress has struggled to pass any Federal legislation related to digital issues), generally prioritises an open and market-oriented approach. In international forums, the U.S. has historically championed minimal government intervention, emphasising innovation, the free flow of data, and the protection of intellectual property rights. Moreover, the U.S. has prioritised addressing security threats, relying on the security powers vested in the Executive branch. It has sought international cooperation to counteract China's influence, combat cybercrime, prevent the misuse of technologies for excessive surveillance, and ensure the resilience of its digital infrastructure. The Trump administration has adopted a course of action based on an "America first" doctrine, undermining multilateral processes and favouring bilateral pressure through unilateral means including tariffs, and promoting a broad deregulation agenda.

China's digital policy reflects its unique socio-political system and aspirations for technological leadership. Prioritising national security and the maintenance of its "social order" and sovereignty, China has been advocating for non-interference and the respect of its cyber sovereignty, emphasising security and control over its digital space at the international level. It has championed the development and international acceptance of its technology standards, positioning itself as the leader of the "Global South" and seeking to shape the global digital landscape in alignment with its interests.

Advancing the EU's approach in international forums has been difficult due to differing priorities and values among its partners. This has been particularly evident in areas such as data and AI, where attempts to make progress on the multilateral front have been limited. However, most advancements to promote the EU international governance priorities have occurred within restricted groupings composed of like-minded countries.

This chapter will delve into the EU and competing efforts to regulate data and AI at the international level, as these issues represent the forefront of attempts to regulate the digital economy internationally. It will examine prominent fora where the EU has been active in projecting its vision and where competition to project different regulatory models has unfolded, notably in digital trade negotiations (about data) and in international forums such as the G20, G7, and the OECD (regarding data and AI).

The Competition to Shape Trade Disciplines on Data: The EU Policy Is Gaining Momentum

Historically, governments attempted to utilise trade agreements to regulate the digital economy at the international level. While cross-border data flows are integral to contemporary international trade, the WTO rule book governing the digital economy—the General Agreement on Trade in Services (GATS)—was established before the advent of the Internet and is ill-suited to regulate cyberspace. As a result, in January 2019, 76 WTO members affirmed their intention to commence negotiations aimed at updating WTO discipline (World Trade Organization, 2019). However, as of January 2024, negotiations for the "Joint Initiative on Electronic Commerce" involving 90 WTO Members have encountered significant challenges, particularly with China and the US in the same room. Progress has been slow, with some contentious topics, such as disciplines for cross-border data flows (and combating data localisation) and protection for Source Code, withdrawn from negotiations due to the difficulty of finding consensus.

Considering the sluggish progress on the multilateral WTO front, trade partners have pursued their e-commerce and digital trade agendas through alternative avenues, notably through preferential bilateral Regional Trade Agreements (RTAs) and Digital Trade Agreements (DTAs). As noted by the OECD, Governments are increasingly using RTAs to facilitate data flows while acknowledging the necessity of accompanying safeguards for personal data protection. Likewise, Academics have observed a "significant jump" in provisions relevant to e-commerce and digital trade in preferential trade agreements, noting that "since January

2020, 49 agreements covering digital trade commitments have been concluded or signed, with more under negotiation" (Casalini et al., 2021, p. 28).

Trade disciplines aimed at promoting cross-border data flows and combating data localisation revolve around three distinct competitive approaches, championed respectively by the EU, CTPP countries[1] (originally including the US), and China. While these approaches share similar features—such as provisions for data flows and anti-localisation, coupled with exceptions for legitimate public policy objectives and/or privacy—they reflect diverse perspectives on digital regulation, privacy, security, and economic interests.

The EU Approach: A Dual Objective

In its latest Trade Policy Strategy paper (COM(2021) 66 final, 2021), the EU Commission—responsible for negotiating trade agreements on behalf of the EU—clarified its approach to data: "With regard to cross-border data transfers and the prohibition of data localisation requirements, the Commission will follow an open but assertive approach, based on European values and interests. (…) In particular, the EU will continue to address unjustified obstacles to data flows while preserving its regulatory autonomy in the area of data protection and privacy".

In fact, the EU pursues a dual objective: as the leader in digital trade (Köhler-Suzuki, 2023), it is resolute in combating "unjustified obstacles to data flows" and ensuring its businesses benefit from the international free flow of data. Simultaneously, the Commission emphasises that new disciplines against digital protectionism must "preserve its regulatory autonomy" to regulate the digital economy. With the adoption, during the Von der Leyen Commission, of numerous regulations applying to cyberspace, the imperative to safeguard the EU's digital regulatory framework from potential trade challenges has become increasingly prominent. In essence, as highlighted in E. Letta's report, the EU seeks to ensure that "Trade agreements should not be used as a trojan horse to weaken legislative frameworks, and the EU should use its economic toolbox to the full, to promote its Single Market regulations as a competitive advantage, positioning the Union as a high-value and high-quality exporter of

[1] Australia, Brunei, Canada, Chile, Japan, Malaysia, Mexico, New Zealand, Peru, Singapore and Vietnam.

safe, secure and human-centric digital technologies and services" (Letta, 2024).

To realise this dual objective, the EU has drafted a model clause that it aims to incorporate into all its trade agreements.

The EU Approach: The Model Clause on Data Flows and Data Protection, Which Has Evolved Over Time and Is Gaining Momentum

In 2018, two years after the adoption of the GDPR, the EU agreed on a model clause for trade disciplines applying to data. The purpose of this language to be included in EU trade agreements was to allow the EU to tackle protectionist practices in third countries while ensuring that such disciplines could not be used to challenge the GDPR. The model clause was, therefore, originally drafted to shield personal data and privacy protection measures (in particular, the cross-border data transfer regime of the GDPR-Chapter V) from trade dispute settlement challenges.

In fact, the EU (unlike notably the US) could not subscribe to an open-ended trade discipline to free cross-border data flows or combat any "restrictions" to data flows. With the GDPR, the EU did put in place a "conditional model" (Marel & Ferracane, 2021) whereby personal data can be transferred outside the EU "only if"[2] certain conditions are met (basically under the condition that the protection continues to apply when the data is transferred). In this situation, the EU could not subscribe to unqualified binding commitments to free data flows that could outlaw the very conditions conditioning cross-border data transfers that the EU did put in place.

The EU model clause comprised two Articles (Art 12.4; Art. 12.5, European Commission, 2024): one with a closed list of four prohibited restrictions to data flows/data localisation measures, and the other one an exception for data protection and privacy.

The EU carefully drafted a discipline consisting of prohibiting four data localisation measures (reflecting barriers identified by EU business) that could not correspond to any scenario of implementation of the GDPR. The prohibited measures comprised: (a) requiring the use of facilities or

[2] See Art. 44 of the GDPR: "Any transfer of personal data which are undergoing processing or are intended for processing after transfer to a third country or to an international organisation shall take place only if, subject to the other provisions of this Regulation (..)".

networks in its territory for data processing, (b) requiring the localisation of data in its territory, (c) prohibiting storage or processing of data in the territory of the other Party, or (d) making the cross-border transfer of data contingent upon the use of facilities or networks in its territory.

Note that this list could be updated (by agreement between the Parties) to tackle additional barriers to data flows. This list-based approach was identified as the best option to address the real-life barriers to data flows identified by EU businesses while shielding the GDPR from any possible challenge before trade courts.

The Commission supplemented these disciplines with a privacy exception (in addition to the General Art. XIV GATS type exception) to safeguard the EU's constitutional right to privacy. This provision stipulated that "Each Party may adopt and maintain the measures it deems appropriate to ensure the protection of personal data and privacy, including through the adoption and application of rules for the cross-border transfer of personal data".

The phrase "it deems appropriate" drew criticism from several negotiators, particularly in the WTO E-commerce negotiations, due to its alleged subjective nature. Some argued that this wording granted excessive discretion to parties and may not be effectively scrutinised by Trade dispute settlement panels. In response to these concerns, the EU has maintained that this language does not provide unchecked authority, citing a previous WTO panel decision (World Trade Organization, 2019a), where similar discretionary language did not preclude review of the measure in question. Furthermore, the EU clarified that the exception could not be invoked to justify any measure, as it is specifically limited to safeguarding personal data and privacy.

The EU approach is gaining traction, both at bilateral and multilateral levels, and recently scored some substantial victories. At the bilateral level, the EU successfully persuaded a few partners to adopt its 2018 model clause. This template, for instance, was incorporated into the EU Free Trade Agreements agreed with New Zealand and Chile. This achievement is particularly noteworthy given that both countries have been advocating for alternative approaches at the WTO.

More recently, as a result of trade negotiations with the UK, Japan and Singapore, the EU's model clause was also endorsed and has undergone two significant developments.

First, in the EU-UK free trade agreement (TCA[3] Art. 202) and, subsequently, in the agreements concluded with Japan and Singapore, the reference to "it deems appropriate" was dropped. Instead, the EU and UK agreed to mention that "Nothing in this Agreement shall prevent a Party from adopting or maintaining measures on the protection of personal data and privacy (…) provided that the law of the Party provides for instruments enabling transfers under conditions of general application". Put simply, the data flow disciplines within the TCA couldn't be employed to challenge data protection measures if the Party has mechanisms in place "enabling" data transfers. This provision could prove valuable in scenarios akin to those observed in China, where countries may have legislation theoretically permitting transfers, but in practice, such transfers don't occur.

Second, in the recently concluded EU-Japan Protocol regarding cross-border data flows (European Council, 2024), the EU and Japan added two prohibitions to the list of the original four agreed in 2018. One addition, which has also been included in the Digital Trade Agreement agreed in July 2024 with Singapore (European Commission, 2024a), applies to incoming data; it forbids "prohibiting the transfer of information into the territory of the Party". The other addition agreed only with Japan (and not with Singapore) governs outbound data, it prohibits "requiring the approval of the Party prior to the transfer of information to the territory of the other Party". With the inclusion of these new prohibitions, the EU, for the first time, accepted to commit to language that does not only prohibit data localisation measures (the 2018 original four prohibitions) but clearly extends to data flows.

It's important to note that, to prevent these additional prohibitions from being used to challenge the EU's legislative framework, and in response to Japan's insistence on maintaining the necessary policy flexibility to regulate data, negotiators also incorporated language to clarify and broaden the scope of the exceptions. Significantly, a footnote specified that the new prohibition regarding outbound data flows does not preclude "requiring the certification or conformity assessment of ICT

[3] See European Union, 2021. Article 2. "Nothing in this Agreement shall prevent a Party from adopting or maintaining measures on the protection of personal data and privacy, including with respect to cross-border data transfers, provided that the law of the Party provides for instruments enabling transfers under conditions of general application for the protection of the data transferred".

products, services and processes, including Artificial Intelligence (..) or for cybersecurity purposes", nor does it prevent ensuring continuity of protection for all data (including non-personal data) when transferred cross-border. Note that this is the first time the EU includes in a trade agreement a reference to the need to preserve policy space to regulate Artificial Intelligence (AI) cybersecurity or to ensure the continuity of protection of non-personal data when transferred cross-borders.

In addition to these clarifications, the texts agreed with Japan and Singapore introduced, for the first time in EU Trade Agreements, a new exception for the pursuance of "legitimate public policy objectives" (LPPOs). This addition was first made at Japan's request, as the Japanese negotiators argued that the General Agreement on Trade in Services (GATS) language on general exceptions, originally drafted in 1947, was inadequate for addressing the contemporary need to regulate the digital economy, notably in alignment with Japan's economic security policies. In the EU-Singapore July 2024 Digital Trade Agreement, a similar exception pertaining to LPPOs was also included and further clarified. In this Agreement, the negotiators specified that this LPPO exception comprises the pursuance of objectives such as the protection of "cybersecurity", "safe and trustworthy artificial intelligence", as well as the protection "against the dissemination of disinformation". Note that this non-exhaustive list of legitimate exceptions applies not only to the data flows and localisation disciplines but also to all the obligations contained in the EU-Singapore Agreement.

At the multilateral level, in the WTO e-commerce negotiations, after years of heated debates over competing data protection approaches, the EU achieved a significant victory. In the final compromise proposal from July 2024, the WTO co-chairs adopted the EU's approach to data protection. The draft compromise includes an article on "Personal Data Protection Exception" (World Trade Organization, 2019, art.25) that mirrors the language used in the EU's trade agreements with the UK, Japan, and Singapore. Notably, it directly replicates the UK agreement's provision, ensuring that trade rules cannot challenge data protection measures if mechanisms are in place to enable data transfers.

The language developed by the EU in 2018, initially crafted to safeguard the General Data Protection Regulation (GDPR), has evolved during trade negotiations to address new restrictions on data flows. Simultaneously, the exception aimed at maintaining policy flexibility to regulate the digital economy has been broadened in scope.[4] With these evolutions, the EU negotiators have brought the EU data trade language closer to the CTPP approach, which enhanced the influence of the EU's model at both bilateral and multilateral levels.

The CTPP/US Approach: A Business Focussed Approach Which Recently Changed

The US approach to digital trade diverged significantly from that of the EU, reflecting differing regulatory contexts. If, in 2018, because of its rules-based approach, the EU could not subscribe to unqualified free data flow commitments, the US came from the opposite direction. The absence of a comprehensive Federal data protection framework in the US (along with the strong advocacy from Silicon Valley) allowed the USTR to pursue a more assertive strategy centred on advocating for a blanket prohibition on restricting data flows.

Turning to trade mechanisms to advance the US business-oriented digital agenda was partly a choice by default: in the absence of a federal data protection law, the US lacked the legal foundation to engage partners in a collaborative regulatory framework. Unlike the EU and China, for instance, the US couldn't pursue "equivalence" or "adequacy" determinations regarding data protection legislation. Additionally, it's important to note the close ties between Silicon Valley and the USTR/Commerce Department, marked by a "revolving door" phenomenon where many high-ranking public affairs officials from US tech companies have previous experience working within the US departments responsible for digital trade. This interconnection may have also fuelled Silicon Valley's interest in influencing the US digital trade agenda (e.g. Office of Senator Elizabeth Warren, 2023).

As a matter of fact, until recently, the United States has played a significant role in shaping and advancing the international agenda on digital trade. It has been a leading advocate for trade principles such as the free flow of data across borders, the prohibition of data localisation, and non-discrimination against digital products and services.

[4] It's worth emphasising that preserving this policy space is crucial not only for enabling the EU to implement its current and forthcoming legislative digital framework but also for allowing foreign partners to adopt regulations like the EU's approach to digital regulation, coined by Professor Bradford in "The Brussels Effect".

The US was a pioneer in developing a digital trade agenda, particularly through the early inclusion of disciplines on data in its trade agreements. The USTR recognised the Trans-Pacific Partnership (TPP) as an opportunity to champion ambitious digital trade disciplines. Coined by Secretary Clinton as the centrepiece of the United States' strategic pivot to the Asia-Pacific region (Clinton, 2011), the TPP marked the first regional deal to incorporate comprehensive rules on digital commerce.

Seizing the opportunity presented by the absence, before 2018, of specific language proposals from both the EU and China regarding data flow discipline in trade agreements, the USTR led the effort to include broad, binding commitments on free data flows in the TPP. These commitments mandated that "Each Party shall allow the cross-border transfer of information by electronic means" (CTPP, Art. 14.11.2) and included robust provisions against data localisation, barring Parties from requiring a covered person to use or locate computing facilities in the territory of a Party as a condition for conducting business there.

Notably, such expansive disciplines could potentially outlaw legislation inspired by the EU data protection regulation model, particularly concerning the prohibition of transferring data across borders when continuity of protection is not ensured.

Importantly, these extensive obligations were accompanied by broad language on exceptions, which, in addition to the General Agreement on Trade in Services (GATS) type exception, stipulated that violations of these obligations could be justified when deemed "necessary" to pursue "legitimate public objectives". Some trade negotiators, notably starting with the EU, criticised this addition, arguing that it would expand the exception to encompass undefined new "legitimate" policies. The EU contended that this would introduce legal uncertainty and undermine data disciplines, potentially enabling countries to justify protectionist policies under the guise of economic or industrial policy-related LPPOs. Supporters of the Trans-Pacific Partnership (TPP) argued that the risk of misuse was mitigated by the application of the "necessity" test. Additionally, they asserted that there was a need to broaden the scope of the language on general exceptions dating back to 1947 to address the contemporary imperative of regulating the digital economy.

After the United States withdrew from the TPP (President Trump's inaugural decision upon taking office), the remaining eleven TPP countries renegotiated the Agreement and finalised the Comprehensive and Progressive Agreement for Trans-Pacific Partnership (CPTPP) in 2018.

The CPTPP final Treaty retained the data-related disciplines and LPPOs exception originally advocated by the US.

Despite President Trump's withdrawal from the TPP, US tech companies continued to advocate for advancements in the digital trade agenda, which were pursued through bilateral agreements. The United States-Mexico-Canada Agreement (USMCA), which took effect on July 1, 2020, introduced several updates to trade rules among the three North American countries. In this agreement, the language on data flows was strengthened, shifting from the CPTPP's affirmative obligation to "allow" data flows to a prohibition (Art. 19.11) on "restricting" data transfers across the three countries. Similarly, the discipline against data localisation was reinforced by eliminating the reference to exceptions for the pursuit of legitimate public policy objectives from Article 19.[5]

While initially, the absence of domestic regulation allowed the US to pursue a more ambitious stance than the EU regarding the trade discipline of free data flows, it has recently become a problem, as the advancement of this agenda could potentially limit the policy space required by the US Congress for legislation. Ambassador Tai recently articulated (Council of Foreign Relations, 2024) that the US no longer wanted trade language to supersede domestic legislation. In fear of negotiating trade disciplines that might pre-empt Congress's legislative work, US trade negotiators withdrew from all trade negotiations related to data, source code protection, and cryptography in 2023. This decision garnered significant criticism from US businesses but was praised by Democrats, trade unions, and civil rights organisations. The repercussions of the US's reversal on digital trade were not only felt in bilateral negotiations but also at the WTO, where this disengagement contributed to a further lowering in the level of ambition of the WTO e-commerce negotiations.[6] The latest developments coming from the Trump administration highlight an attempt to undermine global rules and to give pre-eminence to direct bilateral pressures through trade tariffs, limitations to access to US dominated technologies and the promotion of a broad deregulatory agenda. This

[5] Interestingly, a similar approach to the USMCA was pursued by the US in the Digital agreement reached with the UK and Japan (which however do not comprise biding dispute settlement mechanisms, thereby raising doubts about its legal values).

[6] E-JSI negotiations' chairs have, in April 2024, removed any commitment related to these US-sensitive areas from the text of the draft compromise.

results in alignment with the interests of the very large US digital companies, but it has also prompted reactions from partner countries, in terms of efforts to reduce tech dependencies from the US.

China's Approach

China's stance on digital trade is significantly influenced by its distinctive data governance policy. China views data not only as a production factor but also as a critical element for enabling the government to uphold "social order" and ensure adherence to "core socialist values" (Creemers et al., 2018). By implementing stringent data localisation obligations alongside bans on cross-border data transfers, the Chinese government has warranted that data generated within its borders (which constitutes the largest domestic data pool globally) exclusively serves its digital leaders. This approach also ensures the government's unfettered access to all necessary information to uphold "social morals and ethics" (Rafaelof, et al., 2021) or exercise control over its citizens.

In a recent speech (Ministry of Foreign Affairs of the People's Republic of China, 2023), "Jointly Implementing the Global Security Initiative For Lasting Peace and Security of the World", the Chinese Assistant Minister of Foreign Affairs recalled the fundamentals of China's international digital policy. First and foremost, the Minister insisted that it is key to commit to "respecting the sovereignty and territorial integrity of all countries" and advocated for "non-interference in internal affairs and respect for the development paths and social systems independently chosen by the people of different countries".[7] But, at the same time, the Chinese Minister, who wanted China to be seen as a champion of international law and multilateralism, said that he "rejects the Cold War mentality, unilateralism, bloc politics and confrontation. It calls on all countries to practice true multilateralism".

[7] China's President Xi Jinping repeatedly calls on countries to respect one another's "cyber sovereignty" and different Internet governance models "It is important to respect cyber sovereignty and each country's Internet development path and governance model, abide by international rules in cyberspace and oppose seeking hegemony, bloc confrontation and arms race in cyberspace, deepen practical cooperation in cyber security, effectively crack down on cybercrimes, strengthen data security and personal information protection, and properly deal with the conflicts in rules, social risks and ethical challenges brought about by the development of science and technology".

In trade policy, this dual objective has been pursued through robust support for multilateral trade negotiations (starting with the WTO e-commerce negotiations), coupled with advocating for broad exceptions to safeguard the regulatory space necessary to pursue China's distinct concept of data sovereignty.

A prime illustration of the Chinese approach to data and digital trade can be observed in the E-commerce chapter (Ministry of Commerce of the People's Republic of China, 2020) of the Regional Comprehensive Economic Partnership Agreement[8] (RCEP). This language combines obligations akin to those in the CPTPP (as described earlier in this chapter, which prevent restrictions on data flows and prohibit data localisation) with broad self-judging exceptions. These exceptions ensure that China's own restrictions cannot be subject to review by a trade dispute settlement system. In its RCEP framework, China went so far as to specify that "For the purposes of this subparagraph [re: the interpretation of the language regarding the exception], the Parties affirm that the necessity behind the implementation of such legitimate public policy shall be decided by the implementing Party" (RCEP, Art. 12-15A). Moreover, to ensure that there can be no interference with Chinese data policies, the RCEP included language allowing parties to adopt measures to protect "essential security interests", which "shall not be disputed by other Parties" (RCEP, Art. 12-15b).

Through this digital trade language, China effectively merged its declared backing for the international trade rules-based system with the assertion of its own sovereignty. However, due to the expansive and self-judging nature of the exceptions outlined in this template, RCEP negotiators frequently privately express doubts about the enforceability of these disciplines. In fact, with such a significant exception for legitimate public policy objectives, it is unlikely that these rules will help Chinese businesses tackle foreign digital protectionism.

In light of this context, one can appreciate the challenge China faces in balancing the protection of its digital sovereignty—shielding it from

[8] RCEP entered into force on 1 January 2022 for ten original parties: Australia, Brunei Darussalam, Cambodia, China, Japan, Laos, New Zealand, Singapore, Thailand and Vietnam. RCEP then entered into force for the Republic of Korea on 1 February 2022, for Malaysia on 18 March 2022, for Indonesia on 2 January 2023 and for the Philippines on 2 June 2023. RCEP is the world's largest free trade agreement by members' GDP.

"interference" from trade dispute settlement panels—while also advocating for its business interests beyond its borders. It's noteworthy that China has also applied to join the CPTPP, suggesting a belief that the LPPO exceptions included in this Agreement would afford China the policy space necessary to continue implementing its data localisation measures and restrictions on data flows. Faced with restrictions in terms of access to American technology, China has doubled down in its efforts to reach technological leadership. And increasingly, from automotive to AI, China appears to be winning against the USA.

Is the EU Winning the Competition to Shape Trade Disciplines on Data?

With the US stepping back from digital trade negotiations and China encountering difficulties in establishing enforceable trade data disciplines, the EU has been the only one (amongst these three actors) to be able to effectively conclude Trade agreements reflecting its approach. This has not only been the case with Japan but also most recently with Singapore, with the conclusion on 23 July 2024 of the EU-Singapore Digital Partnership Agreement. As put by EU Executive Vice-President Dombrovskis, this agreement with Singapore represents "a significant step forward for the EU's ambition to be a global standard-setter in the domain of digital trade" (European Commission, 2024a).

As the EU is negotiating a Digital Trade Agreement with Korea as well as digital FTA Chapters with several partners (including India, Thailand, the Philippines, Indonesia, etc.…), there may be more opportunities for the EU to promote its model, building on the language recently agreed upon with Japan or Singapore. This language, which uniquely combines the EU's list-based approach with CPTPP-type LPPO exceptions, could potentially bridge gaps between different approaches.

While digital trade disciplines may be effective in combating digital protectionism, they have limited utility in projecting regulatory models and promoting values. For example, it's worth noting that the EU has effectively promoted its personal data protection template internationally (known as the "Brussels effect") despite privacy and data protection being excluded from its trade template. The "Brussels effect" stems more from the international influence of EU regulations rather than its trade agreements. This projection has been achieved, as described by Professor

Bradford, through both de facto and de jure means rather than through recourse to trade policy (Bradford, 2020).

In reality, the international conversation on how to regulate data and the values underpinning different visions of digital policies primarily unfolds outside trade forums, in particular in the G20 and the G7. With the Trump administration, the pertinence of global rules is however to be questioned, whereas actual tech leadership has become a key argument, probably more important than rule-making.

Progress on International Digital Regulation in Multilateral Fora and the EU'S Role in Shaping G7 and G20 Work on Data and AI

In the absence of an international organisation dedicated to digital policy, discussions on how to regulate the digital space occur across various multilateral forums, including the UN, UNESCO, standards-setting organisations, and initiatives such as the UK-initiated AI Safety Summits. Recently, significant progress on digital governance has been made in the G20, G7, and the OECD, particularly regarding data (a) and Artificial Intelligence (AI) (b).

Progress on Data Governance in the G20, the G7 and the OECD

The G20

Interestingly, despite the differing approaches among its members, the G20 was able to reach a consensus on how to approach international data governance. In their Osaka Declaration (Ministry of Foreign Affairs of Japan, 2019), G20 Leaders endorsed the concept of "Data Free Flows with Trust" (DFFT). This initiative, initially proposed in 2019 by the late Japanese Prime Minister S. Abe, advocates for the idea that data can flow freely across borders while maintaining trust and respecting privacy, security, and other values. While the acknowledgement, in 2019, of this dual objective by leaders may appear intuitive and obvious, it signified a significant shift in perspective.

The DFFT initiative has played a crucial role in redirecting the global conversation away from a narrative promoted by Silicon Valley in the 2000s that treated data as a mere commodity (or "the new oil of the economy"[9]) to be freely exchanged. Instead, it emphasises the recognition, championed by the EU, that data, unlike any raw material, requires protection and should only be transferred along with its protection.[10]

This concept represents a compromise where all G20 partners, representing competing regulatory models in trade negotiations, could see a reflection of their own policy approach to data.

The EU has, from the outset, been a strong supporter of the Japanese-led DFFT initiative. It considered that DFFT reflected the fundamental premise, at the heart of the EU personal and non-personal data regulations (GDPR, the Data Act, the Data Governance Act…), that data protection is not a "restriction" to be combated through recourse to trade disciplines, but an enabler to data flows as it contributes to trust in the digital economy. In particular, the EU was satisfied that its fundamental principle (enshrined in the GDPR, the Data Act and the Data Governance Act) that data can be transferred outside the EU "only if" 46 protected was reflected in the use of the DFFT wording "with trust" (which implies that without "trust" the data cannot be transferred).

The U.S. found satisfaction in seeing its approach reflected in the DFFT concept, particularly with the mention of "free" cross-border data flows, echoing Silicon Valley's advocacy for liberalising international data flows.

Similarly, China welcomed the inclusion of the notion of "trust" at the heart of DFFT, which they interpreted as encompassing the importance of "security". Additionally, Beijing found comfort in the fact that nothing in the DFFT prescribed how sovereign nations should regulate data.

Since its adoption in 1999, the DFFT initiative has been consistently reaffirmed and further developed in all G20 Leaders' Declarations. Notably, in their Rome G20 Declaration, Leaders took a significant step by committing "to work towards identifying commonalities, complementarities, and elements of convergence between existing regulatory approaches and instruments enabling data to flow with trust" (Government of Italy, 2021, paragraph 48).

[9] As coined by Clive Humby in 2006.

[10] The last G7 and G20 Declarations on Digital issues include important references to the ongoing "convergence" in data protection regulations around the world. Contains some significant headways for the EU: with the identification of recourse to "Model contractual clauses" -e.g. as in the GDPR, and the Data Act - as an area of "international convergence", and an issue for future G20 work.

The inclusion of the reference to "convergence" marked a notable evolution from past language, which previously emphasised divergences between domestic privacy frameworks and framed them as economic challenges. With this new language closely aligning with the EU narrative, the international community began to view "convergence" in data protection regulations as essential for facilitating data flows and promoting future interoperability. In other words, the DFFT has shifted the global conversation among leaders from questioning the need to regulate data, initially perceived as a mere "factor of production", towards discussions on how to regulate it in a "converging" manner to enable its optimal and safe utilisation.

While Leaders came to a consensus on the fundamental principle that data can only be transferred with "trust", due to their unique characteristics, the diversity of interpretations regarding the concept of "trust" limited the extent of agreement. It's worth noting that each time G20 Leaders and Ministers mentioned DFFT, they emphasised that such transfers should occur "in accordance with the relevant applicable legal framework", reaffirming their sovereignty to determine what "trust" entails.

Given the varying interpretations of the DFFT concept, especially concerning the notion of "trust", it quickly became challenging to engage in more operational discussions at the G20 level on how to implement DFFT. Further progress was only feasible within more restricted forums involving like-minded partners who share fundamental commonalities regarding the definition of "trust".

DFFT Amongst Like-Minded Democratic Countries: OECD and G7

Interestingly, the imperative for democracies to collaborate in establishing a unified front against techno-authoritarianism was underscored by business leaders as well. Brad Smith, President of Microsoft, emphasised this necessity in his book "Tools & Weapons" (Smith & Browne, 2019), advocating for like-minded countries to join forces in regulating data and AI based on a human rights approach. He stated that "the inexorable course of technology is forcing more international collaboration" and highlighted how "issues like surveillance reform, privacy protection, and cybersecurity have all required governments to deal with each other in new ways" and have compelled governments to engage with each other in new ways. Smith called upon "democratic countries to come together" to address this challenge.

This stance was echoed by the EU, as outlined in its 2020 Communication "A European Strategy for Data" (COM(2020) 66 final, 2020), which expressed its intention to prioritise advancements in data governance alongside like-minded countries that share similar "values". The Communication, which laid out the EU's strategy on data governance, elaborated that "in order to promote the European model around the world, the EU will work with trusted partners sharing the same standards and values, to support others who wish to give their citizens greater control over their data, in line with values they share with Europe".

The OECD: Fight Against Disproportionate Surveillance

While there is a broad consensus among democracies to denounce techno-authoritarian regimes that exploit technologies and personal data to maintain "social order" and perpetuate their rule, until recently, there have been no clear international standards to address this issue. In other words, there was no universally accepted benchmark to distinguish between legitimate surveillance by democratic states to ensure security and the excessive surveillance conducted by techno-authoritarian states to control their population.

Lacking international standards and a dedicated forum to tackle this issue, OECD countries have been regulating and limiting data transfers to techno-authoritarian states in an ad hoc manner. Specifically, in the US, due to the absence of Federal data protection legislation, restrictions on data transfers to China have been imposed by the President, leveraging executive powers for security-related reasons.[11]

To address this gap and respond to the calls from political and business leaders to "operationalise" DFFT by defining what "trust" means, the OECD Committee on Digital Economy Policy (CDEP) decided (OECD, 2020) in December 2020 to establish common principles to combat disproportionate government surveillance.[12]

[11] Note that, on April 24, President Biden signed law, which included a critical provision covering privacy and data transfers known as the Protecting Americans' Data from Foreign Adversaries Act ("PADFA"). PADFA generally prohibits data brokers from transferring personally identifiable sensitive data to certain named foreign adversary countries, including the People's Republic of China ("PRC"), and any entity controlled by certain foreign adversaries.

[12] The Purpose was to address "government access to personal data held by private sector entities that, regardless of the context, is inconsistent with democratic values and the rule of law, and is unconstrained, unreasonable, arbitrary or disproportionate".

These negotiations were particularly intense and difficult because the US and the EU were, in parallel, engaged in difficult negotiations on how to implement the Schrems II judgement (Data Protection Commissioner v Facebook Ireland and Maximillian Schrems, 2020) to agree on adequate guarantees and processes to govern US government access (surveillance) to EU personal data. After 2 years of negotiations, in December 2022, and after the EU and the US found an agreement in principle to implement the Schrems II case, the OECD Ministers agreed on a Legal Instrument "which distinguishes our countries from other countries whose law enforcement or national security access to personal data are inconsistent with democratic values and the rule of law, are unconstrained, unreasonable, arbitrary or disproportionate, or amount to violations of human rights" (OECD, 2022).

This Declaration, which is the first intergovernmental agreement in the area of surveillance, is an important milestone in distinguishing democratic and authoritarian recourse to technologies. To take the OECD Ministers' words, it is an "important expression of our shared democratic values and commitment to the rule of law, which *distinguishes our countries from other countries* whose law enforcement or national security access to personal data are inconsistent with democratic values and the rule of law, are unconstrained, unreasonable, arbitrary or disproportionate, or amount to violations of human rights". (Emphasis added).

This Declaration comprises eleven principles, and some might turn particularly useful to draw a line between techno-authoritarian and democratic surveillance practices.

In particular, the OECD Declaration clarifies that government surveillance must pursue a "legitimate aim". More specifically, this principle provides that "Governments do not seek access to personal data for the purpose of suppressing or burdening criticism or dissent; or disadvantaging persons or groups solely on the basis of characteristics including, but not limited to age, mental or physical disability, ethnicity, Indigenous status, gender identity or expression, sexual orientation, or political or religious affiliation". This language holds an intriguing potential to differentiate from authoritarian practices. For instance, Chinese Government surveillance of the Uyghur minorities could be condemned based on this language.

Likewise, authoritarian regimes where there is no independent oversight nor route for citizen' redress would not comply with the OECD principles defining standards for "oversight[13]" and "redress". In particular, the OECD requirement that national bodies in charge of "oversight" of "surveillance" "*are protected from interference*" could not be met by China, where, pursuant to Art. 60 of the Personal Information Protection Law (PIPL, n.d.), the Chinese government (the State Cyberspace administration) is in charge of "oversight".

Similarly, the requirement, under the OECD "Redress" principle, that "The legal framework provides individuals with effective judicial and non-judicial redress to identify and remedy violations of the national legal framework" would be impossible to meet in countries where there is no independent judicial branch.

While the OECD Declaration is not legally binding, it has the potential to significantly influence OECD signatories and have tangible effects on domestic legal frameworks around the world. Countries can now cite this Declaration within their domestic legal systems to pursue binding enforcement. Similar to the precedent set by the non-binding OECD principles on data protection, nations worldwide may draw inspiration from the OECD Declaration to formulate their surveillance legislation. Additionally, in adjudicating cases involving government access issues, courts may, in the future, refer to the OECD Declaration as a guiding framework.

Moreover, the Declaration could serve as an invaluable international reference for data controllers, processors, and Protection Authorities, particularly in the wake of the Schrems II judgement, as they have to evaluate risks associated with foreign government access to data before authorising cross-border data transfers. Countries may also lend legal significance to the Declaration by incorporating it into international agreements. Notably, the EU and Japan have already taken steps in this direction by acknowledging, in the EU-Japan agreement on Data Flows (Council of the European Union, 2024), that "high standards of privacy and data protection as regards government access to privately held data, such as those outlined in the OECD Principles for Government Access to Personal Data held by Private Sector Entities, contribute to trust in the digital economy".

[13] See definition of VI. Oversight: In the exercise of their functions, oversight bodies are protected from interference and have the financial, human and technical resources to effectively carry out their mandate. They document their findings, produce reports, and make recommendations, which are made publicly available to the greatest extent possible.

Indeed, as the only international standards established by democracies to delineate between "proportionate" and "disproportionate" surveillance and given the growing necessity for such criteria from courts, data processors, and other stakeholders, one could anticipate that these OECD Principles have the potential to evolve beyond mere declarations of intention.

While G7 Ministers have recognised this OECD instrument as "a critical tool to improve trust in cross-border data flows" (Government of Japan, 2023), there currently exists no mechanism for coordinating and monitoring its implementation. This underscores the broader "gap in international governance" (Government of Japan, 2023) regarding data policies, as identified by G7 Ministers in their Takasaki Declaration. To begin addressing this gap, G7 Ministers have recently undertaken some first initiatives.

Progress on Data Governance

Calls to put in place a global forum for governments to cooperate on digital governance issues were already made in 2019 by former US President Sherpa, Dan Price, in a seminal article (Price, 2019) where he called to "look to the post-financial crisis architecture as a model and establish now a 'Data and Technology Board' to anchor global cooperation".

The OECD also recognised that "Moving forward on DFFT requires an integrated policy approach, both domestically and internationally, to build trust. The capacities of governments and regulators, including privacy but also sectoral regulators, to co-operate across silos, borders and at different levels simultaneously are key to supporting organisations in their efforts to build trust and multi-jurisdictional compliance" (OECD, 2023).

In 2023, Japan, as G7 Chair, also identified this issue as a top priority, and, under its leadership, Ministers agreed to "operationalise DFFT through a new institutional arrangement for partnership (IAP)" (Government of Japan, 2023, paragraph 9). Interestingly, this effort was backed by a group of 30 global companies which saw the IAP as "the principal global forum for governments to cooperate on digital governance issues from a cross-sectoral perspective, promote coherent regulatory approaches, enhance transparency and interoperability across jurisdictions, and assess cumulative and systemic risks across the global digital ecosystem. It would also be structured to give stakeholders the opportunity to share their views and expertise on new and emerging technologies" (AMGEN, Applied Materials, APTIV, BMO, Citi, DOW, ENGIE et al., 2023).

In response to the call from G7 Ministers, the OECD has agreed to host the IAP and provide support as a de facto secretariat. Initially, the IAP primarily comprises communities of experts from government, business, and Non-Governmental Organisations convened by the OECD to discuss specific projects, including those related to the implementation of the Principles against unlimited government surveillance.

While this initiative is relatively low-key and currently falls short of meeting the business community's expectations of establishing "the principal global forum for governments to cooperate on digital governance issues", it represents an initial step towards a more structured international dialogue on Data Free Flows with Trust.

China

China has also engaged in international cooperation on data policies with like-minded countries. It launched, in 2020, its "data security initiative" (Park, 2022) aimed at shaping global norms and practices related to data, with a focus on "security". Announced in September 2020, the initiative outlined Chinese principles and proposals for the responsible use and management of data in the international community.

The initiative is a key element of China's efforts to assert its influence in shaping global digital governance and norms, especially amid increasing tensions with the United States over technology and data issues. It was seen as an element of response to the Trump Administration initiatives (notably the "clean network" initiative) to exclude Chinese tech firms perceived as threatening "national security".

Typically, the Global Initiative on Data Security contained the basic features of China's data and digital policy: the principle of non-interference in domestic affairs and respect for sovereignty, insistence on security, support for multilateral cooperation, etc.…

On "sovereignty", it emphasised the rights of nations to manage and govern data within their borders and recalled that "States (…) shall not obtain data located in other States through companies or individuals without other States' permission".

With regard to data security, the initiative stressed the importance of protecting data from unauthorised access and insisted that "States have the responsibility and right to ensure the security of important data and personal information bearing on their national security, public security, economic security and social stability".

Finally, regarding international governance, China called for cooperation and dialogue among countries and stressed that "should States need to obtain overseas data out of law enforcement requirement such as combating crimes, they should do it through judicial assistance or other relevant multilateral and bilateral agreements".

Interestingly, prior to the OECD Ministers reaching a consensus on their collective Principles against disproportionate Government surveillance, China also positioned "surveillance" as a focal point of its key international data initiative. However, China's concern primarily revolved around "mass surveillance against other states" rather than surveillance conducted by states on their own citizens. This language likely targeted US surveillance laws such as the US Cloud Act and Foreign Intelligence Surveillance Act (FISA), which grant US law enforcement agencies access to data stored overseas. In the same vein, the Chinese initiative urged tech companies to refrain from installing "backdoors in their products and services to illegally obtain users' data, control, or manipulate users' systems and devices".

This initiative and insistence on "surveillance" could also be interpreted as a Chinese effort to shift the focus of the international surveillance debate away from China and back to the US, where it originated with the Snowden revelations in June 2013.

Despite China's diplomatic efforts and investments in support of its "digital Silk Road initiative", the "data security initiative" has failed to gain significant traction in foreign countries (Park, 2022). One might question whether a digital governance framework tailored to China's specific needs—based on non-interference and the implementation of protectionist policies aimed at citizen control—is exportable to other nations.

While international data governance has dominated much of the discourse on digital governance in the international arena, the focus has recently shifted markedly towards artificial intelligence (AI).

International Progress on the Regulation of Artificial Intelligence

With the rapid advancement of AI technologies and the increasingly widespread use of generative AI, there is growing recognition of the need for international cooperation and coordination in regulating this space. While some consensus on high-level principles was found at multilateral levels (e.g. Government of the United Kingdom, 2023; United Nations, 2024a) as well as plurilateral levels (e.g. Global Partnership on Artificial Intelligence, 2024; OECD, 2019) there is no single comprehensive international treaty nor international organisation dedicated to AI regulation, and the most advanced initiatives shaping the evolving landscape of AI governance recently took place amongst like-minded partners.

AI Governance at G7 Level

With repeated calls by leading AI developers to swiftly regulate the development of generative AI at the international level and soon after the release of Chat GPT 4 on March 2023, G7 Leaders, in their Hiroshima May 2023 Declaration (European Council, 2023), expressed their determination to "advance international discussions on inclusive artificial intelligence (AI) governance and interoperability to achieve our common vision and goal of trustworthy AI, in line with our shared democratic values". A couple of days after, at their bi-annual of the EU-US Trade and Technology Council (TTC) (European Commission, 2023a), the EU and the US announced their intention to work together to contribute to developing the G7 Principles and the Code of Conduct for trustworthy generative AI.

This G7 initiative called the Hiroshima AI Process (HAIP), is part of a wider range of international discussions on guardrails for generative AI. It builds on the 2019 OECD AI Principles (that were also adopted by the G20) and the GPAI and feeds into global efforts such as the UK-hosted AI Safety Summit, the Council of Europe Convention on AI, Human Rights, Democracy and the Rule of Law (CAI(2023) 01, 2023) and the UN Global Digital Compact (United Nations, 2024).

Under the energetic leadership of Japan, the G7 Working Group on digital and technology issues drafted, in less than three months, twelve Principles and a detailed Code of Conduct (CoC) for developers of generative AI, which were endorsed on 30 October 2023, by G7 Leaders. EVP Vestager qualified (European Commission, 2024b) the results of the Hiroshima process as "the most advanced product of international collaboration [on AI] so far".

It was quite remarkable to achieve such detailed results, especially considering that when the negotiations commenced at the end of August 2023, none of the G7 partners had finalised their national strategies on AI, and initiatives to discipline or regulate generative AI were still underway in each participating partner.

During the G7 Hiroshima process drafting, the EU Institutions were involved in a process of "trialogues" to finalise the text of the AI Act (which was politically adopted in December 2023, after the endorsement of the Hiroshima process outcome). Likewise, the US was elaborating its position domestically: the US President, substituting for Congress inaction, had obtained in July 2023 "voluntary commitments" (White House, 2023a) from seven major AI companies and was preparing his "Executive Order on Safe, Secure and Trustworthy AI" (White House, 2023) (which was issued on 30 October 2023, after Leaders' endorsement of the G7 Hiroshima outcome). Other G7 partners were in similar positions: UK had published in March 2023 its "AI regulation white paper" and was undertaking consultations on "initial proposals to develop a pro-innovation regulatory framework for AI"; Canada was debating about the proposal for "The Artificial Intelligence and Data Act" (AIDA); and, in Japan, the AI Strategic Council (established in May 2023) and the AI Strategic Team (put in place in April 2023) were working on formulating a national strategy on AI.

Indeed, G7 members were grappling with how to fulfil the G7 Leaders' mandate to develop a unified framework governing AI without infringing upon the policy space necessary to finalise ongoing regulatory initiatives at the national level. Interestingly, the outcomes of the Hiroshima process successfully met this objective by capturing commonalities between G7 frameworks while also reflecting some specificities of each member's approach.

As the approaches to AI among G7 partners share many similarities, negotiators were able to swiftly agree to incorporate this common ground into the CoC and Principles. For instance, leveraging the shared aspects of their respective frameworks, the G7 texts advocate for adopting a risk-based approach to guide AI implementation across its lifecycle, beginning with precautionary pre-deployment risk assessments and mitigation measures. They also acknowledge the necessity of continuous monitoring, reporting, and mitigation of misuse and incidents. Among the precautionary measures outlined, the Principles and CoC emphasise the importance of AI developers and deployers implementing risk management policies and procedures, as well as robust security controls that incorporate internal adversarial "red teaming" exercises.

Respective G7 Partners' domestic approach to AI governance could also find some reflection in the Hiroshima process outcome.

The US successfully built on its 21 July voluntary commitments to AI to influence some of the G7 languages regarding safety, security, and trust. For example, on safety, the CoC comprises obligations (similar to the US AI voluntary commitments) for the companies to make sure their technology is safe before releasing it to the public. That means testing the capabilities of their systems, assessing their potential risk, and making the results of these assessments public. Likewise, the CoC indicates that companies have a duty to earn people's trust and empower users to make informed decisions—labelling content that has been altered or AI-generated, rooting out bias and discrimination, strengthening privacy protections, and shielding children from harm.

In the G7 Principles and CoC, the EU also successfully included references to key aspects of the AI Act. The references to notions such as "unacceptable risk"[14] are clearly a reflection of the EU approach. EU negotiators also successfully included in the CoC obligations on developers similar to those put in place in the AI Act, in particular regarding transparency, traceability, testing, incident reporting, and information sharing. CoC language on information sharing with public authorities, or the distinction between "risks for individuals" and "societal risks", was also clearly inspired by the EU approach. This allowed President Von der Leyen "to welcome the G7 international Guiding Principles and the voluntary Code of Conduct, reflecting EU values to promote trustworthy AI" (European Commission, 2023). Notably, the EU and its Member States also effectively pushed for strengthening the G7 language regarding the "monitoring" of the CoC.

While ensuring a reliable monitoring mechanism for the implementation of the HAIP outcome is crucial for its credibility, agreeing on an operational monitoring mechanism has proven to be challenging. This is another example of the "gap in international governance" affecting the digital economy.

[14] See Preamble: "Organizations should not develop or deploy advanced AI systems in ways that undermine democratic values, are particularly harmful to individuals or communities, facilitate terrorism, promote criminal misuse, or pose substantial risks to safety, security and human rights, and are thus not acceptable".

China's "Global AI Governance Initiative"

In October 2023, as a direct response to the Hiroshima process, China, frustrated with being excluded from the AI discussions undertaken by Western democracies, came up with its AI initiative composed of eleven Principles. On October 18, 2023, President Xi Jinping introduced the "Global AI Governance Initiative" in his keynote speech (Xinhua News, 2023) at the opening ceremony of the third Belt and Road Forum for International Cooperation in Beijing.

Initiative (Ministry of Foreign Affairs of the People's Republic of China, 2023a), aimed to use President Xi's words to "jointly promote the sound, orderly and secure AI development in the world", is a set of eleven high-level principles outlining China's approach to international cooperation on AI governance.

As is the case with the Chinese approach to data policy, non-interference and respect for national sovereignty are a priority. "We should respect other countries' national sovereignty and strictly abide by their laws when providing them with AI products and services", the initiative read. Likewise, the preservation (also from foreign interferences) of "social order" is at the core of the Chinese AI strategy. In particular, the text reads: "We oppose using AI technologies for the purposes of manipulating public opinion, spreading disinformation, *intervening in other countries' internal affairs,* social systems *and social order*, as well as jeopardising the sovereignty of other states" (emphasis added).

More generally, the initiative seeks to counter the narrative of the US-China AI arms race by framing China as a facilitator of global AI cooperation. Interestingly, Chinese media depicted the initiative as "offering an open approach in contrast to the U.S. blockade" (Wang & Yin, 2023). China stresses in its Principles that: "All countries, regardless of their size, strength, or social system, should have equal rights to develop and use AI". The contention that "We oppose drawing ideological lines or forming *exclusive groups* to obstruct other countries from developing AI" (emphasis added) implicitly criticised the G7 Hiroshima process. China probably wanted to use this initiative to consolidate its (self-proclaimed) position as a Leader of the "Global South" as it stressed that: "We should increase the representation and voice of developing countries in global AI governance".

It is not clear if and to what extent this initiative will gain traction at the international level beyond the few countries that were reported (by China) to support its 2020 Global Initiative on Data Security.

Conclusion

The internal regulation of the digital economy is at a pivotal moment, with the US trying to torpedo the multilateral rule-based order, and the EU still trying to support it and to shape it.

With its unique, comprehensive, binding regulatory framework applying to EU as well as non-EU stakeholders, the EU has, since the implementation of its 2015 Digital Single Market Strategy, a shaper of the international digital regulatory space. Benefiting from first-mover advantage and sustained digital policy engagements for almost ten years, the EU has managed to successfully project key aspects of its digital policy and convinced partners to embrace its approach to digital trade agreements or implement regulations similar to its GDPR.

The EU's influence has also been filling the vacuum left by other key actors who have been unable to conceive or promote alternative regulatory models. The US, because of its inability to adopt digital legislation at the Federal level, has not been able to propose an alternative regulatory model to foreign countries and has even pulled out of all digital trade negotiations. Its approach of promoting deregulation and undermining multilateral processes by withdrawing massively from international organisations is a very challenge to the European efforts. There are questions about the "exportability" of the Chinese regulatory model (beyond some authoritarian countries), as it prioritises a unique vision of the maintenance of social order and non-interference with digital sovereignty.

The ability of the EU to continue to shape the international digital agenda will also depend on its capacity to enforce its most recent legislative acquis (and notably the DSA, the DMA and the AI Act). For this, the Commission can count on the support of the EU Court of Justice, which has proved, in the past, to be a scrupulous promoter of the strict enforcement of EU digital law, including with foreign companies and foreign countries.

But there are limits to what the EU relying on its own, which lacks digital platforms able to compete with the US ones, can achieve at the international level. Given the divergence in digital policy approaches, particularly between democratic and authoritarian uses of data, progress in asserting a human-centric democratic approach to digital governance can only be achieved through concerted actions among like-minded partners. Recently, with the adoption of the OECD principles against unlimited government surveillance, democratic countries took a significant step in this direction. Similarly, with the adoption of the Hiroshima process' Principles and CoC for AI by the G7, or new AI legislation in Korea or Australia, like-minded leaders have outlined what can be considered "the most advanced product of international collaboration [on AI] so far".

These recent developments represent significant successes for the EU's agenda and for democracies pushing for digital governance respecting Human Rights. However, in the face of divisions between the EU and the US, and with China increasingly winning the technological race, the perspective of global digital rules seems today elusive, and to depend more on like-minded democratic partners than from multilateral fora.

Bibliography

AMGEN, Applied Materials, APTIV, BMO, Citi, DOW, ENGIE et al. (2023, March 29). *Building an institutional framework for data free flow with trust*. https://www.ibm.com/policy/wp-content/uploads/2023/03/G7-IAP-statement-03-29-23.pdf

Bradford, A. (2020). *The Brussels effect: How the European Union rules the world*. Oxford University Press.

Bradford, A. (2023). *Digital empires: The global Battle to regulate technology*. Oxford University Press.

Casalini, F., Lopez-Gonzalez, J., & Nemoto, T. (2021, May). *Mapping commonalities in regulatory approahces to cross-border data transfers*. Retrieved from OECD Trade Policy Paper, no. 248: https://www.oecd.org/content/dam/oecd/en/publications/reports/2021/05/mapping-commonalities-in-regulatory-approaches-to-cross-border-data-transfers_e66a8dc0/ca9f974e-en.pdf

Clinton, H. (2011, October 11). America's Pacific Century. *Foreign Policy*.

Council of Europe. (2023, January 6). *Committee on artificial intelligence: Revised zero draft [framework] convention on artificial intelligence, human rights, democracy and the rule of law*. https://rm.coe.int/cai-2023-01-revised-zero-draft-framework-convention-public/1680aa193f

Council of Foreign Relations. (2024, February). *C. Peter McColough series on international economics with Katherine Tai*. https://www.youtube.com/watch?v=mRDTcTWE2cI&t=2745s

Council of the European Union. (2024, January 23). *Protocol amending the agreement between the European union and japan for an economic partnership*. https://data.consilium.europa.eu/doc/document/ST-16006-2023-INIT/en/pdf

Creemers, R., Webster, G., & Triolo, P. (2018, June). *Translation: Cybersecurity law of the people's Republic of China (Effective June 1, 2017)*. Retrieved from

Stanford University: https://digichina.stanford.edu/work/translation-cybersecurity-law-of-the-peoples-republic-of-china-effective-june-1-2017/

Data Protection Commissioner v Facebook Ireland and Maximillian Schrems, C-311/18 (Court (Grand Chamber) July 16, 2020).

European Commission. (2015). *Communication from the commission to the European parliament, the council, the European economic and social committee and the committee of the regions: Digital single market strategy for Europe*. https://eur-lex.europa.eu/legal-content/EN/TXT/?uri=CELEX:52015DC0192

European Commission. (2020, February 19). *Communication from the commission to the European parliament, the council, the European economic and social committee and the committee of the regions: A European strategy for data*. https://eur-lex.europa.eu/legal-content/EN/TXT/?qid=1582551099377&uri=CELEX%3A52020DC0066

European Commission. (2021). *Communication from the commission to the European parliament, the council, the European economic and social committee and the committee of the regions: Trade policy review—an open, sustainable and assertive trade policy*. https://eur-lex.europa.eu/legal-content/EN/ALL/?uri=CELEX%3A52021DC0066#footnote26

European Commission. (2023, October 30). *Commission welcomes G7 leaders' agreement on guiding principles and a code of conduct on artificial intelligence*. https://ec.europa.eu/commission/presscorner/detail/en/ip_23_5379

European Commission. (31 de May de 2023a). *EU-US trade and technology council enhances cooperation in emerging technologies, sustainable trade and economic security*. Obtenido de. https://ec.europa.eu/commission/presscorner/detail/en/ip_23_2922

European Commission. (2024, March 25). *Free trade agreement between the European union and New Zealand*. https://eur-lex.europa.eu/legal-content/EN/TXT/PDF/?uri=OJ:L_202400866#page=266

European Commission. (2024a, July 25). *EU and Singapore conclude negotiations for landmark digital trade agreement*. https://ec.europa.eu/commission/presscorner/detail/en/ip_24_3982

European Commission. (2024b). *Speech by Executive Vice President Vestager on technology and politics at the institute for advanced study*. https://ec.europa.eu/commission/presscorner/detail/en/speech_24_1927

European Council. (2023). *G7 hiroshima leaders' communiqué*. https://www.consilium.europa.eu/en/press/press-releases/2023/05/20/g7-hiroshima-leaders-communique/

European Council. (2024, January 31). *EU-Japan economic partnership agreement: EU and Japan sign protocol to include cross-border data flows*. https://www.consilium.europa.eu/en/press/press-releases/2024/01/31/eu-japan-economic-partnership-agreement-eu-and-japan-sign-protocol-to-include-cross-border-data-flows/#:~:text=The%20protocol%20will%20provide%20greater,protection%20and%20the%20digital%20

European Parliament. (2024). *European parliament legislative resolution of 13 March 2024 on the proposal for a regulation of the European parliament and of the Council on laying down harmonised rules on artificial intelligence (Artificial Intelligence Act).* https://www.europarl.europa.eu/doceo/document/TA-9-2024-0138_EN.pdf

European Union. (2008). *Consolidated version of the Treaty on European Union.* https://eur-lex.europa.eu/eli/treaty/teu_2008/art_21/oj

European Union. (2016). *Regulation (EU) 2016/679 of the European parliament and of the council of 27 april 2016 on the protection of natural persons with regard to the processing of personal data and on the free movement of such data, and repealing directive 95/46/EC (GDPR).* https://eur-lex.europa.eu/eli/reg/2016/679/oj

European Union. (2021). *Trade and cooperation agreement between the European union and the European atomic energy community, of the one part, and the United Kingdom of Great Britain and Northern Ireland, of the other part.* https://eur-lex.europa.eu/legal-content/EN/TXT/?uri=uriserv%3AOJ.L_.2021.149.01.0010.01.ENG&amp%3Btoc=OJ%3AL%3A2021%3A149%3ATOC

European Union. (2022, October 19). *Regulation (EU) 2022/2065 of the European parliament and of the council of 19 october 2022 on a single market for digital services and amending directive 2000/31/EC (Digital Services Act).* https://eur-lex.europa.eu/eli/reg/2022/2065/oj

European Union. (2022a, September 14). *Regulation (EU) 2022/1925 of the European parliament and of the council of 14 september 2022 on contestable and fair markets in the digital sector and amending directives (EU) 2019/1937 and (EU) 2020/1828 (Digital Markets Act).* https://eur-lex.europa.eu/eli/reg/2022/1925/oj

Global Partnership on Artificial Intelligence. (2024). *Home.* https://gpai.ai/

Government of Italy. (2021). *G20 rome leaders' declaration.* https://www.governo.it/sites/governo.it/files/G20ROMELEADERSDECLARATION_0.pdf

Government of Japan. (2023, April 30). *Ministerial declaration: The G7 digital and tech ministers' meeting.* https://g7g20-documents.org/database/document/2023-g7-japan-ministerial-meetings-ict-ministers-ministers-language-ministerial-declaration-the-g7-digital-and-tech-ministers-meeting#section-1

Government of the United Kingdom. (2023, November 1–2). *The bletchley declaration by countries attending the ai safety summit.* https://www.gov.uk/government/publications/ai-safety-summit-2023-the-bletchley-declaration/the-bletchley-declaration-by-countries-attending-the-ai-safety-summit-1-2-november-2023

Köhler-Suzuki, N. (2023, July). *Mapping the EU's digital trade: A global leader hidden in plain sight?* Retrieved from Jaques Delors Institute: https://institutdelors.eu/wp-content/uploads/2023/08/PP293_Mapping-EU-digital-trade_Kholer-Suzuki.pdf
Letta, E. (2024). *Much more than a market—Speed, security, solidarity. Empowering the SIngle market to deliver a sustainable future and prosperity for all EU citizens*. European Commission.
Marel, E., & Ferracane, M. (2021, May 30). *Regulating personal data: Linking different models to digital services trade*. https://cepr.org/voxeu/columns/regulating-personal-data-linking-different-models-digital-services-trade
Ministry of Commerce of the People's Republic of China. (2020). *Chapter 12: Electronic Commerce*. http://fta.mofcom.gov.cn/rcep/rceppdf/d12z_en.pdf
Ministry of Foreign Affairs of Japan. (2019). *G20 osaka leaders declaration*. https://www.mofa.go.jp/policy/economy/g20_summit/osaka19/en/documents/final_g20_osaka_leaders_declaration.html
Ministry of Foreign Affairs of the People's Republic of China. (2023, October 31). *Jointly implementing the global security initiative for lasting peace and security of the World*. https://www.mfa.gov.cn/eng/xw/wjbxw/202405/t20240530_11343749.html
Ministry of Foreign Affairs of the People's Republic of China. (2023a). *Global AI Governance Initiative*. http://gd.china-embassy.gov.cn/eng/zxhd_1/202310/t20231024_11167412.htm
OECD. (2019). *OECD AI principles overview*. https://oecd.ai/en/ai-principles
OECD. (2020, December). *Government access to personal data held by the private sector: Statement by the OECD committee on digital economy policy*. https://web-archive.oecd.org/2021-10-26/575438-trusted-government-access-personal-data-private-sector.htm
OECD. (2022). *OECD legal insttuments*. https://legalinstruments.oecd.org/en/instruments/OECD-LEGAL-0487
OECD. (2023). *Moving forward on data free flow with trust: New evidence and analysis of business experiences*. https://www.oecd-ilibrary.org/science-and-technology/moving-forward-on-data-free-flow-with-trust_1afab147-en
Office of Senator Elizabeth Warren. (2023, May). *Big tech's big con: Rigging digital trade rules to block antitrust regulation*. https://www.warren.senate.gov/imo/media/doc/USTR%20REPORT.pdf
Park, C. (2022). *Knowledge base: China's 'global data security initiative' 全球数据安全倡议*. https://digichina.stanford.edu/work/knowledge-base-chinas-global-data-security-initiative/
PIPL. (n.d.). *Article 60: Personal information protection law*. https://personalinformationprotectionlaw.com/PIPL/article-60/

Price, D. M. (2019, December 2). *Opinion: Today's tech industry mirrors the pre-2008 financial industry: Have we learned our lesson?* https://www.washingtonpost.com/opinions/2019/12/02/world-leaders-should-act-avoid-digital-crisis-before-its-too-late/

Rafaelof, E., Creemers, R., Sacks, S., Tai, K., Webster, G., Neville, K., & Horsley, J. (2021, June). *Translation: Data security law of the people's republic of China (Effective Sept. 1, 2021).* Retrieved from Stanford University: https://digichina.stanford.edu/work/translation-data-security-law-of-the-peoples-republic-of-china/

Smith, B., & Browne, C. A. (2019). *Tools and weapons: The promise and the peril of the digital age.* Penguin Press.

United Nations. (2024). *Global digital compact.* https://www.un.org/techenvoy/global-digital-compact

United Nations. (2024a, March 21). *General assembly adopts landmark resolution on artificial intelligence.* https://news.un.org/en/story/2024/03/1147831

Wang, C., & Yin, Y. (2023, October 18). *China launches global AI governance initiative, offering an open approach in contrast to US blockade.* https://www.globaltimes.cn/page/202310/1300092.shtml

White House. (2023, October 30). *President biden issues executive order on safe, secure, and trustworthy artificial intelligence.* https://www.whitehouse.gov/briefing-room/statements-releases/2023/10/30/fact-sheet-president-biden-issues-executive-order-on-safe-secure-and-trustworthy-artificial-intelligence/

White House. (2023a, July 21). *Remarks by president biden on artificial intelligence.* https://www.whitehouse.gov/briefing-room/speeches-remarks/2023/07/21/remarks-by-president-biden-on-artificial-intelligence/

Word Trade Organization. (2019, January 25). *Joint statement on electronic commerce.* https://docs.wto.org/dol2fe/Pages/SS/directdoc.aspx?filename=q:/WT/L/1056.pdf&Open=True

World Trade Organization. (2019). *Russia—measures concerning traffic in transit.* https://www.wto.org/english/tratop_e/dispu_e/cases_e/ds512_e.htm

Xinhua News. (2023, October 18). *Full text of Xi Jinping's keynote speech at 3rd belt and road forum for int'l cooperation.* https://english.news.cn/20231018/7bfc16ac51d443c6a7a00ce25c972104/c.html

CHAPTER 21

Conclusion

Thibaut Kleiner and Andrea G. Rodríguez

> It's really hard to design products by focus groups. A lot of times, people don't know what they want until you show it to them.
> Steven Jobs, Former CEO, Apple (1997–2011)

When we sat down to discuss the scope of the book, we asked ourselves the following questions: why has the EU been given this much power to regulate and govern digital? How did this happen, and what lessons can we draw from it for the European project as a whole? How could EU institutions have adopted so many digital policies in the last ten years? The chapters that preceded this final one have been trying to address these issues, offering an in-depth overview of thematic areas as well as initiatives to defend and internationalise a "digital rulebook" based on European values.

T. Kleiner
European Commission, Brussels, Belgium
e-mail: thibaut.kleiner@ec.europa.eu

A. G. Rodríguez (✉)
Centre for European Policy Studies, Brussels, Belgium
e-mail: andrea.rodriguez@ceps.eu

T. Kleiner and A. Garcia Rodriguez (eds.), *The Making of a Global Digital Rulebook*, https://doi.org/10.1007/978-981-95-9226-5_21

In our conversations with the authors, we asked them to reflect, from their expertise and first- experience as either "makers" or "analysts" of this rulebook, on how each topic has been addressed over time, the impact of digital sovereignty in their evolution, the role of interest groups (what we have called "the landscape of forces"), and on its meaning for European integration.

As the book shows, the EU's digital policy agenda has been broadening to incorporate topics with a horizontal effect on society and other areas of the European economy. This "rulebook", often regarded as a book that is written too late, has become a state-of-the-art regulatory framework that aims to address not only market imbalances but also set anticipatory governance frameworks for topics that are yet to become mainstream in policy agendas (Rodriguez, 2022). As the European Union implements a very comprehensive set of rules and regulations, it is also facing new confrontations from international partners like the U.S. and questioning EU digital law and policy as a bureaucratic burden on business and innovation.

Digital technologies are fast-moving, and the development of digital law and policy is certainly not over, and many challenges remain. However, a tipping point has arguably been reached, with a critical mass of digital areas being now governed by EU legislations, policies and governance structures, and with a process in place to manage and enhance digital sovereignty towards 2030 and beyond, with the Commission at its helm.

The previous chapters have offered a rich analysis of the development of the EU digital law and policy over the years. It shows that the path towards further integration has not been uniform or constant. In this conclusive chapter, we try to draw some common lessons from the reflections on the many policy areas the book has covered. We identify some factors that may explain why the EU was able to take a stronger role in some areas and why, in others, the centre of governance remained at the national level, in the hands of the private sector or of international actors. We also found unexpected lessons for EU competitiveness and, overall, a paradoxical message of hope for the European international standing.

The Big Story and the Many Small Steps

The book argues that the European Union has developed a consistent and comprehensive rulebook for the digital space, covering a full spectrum of policies in what has been described as "digital constitutionalism" (de Gregorio, 2021). In the making of this book, our thesis was that EU institutions have managed to advance EU integration further in the digital realm than anywhere else by supplementing the logic of building the single market with objectives linked to citizens' rights and European values. The chapters showed that this overall hypothesis was, by and large, verified. Moreover, Part III of the book explains how this European right-based digital order can also influence other jurisdictions and how international action is necessary to ensure the implementation of the digital agenda at home.

However, these achievements appear also fragile, and subject to effective enforcement, especially in a situation of technological dependency and hostility from the Trump administration. The chapters show that EU digital policy-making has not been uniform or easy, and that—despite successful stories—there are remaining gaps and challenges which illustrate that the EU's digital policy framework might be less consistent than initially projected.

Historically, it is undeniable that the EU has been able to increase its amount of power over the digital space: the body of law of what is considered "digital" has expanded tremendously, having an impact in other policy areas, including trade, healthcare, or competition. The Commission has become a global regulator, supervising the behaviour and market practices of large online platforms and providers of algorithmic decision-making models and developing standards for the whole digital sector, from data to cybersecurity.

This inflexion was concomitant with Brexit, which eliminated a powerful voice opposing integration beyond the single market. And it met the EU governments' need to fight back collectively—as they would be too weak in isolation—against a common democratic challenge coming from very large online platforms. Centuries after Westphalia, Europe is defining a new kind of sovereignty—digital sovereignty—not based on territory and religion but on principles, rules and methodologies that the EU designs as the blueprint for how to tackle complex, cross-border challenges with a unified, agile, and forward-thinking approach.

Nevertheless, a values-based approach will not be enough to ensure that the European model for governing digital remains attractive. Europe has a long-standing fight to ensure that companies can flourish within its territory and compete internationally. In 2024, the European Commission published two very influential reports by the pen of Enrico Letta (April), and of Mario Draghi (September). Though the focus differs, there is one clear common warning: more Europe—and not less—is the only option to bridge sovereignty gaps and ensure it remains an important player in the future in the face of severe challenges like declining demographics and an increasingly uncertain geopolitical order (Draghi, 2024; Letta, 2024). Rules will not be sufficient for the EU to avoid economic decline: it will require proper capabilities, and from European companies developing and marketing the digital products and services that it badly needs to remain competitive without being dependent on other regions. The technology sovereignty package proposed by the Commission in June 2026 illustrates this further: it proposes a series of industrial policy measures to boost EU digital capabilities in areas from micro-chips to cloud and Artificial Intelligence, with the clear motivation that without genuine technological capabilities, the EU lacks the ability to take its destiny into its hands.

Digital sovereignty is the resulting act of balancing competition with cooperation, but since the EU is an economic, and not political, union, regulations must have a widespread impact on the economy and in building the single market. This is one of the unexpected lessons of this book: regardless of the innovative character or forward-looking character of digital policies, those that bring impactful changes are the ones that win legitimacy over time.

In that context, a number of chapters have identified some patterns of success for the EU industry. The data chapter showed that the EU can embrace a different model from the 'as much as you can eat' data model of large US platforms, to create value, and instead work on higher quality decentralised data that is monetised through infrastructures offering discovery and trust building, and open standards. The chapter on China and on semiconductors showed that the EU can build resilience on the basis of excellence and of being indispensable even if this only applies to a small proportion of the value chain or market the EU controls. This shows that the EU rulebook can be a competitive asset too, in the way its underpinnings reflect values and principles that apply to the reality of the EU economy and society, in terms of diversity, openness, small and decentralised entities. As exemplified by ASML, European excellence is also about communities and ecosystems of specialised entities working together thanks to strong regulatory frameworks that build trust and predictability, and open standards that create value through contracts instead of hierarchy. Just like the story of this book (EU digital sovereignty) is about the EU daring to be different and to embrace its common identity, EU competitiveness may also be found through its own unique path rather than through an attempt to copy the success of the USA or China. This would plead for giving a chance to the EU rulebook, which is only nascent, to bring about a quality jump in the way digital technologies are produced and adopted, notably by SMEs. An alternative path that could however emerge from on-going discussions and from the simplification agenda, is that the EU could experience self-doubt, and question the benefits of its regulatory achievements, in a global context where the USA is promoting de-regulation and attacking some of the EU laws, while pushing to accelerate its industrial and technological leadership. Reciprocally, de-coupling from China and from the USA may also boost European independence and reinforce its ability to shape global rule-making. This highlights that digital sovereignty cannot be delivered without a degree of technological self-reliance.

On top of this, this book has shown that the line of what is "digital policy" is very diverse and oftentimes diffuse, with governance pivoting from Member States to the Commission. Emerging technologies and domains, like space or quantum, are primarily governed at the national level, and EU action on them will require breaking internal siloes that will allow different areas to work closer together. Digital is no longer only about data but also about infrastructure, research and innovation, international trade, industrial policy or diplomacy.

In other traditional areas like telecommunication policy, cybersecurity, or electronic identity, the EU is coordinating and providing central resources and standards, where the decision-making power is still largely national. However, it is in domains where the EU has had a "follower" position where the EU Commission has been placed at the heart of governance, such as online platform regulation and artificial intelligence. This confirms that delegation of power happens in moments of urgency of coordination.

The role of the EU is not absent, but it is constantly contested, with multiple actors and forces at play, and unstable equilibrium and unabated efforts needed to keep the EU together. As in cybersecurity, for example, the field will likely stay unfinished (in policy terms) for many years, an "Unvollendete". Interestingly, these tensions also seem to repeat themselves across areas in the process of institution-building: national vs EU-level governance; U.S. online platforms vs EU governments; infrastructure vs content providers; multi-stakeholder vs. state; China vs. EU, etc. From this diversity and these battles emerge a contrasted but equally interesting perspective of forces fighting for power in repeated games that build a common reality over time. Interestingly, these battles and equilibria may lead to either increased regulation, or on the contrary a bigger focus on market freedom and strategic autonomy.

Importantly, the chapters recognise EU digital sovereignty is on the rise, but they also show that the EU is a hybrid sovereign: the governance structures of the EU digital rule book are based on networks of regulators and boards, where the EU is never totally on its own able to rule but always depends from national actors and supplementary structures to derive legitimacy and power over the digital space. Similarly, the analysis shows that whereas there may be a "Brussels effect", the EU is by far not immune to international influence, and there is an "international awareness effect" in the Brussels policymaking too. It takes place through lobbying efforts of international actors, as well as through the interactions with partners to solve common problems and, most importantly, because of the international competition and counter-regulatory models provided by powers like China or the U.S.

Another observation and nuance towards the making of the EU digital rulebook is what could be called the telecom paradox. Whereas across the digital space, the EU has been gaining powers, the institutional set-up seems to be stuck in the area of telecommunications. Instead of sovereignty in terms of continental rules, industrial champions and investment, the consensus among national regulators is that the EU approach should focus on local competition and consumers.

The paradox is that despite this, the same dynamics of principles and values at play in fostering greater EU integration in the digital space apply to the telecom sector. Human-centricity, inclusion, and universal access are professed like in the rest of the digital regulatory areas, but national authorities appear more convinced that they are best pursued through decentralised and national regulations and institutions rather than through pan-European ones: local competition rather than a single market, competition pushing investment instead of profit margins enabling investment, low price and universal access instead of high-speed broadband and universal access. And the list continues. The Commission's proposal of a Digital Network Act, including a European passport and more coordination of spectrum policy is another attempt to break national boundaries, but it is not a given that it will be accepted, nor that it will break this equilibrium of a national-centred model -no matter when it fails to deliver on the Digital Decade targets.

Patterns of EU Integration and Policy-Making: Comparative Analysis and Key Takeaways from the Case Studies

The book describes the interplay between an overall narrative of EU integration and digital sovereignty and a more detailed and sector-specific analysis. This multilevel analysis allows us to reflect more broadly on how some factors have affected the EU's ability to develop its idea of digital sovereignty. Here, we take some inspiration from Anu Bradford, who identified several factors that make up the "Brussels effect" (Bradford, 2020):

- *Large Market Size*: The EU has an extensive consumer market that attracts companies from all over the world. These companies tend to align themselves with the EU's strict regulatory frameworks to secure a place in the European market.
- *Regulatory Capacity*: The EU possesses the institutional structures and the necessary expertise to create and enforce regulations effectively.
- *Stringent Standards*: The regulations accepted by the EU are often more comprehensive and demanding than those in other nations, demonstrating a strong commitment to safeguarding consumer interests, environmental integrity, and societal well-being.
- *Inelastic Targets*: The EU focuses on regulating sectors, such as consumer protection, where the entities subject to regulation have limited ability to relocate and thus avoid EU regulations. Compliance is necessary for companies aiming to penetrate the European market.

Considering these factors, we have identified a set of elements that can be explanatory variables for different levels of integration.

Crises are Catalysts for Change and for Deepening Integration

Several of the chapters provide ample evidence that crises gave legitimacy to joint EU action and increased integration, e.g. showing how the Digital Agenda emerged from a failure of the Lisbon strategy and companies like Nokia Mobile. The COVID crisis was a strong driver towards EU digital industrial policy, as evidenced in the chapter on the digital decade or semiconductors. Regulation in the area of platforms responded to crises and scandals like the Snowden revelations on mass surveillance, Cambridge Analytica on information manipulation and many instances of extremist radicalisation or suicides resulting from social media content, etc.

The EU can Grab Power More Easily in Greenfield Areas

The comparison between telecom and the expansion of the internet vs. AI shows that where there are existing strong actors, it is more difficult for the EU to establish its authority. By contrast, when the EU enters a new policy area, it has more chances to centralise power. Along those lines, the case studies show that it is easier to be tough on foreign actors than on European ones who enjoy political backing. This is illustrated in the case of audiovisual policy or online platforms through the Digital Markets Act. In the negotiations, it was easier to explain that upcoming platform regulation would be a vehicle against U.S. and Chinese platforms than it was to defend the AI Act against the claim that it would hurt European startups.

Reciprocally, the landscape of forces showed alliances of interests and the possibility of bringing equilibrium towards more EU integration, but also showed some multiple geometries. EU influence could align with, for instance, U.S. interests in some areas, like Internet governance. This shows that it is easily imaginable for EU integration to be overturned in situations where it is not stabilised and institutionalised, just like it can more easily advance in settings of low institutional density.

Technological (and Institutional) Maturity Needs to be at the Right Point

The case studies show that the appetite for EU intervention is not universal and that the technology context, as well as the problem definition, has to be at the right point before the EU can exercise authority. EU rules and EU governance have to answer a clearly identified problem to be legitimate and acceptable. This is clear in the case of emerging technologies or in the evolution of EU-China relations, where the analysis shows that the EU must time its actions very carefully.

Sometimes it is too late, and national positions have already built up, like in outer space, and sometimes it is too early to justify EU authority, like in quantum or possibly AI. As illustrated by the case of electronic identity or data, technological solutions offered by the EU can also help justify a pan-European solution and accelerate convergence. This ability to develop an ecosystem approach (instead of white elephant prestige projects) is also an element identified in the ability of the EU to gain international influence through the Global Gateway. The case of China shows that the EU made the mistake of being myopic for too long about the technological development of China and about its ability to become a clear contender with even superior technology than the EU in some areas, leading to dependencies that make de-coupling simply unfeasible.

The Development of High-Quality Rules and Standards is Instrumental in Advancing Integration, Both at the EU and International Levels

The case studies show that in the digital field, standards have become critical elements. As illustrated in the case of the e-Identity Wallet, or data, or AI, or relations with the Indo-Pacific, standards are essential to establish common frameworks based on values and to increase policy alignment between different regions. The quality of the EU law-making and standard development has been a strong asset in the making of the EU digital rulebook: it offered a compelling case to adopt the EU offer, simply because it was simply the best on offer. The GSM standard or the GDPR illustrate this. Furthermore, when the EU offer is of good quality (for instance because it integrates fundamental rights), EU's influence on other regions to adopt its templates can increase, as could be seen in the EU-US relations or in the Indo-Pacific.

In addition, the chapters showed that the very process of developing common standards and common rules is an instrument for consensus building and integration. Just like negotiating legislation is a proxy for granting the EU additional powers in areas of conflicting interests (as shown in the case of the EU Chips Act), standard development offers the opportunity of repeated games (discussion and testing) to come to a consensus and to divide up issues in smaller pieces to advance an integration agenda, as illustrated in the base of cybersecurity. Therefore, we found that standardisation and law-making can be characterised as meta-tools of integration, offering a platform for the landscape of forces to reach equilibrium around guarded outcomes. To some extent, international structures like Digital Partnerships or Trade and Technology Councils have similar potential.

As a corollary, this means that the quality of EU legislation and EU standards is also a factor of stability as well as of contestability of EU integration. If EU laws fail to deliver, for example because policies do not lead to better services or hurt competitiveness, the landscape of forces may lead to questioning their relevance and legitimacy. This is the dilemma at play in the implementation of rules regarding online platforms and AI, for instance, and also the questioning in the Indo-Pacific region towards the appropriateness of adopting more of the EU rulebook, especially given the U.S. offer based on security benefits. If EU competitiveness would be significantly damaged by the EU rulebook, its very maintenance could be put into question.

Principle-Based Legislation is Easier to Adopt and Export but Implementation is Key

Several chapters have outlined the hesitations towards developing legislation in several areas. In contested fields, like cybersecurity, the route of using a Directive instead of a Regulation was instrumental in adopting the first legislation on network and information security. Similarly, the path to reaching consensus in many of the chapters was about compromises that relax the degree of prescription imposed by the EU on the national level or industry and instead about promoting general principles (as observed for the AI Act, electronic identity or media freedom). This 'small steps' approach where the EU gets one bite of the cake, and gets some more at the next round, was at play in a number of areas where consecutive proposals were made (e.g. telecom, eIDAS or cyber). The digital rulebook can claim consistency because it derives from unified elements such as those coined in the Declaration on Digital Rights and Principles, which operate like a constitution. Principles may be flexible enough so that implementation can be tailored to national specificities. This success factor in developing consensus at the EU level, on the basis of common principles, is also an asset when exporting the EU approach internationally. This can be seen in the chapter on the multilateral forum when the G7 or G20 import EU principles to develop codes of conduct.

Conversely, there are various risks at stake with a principles-based rulebook. First, it may be too loose and may require to be supplemented by interpretative guidelines or additional legislative clarifications, leading to complexity, legal costs and inconsistent interpretation. This is a criticism applied to the GDPR already but the chapter on AI identifies it too. Second, principles may require significant monitoring efforts by the EU, as the temptation may be for some national governments to simply pay lip service to high level principles instead of actually enforcing them. Vigorous implementation, using infringement cases and taking Member States to Court could be a signal here, as without implementation, rules will remain on paper only, and their very purpose may be undone. Third, principles may be contested, and competing narratives could undermine the EU rulebook by attacking its very underpinnings or by offering alternatives about how to best deliver them. The telecom paradox presented above falls into this category, as well as challenges to the EU's role in the areas of semiconductor policy and outer space. More generally, tensions around the rule of law could undo the EU efforts in the digital field too.

Prospects for the Future

The EU global digital rulebook is not only an object of study, it is also a reality for students, practitioners and policymakers around the globe to learn about. Digital technologies are fast-moving, but the EU is also a dynamic project. With a new European Commission term led again by President Ursula von der Leyen and a new U.S. Administration led again by President Donald Trump, challenges will continue to multiply, testing the ability of the EU to respond to them while advancing digital sovereignty.

The enforcement of the digital rulebook will be a test for the European Union, something that many chapters have underlined. The laws passed in the last decade will be tested through implementation. Too timid enforcement could undermine the authority of the European Union over digital matters and decrease the credibility of an alternative regulatory model based on fundamental rights and EU values.

At the same time, necessary enforcement, such as sanctions on U.S. or Chinese online platforms, could lead to increased international tensions if they are not properly explained and legitimised. The U.S. Vice President J.D. Vance, for instance, formulated the threat of the U.S. withdrawing from NATO in the case of Elon Musk's *x.com* remains under the sight of EU regulators (Kilander, 2024).

Another implementation challenge will be the ability of the EU to address the criticism about the bureaucratic burden that the industry claims is resulting from the EU digital rulebook. The European Commission has committed to reduce reporting and to make rules simpler, less cumbersome and more understandable. While the intention is commendable, it may not be so easy to realise. One option could be to make the various digital rules and regulations more uniform and to have their governance centralised in fewer structures at the EU level. But will Member States accept to hand over even more control to the EU level for legislation to get simpler? Or will they prefer to stick to imperfect and hybrid governance structures as long as they have a protagonist role?

Beyond implementation, advancing digital sovereignty will require a significant boost in investments, sustained digital industrial policy efforts to develop home-grown technology, and a new leap of faith in the European project. This is the justification behind the technology sovereignty package launched by the Commission in June 2025. Admittedly, some of these objectives are part of the Digital Decade Policy Programme and the call for a competitiveness pact by EU leaders. But results need to be tangible fast. While the EU has many talents, it has failed to transform its innovative potential into industrial (and geopolitical) leadership, and this is homework to catch up on. However, one thing is certain: despite the flaws, we can speak of the EU digital rulebook as a digital constitution.

There is a path, and there is a vision that attracts attention globally. This EU's digital constitution, amended, expanded, and democratic, can become—and to some extent already is—a point of reference for regions trying to come to terms with the power of online platforms or the risks associated with digital technologies, together with issues about how to best develop these technologies and make them successful item in a new world where economic security has become paramount.

At a time where the digital space has become an area of confrontation, where the interests of the US big tech have colluded with those of the Trump administration, and China seems to be on track to become the global technology leader, the EU is facing both risks and opportunities. Building rules will not be sufficient to establish digital sovereignty. Competitiveness and technological independence are also required, which calls for a double de-coupling (from China as well as from the United States). But if the EU is able to chart its own competitive path, it may become a magnet for a number of countries that also strive for digital sovereignty, both in terms of identity and technology.

The promise of EU policy to submit technology to the citizens may well be a return to the original spirit of the Internet. With other regions focusing on preserving money and power, the EU may paradoxically be the best placed to get back to the basics and offer a genuine future-proof vision based on values that shape industrial ecosystems through rules and standards. In a world of confrontation, the spirit of EU policy can offer hope. Without looking for it, in digital, Europe has a soul.

Bibliography

Bradford, A. (2020). *The Brussels effect: How the European Union Rules the world*. Oxford University Press.

Bradford, A. (2023). *Digital empires: The global battle to regulate technology*. Oxford University Press.

de Gregorio, G. (2021). The rise of digital constitutionalism in the European Union. *International Journal of Constitutional Law, 19*(1), 41–70.

Draghi, M. (2024). *The future of European competitiveness: A competitiveness strategy for Europe*. European Commission.

Kilander, G. (2024, September 14). *JD Vance says US could drop support for NATO if Europe tries to regulate Elon Musk's platforms*. Retrieved from The Independent: https://www.independent.co.uk/news/world/americas/us-politics/jd-vance-elon-musk-x-twitter-donald-trump-b2614525.html

Letta, E. (2024). *Much more than a market—Speed, Security, Solidarity. Empowering the SIngle Market to deliver a sustainable future and prosperity for all EU Citizens*. European Commission.

Rodriguez, G. (2022). Una política digital dual para la UE. *Política Exterior* (208).

Kolibri 360 GmbH
Ferdinand-Jühlke-Straße 7
99095 Erfurt, Deutschland
produktsicherheit@kolibri360.de